John Player Art of Cricket

Books by Alastair Smart

THE LIFE AND ART OF ALLAN RAMSAY (1952)
THE ASSISI PROBLEM AND THE ART OF GIOTTO (1971)
THE RENAISSANCE AND MANNERISM IN ITALY (1972)
THE RENAISSANCE AND MANNERISM OUTSIDE ITALY (1972)
CONSTABLE AND HIS COUNTRY (1976) (*with Attfield Brooks*)
THE DAWN OF ITALIAN PAINTING 1250–1400 (1978)

John Player Art of Cricket

Robin Simon

and

Alastair Smart

JPS

First published in England 1983 by
Martin Secker & Warburg Limited
54 Poland Street, London W1V 3DF
in association with Imperial Tobacco Limited
acting for Imperial Group plc

ISBN 0-436-47391-7

Printed and bound in Italy
by Imago Publishing Ltd.

We at Imperial Tobacco Limited have for many years been associated with cricket in its most modern form by sponsoring the John Player League–a competition encapsulating all the action and excitement of limited overs cricket.

As anybody who enjoys a passion for the game will readily tell you, cricket is in itself an art form. As such over the years it has attracted leading artists who have portrayed every aspect of it, and their works now provide a visual record of the game and those connected with it.

We are delighted to be associated with this unique and rare record of the game's heritage and we do not hesitate to recommend the exhibition and this volume to everyone interested in this great game's past. Many of the illustrations depicted in this book are from private collections and have never before been on public display.

The serious student of art and history, as well as cricket enthusiasts, should benefit from this explanation of the game's development and its place in social history.

We congratulate Robin Simon and Alastair Smart on their research, and trust that everyone will enjoy the product of their splendid work.

Imperial Tobacco Limited

This book is dedicated with love to our children

BENET and ALICE,
LYDIA and JULIAN

Contents

Preface

It would have been surprising if the national game – the "manly" sport, as it became in the eighteenth century – had not left its stamp upon English art, especially when one considers the beauty and the grace of cricket: yet its manifold reflections in painting, the graphic arts and sculpture have hitherto received very little attention, let alone systematic study. It is the purpose of the present book to try to remedy this deficiency, and at the same time to offer to the cricket-lover and the art-lover alike what we believe to be a unique anthology of illustrations, many of which have never been published before. We have confined our attention, in the main, to cricket art in Great Britain, although some consideration has been given to a few pictures and drawings relating to cricket as played on the Continent and in America: to have attempted to cover the cricket-playing countries of the world would have been an impossible task–but that terrain lies wide open for others to explore. The book is principally concerned with the art of the eighteenth and nineteenth centuries, and therefore we have not included more than a token representation of modern works–which in our view deserve separate treatment.

The reader will find that, as the story of cricket unfolds, each successive phase is dominated by a representative figure whose eminence in the cricketing world gave him a major role in that story. The first of these, representing the era before the foundation of M.C.C. in 1787, is that influential patron of cricket and prominent player John Sackville, 3rd Duke of Dorset (Plate 1); the second, the eccentric Lord Frederick Beauclerk (Plates 8, 47), the leading all-rounder in the early days of M.C.C. and for a time the game's virtual lawgiver; the third, the cultured Nicholas Wanostrocht (Plates 72, 75), or "Felix"–to give him the name under which he played for Kent and England–who combined supreme skills as a batsman with rare artistic gifts, and who takes us across the threshold of the Victorian Age; and, finally, there stands astride the second half of the nineteenth century, with the commanding inevitability that marked his career at the crease, that immortal symbol of cricket and its place in the heart of England and in English hearts–"W.G." (Plates 97, 100, 103, XXV).

The Catalogue supplies details concerning almost all the examples of cricket art discussed in the introductory narrative. It also includes further works–especially paintings–which had to be omitted from our historical account. It makes no claim to completeness, but it does comprise nearly all the examples of cricket art of the eighteenth and nineteenth centuries that we have found most interesting. We have, however, excluded a large number of representations of cricket subjects and portraits of cricketers which seemed to us to fall more into the category of the historical record than of the work of art.

Pictures of cricketing subjects are frequently illustrated in histories of the game, and yet very few of then have been examined from an art-historical point of view: even when historians of art have discussed them, the writers in question have often appeared oblivious of the subject-matter, or possibly baffled by it, as though cricket were too arcane a cult to lend itself readily to iconographical clarification. One consequence of this neglect is that historians of cricket have been led on occasion to make easy assumptions about the evidential value of pictorial representations whose authorship, dating or even authenticity may be uncertain. It is impossible, for example, that the often-reproduced picture known as *Cricket at the Artillery Ground* (Plate 15) was executed, as is commonly assumed, by the eminent eighteenth-century painter Francis Hayman, whose fine draughtsmanship and subtle handling are on the other hand fully in evidence in the so-called *Cricket in Marylebone Fields* (Plates 10, 11, II-IV), a painting of exceptionally high quality which has been surprisingly neglected in the literature, and to which we now give an overdue place of honour. It is as though the quite unjustified fame of the first of these two pictures–both of them ascribed to the same hand–had obscured the luminous merits of the second. But even apart from such considerations, the traditional or quasi-traditional titles of many cricket pictures are themselves suspect, and none more so than the accepted titles of these two canvases: the cricket historian, therefore, will be batting on a sticky wicket if he takes it for granted that these paintings actually show us the two famous venues of eighteenth-century cricket that are indicated by their present titles; and indeed there is evidence that they do not. As we have tried to show, other historical assumptions may be affected likewise by a study of pictorial evidence–one instance being the question we have raised as to whether the legendary "popping-hole" (a hole supposedly dug in the ground between the stumps of the ancient two-stump wicket, into which the batsman had to "pop" his bat in order to complete a run, and the fielder to "pop" the ball in order to run him out) ever really existed in early cricket.

Whether or not all our conclusions find acceptance, we hope to have shown in positive ways that the study of cricket art can throw new light on the history of the "manly game". Almost at every turn during the preparation of this book we have been surprised by how much there was to discover; and that experience appeared particularly rewarding on the occasions when the "art of cricket" seemed to address us from the past with all the authority of a newly discovered document and to utter something significant not merely about the game itself but also about English society, customs and *mores*. As students of art history, we trust we may be forgiven for hoping that we have also been able to add something, at various points, to the knowledge and understanding of certain aspects of British art of the eighteenth and nineteenth centuries; and there are a few new attributions. Yet we are deeply aware that in an area of inquiry which has not previously received much systematic attention the chances of error are all the greater.

This book is being published to coincide with an exhibition of cricket art–with the same title, *The Art of Cricket*–to which it can perform the function of a companion as well as a catalogue, although only a selection of the works discussed in the book will be available for the exhibition. The whole project–book and exhibition–has been made possible by the generous support of Imperial Tobacco Ltd, and their subsidiary company John Player. The further interest taken in the project by Mr. Tom Rosenthal, Chairman of Secker & Warburg Limited, and by Mr. Bill Neill-Hall, who has seen the book through the press with extraordinary expedition, has also meant much to us. It would have been impossible to write the book at all without long study of the basic collection of works in the Memorial Gallery at Lord's or without the privilege of access to the M.C.C. archives, generously made available to us by the Curator at Lord's, Mr. Stephen Green, to whom we are indebted for many kindnesses. Our work has carried us far afield–to county grounds, museums and libraries and, not least, to private collections–and we have received so much valuable assistance from so many people that our full list of acknowledgements, being a very long one, must appear separately on another page. But we wish here to take the opportunity of expressing our appreciation of the co-operation of Mr. Andrew McIntosh Patrick, Mr. Richard Green and Dr. Richard Schofield, the Directors respectively of the Fine Art Society Galleries in London, the York Art Gallery and the University Art Gallery at Nottingham–the three galleries where the exhibition is being shown.

If we may indulge in a pleasant reminiscence, it was on a blustery day at Trent Bridge, many years ago, that the authors–then colleagues at the University of Nottingham–first conceived the idea of the exhibition and of the survey of cricket art which was to develop into the present book. We had taken refuge in the Long Room in the Pavilion from the chilly beginnings to another English summer, and we found our attention wandering from the field of play to a painting hanging in a corner of the room–Frank Batson's *Playing out time in an awkward light* (Plate XXIX). It was impossible not to respond to the sentiment that the little-known painter had succeeded in expressing–nostalgic certainly, but not less true on that account to feelings that have doubtless been shared by cricketers and cricket-lovers in every age. And because it was so truthful a representation of cricket, this umpretentious–and very English–painting, hanging obscurely in the corner of a pavilion, seemed to provide a fitting background to our thoughts.

Robin Simon
Alastair Smart
London and Nottingham, February 1983

The Art of Cricket

EARLY PATRONS AND PLAYERS

"What is human life, but a game of cricket?" asked the 3rd Duke of Dorset (Plate 1) in an essay published in 1797. Cricket, uniquely among games, is woven into the fabric of British art as well as life. Its place in literature has often been studied: this book celebrates cricket and the visual arts.

Early forms of bat and ball games appear in medieval manuscript illustrations and in stained-glass windows in Canterbury and Gloucester Cathedrals of the twelfth and fourteenth centuries respectively (Plates I, 2, 3). It is not now possible to disentangle these early games and to identify which of the various threads led separately to trap-ball, pell-mell, golf, croquet or cricket. The distinctive feature of cricket is the hitting with a bat by one person of a ball bowled by another. Bat and ball games of this kind can be identified in these early illustrations. Documented at Guildford by the name of cricket in the sixteenth century, the game is referred to by John Florio in *A Worlde of Words* in 1598, and the number of references increases in the following years. It was with the restoration of Charles II in 1660 that cricket really began to flourish, becoming both widely popular and fashionable. It is no coincidence that racing also "took off" in the Restoration court, and the early passion for gambling on both these exhilarating open-air pursuits was to determine many of modern cricket's distinctive features. Not the least of these is the length of time it takes to play.

Cricket is so fluctuating and delicately balanced a contest that it is often impossible to say at any point which side has an advantage which will prove decisive. This factor was especially significant when large sums of money were placed on the outcome: 1,000 guineas a side was quite common in the eighteenth century. The need to play out the game is therefore apparent. Recourse was frequently had to the law when one side was thought to be evading the issue: the motto was "play or pay", and some games lasted not merely for days but months.[1] The constant composition of each side during the match was also crucial and was fully incorporated into every early agreement and code of laws. A related practice was that of adjusting the odds–handicapping as in racing, in effect. Thus a player would be moved from one side to the other by the patrons: this happened to the great "Lumpy" Stevens (Plate 4) on many occasions, and we find "Hambledon (with Lumpy)" *versus* Kent, or "Kent (with Lumpy) *versus* Hambledon" in 1786, or White Conduit Club "with six given men". A vivid example concerns Lumpy and the 3rd Duke of Dorset in 1774. Kent (the Duke of Dorset's team) lost to Hambledon (with Lumpy) on 13-14 July, and the Duke lost 500 guineas. He made a return challenge for double the money, on condition that Kent had Lumpy this time "and two other men from any part of England, except Hampshire". The match took place the nexth month, on 8-9 August. Not only did Kent win and the Duke more than recover his money, but he showed his determination by scoring 77 (which is apparently his highest recorded score).[2]

Betting was included in the 1774 "Laws of the Noble Game of Cricket", and, curiously enough, cricketers throughout the eighteenth century were referred to as "gamesters".[3] This is a coincidence, for, although so suggestive of compulsive gambling, in this context the term was simply the normal usage, as we would say "players". For our purposes there is a further significance in gambling's importance to cricket. The money and the taste for gambling were largely confined to the aristocracy. Those with money for gambling on racing and cricket were those with the money and the taste for the patronage of artists. Instances of patrons who were equally remarkable for their expenditure on both cricket and the arts can be adduced: the 3rd Duke of Dorset was conspicuous in this respect. He patronized Reynolds, Gainsborough (Plate 1), Opie, Humphry, Hoppner and Romney, as well as filling his house at Knole with sculptures and Old Master paintings. But the coincidence of interests can almost be taken, in the eighteenth century, as axiomatic.[4]

The earliest records suggest that cricket was played casually by the population at large, and games between villages are recorded in the seventeenth century.[5] When it was patronized by the aristocracy and by royalty, from the Restoration onwards, the rise of cricket–in its fashionability, and in its organizational structure–was as great as that of horse-racing. And there are further ramifications here, particularly concerning the democratic character of cricket. Because of the money resting on a horse, the best jockeys came to be used, regardless of class; and there the relationship between owner and jockey began and ended. But cricket, unlike racing, is a team game, and also lasts much longer. Thus, the best batsmen and bowlers were employed to strengthen a team's chances, from whatever station in life they came, and in cricket this custom has always led to a strange alliance of widely different parts of society in the game–fleeting and occasional perhaps, but nonetheless real. The 3rd Duke of Dorset kept, somewhat notoriously, a "stable" of cricketers, as others might keep a string of racehorses: it cost him at least £1,000 a year. But in cricket matches, these men - who were employed on his estates - would play alongside him and against his fellow peers. The scorecard of Kent *v.* Hambledon of 8 - 9 August 1774 reveals the humble names of "Lumpy", the unlovely-sounding "W. Hogsflesh", and "Jas. Fuggles", mingling with some of the great names in the land.[6]

Much of the appeal of cricket lay in the fact that, like racing, it was hard open–air exercise. The key word used to commend it in the eighteenth century is "manly"; and "Hail Cricket! glorious manly British Game!" is the opening line of James Love's poem on the first fully recorded game of cricket (i.e. with a full scorecard), which was played on 18 June 1744 — "Kent against All England."

Cricket could be very hard indeed: the bats were often large and heavy (for example, 5 lbs. 5 oz. is the weight of one of about 1750 which survives at Lord's); they were unspliced and unsprung; and the game could lead to violence and death. Such an outcome was likely even if the laws were obeyed, for deliberate obstruction was written into the Laws of 1744 and 1755:

> When the ball is hit up, either of the Strikers may hinder the catch in his running Ground, or if it is hit directly across the Wickets, the other Player may place his Body anywhere within the Swing of the Bat, so as to hinder the Bowler from catching it; but he must neither strike at it, nor touch it with his Hands.[7]

Accidents would happen in these circumstances:

> John Boots, killed at Newick by running against another man on crossing the wicket. Buried May 14. (1737–Parish Register of Chailey.)[8]

William Waterfall was convicted of manslaughter at Derby Assizes in 1775 for "unlawfully killing George Twigg in a cricket match" and was sentenced to be burnt in the hand and to nine months' imprisonment.[9]

In addition to the rough and tumble of the game itself, trouble was often close at hand, whether or not in conditions exacerbated by the wagering involved. A riot ensued in an Essex *v.* Kent match at Tilbury in 1776 because of an alleged "ringer" in the Kent team. Shots were fired, one Essex player was killed, a sergeant shot dead, and an invalid run through with a bayonet.[10] Deaths followed a quarrel in 1786, on an occasion when money can hardly have been involved, in an impromptu game at Haverhill, Suffolk, between a farmer's servants "playing at cricket".[11]

Even the grandest aristocrats could get caught up in the prevailing tensions. On Monday, 23 August 1731:

> The Duke of Richmond and his Cricket players were greatly insulted by the mob at Richmond, some of the men having the shirts tore off their backs; and 'tis said a law suit will commence about the play.[12]

And some were apparently just as likely to quarrel amongst themselves:

> During the cricket match between the Duke of York and Col. Tarleton [later General Sir Banestre Tarleton] a smart altercation ensued respecting the game, that had nearly put an end to it... The Duke of York fetched 19 from his own bat.[13]

A match between Surrey and Kent on 19 July 1762

> ...was brought to a sudden conclusion owing to a dispute concerning the dismissal of a batsman in the first innings of Surrey. "From words they came to blows, which occasioned several broken heads, as likewise a challenge between two persons of distinction."[14]

The more positive side of things is that at least one notorious quarrel, which had nothing to do with the game, could be healed through cricket. Colonel Charles Lennox, later 4th Duke of Richmond (Plates 5, 7), fought a duel with the Duke of York, on 26 April 1789: they were reconciled a year later at Lord's (Thomas Lord's first ground, in present-day Dorset Square) at the match between the Hambledon Club and England. Incidentally, Charles Lennox was held in such high esteem as a batsman that he and another famous bat, The Hon. Mr. J. Tufton, "had to be put on different sides. If not separated, there is no probability of their being beaten in this kingdom."[15] This Duke of Richmond died as the result of being bitten by a pet fox in Canada, where he is also known to have played cricket. It was his Duchess who gave the famous ball on the eve of Waterloo, and the Duke himself took part in a cricket match played earlier that day.

As the eighteenth century progressed, a strong sense developed of cricket as having been a pure, simple and "manly" game of ancient English tradition, this within a hundred years of the

Restoration period. There has always been a "golden age" to look back to, and this sweaty pursuit, with its tinge of toughness and violence, in the midst of the extreme elegance of manners which characterized eighteenth-century high society, seems to have sounded an appealing note of lost innocence.

Thus, in 1774, betting was felt to have corrupted the game from its pristine form, even though the prevailing popularity of cricket was so much due to its very potential for gambling. As the *Chelmsford Chronicle* reported:

> The game of cricket, which requires the utmost exercise of strength and agility, was followed until of late years for manly exercise, animated by a noble spirit of emulation. This sport has too long been perverted from diversion and innocent pastime to excessive gaming and public dissipation. Cricket matches are now degenerated into business of importance. The increasing evil our magistracy ought to suppress in the Artillery Ground. It is confidently said that a set of idle fellows, or more properly a gang of dextrous gamblers, are hired and maintained by a most noble Lord at so little expense as 1,000 a year.[16]

This last sarcastic stroke was a hit at the 3rd Duke of Dorset; and the so-called "dextrous gamblers" were some of the most famous players of the Hambledon period. More sympathetically, the 3rd Duke of Dorset is commended in 1782 because "his Grace is one of the few noblemen who endeavour to unite the elegances of modern luxury with the more manly sports of the old English times".[17] He was often, however, on the receiving end of attacks from people who thought he should be spending his time more seriously. A particularly sarcastic one came in 1783:

> In the estimation of many people, the Duke of Dorset is the most extraordinary accomplished nobleman we have–at cricket, tennis, and billiards his Grace has hardly any equal.[18]

Nonetheless, in one summary of the position which cricket had achieved by 1789, the main threat, as has so often been the case, was thought to be from the weather. The only threat from the French Revolution, which broke out in that year, had in fact been to the Duke of Dorset's plan to introduce a team to Paris, where he was a somewhat reluctant Ambassador. He had already managed to assuage his passion for the game by commuting from Paris to England for cricket matches. One game was delayed to await his arrival from across the Channel until 22-24 June 1786: this was the Star & Garter or White Conduit Club *versus* Kent: he was back again in August the next year.[19] It was the weather which was really bothersome in 1789:

> Cricket. This game, at present so fashionable, at all times so creditable and manly, will, it is feared, receive a check from the variable state of the weather.. the frequent showers are preventing cricket from being played so often as it otherwise would.[20]

However this may have been, Colonel Charles Lennox scored 136 at Aberdeen as late as 7 October in that very year.

A little earlier, the unattractive Lord Chesterfield injected some characteristically sarcastic sneers about cricket into the famous *Letters to his Son:*

> Though I need not tell one of your age, experience and knowledge of the world [the boy was at

> Westminster School, aged about ten] how necessary good-breeding is to recommend one to mankind; yet, as your various occupations of Greek and cricket, Latin and pitch-farthing, may possibly divert your attention from this object, I take the liberty of reminding you of it.[21]

One of the main reasons why cricket had become so fashionable by this stage was the interest and patronage of the Royal princes. In this, at least, Hanoverian and Stuart blood combined, for several of Charles II's descendants (ducal offspring of his mistresses) were conspicuous players as well as patrons of the game and continued to be court and cricket allies of the Hanoverian princes.[22] The 2nd Duke of Richmond (grandson of Charles II *via* Louise de Kérouaille) was one of the greatest of all early patrons, and the 4th Duke was one of the greatest players.

The 2nd Duke of Richmond, a close associate of George II, was presumably responsible for that monarch's entertainment (while Prince of Wales) of the London and Surrey teams at Hampton Court in 1723 after a match at nearby Molesey Hurst. This move was, no doubt, calculated further to infuriate his estranged father, George I. When Prince George was crowned king in 1727, the Duke of Richmond was High Constable of England for the day. During George II's absences from the kingdom to slake his passion for his Hanoverian mistress Walmoden, Richmond was one of the regent council.

There is a parallel to this position of the Duke of Richmond in the case of George II's own son, Frederick, Prince of Wales; for the cricket-mad Sackvilles, Dukes of Dorset, were key figures in this princely court–a court set up often in open opposition to the King, who had continued the Hanoverian tradition of paternal loathing for his heir. The future 2nd Duke of Dorset, then Earl of Middlesex, was Master of Horse to Frederick: he was also M.P. for East Grinstead, and, as one of the most prominent of cricket patrons, he duly staged cricket matches there. His wife was Mistress of the Robes to Augusta, Princess of Wales. The Sackvilles chose especially well in their alliances, for it was Frederick's eldest son who succeeded in 1760 as George III, and the influential 2nd Duke lived on until 1769. His nephew, the 3rd Duke, was accordingly treated with indulgence, and, despite his reputation as one of the two idlest peers in the realm, was sent as Ambassador to France. An accurate gauge of the 3rd Duke's political acumen is undoubtedly the fact that, at the very moment that the French Revolution was about to sweep Paris, his energies had been directed towards getting a cricket team ready in Dover to embark for France. But these solemn plans were taken by surprise. In mitigation of the Duke of Dorset, it must be said that his detachment from political reality was surpassed by that of the French King, Louis XVI, whose diary for the day in July 1789 when the Revolution broke reads simply "Rien": a just, if inadequate, observation from his point of view, as he had not been able to go hunting.

Both the Lennox and Sackville families carried their passion for cricket from generation to generation. Through their key positions in the princely and royal courts they ensured its inheritance by successive kings and princes who fell under their influence. By far the nicest of these was George III, who also broke with family tradition by loving his children. Thus, in 1770, it is recorded that:

> His majesty has given a silver cup to be played for at cricket on the 20th inst. on Richmond Green, on account of the Princes having been much pleased with a cricket match there on Monday last.[23]

This *tendresse* is all the more poignant because his own father, Frederick, was supposed to have died as a result of playing cricket with George and his other children at Cliveden House, near

Maidenhead. He was struck on the chest by the ball and died a month or so later after collapsing while dancing: an abscess was found to have formed.[24] (This was a sufficiently bizarre death, but was at least more dignified an exit than that of his father, George II - the only English monarch to have died in the privy.) The interest in cricket of George III's young princes continued as they grew up, and both the Prince of Wales (later Prince Regent and George IV) and his brother, the Duke of York, were keen players.

Countless early eighteenth-century cricketers were of great social distinction, and can be identified today in contemporary portraits. These included, in the first half of the century alone, the Dukes of Devonshire, Richmond, and Dorset; the Earls of Albemarle, Sandwich, and Middlesex (son of the lst Duke of Dorset); Lord James Cavendish (son of the Duke of Devonshire), and Lord John Sackville (younger brother of the Earl of Middlesex and father of the 3rd Duke of Dorset). Of the royal family, active participants or patrons included George II, Frederick, Prince of Wales, and the Duke of Cumberland (the "Butcher" of the Forty-Five Rebellion, who was assisted in the campaign which gave him that nickname by the 2nd Duke of Richmond). Baronets and other prominent landowners included Sir William Gage, 7th Baronet, of Sussex (who introduced the greengage, called after him, to England); Mr Edwin Stead, of Kent, whose team played a match in 1733 against the Prince of Wales's team; and the Revd Charles Powlett, who was so prominent in the development of the Hambledon Club. Powlett was the illegitimate son of the Duke of Bolton and Lavinia Fenton (the original Polly Peachum in John Gay's *Beggar's Opera*), having been born before she succeeded in getting the Duke to marry her.

THE FIRST CRICKET PICTURES

Contemporary paintings and prints do not show these early "stars" of the game as cricketers: paintings of cricket matches or of individuals as cricketers only begin to appear from about 1740 onwards. It was at this time, in 1744, that a famous Code of Laws was drawn up, and in that same year also the full recording of the score would appear to have begun. And yet we know that cricket was well established before this date. The reason for the fact that it appeared in art only now is therefore something of a happy coincidence: it was only in the 1740s that the first generation of British professional painters came to maturity.

Until this time, painting in England had been dominated by foreigners – notably Sir Peter Lely (1618-1680), Antonio Verrio (?1639-1707), Sir Godfrey Kneller (1646-1723) and Louis Laguerre (1663-1721). None of these was likely, by temperament or in his usual line of work, to show any interest in cricket. William Hogarth (1697-1764) was the single most important figure in the revolution whereby British artists came to flourish (which was from about 1730 onwards), and it is in the work of the artists of the St Martin's Lane Academy, which Hogarth had furnished and which he helped to run, that we find the first representations of cricket.

It is therefore not so odd, after all, that what is generally agreed to be the first modern representation of cricket should be by a Frenchman, Hubert Gravelot (1699-1773) (Plate 9). Gravelot taught drawing at the artists' academy in St Martin's Lane and was a close associate of Francis Hayman (1708-1776), who taught painting there: Hayman's pictures of cricket in the 1740s are, as we shall see, key works. Close at hand by this academy was the "best shop" of John Boydell, the most successful engraver-publisher of the century. His shop was "at the sign of the Cricket Bat" in Duke's Court, St Martin's Lane. The choice of this symbol, apparently quite unrelated to Boydell's trade, shows how far cricket had become a natural part of eighteenth-century life, and indicates a remarkable enthusiasm for the game at the heart of the artists' community.

Gravelot's little design–for that is all it is–was published on 7 May 1739. It forms part of a series of decorations in his typically French rococo manner. The decorative character of this style is reflected in the fact that Gravelot's cricket design was used on a sugar bowl in a set of contemporary porcelain. Not too much should be made of this engraving as documentary evidence, save that the wicket looks like a two-legged, flat-sided stool of a type familiar in churches of the time and known as a "cricket". In fact, Dr Johnson gives this definition of the word "cricket" in his *Dictionary* of 1755 after defining the game. This eighteenth-century definition of "cricket" as "a low stool" should be noted in the never-ending discussion of the origin of the game, in which the two-legged church stool has sometimes been suggested as the original "target".

Francis Hayman's two known pictures of cricket were far more substantial than Gravelot's design, and, in their engraved form, both paintings were frequently reproduced. However, it must be pointed out that only one authentic painting of cricket by Hayman still exists, the so-called *"Cricket in Marylebone Fields"*, which hangs in the Long Room at Lord's (Plates II, 10). The better-known *"Cricket at the Artillery Ground"* (M.C.C. Memorial Gallery) (Plate 15) is of poor quality, and is clearly a crude version taken from an engraving by Benoist of 4 April 1743 (Plate 14). The original painting from which Benoist's engraving was made used to hang in a supper box at Vauxhall Gardens but is now lost. The other important distinction to make is that this latter picture is of single-wicket cricket (another good view of which is by Thomas Sandby, in a drawing of about 1750).[25] *"Cricket in Marylebone Fields"* (Plates II, 10), on the other hand, is an invaluable record of the proper double-wicket game. As such, it was enormously influential, and, through its frequent reproduction at the head of editions of the Laws, was the model for many later paintings and engravings of cricket matches.

Little significance can be attached to the names by which both these pictures are known. *"Cricket at the Artillery Ground"* (Plate 15) gets its name from the fact that it was reproduced, in its second engraved form, in the *New Universal Magazine* for November 1752, where the Laws of cricket were published. There, the title of the engraving was *The Game At Cricket as Played In The Artillery Ground, London*. The words "as played" suggest that this was just a convenient method of identifying cricket by reference to the most famous site in London where the game might be witnessed. There was probably a stronger connection, however, between the Laws themselves and the Artillery Ground: they are described in the text as those "settled by the CRICKET-CLUB, and play'd at the ARTILLERY-GROUND, LONDON". In fact, the picture had already been reproduced in its first engraved form on 4 April 1743, the engraving being inscribed *F. Hayman Pinxt. Benoist Sculpt. after the Painting in Vauxhall Garden* (Plate 14). There is no suggestion that there is any connection with the Artillery Ground. Underneath this first edition of the engraving is the following verse:

Cricket

To exercise their Limbs, and try their Art
Forth to the verdant Fields the Swains depart:
The buxom Air and chearfull Sport unite
To make Hulse useless by their rough Delight.

Britons, whom Nature has for War design'd
In the soft Charms of Ease no Joy can find:
Averse to wast in Rest th' inviting Day
Toil forms their Game & Labour is their Play.

The odd thing about the use of this engraving in 1752 is that it does not illustrate the game as described in the Laws. As has been pointed out, the picture showed a single wicket form of cricket, and the context in which it was displayed in Vauxhall Gardens, in a dimly lit supper-box, suggests that it was not in any way intended to be a serious illustration of the fully developed contemporary game. The subjects of its companion pieces in the supper-boxes were appropriately frivolous: "the play of hot cockles"; "an old gypsy telling fortunes"; "the cutting of flour" (a Christmas game); "a Northern chief".[26] For a fully informative and accurate representation of a contemporary game in its developed double-wicket form, we must turn to Hayman's surviving painting of a cricket match, known as "*Cricket in Marylebone Fields*" (Plates II, 10).

There would appear to be no particular justification for identifying the scene as taking place in Marylebone Fields. In fact, rather confusingly, it has also been argued that the picture shows the Artillery Ground.[27] Against that suggestion must be held the fact that no wall is depicted, whereas the Artillery Ground had been walled in at a very early date, shortly after the Restoration, and an admission charge of between twopence and sixpence could be levied.[28]

In his classic work on the Laws of Cricket, R.S. Rait Kerr pointed out that "*Cricket in Marylebone Fields*" was used for the illustration of the earliest printed version of the Laws, on a handkerchief in the collection of M.C.C. Rait Kerr dated the handkerchief to about 1744; the same representation was used for a handkerchief on which the Laws were printed in about 1785 (Plate 12), and for later editions of the Laws, for example in 1809 (Plate 13). The Laws had indeed been revised in 1744, and the game of cricket as illustrated in Hayman's picture conforms precisely to that code. A very fine mezzotint by Grignion (Plate 11), published on 16 July 1748, was engraved after Hayman's painting, and the style suggests a date for the painting in the mid-1740s. Another painting of a cricket match, attributed to W.R. Coates and datable about 1743-5, is in the Tate Gallery (Plate VIII, 16), and provides full confirmation of the accuracy of Hayman's representation, as well as adding some further fascinating and specific details.

Hayman's painting shows that cricket had not changed substantially since 1706. In that year we find the earliest detailed description of a game, in a Latin poem by William Goldwin. The key passage of the poem is as follows:

the Lists are set where, (happy chance!)
the meadow yields a smooth expanse;
opposed, on either hand, appear
twin rods that forkéd heads uprear,
with ends set firmly in the green,
(nor wide the middle space between),
and next a milk-white Bail is laid
from fork to fork, whereby is swayed
the dubious issue of the fight,
and all must guard it with their might.
the Leathern Orb speeds forth like fate,
and should its destined line be straight
and raze the bail's support, defeat
ensues and sorrowful retreat.

each at his wicket, near at hand,
propped on his staff, the Umpires stand,
the runner's bat must touch their pale,
or else the run will nought avail.

on a low mound, whence clear the view,

repose a trusty pair and true:
their simple task, with ready blade,
notches to cut, as runs are made.[29]

A comparison of the painting with the poem shows how closely the two descriptions agree. The main features of the game as described in the poem are: the double-wicket; the two umpires; the shape of the wicket; the choice of level-ground; scoring with notches on sticks; and the touching of the umpire's bat to score a run. The mention in the poem of this last detail explains why, in so many early pictures of cricket, each umpire carries a bat and stands close to the wicket at either end (Plates III, IV, VIII, IX, 20). Further confirmation of this system is to be found in the agreement for a game played in 1727 between the 2nd Duke of Richmond and a Mr Broderick:

> Fourteenth. The batt Men for every one they count
> are to touch the umpire's stick.[30]

The question is here raised as to whether the presumed existence in early cricket of a so-called "popping-hole" is a correct explanation of the term "popping-crease". It is quite clear that by 1755, when the laws of cricket were first issued in pamphlet form, a crease had been introduced to measure runs, and it was no longer required that the batsmen should touch the umpire's bat or stick (though the practice whereby umpires held bats, as a sort of badge of office, continued into the nineteenth and twentieth centuries). The 1748 engraving by Grignion after Hayman's *"Cricket in Marylebone Fields"* (Plate 11) clearly delineates a popping crease at each end, as is also the case with the handkerchief dated by Rait Kerr to about 1744. The Laws which are printed as a border to this handkerchief also establish a popping-crease.

There is one main source for the idea that a popping-hole existed: John Nyren, in *The Young Cricketer's Tutor*, published in 1833, which incorporates recollections of Hambledon players and other early cricketers, refers to Mr Ward (the owner of Lord's) as having

> obligingly furnished me with a small manuscript, written some years since by an old cricketer, containing a few hasty recollections and rough hints to players, thrown together without regard to method or order.

He continues:

> From the authority before me, it appears that 150 years since...between the stumps a hole was cut in the ground large enough to contain the ball and the butt end of the bat. In running a notch, the striker was required to put his bat into this hole, instead of the modern practice of touching over the popping-crease. The wicket-keeper, in putting out the striker running, was obliged, when the ball was thrown in, to place it in this hole before the adversary could reach it with his bat. Many severe injuries of the hand were the consequence of this regulation; the present mode of touching the popping-crease was therefore substituted for it.[31]

Rait Kerr developed this idea by suggesting that the word "pop" had to do with the ball's being popped into the hole to run the batsman out.[32] That there had been some nineteenth-century derivation of the term, based on these vague semantic grounds, cannot be doubted. Nonetheless, it would appear that the word "pop" was used in quite a different sense in the eighteenth century, and had nothing to do with a hole to pop anything into.

In the pamphlet edition of the Laws of 1755 the "popping-crease" is defined as the line 3 feet 10 inches in front of the line of the wicket (as had also been the case in the 1744 Laws), and the word "pop" is used only of the bat: "If a striker nips a ball up just before him, he may fall before his wicket, or pop down his bat, before it comes to the wicket, to save it." This usage is supported by the definition of the word "pop" in the *Oxford English Dictionary*: "to strike with a slight rap or tap...to put promptly, suddenly, or unexpectedly; usu. with *down, in, on...*" "Popping", in its intransitive form, could describe the simple act of running: "to pass, move, go or come promptly..."; it could also indicate the crease itself: "a mark made by a slight rapid touch..." Thus the word "pop" could apply to touching "the umpire's stick" with the bat, or touching the bat down behind a line. The *Oxford English Dictionary* , in its derivation of the popping-crease itself, suggests that "popping" is used in the sense of "striking".

None of the pictures we have discussed so far shows any sign of a "popping-hole", and no pictorial representations of it exist which can be dated to the eighteenth century or before. There are a number of paintings which purport to show popping-holes, but they can all be dated to a later period, presumably post-Nyren; they can be viewed as inaccurate antiquarian reconstructions.

In Hayman's painting (Plates II-IV), the stumps are two forked sticks, with a bail resting on the fork and extending a little way beyond the uprights. Other paintings of the time show the same method of construction of the wicket, among them the important portraits of *Sir William Benett of Fareham* by Edward Penny (Plate V), and *Lewis Cage* by Francis Cotes (Plates XVI, 17). In a portrait ascribed to Thomas Hudson of *Walter Hawkesworth Fawkes* (Plate 27), which can be dated about 1760, we may note the two stumps in their most developed form, shortly before they were superseded by the introduction of the third stump in 1776.[33] In this painting the stumps are no longer forked twigs, but are flat in section with notches carved in the top. The three-stump version of this method of manufacture is to be found a little later in the painting of *William Wheateley at the age of fourteen*, of 1786, by Francis Alleyne (Plate VI). The stumps are also flat in Thomas Henwood's memorable portrait of *The Scorer* of 1842 (Plate 98).

In "*Cricket in Marylebone Fields*" Hayman shows how the ground around the stumps has become well-worn at either end, extending into the bowler's run-up (Plates II-IV). There is not a mown pitch, but the "level ground" has been worn where the batsmen have run up and down between the wickets. The cricket dress of specific clubs is indicated, for most of the players wear caps, which are, interestingly enough, rather like jockey's caps. They are dressed in smart breeches and loose white shirts of a type which remain familiar as cricketers' clothing in the eighteenth century.

Almost all the players in Hayman's painting strike particularly elegant poses, of a kind which shows them conforming to current notions of the correct deportment of a gentleman. The position of the feet and of the hands would invariably mark the social class of an individual: a gentlement was expected, for example, to stand with his feet turned outwards, the one foot at right angles to the other, with the hands performing distinct, as well as graceful, gestures. The exceptions here are the figure with hands on hips in the centre foreground, and perhaps the fielder at the extreme left. The centre foreground figure is noticeably scruffy in comparison with the other players: he is dressed in blue breeches, and has one stocking falling down. He wears his own hair, in contrast to the figure at the extreme right, who, wearing neither wig nor cap, has a skull-cap on his shaven head. The rather lumpish posture of this figure in the centre seems to indicate that he is to be distinguished from the gentlemanly players on the rest of the field. It is likely that he is one of the servants who were included in club games because of their special prowess. A further comparison might be made with the player who stands elegantly to his right, and who is dressed in a frilled shirt, with a pink sash around his waist.

Hayman's use of colour in this picture is characteristically refined, and what little marked local colour he employs is ingeniously designed to focus attention on the batsman. The striker wears grey-pink breeches, and to his left is the umpire in a coloured frock-coat. To the right, the centre foreground figure wears dark blue breeches, and to his left is a close fielder, again with grey-pink breeches.

Coates's *Cricket Match* (Plate 16) must be very close in date to Hayman's picture, being datable on grounds of style to about 1740-5. It is of great documentary interest, for, although primitive to a degree in overall conception, it is painstakingly accurate and technically accomplished in its detail. It is surprising that this painting has had such little attention paid to it, for in an attractive way it can tell us much about the game as it was played in the 1740s, which was such a significant decade in the history of cricket.

An important point to make about Coates's painting is that it is derived from an engraving by H. Roberts after L. Boitard, entitled *An Exact Representation of the Game of Cricket & Inscrib'd to all Gentlemen Lovers of that Diversion*, and published in 1743 (Plate 20). This latter print is contemporary with the first engraving after Hayman's lost Vauxhall picture, but it is of far greater interest, since it shows the full double-wicket game. It was this same Boitard print that provided the model for the design of a Match Ticket of 18 June 1744, which still survives (Plate 21). Comparison between Boitard's *Exact Representation* and Hayman's *"Cricket in Marylebone Fields"* reveals, as we should expect, Hayman's greater subtlety and realism: Boitard shows a number of fielders all with their hands raised for a catch, even before the ball has been bowled, which is quite unrealistic. Hayman, on the other hand, depicts a variety of attitudes consonant with the fielders' positions on the field. The sense of urgency in the striker is captured by Hayman only, as also the precise action of the bowler. Nonetheless, Boitard has scrupulously attempted to record the details of the game, and comparison, on the other hand, with Coates's painting reveals the latter to be more static and lifeless.

The scorers in Boitard's engraving are shown comparing the score, notched on their respective sticks. Coates has not fully understood this detail, or perhaps has not noticed it, and as a result has omitted it. Nonetheless, although Coates is a considerably less sophisticated artist, he has added as well as omitted. Some of the figures are individually characterized – the wicket-keeper being a case in point. But the depiction of the construction of the wicket is less satisfactory, and its proportions are not so convincing when we consider the evidence afforded by the Boitard engraving, the match ticket derived from it, and Hayman's *"Cricket in Marylebone Fields"* in both its painted and engraved forms.

In the three closely related representations, the Boitard print, the painting by Coates (Plate IX) and the match ticket, the bowler can be seen "presenting" the ball, which he holds high in his hand immediately before moving into the delivery. A similar but very high pose is visible in the remarkable drawing by George Shepheard of David Harris (Plate 6). This sketch is one of a number by Shepheard in which he captured the characteristic movements of several great players of the end of the eighteenth century (Plate 5). A little later, in Henry Rossi's sculpture of *The Bowler*, carved in 1825, the same bowling stance is adopted (Plate 53). The holding-up of the ball is partly to take aim but also to impart speed to the delivery, and is a method still in use today for a fast attacking ball among certain players of bowls. A slightly different method is shown by Francis Hayman, for in *"Cricket in Marylebone Fields"* the bowler has one hand on his knee and is, we may surmise, about to deliver a rather slower ball (Plate IV).

In early days the ball was rolled along the ground when bowled, as is described in a piece of doggerel which also implies the close relationship between racing and cricket:

> With horses some for glory seek
> And shine away Newmarket week:
> Others for fame erect a wicket
> And roll and strike the ball at cricket.[34]

A variety of deliveries must have been used, but the main development, of bowling "to a length", was the work of "Lumpy" Stevens (Plate 4) and of David Harris (Plate 6), particularly in the 1770s. This naturally led to a swift change in the methods of batsmen, who now had to get to the pitch of the ball. Nyren wrote of Harris:

> In bowling, he never stooped in the least in his delivery, but kept himself upright all the time. His balls were very little beholden to the ground when pitched; it was but a touch, and up again; and woe to the man who did not get into block them, for they had such a peculiar curl that they would grind his fingers against the bat: many a time have I seen blood drawn in this way from a batter who was not up to the trick...It was utterly impossible to remain at the crease when the ball was tossed to a fine length.

"Lumpy", although according to Nyren bowling "the greatest number of length balls in succession", chose to make the ball shoot, forgoing the possibility of catches, for "nothing delighted the old man like bowling a wicket down with a shooting ball".[35]

The Boitard engraving (Plate 20) and the Coates painting (Plate 16) show a roped-off area for play (which was usually known as "the ring"), together with a number of spectators.[36] The scorers, interestingly enough, are well within the "boundary", but the idea of a boundary as such did not exist at this time. The scorers must have had to move out of the way on frequent occasions. It was also usual not even to rope off the playing area at all. The existence of the "ring" suggests that Boitard's engraving is of a highly organized cricket match, and the Match Ticket of 1744 (Plate 21), which is derived from the same view and numbered "113", is probably related to the same ground as that depicted by Boitard. We know that admission was charged at the famous Artillery Ground in Finsbury from Restoration times. The superscription here indicates that the ticket on this occasion cost no less than two shillings and sixpence.

The remarkable survival of this Match Ticket, which was no doubt for a special seat, must be due to the outstanding importance of the game, which was England *v.* Kent, 18 June 1744. On that occasion, Lord John Philip Sackville, younger son of the 1st Duke of Dorset (and father of the 3rd Duke) opened the innings for Kent and, in a low-scoring game, made 5 and 3. The match was the subject of James Love's mock-epic, *Cricket: An Heroic Poem*, and was the playing out of a challenge from Lord John Sackville at which the Prince of Wales, his brother the Duke of Cumberland, the Duke of Richmond, and Admiral "Old Grog" Vernon were present. It is the first match of which a full scorecard survives and it was played at the Artillery Ground. The name "Smith" so prominently displayed in the centre of the card is the same George Smith who sold the Grignion engraving of 1748 (after Hayman) from the Artillery Ground, of which he was the proprietor. There is, therefore, every likelihood that the match ticket and Boitard's engraving show us cricket as it was played at the Artillery Ground.

Smith, the keeper of "The Pyed Horse" in Chiswell Street (the Artillery Ground backs on to this street), was celebrated in heroic couplets in the course of Love's poem, where the poet describes the roping-off of the ground to form "the ring".

> Wide o'er the extended Plain, the circling string
> Restrains th' impatient Throng, and marks a Ring.
> But if encroaching on forbidden ground,
> The heedless crowd o'erleaps the proper Bound,
> Smith plies, with strenuous arm, the smacking Whip.
> Back to the line th' affrighted Rebels skip.[37]

The ground and the public house clearly went together – a situation paralleled today, for example, in the case of crown bowling greens – for Smith was succeeded by one Read, whose death as "master of the Pyed Horse in Chiswell Street and also of the Artillery Ground" was recorded on 25 September, 1766.[38]

The Match Ticket issued by George Smith is a particularly good design. The fielder second from the left in Boitard's engraving has been reversed (Plates 20, 21). This trick aids the balance of the composition, which shows a simplified view of the game suitable for small-scale reproduction. At the foot of the ticket, and framing the word "SMITH", is a witty parody of French-inspired rococo decoration of a type common in the work of Gravelot, Grignion, and Boitard. Curved bats have replaced cornucopias, and baskets of cricket balls take the place usually occupied by piles of fruit.

THE CRICKET PORTRAIT

In view of the fact that it became so fashionable for young men and boys to be depicted holding a cricket bat–a fashion which also started in the 1740s–it is odd that one of the first two or three cricket portraits of an individual, *Sir William Benett of Fareham at the age of twelve*, should show the sitter next to a wicket but without a bat (Plate V). This painting can be attributed to Edward Penny. Penny had been a pupil of Thomas Hudson, by whom several cricketing portraits are known; he went to Italy to study, returning home in 1743. As the costume can be dated about 1740-3, it would seem that the portrait should be dated to the end of 1743 or the beginning of 1744. It is, of course, no surprise that one of the earliest of all individual cricket portraits should be of a sitter from Hampshire, where the game had long been popular.

Unlike so many of the young subjects of cricket portraits, Sir William Benett grew up to occupy a distinguished place in the contemporary game. In 1778, he became Steward of the Hambledon Club (Hambledon being not far away from his native Fareham), and, in 1786, President. He first appears in the Club accounts in 1777, but had obviously been a member beforehand, and probably for some time; the relevant minute of that year records that "Sir Wm. Benett and Mr Garnier be desired to accept the Office of Stewards for the ensuing year". He subscribed his three guineas a year faithfully until 1796, and invariably headed the list of "gentlemen subscribers" from 1791 onwards.[39] Benett was at one time Sheriff of Hampshire, and was knighted in 1760. It would appear that at this early stage in his life he was already closely involved with the game, and no doubt this picture celebrates some specific incident, the meaning of which, however, is now obscure.

Benett is not in cricket clothes, for he has his top-coat on and holds his tricorn hat under his left arm, while his collar is fully done up. He stands in the classic pose of a gentleman, with the feet placed elegantly at right-angles and the hands pleasingly differentiated by their varied attitudes. In his right hand he holds a prominent red kerchief, and seems to be holding it in direct relationship to the wicket below. A figure in the background climbs a fence towards us, and has dropped a red bundle on the ground similar in colour to the kerchief held by Benett. In the background we see a church with a spire, and a cottage with a figure in the doorway, before which there appears to be a stream. It is fitting that this lifelong, assiduous and faithful supporter of the game should now be identifiable in such a lovely painting, when his name has been so long forgotten.

There appear to be no other eighteenth-century portraits of individuals with a wicket alone:

the sitters invariably carry bats if a wicket is shown, and there is usually a ball alongside. It is only with the portraits of umpires which begin to appear in the nineteenth century that we see the former combination again. It is noteworthy that in Penny's portrait the wicket is pitched on as level a piece of ground as could be found, but it appears to have a slope immediately behind it. In this respect the picture is likely to be perfectly accurate, and Windmill Down at Hambledon forced such an arrangement on the players. In Benett's day it was the right of "the party going from home" to pitch the wicket anywhere within thirty yards of a spot designated by the umpires, an opportunity notoriously exploited by "Lumpy" Stevens, who used to choose a place where the ball would shoot. The painting is of the highest quality, and its exquisite execution suggests that we may trust it in detail. It is one of the very earliest painted representations of a wicket to have survived, and the wicket is of the type constructed from two forked twigs with another laid across as a bail. The wicket is not very high, but even in the 1744 Laws the height of the stumps was only twenty-two inches. Other pictures of the time show noticeably low wickets, for example a drawing of *The Free School at Maidstone* in a sketch-book by William Jefferys (Plate 22), datable about 1750, and a water colour by James Miller of *Carmalt School, Putney* (Plate 23) of about 1780.

Individual cricket portraits with bats begin to appear in the same decade. A painting by Robert Scaddon of *William Rice* (Plate 18) dates from 1744, but is curiously awkward in comparison with an anonymous portrait of *A Boy of the Lansdowne Family* (Plate 19) which is datable to about the same time. Each sitter holds a cricket bat, and each is fashionably, even richly, dressed. The game was considered "manly" and appropriate to portraits of young men, and the cricket bat lent itself particularly well to acting as a prop in the theatrical sense. But sometimes it is used as a prop to hold someone up, allowing the sitter to strike an elegant cross-legged pose. The bats chosen for these early single portraits are remarkably large in relation to the sitter, and we continue to find boys portrayed with bats reaching above their waists, and even up to their armpits – as, for example, in Wright of Derby's portrait of *The Wood Children* of 1789 (Plate X).

Certainly, eighteenth-century bats could be very big (Fig. 1), and even if they did not always reach the 5 lbs. 5 oz. of the one in the M.C.C. Collection from this time (*c.* 1750), they regularly weighed over 4 lbs., as is clear from a letter written to Fanny Burney (Mrs d'Arblay) on 6 June 1773:

> Mrs Rishton begs Miss Burney to Buy Mr Rishton two cricket batts made by Pett, of 7 Oaks [i.e., where the 3rd Duke of Dorset maintained his great Sevenoaks Vine ground]. You will get them at any of the great toy shops, the maker's names always stamp'd upon them. Ask for the very best sort, which cost 4s. or 4s. 6d. each. Let them weigh 4 oz. [i.e. 4 lbs.] and a quarter, or 4 oz. and half each. Send them by the Exeter post coach.[40]

It may well be that their great weight was one of the reasons that bats were carried on the shoulder, as is shown in Thomas Hudson's several portraits of boys with bats (Plates 24-27). This habit was also customary during the game itself in the case of the non-striker, to judge from Boitard's *Exact Representation* and the painting by W.R. Coates (Plates 20, IX). Nonetheless, bats also came in smaller sizes for men. Children's sizes, too, were available, as we can see from Wright of Derby's *Wood Children* , where both sizes of bat appear simultaneously (Plate X). In John Morgan's painting of 1869 (Plate XXVI) the young cricketers who approach the scene of a fight between two other boys still hold their bats on their shoulders; but long before the date of this picture the excessively heavy implements of former days had of course ceased to be made.

While it was proper and "manly" for a boy to be portrayed with a bat, as a dashing officer might be represented with a sword, or an imperious field-marshal with a baton, a ball was usually considered more appropriate for a girl, as we find in such group-portraits as Wright of Derby's *Wood Children*, which we have just been considering, and Thomas Beach's *Children of Sir John William de la Pole* (Plate 28).

The Lansdowne Boy (Plate 19) is a particularly elegant picture, and gives a rather better idea than Scaddon's portrait of *William Rice* (Plate 18) of the rules governing correct "gentlemanly" posture. To appreciate the significance of the boy's graceful attitude–and indeed of similar poses in many other such pictures of the period–we must bear in mind the importance attached in the eighteenth century to correct deportment. The peasantry and other members of the lower classes might hunch their backs or stand inelegantly with their feet parallel to one another, but a gentleman was supposed to stand erect with arched back and with his feet turned outwards to make a right-angle. Instructions on how artists should distinguish the manners of the different classes were given at length in Gérard de Lairesse's influential *Art of Painting in All its Branches*, first published in Amsterdam in 1707 and in London in 1738; and Nivelon's *Rudiments of Genteel Behavior*, which addressed itself to polite society in general, appeared in 1737.[41] Both these works contained engraved illustrations, in the latter case by L.P. Boitard after Bartholomew Dandridge (Fig. 2). One has only to turn to Lord Chesterfield's letters to appreciate how seriously the members of high society regarded such matters. As Nivelon explained, his purpose was to provide "an introduction to the method of attaining a graceful attitude, an agreeable motion, an easy air, and a genteel behaviour"; and eighteenth-century portraiture reflects the same ideal. In *The Lansdowne Boy*, accordingly, the young cricketer stands with his feet correctly at right-angles, so that one foot is advanced (Plate 19).

Indeed, this pose, originating in the rules of eighteenth-century deportment, seems to have exerted a long-lasting influence upon the stance adopted by the striker at the wicket as he waited to receive the ball; and it was evidently still being used – by A.C. MacLaren, for example – well into the twentieth century (Fig. 3). The same stance can be identified very early on in the paintings of the 1740s by Coates and Hayman, where it is also adopted by the non-striker, by fielders and by the umpires (Plates III, IV, VIII, IX). It can be traced continuously through the later eighteenth century and much of the nineteenth century in a variety of paintings, drawings, prints and photographs: we see it, for instance, in Henry Walton's *Cricket Scene at Harrow School* (Plate 30) and in Watts's illustrations of correct batsmanship; and it is still present in Stuart Wortley's famous full-length portrait of W.G. Grace at the wicket (Plate XXV). When cricket was growing up in the fashionable clubs of eighteenth-century England, to have had one's feet parallel at the batting crease (as is recommended today) would have been to commit a social solecism, and to indicate one's essentially peasant nature. The placing by an umpire of one hand inside his coat or vest, which we also see in some of the early cricket pictures, conformed no less to Nivelon's instructions concerning elegant deportment (Plates III, 20); and when this attitude appears in eighteenth-century portraits, as it frequently does, we should not fall into the common error of assuming that it was chosen by the artist as a means of avoiding the difficulty of painting a hand.

Scaddon's portrait of *William Rice* (Plate 18) shows a game of cricket in progress in the background. The Late Baroque props which surround the boy give way to a view of the exercise he may be about to take. Even the *Lansdowne Boy* (Plate 19) is nearly in the open air, although the arrangement is, to be sure, more a matter of studio convention, complete with marble urn. No such hints of the open air exist in Thomas Hudson's painting, of about 1757-8, of *Mrs Matthew*

Michell and her two children (Plate 26). Hudson's portrait group is set in the grand interior of a house, and the painting demonstrates to a remarkable degree how fully cricket had become absorbed into the everyday life of upper-class English families.

Thomas Hudson, for a time the most successful portrait painter of his day, seems to have been particularly sympathetic to cricket. Even within the close-knit artistic community, the relationships of some of the artists who portray cricket are especially striking. Hudson was a close associate of Francis Hayman; he taught Wright of Derby, and also J.H. Mortimer, a keen player,[42] who in turn was the pupil of Robert Edge Pine. Hudson introduced cricket into the very grandest of his commissions, the vast *Family of the 3rd Duke of Marlborough*, of about 1753-5, designed for Blenheim Palace.

Hudson's preliminary sketch in oils for *The Marlborough Family* has also come down to us (Plate 24); and both in the sketch and in the final painting the two boys at the left are about to go out and play cricket. The older boy holds a ball and a bat, the other only a bat; the former carries the bat on his shoulder; and both are dressed in identical rig to that of Matthew Michell in Hudson's group-portrait of the Michell family (Plate 26).[43]

Despite the fact that the finished version of *The Marlborough Family* is on such a large scale, its conception is that of a "conversation piece" – a term used for rather informal, small-scale group portraits. And in the following decades cricket was frequently introduced into group portraiture of this kind, lending an appropriately informal touch. Even when the pictures were on the scale of life, as in Thomas Beach's painting of *The Tyndall Family* (Plate 29), cricket could play a prominent part in striking the right emotional note. More strictly typical of the "conversation piece" are *The Children of George Bond of Ditchleys* (Plates XII, 33), painted in 1768 by Hugh Barron, and *The Sondes Children* by Johan Zoffany painted a few years earlier (Plate XI) – two of the most enchanting of all works in this genre.

As he painted this picture at the age of twenty-one, Barron must have been as precociously accomplished an artist as he was a violinist: as a musician he was a child prodigy, and later largely abandoned painting for music and travel. Despite being one of Sir Joshua Reynolds's most gifted pupils, he was altogether a "gentleman" rather than a "player" – except in the strictly musical sense. Barron finished comparatively few paintings, and it is notable that there is at least one other cricket portrait attributed to him, of *Edmund Butler and his son* (Plate 32). Perhaps Barron shared a love of playing both cricket and the fiddle with his contemporary, John Small of Hambledon, who was presented with a violin by the 3rd Duke of Dorset on 22 May 1775 after batting to win a match.

Although the setting is within in a part of the early home of cricket, which had long flourished in the South Weald, we must assume that the children in Barron's painting are finding it difficult to find a suitable pitch. The two-stump wicket has been erected on a particularly uneven piece of ground. Nonetheless, the game is not yet in progress, as the boy on the right is merely throwing the ball to his brother, who, having taken off his hat, which lies under the bat to the left, is kneeling in the centre. The centre figure is indicating where the ball is so that the game can start: he is ready to bat, and his brother has just set the wicket up. This interpretation is confirmed by the similarity of the centre pair to the boys in Wright of Derby's portrait of *The Thornhill Children* (Plate 31), where the boy kneeling is in the very act of positioning the bail. In Barron's painting the game may therefore be about to commence to the left-hand side. The girls in this altogether charming picture are associated, as so often in these eighteenth-century groups, with flowers.

At this time, of course, George III had not yet presided (if that is the word) over the loss of the American colonies, and cricket was enjoyed and understood on both sides of the Atlantic. One of the most unusual portrait groups, *The Cricketers*, painted in 1763, five years earlier than Barron's *Bond Children*, is by an artist from Pennsylvania, Benjamin West, P.R.A. (1738-1820), and shows five young Americans (Plate 34).

West left America for good in 1760, and it was shortly before he painted this picture that he had come to London from Italy and decided to remain. The young Americans of West's picture were completing their education in this country, but both they and West would have come across cricket beforehand. The same is true of West's fellow-American John Singleton Copley, who also came to this country, and, while here, painted *Richard Heber as a boy with bat and ball* in about 1783 (Plate 44).

Pennsylvania—with Philadelphia pre-eminent—has the strongest cricket tradition of all American States. The game is shown in a number of paintings - notably in John Wollaston's portrait of *Warner and Rebecca Lewis*, of about 1760 - as well as in prints and drawings throughout the eighteenth and nineteenth centuries in Pennsylvania, and also in other New England States such as Virginia. Haverford College, Pennsylvania, where the C.C. Morris Cricket Library is flourishing today, makes an early appearance, but the first mention of cricket in America is to its being played in Virginia as early as 1709-10.[44] As is better known, the oldest recorded international match is that between America and Canada in 1844.[45] It was perhaps because of the unusual survival of Philadelphian cricket, which was particularly strong at the end of the nineteenth century, that Eadweard Muybridge, the pioneer of photography, included cricket in his first sequences of moving pictures. Muybridge's main interest was in studying movements of the body, and so he apparently found it quite natural to show his University of Pennsylvania volunteer dressed in nothing at all for either batting or bowling.[46] At least one of the several different methods of early cricket ball construction appears to be preserved in the modern baseball. The same pattern is impressed on the surface of the modern lawn-tennis ball, and this S-curved system of stitching appears on a cricket-ball in one of the loveliest of all cricket portraits, that by Daniel Gardner of *Frederick Francis Baker* (Plate XIV), which was perhaps painted in 1778.[47] Near the boy on the bank is a small curved bat, and under his arm he has a folio – one of many instances in which artists show books and cricket together in close conjunction, no doubt illustrating the theme *mens sana in corpore sano* (Plates 33, 54). In this case, the suggestion of intellectual as well as athletic resource was to be amply fulfilled, for Frederick, later Sir Frederick Baker, son of George III's physician, the 1st Baronet, became a Fellow of the Royal Society. He was killed in tragic circumstances, being decapitated by a windmill while out riding with his children.

A portrait of a far more robust child, who seems to have lacked the delicate blue-eyed charm of the young Baker so brilliantly evoked by Gardner, the *Revd John H. Chandler as a Boy*, painted in 1767 by John Russell, shows clearly that the red cricket ball with the hemisphere seam was then being made. In 1793, Thomas Beach depicted a cricket ball of the modern type in his portrait group *The Children of Sir John de la Pole* (Plates XIII, 28). Indeed, in W.R. Coates's painting of a cricket match (of about 1740-5), the bowler already holds a conspicuously bright red ball aloft (Plate IX). Cricket balls were not, however, always dyed red at this time. The one shown in Gardner's portrait of Frederick Francis Baker is not (Plate XV); nor is the more conventionally stitched ball shown in Francis Alleyne's portrait of *John Call with Bat and Ball* of 1784 (Plate 37).

The artist and diarist Joseph Farington, indefatigable recorder of bits and pieces, noted in his journal in 1811 that the Duke family in Kent had then been making cricket balls for 250 years. If true, this is a remarkable fact, and takes us back to about 1560, the period of the earliest record of cricket, at which time it is known to have been played at Guildford. Duke manufactured a six-seamed ball of the modern type, with raised hemisphere seam, in 1780, and presented one to the Prince of Wales (later Prince Regent and George IV), that great swimmer and cricketer. As a newspaper of the time reported:

> The two prevailing amusements of the Prince of Wales at Brighton are swimming in the sea and cricket; in both of which H.R.H. is said to excel.[48]

If the Duke family were in the forefront of cricket-ball manufacture, other constructions than theirs were clearly possible. In an early portrayal of a lady cricketer, John Collet's engraving of *Miss Wicket and Miss Trigger* of 1778 (Plate 90), the ball is seen to have two double seams crossing at right angles. Miss Trigger sternly treads underfoot a pamphlet entitled "effeminacy", and underneath is the following doggerel:

> Miss Trigger you see is an excellent shot,
> And forty-five notches Miss Wicket's just got.

The quasi-feminist note struck here was humorously, but sympathetically, repeated by John Collet in what amounts to a series of related paintings (of rather rough quality) and in mezzotints derived from them. Thus we have *The Female Foxhunter* (Bearsted Collection, Upton House), *Miss Tippapin* (playing skittles) and so on. The slightly risqué *Summer* (Bearsted Collection) has a link with cricket, for there is a sign to "White Conduit F[ields]" – by now a famous cricket ground in London – visible on the right, leading away from the more dubious preoccupations of these particular young women (one of whom is looking through a telescope at a muscle-bound labourer). There is a more concealed joke in *Miss Wicket and Miss Trigger*, for Miss Wicket is shown in a cross-legged pose – leaning on her bat – of a kind unthinkable for eighteenth-century ladies but common in portraits of men. A good comparison is provided by David Martin's portrait of *John Campbell of South Hall*, painted in 1771 (Plate 38): the male portrait with a cricket bat was becoming enough of a *cliché* to be parodied.

Women played cricket in the eighteenth century as a matter of course. As early as 26 June 1745, the *Reading Mercury* noted:

> The greatest cricket match that was ever played in the South part of England was on...Gosden Common, near Guildford, in Surrey, between eleven maids of Bromley and eleven maids of Hambledon, dressed all in white...The girls bowled, batted and catched as well as most men can in that game.

There are many other records of women's cricket. Elizabeth Anne Burrell was top-scorer in one match in 1777, and found that the Duke of Hamilton was inspired with love for her. Alas, they were separated after a fairly short married life: it was evidently not such a good match after all. Her brother was Sir Peter Burrell, a prominent member, like the Duke, of the Star and Garter Club in Pall Mall, the club which had been chiefly responsible for drawing up the Laws of Cricket in 1755.

The 3rd Duke of Dorset (Plate 1) encouraged the ladies of his circle to play cricket. In his essay of 1797, which includes that memorable rhetorical question, "What is human life but a game of cricket?", he continues: "And if this be so, why should not the ladies play it as well as we?"[49]

There is a persistent legend that his ravishing mistress, Giovanna Baccelli, ran him out at cricket and was dismissed from his keeping. This is a difficult story to track down. At the date usually given, 1754, even allowing for precocity in a famous connoisseur of female beauty, it should be pointed out that the Duke was only a boy of nine. Nor was *la Baccelli* in England at that date; nor did she leave the Duke until 1789, just before he made a respectable dynastic marriage. (She had been with him since 1779 at least.) Her naked body (in plaster by Locatelli) still lies curled at the foot of a staircase in the Sackville family home at Knole. The Duke had her painted by Gainsborough (Fig.4) and, more decorously, by Reynolds.

In Gainsborough's famous portrait, Giovanna Baccelli displays a vivacity which would have helped on the cricket field, and it seems certain that she played the game, as did most of the other ladies of the Duke's jolly *ménage* at Knole. A fellow-peer made a waggish remark which seems to indicate that part of Baccelli's way to the Duke of Dorset's heart lay in her readiness to play cricket: "The Duke would have batted till Baccelli ran him out." It may well have been this observation that gave rise to the story that she had run him out in actual fact. Certainly, her son by the Duke, who was given the same names as his father, was being trained as a cricketer before the age of ten. In 1788 the Knole accounts concerning *la Baccelli* show a payment for "Batts and Stumps – 0.8.6."[50] There were enough professional cricketers employed at Knole to give the boy a lot of coaching. Not the least of them, by this time, was presumably the great "Lumpy" Stevens, whose portrait the 3rd Duke had commissioned in 1783 from an artist named Almond, a portrait which, along with those of other servants of the Duke, still hangs at Knole today (Plate 4). The old inscription on the back of the painting identifies his occupation as "the famous player at cricket", and Lumpy must therefore have a claim to be the first professional cricketer recorded solely in that capacity.[51]

Other artists showed women playing cricket, among them Thomas Rowlandson, who took the opportunity for some mild scurrility in his drawing of *Rural Sports, or a Cricket Match Extraordinary,* of 1811 (Plate 91). An odd feature of Rowlandson's drawing is that it shows two stumps, even though this arrangement had been abandoned in top-flight cricket in favour of three by 1776-7. It seems that, especially in its more rural or rustic context, cricket was thought of as a game of two stumps, played with curved bats, for at least a generation after these fashions had changed. Three stumps and straight bats were introduced in the late 1770s in Hambledon and London circles. But in genre portrayals of humorous or rustic scenes the older forms were used for a long time. Richard Barrett Davis was an accomplished sporting artist, but as late as 1827 he showed country children using a curved bat (Plate 40). No doubt these weapons did survive, and there are famous instances of a single bat being treasured, and used, for a lifetime among cricketers of this period. It is certain that comparatively soon after these changes had been made at the centre of things, the old methods continued in provincial areas. One of Rowlandson's cronies, John Nixon, depicted single-wicket cricket at Harwich in 1784 with an "old" wicket (Plate 41).

To an extent, the standardization of cricket equipment was in its infancy. But all the laws made attemps at it, and at the highest level considerable uniformity was undoubtedly achieved. In this respect, M.C.C., founded in 1787, can be seen as the last in a series of major clubs which had taken the lead in the matter of rules governing the game and the equipment with which it should be played. In 1744 the London Club at the Artillery Ground was probably in a dominant position concerning these matters; in 1755, the Star and Garter Club in Pall Mall had taken over the same role, while the White Conduit Club at Islington (Plates 56, 57) became increasingly fashionable until some of its members founded M.C.C. From 1755 until 1787 the crucial innovations, which by now were largely confined to adjustments in equipment in line with vast technical advances in batting and bowling, were made at the Hambledon Club. John Small forms a real and symbolic link between the two eras: he was a star of the Hambledon Club (where he had his workshop) and made the new equipment as it evolved. His shop-sign carried the legend:

Here lives John Small
Makes bat and ball,
Pitch a wicket, play at cricket
With any man in England.

When he died, he handed on his tools and knowledge to Robert Dark of Lord's.

The three main innovations during the Hambledon period were the regulation of the size of the bat to 4¼ inches wide in 1771; the introduction of "length" bowling and the development of the straight bat from the curved in the 1770s; and the introduction of the third stump in 1776.[52] Much wonder and mystery–and rightly–surround the story of Hambledon, although some of this arises from confusion about the Hambledon Club's precise character. Although many in the club team were Hampshire players (and part-time professionals), few were Hambledon villagers as such. The members of the Hambledon Club were elected and were exclusively "gentlemen"; the players were paid by the club members for practising and playing.[53] The use of the term "Hambledon *versus* All-England" ought not to be understood as indicating a tiny village taking on an England team: Hambledon was a club run by many of the most influential patrons who employed the best players; "All-England" was a term used to indicate a team chosen by the opposing punter from players anywhere else in England—as we would say "The Rest". The precise attitude of the grandees who ran the Hambledon Club is aptly summed up by the pointed outrage of the Revd Charles Powlett on the occasion of an unexpected defeat: "Here have I been thirty years raising our Club, and are we to be beaten by a single parish?" Hambledon was not, in the world of cricket, "a single parish", although there was, nevertheless, a real sense of the team as the county team of Hampshire.[54]

The proceedings of the club can easily be studied in *The Hambledon Chronicle*, and the continuity in the changes whereby the primacy passed from Hambledon to M.C.C. is well represented by the fact that the chief founder of M.C.C. in 1787 was the Earl of Winchilsea, who in that year was President of the Hambledon Club. He had also been, up to that point, a member of the White Conduit Club. It appears that the spirit of innovation was strong in him, for in 1797 he decided to introduce a fourth stump and raise the wicket by two inches. This attempt to shorten the game "by easier bowling out" was mercifully short-lived.[55]

The great Hambledon era thus looked forward to modern times. But it also looked back, as the very reason for the spectacular growth of this rather remote club must have been its position in the heartland of much early cricket. Certainly Slindon, early object of the cricket patronage of the 2nd Duke of Richmond, was not far away (Goodwood, home of the Richmonds, is nearby). And a happy relationship grew up in the next generation of Richmonds and Sackvilles, as between Hambledon (or Hampshire) and Kent (the Duke of Dorset). The Hon. Charles Lennox, later 4th Duke of Richmond (Plate 7), was a member of Hambledon; the 3rd Duke of Dorset (Plate 1) was apparently not, and yet he was entitled to have Hambledon players in his teams, if they were free from Club commitments. The same compliment was extended to that other great patron, Sir Horatio Mann. In fact, the move to Windmill Down from Broadhalfpenny Down was made at the request of the 3rd Duke of Dorset and "other gentlemen who complained of the bleakness of the latter".[56]

When we look back over the period up to the founding of M.C.C., it is not surprising to find that two of the earlier portraits we have considered were from Hampshire, those of *The Lansdowne Boy* (Plate 19) and of *Sir William Benett of Fareham* (Plate V). The early pictures of cricket matches from the same time are identified with London, and all these first paintings therefore represent the polarities of early organized cricket, evenly poised between the counties of Hampshire, Sussex and Kent on the one hand, with their individual patrons, and the London clubs on the other. Paintings, drawings and prints of cricket then multiply so rapidly that we can obtain an accurate picture of its fashionable spread through "society" and through the country. When David Allan painted *The Cathcart Family* in 1784 (Plate 42), cricket was already established in Scotland.

This painting has sometimes been known as "The First Cricket Match in Scotland", an assertion for which there is little justification. Nonetheless, it was clearly an important occasion: there was a glass engraved with the same scene, and a papier mâché tray decorated with it. Furthermore, although the picture clearly falls into the type of "conversation piece" which we have noticed before, here cricket is not an adjunct, but the main subject of the picture, which thus approaches the kind of genre subject so beloved of painters of a later age. The rather elusive compliment to Allan, that he was the "Scottish Hogarth", also seems fitting in this instance.

The Cathcart Family has a wealth of precise detail. Here David Allan's reputation for "accurate recording of the contemporary scene" and "the sincerity of his observant eye" is not only a compliment but seems amply justified.[57] The moment captured in the foreground (while the match continues in the background) will be familiar to any cricketer. The man on the right has clearly just been out: he sits rather dejectedly on his coat; his bat lies where he has thrown it down, and he has been mopping his face. His friend opposite points to his score on the stick in which the notches have been cut. At this inopportune moment, in a way typical of children, a little boy holds out a ball for the vanquished and rather tired-looking batsman to bowl. Incidentally, the child is holding a thin, rather flimsy bat. It is not clear precisely what game is indicated, but this type of bat is frequently represented in eighteenth-century paintings. In 1749, *The Andrews Family* by the Revd J. Wills (Plate 43) shows two such bats, the size and weight of which can be accurately gauged from that held by the boy at the right. Towards the end of the century *The Masters Foster* by H.P. Danloux shows the same type of bat again. The ball is smaller than a cricket ball in these examples, as it is in *The Cathcart Family*. A solitary pursuit such as golf or pell-mell is surely not indicated, for the Cathcart child is holding the ball out for some one else to bowl.

Other technical details shown in *The Cathcart Family* are of interest. The cricket bats themselves are straight and therefore very up-to-date for 1784. They are noticeably thick, in comparison with the modern bat with its tapered edges. Pictures of the same period show a number of thick bats of this kind: that in the portrait of Lord Hay (Plate XVII) (also painted in Scotland) is a good example. The close relationship of this type of bat to its chunky, curved predecessor is thus apparent. Sometimes one shoulder remained higher than the other – reflecting the earlier curve of the blade – and such bats are preserved in the M.C.C. collection. An example of a "bow-shaped" bat, a short-lived variant of this development, also survives at Lord's; examples can be seen in the painting by Thomas Beach of *The Children of Sir John de la Pole* of 1793 (Plate 28). We can tell that Beach took care to depict these bats accurately, for in another, even larger, portrait group, *The Tyndall Family* of 1797 (Plate 29), he shows a bat with a straight blade (in addition to a cricket ball with a modern seam).

Both paintings by Beach are of West Country families: Beach lived in Bath, and usually made a tour of country houses in the summer. Cricket was becoming widely spread, but it must have been long familiar in the West Country before the date of the first of Beach's paintings, just as it was in Scotland well before Allan's *Cathcart Family* of 1784.

Cricket seems to have been known in Scotland by the early eighteenth century,[58] and shortly after the Battle of Culloden the Duke of Cumberland's troops played a game of ball on the Inch at Perth which is likely to have been cricket: as the game took place on the Sabbath it elicited much the same adverse comment as another game of "ball" observed on a Sunday by the Scottish diarist Margaret Calderwood of Polton.[59] The Inch at Perth was to become one of the principal homes of cricket in Scotland, along with the Grange Club in Edinburgh and the West of Scotland Club at Glasgow, and it has remained so to this day. As early as October 1789, Charles Lennox (Plate 7), himself a Scot born in Scotland, is recorded as playing in a match at Aberdeen, on which occasion he scored a century. (The playing of cricket as late in the year as October does not appear to have been unusual in this period.) But an indication of the extent to which cricket had already taken hold in Scotland well before this date is provided not so much by documentary as by visual evidence, in the form of the portrait of *John Campbell of South Hall* painted in 1771 by the Scottish artist David Martin (Plate 38).

In this portrait John Campbell adopts a cross-legged pose common in fashionable portraiture of the eighteenth century – for instance in the work of Hudson, Ramsay, Reynolds, Cotes, Gainsborough and Wright of Derby – and it is also to be found, for example, in Giovanni Batista Guelfi's *Craggs Monument* in Westminster Abbey. One such example is provided by the portrayal of the Duke of Marlborough in Hudson's great family group at Blenheim (see Plate 24). This pose derives ultimately from classical antiquity, and eighteenth-century artists would have found two prime examples of it in the figure of *Mercury* in the Uffizi in Florence (Fig. 5) and in a marble figure of a *Faun with Pipes* now in the Louvre but formerly in the Villa Borghese in Rome.[60] In both these statues the crossed legs – one supporting the body and the other bent at the knee so that the toes rest lightly on the ground – are models of gracefulness, and it is understandable that the attitude should have made so strong an appeal in an age of elegance. The first British painter of the period to have adapted it to a full-length portrait was probably Allan Ramsay[61] (who, it may be noted, was David Martin's master).

In Wright of Derby's *Wood Children* (Plate X) one of the two cricketing boys is portrayed with his legs crossed in this manner. The boy also holds his bat under his right armpit, and there seems to be little doubt that a further classical allusion is present here; for no eighteenth-century artist could have conceived or represented such an attitude without calling to mind the ancient sculptures of Hercules leaning on his club, of which the *Farnese Hercules* (Fig. 6) was the best known.[62] In view of the often massive bats displayed by their youthful owners in such pictures, the source was not inappropriate, and even in a portrait of a boy a playful reference to the herculean strength that might be required in the manly game of cricket would have been appreciated as a pleasing form of "wit".

Another feature of David Martin's picture (Plate 38) deserves attention. The young John Campbell is scarcely dressed for cricket, for he wears a seventeenth-century costume reminiscent of portraits by Van Dyck: the pose suggests in particular a derivation from a portrait by Van Dyck of Charles II when Prince of Wales. Here again we touch upon a fashion much favoured by eighteenth-century society (especially from the early 1740s), whereby sitters chose to be represented in "Van Dyck costume".[63] Evidently such costumes were often worn at masques, whether by ladies or by their escorts, and when they were introduced into a portrait they had the added value of giving the picture a prestigious "look" of a Van Dyck, that is to say of the highest class of portraiture. It is not, therefore, to be imagined that the young John Campbell ever dreamt of playing cricket in such attire, which is rather to be understood as an attribute of his family's social status or aspirations. We may observe finally of this portrait that it takes its place within a still further tradition. By the second half of the eighteenth century full-length portraits of children were increasingly given an open-air, landscape setting, a notable and evidently influential example being Allan Ramsay's *John, Lord Mountstuart* of 1759;[64] and it is to the same tradition that Gainsborough's famous *Blue Boy* belongs. Such a convention was naturally suited to portraits of boy cricketers, such as is exemplified by Francis Cotes's masterly painting of *Lewis Cage* (Plate XVI).

In Cotes's portrait of *Lewis Cage*, of 1768, which was one of the works shown in the first-ever exhibition of the newly founded Royal Academy in 1769, the landscape is now wholly uncluttered by those late-Baroque props of an urn or a pillar which "dignify" so many earlier portraits set in the open air. The sky is clouding over, the sun is setting (as so often in paintings of cricket subjects), and the whole feeling looks forward to the more Romantic portraiture of the end of the century. A fascinating example of this new, more relaxed mode is a painting by Robert Edge Pine of *The Revd Robert Waugh as a boy*, of about 1777 (Plate 39). The sitter's figure is animated by a graceful rhythmic movement perhaps inspired by the *Apollo Belvedere* in Rome (Fig. 7), a classical statue which represented, in eighteenth-century eyes, the epitome of male perfection. The picture is endowed, besides, with a rococo grace worthy of Hogarth's famous "Line of Beauty".

A more definite example of the adaptation of the *Apollo Belvedere* (Fig. 7) to eighteenth-century cricket portraiture is to be found in Hudson's imposing portrait group of *The Marlborough Family* (see Plate 24), evidently painted in the early 1750s, in which the attitudes of the two oldest sons, isolated in the left-hand section of the composition, together reflect the influence of this celebrated antique sculpture. The allusion is all the more interesting because it is clear that Hudson's attention was drawn to the antique statue by the example set by his former pupil Joshua Reynolds, who had adapted it to the design of his famous full-length of *Commodore Keppel* (Fig. 8). Reynolds's portrait is a landmark in his career and in the development of eighteenth-century portraiture as a whole, for Reynolds had just returned from his studies in Italy and was demonstrating how portraiture could be "elevated" by learned allusion and by an air of the "Grand Manner". The dramatic lighting in Reynolds's picture heightens the effect, and the virtual repetition by Hudson of the same lighting in the figures of the two boys demonstrates that his own adaptation of the *Apollo Belvedere* was mediated by Reynolds's example. The influence of the *Apollo Belvedere* is particularly apparent in the very oldest boy (on the extreme left of the picture), but it also present in the turned head of his younger brother. The rest of the picture is entirely in Hudson's more conventional manner, showing nothing of the same dramatic contrast of light and shade. Hudson's portrayal of the two older children–who are given a section of the composition all to themselves–is therefore a fascinating example of the way in which an artist can be led to revise his style on encountering the new ideas of a gifted pupil.

If two artists might be taken to represent the full development of the British School, of which Hudson and Reynolds are such prominent representatives, they would be William Hogarth (1697-1764) and J.M.W. Turner (1775-1851): we have a combination of Augustan sensibility and rococo grace on the one hand; the Romantic imagination on the other. In the individual cricket picture this contrast between the styles of the two periods can be demonstrated by comparing the portrait by Pine (Plate 39) which we have just been discussing with the portrait of

Lord Hay of about 1810 (Plate XVII). The latter picture is supposed to have been painted when Lord Hay was at Eton, and the distant view is traditionally thought to be Windsor Castle; but it can be more plausibly interpreted as a representation of the family home in Scotland of Slains Castle (near Peterhead) and the coast above which it stands (Fig. 9) – as seems to be confirmed by an early engraving of the site, which shows similar landscape and architectural features. The style of this picture, which is close to that of John Hoppner, is essentially "Romantic", and a threatening sky adds an effectively dramatic note. It is common for full-length portraits of cricketing children to contain a suggestion of evening light in the sky, as though play were over for the day and night were drawing on. In the portrait of the young Lord Hay, however, the mood has changed subtly from that of Cotes's full-length of Lewis Cage (Plate XVI): the painter now seeks to express the full intensity of his feelings in front of Nature, which assumes a greater pictorial importance in the composition as a whole; and there is something touching in the resulting contrast between the vulnerability of youth and the untamed wildness of sky and sea. Further such comparisons could be made. The lovely double portrait by John Russell of *The Sons of Thomas Pitt* (Plate 45), painted in 1804, has more in common with Danloux's *The Masters Foster*, of 1792, than either has with the Augustan restraint displayed by the *Courtenay Brothers* of about 1751-3 (Plate 25) or their pictorial "twins" in Hudson's *Family of the 3rd Duke of Marlborough* of about 1753-5 (see Plate 24).

Cricket features in several landscapes by Turner. Two of these are *Wells Cathedral* (Plate XVIII), of about 1795, and *Petworth Park and Bucks Fighting* (Plates XIX, 48), of about 1830. The contrast between the two pictures is revealing in many respects. For the historian or connoisseur of art there is the revelation of Turner's development from painstaking seeker after the "picturesque" or the "sublime" to Romantic visionary, and from accomplished watercolourist to virtuoso in oil painting. To the cricketer the pictures display the extremes of rustic single-wicket in front of Wells Cathedral (with out-of-date curved bats and two-stump wickets) and the sunset romance of white-flannelled cricket in the perfect surroundings of a Capability Brown landscape before a country house.

The developments in art which these various comparisons reveal can be paralleled in some ways by the great changes which cricket underwent in the same period. One of the most significant factors in these latter developments was the founding of the Marylebone Cricket Club in 1787.

THE M.C.C.

The "age of M.C.C." was to see profound changes in the structure of the game, and there were equally great changes in the relationship between art and cricket. In the early days of cricket there was a natural alliance between the aristocracy and the labouring or yeoman classes in the pursuit of cricketing success. The two-level structure of the Hambledon Club exemplifies the relationship, which was apparently harmonious on the field and off it, in its rigid but mutually accepted distinctions. The middle class really seems to have played very little part. At first, the M.C.C. perpetuated this member-player relationship in the context of the same social divisions. But the tensions consequent upon the Industrial Revolution, and the resultant growth of an *haute bourgeoisie* of a kind new to English society, gradually created certain problems. Such a quasi-feudal structure as M.C.C. was at its inception was only likely to react by becoming increasingly conservative. Its members were, no doubt, only too aware of the economic changes involved and of the existence of "new" money, but, not surprisingly, they were unable (or unwilling) to absorb them socially.

In cricketing terms, the most serious result was that the M.C.C. became alienated from its natural allies, the cricket professionals, whose final emergence as independent money-earners in the 1840s was a natural and healthy consequence. These changes also meant that the law-givers or law-makers were no longer the players. In Hambledon the laws had developed, as it were, from within, as the result of new skills and new difficulties encountered on the field which demanded urgent consideration. Under M.C.C., pronouncements on the laws were delivered *de haut en bas*, more slowly, and sometimes nearly too late. The resistance to round-arm and over-arm bowling is a case in point.

In terms of art, one consequence was the temporary disappearance of the large-scale individual cricket portrait in oils, which had invariably been of a gentleman. Almost the last of these–as it is also one of the finest–is the portrait of *Lord Hay* of about 1810 (Plate XVII). There is then a hiatus until we find the large-scale oil portrait reappearing at the end of the century, examples being *A.N. Hornby* by the Hon. John Collier (1893) (Plate XXXI), *W.E. Roller* by G.R. Roller (1896) (Plate 108), and *W.G. Grace* by Archibald Stuart Wortley (1890) (Plate XXV). These were all painted because the sitters were cricketers first, although they were also, of course, gentlemen. Nothing could be more different from the situation pertaining in the eighteenth century. The nineteenth-century oil portraits in which non-players as such are portrayed as cricketers, as in Richard Dagley's portrait of *Benjamin Disraeli* (1824) (Plate 51), are small-scale and unheroic.

Another example is a portrait of *George Whieldon* (Plate XXI), painted on his visit to Lord's in 1845. Whieldon was, in fact, a first-class amateur cricketer, but this is again a small-scale picture, as is a closely contemporary painting of *An Unknown Batsman* (Plate 50), which shows the newly invented splice in the bat. A portrait of *Sir Emilius Bayley, Bart.* (son of Sir John Bayley, Bart., who was President of M.C.C. in 1844), painted while he was a boy at Eton, is of a similar type (Plate 51).

It seems possible that one reason for the fact that the large-scale cricket portrait fell out of fashion between about 1820 and 1860 was the growth of professionalism, which would have made it, for the nonce, rather "non-U". Its return to fashion in the latter part of the century, with the portrayal of great amateur players of the game, must have been largely due to the Victorian establishment of cricket as part of the public school, imperial, and chivalric *ethos*. Its utter propriety in that world is nowhere better captured than in the meaningfully entitled *Young England* (Plate 54), a Parian-ware sculpture by George Halse produced in 1874. The theme *mens sana in corpore sano* is reiterated in the bat and book incorporated in the design, and sounds a pleasing echo of the similar sentiment evoked by Daniel Gardner in his portrait of Frederick Francis Baker (Plate XIV), painted a hundred years earlier.

In the nineteenth century by far the most common cricket portraits were of those who made their living from the game: in the eighteenth century, however, we can point to the solitary head-and-shoulders of "Lumpy" Stevens among the professionals (Plate 4). In the early nineteenth century we find an increasing use of pencil, watercolour and pastel; and during the same period the development of the lithographic process facilitated reproduction, making possible the widespread dissemination of images of cricketers who were increasingly seen as national heroes. The attractive person of "Felix" embodies many of these factors. He was a gentleman, Nicholas Wanostrocht, but played cricket as a professional and had therefore to play under his happy *alias*, the choice of which came naturally to a classical scholar and headmaster. He was also an artist, and his portraits of cricketers are almost exclusively carried out in pencil, watercolour or pastel – for these are media in which relative simplicity of line would ensure easy adaptation to printing (Plates 68, 69). When M.C.C. was founded, however, all these developments lay ahead. Encompassing this time was the long reign of George III, stretching from 1760 to 1820, the last twenty years of which were in the hands of a keen cricketer, the Prince Regent.

The reigns of few British monarchs can have seen so many changes in the social, political and cultural life of the nation as that of George III. This is the period of the American and French Revolutions and of England's long struggle with Napoleon, of the Industrial Revolution and agricultural reform, of the Romantic movement in literature and the arts, and of Regency architecture and taste. For the historian of art the most significant event of all must be the foundation of the Royal Academy in 1768 under the Presidency of Sir Joshua Reynolds. For the historian of cricket a comparable importance attaches to the year 1787, when Thomas Lord (Plate VII), on the prompting of the 8th Earl of Winchilsea and his cricketing friend Charles Lennox, afterwards 4th Duke of Richmond (Plate 7), acquired his first cricket ground at Dorset Fields (today's Dorset Square), an event which coincided with the foundation of the Marylebone Cricket Club.

It may be said that with the foundation of the Royal Academy the British School rose above its former provincialism and acquired a truly European stature, to which the reputation of its great Presidents Reynolds, West and Lawrence greatly contributed. So it was that with the establishment of the M.C.C., of which Lord Winchilsea was the principal founder and Charles

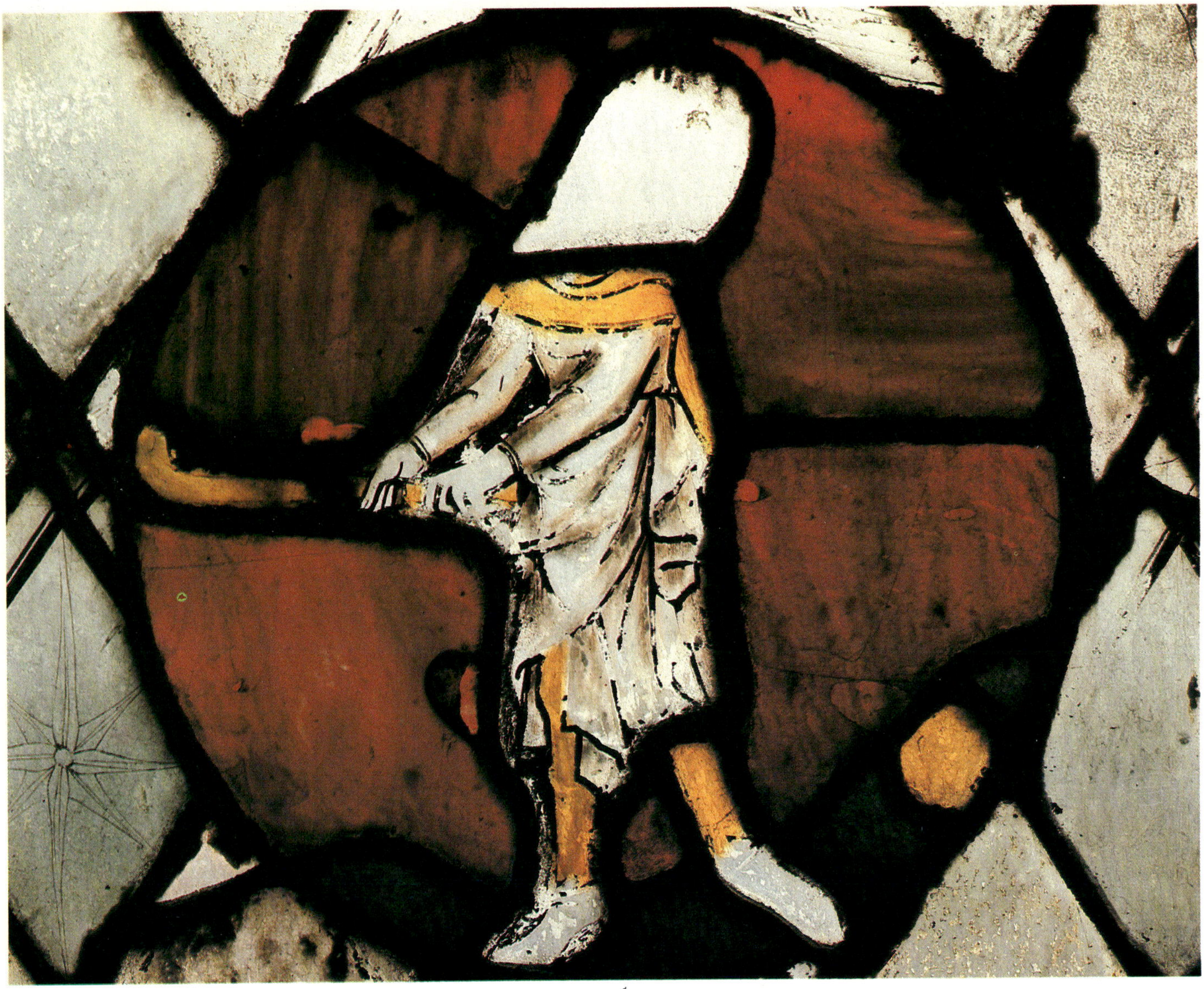

I. Window, Gloucester Cathedral, *c.* 1350.

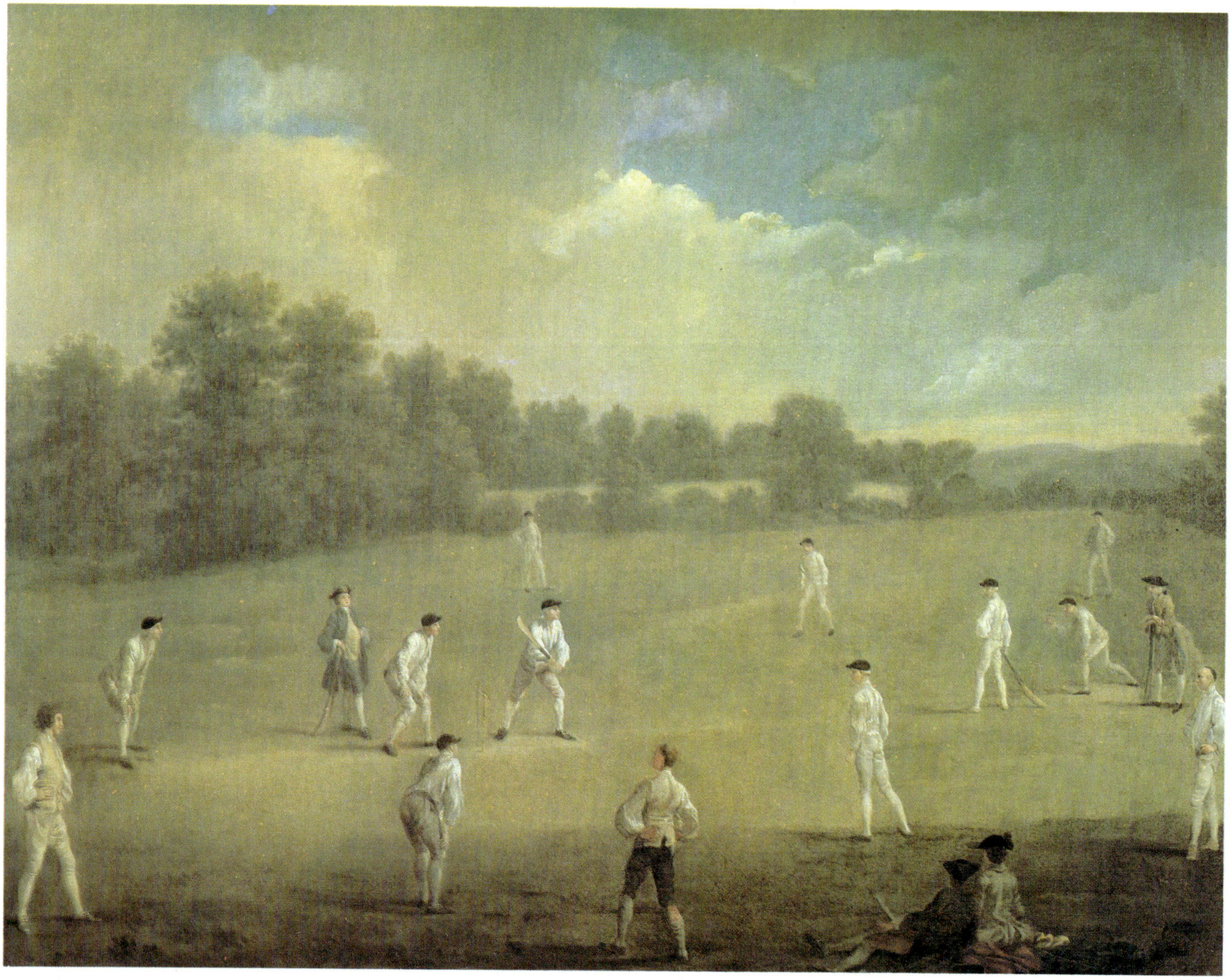

II. Francis Hayman, R.A.: "*Cricket in Marylebone Fields*" (M.C.C.).

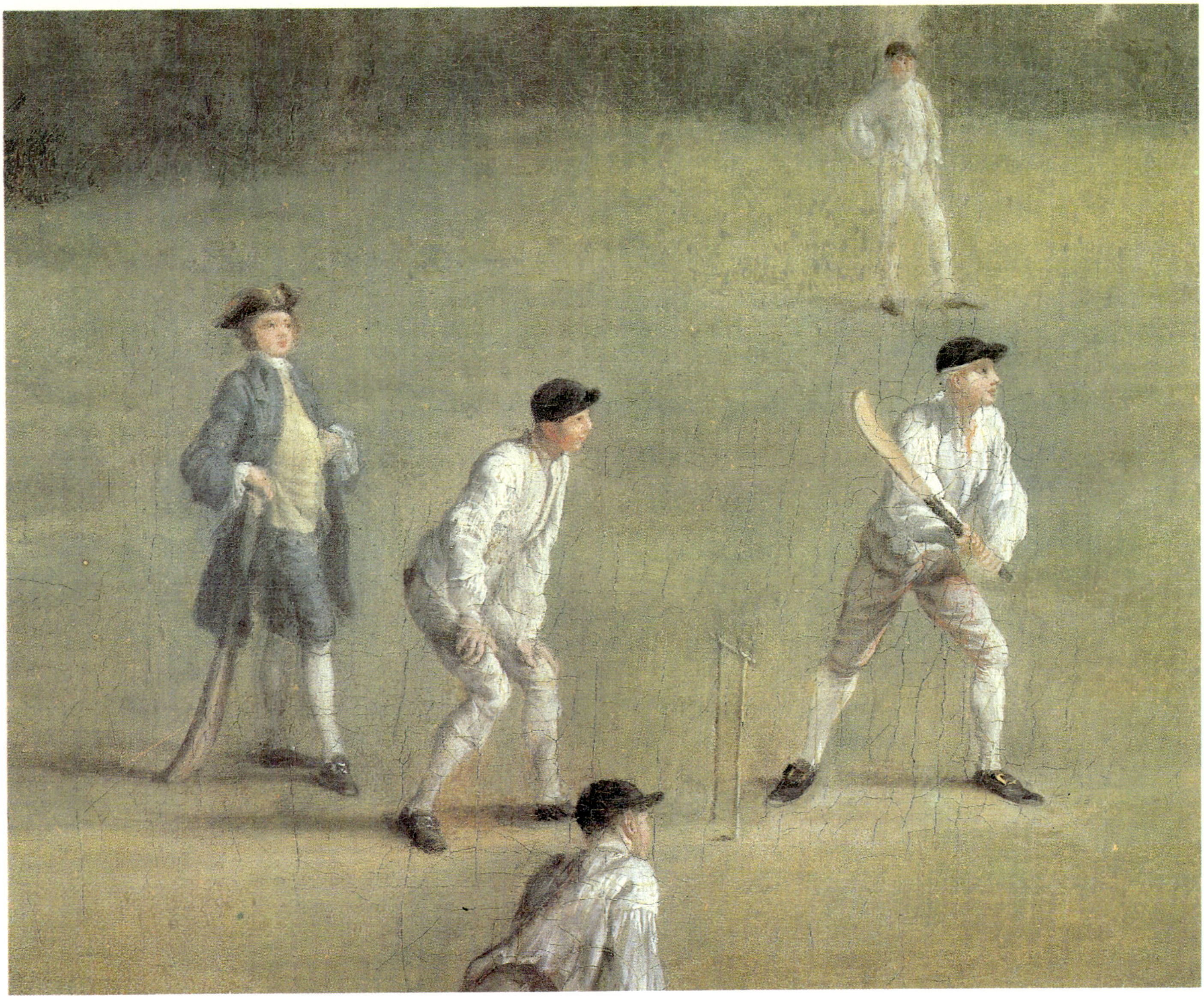

III. Francis Hayman, R.A.: *Batsman, umpire and three fielders*: detail of Plate II (M.C.C.).

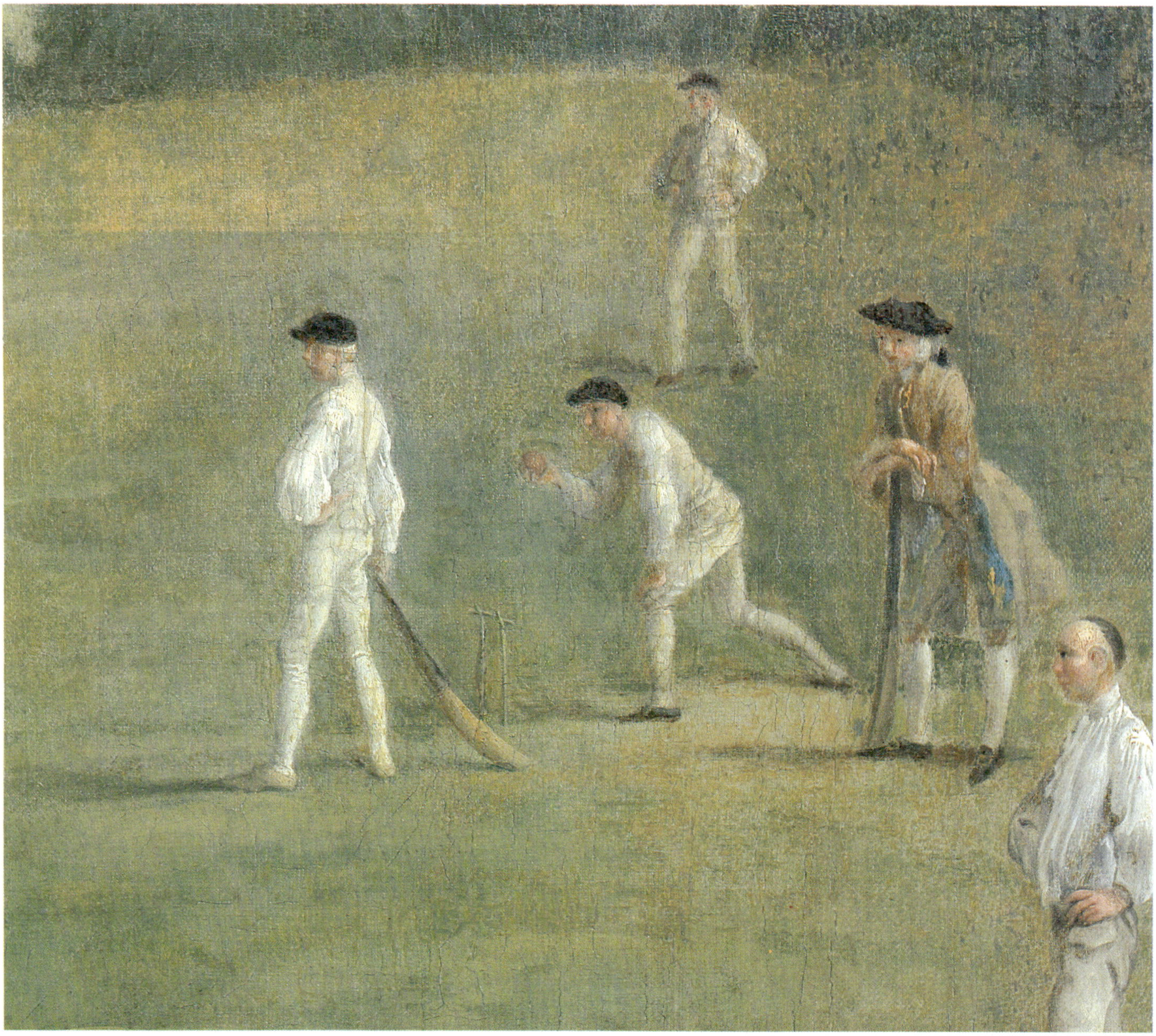

IV. Francis Hayman, R.A.: *Bowler, non-striker, umpire and two fielders*: detail of Plate II (M.C.C.).

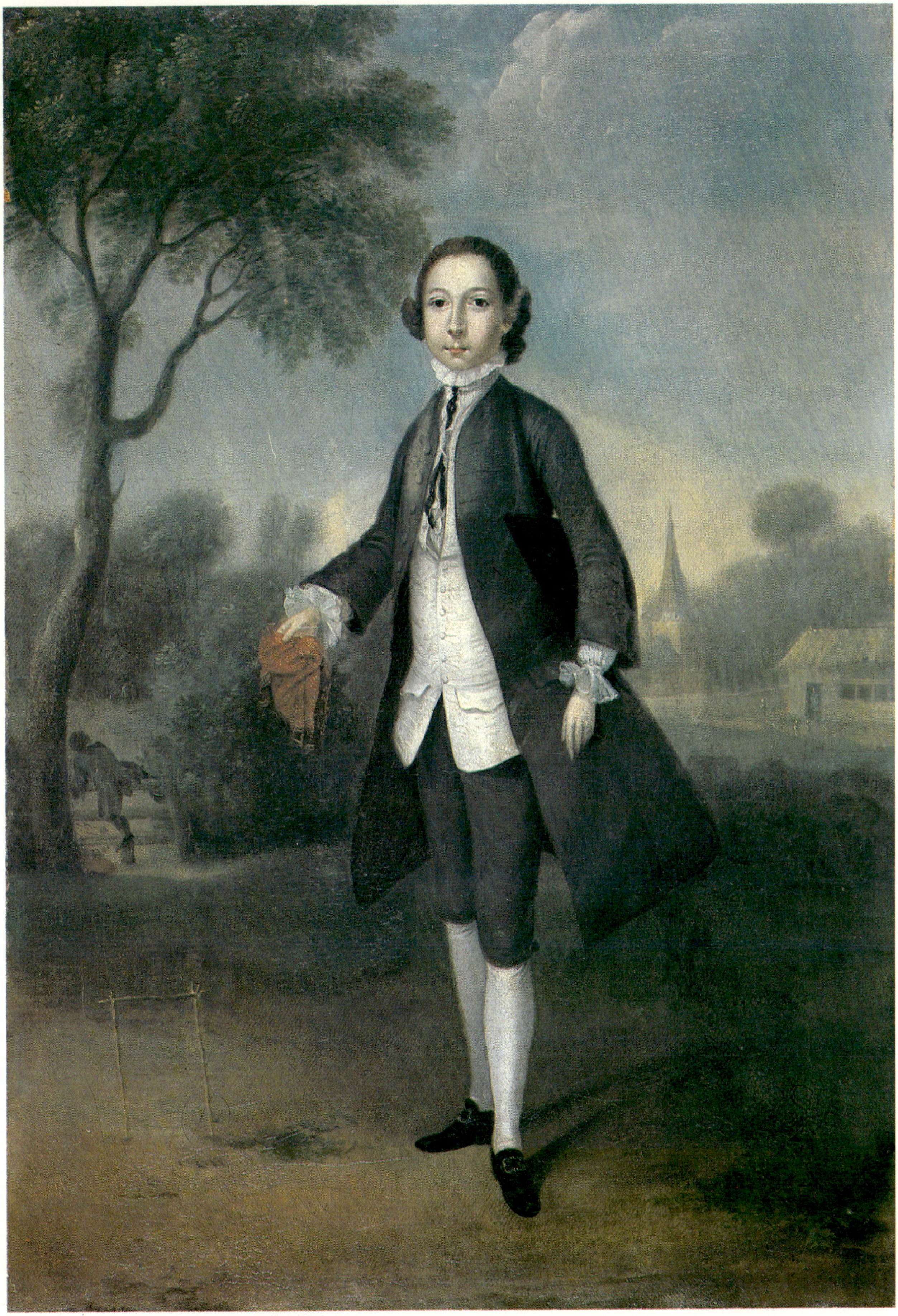

V. Edward Penny, R.A.: *Sir William Benett of Fareham* (Laing Art Gallery, Newcastle upon Tyne).

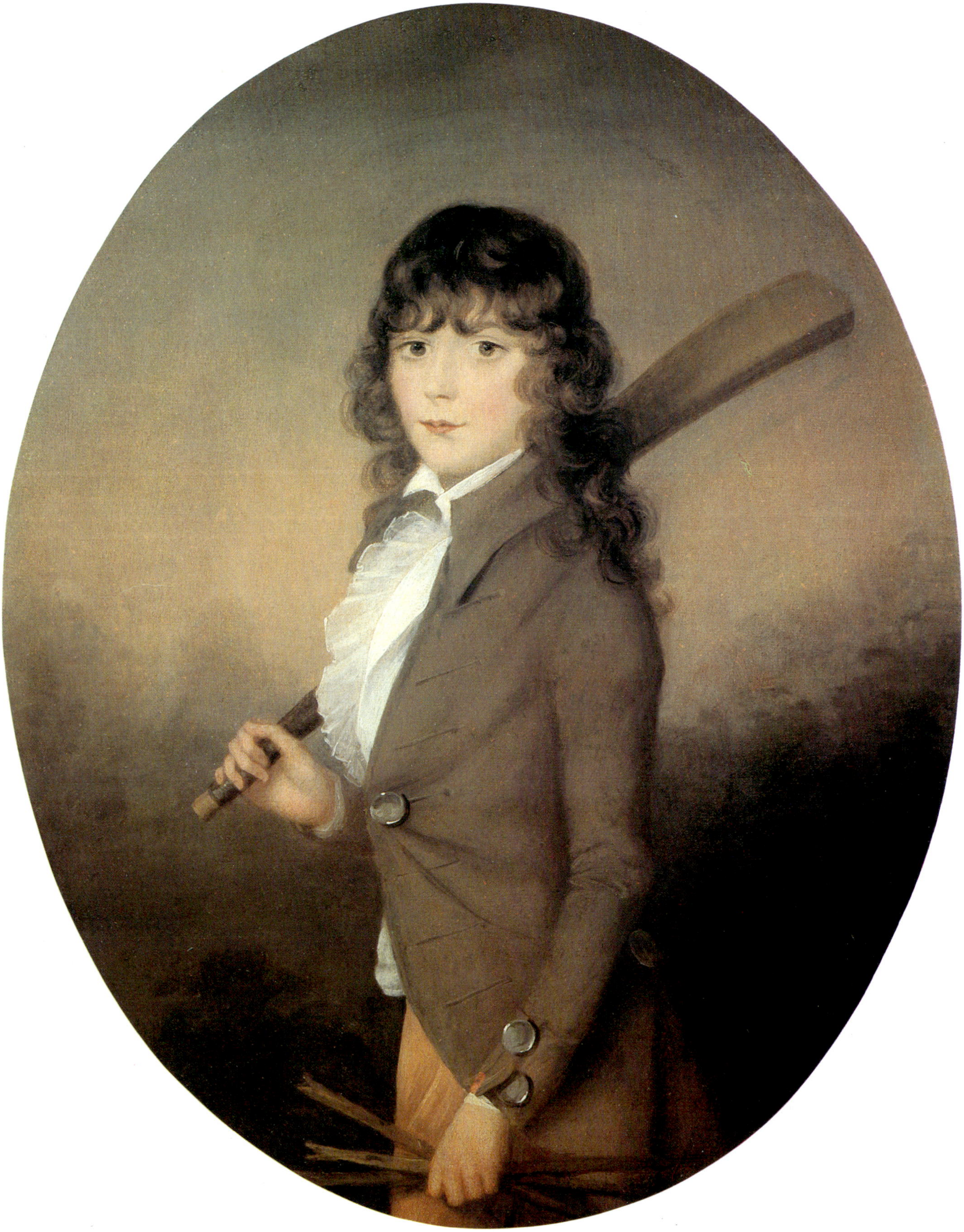

VI. Francis Alleyne: *William Wheateley at the age of fourteen* (1786) (M.C.C.).

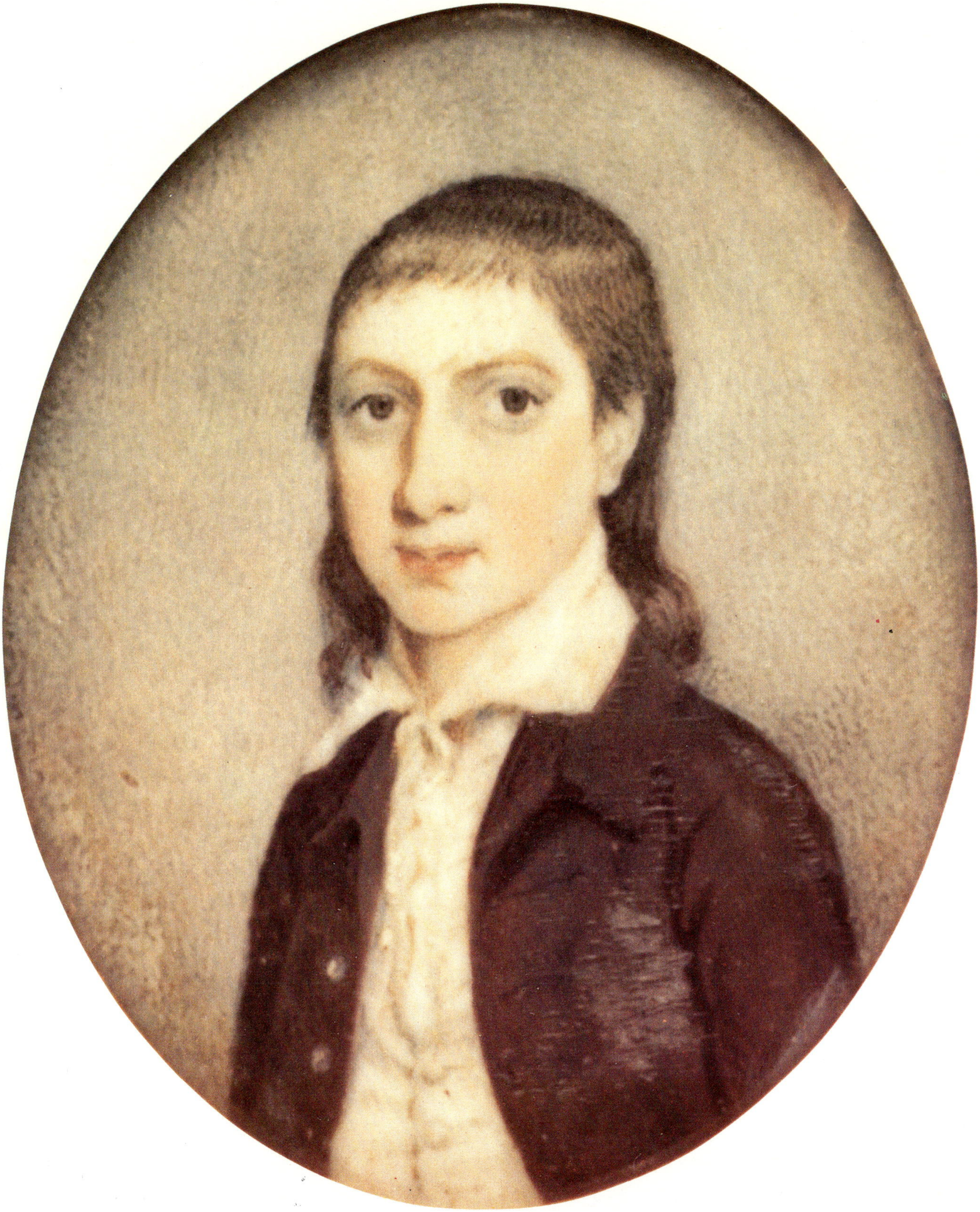

VII. British School: *Thomas Lord as a boy* (enlarged) (Private Collection).

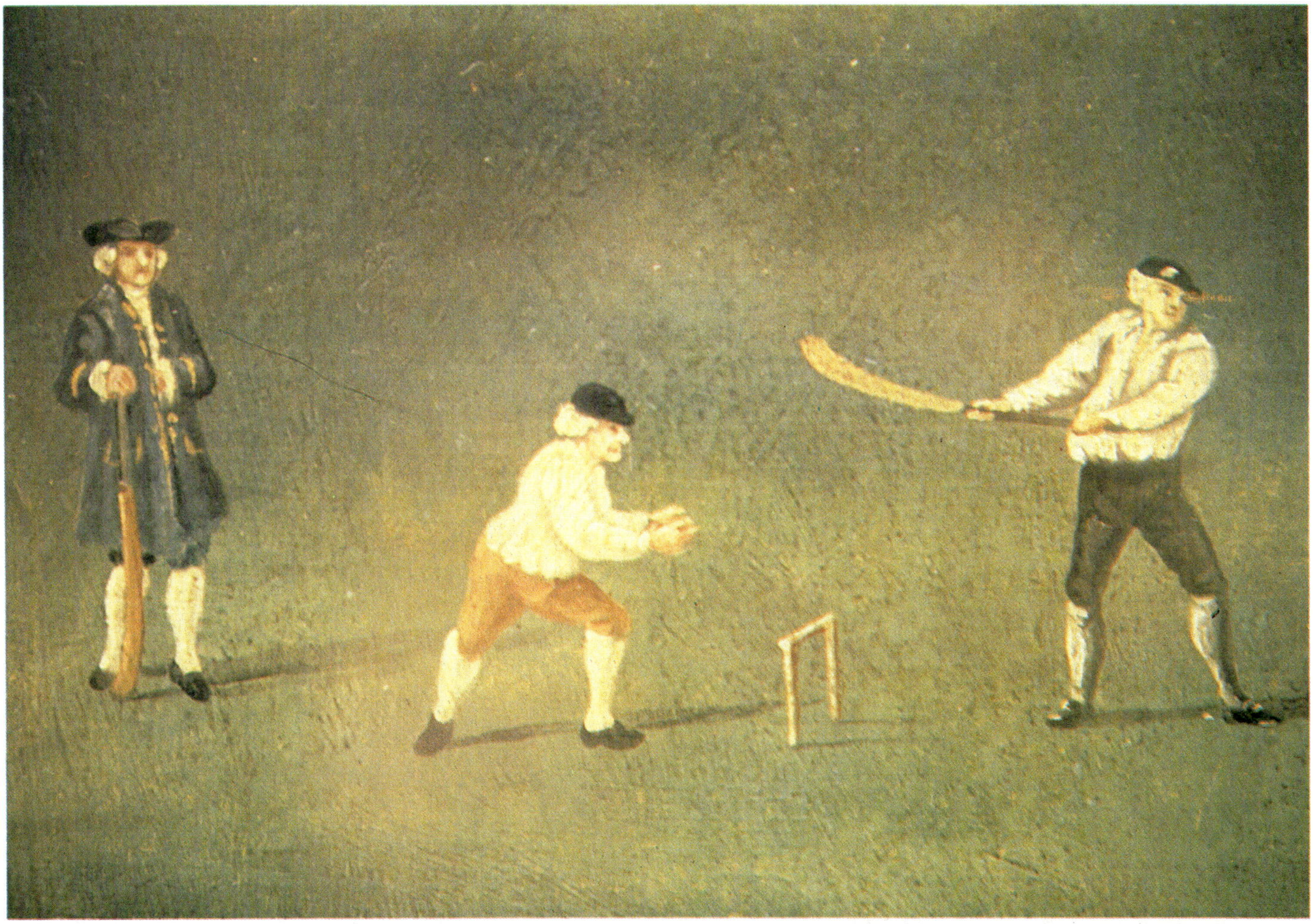

VIII. *Attributed to* W.R. Coates: *Batsman, wicket-keeper and umpire*: detail of Plate 16 (Tate Gallery, London).

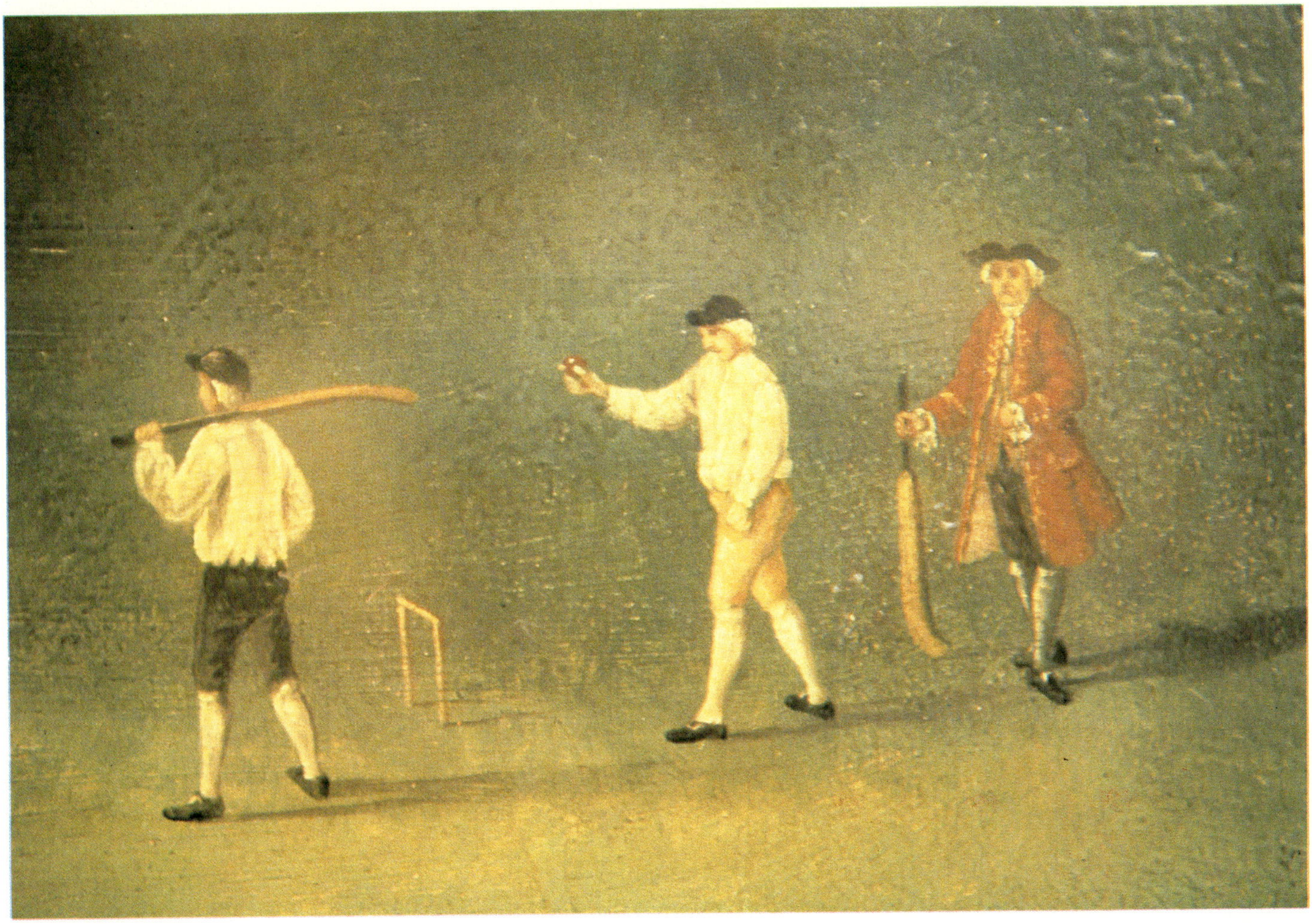

IX. *Attributed to* W.R. Coates: *Bowler, non-striker and umpire*: detail of Plate 16 (Tate Gallery, London).

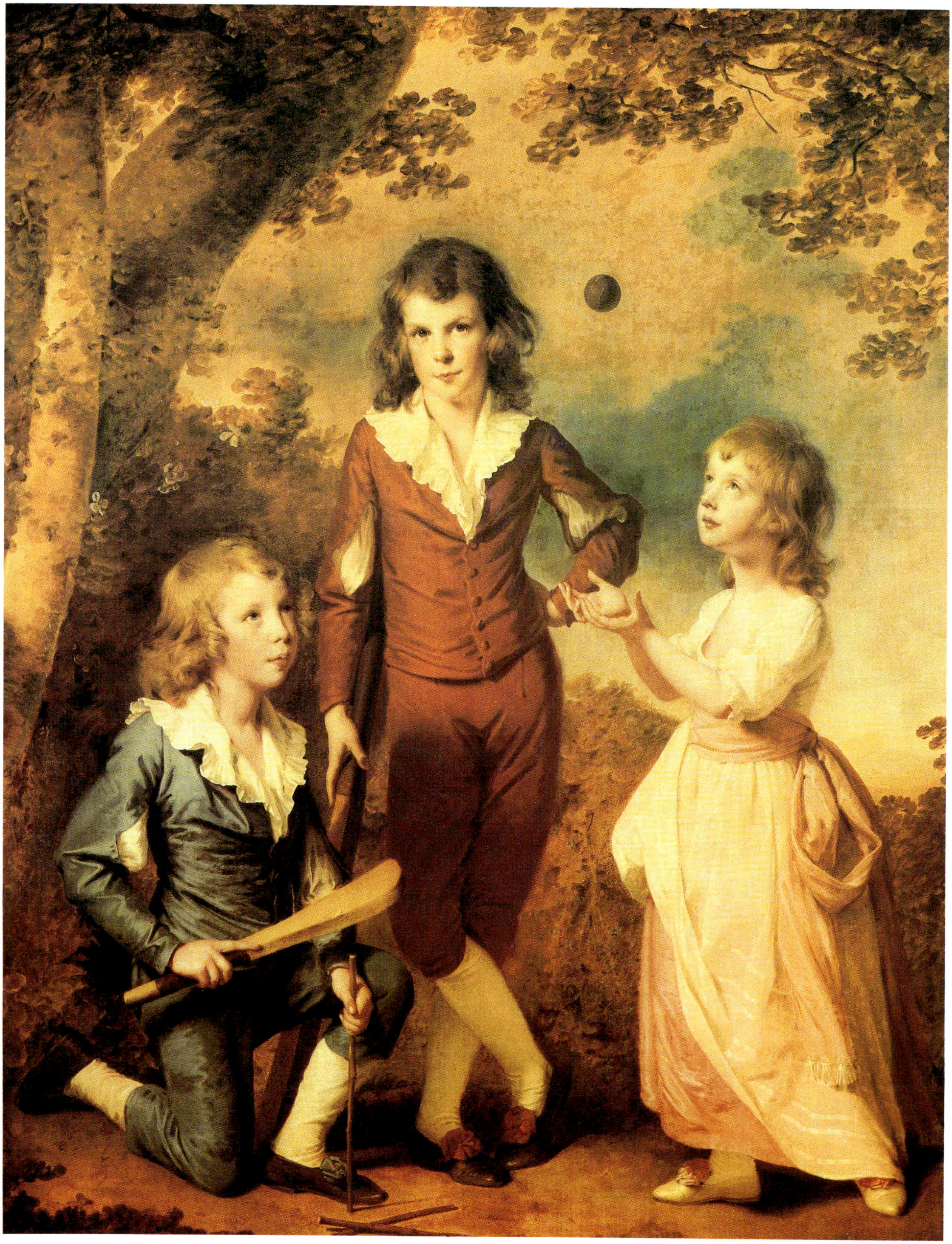

X. Joseph Wright of Derby, A.R.A.: *The Wood Children* (1789) (Derby City Museum and Art Gallery).

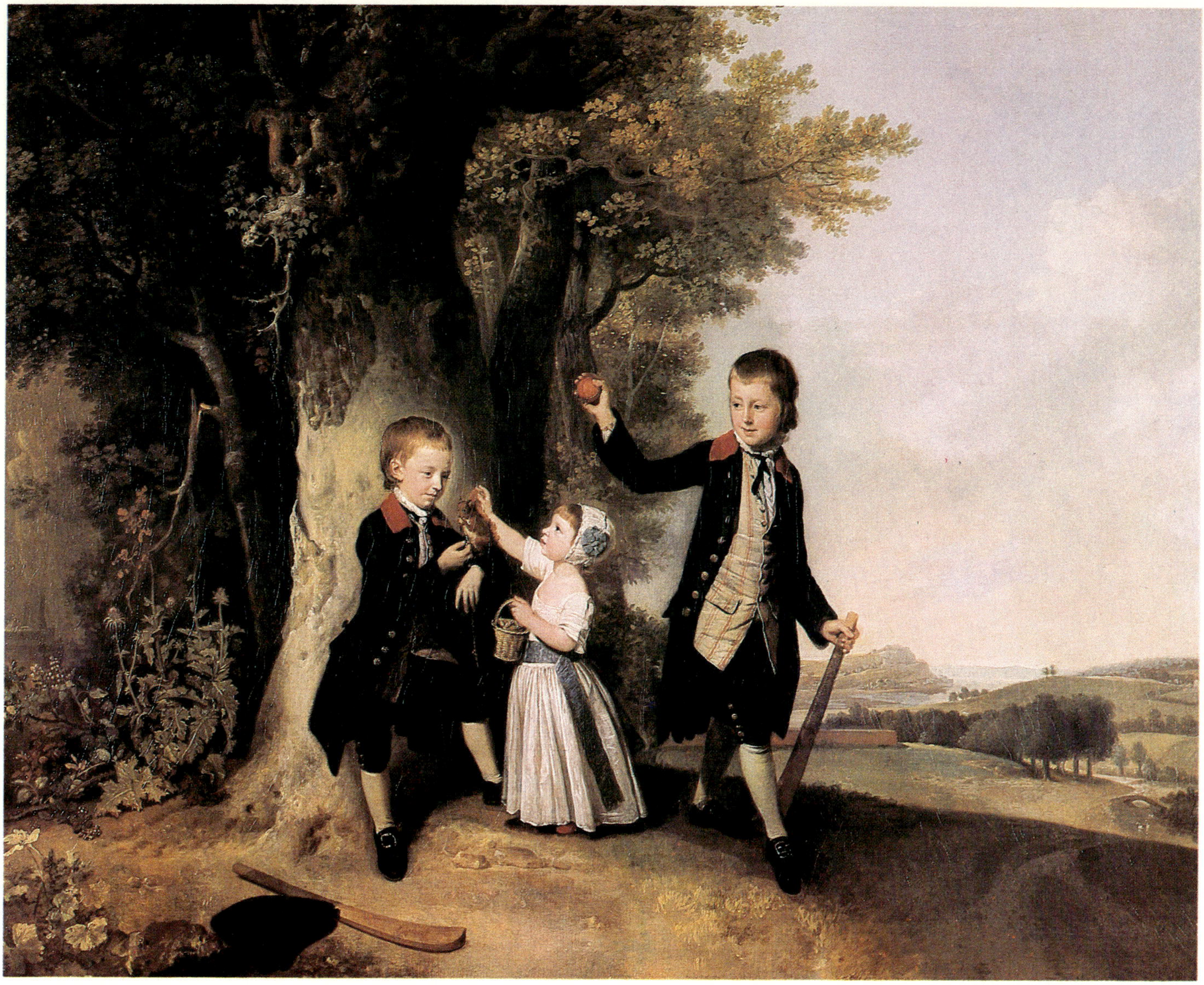

XI. Johan Zoffany, R.A.: *The Sondes Children* (c. 1764-5) (Commander Michael Saunders-Watson).

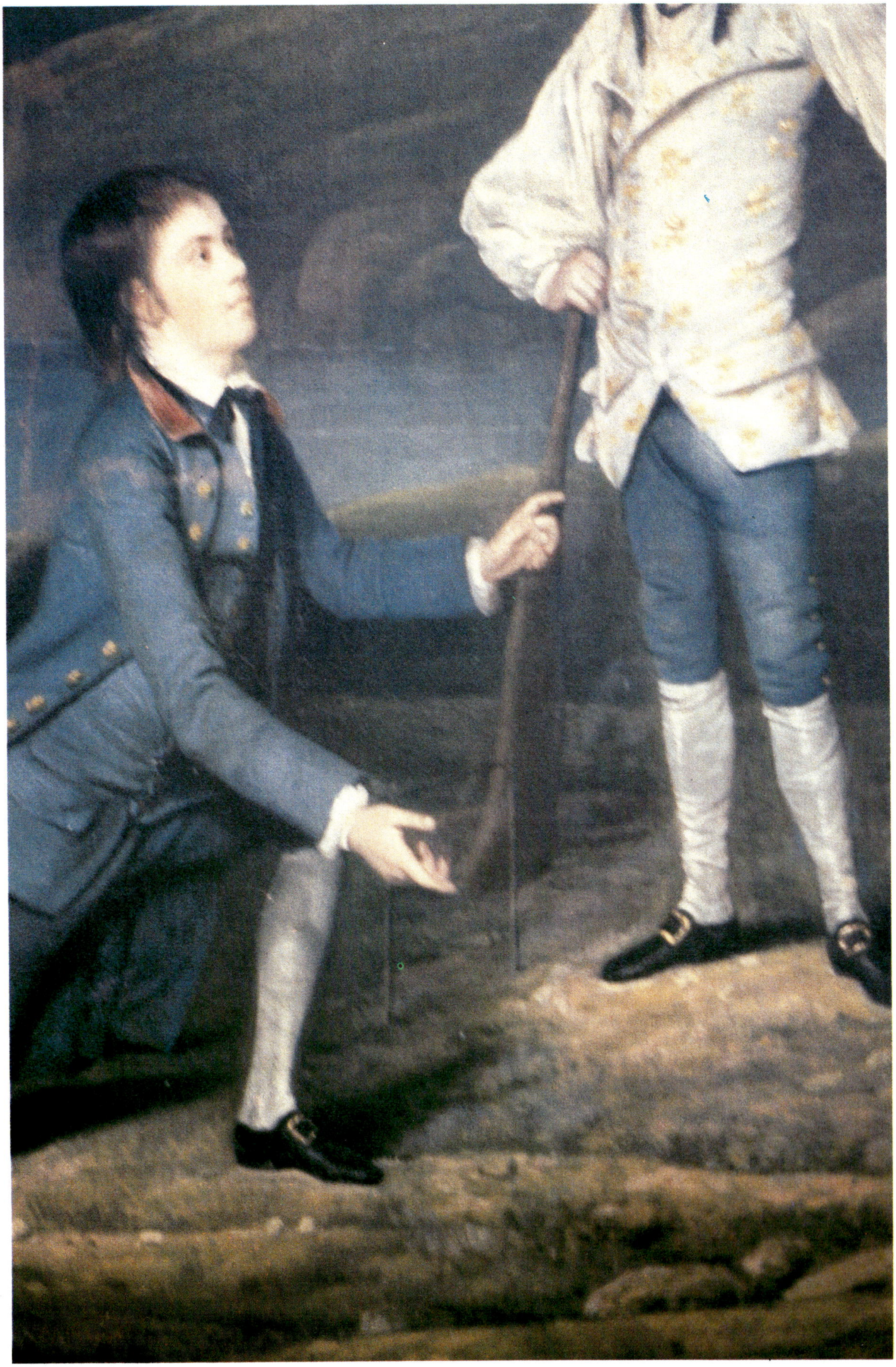

XII. **Hugh Barron: *Boy cricketers and wicket*: detail of Plate 33 (Tate Gallery, London).**

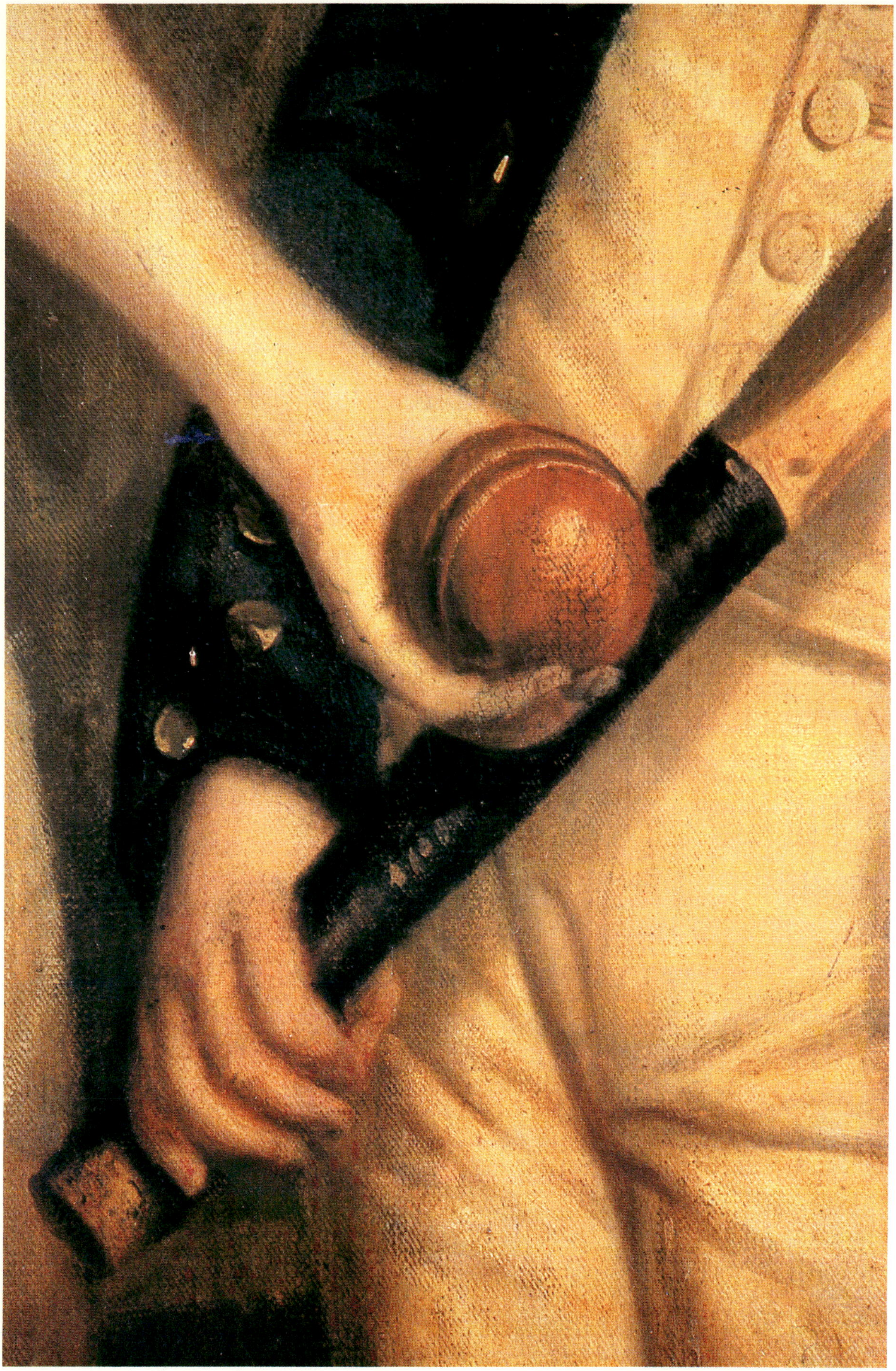

XIII. Thomas Beach: *A cricket ball of 1793:* detail of Plate 28.

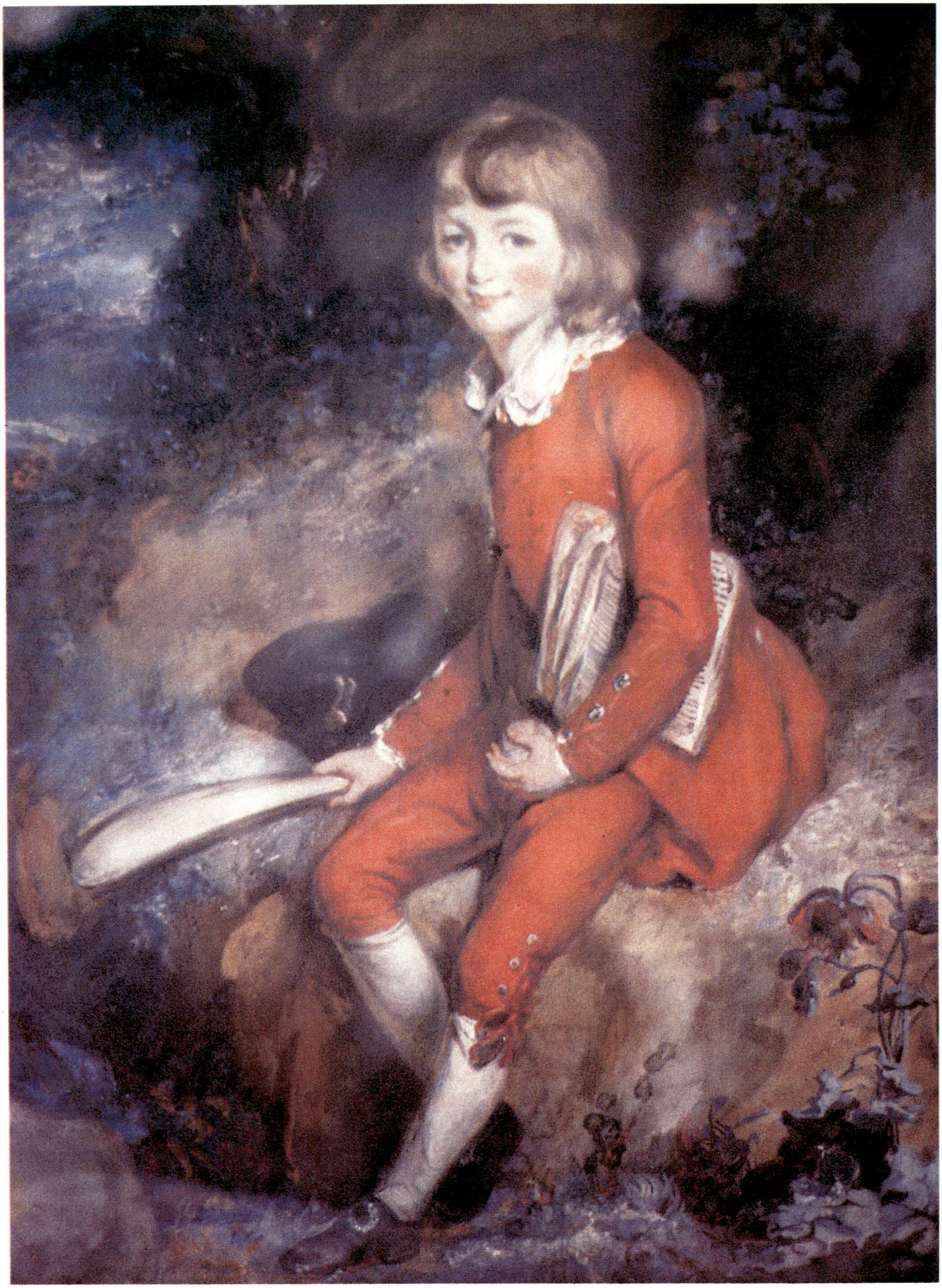

XIV. Daniel Gardner: *Frederick Francis Baker* (Private Collection).

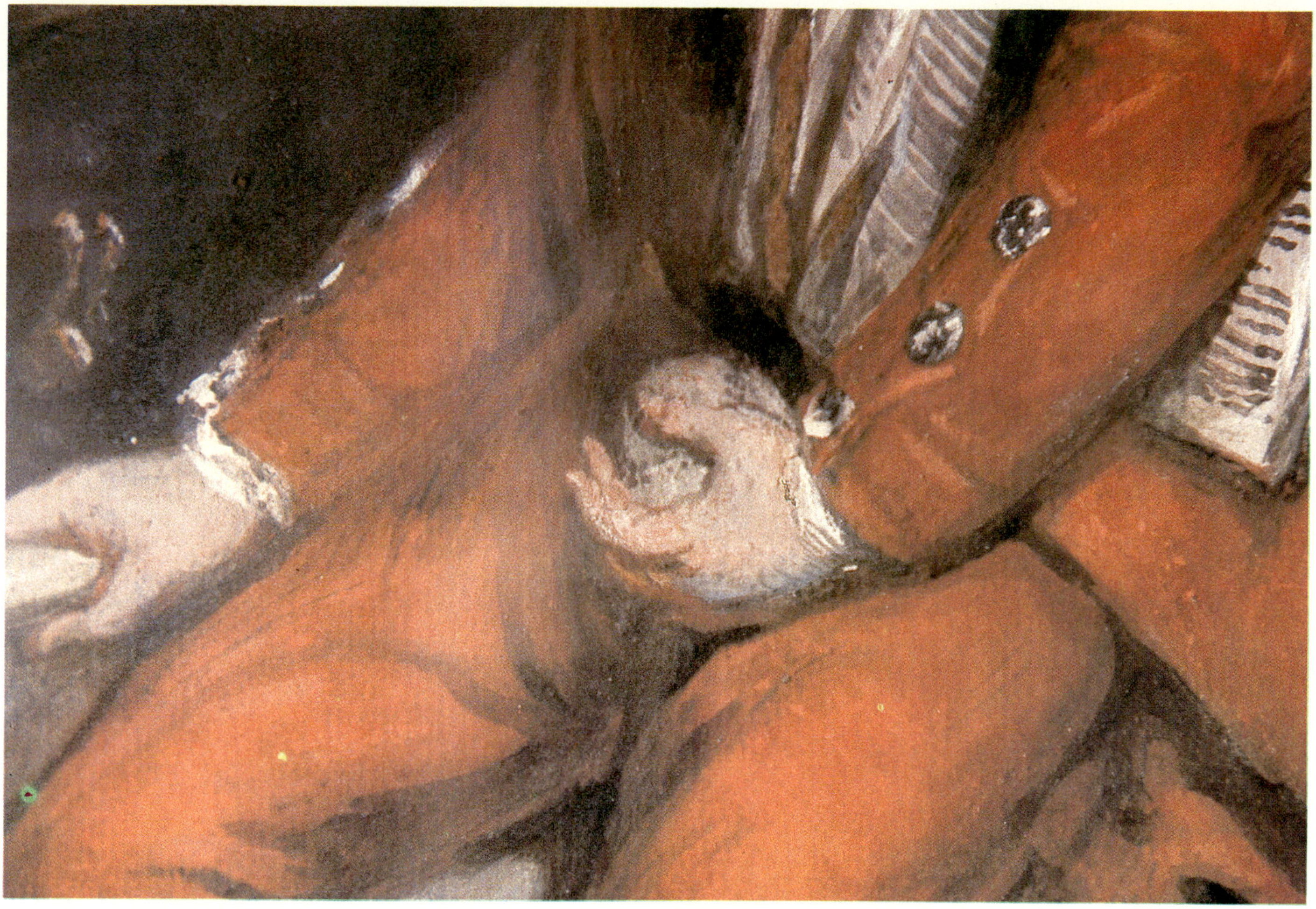

XV. **Daniel Gardner: detail of Plate XIV, showing cricket ball.**

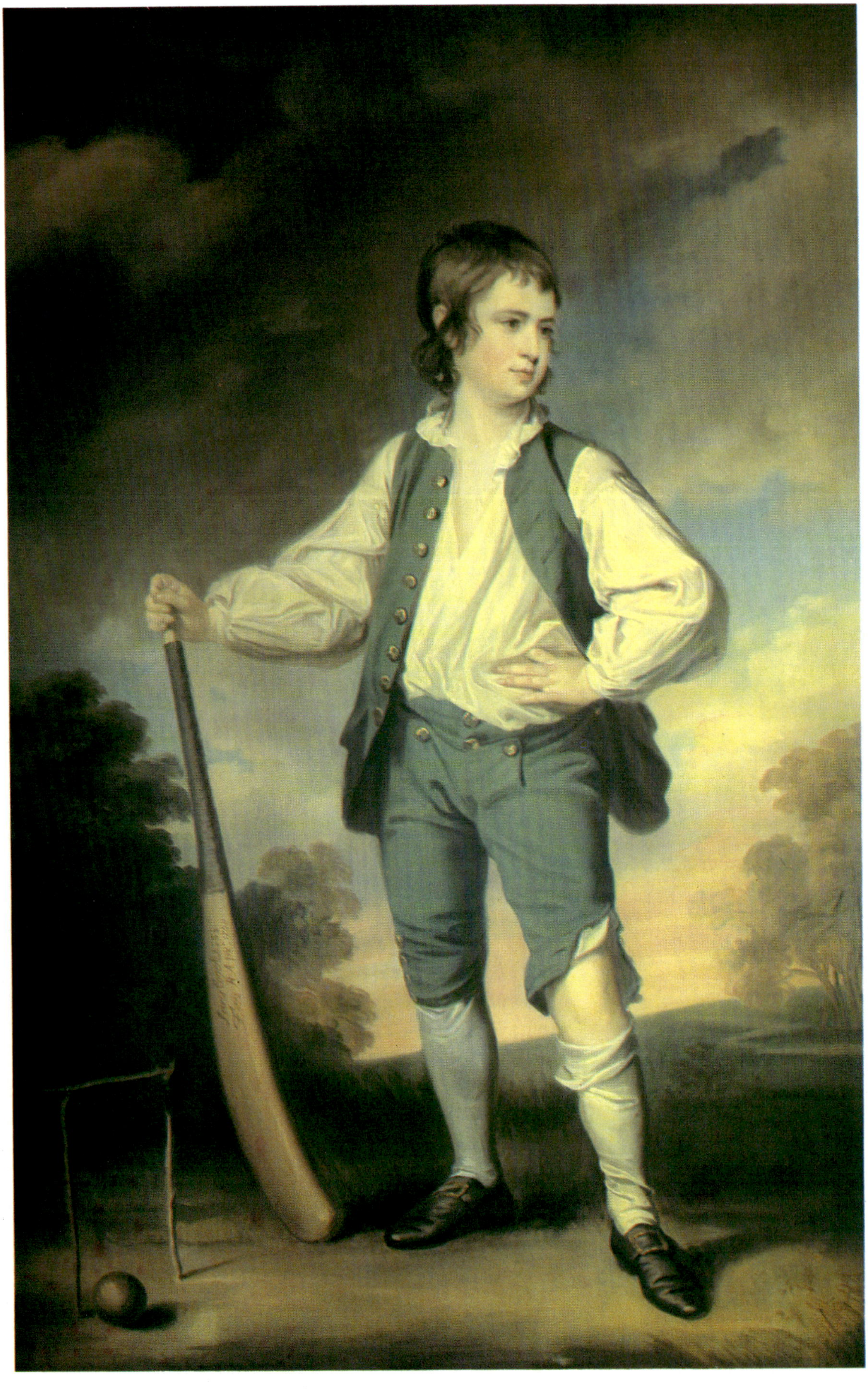

XVI. *After* Francis Cotes, R.A.: *Lewis Cage as a Batsman* (John Nutting, Esq.).

Lennox a scarcely less enthusiastic promoter, English cricket came of age. And although, unlike the Academy, the M.C.C. was never granted, nor sought, a Royal Charter, it enjoyed the interest of the King and the active participation in its affairs of his son the Duke of York, one of the earliest members of the Club. The standing of the M.C.C. was such that it gradually assumed the status of a central authority to which points in dispute could be referred; and it was soon after its establishment that the Laws of Cricket – apart from those relating to round-arm and, subsequently, to over-arm, bowling – were promulgated in virtually their modern form. The importance of royal patronage to the early rise of cricket has already been discussed; it was no less significant in the period when M.C.C. was just taking hold. It has been said of Frederick, Prince of Wales that he "revolutionized cricket"; and George III, in turn, although no keen player like his father, inherited his deep interest in cricket and inculcated the same passion in his own sons. He enjoyed watching a match, and a player who missed a catch or was slack in the field could often expect an admonition from the Royal tent: on the other hand, if he did well, he might find himself rewarded with a sovereign.[65]

It was at Kew, his favoured and most modest residence, that George III's many sons developed their skills in the game, at which they were considered as children to be outstanding. The young princes had their own houses on Kew Green, where their grandfather, Frederick, had patronized the game, and the Green became the scene of many games between them of single-wicket cricket. These contests would often have been witnessed by the crowds that flocked to the Gardens, and for which a glimpse of the Royal children at play was not to be missed.[66] Of all the sons of George III, the eldest, George, Prince of Wales – afterwards George IV – and Prince Frederick, Duke of York, were to become the most active players and promoters of the game in later life; but the younger Prince William, who was to come to the throne as William IV, and Prince Augustus Frederick, Duke of Sussex, the King's sixth son, who was elected a member of M.C.C. towards the end of his life, both took a keen interest in cricket as patrons if not as players.

The most enthusiastic cricketer of all was the Prince of Wales, the future George IV, who showed on the cricket-field all that geniality and good-heartedness which characterized him in society and among his personal friends. When on a sea-water cure for swollen glands in 1783, he took up residence at Brighton, and he loved nothing more than to play cricket on the Downs with the members of his "set", notably Lord Darnley and Lord Barrymore, excelling as a batsman: a report of August 1790 describes him as making "a party at cricket almost every day". The natural affinity between cricket and art may be said to be exemplified in the person of the Prince Regent. Like his predecessor as Prince of Wales, "poor Fred", he may not have been possessed of many virtues, but he loved and patronized both cricket and the arts, and displayed a personal discrimination and taste of a quality decidedly unusual in a king of England.

Undoubtedly, the patronage of the Royal Family greatly enhanced the prestige and popularity of cricket in the country as a whole, and the establishment of the M.C.C. in 1787 must be seen against this background. The founders of M.C.C. were aristocrats close to the Court and intimates of the King–not least among them the Hon. Charles Lennox. But, as we have noted, it was Lennox's close friend the Earl of Winchilsea who was the Club's real founder.

An enthusiastic cricketer, Lord Winchilsea was an *habitué* of the famous White Conduit Club, which took its name from the White Conduit House, celebrated for its tea-gardens, whose members played cricket from about 1780 in White Conduit Fields. An impression of a match there was published in 1784 in a series of coloured engravings after Robert Dighton entitled *British Sports*: Dighton's original drawing of the scene in pen and watercolour has survived (Plate 56). Among the other playing members of this club were the Hon. Charles Lennox himself, the

3rd Duke of Dorset, the 7th Earl of Barrymore, Sir Horatio Mann and Sir Peter Burrell. And it was at the White Conduit Club that there was also to be seen a retainer and general factotum of Lord Winchilsea's –Thomas Lord.

If Lord Winchilsea may properly be called the founder of the M.C.C., it is right that a wider fame should be attached to the name of Lord. A Yorkshireman, Thomas Lord came from a good family whose fortunes had been ruined by its support of the Young Pretender. A miniature of him as a boy survives (Plate VII). His later fortune was made entirely by his own qualities of character and sound business sense, and his prosperous middle age is captured in a portrait preserved at M.C.C. fomerly attributed to George Morland. In 1786, Lord leased a piece of land in Dorset Fields, and the appearance of this first ground is recorded in an engraving of 1793. It was there in the following summer of 1787 that the first match–between Middlesex and Essex–was played "at Lord's". Because there were plans for building on the site, Lord was obliged in the year 1808 to give up this ground for another at North Bank, Regent's Park, taking with him turf from the old field. But not long afterwards, in 1812, his tenure of this second site became insecure: as a recent writer has put it, expressing the gravity of the threat in terms which any cricketer will appreciate: "Plans for a Regent's Canal showed that the new waterway was destined to cross the main wicket at a point just short of a 'good length'."[67] And so the present Lord's Cricket Ground at St John's Wood came into being: once again the sacred turf was carried to this third and immortal site.

The M.C.C. gradually assumed the role of a recognized legislative body more powerful than any of the clubs which had preceded it. About 1800, for example, we find the Laws printed below an engraving derived from Hayman's "*Cricket in Marlyebone Fields*" with the caption *The Laws of the Noble Game of Cricket, as revised by the Club at St. Mary-le-bone.* In July 1818 a dispute between the Oakham and Melton Mowbray Clubs about "the rules of play"– as to whether it was required of both umpires to make a decision in response to an appeal – was referred to the Marylebone Club. Lord Frederick Beauclerk answered on behalf of the Club.

In Lord Frederick Beauclerk (Plates 8, 47) we meet one of the most extraordinary personalities in the period of cricket history immediately preceding the advent of the "three Graces".[68] The features of the Revd Lord Frederick Beauclerk are known to us from the striking picture by Sir William Beechey (Plate 47) and from other portraits. Beauclerk was the fourth son of Aubrey, 5th Duke of St Albans. Like Charles Lennox, he was descended from Charles II (*via* Nell Gwyn), and his haughty bearing and conduct witnessed to his pride in his lineage. He was a natural athlete, and he had the good fortune to be discovered by Lord Winchilsea, who brought him to Lord's to play for the M.C.C. Cricket remained his passion, if not quite his religion. His lithe and graceful figure as he appeared on the cricket-field has been captured for us in Shepheard's remarkable sheet of sketches, in which Charles Lennox, Beldham and other famous players of the time are also portrayed (Plates 5-8).

Born in 1773, Beauclerk lived on until the year 1850, and therefore forms a link between the "Hambledon era" and the "Age of Grace". He became the outstanding all-rounder among gentlemen players of his time, and indeed he has been aptly described as "an earlier incarnation of W.G. Grace". He played regularly for All-England, and he made eight centuries on the first Lord's. In 1827, at the age of fifty-four, he compiled a score of 78, which Sir Pelham Warner has compared with Grace's 74 at the age of fifty-eight at The Oval (in 1906). As a bowler, he was impatient of the slow defensive batting which a number of the professionals would sometimes indulge in; and on one occasion, when he had bowled interminably at a notorious stonewaller, Tom Walker of Hambledon (known as "Old Everlasting"), he threw his white hat on the grass in his frustration, and expostulated to the batsman, although the words he is said to have addressed to him –"You confounded old beast!"– were restrained enough, as befitted a gentleman and a parson.

The name Beauclerk will always be associated with that of his engaging but temperamental enemy, George Osbaldeston, whose appearance is known to us from contemporary paintings. "Squire" Osbaldeston, as he was always called, came from a Yorkshire family, though born in London, and was educated at Eton and Oxford, going down from Brasenose without a degree.[69] There was no finer man, it was said, to hounds, and he was successively Master of the Quorn, the Pytchley, and the Athelstone. He loved a fight, and was a dangerous man to cross–the fastest bowler yet seen, or not seen. Having as his partner at double-wicket William Lambert, a fine all-rounder, he was able to challenge any pair in England, especially as he was himself not only a great bowler but also a hard-hitting bat. It was such heroes of the game that the young cricketers so frequently represented in portraits of the period would have looked up to and attempted to emulate. And they imitated them in their elegant cricketing dress, which frequently included an open-necked silk shirt, a cricket-jacket and black shoes with those dangerous buckles which sometimes caused injuries to the hands of fielders, and which were to disappear by the time of Felix and Mynn.

If Beauclerk was a more distinguished figure than Osbaldeston, there was nevertheless a similar streak of ruthlessness in him, which is exemplified most strikingly by his refusal in 1810 to cancel a double-wicket match against the Squire, who had as usual William Lambert for a partner, but who was so ill that he pleaded that he was incapable of playing. "No! Play or forfeit!" replied Lord Frederick; "I won't forfeit: Lambert shall play for you both, and if he wins have the money." It was poetic justice that Lambert won the game singlehanded. The name of Lambert himself was linked to one of the scandalous practices of the time, for in 1817 he was "warned off the Turf" at Lord's, when taking part in a match between All-England and Nottinghamshire, on the charge of not playing his best in order to profit from a bet. In fact, by this time, the very interest in gambling which had ensured the rise of cricket now threatened its survival.

The evils of betting at cricket were by now becoming very clear to many lovers of the game; and Beauclerk himself was active in stamping out its abuse, securing the dismissal of two M.C.C. cricketers who had succumbed to its pecuniary temptations. Neither Lord Frederick, however, nor his old enemy Osbaldeston would have approved of its abolition, for betting had long been such a natural adjunct to cricket that a wager won was regarded as a well-deserved prize for a good performance: indeed Lord Frederick boasted that he reckoned to make 600 guineas a year out of cricket. Gambling, moreover, was a normal pleasure of the period, and had its own etiquette. We read for example, of how Osbaldeston, having won a bet from Lord George Bentinck, immediately challenged him to a duel, simply because, on paying the debt, Bentinck had muttered, "This is robbery." According to one account of the duel which followed, Osbaldeston fired in the air; according to another, the Squire's ball went through Bentinck's hat, narrowly missing his brain.[70]

Ruthless Beauclerk may have been on occasion, but he seems to have been naturally generous, and he was also a man of some distinction as a scholar. His oddities have become legendary: he raced and rode horses under a pseudonym, in order not to fall foul of the Bishop of Rochester; and, still more remarkably, he arranged for the pulpit in his church at St Albans to be fitted up with a saddle, from which he would preach, on the grounds that thus seated he felt more confident. Beauclerk appears to us today as the epitome of the high-born sporting parson of those indulgent times; but while to combine a love for cricket with a passion for the chase was common enough, and even traditional, Beauclerk's habit of mounting the pulpit and saddle at one and the same time seems extreme. It has been well said of Lord Frederick that "long before Charles Kingsley had ever heard of the phrase, he embodied the sternly Victorian ideal of muscular Christianity".[71] In 1824, the University of Cambridge bestowed upon him the degree of Doctor of Divinity–an honour which may well have compensated him for having in the same year missed a century by only one run when playing, though over fifty years old, for the famous "Bs"–an eleven composed of cricketers whose names began with a B, such as Beldham, Beagley (both celebrated players) and Beauclerk himself. As a Doctor of Divinity, however, he could be less excused his notorious weaknesses, and indeed a clergyman friend of Osbaldeston's, on learning of Beauclerk's refusal to have the Squire readmitted to the M.C.C, remarked to him, "I should not have thought him capable of so mean an act, and he a D.D., too!"–to which the Squire replied darkly: "D.D. can stand for many things besides Doctor of Divinity." Beauclerk himself, however, may well have been as much pleased by his election in 1826 to the Presidency of the M.C.C. as by any academic honour. When he retired from cricket, Lord Frederick was to be seen at Lord's on a seat just within the pavilion gate, smoking his cigar and watching the play, and accompanied by his faithful dog, which, it is said, "barked the batsmen in and out".

Lord Frederick, as a member of an All-England or M.C.C. side when it travelled into the country to play local teams, was one of the stars whom the populace flocked to watch in great numbers. He played, for example, in the great contest of 1817 between Eleven of All-England and Twenty-two of Nottinghamshire, which took place on the Forest Ground at Nottingham (where cricket is still played), and which was won by the Nottingham team through their brilliant fielding.[72] The crowds on this occasion were frighteningly large, and one of the All-England players (Budd) has described the scene:

> The concourse of people was very great. These were the times of the Luddites, and the Magistrates warned us that unless we could stop our game at 7 o'clock, they would not answer for keeping the peace. At 7 o'clock we stopped, and simultaneously the thousands who lined the ground closed in upon us. Lord Frederick lost nerve and was very much alarmed; but I said they did not want to hurt us. They simply came to look at the Eleven who ventured to play two to one.[73]

A different sort of intrusion upon the field is depicted in a curious representation of *Cricket at Kenfield Hall* (Plate 49), of about 1780, which shows a horseman approaching the wicket while play is in progress. This image may well be merely the product of the artist's imagination; but it brings to mind a strange type of cricket–"polo-cricket" perhaps–which appears to have enjoyed a brief vogue at about this time, although no doubt within a small coterie. Sir Horatio Mann, that great patron of Kent cricket and enthusiastic player, is known to have organized a cricket match to be played on horseback; and Osbaldeston was not only famous as a huntsman but was said to have "batted as well on four legs as most men on two".[74] Specially long bats had to be devised for these eccentric contests, one of which was advertised in the *Kentish Gazette* of 29 April 1794:

> Cricketing on Horseback. A very singular game of cricket will be played on Tuesday, the 6th of May, in Linsted Park, between the Gentlemen of the Hill and the Gentlemen of the Dale, for one guinea a man. The whole to be performed on horseback. To begin at nine o'clock, and the game to be played out...

After the Nottingham *v.* All-England match of 1817 the *Nottingham Journal* reported that "men and boys, young and old alike", were now emulous of becoming "proficient at the game", and that bats and balls were "held in perpetual requisition".[75] By the 1840s, with the development of the railways, matches between distant clubs became a realistic proposition, and the greater ease of travel undoubtedly exerted a particularly beneficial influence upon the development of cricket in such counties as Gloucestershire and Yorkshire, even though the teams themselves seem more often to have travelled by coach.

By the end of the eighteenth century, cricket had become established up and down England, and its wide dispersion is reflected in the many portraits of cricket-playing patrons which were executed in diverse parts of the country and even in Scotland; but it had long been popular in such areas as the West Country, where its informal and rustic character was sympathetically captured by Turner in his watercolour of *Wells Cathedral* (Plate XVIII). In a fine drawing by Edward Bradley of 1849 (made for an engraving) cricket is being played against the majestic background of Durham Cathedral and Castle (Plate 59). That cricket was being played in the square in front of Durham Cathedral as early as the mid-eighteenth century is suggested by a reference to small boys "playing at ball" in the *Journal* of Margaret Calderwood of Polton, a Scotswoman of literary tastes who recorded a journey which she made in the summer of 1756 from Edinburgh to London and thence to the Low Countries:

> June the 6th, we Din'd at Durhame, and I went to see the Cathedrall; it is a prodigious Bulky Building; it was on a Sunday betwixt Sermons, and in the Piazza there were Small Boys playing at Ball. I ask'd the girl that attended me, if it was the Custome, for the Boys to play at Ball on Sunday. She said they play on other days as well as on Sundays.[76]

(The playing of cricket on Sundays was to be featured in a steel engraving of *Sabbath Sports*, published in 1827.) In a painting of about 1848 by that fine Scottish landscape painter Sam Bough, the scene has shifted to Carlisle (Plate 63); and the watercolours made by Felix - again in the middle years of the nineteenth century - take us to cricket grounds at Oxford, Ilkeston in Derbyshire, and elsewhere (Plate 60).

Many of the matches of this era were still being organized under noble patronage, and there was a strong tradition of local club cricket played on the many grounds situated beside great houses–a tradition which still survives to some extent. The relationship of country houses and cricket grounds shown in the picture of *Kenfield Hall* (Plate 49), and in Turner's *Petworth Park* (Plates XIX, 48), was to become stronger and stronger until, in the late Victorian and Edwardian eras, some houses even had special wings added to them specifically for two cricket teams.[77]

Aristocratic patronage continued, but paradoxically became less important after the foundation of M.C.C. Instead, the nineteenth century witnessed the rise of professionalism, the fruit of the deep roots which cricket had let down in the life of the simple English yeomanry. There is no finer illustration of this ancient tradition than Peter De Wint's delicate watercolour of *The Cricketers* (Plate 62), showing a game played in a field in the heart of the countryside, where the cricketers seem to be as natural a part of the scene as any flock of cows or sheep. John Ritchie's evocative painting of *Village Cricket* (Plate 65), which expresses so well the atmosphere of countless contests such as are still engaged all over rural England, and John Robertson Reid's rather later depiction of *A Country Cricket Match* (Plate 96), while sharing a greater interest in the game itself, belong to much the same tradition.

Nonetheless, as country house cricket was to show, cricket had equally deep roots in the upper classes. Through its increasing hold in the Public Schools, which underwent a notable expansion during the nineteenth century, it spread through the aspiring middle classes as well. Winchester, Eton and Westminster are all recorded as cricket-playing schools by the middle of the eighteenth century, while the first Eton and Harrow match was held at Lord's in 1805.

This first match in the great series is particularly memorable because Lord Byron played in the Harrow XI, batting with a runner on account of his lameness, his deformed foot being supported by an inner shoe. A rough scoresheet of the match credits the poet with seven runs in the first innings and two in the second innings; but as he himself claimed, in a letter written shortly after the game, to have achieved "eleven notches" in the first innings and "seven the second", it has been suggested that the runner confused the scorer. "After the match," Byron recollected, "we dined together, and were extremely friendly; not a single discordant word was uttered by either party. To be sure, we were most of us rather drunk, and went together to the Haymarket, where we kicked up a row ... How I got home after the play God knows."[78] That he loved the game is evident from his poem "Cricket at Harrow", in which he extols the friendships he made there, among them that of the young 4th Duke of Dorset, who was yet another cricketing Sackville:

> Our sport, our studies, and our souls were one:
> Together we impell'd the flying ball;
> Together waited in our Tutor's hall;
> Together join'd in cricket's manly toil.

The scorecard has come down to us of a match played by the Winchester boys as early as 1746; and in 1796 the school played Eton on Hounslow Heath, as also in the three years from 1799 to 1801. Winchester first appeared against Harrow at Lord's in 1825. It is not surprising, therefore, that portraits of school cricketers should have become as fashionable as they did, although in the nineteenth century these were usually on a small, rather intimate scale. An example is the pencil portrait of Philip Woodhouse at the age of thirteen, drawn by Henry Edridge in 1802. It shows a view of Harrow School in the background, and another such highly-finished pencil drawing by Edridge portrays an anonymous schoolboy of the same period (Plate 64). Later in the century we find a number of representations of school cricket, such as William Evans's beautiful watercolour of *Cricket on College Field, Eton* (Plate XXII). As early as 1771 Henry Walton had painted *A Cricket Scene at Harrow School* (Plate 30), incorporating a portrait of a master whose imperious aspect suggests that the Laws will be obeyed.

Byron was not the only Romantic poet to celebrate cricket. William Blake, besides perpetrating, in "The Song of Tilly Lally", some of the worst doggerel ever written about the game,[79] included in his *Songs of Innocence* the lovely poem "The Echoing Green", with its nostalgic recollection of childhood pastimes, surrounding the two pages of the verses with an emblematic illustration in which boys with cricket bats are a prominent feature. The most interesting of these figures appears in the illustration on the second page (Plate 66). This figure belongs to a group of three children, accompanied by a mother holding an infant and leading a small boy, who are being shown the way home by the "old John, with white hair" of the poem. The day is drawing to an end and it is time for repose:

> Such, such were the joys
> When we all, girls and boys,
> In our youth time were seen,

On the Echoing Green.

Till the little ones, weary,
No more can be merry;
The sun does descend,
And our sports have an end;
Round the laps of their mothers
Many sisters and brothers,
Like birds in their nest,
Are ready for rest;
And sport no more seen,
On the darkening Green.

The illustration exists in two main versions, and one difference between them demonstrates Blake's recognition of an important development in cricket–the change from a curved to a straight bat. *Songs of Innocence* first appeared in 1789, and in the illustration to "The Echoing Green", as then published, the boy cricketer has a curved bat, such as was in use at that time (Plate 66). In 1794, however, Blake reissued *Songs of Innocence* in a volume incorporating his *Songs of Experience*. In the interval the curved bat had fallen out of use, and in a later edition of the 1820s Blake now represented the boy's "implement" as a straight bat (Plate 67). Nevertheless, in "updating" his composition in this manner, Blake did not necessarily improve it, for the earlier form of the bat harmonizes more with the curvilinear rhythms of the design.

It is conceivable that Ford Madox Brown had Blake's illustration in his mind when he painted in 1886 his mural of *Chetham's Life Dream* for the Manchester Town Hall (Plate 61), for in both compositions children are seen climbing trees whose function in the design as a whole is very largely decorative. There cricket, or a form of it, makes its appearance in a well-meaning but dubious attempt at archaeological accuracy. The composition is one of twelve symbolic scenes illustrating the history of Manchester from its origins in ancient Roman times; and the eighth scene pays tribute to the philanthropist Humphrey Chetham, by the terms of whose will the boys' school was established in 1656. In Madox Brown's picture Chetham is seen in the College garden studying his will; in his mind's eye he has conjured up the "forty healthy boys" of his life's dream, together with their schoolmaster. The scholars are engaged in various games and other activities, and a sort of mixture between those legendary precursors of cricket, "stool-ball" and "club-ball", provides the central *motif* in the design (Plate XXIII).

Like his Pre-Raphaelite associates, Madox Brown was a stickler for historical accuracy, and his problem was how to represent a game of the seventeenth century. In the foreground a somewhat awkward-looking and lumpish boy stretches forward with his right hand, towards the spectator, to retrieve a ball struck by another boy who holds a bat in his hands. It is probable that Madox Brown consulted old prints of cricketers, for the young batsman has his left foot pointing correctly down the pitch, his manner of holding his bat leaves nothing to be desired, and the bat itself is long and curved: even the ball is shown as stitched in the manner of early cricket-balls, as in the painting by Gardner of *Frederick Francis Baker* (Plate XV). But the wicket is composed not of two sticks, or stumps, but of an upturned three-legged stool. By Madox Brown's day the third stump had, of course, been introduced, and, if one were ignorant of the vital fact that originally only two had been the rule, it could seem a plausible explanation of the three stumps that they had originated in the three legs of a stool. The old term "stool-ball" must have encouraged Brown in this idea. It must be remembered that Madox Brown's picture was painted at a time when the history of cricket was attracting considerable interest while remaining still more obscure than it is now. This interest was stimulated above all by the successive editions of Joseph Strutt's *Sports and Pastimes of the People of England*, of 1801, in which a serious attempt is made to trace the origins of the game.[80] As many as five new editions of this work appeared between 1810 and 1875. Strutt had traced the origin of cricket to club-ball[81], in which the ball was struck with a club-like implement but in which there was evidently no "target" or "wicket" such as the stool of stool-ball provided. On the other hand in stool-ball the player defending the stool, at which the ball was thrown, did so with his hand alone. It became possible, therefore, to argue that cricket arose from a marriage of the two games - a theory accepted by Charles Cox in his edition of Strutt of 1903[82] and perhaps generally current before Madox Brown painted his mural.

The literature of cricket was growing fast. In 1833 John Nyren had published his *Young Cricketer's Tutor*, with its delightful accounts of the Hambledon Club, led in those days by his father Richard Nyren, the great left-arm bowler who was held in such esteem for his experience and judgement that, in John Nyren's words, "he was uniformly consulted on all questions of law or precedents". The literary style of this volume, which is of a high order, seems to have owed almost everything to Chales Cowden Clarke, who may well have written the book on the basis of conversations with Nyren, as Andrew Lang suggested. And in another work of literature, Mary Russell Mitford's *Our Village*, of almost the same date, there was to be found a description of a village match written with all the perception of a true lover of cricket–an account to be equalled in the fiction of the period, in terms of Public School cricket, by the famous chapter in Thomas Hughes's *Tom Brown's Schooldays* of 1857, in which one of the great cricket personalities of the Beauclerk era is immortalized. This was Benjamin Aislabie, a member of the Homerton Club, which in 1808 was absorbed into the M.C.C., whose secretary he became from 1822 until his death twenty years later. Aislabie was a genial man and a fair batsman, but as he weighed nearly twenty stone towards the end of his career, he was permitted to have a runner. John Mitford, who was devoted to the game and excelled as a player, called him "the Father of Cricket". Aislabie's great pleasure was to play against the Public School elevens, and in *Tom Brown's Schooldays* he faces slow lobs bowled by Tom. Before going in to bat he is described as "looking on in his white hat", and "leaning on a bat" (as cricketers have always done) "in benevolent enjoyment". Besides his love of cricket, he was the author of several verses on cricket, and of cricket songs which he would sing at the Anniversary Dinners of the M.C.C. There are three likenesses of him at Lord's–a bust and two paintings, in one of which he is portrayed on horseback in his evidently slim youth. He was also one of the M.C.C. members to whom Felix was to dedicate the famous lithographs of cricket actions which he had commissioned from George Frederick Watts.

A number of the pictorial representations of cricket of this period strike us by the serious air of the players in their trim cricketing attire, as in the vivid impression by an unknown painter of a match of around 1830 between Nottingham and Leicester – the supposed site of which has generally been identified with the old Forest Ground in Nottingham. All the players, who wear tall black hats, are uniformly dressed in white shirts and trousers, much as we see in the portraits by Felix (Nicholas Wanostrocht), including his group portrait of *The Eleven of England* of 1847 (Plate 68). Similar attire is still worn by the players in the print of *A Victorian Cricket Match at Brighton between Surrey and Kent*, published by W.H. Mason in 1865. The simple clothes worn by the boy disporting himself on the village green must always have presented a contrast to the elegance of the aristocratic youth at cricket in his park; but even in the 1820s, before cricketing jackets fell out of use and white trousers replaced breeches and silk stockings, the sartorial affectations of famous cricketers did not please everyone: they certainly offended the sensibility of that enthusiastic devotee of the game, Mary Russell Mitford, who found herself wondering how the Apollo Belvedere (Fig. 7) would look in such gear. Her remarks reflect a new division which had opened, that between the M.C.C. and the professionals on the one hand and the village players on the other – a distinction hitherto unfelt. Writing in August to the painter Benjamin Robert Haydon, she described her disappointment over a match which she had recently watched at Bramshill between Hampshire and All-England, and in which Lord Frederick Beauclerk himself (Plate 47) and William Ward of Lord's–neither of them now in his prime–had taken part as members of the All-England Eleven:

> I anticipated great pleasure from so grand an exhibition, and thought, like a simpleton, the better the play the more the enjoyment. Oh, what a mistake! There they were - a set of ugly old men, whiteheaded and bald-headed (for half of Lord's was engaged in the combat, Mr Ward and Lord Frederick, the veterans of the green) dressed in tight white jackets (the Apollo Belvedere could not bear the hideous disguise of a cricketing jacket), with neckcloths primly tied round their throats, fine japanned shoes, silk stockings, and gloves, instead of our fine village lads, with their unbuttoned collars, their loose waistcoats, and the large shirt-sleeves which give an air so picturesque and Italian to their glowing, bounding youthfulness: there they stood, railed in by themselves, silent, solemn, taciturn as chess players—a sort of dancers without music, instead of the glee, the fun, the shouts, the laughter, the glorious confusion of the country game. And there we were, the lookers-on, in tents and marquees, fine and freezing, dull as the players, cold as this hard summer weather, shivering and yawning and trying to seem pleased, the curse of gentility on all our doings, as stupid as we could have been in a ball-room. I never was so much disappointed in my life. But everything is spoilt when money puts its ugly nose in. To think of playing cricket for hard cash! Money and gentility would ruin any pastime under the sun.[83]

Miss Mitford goes on to lament the attempt to turn cricket into a "science". She was consoled only by the fact that the match had ended unsatisfactorily to both sides, in consequence of Beauclerk's having absented himself from the game, "on some real or imaginary affront", during the second innings, "so that the last two were played without him, by which means his side lost, and the other could hardly be said to win". As Miss Mitford was to explain in *Our Village*, neither the cricket promoted at Lord's nor private matches "at a pretty fête in a gentleman's park, where one club of cricketing dandies encounters another", would do for her: "No! the cricket I mean is a real solid, old-fashioned match between neighbouring parishes, where each attacks the other for honour and a supper, glory and half-a-crown a man."[84]

The cricket dear to Miss Mitford's heart provided artists with particularly attractive subject-matter on account of its very picturesqueness. Indeed, the formality of first-class cricket had much less to offer the painter. As the century advanced and important matches were acted out in great arenas, in front of vast crowds, one such occasion had little to distinguish it from another, and panoramic views of modern cricket fields like Lord's or The Oval have rarely been successful in a purely artistic sense. Usually, it has only been by some ingenious device of emphasis that the difficulties have been overcome. When, in 1887, Barrable and Ponsonby Staples painted their large picture of an imaginary Test match (Plate 70), they solved the problem by concentrating attention upon the action of the bounday fielder (compare Plate 71) and by filling the foreground with portraits of distinguished spectators.

Rather than represent a game, the Victorian painter tended to prefer a genre-like portrayal of a group of young cricketers or of an individual, in which justice could be done to character and sentiment. Miss Mitford would surely have delighted in W.H. Hunt's enchanting watercolour studies of youthful cricketers – "characters" of robust peasant stock who, whether represented in heroic action at the wicket (Plate 73) or in stolid mood before or after play (Plate 74), have so little in common with the elegant young "aristocrats of the bat" seen in eighteenth-century portraiture (Plates XVI, 18, 19, 44). The rough-and-tumble of the genre paintings by Thomas Webster and John Morgan reflect the same development (Plates XXVI, 94), which was to produce its masterpiece in one of the most memorable of all cricket images–Robert James's variations on the theme of *Tossing for Innings,* in which a group of ragged Nottingham chimney-sweeps is preparing to play a game on a desolate common (Plates XX, 77).

Yet one of Hunt's watercolours of boy cricketers possesses an iconographical interest of its own which illustrates the way in which memorable imagery tends to survive. The rustic batsman portrayed by Hunt (Plate 73) stands at a makeshift wicket composed of piled-up clothes, much as we also see in James's picture. He stands with his bat raised behind his shoulders to smite the ball, and looks at the bowler with an intense expression of concentration. His attitude has been borrowed from one of the most celebrated of all representations of cricketers – the lithograph of *The Cut* executed in his youth by the great painter George Frederick Watts for his friend and mentor Felix (Nicholas Wanostrocht) (Plate 72).

In Watts's lithograph the batsman is Felix himself (Plate 75), one of the supreme batsmen of his age, and the intention was to show the correct way to play this particular stroke. Hunt's rustic cricketer, therefore, is playing very correctly indeed: but a frowning and somewhat anxious expression has replaced the bland confidence, as well as the breeding, reflected in Watts's portrayal of Felix. Nor, of course, is there any less a contrast between Felix's elegant cricketing attire and the boy-batsman's rough country clothes: the boy's trousers are torn at the left knee, and one of his leggings has slipped down to his boot; yet even here there is an echo from an older tradition, for as early as the 1760s Francis Cotes had alluded in the same manner, in his full-length of *Lewis Cage* (Plate XVI), to the natural "disorder in the dress" that was to be expected from exertions on the cricket-field.

Miss Mitford had objected to any attempt to turn cricket into a "science". To demonstrate that it was indeed a science was one of Nicholas Wanostrocht's principal objects when, in 1845, he published his celebrated *Felix on the Bat.*[85] Watts's representation of a batsman executing "The Cut" belonged to a series of five lithographs by Watts which Felix published in 1837, and which were intended to illustrate some of the principal actions in cricket. Watts's original drawings for these lithographs have also come down to us (Plates 78, 79). The pages of Felix's book are decorated wth similar drawings demonstrating the various batting strokes, together with some comic end-pieces showing how *not* to play (Plates 80, 81). These drawings are all outstanding in their graceful qualities of draughtsmanship, and it would appear that, apart from two pages containing fourteen action studies, they are the work of Felix himself. As the author explained at the beginning of his book, "My great aim is to discover whether this splendid game is or is not so connected with some of the beautiful laws of motion as to deserve the appellation of a science." For the connoisseur of cricket art a particular interest must attach to Felix on account of his association with Watts, even if, at the time that the drawings for the five lithographs were executed, Watts had yet to establish himself as one of the supreme painters of his age. Moreover, as we shall see, there is evidently a further connection, although an obscure one, between Felix and another of the leading artists of the period–the historical painter and illustrator Sir John

Gilbert.

Nicholas Wanostrocht (Plate 75) was born, of Flemish descent, at Camberwell in 1804.[86] In his early twenties, shortly before his first marriage, he became headmaster of a school at Camberwell, the Alfred House Academy, which an uncle of his had founded. When, in 1832, he moved the school to Blackheath, it became possible for him to combine schoolteaching with membership of the Kent Eleven. Perhaps because of the risk that parents might be offended at seeing the name of their sons' headmaster on a score-sheet–for cricket was still associated in many people's minds with gambling and was now increasingly "professional"–he played cricket under the name of Felix. A left-handed batsman, Felix served the Kent team for nearly twenty years alongside such great cricketers as Fuller Pilch and Alfred Mynn. He had already played at Lord's in the late 1820s, and in 1834 he made his début for Kent. (Later on he was also to play for Surrey.) Fuller Pilch describes him appropriately as one who "knew the whole science of the game", and praised his off-driving–his right foot thrown forward–as "a beautiful thing". The crown of his distinguished career as a cricketer was a match played in his honour at Lord's in June 1846–Felix's XI *v.* Fuller Pilch's XI–which was visited by Prince Albert, "who came on horseback, attended by some of the élite of the land, and was invited to inspect the Pavilion and the implements of war". Felix's scientific bent led him to invent a bowling-machine which he named (after the Roman artillery weapon) the Catapulta, and against which he would practise, though this does not seem to have been an invention that caught on generally.

A man of exceptional charm, with a rich vein of humour, Felix had many gifts, and besides being a sound classical scholar he was a talented musician and–what is more important–a fine draughtsman. As an artist he had a *penchant* for portraiture in pastel or watercolours, although he occasionally worked in oils. In addition to what he must have learnt from the young Watts, he received some training from John Baverstock Knight, whose widowed daughter he was to marry in 1863, his first wife Elizabeth Heale having died in the same year. Brodribb has listed over two hundred works by him, and as many have been lost his total *oeuvre* must have been far more extensive than this.[87] It includes two sketch-books used during the All-England tours of 1851 and 1852 and depicting, for the most part, the grounds that the team visited (Plate 60). He also made a number of drawings for an unpublished book of instruction for artists, the *Vade Mecum of Art*. But to assess his powers as an artist we do not have to go beyond his portrait drawings of his fellow-cricketers and his many self-portraits. These are not only accomplished, but reveal a true portraitist's feeling for the character of the individual. When, about 1855, Felix retired to Brighton, he was able to devote himself to portraiture, and he was beginning to enjoy considerable success when, two years later, he suffered a stroke which impaired his powers. After his second marriage he retired finally to Wimborne Minster, in Dorset.

No doubt Felix's artistic ambitions were greatly stimulated by his association with the young Watts, who after attending the Royal Academy Schools for a period of two years had taken a studio in Blackheath. Watts was eager to improve his education by attending classes at the Alfred House Academy in music, French, Italian and Greek, and he soon developed a close friendship with its engaging headmaster. According to Watts's widow, writing of the year 1837, the evenings which the young painter spent with Felix at Alfred House were "amongst the happiest of the recollections of this time", Felix and he finding "much pleasure in each other's society".[88] Felix posed for the five drawings of 1837 in a unique alliance of cricketer and artist. As Felix was a left-handed bat, Watts was able to draw directly on the lithographic stone to produce a reversed image, so that in each case the batsman is shown in the finished print as the more usual right-handed player[89] (Plates 72, 78, 79).

The publication of the lithographs was sponsored by Felix, who dedicated them to a number of members of the M.C.C. At much the same time (the precise date is not known), Watts executed two further drawings and lithographs – *The Batsman,* for which Fuller Pilch was the model, and *The Bowler,* a representation of Alfred Mynn, – and these were also published by Felix. In 1895 Watts offered the five original drawings for the batting lithographs to Lord Harris, as President of the M.C.C., and they can now be seen at Lord's. Six years after the publication of the first set of five lithographs, Watts and Felix are again found together; and the occasion was a memorable one. Watts had entered his cartoon of *Caractacus led in Triumph through the Streets of Rome* in the competition, announced in 1842, for the decoration of the new Palace of Westminster, and out of 140 competitors he was one of three prizewinners. The premium of £300 awarded to him now enabled him to plan a period of study in Italy; and on 3 July 1843, on the eve of his departure, he was given a reception at the Alfred House Academy in honour of his triumph. Felix awarded the boys a whole day's holiday, and all the school was assembled to congratulate the young painter. Wilfrid Blunt has written of Watts's time with Felix:

> At Alfred House Watts trained his voice and throughout his life was a happy songster...No doubt he also played a good deal of cricket, for even in old age the sound of bat on ball would bring him running (or his nearest equivalent) from his studio to see the sport...In short, the hours he spent at Felix's Academy were to be often recalled as "happy old times ... I think they were to many of us happier than any of our later years".[90]

Gerald Brodribb has rightly emphasized, in contradiction of what is often stated, that Watts's lithographs, as such, have no apparent connection with *Felix on the Bat,* which was not published until 1845; nor, it may be added, did Watts's widow, in her life of the artist, maintain that there was any such connection[91]: the many illustrations in *Felix on the Bat* are indeed quite different. Yet Felix himself, writing to Frederick Gale about 1870, gives the following confusing account:

> When I published my little book of Felix on the Bat I was determined to use every means in my power to make it palatable to cricketers by reducing the glorious game to a system of attack and defence, and having received the approving opinion of so great a cricketer as W. Ward, Esq., I felt I had nothing to do but secure artists of well-known reputation. Accordingly I secured the services of G.F. Watts and John Gilbert, then in their youth, but now occupying the highest seats in the Temple of Fame.

As Brodribb has pointed out, the only connection between Watts's lithographs and the coloured plates in *Felix on the Bat* is that, apart from *The Home Block,* which did not feature in the Watts series, they represent similar actions. Brodribb suggests that all the coloured illustrations in the book may have been executed by Felix himself, and that Gilbert, who lived all his life in Blackheath, may have been responsible for the two pages demonstrating the fourteen stances.[92] The style of the latter drawings, which are extremely expressive, seems to make an attribution to Gilbert very possible; and the other illustrations in the book strongly recall Felix's own style in his authenticated portraits. It may well be that, having modelled his own drawings on Watts's originals, Felix was sufficiently conscious of his indebtedness to the young painter to wish to acknowledge it in his letter to Frederick Gale. Brodribb gives as possible reasons for the fact that Felix did not use the original illustrations in his book his consciousness that they were now too old and well known and, secondly, a reluctance on Watts's part, once he had become established as an artist, to allow his work to appear in a cricket book. Whatever the truth of the matter, the drawings by Watts survive as the most beautiful of all graphic representations of action in cricket, as well as conveying to us a very clear idea of how strokes were played in the period just before the appearance of W.G. Grace, and of how Alfred Mynn bowled. But when this has been said, lovers of cricket will probably find still greater pleasure in the lively renderings of action on the field–whether demonstrating how to play or how not to–which we must ascribe to Felix himself. They show a very complete understanding of the human figure in the expression of movement which is quite extraordinary for an amateur (Plates 80, 81).

A signed sketch made by another major artist of the Victorian period, Sir Edwin Landseer, representing a view of Lord's, was formerly in the M.C.C. Collection, but unfortunately no photograph exists. Landseer executed this sketch about 1868, when he had been living at 1 St John's Road for some forty years, and he made it from the "Nursery" end, showing a prospect of the ground with the pavilion and grandstand.[93]

The names of Felix, Fuller Pilch and Alfred Mynn introduce us to one of the legendary periods of cricket history. It was these great players who dominated cricket in the second quarter of the nineteenth century, and there were others of comparable fame. Pilch was the most celebrated batsman of his time, being noted for his forward play. It is fitting that in later life, as an umpire, he stood in the first representative match played by W.G. Grace,[94] although Mynn, the "Lion of Kent", bore the greater resemblance to Grace in being an all-rounder – a high-scoring batsman and a terrifyingly fast round-arm bowler. The epitaph on Mynn composed by the sporting writer William Jeffrey Prowse, who for a short time had been a pupil at Felix's school, where he must first have developed his love of the game, is one of the most evocative and moving of all cricket verses. The echo in the last line of the Roman poet Martial may well testify to the soundness of Felix's teaching of the classics:

> With his tall and stately presence, with his nobly moulded form,
> His broad hand was ever open, his brave heart was ever warm.
> All were proud of him, all loved him. As the changing seasons pass,
> As our champion lies asleeping underneath the Kentish grass,
> Proudly, sadly we will name him–to forget him were a sin:
> Lightly lie the turf upon thee, kind and manly Alfred Mynn.[95]

This was the period also of William Lillywhite of Sussex, called "the Nonpareil", whose adoption of the new style of round-arm bowling was largely instrumental in compelling a change in the Laws; of William Clarke of Nottingham, another great bowler but remembered besides for having established the Trent Bridge ground and for his imperious leadership of the All-England Eleven;[96] and of the handsome George Parr, again from Nottingham, famous for his unorthodox leg-hits into a tree which stood until recently at Trent Bridge, and which was called "Parr's Tree" after him. It is the eminence of Clarke of Nottinghamshire that explains the choice of his likeness for the decoration of some notable Staffordshire ware and its derivatives (Plates 84, 85).

We must pass over, with only a brief mention, the notorious rift in the 1860s between the northern and southern players which was caused by the southerners' justified suspicion that Clarke, as the manager of the All-England XI, was lining his own pocket with the profits, and which led to the formation of a new representative team, the United England XI: but it is worth recalling that it was this new team that numbered among its leading players John Wisden, the founder of the *Cricketer's Almanack* (sometimes known as "the Cricketer's Bible").

The appearance of many of these players has been captured for us by the fluent pencil of Felix. The group by Felix of *The Eleven of England*, showing the All-England team of 1847, stands by its quality far above the run-of-the-mill print of the period (Plate 68). The draughtsmanship is of no mean order: the same hand was surely capable of executing the lively studies of players in action which decorate the pages of *Felix on the Bat* (Plates 80, 81), and the characterization is that of a born portraitist. Furthermore, in *The Eleven of England* the disposition of the figures and the management of the varied lighting are extremely skilful, and monotony is avoided by the fact that not one attitude or gesture is repeated. The result, although on a minor scale, is a satisfyingly unified group-portrait in the best tradition of a genre which Hogarth and Zoffany had brought to perfection in England in an earlier age. Felix was indeed an "all-rounder" – as cricketer, classical scholar, musician and, by no means least, as artist.

The pattern of modern cricket was woven in the second half of the nineteenth century. To change the metaphor, it was then that its structure took on the clear form described by Sir Home Gordon: "English cricket may be compared to an imposing edifice. The spacious foundations are formed by village matches. On that is raised the charming ground-floor of club cricket. The more austere and less irresponsible superstructure of county cricket appears majestic but severe. The cupola consists of Test Matches and is so elevated as to excite ambitious aspirations, but also so bleakly exposed as to lose recreative consciousness."[97]

AT HOME AND AWAY

The rapid increase in the number of cricket clubs during the latter half of the nineteenth century must have been encouraged in great measure by the prestige and the missionary enterprise, as we may call it, of the M.C.C. In addition to the innumerable local clubs, the middle and later years of the century saw the creation of the famous wandering clubs which possessed no ground of their own and engaged in peripatetic cricket against the clubs and schools. Their story – which now decorated the game with such picturesque names as I Zingari, The Free Foresters, The Incogniti, The Wanderers, The Harlequins and The Quidnuncs – lies outside the scope of these pages; but the continuity of cricket history is reflected once again in the fact that it was Lord Frederick Beauclerk's nephew by marriage, Sir Spencer Ponsonby-Fane, who, together with his brother Lord Bessborough and J. Loraine Baldwin, founded that most celebrated (and most quaintly mispronounced) club I Zingari. In a tiny watercolour by A.F. Payne of *Cricket at Cowley*, the flag of I Zingari flies proudly over the pavilion (Plate 83).

Sir Spencer, besides holding an office in the Lord Chamberlain's Department, was treasurer of M.C.C. for many years, declining the Presidency on several occasions, and he earns our particular gratitude for having begun the collection of cricket pictures now at Lord's. That was around the year 1864, when the only two paintings owned by the M.C.C. were the fine picture by Hayman of "*Cricket in Marylebone Fields*" (Plates II, 10) and the version (wrongly ascribed to Hayman himself) of the same artist's composition for the Vauxhall decorations (Plate 15). Sir Spencer's passion was to visit auction-rooms and dealers' galleries in search of cricket pictures and portraits of cricketers, and in the Diamond Jubilee year the M.C.C. commissioned a portrait of him from the Royal Academician W.W. Ouless, so that it could be hung in the Long Room along with the portraits of former Presidents which he had been instrumental in acquiring for the Club. He also had the further honour of being portrayed by Felix.

Although what Andrew Lang called "the cosmic movement"[98] did not commence until 1862, when a party of twelve English cricketers visited Australia, to be followed two years later by another national team (whose members included George Parr and Dr E.M. Grace), cricket had long been played by Englishmen abroad, notably when they were making the Grand Tour in Italy or, for instance, if they were on military or diplomatic service. As we have seen, the 3rd Duke of Dorset would have played cricket in Paris, if the French Revolution had not stopped play. But earlier still, the game had been played in Belgium, and we find the young Earl of Carlisle writing from Spa in August 1748 to his friend George Selwyn: "I rise at six, am on horseback till breakfast, play at cricket till dinner [often in this period taken at four o'clock], and dance in the evening till I can scarce crawl to bed at eleven. There's a life for you!" As Robert Streatfeild's watercolour shows, cricket was still being played at Spa in the 1840s (Plate 86).

During the wars against Napoleon, cricket was revived in Belgium by officers in the British Army. Colonel Basil Jackson, in his *Notes and Reminiscences of a Staff Officer*, refers to cricket matches in Brussels in 1814, and Pycroft tells us of a game among officers on 12 June 1815, in which the Duke of Richmond participated, and which was interrupted by the arrival upon the scene of the Duke of Wellington.[99] It was this match that was followed by the famous Ball given by the Duke and Duchess of Richmond on the eve of Quâtre Bras – the engagement which developed into the Battle of Waterloo, and in which fell the young Lord Hay, who had sat for one of the finest of "cricket portraits" (Plate XVII). Although it appears that Wellington never uttered the saying attributed to him that the Battle of Waterloo "was won on the playing fields of Eton", he is associated with cricket in more than one political caricature of the period. In the imagination of one cartoonist, thought to be Charles Landseer, it was the Iron Duke's superior batsmanship that, as the late Viscount Montgomery would have said, "hit Napoleon for six". The cartoonist shows him (somewhat prophetically) in the act of defending, not a wicket, but the Three Graces, who display a banner with the legend, "Down with the tyrant" *(à bas le tyran)* (Plate 82).

If only because Felix's forebears had been Flemings, it is appropriate that Belgium should have become, long after the Napoleonic Wars, a fertile ground for the indigenous growth of cricket; and the year 1866 saw the foundation, with the support of the Count of Flanders and the British Ambassador, of the Brussels Cricket Club, whose beautiful ground in the Vallon des Anglais, Bois de la Cambre, can be seen in an anonymous sketch of about 1870 (Plate 87).

At about the same time we hear of a Cricket Club in Paris; and in 1867, on the suggestion of R.A. FitzGerald, the eminent secretary of the M.C.C., who was then on a visit to France, a twelve-a-side match was played in the Bois de Boulogne between a team from Lord's and the Paris Club. But the game has put down few lasting roots in France (even if it be allowed that the word *umpire* comes from the French *non pair*, meaning "odd man"), and "French cricket" has a connotation of its own. We learn indeed without surprise that after the match of 1867 a French onlooker remarked to FitzGerald: "It is a truly magnificent game, but I cannot understand why you do not engage a servant to field for you instead of having so much running about to do yourself".[100]

It was the scion of a British banking family resident in Holland, Thomas Hope "of Amsterdam", who posed for the most memorable of cricketing pictures associated with the Grand Tour. J. Sablet's small full-length portrait (Plate XXIV), painted in 1792, shows him as a batsman at the wicket, and Thomas Hope is holding one of those curiously long – but by now archaic – bats which players somehow knew how to manipulate in the early period of cricket history. The picture was painted in Rome – where Sablet was resident at this time. Thomas Hope, on his retiring, in uncomfortable circumstances, from Amsterdam to his fine country seat in Surrey in 1794-5, was to become a leading promoter of the Neoclassical style in architecture and the arts and had Sablet's advice on the decoration of his London house in 1800. He was the patron of West and Haydon among painters, and of Flaxman and Thorvaldsen among sculptors. A furniture designer and a collector, as well as being the author of a novel, Hope was a man of unusually wide interests and varied abilities. Among his passions was a fondness for things oriental (most notably Turkish dress), a taste that relates him, in this respect, less to the Neoclassical than to the Romantic movement.[101]

An illuminating insight into the manner in which the English imported cricket, and even hunting, into foreign lands is supplied by Henry Matthew's *Diary of an Invalid,* in which the author describes his travels in Italy. When he arrived in Naples in February 1818 an agreeable surprise was awaiting him:

> The weather is beautiful, and as warm as a June day in England...Drove after breakfast to the *Campo di Marte;* where to my great surprise, I found myself transported ten years backwards, into the middle of old school-fellows. There was a regular double-wicket match going on;–Eton against the world; and the world was beaten in one innings! This disposition to carry the amusements of their own country along with them is a striking characteristic of the English. One of them imports a pack of hounds from England to Rome, and hunts regularly during the season, to the great astonishment of the natives. At Florence, they establish races on the Cascine, after the English manner, and ride their own horses, with the caps and jackets of English jockeys; and everywhere, they make themselves independent of the natives, and rather provide entertainment for themselves, than seek it from the same sources with the people amongst whom they happen to be.[102]

The artist Benjamin Robert Haydon wrote in similar vein to his painter friend Seymour Kirkup in Florence:

> Wherever they [the English] go, racing, cricket, trial by jury, fox-hunting and portraits are the simple commodities first planted or thought of. Blessed be the name of John Bull![103]

Such customs are well illustrated by two fascinating watercolours (Plates 88, 89) by the German artist Carl Werner, who was later to work for some time in England, becoming a member of the New Watercolour Society and exhibiting in the 1860s at the Royal Academy. Werner travelled extensively in Europe, and, while in Rome in the year 1850, he watched and drew a cricket match played by a party of English gentlemen in the grounds of the Villa Doria-Pamphili, and also sketched them as they took refreshments during the luncheon interval. The connection of the noble Doria family with cricket continues to this day, for the Principessa Doria and her English husband Don Frank Pogson still patronize cricket matches at the Villa.

It may be noted that in Werner's view of the match the scorer (there is only one) is no longer seated on the ground within the field of play, as in eighteenth-century representations (Plates II, 16, 20), but sits, top-hatted, at a table at which three of the English party – a gentleman and two ladies – are also gathered. It is clear from other pictures that by the early nineteenth century this arrangement had become the rule, as, for instance, in Thomas Henwood's famous picture *The Scorer,* of 1842, where the mathematical task is lightened further by an ample provision of claret (Plate 98).

WOMEN'S CRICKET

The attendance of fashionable ladies at cricket matches was common in the late eighteenth century and throughout the nineteenth, as we know from contemporary letters and other written accounts (such as those of Mary Russell Mitford) and also from many paintings of the period. It must not be supposed, however, that women did not often participate directly in the game, and in the eighteenth century they had, as we have indicated, a formidable advocate in the 3rd Duke of Dorset. Some of the leading ladies in fashionable society were known for their interest in cricket. For example, the beautiful Lady Sarah Bunbury, whom Reynolds immortalized in the act of sacrificing to the Graces, was the subject of a characteristically trenchant observation on the part of Mrs Piozzi: "She never did sacrifice to the Graces: her face was gloriously handsome, but she used to play cricket and eat beefsteaks on the Steyne at Brighton."[104] Lady Sarah, a Lennox, was the daughter of "the Duke who was cricket", as the 2nd Duke of Richmond was called. She was the aunt of Charles Lennox, the famous cricketer (Plate 7). Eighteenth-century newspapers contain a number of reports of ladies' matches: sometimes, for example, a game might be arranged between the married and the unmarried women of a village; sometimes there would be a much grander match under noble patronage. In 1775 the *Annual Register* reported an "extraordinary" game played on 3 August of that year at Molesey Hurst:

> An extraordinary match at cricket was played at Moulsey-Hurst, between 6 unmarried against the same number of married women; and was won by the former, though one of the latter ran seventeen notches. There were great betts depending.[105]

An account in the *News* of 1811 of a cricket match played at Newington, in Middlesex, between eleven women of Hampshire and eleven women of Surrey, is no less patronizingly headed *CRICKET MATCH EXTRAORDINARY* – a title also adopted for a well-known coloured print, of about the same date, after Rowlandson (which gives most of the players an unseemly and probably misleading appearance of blowsiness) (Plate 91). The match of 1811 had been arranged by two noblemen for 500 guineas a side, and we may agree with Marjorie Pollard that the occasion "savours of exploitation".[106] Attention would appear to have been focused in this period very much upon the appearance and attire of the lady cricketers, and in this particular instance the author of the newspaper account noted that the players were "of all ages and sizes" and that the Hampshire ladies wore purple ribbons and their Surrey rivals orange and blue. He did, nevertheless, consider the play interesting enough to inform his readers that the outstanding performer was "a Hampshire lass" who scored 41 before being run out. A rather amateurish – and perhaps suspect – painting reputed to be of 1838 (in the M.C.C. Collection) shows what a ladies' match may have looked like at the beginning of the Victorian Age, when the need for a greater propriety in dress than was acceptable in Rowlandson's day must have somewhat encumbered the players.

The principal change in the status of women's cricket came with the foundation, in the summer of 1887, of the White Heather Club at Nun Appleton, in Yorkshire (of which, before her marriage, Stanley Baldwin's wife was a member). In 1892 the English Cricket and Athletic Association announced the formation of two women's elevens under the title of "The Original English Lady Cricketers", who were to be trained by leading male professionals and to be "elegantly and appropriately attired" (one of their cricketing dresses can be seen at Lord's). The advertisement added:

> N.B.–Every effort is made to keep this organization in every respect select and refined. A matron accompanies each eleven to all engagements...

W.G. Grace was not impressed, and foretold the early demise of such associations; but in the late 1890s, when the "Clifton Ladies" team was formed, Grace's daughter Bessie became a member of it, establishing a reputation for strong hitting.

The slow progress of women's cricket accounts for its rarity in cricket art of the Victorian period; but women – and especially great ladies – became more and more prominent as members of crowds in paintings or engravings of cricket matches, whether they represent major events or village games: typical examples are provided by the famous *England v. Australia at Lord's*, painted by George Barrable and Sir Robert Ponsonby Staples in 1887 (Plate 70), and by the well-known print by William Drummond and Charles Basèbe (published by W.H. Mason) of a county match at Brighton played in 1865 between Sussex and Kent, although this latter composition was, perhaps, more of an idealistic reconstruction.

HIGH VICTORIAN ART AND CRICKET

It was the Victorians who made cricket art "point a moral, or adorn a tale". The language lay ready to hand: it was the language of down-to-earth genre painting as it had been developed earlier in the century by Sir David Wilkie and William Mulready, who had taken their inspiration from the Dutch seventeenth-century masters. The paintings of Thomas Webster and John Morgan, with their anecdotal reflections of everyday English life, are typical of this tendency, and both painters delighted in depicting the games and amusements of children. Direct or indirect allusions to cricket found their natural place in this homely and realistic style (Plate 92). Morgan's variations on the theme of *The Fight* (Plate XXVI) are among the most enchanting of such pictures from the Victorian period, and have rarely been excelled for their sympathetic insight into the world of childhood. Webster, on the other hand, preferred to allude to cricket much less directly: often he places in the foreground of a scene of boyish activity a discarded bat and perhaps a ball, as though these were the recognized "props" in the theatre of sport that should designate the greatest and noblest of English games. In the schoolhouse scene of *The Boy with Many Friends* (Plate 94) such a foreground detail suggests that even cricket is forgotten when the heart of a boy is seduced by the prospect of "tuck" – indicated by the hamper belonging to the pampered child at the centre of the inquisitive throng.

This genre tradition survived into the twentieth century. Other relatively early examples from the Victorian period include Alexander Burr's charming confrontation of old age and extreme youth on a makeshift cricket pitch (Plate 95) and John Robertson Reid's splendid picture of *A Country Cricket Match* (Plates XXVII, 96), which was painted in 1878. The old man about to bowl underarm to a small boy in Burr's painting would have remembered the Beauclerk era.

That Reid knew his cricket will be evident from a glance at the details of the actual play shown in the top right-hand corner of the painting; but the artist has focused his main attention on the group of spectators and cricketers gathered by the marquee at the edge of the field. Not all the players appear to possess cricket gear, and some have turned out in braces: others, however, are very correctly attired and are wearing striped caps of various colours. Old men look wisely on; the young enjoy the festival spirit that pervades the scene. Prominent in the foreground, a pretty village girl is carrying a tray of drinks, while an elegant cricketing beau teases her by pulling at her neck-ribbon and murmuring, no doubt, some sweet nothing in her ear (Plate XXVII). This masterpiece of cricket art contains brilliant passages of painting, including a finely rendered "still-life" of bat, pads, gloves and other cricketing equipment. What could be more evocative than this happy picture of country cricket on a summer's day, and what could be more true as a depiction of its times? Indeed, the artist's eye has caught a detail that he could not have guessed would be of interest long afterwards to the cricket historian–the fact that the square-leg umpire still stands with a bat in his hand like his eighteenth-century predecessors: in the heart of England the old customs die hard; and in the hands of the truthful and observant artist cricket art can show an intriguing continuity.

Mark Girouard has brilliantly illuminated the development in Victorian England of a chivalric code inspired by the Arthurian legend, and has shown how the games played at school–and especially cricket–were regarded not only as pastimes or forms of exercise but also as the means whereby the "manly virtues" were encouraged.[107] A joint memorial at Harrow School to the Hon. Robert Grimston and the Earl of Bessborough, who had both coached the boys in cricket, pays tribute to them in a manner typical of this chivalric ideal: "While teaching skill in cricket, they taught manliness and honour." [108]

Sir Henry Newbolt's poem *Vitaï Lampada* (first published in 1897) is only the best-known and most frequently quoted expression of the relationship between the manly virtues learnt at school on the cricket field and the courage and discipline required of a true son of the Empire in the sterner engagements of life.[109]

We may take as a pictorial counterpart of Newbolt's poem Henry Garland's painting *The Winner of the Match*, of 1864 (Plate XXVIII), not because any heroic deed on the frontiers of Empire is represented, but because we are led to assume that the boy-hero of the cricket match, carried in triumph on the shoulders of his fellows, and receiving admiring glances on every hand from old and young alike, the flag of his team–*Excelsior* (no less!) – raised proudly above his head, will acquit himself no less well in the lists of life.

There is a hint of the same heroic ideal in that most popular of nineteenth-century paintings of boy cricketers, P.H. Calderon's *Captain of the Eleven* (Plate XXX). Calderon was an artist who exemplified Victorian "high seriousness", and the painter of such pictures as *Renunciation* and *Broken Vows* was essentially a storyteller who was particularly fond of subjects which could carry moral overtones. Thus in *Broken Vows* we share the heartbreak of a young woman who overhears, from the other side of a garden wall, the treacherous advances made by her fiancé to a fair rival. Where the subject is the universal passion, as it is here, such a picture can present no problem of interpretation: the meaning is clear. But it is questionable whether the essential meaning of *Captain of the Eleven* could be fully understood by any one who was not conversant with the place of cricket in English life or of what its values represented to the Victorian mind. The boy captain is evidently practising in a garden, and it is a serious activity. And the painting would be nothing without the boy's determined expression of concentration or the correctness with which, in evident obedience to the expert coaching of the time, his hands grasp the bat and, above all, keep it *straight*.

A similar suggestion of the young cricketer on the threshold of life – for which the game will better prepare him – is to be found in Joseph Durham's sculpture of Basil Edwin Lawrance, entitled *Waiting his Innings* (1866) (Plate 55). And Halse's Parian-ware model of *Young England* (1874) has similar, more plainly expressed connotations (Plate 54).

Even still-life paintings can tell a story or point a moral; and in this sense, as well as in their realism, the still lifes of the obscure Edward George Handel Lucas, who lived and worked in poverty in Croydon, revive a Dutch seventeenth-century tradition. Lucas's groups of meaningfully selected objects, such as bottles, glasses, dice and clay pipes, offered to visitors to the Royal Academy stark sermons upon the evils of drink, gambling or smoking; and an air of melancholy usually hangs like a shadow over these pathetic assemblages. The same melancholy pervades the picture which he entitled *When We Were Boys Together* (Plate 93). Here the still-life group includes a cricket bat and ball, books and marbles, a slate bearing a chalk sketch of a schoolmaster in a mortar-board and with a cane raised in his right hand, and a tawse hanging ominously from a nail on the wall. The artist seems to have been fond of the subject, for he repeated it, and perhaps he found that it sold. But the feeling that is evoked is scarcely one of unalloyed delight in recollections of boyhood years, for there is a grimness in the nostalgia, as though it were oppressed by memories of the tawse and the schoolmaster's cane, and as though the lesson to be learnt was that in order to grow to man's estate a boy must be licked into shape. A cricketer, however, may perhaps be reassured by the evidence provided by the edge of the bat represented in the picture that it has been much in use.

The reign of Queen Victoria may be called the Age of the Graces, for when she ascended the throne in 1837 the eldest of the five celebrated cricketing brothers, Henry, was already four years old and his mother, the remarkable Martha Grace, who knew everything there was to know about cricket, would already have placed a bat in his hand. Alfred, the next boy, was born in 1840, and the three youngest sons, who, as well as following their father into the medical profession, were to become the most eminent in the game, arrived respectively in 1841, 1848 and 1850: they were, of course, E.M. (Edward Mills), W.G. (William Gilbert) and G.F. (George Frederick), great cricketers all and the champions of the Gloucestershire side, which by their prowess now rose up to challenge the supremacy of Nottinghamshire, and all of them England players. When Queen Victoria died in 1901, "W.G." was still playing for the London County Eleven, but his career was now drawing to an end. The manner in which, as a player and as a national figure, "W.G." dominated Victorian cricket – even in an age that saw such players as Arthur Shrewsbury, the Hon. Alfred Lyttelton, Gilbert Jessop and E.M. himself – is too much part of our heritage to require retelling here.[110] The best-known painting of him at the wicket – by Archibald Stuart Wortley (Plate XXV) – emphasizes his colossal bulk and strength, while suggesting something more – that mental concentration and that co-ordination of hand and eye which made him (as the statistics of his performances are alone sufficient to prove) the greatest all-round player ever to appear on a cricket field. Lord Ullswater's account of this picture could scarcely be bettered:

> It depicts W.G. at the wicket in the centre of Lord's ground, standing ready to play the ball, in the correct position, his right foot behind the popping-crease, left foot slightly advanced, with toes off the ground, his left shoulder well forward and head slightly turned to the bowler. His browned, brawny arms (sleeves turned up above the elbow), his massive frame and powerful shoulders, look like the embodiment of strength and drive. Woe betide a loose ball!...It has been critically observed that the clock appears to point to 2.30, an hour at which there was never any play in W.G.'s time at Lord's. But this is hyper-criticism![111]

It may be observed that W.G. wears brown shoes. Dark shoes for cricket were in fact traditional, and most frequently they are shown in early cricket pictures as black (Plate III). But often brighter footwear had been preferred by eighteenth-century gentlemen, and the poet Huddesford, writing in 1791, hails the advent of Whitsuntide in anticipation that it will see the return of cricket "in slippers red and drawers white".

We are now far removed from eighteenth-century elegance. Batsmen's pads, first tried out in a crude form by Robert Robinson of Fareham at some time between 1792 and 1819, had been in wide use since the 1830s and probably earlier; and gone now were the days when Lord Frederick could denounce any form of "leggings" as being "so unfair for the bowler", as he meaningfully put it. Batting gloves were longer in appearing, and although Benjamin Aislabie mentioned them in 1839 in a speech at the Anniversary Dinner at Lord's, there had been much opposition to their use. But once–by the Age of Grace–pads and gloves had been introduced, the iconography of cricket art could never be the same again, and an artist like Watts or Felix would have regretted the armour that obstructed the natural rhythms of the human frame. The full-length portraits of Grace (Plate XXV) and of Hornby (Plate XXXI) represent in this important respect a break with the older images of physical elegance by which we remember Mynn and Clarke. It is significant that in the 1830s, before pads and gloves had been universally adopted, artists preferred to portray cricketers without them.

Another picture of Grace, at half-length, in the National Portrait Gallery, which is the work of an unidentified but very competent portraitist (Plate 97), reveals perhaps more of the innate friendliness of the man, which showed itself in many acts of generosity on and off the cricket-field. One would not, perhaps, search in "W.G.'s" familiar countenance for signs either of great intellectual powers or of refined sensibility, but rather for a frank openness of disposition and for the manly virtues of a natural athlete. It is a strong face, that of a man who while enjoying life to the full maintained an exemplary self-control. Bernard Darwin, his biographer, has written of him:

> His interests were all of the open air. If people wanted to read books, no doubt they got pleasure from it, but it was a pleasure that he could not really understand. *Wisden*, yes, perhaps, to confirm a memory or refute an argument, or in winter as an earnest of the summer to come; but in a general way, books were bad for cricket. "How can you expect to make runs," he said to one of the Gloucestershire side, "when you are always reading?" [112]

And again, with regard to his constitution:

> A whole bottle of champagne was a mere nothing to him; having consumed it he would go down on all fours, and balance the bottle on the top of his head and rise to his feet again. Nothing could disturb that magnificent constitution, and those who hoped by a long and late sitting to shorten his innings next day often found themselves disappointed. His regular habit while cricketing was to drink one large whisky and soda, with a touch of angostura bitters, at lunch, and another when the day's play ended; this allowance he never varied or exceeded till the evening came, and despite his huge frame, though he never dieted, he ate sparingly. [113]

As a man of sixty, Grace sat for an unusual watercolour study by Henry Tuke, the portrait and genre painter. The occasion was the evening after a match played in the summer of 1908 at Ranjitsinhji's country home in Sussex, and–perhaps at the artist's request–Grace posed in the great Indian batsman's turban. It may well be that the characteristic slant of Grace's often narrowed eyes had suggested to Tuke a resemblance to some Eastern potentate. The expressive freedom of Tuke's style was, at all events, worthy of his subject, and Grace's reflective, sideways glance, combined with the oriental aspect imposed upon him, helps to give the portrait its undeniable power. More sinister than this is Max Beerbohm's caricature *The Doctor* (Plate 103), in which Grace is shown holding a proportionately tiny bat in one hand as he stands on the field at Lord's, and with the other accepting a large cheque from the cricket-loving editor of the *Daily Telegraph*, while the funeral of one of his patients passes in the distance. "W.G." did, of course, practise as a doctor, but there were other duties in the season of summer.

Cricket and cricketers frequently became targets for cartoonists during the nineteenth century; but they were more often shown by caricaturists in a favourable light, as in the famous series of "Ape" and "Spy" cartoons contributed to *Vanity Fair* by Carlo Pellegrini ("Ape"), a descendant of the Medici family who had settled in London in the 1860s, and Sir Leslie Ward ("Spy"), a great-grandson of the Romantic painter James Ward and a *protégé* in his early days of Sir John Everett Millais. We have from the hand of "Ape" caricatures of Spofforth, the "Demon Bowler" from Australia, and of the Hon. Alfred Lyttelton, and from that of "Spy" portrayals of "W.G."; of Albert Neilsen Hornby–the Hornby of Francis Thompson's famous line, "O my Hornby and my Barlow long ago!";[114] of Lord Hawke, the great Yorkshire cricketer (Plate 102); of Ivo Bligh (the Earl of Darnley), for ever to be associated with "the Ashes"; of Charles Fry, that all-rounder in life itself; of Gilbert Jessop, the great hitter; of (Sir) Pelham Warner, cricketer and afterwards historian and elder statesman of cricket; and of many others, the series culminating from a cricketing point of view in the portrait of one of the bright new stars of the "Golden Age", (Sir) Jack Hobbs. The quality of these drawings, and especially of the cricket caricatures of "Spy", which are by far the more numerous, gives them a place of their own in the history of cricketing art, not least because of the artist's ability to create an image that is at once memorable and convincing.

The series as a whole reminds us that many of the other subjects of the *Vanity Fair* caricatures, whether they were statesmen or writers, or dignitaries of the Church, were also cricketers, or had played in their earlier days. It is not, however, possible to associate many of these eminent Victorians with specifically cricket art. There was of course Disraeli, who was once portrayed as a batsman at the wicket, albeit a rather distracted-looking one (Plate 101); and Dickens is represented in one picture of a cricket match in the role of the scorer and on another occasion in the act of bowling the first ball (Plate 99). It may be added that Dickens's appreciation of cricket and its humane influence is reflected in a letter which he wrote home from Baltimore in February 1868 about the formation and management of a cricket club, to which he subscribed £5 besides offering his services as Chairman:

> It [cricket] really places a thousand joys of life within the reach of those who, without their powers with the bat and ball, would find existence a very humdrum and monotonous affair. It acts as the social cement of classes ... It is no exaggeration to say ... that more valuable acquaintances, more permanent and faithful friendships, have been made in the cricket field than in any other social rendezvous of the United Kingdom.[115]

Among the poets, Francis Thompson, who merits special mention as the author of the finest cricket poem in the language, was never, so far as we know, portrayed as a cricketer despite his passion for the game. A.N. Hornby, one of the two Lancashire heroes of the match recollected in Thompson's poem, whose brilliant batting style contrasted so strongly with the more plodding manner of his professional partner, Barlow, was as fortunate in the painter for whom he sat at the height of his career as in the poet who celebrated him. The full-length portrait of Hornby by the Hon. John Collier (Plate XXXI) shows him accoutred in flannels and pads, like a knight ready for a tourney (as Mark Girouard has suggested), a bat in his right hand and a tubular batting-glove in his left; his bearing and expression convey both dignity and alertness, and the whole portrait is alive.

In "At Lord's", Francis Thompson, sitting at the ground, finds himself, as a Lancashire

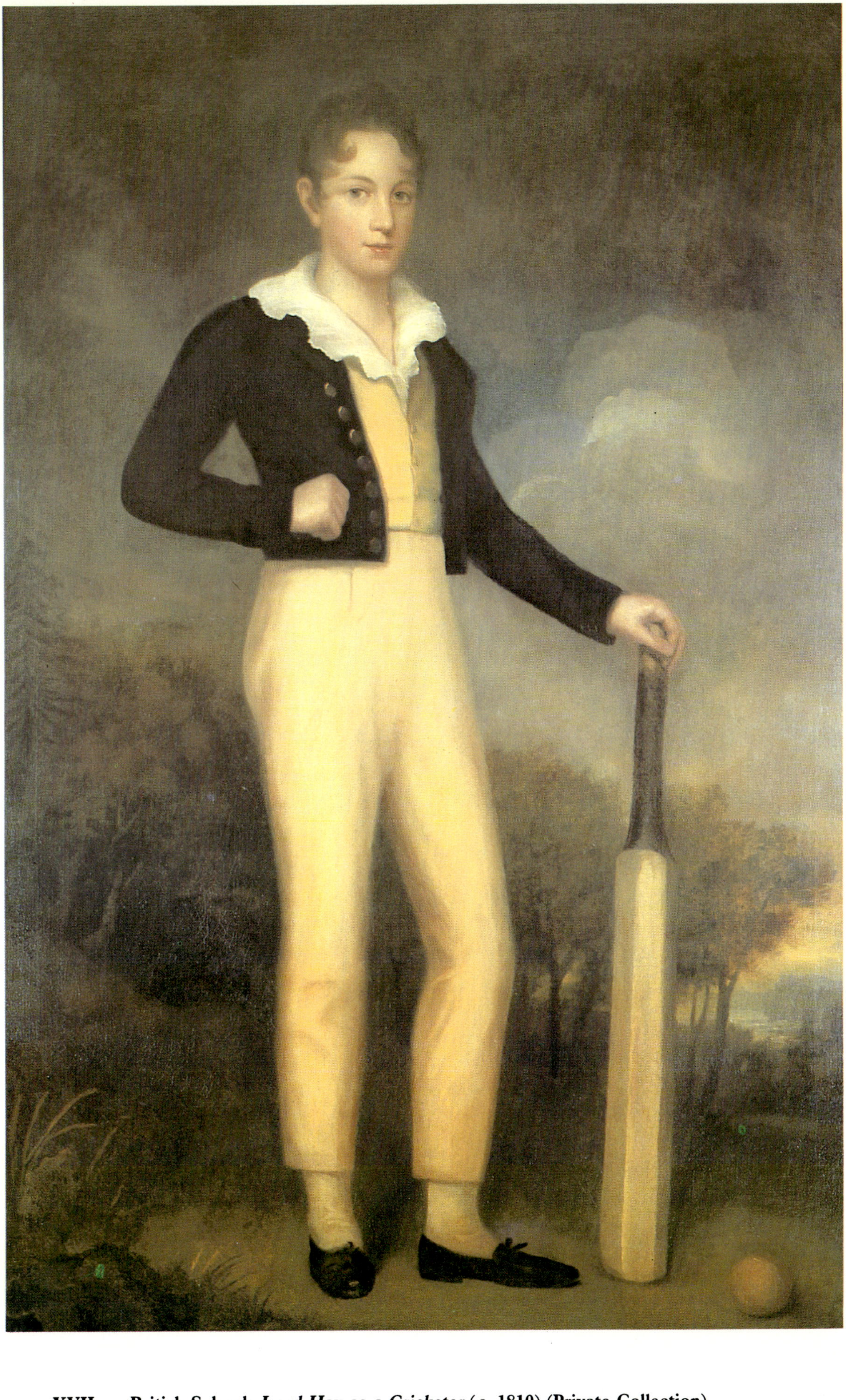

XVII. British School: *Lord Hay as a Cricketer* (c. 1810) (Private Collection).

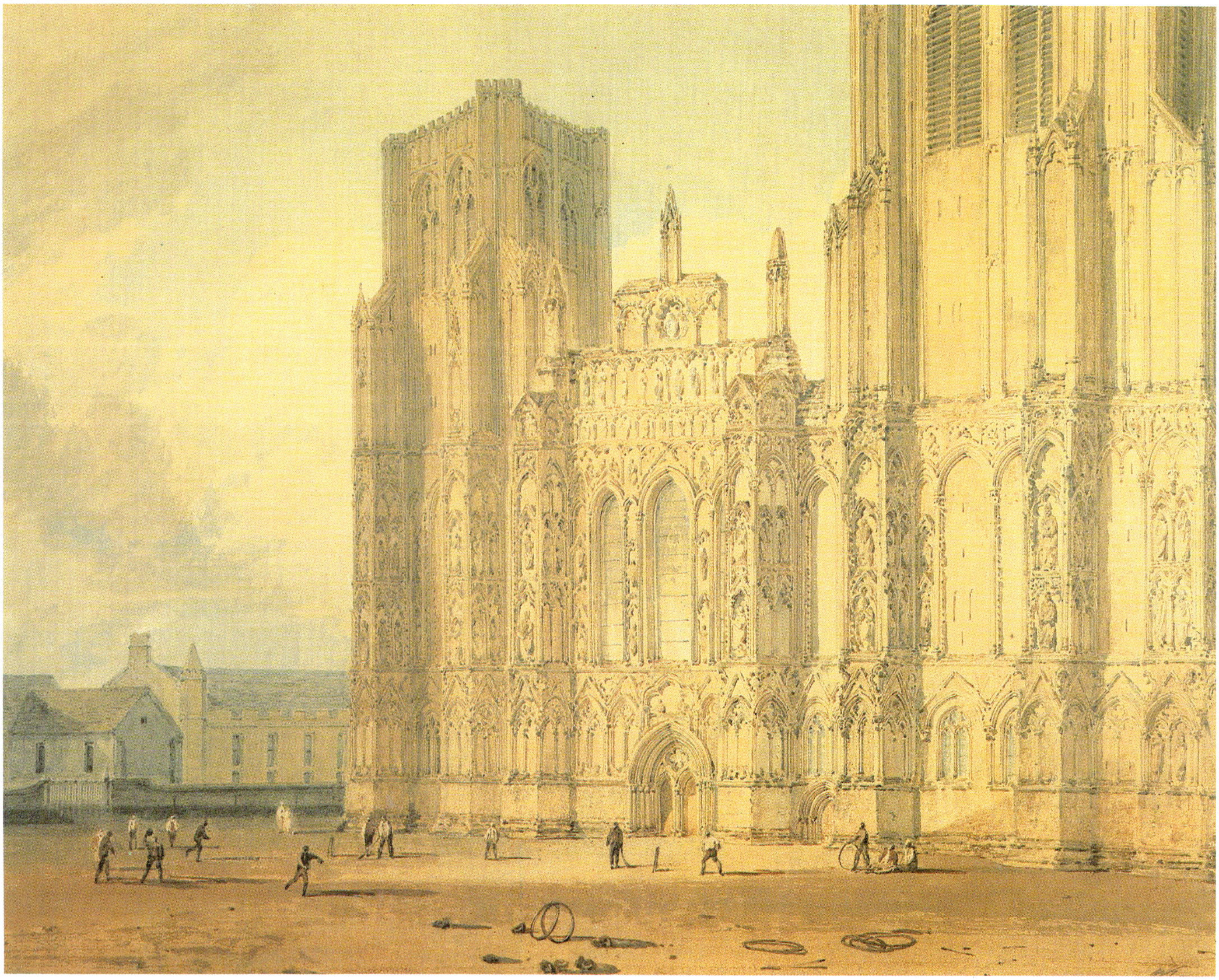

XVIII. J.M.W.Turner, R.A.: ***Wells Cathedral with a Game of Cricket*** **(c. 1795) (Lady Lever Art Gallery, Port Sunlight).**

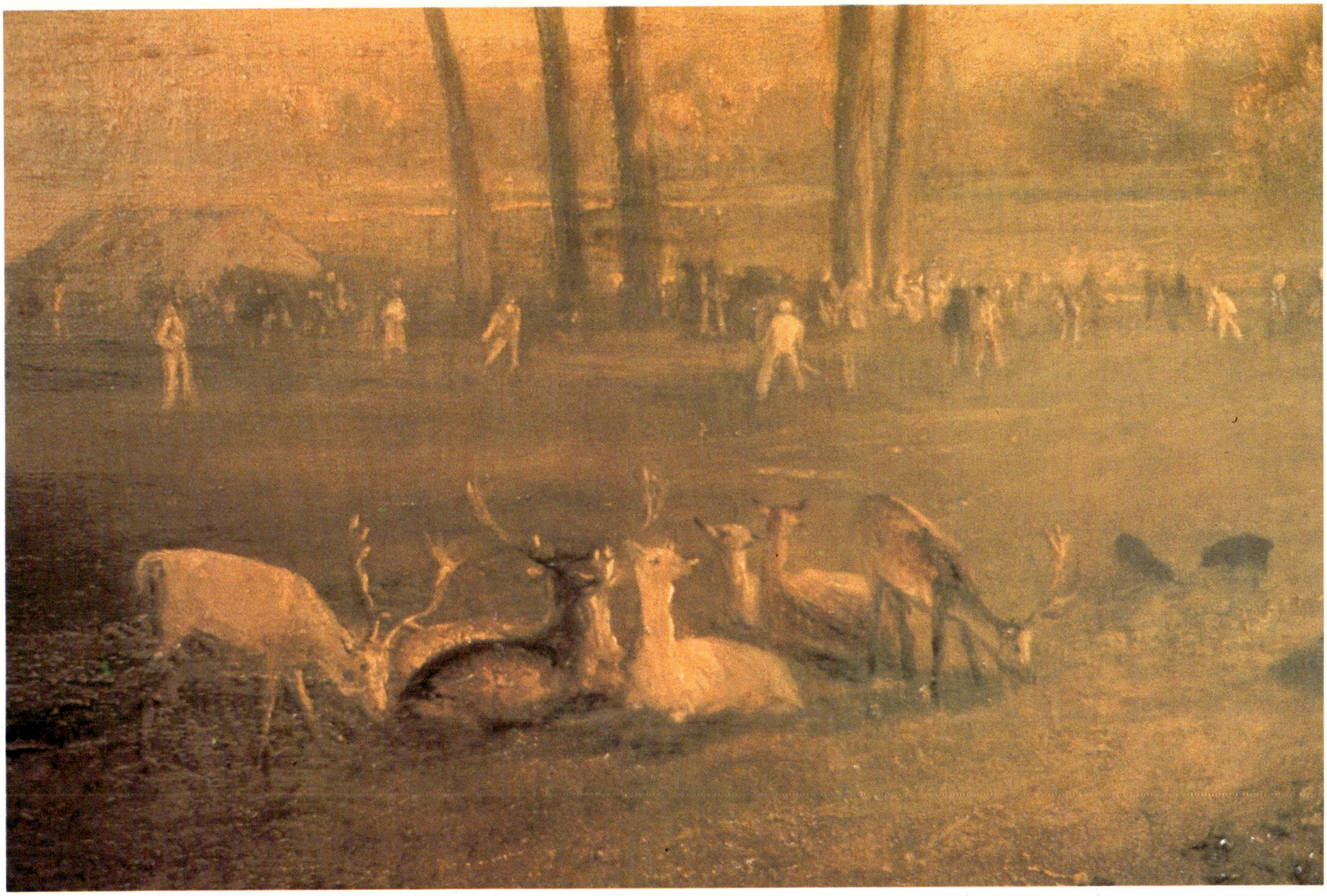

XIX. J.M.W.Turner, R.A.: *Cricket Match*: detail of Plate 48 (Petworth).

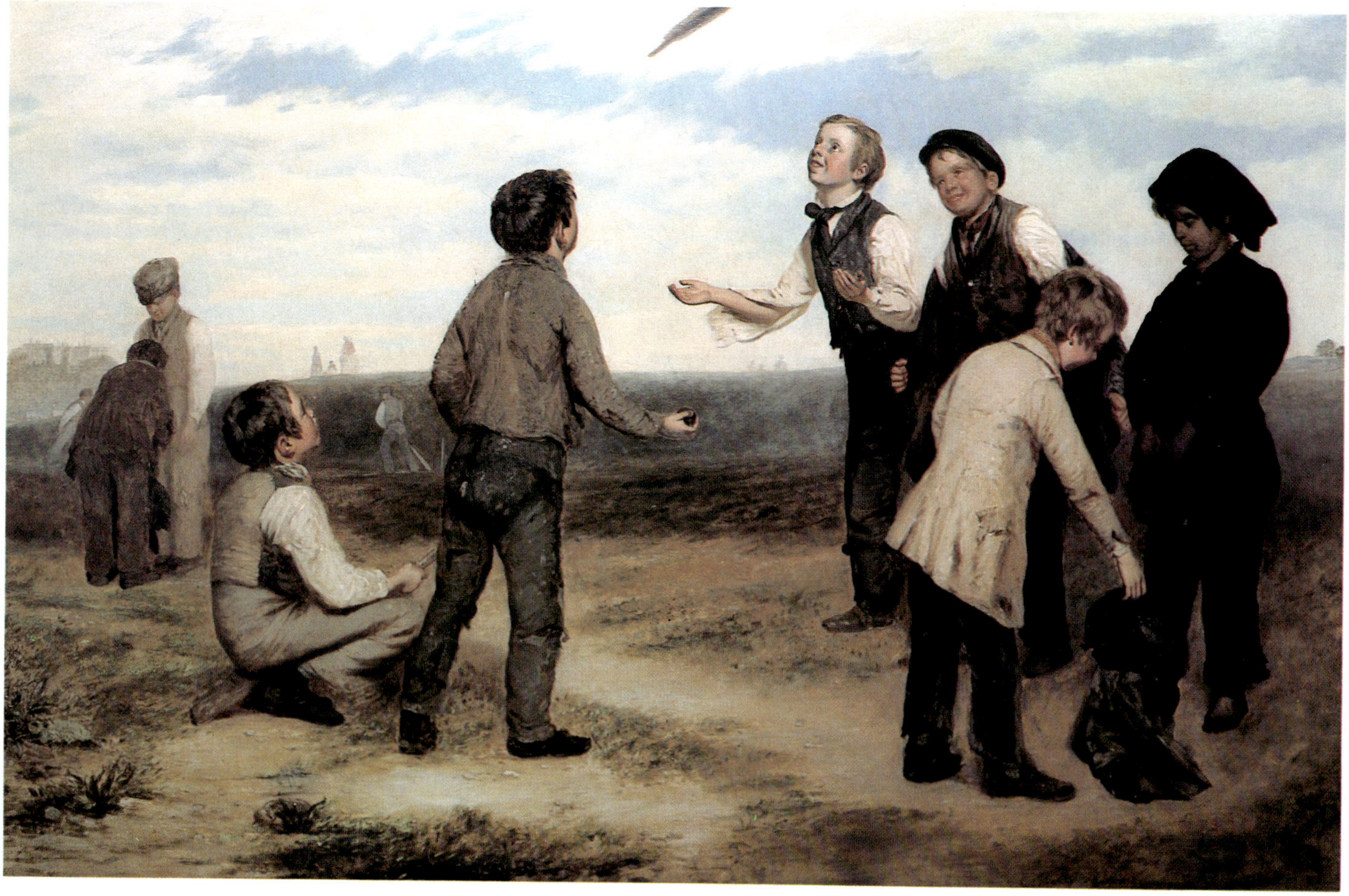

XX. Robert James: *Tossing for Innings*, II (Private Collection).

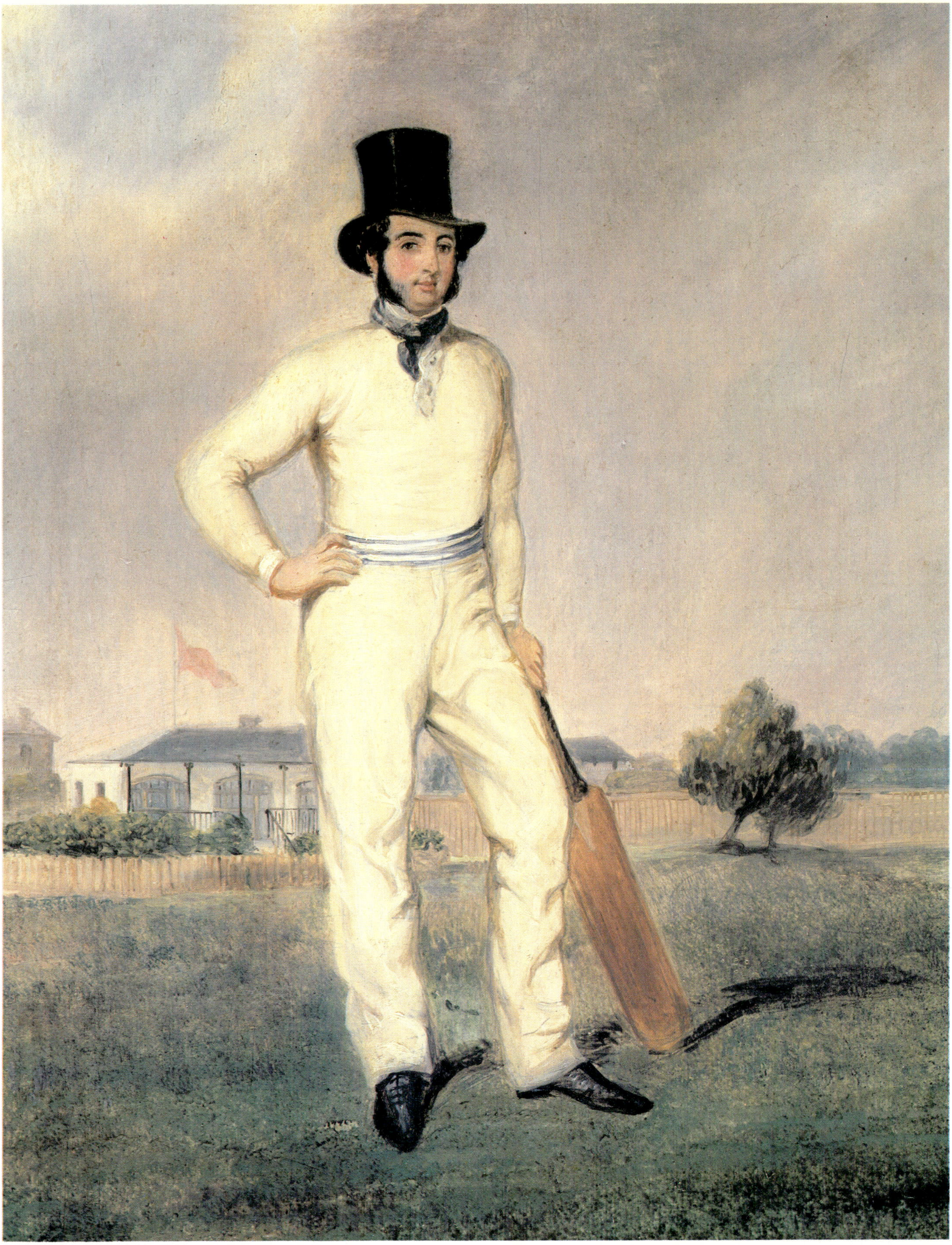

XXI. British School: *George Whieldon at Lord's* (1845) (Simon Tindall, Esq.).

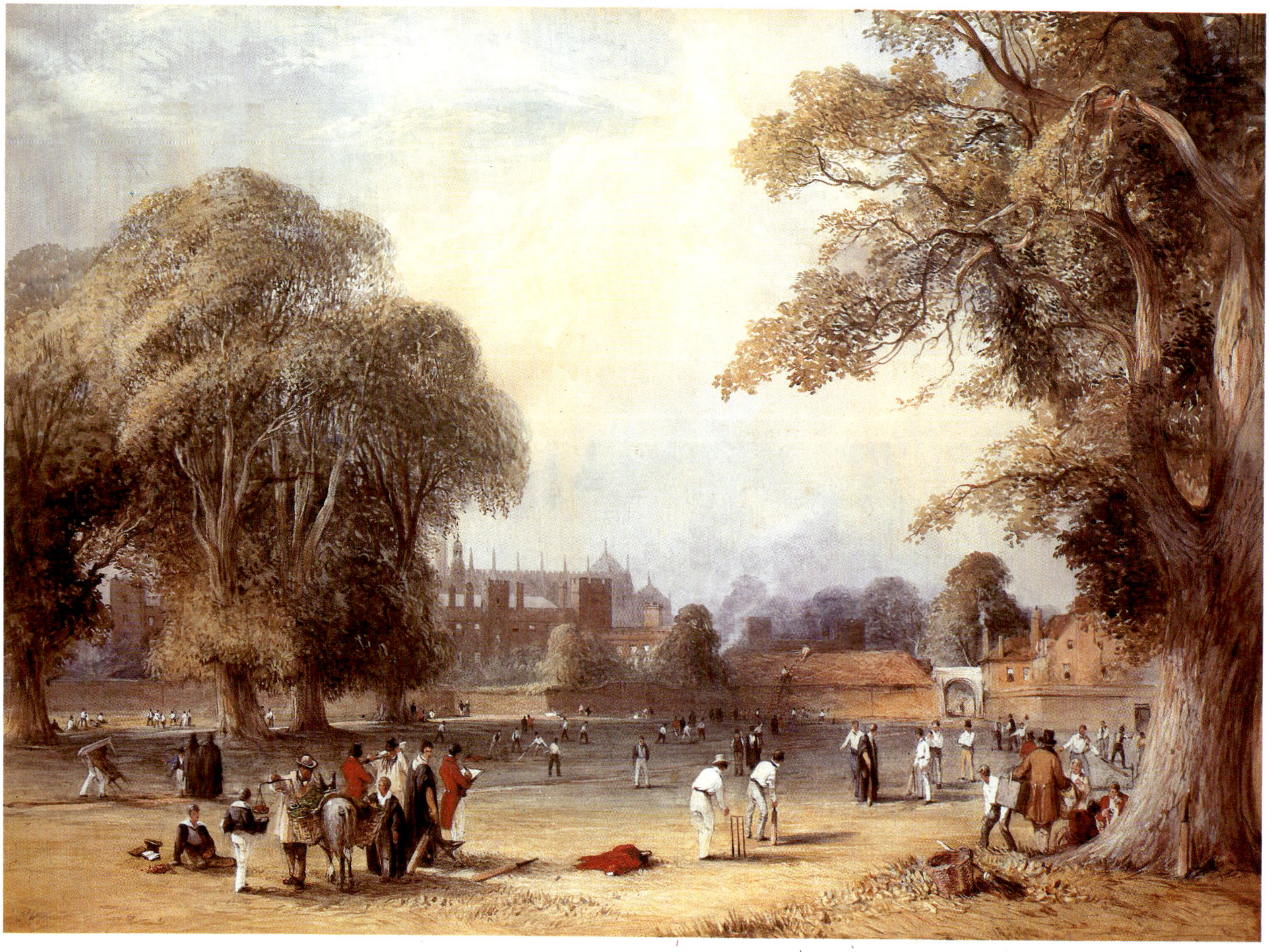

XXII. William Evans: ***Cricket on College Field, Eton*** **(Eton College) (reproduced by permission of the Provost and Fellows of Eton College).**

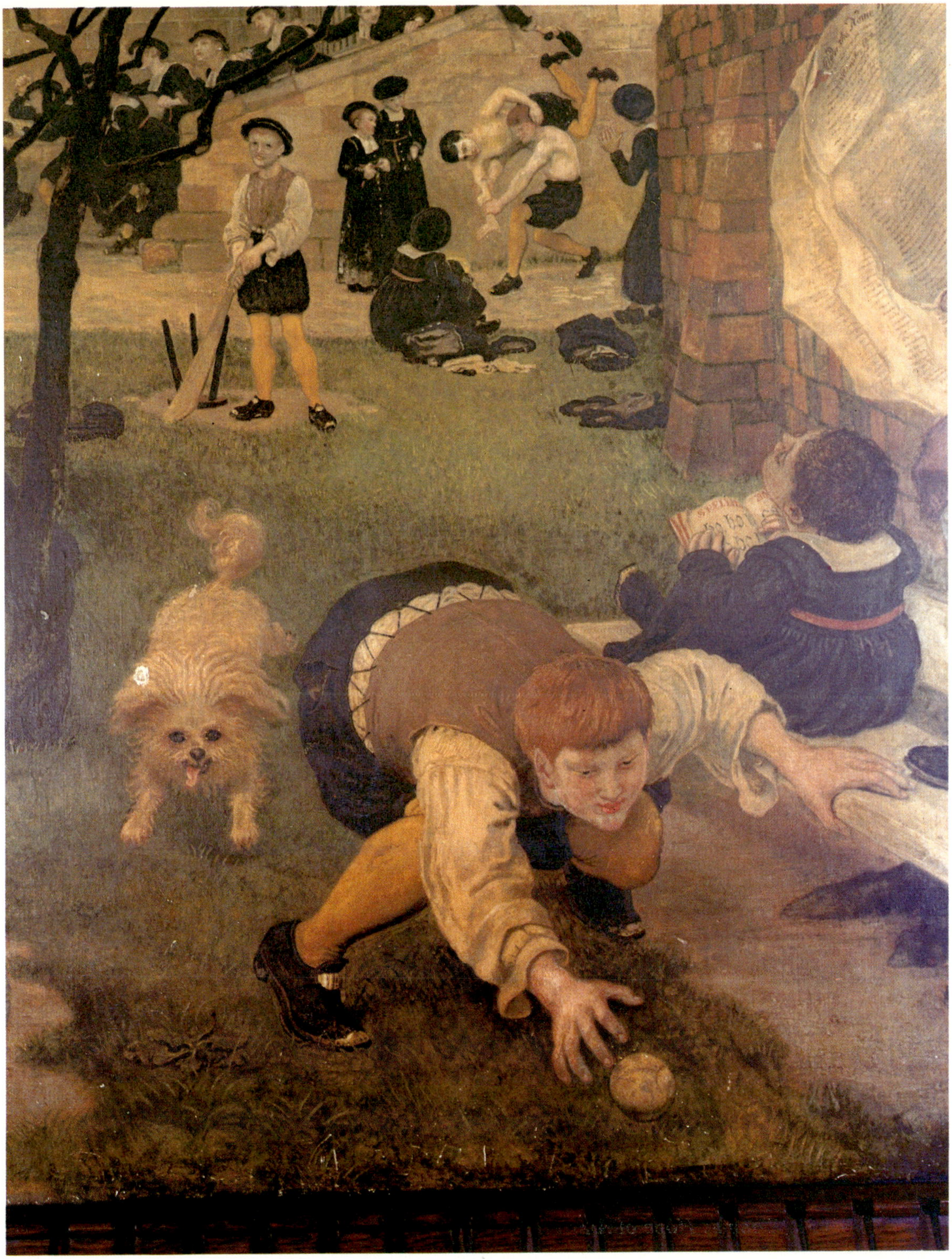

XXIII. Ford Madox Brown: ***Humphrey Chetham's Life Dream*** (1886): detail of Plate 61 (Manchester Town Hall).

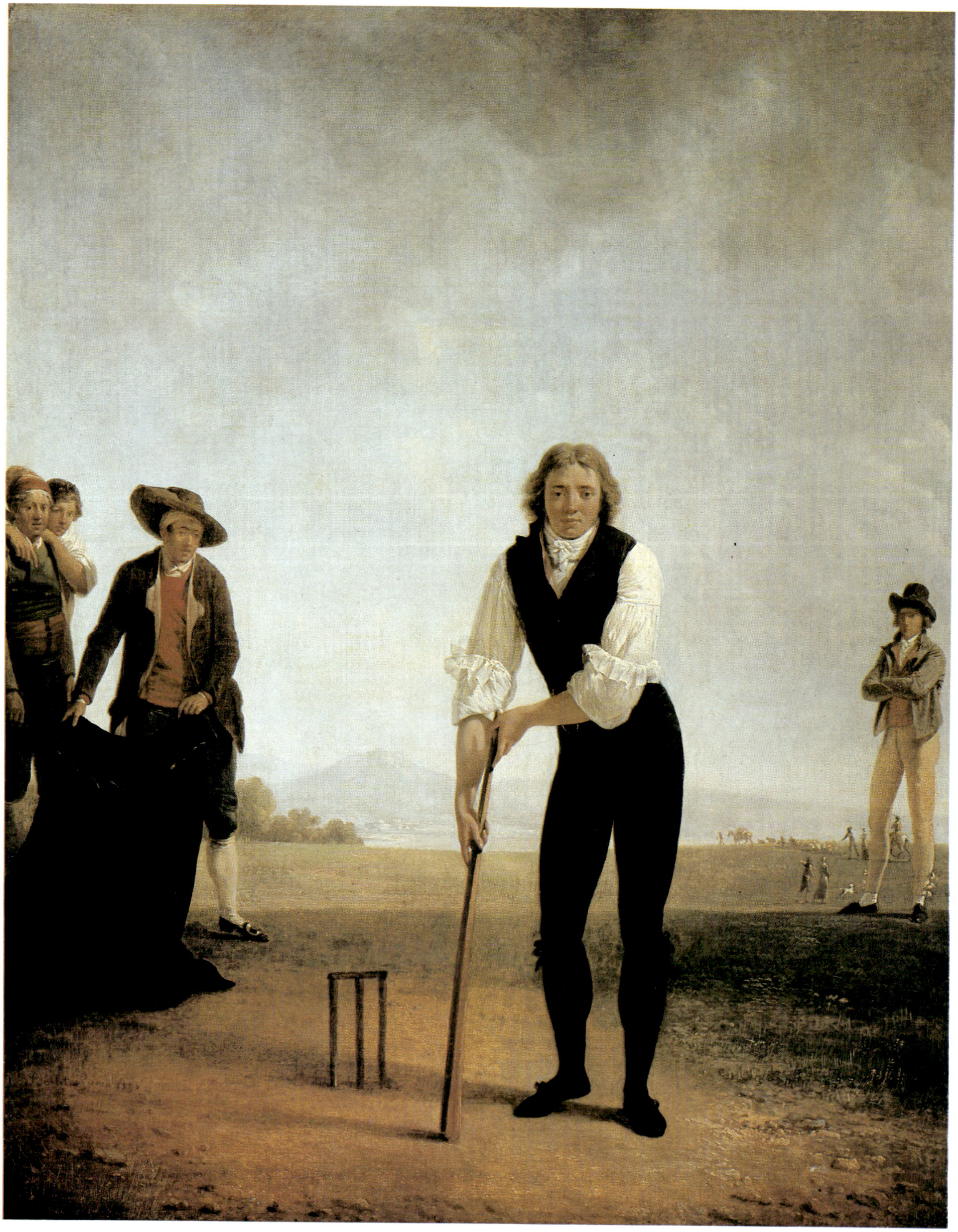

XXIV. J. Sablet: *Thomas Hope of Amsterdam* (1792) (M.C.C.).

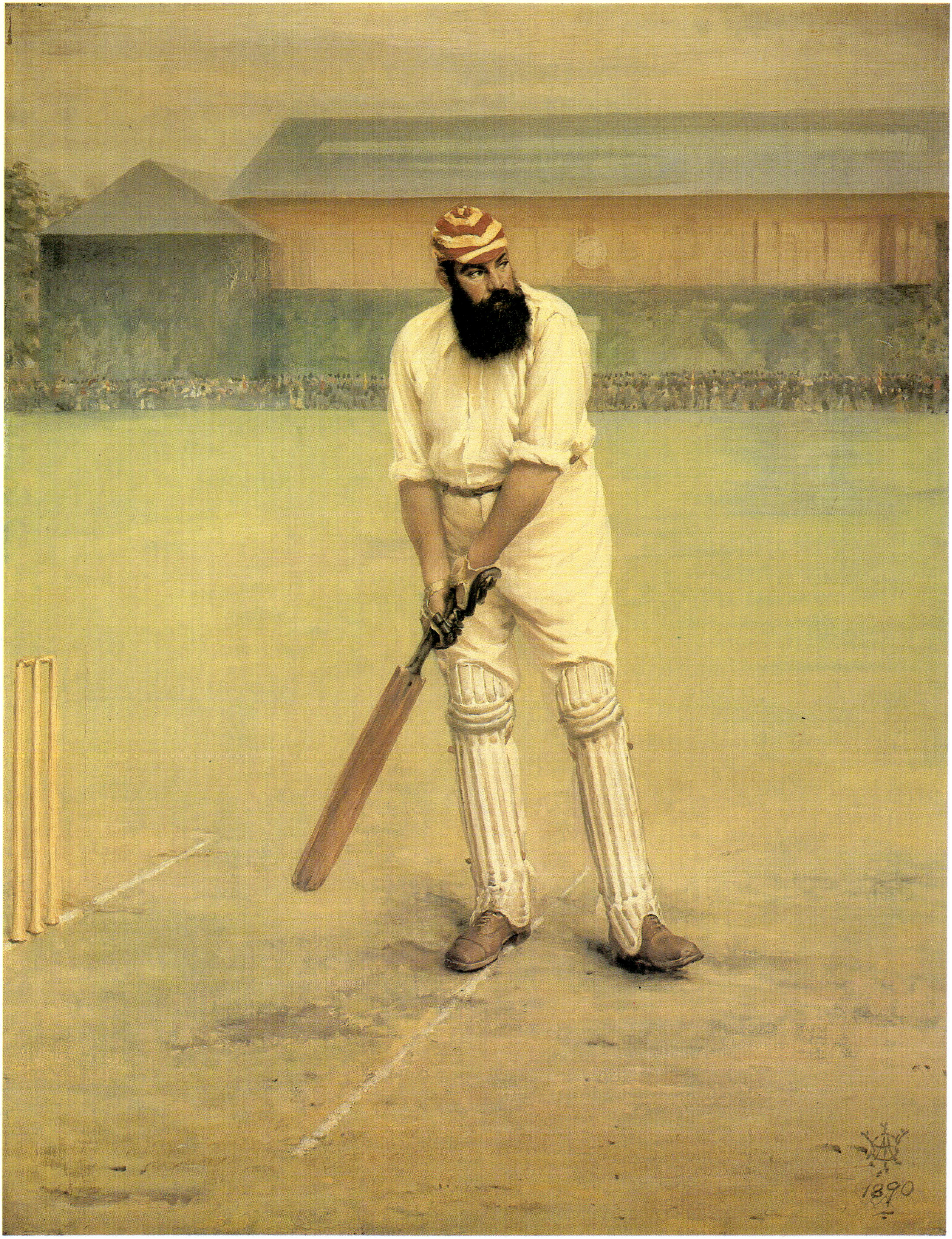

XXV. Archibald Stuart Wortley: *W.G.Grace at the Wicket* (1890) (M.C.C.).

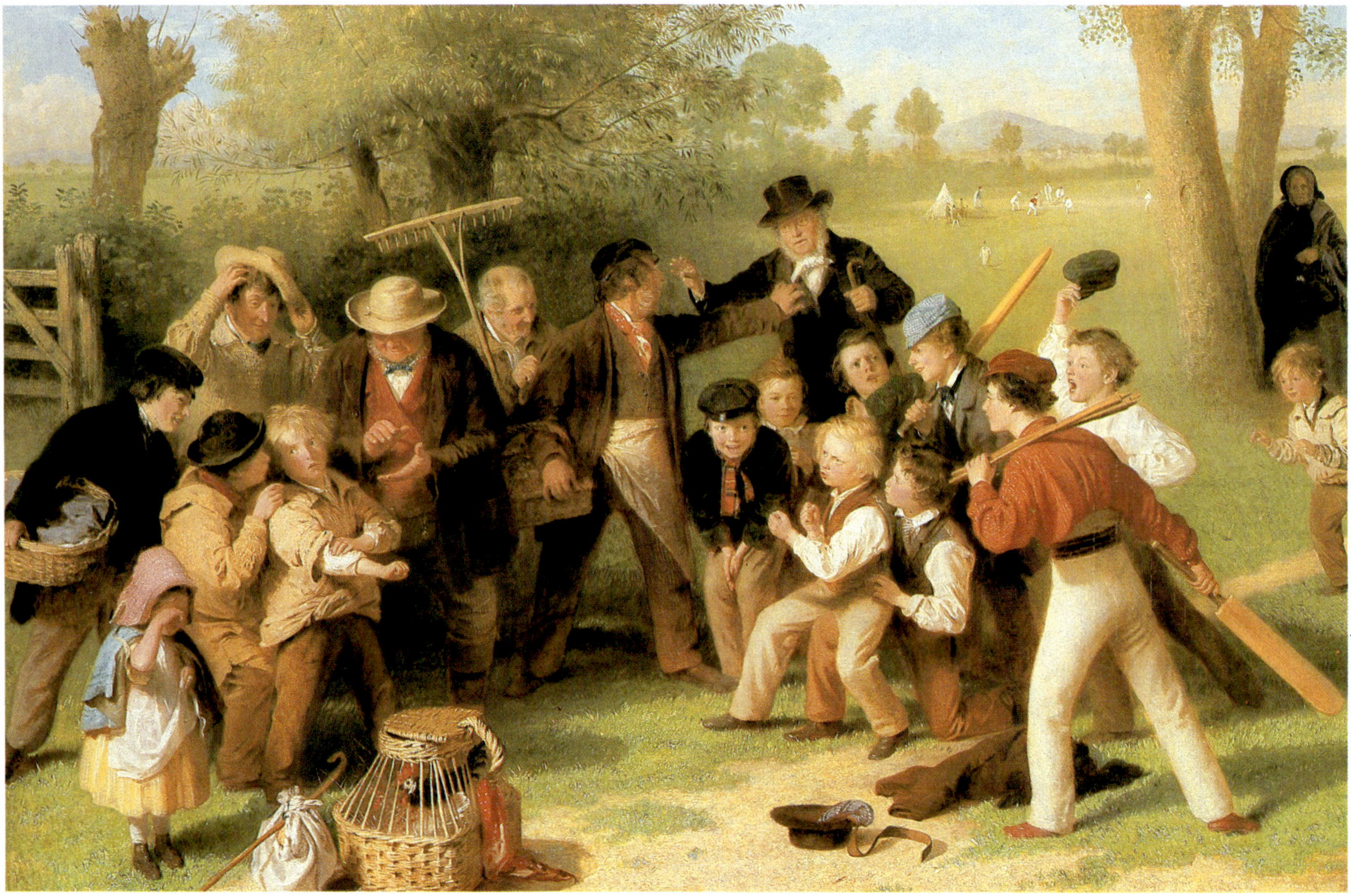

XXVI. John Morgan, R.A., R.B.A.: *The Fight* (1869) (formerly with Roy Miles, London).

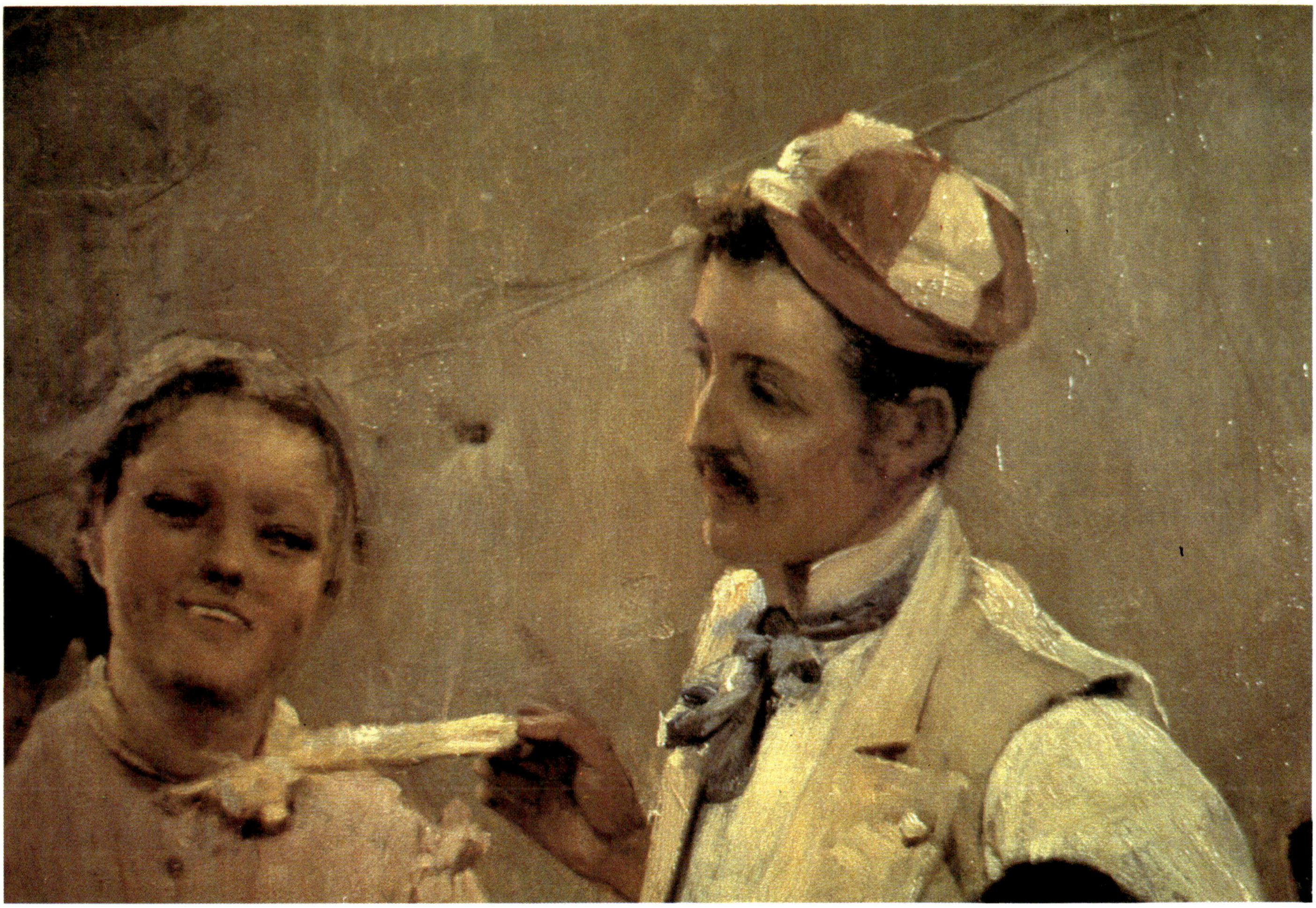

XXVII. John Robertson Reid: *A Country Cricket Match* (1878): detail of Plate 96 (Tate Gallery, London).

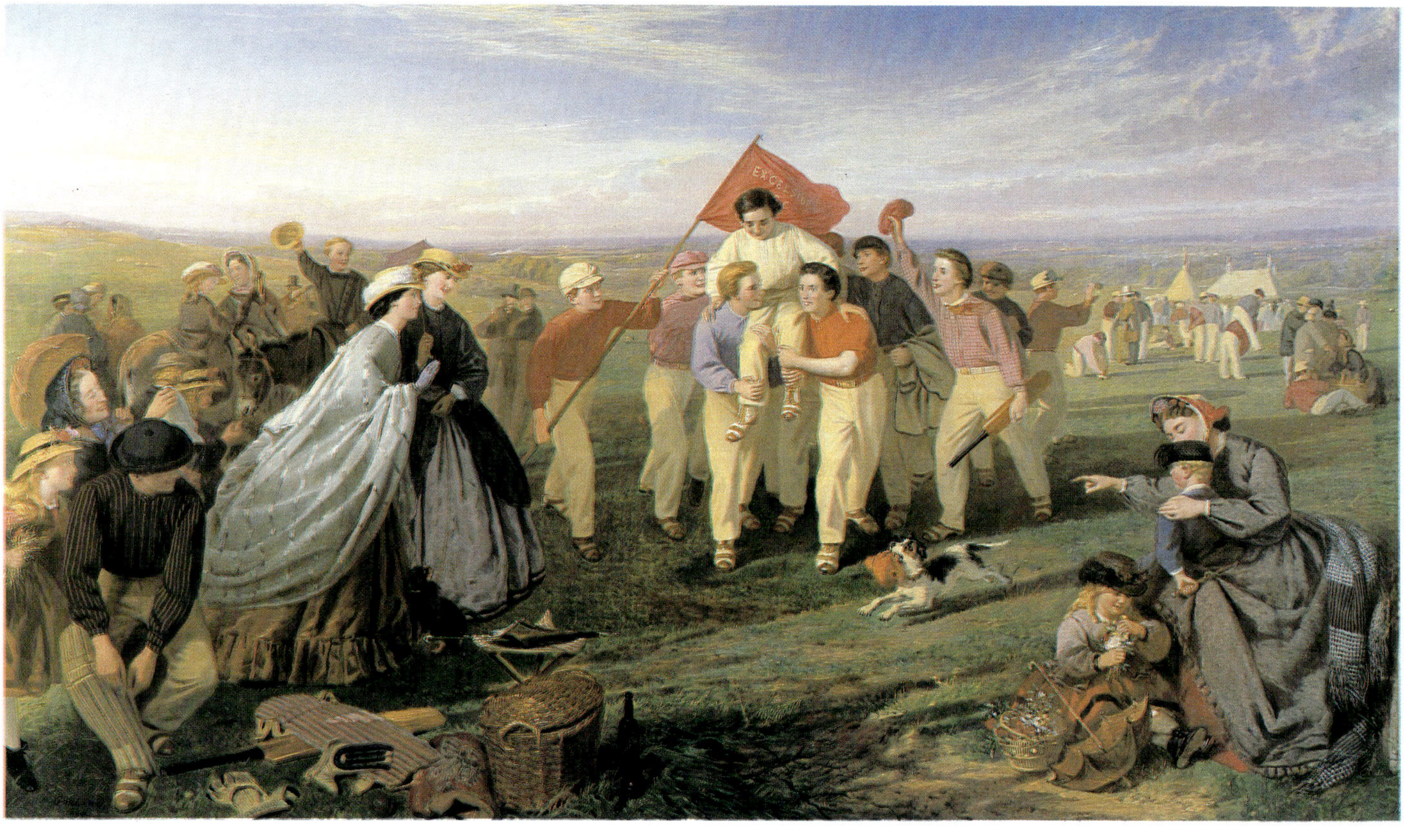

XXVIII. Henry Garland: ***The Winner of the Match: Excelsior Cricket Club, Islington*** **(1864) (M.C.C.).**

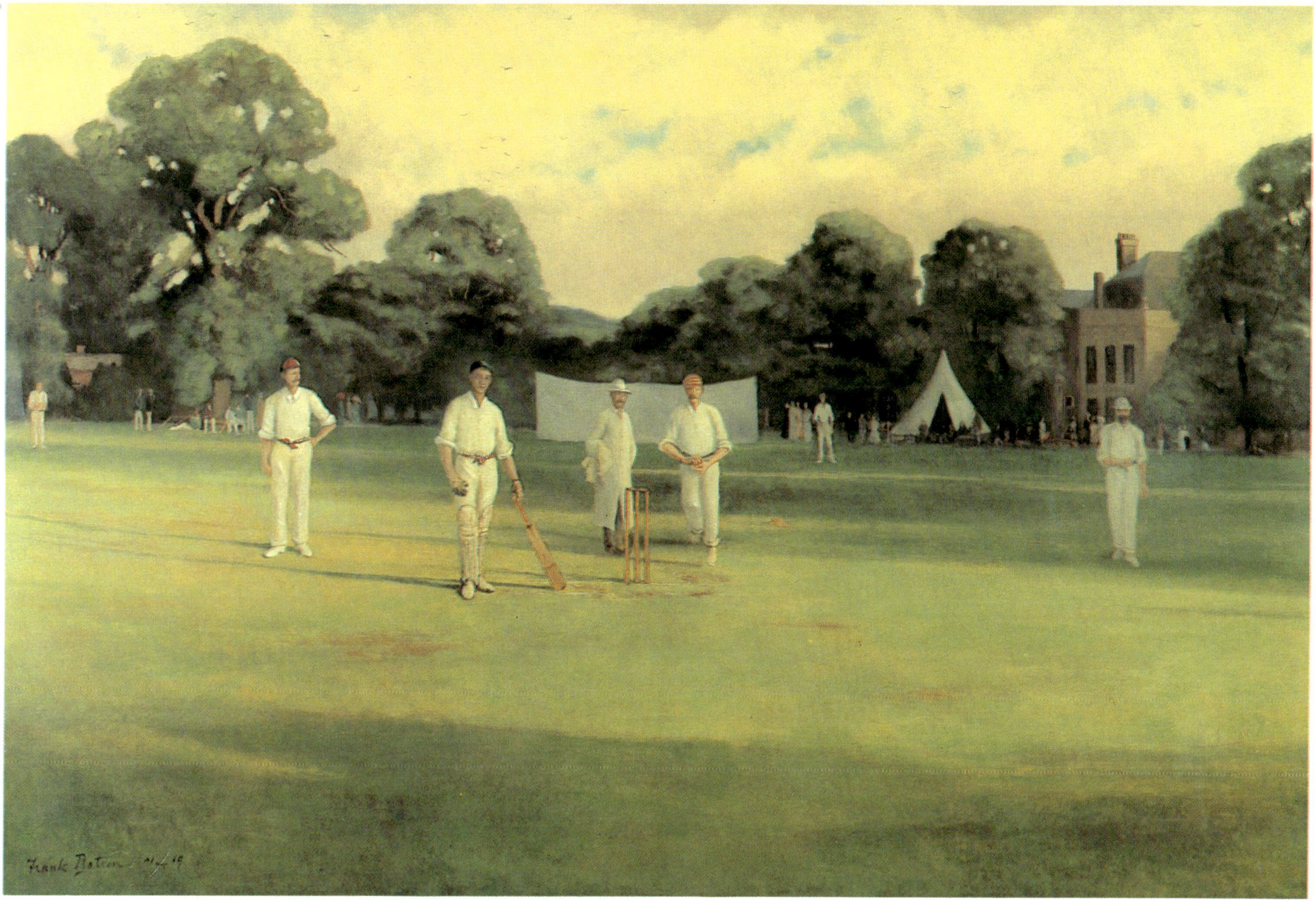

XXIX. Frank Batson: ***Playing out time in an awkward light*** **(Nottinghamshire C.C.C.).**

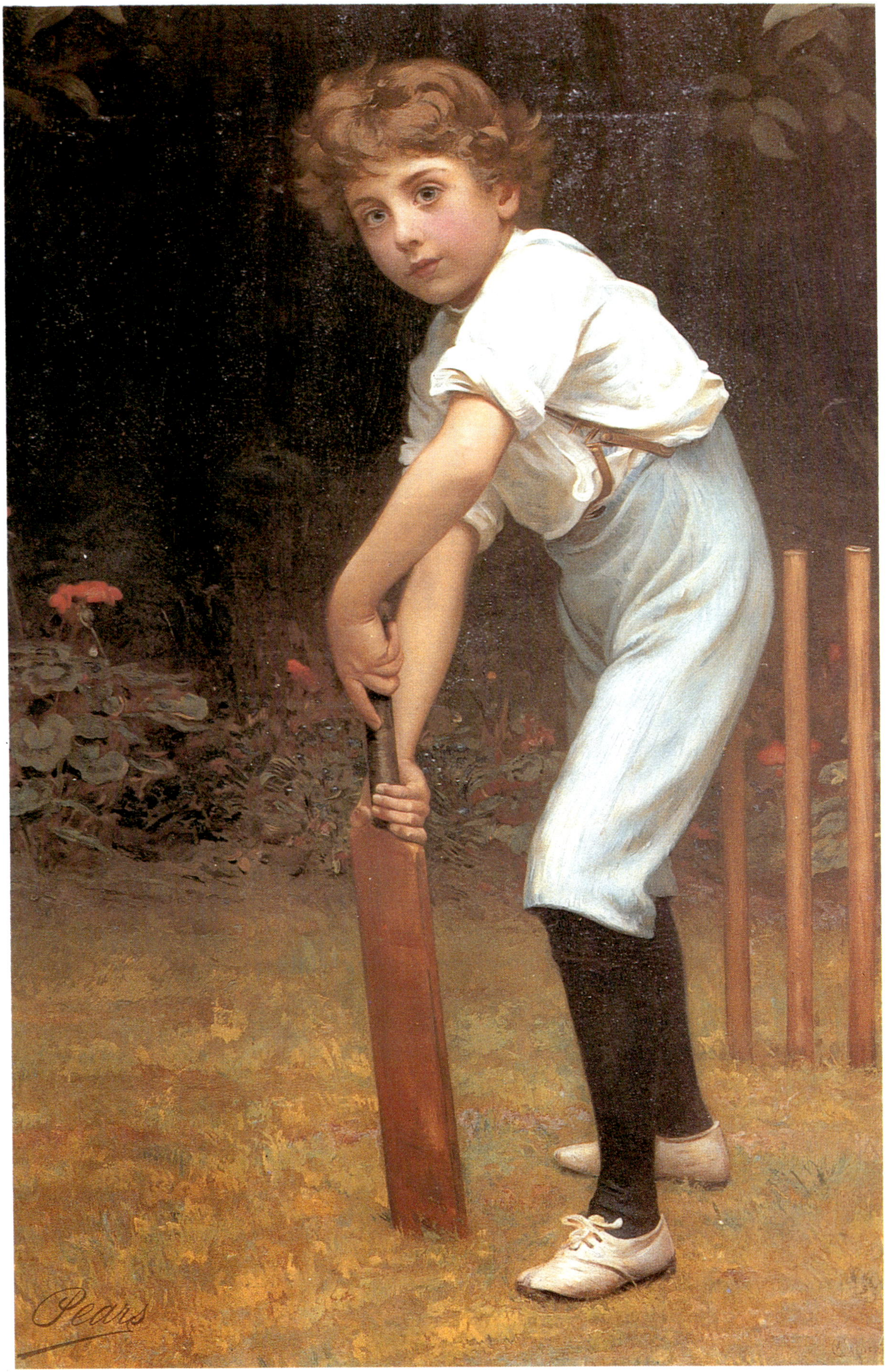

XXX. **Philip Hermogenes Calderon, R.A.:** ***Captain of the Eleven*** **(Thames County Primary School, Blackpool).**

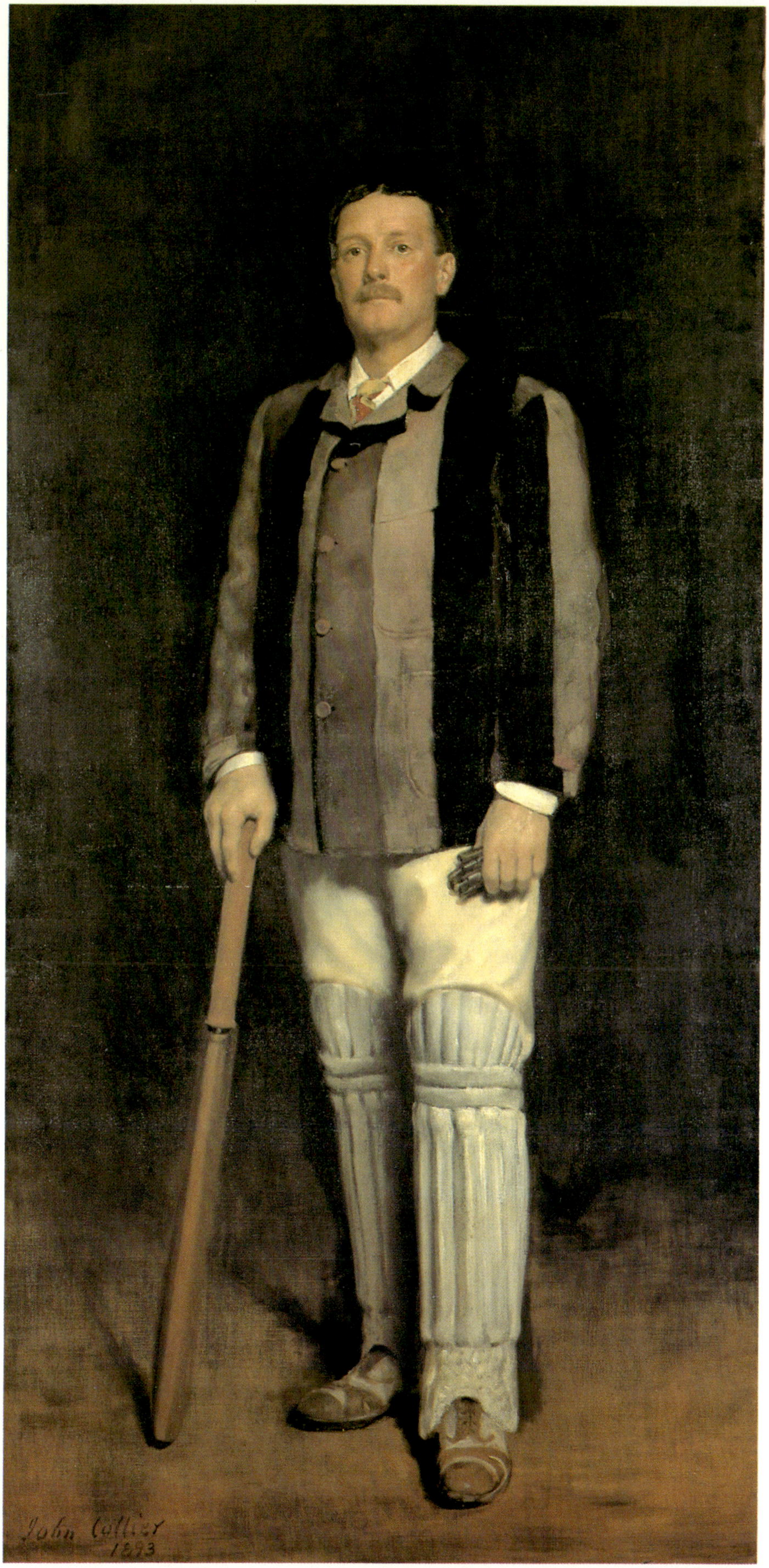

XXXI. The Hon. John Collier: *A.N. Hornby, Esq., Captain of the Lancashire Eleven* (Blackburn Museum and Art Gallery).

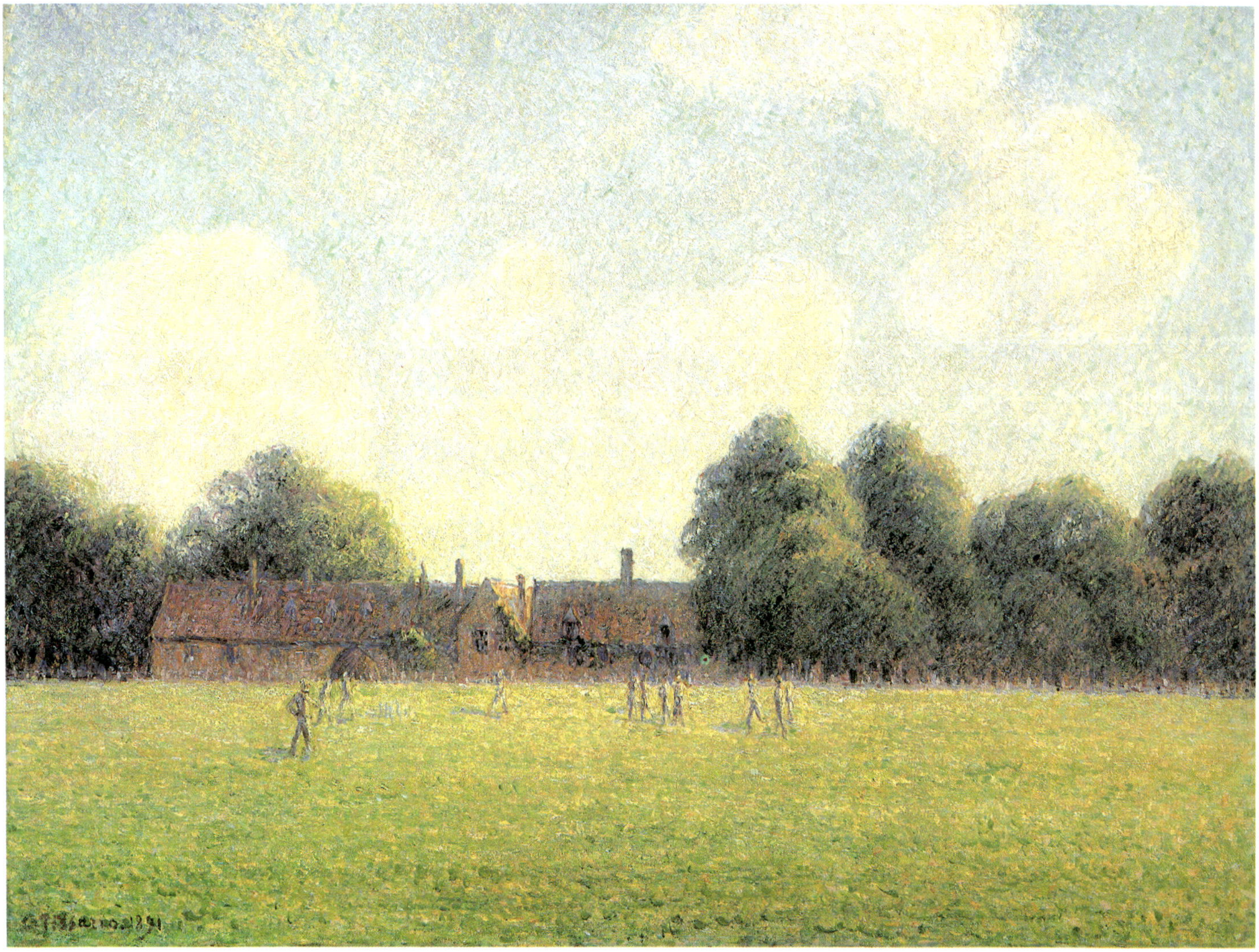

XXXII. Camille Pissarro: *Cricket on Hampton Court Green* (1890) (The Ailsa Mellon Bruce Collection, National Gallery of Art, Washington).

supporter, thinking back to a day at Old Trafford when he had watched his county take on Gloucestershire and the Graces;[116] and the match seems to be re-enacted before his eyes:

As the run-stealers flicker to and fro,
    To and fro:-
O my Hornby and my Barlow long ago!

The dreamy nostalgia of Thompson's lines cannot perhaps be truly matched in cricket art; and yet a sensitive painter faced with the inherent beauty of a cricket match in green surroundings, where the white flannels can shimmer in a flickering haze under the hot sun or gleam in the light of early evening, may consciously or unconsciously evoke an analogous poetry. We may instance Sir David Murray's *Cricket on the Village Green* (Plate 104), painted not long after the foundation in 1886 of the New English Art Club, which was the principal channel in England for the promotion of the ideas of the French Impressionists. Murray was a member of this group of painters, which included Whistler and Wilson Steer. And is there a cricketer, or cricket-lover, who will fail to respond to Frank Batson's evocation of the end of a day's play in his memorable *Playing out time in an awkward light* (Plate XXIX), in which the viewpoint is that of the batsman as he awaits the delivery of the ball? Both these paintings are cricket pictures in the fullest sense, being concerned with the game itself and not merely with the landscape setting. On the other hand, in *The Cricket Match* by Spencer Gore (Plate 107), less interest is shown in the players themselves as individuals or as members of a team: the tradition of the precise representation of a game in progress has been cast aside in favour of a general impression; and indeed it is Impressionism that is directly responsible. The light is hazy, the players take on a ghostly appearance, and the effect is that of an idyllic landscape of which the figures happen to be a component.

On visits to England, Camille Pissarro himself, one of the leaders of Impressionism, painted two scenes of cricket matches, at Hampton Court Green (Plate XXXII) and Bedford Park (Plate 106), and no doubt he was particularly conscious of the white-and-green loveliness which is so inseparable from cricket and cricket-grounds. When he painted the earlier of the two pictures in 1890 he must, we suppose, as a Frenchman, have known nothing whatsoever about the English game, as seems to be proved by the uncertain field-placings; and if we should detect in the second picture, painted seven years later, an advance on his part in such arcane knowledge, it is probable that we shall have been deceived by his simple concern for truth to appearances. No, his intention, like that of Spencer Gore (Plate 107), lies outside cricket as a contest: it resides rather in the normal response of a landscape painter to the particular beauty of a particular scene–and yet the fact that it is a cricketing scene helps to give it its peculiarly English charm and character.

ENVOI: THE MODERNS

In Impressionism lay the seeds of a revolution in art in which the artist tended to turn his back on traditional forms and to explore entirely new modes of expression. The early twentieth century saw not only an extraordinary and unprecedented proliferation of styles but the emergence of abstract, or non-figurative, art. In so chaotic an aesthetic climate, it would be vain to expect the older traditions of cricket art to survive, except there and there. Further, the role of the painter has been diminished by the development of action photography, of which the great pioneer in terms of sport was the Middlesex batsman George William Beldam: it is instructive to compare the artificially posed photographs of cricketers published in 1897 in Ranjitsinhji's *Jubilee Book of Cricket* with the marvellous action photographs in Beldam's *Great Batsmen* of 1905 and in his *Great Bowlers* of the year after. Beldam's famous shot of Trumper leaping out to drive remains, indeed, one of the most memorable of cricket images. The development of cricket photography has been taken a stage further by Patrick Eagar, who has exploited with great skill, and with remarkable results, the possibilities opened up by the telephoto-lens. Painters, however, have continued to execute cricket scenes, and, of course, portraits of cricketers–among the most notable of which, in modern times, are A.R. Thomson's *Sir Pelham Warner,* John Ward's *G.O. Allen* and Ruskin Spear's menacing full-length of *F.S. Trueman* (Plate 109); but increasingly one finds the painter's individual style taking precedence over the subject itself: we have more and more personal interpretations of cricket, and less and less respect for its nature and character.

Attempts at personal expression of this kind are usually in vain, for there is a sacrosanctity about cricket which is not to be ignored. In a few rare instances, however, personal expression and a true feeling for the game come together in paintings comparable in quality, both as works of art and as "cricket pictures" in their own right, with some of the best works of the "Old Masters" of cricket subjects. It may be added that contemporary painters have often availed themselves of photography, with advantage to the authenticity of the action or actions depicted. It is not within the compass of these pages to attempt to trace developments after the end of the Victorian period; but there is one painter who seems to us to combine in a contemporary figurative style many of the virtues of cricket art at its best. This is Lawrence Toynbee, whose *Cricket Match at Hovingham Hall* (Plate 110) not only captures the atmosphere of one of the great Yorkshire homes of country house cricket but expresses in quite masterly fashion the true character of cricket as it is actually played. We recognize the scene by its general familiarity, not considering it simply as belonging to a particular place or time, but as an evocation of our experience of many remembered fields of play.

The best cricket art–and we confine ourselves to this country–is not necessarily the most "fashionable" in terms of contemporary aesthetics, for it must be truthful to a peculiarly English invention and cultural phenomenon which has its own canons of style. In the summer, cricket will never be far out of sight, whether for artists or for others, and a poet looking out of a train window will not be surprised to glimpse "someone running up to bowl";[117] and although he may note the beauty of it, he will still wonder what ball was bowled. Philip Larkin's line calls to mind a passage in Neville Cardus's *Cricket:*

> Has any true Englishman ever resisted the temptation, while travelling on the railway, to look through the carriage window whenever the train has been passing a cricket field? The train rushes round a curve just as the bowler is about to bowl; in a flash we are swept out of sight of the game, and never can we know what happened to that ball![118]

True cricket art must satisfy the same curiosity, the same concern for the essential realities of the game, which, although basically a physical contest between bat and ball, is an art in itself, exacting in its demands on technical proficiency as well upon character and personal courage, and spiritually rewarding in its unique power to enhance the brief summer of our days.

NOTES TO TEXT

Some of the books to which reference is made have a chronological arrangement; page references will be omitted in these cases.

1 In 1719 Kent and London played the same match in May and in July. It had to be played over again as was ordered by Lord Chief Justice Pratt; it was for £60"played for at cricket", and London were taken to court by Kent. It may even be that this is the game begun the previous year which itself had been played on two separate days in September, the 6th and 20th. Cf. G.B. Buckley, *Fresh Light on 18th Century Cricket: a collection of 1000 new cricket notices from 1697 to 1800 A.D.* (Birmingham, 1935), hereafter referred to as Buckley, 1; Lord Harris and F.S. Ashley-Cooper, *Kent Cricket Matches 1719-1880* (London, 1929). Lord Chief Justice Pratt had a busy time with cricketers, having to deal with them again in 1722, and again in 1726 "when the merits of the cause appeared to be, that at a match [between Dartford Heath and Chinkford] the Chinkford men refused to play out the game at a time the other side had the advantage" (quoted by E. Parker, *The History of Cricket* [London 1950], p.59). Another case was the often fraught fixture between Leicester and Coventry: in 1788 it began on 22 September and ended on 20 October. The previous year's game had ended in great violence, with the victorious Leicester team being attacked by infuriated Coventry colliers (Buckley,1).

2 Cf. Lord Harris and F.S. Ashley-Cooper, *op. cit.*

3 E.g., see the 1727 "Articles of Agreement" drawn up between the 2nd Duke of Richmond and Mr Broderick, illustrated in the standard work, R.S. Rait Kerr, *The Laws of Cricket* (London, 1950), opp. p. 10, where the 1774 laws are also discussed in great detail (hereafter referred to as Rait Kerr). The use of this term, incidentally, lends weight to G.B. Buckley's supposition that a reference to "two umpires" as early as 1680 indicated cricket, for we find the word "gamesters" used in the same report, thus confirming Buckley's conclusion that the "double-wicket form of the game was well known about London at this time" (Buckley, 1, where the author quotes from *Poor Robin's Intelligence Revived*, 28 April 1680).

4 An attractive account of the 3rd Duke of Dorset is to be found in Elizabeth Einberg's *Gainsborough's "Giovanna Baccelli"* (Tate Gallery, London, 1976). The Duke was a pall-bearer at the funeral of Sir Joshua Reynolds in 1792. The 3rd Duke of Richmond, although not so mad on cricket as his father, whom he succeeded in 1750, established an academy for artists in which they could study, in particular, a collection of classical sculptures. His nephew was Col. Charles Lennox, the great cricketer, who succeeded him as 4th Duke of Richmond in 1806.

5 E.g., cf. E.L. Padwick, *Bibliography of Cricket* (1977), No. 846–a wager on a cricket match at Coxheath, 28 May 1646. Also, in B.M. Egerton MS., fol. 108-522 b we find (in a Kentish farmer's diary) that the writer records, "Memorandum, June ye 23rd, 1708, wee beat Ash Street at Creckits" (cited by E. Parker, *op. cit.*, p. 58).

6 Cf. Lord Harris and F.S. Ashley-Cooper, *op. cit.*

7 Cf. Rait Kerr, pp. 91-8, where the 1755 Laws are reproduced.

8 Cf. F.S. Ashley-Cooper, *Cricket Highways and Byways* (London, 1927), p. 180.

9 Cf. G. Buckley, *Fresh Light on Pre-Victorian Cricket: a collection of more cricket notices from 1709 to 1837*... (Birmingham, 1937), hereafter referred to as Buckley, 2.

10 *Ibid.*: cf. *London Chronicle*, 31 October 1776.

11 *Ibid.*

12 *Ibid.*:cf. *Fog's Weekly Journal*, 28 August 1731.

13 Cf. Buckley, 1.

14 Cf. F.S. Ashley-Cooper, *Curiosities of First-Class Cricket* (London, 1901), p.3.

15 Cf. Buckley, 2.

16 *Ibid.*:cf. *Chelmsford Chronicle*, 1774.

17 *Ibid.*:cf. *Morning Chronicle*, 1 July 1782.

18 *Ibid.*:cf. *Whitehall Evening Post*, 8 July 1783.

19 Cf. A. Haygarth (ed.), *Frederick Lillywhite's Cricket Scores and Biographies of Celebrated Cricketers* (14 vols., London, 1862-1895), Vol.I (1746-1826), 65 f.

There is any amount of evidence to show the Duke's lasting and active interest in cricket, despite a stroke probably suffered in 1785 and increasing ill health. It is odd, therefore that H.S. Altham, in *A History of Cricket* (with E.W. Swanton, 4th Edition, London, 1948), p. 37, states that the Duke's "active participation in the game ended with his appointment as Ambassador". This erroneous opinion has been reasserted recently by Christopher Brookes, *English Cricket* (London, 1978), p. 47, where the author also says that the Duke's interest was "never to be rekindled". The Duke's great friend and rival on the cricket field, Sir Horatio Mann, is also stated by Dr Brookes to have lost interest in cricket, again erroneously. Dr Brookes (*op. cit.*, pp. 47-8) says that Sir Horatio gave up cricket in 1782. The evidence is all to the contrary, and it was with Sir Horatio, or against him, that the Duke played in the 1786 and 1787 games cited above, on visits specially arranged from Paris. Sir Horatio kept watching the game faithfully to the very end of his life, and was, of course, like the Duke of Dorset, a founder member of M.C.C. As late as 1800, he organized his curious game of cricket on horseback. (Cf. Lord Harris and F.S. Ashley-Cooper, *Lord's and the M.C.C.* [London, 1903].)

The Duke of Dorset played against Sir Horatio in 1788 in an "Alphabetical Match", A-M *versus* N-Z (Buckley, 1); in 1789, the Duke's team (England) played Sir Horatio's (Hampshire): "After the match was over, the Duke expressed a wish to have it played again, placing himself in the room of Lumpy who was ill" (*ibid.*, *Kentish Gazette*); in 1791 we hear that "Sir Horatio Mann, though no longer a player, is one of the most eager spectators, remaining the whole day on the ground with his book and pencil" (*ibid.*, *Kentish Post*).

20 Buckley, 2: cf. *The Diary, or Woodfall's Register*, 25 July 1789.

21 *Letters written by the Earl of Chesterfield to his son, Philip* (2 vols, London, 1774); for this quotation cf. letter of Saturday after 6 August 1741. In Chesterfield's next reference to cricket is to be found some of the ammunition for Dr Johnson's famous hit, that Chesterfield's letters "taught the morals of a whore, and the manners of a dancing-master":

"...though I would not have you a dancer, yet when you do dance, I would have you dance well... There is no one thing so trifling but which (if it is to dance at all) ought to be done well. And I have often told you, that I wished you even played at pitch, and cricket, better than any boy at Westminster."

This remark at least confirms cricket's early hold at Westminster School, and also that Chesterfield thought of it in connection with a trivial gambling game such as pitch-and-toss. In the school the gambling connection persisted, though for less trifling sums, and we find that Westminster played Eton for 100 guineas a side in 1796 (Parker, *op.cit.*, p. 87).

22 In addition to those mentioned here, the Old Pretender is supposed to have played in Rome in 1718. Lord Frederick Beauclerk, that great figure of the early days of the M.C.C., was a direct descendant of Charles II *via* Nell Gwynn.

23 Buckley, 2: cf. *General Evening Post*, 7 August 1770.

24 It is difficult to be sure of the facts, as contemporary accounts were varied, but the source would seem to be Sir Nathaniel Wraxhall in his famous *Historical and Posthumous Memoirs*, ed. Wheatley (London, 1884), I, 408. Cf. *Scores and Biographies, op. cit.*, I, xvii.

25 Mr Brian Allen, who is completing a doctoral thesis on the work of Francis Hayman, is of the same opinion as we are regarding the M.C.C.'s painting of *Cricket at the Artillery Ground*. We are indebted to him for communicating this view to us, together with other informative details on the two Hayman cricket pictures here discussed. Vauxhall, the celebrated pleasure gardens, had been opened in the 1730s by Jonathan Tyers, and became the fashionable resort of high society. The numerous supper-boxes and pavilions were decorated with paintings, most of them by Hayman.

26 Cf. L. Gowing, "Hogarth, Hayman, and the Vauxhall Decorations", *The Burlington Magazine*, XCV (January, 1953), 4-19.

27 E.R. Wilson, "Early Cricket Prints", *The Cricketer Spring Annual*, XXII (1941), pp. 74-7. There appear to be no records of cricket in "Marylebone Fields" at this time.

28 Rait-Kerr, p.2

29 William Goldwin, "In Certamen Pilae, *Anglice*, A Cricket Match", in his *Musae Juveniles* (1706), translated by H.A. Perry, *Etoniana*, 30 December 1922; reprinted in Rait Kerr, pp. 4-8. Another translation was published by "H.P.–T." (P.F. Thomas) in *Early Cricket* (Nottingham, 1923), pp. 8-17.

30 The Articles are reproduced by Rait Kerr, opp. p. 10. Since being exhibited at the Sussex County Ground at Hove some years ago the whereabouts of the Articles cannot now be traced. Incidentally, there is a Poppinghole Lane near Fordingbridge, Sussex (running to Cripp's Corner), but we are kindly informed by Professor Kenneth Cameron, of the English Place Name Society, that this was originally "Poppa's heath", from an Old English name, *Poppa*.

31 John Nyren, *The Young Cricketer's Tutor to which is added The Cricketers of My Time*, ed. Charles Cowden Clarke, reprinted with an introduction by John Arlott (London, 1974), pp. 89-90.

32 Rait Kerr, p. 67.

33 See, for example, F.S. Ashley-Cooper, *Cricket Highways and Byways*, p. 116. There was a game at Chertsey on 6 September 1776 which was played with three stumps and two bails. On 7 September 1776 the *Hampshire Chronicle* announced a game to be played on the Monday at Broadhalfpenny Down, Hambledon, "after a new plan, when they are to have three stumps instead of two, in order to shorten the game". This change was born of a game the previous year, played on 22 May 1775, when John Small was consistently beaten by "Lumpy" Stevens, only for the ball to go harmlessly through the middle of the wicket. (Cf. Rait Kerr, pp. 22f.)

34 Buckley, 2: cf. *London Chronicle*, 1757.

35 J. Nyren, *op.cit.*, pp. 79f.

36 See Parker, *op.cit.*, p. 61, for the roping-off of the playing area in 1731.

37 James Love (1722-1774), playwright and actor, was the son of George Dance (1700-1768), the architect who designed, *inter alia*, the Mansion House. In the course of a somewhat chequered career he changed his name to Love. His poem was first published in 1744, and in second and third editions in 1754 and 1770. It was dedicated to the Earl of Sandwich, the inventor (while gambling) of the

eponymous snack. A keen cricketer, and also a member of the Hell-Fire Club, Lord Sandwich once wrote to his colleagues at the Admiralty: "I'll at your Board when at leisure from cricket."

38 Buckley, 2: 1766 was evidently a bad year for "masters" of cricket grounds, for on 6 February that year also died "Robert Bartholomew, a wealthy farmer, master of the Angel Inn at Islington and likewise of the White Conduit House". The honourable tradition of keeping pub and ground was maintained by Thomas Lord at his first ground : in 1791 he is recorded as the lessee of the Allsopp public house which stood at the corner of Upper Gloucester Place on the Marylebone Road, i.e., backing on to Dorset Fields, where he had laid out his first ground in 1787 (information from F.W. Hunt, agent to Lord Portman, quoted by E. Parker, *op. cit.*, p. 69). The site of the public house is now occupied by No. 172 Marylebone Road.

39 See F.S. Ashley-Cooper, *The Hambledon Cricket Chronicle 1772-1796* (1924).

40 *The Early Diary of Frances Burney...with Selected Correspondence*, ed. Annie Raine Ellis (2 vols., London, 1889), Vol. I.

41 For the influence of Lairesse's *Art of Painting in All its Branches* on eighteenth-century English painting see Alastair Smart, "Dramatic Gesture and Expression in the Age of Hogarth and Reynolds", *Apollo*, LXXXII, 42 (August, 1965), 90ff. For reflections in eighteenth-century English portraiture of the manners recommended in Nivelon's *Rudiments of Genteel Behavior* see David Mannings, "A Well-Mannered Portrait by Highmore", *The Connoisseur,* CLXXXIX (June, 1975), 117 ff.

42 Cf. James Gandon, *The Life of James Gandon* (Dublin, 1846), p. 203.

43 See Ellen G. Miles and Jacob Simon, *Thomas Hudson 1701-1779, portrait painter and collector: a bicentenary exhibition* (exhibition catalogue) (The Greater London Council, The Iveagh Bequest, Kenwood, London, 1979).

44 See *The Secret Diary of William Byrd of Westover, 1709-12,* ed. Louis B. Wright and Marion Tinling (Richmond, Va., 1941).

45 For American cricket, see e.g., John A. Lester, *A Century of Philadelphia Cricket* (Pennsylvania, 1951). Pl. 1 shows cricket in a print of 1800 being played behind the State House, Philadelphia: a curved bat is being used.

46 Cf. E. Muybridge, *Animal Locomotion: An electrophotographic investigation of consecutive phases of animal movements* (11 vols., Philadelphia, 1887), II, Pls. 289-293.

47 Ford Madox Brown, in his Victorian re-creation of a seventeenth-century cricket game in Manchester Town Hall (Plate XXIII), shows a ball stitched in the same manner.

48 *Kentish Gazette*, 13 August 1790. The entry from Farington's diary is as follows:
"I called upon – Duke, a person who resides near Redleaf and is remarkable for making Cricket Balls of the best quality. He has only one Competitor in England for the reputation of making the best Balls. He told me that his family had been famous for this art for 250 years past. The great secret of it is to wind the thread round an octagon piece of cork which forms the Kernel of the Ball. This art he does not disclose but to His own family & now had a Son, a lad, working with Him. When the Ball is perfectly formed with Cork and thread, he delivers to men who work in a room adjoining and they put on the Leather cover which is made of Bull Hide. The weight of a Ball according to the rules of the game is not to be less than 5 ounces and a Half, or more than 5 ounces and Threequarters...The Price of a Ball of the best kind is Seven Shillings...He showed me the rules of the game. The wickets are to be pitched at the distance of 22 yards; a long list of rules follows."
(*The Farington Diary,* by Joseph Farington, R.A. [8 Vols., 1922-8], VII [1927], 54, Oct. 21, 1811.)

49 The Duke of Dorset's essay was in the form of a letter to the "Ladies", and exhorted them to follow the example recently set by the Countess of Derby and "some other ladies of quality and fashion" in playing cricket. It was accompanied by a drawing by the Duke himself of these ladies on the cricket field. The drawing has since been lost. The essay was published, after the Duke's death, in *The Sporting Magazine* for April 1803, and was reproduced in *Scores and Biographies, cit.*, I, xxii - xxiii.

50 Einberg, *op. cit.*, p. 34.

51 Lumpy Stevens was certainly employed as a gardener by the 4th Earl of Tankerville before this date. While the 3rd Duke of Dorset knew him, and especially included him in his teams when he could, it would seem to be only an inference that he was actually employed by the Duke. Both the Earl of Tankerville and Lumpy were in the Duke's team due to play in Paris in 1789.

52 For the width of the bat and the introduction of the third stump cf. Rait Kerr, pp. 21 f., and n. 33 above. The development of the straight bat is usually attributed to John Small of Hambledon, and was partly born of necessity in the face of bowling to a length.

53 Strictly contemporary information on the workings of the club is to be found in *The Hambledon Cricket Chronicle*. Perhaps the most lucid and balanced short account is to be found in John Arlott's introduction to the 1974 reprint of John Nyren's *Young Cricketer's Tutor (cit.)*.

54 E.g., *Hambledon Cricket Chronicle*, p. 81. This sense of "county matches" was strong from early times, usually as a means of limiting the terms of a wager: cf. 1727 "Articles of Agreement", Rait Kerr, *op. cit.*

55 *Hambledon Cricket Chronicle*, p. 161; *Hampshire Chronicle*, 15 July 1797.

56 Lord Harris and F.S. Ashley-Cooper, *Kent Cricket Matches*. The first game on Windmill Down was played on 8, 9, 10 August 1782.

57 The phrases are those of Sir Ellis Waterhouse, *The Dictionary of Eighteenth-Century British Painters* (London, 1981).

58 Cf. John Lang, "Cricket across the Border," in *Imperial Cricket*, edited by P.F. Warner (London, 1912), pp. 229 ff.

59 See p. 33.

60 For these statues see Francis Haskell and Nicholas Penny, *Taste and the Antique: The Lure of Classical Sculpture 1500-1900* (Yale University Press, New Haven and London, 1981, 2nd printing with corrections, 1982), pp. 266 f., fig. 138 (*Mercury*); pp. 212 f., fig. 110 (*Faun with Pipes*). The classical origin of the cross-legged pose and its adaptation to 18th-century English sculpture and painting have been discussed by Joseph Burke, who, however cites the *Pothos* (or "Longing") statue in the Conservatori, Rome, as the prime exemplum in antique art: see Joseph Burke, *English Art 1714-1800* (The Oxford History of Art, edited by T.S.R. Boase [Oxford, Clarendon Press, 1976], pp. 106f.).

61 Portrait of the Hon. John Bulkeley Coventry, *c.* 1740 (Private Collection, England): reproduced in Alastair Smart, *The Life and Art of Allan Ramsay* (London, 1952), Pl. V.

62 See F. Haskell and N. Penny, *op. cit.*, pp. 229 f., fig. 118.

63 Cf. John Steegmann, "A Drapery Painter of the Eighteenth Century", *The Connoisseur*, XCVLI (June, 1936), 390 ff.; J.L. Nevinson, "Vandyke Dress", *The Connoisseur*, CLVII (September-December, 1964), 164 ff.; Aileen Ribeiro, "Some Evidence of the Influence of the Dress of the seventeenth century on Costume in eighteenth-century Female Portraiture", *The Burlington Magazine*, CXIX, 897 (December, 1977), 834 ff.

64 Reproduced in Smart, *The Life and Art of Allan Ramsay*, Pl. XVI, and in Edward Mead Johnson, *Francis Cotes* (Oxford, 1976), Pl. 73.

65 F.S. Ashley-Cooper, "Cricket and the Royal Family", in *Imperial Cricket*, edited by P.F. Warner (London, 1912), p. 14.

66 Cf. Roger Fulford, *Royal Dukes : The Father and Uncles of Queen Victoria* (London, 1973), p. 22.

67 Brookes, *op. cit.*, p. 68. For some details of Lord's first ground see n. 38 above.

68 See Donald Adamson and Peter Beauclerk Dewar, *The House of Nell Gwyn : The Fortunes of the Beauclerk Family 1670-1974* (London, 1974).

69 See *Osbaldeston : His Autobiography*, edited by E.D. Cuming (London, 1926).

70 Sir Pelham Warner, *Lord's, 1787-1945* (London, 1946), p. 25.

71 Adamson and Beauclerk Dewar, *op. cit.*, p. 95.

72 Brookes (*op. cit.*, p. 89) gives the victory to the All-England XI, but the record should be put straight.

73 E. Browne, *A Short History of Nottinghamshire Cricket Including the Season of 1887* (Nottingham, 1887), p. 6.

74 Warner, *Lord's, 1787-1945* p. 25; Brookes, p. 71.

75 Brookes, p. 90.

76 Arniston MSS.: Box 24, Vol. No. 3: *Narrative of a Journey from Edinburgh to London, Rotterdam, Amsterdam, Antwerp & Spa. With a Residence at Spa and Brussels, in 1756, by Mrs. Calderwood of Polton. Born Margaret Steuart of Coltness.*

77 *Cf.* Mark Girouard, *The Return to Camelot : Chivalry and the English Gentleman* (Yale University Press, New Haven and London, 1981), p. 236.

78 *Byron: A Self-Portrait. Letters and Diaries 1798 to 1824*, ed. Peter Quennell (London, 1950), pp. 17 f.; Elizabeth Longford, *Byron* (London, 1976), p. 11. Two years later Byron was trying to lose weight by playing cricket in seven waistcoats and a greatcoat.

79 That Bill's a foolish fellow;
He has given me a black eye.
He does not know how to handle a bat
Any more than a dog or a cat;
He has knock't down the wicket,
And broke his stumps,
And runs without shoes to save his pumps.

80 Joseph Strutt, *Glig-Gamena Angel Dead, or The Sports and Pastimes of the People of England: Including the Rural and Domestic Recreations, May-games, Mummeries, Pageants, Processions and Pompous Spectacles, from the Earliest Period to the Present Time illustrated by Engravings selected from Ancient Paintings in which are represented most of the Popular Diversions* (London, 1801).

81 *Ibid.,p.97ff.*

82 Strutt, *The Sports and Pastimes*... new edition, enlarged and corrected by J. Charles Cox (London, 1903),p. 101.

83 *The Life of Mary Russell Mitford, related in a selection from her letters to her friends*, edited by the Rev. A.G. L'Estrange (3 vols., London, 1870), II, 168 ff.: Mary Russell Mitford to B.R. Haydon, 24 August 1823.

84 Mary Russell Mitford, *Our Village* (London, 1832).

85 *Felix on the Bat : Being a Scientific Inquiry into the Use of the Cricket Bat; together With the History and Use of the Catapulta* (London, 1845).

86 For Wanostrocht (Felix) see especially Gerald Brodribb, *Felix on the Bat : being a memoir of Nicholas Felix* (London, 1962), which supersedes earlier accounts, such as that in G.D. Martineau's excellent *Bat, Ball, Wicket and All* (London, 1950).

87 Brodribb, *op. cit.*, Appendix C : "Notes on the Illustrations to *Felix on the Bat*".

88 M.S. Watts, *George Frederick Watts* (3 vols., London, 1912), I (*The Annals of an Artist's Life*), 28 ff.

89 Sir Spencer Ponsonby-Fane thought that his brother, the Hon. Fred Ponsonby, posed for one of the drawings–"Leg Half Volley": cf. Brodribb, *op. cit.*, p. 144 (Appendix C).

90 Wilfrid Blunt, *"England's Michelangelo"* (London, 1975), p. 11.

91 M.S. Watts, *op. cit., loc. cit.*

92 Brodribb, *op. cit.*, pp. 142 f.

93 Sir Edwin's brother Charles Landseer, the illustrator and engraver, has also been associated with cricket art, a well-known caricature of the Duke of Wellington at the wicket having been ascribed to him, although somewhat doubtfully (Plate 82). See p. 42.

94 Cf. A.A. Thomson, "Lord's and the Early Champions, 1787-1865", in *Barclays World of Cricket: The Game from A to Z*, edited by E.W. Swanton, John Woodcock and others (London, 1980), p. 10.

95 Martial's epigram was adapted, for example, by Ben Jonson to the last lines of his poem "On My First Daughter", and the sense was wittily reversed in an eighteenth-century epitaph on the architect Sir John Vanbrugh:

"Lie heavy on him, Earth, for he
Laid many a heavy load on thee."

The original runs as follows:

"mollia non rigidus caespes tegat ossa, nec illi
terra gravis fueris : non fuit illa tibi." (V, 34).
("Let not hard turf cover her soft bones; nor, O Earth, be heavy upon her : she was not so upon you.")

96 See especially F.S. Ashley-Cooper, *Nottinghamshire Cricket and Cricketers* (London, 1923), and E. V. Lucas, *A Hundred Years of Trent Bridge* (Nottingham, 1938).

97 Sir Home Gordon, "Club Cricket in England", in *The M.C.C. 1787-1937; reprinted from "The Times" M.C.C. Number : May 25, 1937* (London, 1937), pp. 67 ff. (p 67).

98 Andrew Lang, "The History of Cricket", in *Imperial Cricket*, edited by P.F. Warner (London, 1912), pp. 53 ff. (p. 69).

99 The Revd James Pycroft, *The Cricket Field*, edited by F.S. Ashley-Cooper (London, 1922).

100 Lord Harris and F.S. Ashley-Cooper, *Lord's and the M.C.C. : A Cricket Chronicle of 137 years, based on official documents, & published, with the knowledge and sanction of the Marylebone Cricket Club, to commemorate the centenary of their present ground. With an Introduction by the Rt. Hon. Sir Spencer Ponsonby-Fane, G.C.B.* (London, 1914), p. 167.

101 For Thomas Hope see David Watkin, *Thomas Hope 1769-1831 and the Neo-Classical Idea* (London, 1968).

102 Henry Matthew, *Diary of an Invalid* (5th edition, London, 1835), pp. 160 f. We are indebted to Dr Edward Chaney for drawing this reference to our attention.

103 Quoted by Wilfrid Blunt, *op. cit.*, p. 30.

104 Quoted by C.R. Leslie and Tom Taylor, *The Life and Times of Sir Joshua Reynolds* (London, 1865), I, 247.

105 *The Annual Register*, 3 August 1775 (p. 143).

106 Marjorie Pollard, "Women as Cricketers", in *The M.C.C. 1787-1937; reprinted from "The Times" M.C.C. Number : May 25, 1937* (London, 1937), pp. 119 ff.

107 Mark Girouard, *The Return to Camelot : Chivalry and the English Gentleman* (Yale University Press, New Haven and London, 1981).

108 *Ibid.*, p. 233.

109 Newbolt's poem begins :

There's a breathless hush in the close to-night,
Ten to make and the match to win–
A bumping pitch and a blinding light,
An hour to play and the last man in.
And it's not for the sake of a ribboned coat,
Or the selfish hope of a season's fame,
But his captain's hand on his shoulder smote–
"Play up ! play up ! and play the game !"

The scene changes to a field of battle many years later. When all seems lost –
The voice of the schoolboy rallies the ranks:
"Play up ! play up ! and play the game!"

110 For "W.G." and his family see especially Bernard Darwin, *W.G. Grace* [1934], with an introduction by John Arlott (London, 1978; 1981).

111 Viscount Ullswater, "The Long Room Pictures", in Sir Pelham Warner, *Lord's 1787-1945* (London, 1946), pp. 265 f. (Appendix II).

112 Bernard Darwin, *op. cit.*, p. 89.

113 *Ibid.*, p. 91.

114 Cf. Russell March, *The Cricketers of Vanity Fair*, with an introduction by John Arlott (Exeter, 1982).

115 Quoted in F.S. Ashley-Cooper, *Cricket Highways and Byways* (London, 1927), pp. 107 ff.

116 For Thompson's love of cricket see especially Everard Meynell, *The Life of Francis Thompson* (London, 1913), pp. 13, 39 ff., 43 ff.; also J.C. Reid, *Francis Thompson, Man and Poet* (London, 1959), pp. 17, 171 f. Besides "At Lord's", Thompson wrote several other cricket poems. See p. 76 (Cat No. 30). He also reviewed Ranjitsinhji's *Jubilee Book of Cricket* in *The Academy*, 4 September 1897.

117 Philip Larkin, "The Whitsun Weddings".

118 Neville Cardus, *Cricket* (London, 1930): "Prelude".

CATALOGUE

The Catalogue does not aim at completeness, but besides containing entries on almost all the works mentioned in the text, it lists most of the important examples of cricket art of the British School, especially of the eighteenth and nineteenth centuries, that the authors have been able to trace. Only a few modern works have been included.

1 Henry Alken, *junior*: *The Cricket Match between the Greenwich and Chelsea Hospital Pensioners*

M.C.C.

Pencil and watercolour: 9¼ × 14¼ in.

Provenance: Colman Gift, 1952.

Exhibited: Nottingham Castle Museum, *Exhibition of Cricket Pictures*, 1930 (34); London, Tate Gallery, 1934; Manchester, 1937.

Henry Alken, *junior* (*fl.* 1816-1831), sporting painter; son of Henry Alken (1785-1851), the sporting painter and watercolourist; imitated the style of his father.

2 David Allan: *The Cathcart Family* (Plate 42)

Collection of The Earl Cathcart.

Oil on canvas: 47½ × 61½ in.

Painted at Schawpark, near Alloa, 1784-5.

Provenance: By family descent.

Exhibited: Arts Council, *British Life*, 1953 (4); R.A., *British Painting*, 1956-7 (346).

Literature: D. Crouther Gordon, *David Allan* (Alloa, 1951), p. 38 (repr.); C. Aspinall-Oglander, *Freshly Remembered*: *The Story of Thomas Graham, Lord Lynedoch* (London, 1956), pp. 27f.; *The Indefatigable Mr. Allan*, Scottish Arts Council Exhibition, 1973.

David Allan (1744-1796), portrait and history painter, known as "the Scottish Hogarth"; much patronized by the Cathcart family, who paid for him to go to Rome in 1767; returned from Italy in 1777. The then Lady Cathcart (wife of the 9th Earl) was the sister of Sir William Hamilton (husband of Nelson's Emma), who helped Allan in Rome and Naples.

The sitters are, *from left to right*: Archibald Hamilton (1764-1841), fourth son of 9th Lord Cathcart, later Prebendary of York; William (1782-1804), Master of Cathcart, eldest son of 10th Lord Cathcart; William (1755-1843), 10th Lord and later 1st Earl Cathcart; the latter's wife Elizabeth (d. 1847), daughter of Andrew Elliott, last Lieutenant-Governor of New York; and Charles, second son of the 9th Lord Cathcart.

Lord Cathcart was then commanding a company of the Coldstream Guards, and had borrowed a tent from his regiment, which can be seen in the right foreground serving as a pavilion for the match which is being played in the distance.

The mobility of the Army was an important factor in the spread of cricket through the British Isles in the eighteenth century.

The picture was sometimes known as "the first cricket match in Scotland", a title which is not strictly accurate. The legend *The First Cricket Match in Scotland* appears on a contemporary engraved glass which features the same scene, as does a papier mâche´ tray, and the match was clearly an important occasion. The family house is shown in the background: compare Allan's painting of *The Family of the 7th Earl of Mar at Alloa House* (1783). Sir Ellis Waterhouse remarks of the latter, in words which are applicable to our painting, that "Allan was at his best in these informal groups in the open air, with a view of the house and park in the background." He continues: "The sincerity of his observant eye and his accurate recording of the contemporary scene make him a precious witness of the past" (*The Dictionary of British 18th Century Painters*[London, 1981]). The latter statement is amply borne out by this picture.

3 Francis Alleyne : *John Call with Bat and Ball* (Plate 37)

Arthur Ackermann & Son Ltd., London.

Oil on panel transferred to canvas: 10 × 8 in. Painted in 1784.

Provenance: R.F.B. Prior; his sale, Christie's, 20 November 1981 (124).

Francis Alleyne (*fl.* 1774-1790) exhibited a single picture at the Royal Academy in 1790; he was itinerant and presumably painted the portraits of the Call family on one of his journeys among country houses.

An old label on the back reads: *John Call b.1778 Painted in 1784 when 6 years old. Died in 1786 when 7 years, 4 months*. The picture is one of a series of eight portraits of the Call family in the possession of Arthur Ackermann and Son Ltd. John Call was the eldest son of Sir John Call, Bart. (1732-1801).

The boy wears a bright red jacket and trousers

and carries a child's bat and a small buff-coloured, un-dyed cricket ball with a double hemisphere seam.

4 **Francis Alleyne** : *William Wheateley at the age of fourteen* (Plate VI)

M.C.C.

Oil on panel (oval) : 14 × 11 in. Painted in 1786.

Provenance: Colman Gift, 1952.

Exhibited: National Gallery of British Sports and Pastimes, Hutchinson House, London, *Cricket Exhibition*, 1950.

In 1786 Alleyne painted Mr Wheately of Lesney House, Kent, Mrs Wheateley and each of the two Wheateley children. "Alleyne probably moved round Kent in 1786, going from family to family" (Ellis Waterhouse, *The Dictionary of British 18th Century Painters* [London, 1981]). The portraits of Mr and Mrs Wheateley were sold at Sotheby's, 14 March, 1962 (175).

This picture may be compared with Alleyne's portrait of *John Call* (1784) (No. 3, Plate 37).

5 **Almond** (*itinerant painter*) : *Edward ("Lumpy") Stevens* (Plate 4)

Collection of Lord Sackville, Knole Park.

Oil on canvas: 11½ × 9½ in. (in an oval). Painted in 1783.

Inscribed on the back: *Stevens, alias Lumpy the famous player at cricket.*

Almond visited Knole, the residence of the 3rd Duke of Dorset, in 1783, when he painted a series of portraits of the servants. On the back of one of these is the following inscription:

These portraits were painted at Knole in 1783 by a Mr Almond, an itinerant painter–I have to each name subjoined the county, the office, and the year he or she came into His Grace's service. J. Bridgman, 1793.

Bridgman was Steward at Knole.

Almond: *fl. 1775-1783.* For Almond at Knole, see C.J. Phillips, *History of the Sackville Family* (London, 1929), II, 444, and Elizabeth Einberg, *Gainsborough's "Giovanna Baccelli"* (Tate Gallery, London, 1976), p.33.

As there is a portrait by Almond at Knole inscribed *Vallet to Madam Baccelli 1775* it is possible that Miss Baccelli (Fig. 4), who was the mistress of the 3rd Duke of Dorset, was already established there at that date, although the first reference in the documents to her residence at Knole is in 1779.

This is the first portrait of a cricketer identified solely in that capacity. "Lumpy" Stevens had already played in the Duke of Dorset's side before being retained by him at Knole, an employment which the painting of this portrait implies. The only records of his being retained on an estate, however, indicate that his employer for most of his career was the cricket-loving Earl of Tankerville.

For "Lumpy" Stevens, see pp. 1f.,13ff.

6 *attributed to* **John C. Anderson** : *? Thomas Barker of Nottingham*

Formerly in the collection of G.H. Weston, Esq.

Oil on canvas: 21 × 16½ in. *c.* 1845.

Literature: *Country Life*, 20 September 1956, p. 591.

The attribution to John C. Anderson, watercolourist, oil painter and lithographer, and painter of a series of famous cricket personalities of the mid-nineteenth century, was made in *Country Life*, 20 September 1956, p. 591, in reply to a letter from the owner, Mr Weston. At the same time it was suggested that the sitter might be Thomas Barker (1798-1877), who played for Nottinghamshire, and was a bowler on the M.C.C. ground staff, and who later became a notable umpire, in which capacity he is shown here. Instead of the sweater we might expect to see today, he carries a waistcoat over his arm. Small-scale individual portraits in oil of this type are typical of mid-19th-century cricket pictures.

7 **George Hamilton Barrable** and **Sir Robert Ponsonby Staples, Bart.**: *England v. Australia at Lord's* (Plate 70)

M.C.C.

Oil on canvas: 58 × 117 in. 1886.

A photogravure with a key was published by

Boussod Valadon.
Below, 22 panels containing the portrait-heads of 22 players, representing England and Australia: 10 × 139½ in. (overall).

Provenance: Purchased from Sir Robert Ponsonby Staples in 1927.

George Hamilton Barrable (*fl.* 1873-1887), London painter of genre subjects; exhibited at the Royal Academy and the Society of British Artists.

Sir Robert Ponsonby Staples, 12th Bart. (1853-1943), Irish painter of portraits, landscapes and genre subjects; studied at Louvain and Dresden; visited Paris in 1869, and Australia in 1879-80; exhibited at the Royal Academy, the Society of British Artists and elsewhere.

Lord's is here seen from the "A" enclosure, the view being towards the Tavern. The scene is imaginary, and the cricketers portrayed did not represent England and Australia together in any Test match at Lord's or elsewhere, although they all represented their country at some time.

The teams are: *England*–R.G. Barlow, W.Scotton, W.Barnes, A.N.Hornby, the Hon. A.Lyttelton, W.G.Grace, A.G.Steel, Lord Harris, G.Ulyett, W.W.Read, A.Shrewsbury; *Australia*–T.W.Garrett, P.S.McDonnel, S.P.Jones, A.C.Bannerman, H.J.H.Scott, F.R.Spofforth, G.Griffen, C.F.Palmer, J.M.Blackham, W.L.Murdoch, C.J.Bonnor.

The most striking feature of the painting–the fielder reaching down to field the ball–was "lifted" from the slightly earlier print of *The Eton and Harrow Cricket Match* by V.W.Bromley (No. 22, Plate 71). Much attention is concentrated on the group of spectators in the foreground, which includes portraits of the Prince and Princess of Wales (the future Edward VII and Queen Alexandra), Lord Harris, Sir Arthur Blyth, the Earl of Bessborough and the Duchess of Leinster.

8 **Henry Barraud** : *Portrait Group of Members of the Marylebone Cricket Club outside the Pavilion at Lord's*

Museum of London (A 25329).

Oil on canvas: 28 × 60 in. Painted about 1870-4.

Provenance: Henry Barraud sale, Christie's, 24 June 1875 (112), bought in; purchased by the Museum in 1923 (without attribution).
Literature: John Hayes, *Catalogue of the Oil Paintings in the London Museum* (London, 1978), pp. 198, 200 (No. 114) (Pl. 114).

Henry Barraud (1811-1874), portrait and animal painter and photographer, specializing in large group portraits, in which his brother William Barraud (1810-50) sometimes painted the backgrounds; studied under J.J. Middleton; worked in London, residing finally at St. Marylebone. Barraud was best known in his own day by this picture and two others–*The Lobby of the House of Commons* of 1872 and a view in Hyde Park entitled *The London Season*.

In this elaborate group portrait about ninety members of M.C.C. and patrons of cricket are represented in the foreground, with other figures seen in the area of the Pavilion. They include Sir R. Ponsonby-Fane (15th from the left), the Earl of Darnley (16th from the left), the Prince of Wales, later Edward VII (21st from the left), E.M. Grace (35th from the left), R.A. FitzGerald (Hon. Secretary) (36th from the left), and W.G. Grace (38th from the left). The Pavilion, which had been enlarged by H. Newton in 1866, was replaced in 1889-90 by the present building, designed by F. Verity. The Union Jack and the M.C.C. flag are being flown. The style of dress being worn dates the picture to the early 1870s.

The painting is related to two photographs by Barraud, both of them portrait-groups in which a separate photograph of each individual was stuck on. One of these is signed by Barraud and shows substantially the same group, but from a different viewpoint. The latter was published as an autotype photograph by Barraud and Jerrard on 1 May 1874. Considerable use was generally made of photographs by many nineteenth-century portrait painters, and the photo-montage method in particular was used in a drawing of *The Chute Family* which survives at The Vyne, Hampshire (The National Trust); in which picture, incidentally, a box for cricket equipment, of a type usually associated with croquet, can be seen.

9 **Hugh Barron:** *The Children of George Bond of Ditchleys, South Weald, Essex* (Plates XII, 33)

Tate Gallery, London (T. 1882).

Oil on canvas: 41¾ × 55 in.

Inscribed (bottom right): *H. Barron Pinxt 1768.*

Provenance: Warland Andrew; sold Christie's 24 July, 1914 (24), bought Huggins; the Hon. Frederick Wallop by 1930; by descent to Alan Evans, who bequeathed it to the National Gallery; whence transferred to the Tate Gallery in 1974.

Exhibited: ? R.A. 1768 (4) (as "Young Gentlemen at Play"); London, 25 Park Lane, *Conversation Pieces*, 1930 (repr. p. 7 in souvenir booklet).

Literature: G.C. Williamson, *English Conversation Pictures* (London, 1931), p. 24, Pl. LXX11.

Hugh Barron (1747-1791), portrait painter, pupil of Sir Joshua Reynolds; began as a musical prodigy; showed great promise as an artist; exhibited at the Society of Artists from 1766 to 1778, and at the Royal Academy in 1782, 1783 and 1786; reputedly the best amateur violinist of his day.

The title is traditional, but nothing is known of the family except of their residence at Ditchleys (which is not very far from Romford). The boys are about to play cricket; the boy at the right is not about to bowl, but to toss the ball to his brother, who has just set up the wicket. The hat worn by the boy with a bat may be compared with those in the portrait of *Walter Hawkesworth Fawkes* (No. 70, Plate 27) and in the portrait attributed to Barron of *Edmund Butler and his Son* (No. 10, Plate 32).

10 *attributed to* **Hugh Barron:** *Edmund Butler and his son* (Plate 32)

Private Collection.

Oil on canvas: 35½ × 28 in. *c.* 1767-8.

Provenance: Anon sale, Christie's, 6 April 1973 (48), bought Whitcomb.

Exhibited: Bradford, 1930 (129); Manchester, *Works of Art from Private Collections in the North-West and North Wales*, 1960 (149) (as by Romney).

A comparison with Barron's *Children of George Bond* (No. 9, Plates 33, XII) reveals an identity of authorship. This painting appears to be even earlier: there are *pentimenti* around the legs and bat of the boy which seem to suggest some difficulties, and its obvious dependence upon the manner of Barron's master Sir Joshua Reynolds, both in the figure style and in the general design, argues for an earlier date than that of the *Children of George Bond*. The boy wears a hat of the same kind as the central child in the Bond picture; it must have been generally worn for cricket, for the same type of hat can be seen in the portrait of *Walter Hawkesworth Fawkes* (No. 70, Plate 27).

11 Frank Batson: *Playing out time in an awkward light* (Plate XXIX)

Nottinghamshire County Cricket Club.

Oil on canvas: 48 × 72 in.

Signed in the bottom left corner: *F. Batson.*

Provenance: Presented by the artist's daughter in 1904.

Exhibited: R.A., 1901 (571).

Literature: Christopher Wood, *The Dictionary of Victorian Painters* (2nd edition, Woodbridge, 1978), p. 40.

Frank Batson (*fl.* 1892-1904), landscape painter; worked at Ramsbury, Hungerford and Penzance; exhibited at the Royal Academy and the Royal Institute of Painters in Watercolours from 1892 to 1904.

The bowler is seen through the eyes of the batsman. The painting was cleaned and restored in 1982.

12 Thomas Beach: *The Children of Sir John William de la Pole* (Plates XIII, 28)

Collection of Sir John Carew Pole, Bart.

Oil on canvas: 79½ × 55½ in.

Signed and dated on the bat of the elder boy (William) : *T. Beach pinxit 1793.*

Provenance: By family descent.

Exhibited: Royal Academy, *British Art*, 1934 (693).

Literature: E.S. Beach, *Thomas Beach, a Dorset portrait painter, favourite pupil of Sir Joshua*

Reynolds (London, 1934).

Thomas Beach (1738-1806), portrait painter; after studying under Reynolds settled at Bath, where he enjoyed a successful practice; often made summer tours in the West country, executing commissions for portraits in country houses. Apart from James Northcote, who excelled as a history painter, Beach was the most distinguished of Reynolds's pupils.

The children are *(from left to right)*: William (b.1784), later Sir William Templer Pole, 7th Baronet; Marianne (b. 1784), who married J.M. West; and John George (1787-1803). The boys wear blue coats and cream breeches and hold bats, while Marianne carries a basket of flowers and a cricket ball. The bats are the unusual "bow-shaped" sort. The elder boy's hat lies on the ground at the right and is inscribed: *W.T. de la Pole*. Old Shute House, Axminster, the Poles' family house, is shown in the background, and Beach painted a number of portraits of members of the family there in the 1790s–three of the mother of these children in 1793; and two of their father in 1794.

13 Thomas Beach: *The Tyndall Family* (Plate 29)

University of Bristol.

Oil on canvas: 104 × 74 in.

Inscribed: Painted by T. Beach 1797.

Provenance: Mrs Laura F. Walwyn of Croft-y-Bwla, Monmouth, in 1921 (last surviving daughter of T.O. Tyndall, Esq), when the picture was at The Fort, Bristol.

Literature: see no. 12.

Thomas Tyndall (1764-1804) of The Fort and his wife Marianne Schimmelpenninck are shown with their children. The picture still hangs at The Fort. As in Beach's portrait of *The Children of Sir John de la Pole* (No. 12 Plate 28), one boy props his bat on the ground, and the other has his bat on his shoulder, while a girl holds the cricket ball (which is a good illustration of the modern type). The boys' blue jackets with gilt buttons and their shirt collars may be compared with those worn by Lord Hay in the portrait of him datable *c.* 1810 (No. 151, Plate XVII), and by other sitters for cricket portraits during this period.

This portrait group by Beach is on a very large scale, and is evidence of the way in which cricket had survived as a suitable subject to be incorporated in groups of this type some 40 years after its introduction by Hudson into his painting of *The Family of the 3rd Duke of Marlborough* (No. 67) (see Plate 24).

14 Sir William Beechey, R.A.: *The Revd Lord Frederick Beauclerk* (Plate 47)

M.C.C.

Oil on canvas: 28¾ × 23¼ in. *c.* 1789.

Provenance: The Duke of St Albans sale, Christie's, 23 June 1978 (124).

Sir William Beechey (1753-1839), portrait painter, born in Oxfordshire; received some instruction under Zoffany; beginning with small-scale portraits and conversation pieces, he established a thriving full-scale portrait practice from 1787 onwards, and reached his highest point of success with a number of royal portrait commissions in the late 1790s.

The portrait would have been painted *c.* 1789, the date of a group of portraits at Bowhill with which this painting is comparable. Lord Frederick is wearing a blue coat with a red waistcoat and white cravat. See also under Nos. 101, 149.

For Lord Frederick Beauclerk see pp. 30ff.

15 Sir Max Beerbohm: *W.G. Grace* (Plate 103)

M.C.C.

Pen and ink: 8 × 12¾ in.

Provenance: Bought in December 1946 from Col. H. D. Whittick.

Sir Max Beerbohm (1872-1956), critic, essayist, wit and caricaturist, author of *Zuleika Dobson*.

In 1895, when "the Doctor" made 1000 runs in May, the *Daily Telegraph* organized a sitting fund for him, which realized £10,000. In Beerbohm's cartoon, "W.G." is receiving with his right hand a cheque for £10,000 bearing the signature of the editor of the *Daily Telegraph*, Edward Lawson; in his left hand he holds a diminutive bat; behind on the left, Lord's, and on the right the funeral of one of his patients. This cartoon is an early work by

Beerbohm, who had not long come down from Oxford (but who nonetheless contrived to call his first book, published in the following year, *The Works of Max Beerbohm*).

16, 17 William Blake: *The Echoing Green* I *and* II: from *Songs of Innocence* (1789) and *Songs of Innocence and of Experience* (1820s). (Plates 66, 67).

Literature: *The Illuminated Blake*, annotated by David V. Erdman (London, 1975), pp. 47-8.

William Blake (1757-1827), poet, painter, engraver and visionary; studied engraving under James Basire and at the Royal Academy Schools; influenced by the Neoclassicists and was violently opposed to the ideals of Reynolds; for a time an enthusiastic supporter of the French Revolution; published his poems by means of his invention of "illuminated printing", in which text and illustrations were first engraved in monochrome and afterwards coloured.

Song of Innocence was first published in 1789 and then re-issued in 1794 in *Songs of Innocence and of Experience*. In a late edition of the latter volume, of the 1820s, Blake revised the illustration to *The Echoing Green*, substituting a straight bat for the older type of curved bat (Plate 67), thus reflecting one of the major developments in cricket. See pp.34 ff.

18 H. Roberts after **Louis P. Boitard:** *An Exact Representation of the Game of Cricket* (Plate 20)

Engraving by H. Roberts, 1743.

Literature: G.D. Martineau, *Bat, Ball, Wicket and All: An Account of the Origin and Development of the Implements, Dress and Appurtenances of the National Game* (London, 1950), p. 89 (repr. opp. p. 33).

Louis Phillippe Boitard (*op.* 1737-1763), French draughtsman and engraver working in London; engraved prints after Bartholomew Dandridge for F. Nivelon's *Rudiments of Genteel Behavior*, of which Plate 1 (see Fig. 2) illustrates a gentlemanly attitude often seen in eighteenth-century representations of cricketers (see pp.11f.17ff.).

As a documentary record of cricket in the 1740s this engraving is only surpassed by Francis Hayman's *"Cricket Match in Marylebone Fields"* (No. 60, Plates II-IV, 10, 11). It has the additional interest of showing a roped-off "ring". The *Match Ticket* of 18 June 1744 (No. 19, Plate 21) is derived from it, and it is likely that the Artillery Ground is indicated. The *Cricket Match* in the Tate Gallery attributed to W.R. Coates (No. 28, Plates VIII, IX, 16), and datable in the early 1740s, is a version in oil, with variations, but is less precise. The M.C.C. possesses another, much more primitive, oil painting, of uncertain date, which is also derived from it (24½ × 38¾ in.).

It is difficult to prove, but there are sufficient similarities between this engraving and Hayman's *"Cricket Match in Marylebone Fields"* (No. 60, Plates II-IV, 10, 11) to make one suspect that Boitard's less realistic portrayal of cricket is derived from Hayman's picture. The presence in both works of the man with a skull-cap at the extreme edge of the composition is a case in point, if we allow for the reversals consequent upon copying and engraving; and the fielder who stands with hands on hips in the centre foreground of the engraving is remarkably similar to the figure in the corresponding position in the painting (and we may compare the *Match Ticket* of 18 June 1744 [No. 19, Plate 21]).

19 *after* **L.P. Boitard:** *Match Ticket for 18 June, 1744* (Plate 21)

M.C.C.

Engraving.
Inscribed in ink: *June 18th. 1744 No. 113/A ticket to see a Cricket match/price 2s–6d.*

The design is an adaptation of Louis Boitard's *Exact Representation of a Game of Cricket* (No. 18, Plate 20), published in the preceding year. "Smith" is George Smith, "Keeper of the Pyed Horse in Chiswell Street and of the Artillery Ground". The Ticket was for England. Kent, the first cricket match for which a full scorecard survives and which was the subject of James Love's *Cricket: an Heroic Poem* (1744). The superscription with the price appears to be in a slightly later hand. The price of 2*s* 6*d* was a considerable one at the time. The design of the ticket includes a droll cartouche around the name "Smith", which parodies the work of such Huguenot emigré engravers as Boitard, from whom the scene above derives. The curved bats of the time take the place of the curling cornucopias usual in such rococo decorations, and the fruit-baskets are filled with cricket balls.

20 Sam Bough, R.S.A.: *Cricket at Edenside, Carlisle* (Plate 63)

Carlisle City Art Gallery.

Oil on canvas: 24 × 35 in. *c.* 1848.

Provenance: William Howe; Sir Benjamin Scott.

Exhibited: Carlisle, 1896; Sheffield, *Two Centuries of Cricket Art*, 1955 (3).

Samuel (Sam) Bough (1822-1878), Scottish landscape painter and watercolourist; born in Carlisle the son of a shoemaker; painted theatre scenery in Manchester and Glasgow before devoting himself to landscape; worked in Glasgow from 1848 to 1855, afterwards moving to Edinburgh; elected R.S.A. in 1875; exhibited at the Royal Academy and Royal Scottish Academy

The match is being played at Edenside, Carlisle, and the painting was commissioned by one of the umpires, a Mr Howe. The nearest fielder is wearing a rather dashing hooped shirt : there were passing fashions for such fancy clothes in the nineteenth century, and even polka-dots appeared on cricket shirts. The bowler is bowling round-arm, and his pose is comparable with that of Alfred Mynn in the lithograph by G.F. Watts of about 1837. It is noticeable that the umpire at the bowler's end is carrying a bat, a habit which continued to be followed by some umpires in the nineteenth century; his colleague at square leg does not appear to be holding one.

21 Edward Bradley: *Durham* (Plate 59)

M.C.C.

Pen and some body-colour on white paper: 14½ × 11½ in. 1849.

Signed (lower centre): *Edward Bradley delt.*

Inscribed below in the artist's hand:

On the cricket ground, the nearest tent to the right is that of the Gentlemen of the University, the central one profusely decorated with flags is that of the All England Eleven, the 3rd. is that of the Durham Club. Lillywhite's Printing Press Tent is seen to the centre of the far side. Of the tents to the left, the nearest is the spacious dinner tent, in front of which the Brass Band was stationed. The central one is the Grand Stand erected for the accommodation of ladies, beyond which are other refreshment tents, all gleaming in snowy white canvas and covered with flags of all colours.

The sketch is taken from an eminence in Pellaw Wood commanding a fine view of the cricket ground, backed by the irregular but picturesque city of Durham...

Edward Bradley (*fl.* 1824-1867), painter of landscapes and still lifes; worked in London; exhibited at the British Institution, the Society of British Artists and the Royal Academy. His pictures include scenes in various parts of England and Scotland and some in Italy.

A cricket match is taking place in a field in the foreground. Durham Cathedral, with the Castle to the right, dominates the background.

22 Valentine Walter Bromley: *At the Eton and Harrow Match* (Plate 71)

Engraving. *c*1877.

Signed, lower right: *V W Bromley* (*V* and *W* in monogram).

Valentine Walter Bromley (1848-1877), historical painter, watercolourist and illustrator, was an assistant on the *Illustrated London News*; son of the impressive Victorian genre painter William Bromley III (*fl.* 1835-1888), he inherited few of his father's gifts, a fact which did not prevent his producing "histories" and "ideal" paintings such as *Spring* (Christie's, 29 February 1980)–a painting of a feebly pornographic kind much indulged in by respectable Victorians.

The most striking feature of this print–the fielder who is bending down to retrieve the ball on the boundary–inspired Barrable and Staples to incorporate the same pose in their well-known painting of *England v. Australia at Lord's* (No. 7, Plate 70), which they produced in 1887, some dozen years after the appearance of this print.

23 Ford Madox Brown: *Humphrey Chetham's Life Dream* (Plates 61, XXIII)

Manchester Town Hall, Great Hall.

Mural: No. 8 in a series of 12 panels illustrating the history of Manchester.

Oil on canvas laid on wall.

Painted in 1886.

Literature: Particulars relating to the Manchester Town Hall and Description of the Mural Paintings in the Great Hall (Manchester, n.d.), p. 10; Ford M. Hueffer, *Ford Madox Brown: A Record of his Life and Work* (London, 1896) pp. 302ff., 362ff., 369, 371f., 385, 444.

Ford Madox Brown (1821-1893), painter of literary and religious subjects and landscapes; a precursor of the Pre-Raphaelites, becoming the teacher of D.G. Rossetti and being influenced in turn by the ideals of the Brotherhood; born in Calais; studied in Bruges, Ghent and Antwerp; visited Rome in 1845, coming under the influence of the German Nazarenes; exhibited at the Royal Academy and at the British Institution. Madox Brown is celebrated for such pictures as *Work* and *The Last of England*.

The Boys' School in Manchester was established in 1656 in accordance with the terms of the will of Humphrey Chetham, a cloth merchant of great wealth. His Will directed that the College buildings annexed to the present Cathedral were to be purchased for their conversion into a school and library. Chetham boarded out and educated 22 poor boys, and after his death the number increased to 40. In Madox Brown's mural Chetham is shown in the garden of the College, studying his will, and in his imagination he has peopled the garden with the "forty healthy boys" of his will, together with their schoolmaster. While the school cook awaits the arrival of the butcher, the scholars engage in various activities, from reading to playing leap-frog. At the centre, a game similar to "stool- ball", which has been thought to have been an early form of cricket, is being played by two boys–a "bowler", who is retrieving the ball in the near foreground, and a "batsman" who stands at a "wicket" formed by a three-legged stool placed on the ground upside down. The ball is stitched in the manner of a modern baseball; the bat is curved. For comments see pp.35f.

The series of twelve pictures, together with the preliminary cartoons, was painted between 1878 and 1887. The cartoon for *Chetham's Life Dream* was executed in 1885, the finished painting being completed in the following year. This was the first in the series to be painted on canvas which was then stuck to the wall by the French process known as *maroufler*.

24 *after* **William Burgess:** *Kent v. All England at Canterbury, 1845*

Coloured lithograph: 13½ × 19½ in.

Lettered: *W. Burgess del. Published by H. Ward, Mercery Lane, Canterbury / To the President & Members of the Beverley and East Kent Cricket Club / This Print, representing the Match played at Canterbury on Monday, August 4th. 1845, between Kent and All England,/is respectfully dedicated by their obedient servant / Henry Ward.*

Signed with initials on hamper in bottom left corner: *WB*.

William Burgess (1805-1861), painter of coastal scenes, landscapes and other subjects; worked at Dover; exhibited at the Royal Academy and the Society of British Artists; a friend of the animal painter Thomas Sidney Cooper, R.A. (1803-1902).

25 Alexander H. Burr: *A Game of Cricket: Youth and Age* (Plate 95)

Harvert Consultancy (Holdings) Ltd, Dundee.

Oil on canvas: 18 × 26 in. *c.* 1860-70.

Alexander Hohenlohe Burr (1835-1899), a Scottish painter of genre and historical subjects; younger brother of the painter John P. Burr, R.B.A. (1831-1893); studied in Edinburgh under John Ballantyne; specialized in pictures of children.

There are other versions by Burr of this composition. The wicket looks odd, since the bails are on two levels, and the intention may well have been to suggest a wicket-gate. An old man–perhaps a cricketer of the Beauclerk era – is about to bowl an underarm lob to a small boy.

26 Philip Hermogenes Calderon, R.A.: *Captain of the Eleven* (Plate XXX)

Thames County Primary School, Thames Road, Blackpool.

Oil on canvas: 84 × 48 in.
Engraved in mezzotint by R. Josey: engraving

published by the Fine Art Society Ltd, 1 June 1883.

Provenance: A. & F. Pears, Limited; presented to the School by Councillor Halstead in 1926.

Philip Hermogenes Calderon (1833-1898), painter of genre and historical subjects and portraits; leader of the St John's Wood Clique; born at Poitiers the son of a former Spanish priest, the Revd. Juan Calderon, who became Professor of Spanish Literature at King's College, London; studied in London and Paris; achieved early fame with his *Broken Vows* (1857) (Tate Gallery); won a gold medal at the International Exhibition in Paris in 1867; exhibited at the Royal Academy, of which he was elected Keeper in 1887; after 1870 worked chiefly as a portrait painter; died at Burlington House.

27 James Warren Childe: *Two Young Cricketers* (Plate 46)

Present whereabouts unknown.

Miniature: 7 × 5½ in. Painted in 1817.

Provenance: Christie's, 11 October 1977 (67) (repr.).

James Warren Childe (1778-1862), portrait miniaturist.

In contrast with large-scale portraits of the eighteenth century, in which the bats sometimes look too large for their boy-owners, the bat here appears disproportionately small. The sitters are dressed in typical clothes of the period, and such loose-fitting trousers had begun to overtake knee-breeches for playing cricket.

28 *attributed to* **W.R. Coates:** *A Cricket Match* (Plates VIII, IX, 16)

Tate Gallery, London (5383).

Oil on canvas: 19¼ × 23¼ in. *c.* 1740-5.

Provenance: T. Grange.

Exhibited: Sheffield, *Two Centuries of Cricket Art*, 1955 (2), as attributed to L.R. Boitard (*sic*).

The attribution to the obscure W.R. Coates has been made by the Tate Gallery.

This painting derives from L.P. Boitard's picture of *An Exact Representation of the Game of Cricket* (No. 18, Plate 20), but is enlivened by the heightened characterization of the participants.

For comments see pp.9 ff.

29 *after* **John Collet:** *Miss Wicket and Miss Trigger* (Plate 90)

Mezzotint: 13 × 10 in.

Published by Carrington Bowles, 1778.

Inscribed with the following verse:

Miss Trigger you see is an excellent shot
And forty-five notches Miss Wicket's just got.

John Collet (*c.* 1725-1780), painter of low life subjects; studied at the St Martin's Lane Academy.

This print is one of a series engraved after paintings by Collet, showing "Ladies' Recreations". Other titles are: *The Female Foxhunter*; *Miss Tippapin*; *The Ladies' Shooting Party*; and *The Pleasures of Skating*. Some of the original paintings survive, but that of *Miss Wicket and Miss Trigger* has been lost.

A two-stump wicket and curved bat are shown, as well as a cricket ball with two double-stitched seams crossing at right-angles. Miss Wicket is dressed in ladies' cricket costume, together with one of the high bonnets fashionable at the time. She is shown striking a masculine cross-legged pose of a kind often seen in eighteenth-century portraits of male cricketers, for example in David Martin's painting of *John Campbell of South Hall* of 1771 (No. 79, Plate 38).

30 The Hon. John Collier: *A.N. Hornby, Esq., Captain of the Lancashire Eleven* (Plate XXXI)

Blackburn Museum and Art Gallery.

Oil on canvas: 84 × 43 in.
Signed, bottom left: *John Collier/1893.*

Provenance: Presented by A.N. Hornby.

Exhibited: Royal Academy, 1893 (921).

Literature: Mark Girouard, *The Return to Camelot: Chivalry and the English Gentleman* (Yale University

Press, New Haven and London, 1981), p. 167 (repr.).

The Hon. John Collier (1850-1934), portrait and history painter, son of Robert Collier (afterwards Lord Monkswell), the eminent judge; educated at Heidelberg before studying under Sir Edward Poynter, P.R.A. (1836-1919), at the Slade School; continued his studies in Paris and Munich; exhibited at the Royal Academy from 1874. Collier was the author of three manuals on painting; he is best known for his domestic scenes of upper-class life; he also exhibited a picture at the Royal Academy in 1893 with the interesting title of *A Glass of Wine with Caesar Borgia*, which is now in the Ipswich Museum. He was the illustrator of Thomas Hardy's *The Trumpet-Major* when the novel was serialized in *Good Words*.

It is easy to imagine from this alert full-length portrait of the great Lancashire batsman and captain why Hornby's stylish play so excited the crowds who saw him. Albert Neilsen Hornby (1847-1925) was educated at Harrow, where owing to his small stature he was known as "Monkey", a nickname he retained in later life. He played for Lancashire and England. Hornby is immortalized in Francis Thompson's poem "At Lord's", in which the poet, sitting at Lord's, sees in his mind's eye the famous match of July 1878, when Gloucestershire, with the Graces in their Eleven, met Lancashire for the first time at Old Trafford. As a keen Lancashire supporter, Thompson had watched this match, in which Barlow, Hornby's stolid opening partner, was last man out for 40 in the Lancashire first innings, and in which Hornby made a scintillating century. This was very much Hornby's and Barlow's match; and hence Thompson's nostalgic lines:

It is little I repair to the matches of the Southron folk,
  Though my own red roses there may blow;
It is little I repair to the matches of the Southron folk,
  Though the red roses crest the caps, I know.

For the field is full of shades as I near the shadowy coast,
And a ghostly batsman plays to the bowling of a ghost,
And I look through my tears on a soundless-clapping host,
  As the run-stealers flicker to and fro,
  To and fro:-
O my Hornby and my Barlow long ago !

The evocative word "run-stealers" was inspired by the manner in which Hornby and Barlow, who had a good understanding (though the styles of the great amateur and the reliable professional were so different), responded to one another's calls for quick singles. (For Francis Thompson's poem and his love of cricket see especially Everard Meynell, *The Life of Francis Thompson* (London, 1913), especially pp.13, 39 ff., 43 ff.) Thompson reviewed Ranjitsinhji's *Jubilee Book of Cricket* in *The Academy*, 4 September, 1897, and he contemplated writing his own cricket memoirs. In addition to the famous "At Lord's", Thompson wrote other cricket poems, including a parody of Edward FitzGerald's *Rubáiyát of Omar Khayyám*, of which the following quatrain is characteristic:

O Love, if Thou and I could but Conspire
Against this Pitch of Life, so false with Mire,
  Would we not Doctor it afresh, and then
Roll it out smoother to the Bat's Desire ?

See also No. 88 and pp,52f., 63 (note 116).

31 John Singleton Copley, R.A.: *Richard Heber as a boy* (Plate 44)

Yale Center for British Art, Paul Mellon Collection (B1981, 25. 745), New Haven, Connecticut, U.S.A.

Oil on canvas: $65\frac{1}{4} \times 51\frac{3}{16}$ in. *c.* 1783.

Provenance: Agnew, 1978.

John Singleton Copley (1738-1815), American painter, largely self-taught; influenced by John Smibert, a Scottish artist who had settled in the American colonies; left for Europe in 1774, coming to London in 1775; influenced by Reynolds and the Grand Manner; achieved great success with such history pictures as *Brook Watson and the Shark* (1778) and *The Death of Chatham* (1780). His son, also John Singleton Copley, became Lord Chancellor and was ennobled as Lord Lyndhurst.

Richard Heber (1773-1833), brother of Bishop Reginald Heber (author of "From Greenland's Icy Mountains"), was a great bibliophile, and was described by Sir Walter Scott as "Heber the magnificent, whose library and cellar are so superior to all others in the world". The series of sales of his 146,827 books lasted three years (cf. Osbert Sitwell, *Left Hand Right Hand!* (London, 1945), pp. 42 f.). The sitter would appear to be about ten years old. He holds a long curved bat and is holding a cricket ball with a prominent seam. There seems no doubt that the curved bat was considered more picturesque than the bat with a straight blade which had been developed in the previous decade. It would also appear that the straight bat, as yet, had superseded the curved only at the highest levels of the game. The two-stump wicket which is shown here had also given way to the three-stump wicket by the time this picture was painted, but, in the same way, only in the grandest circles. The wicket represented by Copley is, in any case, much too low for an official wicket of the eighteenth century. Its primitive form, however, can be paralleled in other paintings of the period, and rudimentary shapes of wicket of the kind seen here must have been common in *ad hoc* games among children.

32 Francis Cotes, R.A.: *Lewis Cage as a Batsman* (see Plates XVI, 17)

Collection of The Lord Brocket.

Oil on canvas: 66½ × 43½ in.

Inscribed, signed and dated, lower left, on the cricket bat: *Lewis Cage Act: 5½/ F Cotes R.A. px^t 1768* (*F* and *C* in monogram).

Engraved in mezzotint by L. Busière.

Provenance: By family descent from the sitter to the present owner.

Exhibited: R.A. 1769 (No. 23) (probably) (No. 23 appeared in the catalogue as "A Young Gentleman", and was described by Horace Walpole as "very pretty"); R.A., *British Art*, 1934 (368); Montreal, *British Painting in the 18th Century* (Arts Council), 1957, then Ottawa, National Gallery of Canada, 1957-8, and then Toronto, 1958.

Literature: James Northcote, *The Life of Sir Joshua Reynolds*, (London, 1819), I 184 ("a boy playing at cricket by Mr Cotes"); Sir Pelham Warner, *Lord's 1787-1945* (London, 1946), p. 268; Edward Mead Johnson, *Francis Cotes* (London, 1976), pp. 36 (No. 255), 160, Pl. 72.

A replica is in the collection of John Nutting, Esq (reproduced here, Plates XVI, 17). A modern copy (1950) is in the Long Room at Lord's.

Francis Cotes, R.A. (1726-1770), English portraitist in pastel and oil; born in London and trained under George Knapton (1698-1779); first established his reputation as a crayon painter (pastel painter in modern parlance), but gradually came to work more and more in oils; became a founder-member of the Royal Academy, being the artist chosen to present the Instruments establishing the Academy for the royal signature; was attracting favourable notice at Court at the time of his early death, which was due to his choking on a soap cure for the stone. His portrait of *Queen Charlotte with the infant Charlotte, Princess Royal* (Collection of H.M. The Queen) earned him particular praise. Apart from Gainsborough and Ramsay, he may be considered the most distinguished of Reynolds's rivals in portraiture.

The sitter is Lewis Cage of Milgate Park, Maidstone, Kent (born 1763), and is represented at the age of 5½, standing by a wicket made of two forked sticks and a bail laid across them. He wears a white shirt open at the neck and suitable for active cricket, a green waistcoat and green breeches. The fact that his breeches have become unbuttoned at the left knee indicates that he has just been playing cricket, and it appears that it is now early evening. He holds a long curved bat such as was in use in 1768, the year in which he posed for this picture. Full-length portraits of boys in landscapes became popular in late eighteenth-century England, and several of them, including this one, seem to show an awareness of a full-length by Allan Ramsay (1713-84) of *John, Lord Mountstuart*, begun in 1758 and completed in 1759.

Lewis Cage's sister Catherine (born 1771) married the notable county cricketer Richard Fielder (probably 1758–*c.*1826), a horsebreaker and trainer by trade, who played for Richard Leigh's cricket team at Dartford. She eloped with him after receiving lessons from him in riding. Fielder afterwards became landlord of the Woolpack Inn at Tenterton.

There is no connection between the Lewis Cage of Cotes's portrait and the cricketer named C. Cage who played in the London area (e.g. for the Montpelier Club) in the late eighteenth century (cf. *Sports Quarterly*, No. 3, autumn 1977).

Lewis Cage is mentioned in the correspondence of Jane Austen, who met the Cages at Rowley.

33 Francis Cotes, R.A.: *The Revd Charles Collyer as a boy* (Plate 36)

Yale Center for British Art, Paul Mellon Collection (B1981.25.166), New Haven, Connecticut, U.S.A.

Oil on canvas: 35¾ × 27⅜ in.

Signed and dated, lower left: *FCotes px[t] 1766 (F* and *C* in monogram). A label on the back is inscribed: *Charles Collyer/of Gunthorpe/2[d] son of Danl Collyer/of Wok & Anne his wife.*

Provenance: By family descent from the sitter to Brigadier-General J.J. Collyer; Thos. Agnew & Sons, 1930, from whom bought by Mr L.K. Thorne, U.S.A.; Knoedler and Co., London; Thos. Agnew & Sons, London, 1966; from whom bought by Mr and Mrs Paul Mellon.

Literature: Prince Frederick Duleep Singh, *Portraits in Norfolk Houses* (2 vols., Norwich, 1928), I, 202 (No. 10); Walter Heil, "Portraits by Francis Cotes", *Art in America*, XX, No. 1 (December, 1931) (pp. 2-12), 6; Edward Mead Johnson, *Francis Cotes* (London, 1976), p. 81 (No. 195), fig. 70.; J. Egerton, *The Paul Mellon Collection: British Sporting and Animal Paintings* (1978), No. 103, Pl. 38, pp. 107 f.

Charles Collyer (1755-1830) was the second son of Daniel Collyer of Wroxham Hall, Norfolk; he married Sarah Astley, eldest daughter of Sir Jacob Astley, Bart.; in 1798 he became Rector of Gunthorpe. In this portrait he wears a white open-necked cricket shirt, a green waistcoat and green breeches; he holds a curved cricket bat in his right hand and a black tricorn hat in his left. The sky suggests evening, after the match, as in the portrait by Cotes of *Lewis Cage* (No. 32, Plate XVI). The sitter's attitude of placing one hand on his hip is frequently found in eighteenth-century British portraiture, and derives ultimately from pictures by Van Dyck. The bat is held in the crook of the arm–a variation of pose occasionally seen, in addition to those where the sitter leans on the bat or carries it on his shoulder.

The picture is a companion to a portrait by Cotes of the sitter's elder brother Daniel Collyer (1752-1819), who also entered the Church, becoming Rector of Wroxham.

Another cricket portrait ascribed—although unconvincingly—to Cotes is a painting, in a private collection, of *The Young Lord Manners* (50 × 38in.).

The sitter, who leans on a cricket bat, wears fancy dress as though of the seventeenth century–a fashion in eighteenth-century England, especially from the 1740s onwards. Such costumes gave eighteenth-century portraits a "look" of the work of Van Dyck. A ball lies on the ground at the sitter's feet, but it is of a decorative kind not known from representations of cricket balls. The cricket bat, however, is a solid, curved weapon of a type familiar from pictures of *c.* 1760-1770.

34 Charles Cundall, R.A., R.W.S.: *A Hastings Cricket Festival*

Hastings Borough Council: on loan to the Museum and Art Gallery from the Town Hall.

Oil on canvas: 50 x 30in.

Provenance: Anonymous gift, 1954.

Exhibited: R.A., 1953.

Charles Cundall (1890-1971), painter in oil and watercolour of landscapes, townscapes and portraits; born in Stretford, Lancashire; began as a designer of pottery and stained glass for Pilkington's Pottery Company; studied at the Manchester School of Art, obtaining a scholarship to the Royal College of Art; severely wounded in the First World War when serving with the Royal Fusiliers; elected A.R.A. in 1937, R.W.S. in 1941, and R.A. in 1944; appointed official artist to the Air Ministry in 1940; was widely travelled on the Continent; worked in Chelsea.

35 J.D. Curtis: *A Cricket Match at Newark-on-Trent*

M.C.C.

Oil on canvas: 22 × 36 in. 1823.

Provenance: Colman Gift, 1952.
John Digby Curtis (*fl.* 1790-1827), son of the painter John Curtis.

There are lists of Newark cricketers dating back to *c.* 1815, and the same ground is in use today. It seems clear that the portrait of *Walter Hawkesworth Fawkes*, attributed to Thomas Hudson and datable about 1760 (No. 70, Plate 27), shows the sitter on his way back from this same ground, which would suggest that the history of cricket in Newark predates, by some decades, the surviving written records.

36 R.D. [Richard Dagley]: *Benjamin Disraeli at the Wicket* (Plate 101)

M.C.C.

Oil on canvas: 21½ × 11⅜ in.

Provenance: Charles Dickens; Sir Jeremiah Colman.

Datable in 1824, when Disraeli was staying with his publisher John Murray. At that time Disraeli was writing his first novel, *Vivian Grey*.

The inscription almost certainly indicates that the artist is Richard Dagley (1765-1841), who is known best for his melancholy *Death's Doings* of 1826, comprising a series of etchings. One of these is entitled *Death among the Cricketers*, and shows a skeleton (Death) bowling at a boy batsman, behind whom a winged wicketkeeper waits.

Benjamin Disraeli (1804-1881), the statesman and novelist, stands with a bat by a wicket, wearing white cricket clothes and a top hat, such as were commonly worn on the cricket field in the middle years of the nineteenth century.

In 1844 Disraeli played in one of the cricket matches organized by William Busfield Ferrand, the Radical Tory politican, at the Bingley Cricket Club in Yorkshire, to mark the opening of the Cottingley allotment gardens. The land for the allotments had been presented by his aunt, Mrs Walker Ferrand, after Parliament had rejected his "Bill for the Allotment of Waste Lands", which he had proposed as "an act of justice to the poor". The celebrations were attended by Disraeli and Lord John Manners, and included a parade and a dinner. "Manners is said to have captained one of the teams, and Disraeli to have gone in to bat with a local shoemaker" (Mark Girouard, *The Return to Camelot: Chivalry and the English Gentleman* [Yale University Press, New Haven and London, 1981], p. 245).

See also under No. 161.

37 Henri Pierre Danloux: *The Masters Foster*

Private Collection.

Oil on canvas: 45½ × 37½ in.

Signed and dated (bottom right): *H Danloux f ano 1792.*

Provenance: Foster and Elmslie families; Sir James Bowker; his sale, Christie's, 26 June 1981 (148).

Exhibited: R.A. 1793 (213); R.A. *France in the 18th Century*, winter, 1968 (174).

Henri Pierre Danloux (1753-1809), a French portraitist, came to England in 1792, when this picture was executed, and became a fashionable portrait-painter in London.

The two children were the sons of Constantia and Richard Foster. It is a question whether in this picture they hold cricket bats. These small, slim weapons are similar to those in the picture by Wills of *The Andrews Family* (No. 136, Plate 43), in David Allan's *Cathcart Family* (No. 2, Plate 42), and in some other eighteenth-century paintings. However, it may be noted that the boy on the right carries his implement over his shoulder in the cricketing manner.

38 Richard Barrett Davis, R.B.A.: *Landscape with Children playing Cricket* (Plate 40)

Present whereabouts unknown.

Oil on canvas: 18 × 21 in.

Signed and dated (bottom right): *R.B. Davis 1827.*

Richard Barrett Davis (1782-1854), landscape and sporting painter; studied under Sir Francis Bourgeois and Sir William Beechey; exhibited at the Society of British Artists and at the Royal Academy; patronized by George III, George IV, William IV and Queen Victoria.

Three yokels are playing cricket under a tree, and their use of a curved bat at this late date is an appealing instance of the survival of outmoded cricket equipment in rural areas.

39 Peter De Wint: *The Cricketers* (Plate 62)

Victoria and Albert Museum, London (F.A. 515).

Watercolour: 22¼ × 34¾ in. Probably 1815.

Literature: Martin Hardie, *Water-colour Painting in Britain* (3 vols., London, 1966-8), II (*The Romantic Period*) (1967), 214, Pl. 199.

Peter De Wint (1784-1849), landscape painter in watercolour; born at Stafford, the son of a Dutch-American; settled in London in 1810, coming to know the amateur and connoisseur Dr Thomas Monro, who had encouraged Turner and Girtin in their early days; became a close friend of the Lincoln painter William Hilton (1786-1839), whose sister he married. De Wint devoted himself principally to Lincolnshire scenes, but he also travelled extensively in various parts of England.

This is probably the watercolour exhibited by De Wint as *A Cricket Match* at the Old Water-colour Society in 1815. It is related of the latter drawing that, having failed to find a purchaser, De Wint strained another piece of paper over it in order to save the cost of purchasing a new stretcher. The hidden watercolour was not discovered until after his death, when preparations were going forward for the sale of his work at Christie's.

40 Robert Dighton: *Cricket played by the Gentlemen's Club, White Conduit House* (Plate 56)

Paul Mellon Collection.

Pen, ink and watercolour: 5¾ × 7¾ in. (in an oval). 1784.

Inscribed: *Cricket played by the Gentlemen's Club Whiteconduit House.*

Provenance: Executors of the late Mrs Charles E. Dunlap; Sotheby Parke Bernet, Inc., New York, 4 December 1975 (342).

Preliminary drawing for one of a series of six engravings of *British Sports*, published in 1784. The other games represented are "Four Corners", "Coits", "Trap Ball", "Football", and "Fives".

Literature: *The Illustrated London News*, 22 August, 1931 (with the whole series reproduced in colour); J. Egerton and D. Snelgrove, *The Paul Mellon Collection: British Sporting and Animal Drawings, c. 1500-1850* (The Tate Gallery for the Yale Center for British Art, 1978), p. 32; D. Rose, *The Life, Times and Recorded works of Robert Dighton (1752-1814) and three of his Artist Sons* (London,1981).Robert Dighton (1752-1814), portrait painter and caricaturist; exhibited at the Free Society of Artists and at the Royal Academy; in 1779, published a *Book of Heads*, thereafter devoting himself chiefly to caricature.

White Conduit House in Islington was a tea and coffee hour with small pleasure gardens. The White Conduit Club was formed of members from the Star and Garter Club who used to play cricket in White Conduit Fields. The "master of the Angel Inn at Islington and likewise of the White Conduit House" was recorded in 1766 as being Robert Bartholomew, a wealthy farmer, and H.S. Altham states that "the proprietor of the tavern of that name [i.e. White Conduit]...as early as 1766 had advertised 'Bats and Balls for Cricket and a convenient field to play in' " (H.S. Altham and E.W. Swanton, *A History of Cricket* [London, 1948], p. 53). The aristocratic members of this club formed the Marylebone Cricket Club in 1787. Thomas Lord had been an employee of the White Conduit Club, and the first game played by the M.C.C. was at Lord's new ground in June 1787 in what is now Dorset Square: M.C.C. played the White Conduit Club and won by 83 runs. Dighton's drawing portrays well the fashionably dressed and bewigged cricketers of the club. As befits the future founders of the M.C.C., their equipment is up-to-date for 1784: three-stump wickets and a straight-bladed bat can be seen. Thomas Rowlandson also depicted cricket in White Conduit Fields (No. 100, Plate 57).

41 Mary Drew: *A Woolwich Cadet (?) in a cricket cap*

Private collection.

Oil on board. *c.*1890.

Mrs Rosemary Treble has convincingly attributed this painting to the rather obscure Mary Drew (*fl.* 1880-1901), a London painter of portraits and domestic subjects who exhibited at the Royal Academy, the Royal Society of British Artists and elsewhere. No. 41 is characteristic of Mary Drew's habit of posing a half-length figure against a neutral background. Many of her pictures are of children. A painting by her of a girl with a badminton racquet and a shuttlecock, entitled *"I cannot play alone"*, is in the Southampton Art Gallery.

No. 41 has previously been thought to represent a boy cricketer taking a catch, but it seems more likely that he is applauding. He can perhaps be identified as a cadet at the Royal Military Academy, Woolwich. He is wearing a cricket cap of the type visible in John Robertson Reid's *Country Cricket Match* of 1878 (No. 95, Plates XXVII, 96).

42 William Drummond: *A Young Batsman*

Present whereabouts unknown.

Pencil and watercolour: 18¼ × 12½in.

Signed and dated 1848.

Provenance: Sotheby, 22 November 1979 (99) (repr.).

For William Drummond see under No. 43.

43 W.H. Mason *after* **William Drummond and Charles J. Basèbe:** *Sussex versus Kent at Brighton*

Coloured lithograph published by by W.H. Mason, 1849. Dedicated to H.R.H. Prince Albert.

Literature: John Arlott, "Art", in *Barclay's World of Cricket*, ed. E.W. Swanton and others (London, 2nd edition, 1980), p. 570.

William Drummond (probably *fl.* 1830-1865), painter of figure subjects and portraits; exhibited at the Royal Academy, the British Institute and the Society of British Artists; painted a picture of *A Young Batsman* in 1848 (No. 42).

Charles J. Basèbe (*fl.* 1849-1865), painter of cricket pictures and cricket portraits; sometimes referred to in the literature as *Basbe*.

William Henry Mason (*fl.* 1858-1888), painter mostly of marine subjects; worked at Chichester and Worthing; exhibited at the Royal Academy from 1863 to 1888, and also at the British Institution, the Society of British Artists and elsewhere.

The portraits of spectators in the foreground are by Drummond; the cricket scene further back is by Basèbe. A key identifying the portraits exists.

44 Joseph Durham, A.R.A.: *Waiting his Innings* (Plate 55, Fig. 10)

City of London School.

Marble.

Inscribed at the front: *WAITING HIS INNINGS*. Inscribed at the back: *J. DURHAM. R.A./1866*.

Provenance: Presented by the sitter, Basil Edwin Lawrance, in memory of his father.

Exhibited: R.A., 1866 (853); London, Holland Park, 1957.

Literature: Benedict Read, *Victorian Sculpture* (Yale University Press for the Paul Mellon Centre for Studies in British Art, New Haven and London, 1982), p. 212, Pl. 273.

Joseph Durham (1814-1877), sculptor of statues, ideal subjects and portrait busts; born in London; first exhibited at Royal Academy in 1835; he won the competition for a memorial for the Great Exhibition, and his statue of the Prince Consort, of 1863, ended up on the front of the Albert Hall. His bust of Hogarth (1875), after Roubiliac, can be seen in Leicester Square.

The sitter was Basil Edwin Lawrance (1853-1928), whose family lived at Abbey Farm Estate, South Hampstead. Lawrance was educated at King's College, London, and at Trinity College, Cambridge; he was a writer on legal history and a Fellow of the Society of Antiquaries.

An interesting feature of this beautiful work is the care taken by the sculptor to show–with evident accuracy–the type of cricket-boot then in use: four studs can be seen, three on the sole and one on the heel (Fig. 10).

45 Henry Edridge, A.R.A.: *A Young Cricketer* (Plate 64)

Private Collection.

Pencil and watercolour: 14¾ × 10¼ in. Early nineteenth century.

Exhibited: Thos. Agnew & Sons, *150th Anniversary*, February 1978 (180).

Henry Edridge, (1769-1821), miniaturist; apprenticed to William Pether (1731-1795); painted miniature portraits executed in black lead and Indian ink to which he added watercolour; exhibited at the Royal Academy, showing there in

1803 portraits of George III and Queen Charlotte; elected A.R.A. in 1820. His portrait of the poet Southey is in the National Portrait Gallery.

46 Henry Edridge, A.R.A.: *Philip Wodehouse at the age of 13*

Present whereabouts unknown.

Pencil and grey wash: 13 × 9 in.

Signed and dated (lower right): *Edridge 1802.*

Provenance: L.G. Duke sale, Sotheby's 16 July, 1970 (62).

Philip Wodehouse is shown at full-length with a cricket bat. There is a view of Harrow School in the background. This picture is an early indication of the role cricket was to play in public school education in the nineteenth century.

47 William Evans, R.W.S.: *Cricket on College Field, Eton* (Plate XXII)

Eton College.

Watercolour: 26 x 37 in.

Literature: Eton College, *The Treasures of Eton* (London, 1976), Plate 3.

William Evans of Eton, (1798-1877), born and educated at Eton College; in 1818 followed his father Samuel Evans as drawing master at Eton; exhibited many works at the Old Watercolour Society. Four generations of his family held the post of drawing master at Eton: he was the second. His style has affinities with that of David Cox.

Several games of cricket are in progress. The masters who are acting as umpires are carrying bats–an example of the interesting survival of this tradition in the nineteenth century.

48 Edward Eyre: *The Cricket Match*

Present whereabouts unknown.

Watercolour, heightened with white: 7¾ × 10½ in. Presumably 1798.

Provenance: L.G. Duke; Sotheby's, 22 October 1970 (70); with Oliver Sutton Antiques, London.

Exhibited: Sheffield, Graves Art Gallery, *Two Centuries of Cricket Art*, 1955 (65).

Edward Eyre, of whom little is known, exhibited landscapes and architectural views at the Royal Academy between 1771 and 1786.

The match represented is said to be that played between the Kingscote Club and Eleven Gentlemen of Oxford on 7 August 1798, for 100 guineas, at the Kingscote Ground, Sussex. The former team won by 6 notches (scoring being recorded at this time by notches cut in a wooden stick).

49 N. Ploszczynski *after* **Felix (Nicholas Wanostrocht):** *The Eleven of England, Selected to contend the Great Cricket Matches of the North for the Year 1847* (Plate 68)

Coloured lithograph: 19 × 24 in. (arched top).

Lettered: *Drawn by N. Felix Esqr. London. Published Novr. 20th 1847, by Baily Brothers, No. 3 Royal Exchange Building, Cornhill. N. Ploszczynski Lithog./Guy. Parr. Martingell. A. Mynn Esqr. W. Denison Esqr. Dean. Clarke. N. Felix Esqr. O.C. Pell Esqr. Hillyer. Lillywhite. Dorrington. Pilch. Sewell.*

Nicholas Wanostrocht (1804-1876), or "Felix", artist, first-class cricketer, musician, and schoolmaster, who adopted the pseudonym Felix (often appearing in the form "N.Felix") for reasons of propriety in his activities as a professional cricketer (which was not normally the occupation of a gentleman like himself); author of *Felix on the Bat* (1845), which he illustrated with his own drawings (Plates 80, 81).

N. Ploszczynski (active in the 1840s) worked as a painter and engraver in London.

The original watercolour by Felix from which this lithograph was made was lately with the fine art dealer Messrs. Sabin: cf. *The Connoisseur*, December 1976. Felix had a happy knack for group portraiture of this extended kind: for example, in *The Two Elevens of the University of Cambridge* (M.C.C.), a water-colour also executed in 1847 (measuring 24 × 36 inches) (Plate 69), each player is shown distinctly, and yet the overall effect is remarkably melodious and serene.

In addition to his portraits and his illustrations to

Felix on the Bat, Felix made many watercolour drawings of the cricket fields on which he played (M.C.C. Collection) (Plate 60).

50 Felix (Nicholas Wanostrocht): Self-Portrait (Plate 75)

M.C.C.

Pencil: 8 × 6 in.

Provenance: Presented by Delamark B. Roffey in 1913.

51 Myles Birket Foster, R.W.S.: Landscape with a Cricket Match in Progress

Present whereabouts unknown.

Watercolour: 1⅜ × 5½ in.

Provenance: Sir Hugh Beaver, K.B.E.; Appleby Bros. Ltd, 1966; Sotheby's, 5 April 1973 (110).

Literature: *Country Life*, 3 March 1966 (advertisement, repr.).

Myles Birket Foster (1825-1899), watercolourist, illustrator and engraver, specializing in landscapes and rustic scenes; apprenticed to a wood-engraver before being employed as a draughtsman under Henry Vizetelly; set up as an illustrator in 1846; turned to painting in watercolours about 1859; elected R.W.S. in 1862; travelled frequently on the Continent, especially in Italy—in 1868 in the company of W.Q. Orchardson (1832-1910) and Frederick Walker (1840-1875). Birket Foster is most famous for the watercolours of the Surrey landscape which he executed after settling at Witley, near Godalming, in 1863.

This tiny watercolour is an impressive and evocative depiction of a rural cricket scene. The batsman has just played a square cut, and, in an unusual and striking manner, the ball is shown in mid-air, travelling towards the viewer.

52 Thomas Gainsborough, R.A.: *John Frederick Sackville, 3rd Duke of Dorset* (Plate 1)

Collection of Lord Sackville, Knole Park.

Oil on canvas: 30 × 25 in. Painted in 1782.

Engraved by J. Scott.

Provenance: Commissioned by the sitter; then by family descent.

Exhibited: Tate Gallery, *Gainsborough's "Giovanna Baccelli"*, 1976 (9).

Literature: E.K. Waterhouse, *Gainsborough* (London, 1958), p.203, No. 203, Pl. 251.

Thomas Gainsborough (1727-1788), portrait and landscape painter born in Suffolk; after early training in London, and subsequent return to Suffolk, settled in Bath in 1759; moved to London in 1774; became the great rival of Sir Joshua Reynolds, whose complete opposite he was in nearly every respect. Gainsborough was a great favourite with the Royal Family; his first love was landscape painting.

This portrait of the 3rd Duke of Dorset (1745-1799) was partly paid for in 1784, the receipt showing that the Duke had commissioned two versions of the painting, together with the full-length of Giovanna Baccelli (Tate Gallery) (Fig.4), two landscapes, and a "sketch" of "a Beggar Boy and Girl". The discerning choice of artist, and the unusual variety of the commission, are indicative of the Duke's refined taste. Gainsborough captures the Duke's famed good looks. The Duke seems to have suffered a stroke in 1785, and was gradually overcome by melancholy, from which cricket, evidently, was able to rouse him: records of his still active interest in the game persist until the 1790s. He is supposed to have died "in a state of intellectual decay or mental alienation". Nyren records that his favourite position on the field was at slip: "This station was the Duke's *forte*. He was in height about five feet nine, very well made, and had a peculiar habit, when unemployed, of standing with his head on one side." It is possible that this latter characteristic may have been a result of the stroke, the effects of which, together with an insight into his sympathetic nature, are described by his steward William Humphry in a letter of 7 December, 1785 to his brother, the painter Ozias Humphry, R.A.:

> [The Duke of Dorset] is far from well you hardly ever saw any person more alter'd than he is,–he has a catching in his right Eye, as if he had had a paralytic stroke, and in order to conceal it he constantly carries a Handkerchief to his face...His Behaviour to me is at all Times the Kindest in the

World.

(E. Einberg, *Gainsborough's "Giovanna Baccelli"*, *.cit.*, p. 11.)

The Duke was both a batsman and a bowler, and although he and the Earl of Tankerville were described by Nyren as not being in the same class as Lord Frederick Beauclerk, "yet", Nyren assures us, "they were pretty players". In John Burnby's *The Kentish Cricketers: A Poem*, published in 1773, he was described thus:

. . . Far unlike the modern way
Of blocking every Ball at Play
He firmly stands with Bat upright
And strikes with his athletic Might;
Sends forth the Ball across the Mead,
And scores six Notches for the Deed.

Such records as exist rather suggest that the Duke did not often score so impressively, at least at the highest level. Nonetheless, he did score a match-winning 77 in a return match between Kent and Hambledon in 1774 on which he had placed 1000 guineas. His father was Lord John Philip Sackville (1713-1765), another very keen (and successful) cricketer, with whom he has sometimes been confused. Lord John Philip was the younger brother of Charles, Earl of Middlesex (1710/11 [O.S.]–1769), another famous early patron and player. The passion for the game would seem also to have touched Lionel, the lst Duke (1687/8 [O.S.]–1765), to whom a poem describing the famous Sevenoaks Vine cricket ground was dedicated in 1753 (*Sevenoke: A Poem*, by A. Harrod). It is appropriate that the first fully recorded game of cricket, that played between England and Kent on 18 June 1744, should have been the result of a challenge from Lord John Philip, who opened the innings for Kent: in a low-scoring game he scored 5 and 3 (he features in James Love's poem about this match).

The 3rd Duke of Dorset was a founder member of the M.C.C. He was British Ambassador to France from 1783 until the outbreak of the French Revolution in 1789, an event that spoilt his plans for a cricket match that year in Paris (see pp.4f.). After his appointment as Ambassador an engraving published in the *Rambler's Magazine* for 1 February 1784 satirized the choice for that office of a peer who never spoke in the House of Lords and was celebrated only as a cricketer. This shows the Duke standing at the wicket with a bat in his hand and with his back to the bowler as he remarks, over his shoulder, "My Notches against any Man in France for 1,000." As a hunting Englishman, he wears riding-boots whereas the bowler, who is French, wears jack-boots. The bowler promises to "knock down his Stumps", while four French fielders comment as follows: "Me vill catch him out at first Stroke"; "He plays well at de Cricket, he be one very good Ambassadeur"; "He be very clever at getting de Notches"; and "He no speak in de Senate but he be one bon Cricketer". A fifth fielder, who has a tuft of feathers on his head to denote that he is an American, observes: "If you play'd for 13 Provinces you'd lose." (Cf. Mary Dorothy George, *Catalogue of Political and Personal Satires preserved in the Department of Prints and Drawings in the British Museum*, VI [London, 1938], 24 No. 6397.)

53 Daniel Gardner: *Frederick Francis Baker* (Plates XIV, XV)

Private Collection.

Gouache and pastel: 20 × 16 in. *c. 1780.*

Provenance: By family descent.

Daniel Gardner (1750-1805), portrait painter; born in Kendal, where he was taught as a boy by the portraitist George Romney, a family friend; moved to London in 1767 or 1768; entered the newly opened Royal Academy Schools in 1770, where he stayed for two years; silver medallist in 1771; exhibited at the Royal Academy in the same year; was invited by Reynolds to join his studio; left shortly afterwards and rapidly established a vigorous practice; married Ann Haward in 1767 or 1768, and after her early death he became rather more eccentric than before, gaining a reputation with some for being "difficult"; but he had loyal and close friends, among them the young John Constable, whose portrait he painted. Gardner experimented with techniques, especially in the use of gouache. This picture is a good example of his adventurous approach.

The sitter, later Sir Frederick Francis Baker, 2nd Bart., F.R.S., was the son of George III's physician, the first baronet. This enchanting picture demonstrates Gardner's fitful brilliance, and the delicate pastel painting of the face is in charming contrast to the rough impasted gouache of the rest of the picture. The stitching on the un-dyed ball is of especial historical interest.

54 Daniel Gardner: *The Rumbold Family*

Collection of Miss D.A. Puigoerver-Rumbold. Gouache and pastel: 45¼ × 31½ in.

Provenance: By family descent.

*Exhibited:*Kendal, Abbot Hall Art Gallery, *Four Kendal Portrait Painters*, 1973 (38).

The sitters are Lady Rumbold, wife of Sir Thomas Rumbold, and her two sons.

55 Henry Garland: *The Winner of the Match: Excelsior Cricket Club, Islington* (Plate XXVIII)

M.C.C.

Oil on canvas: 31 × 53 in.

Signed and dated (bottom left): *H. GARLAND P./1864.*

Provenance: R.B.A., March 1865; bought probably by a Mr Saire; from whom bought by Mr Thomas Laurence, father of the donor, Mrs H.A. Doubleday, who gave the picture in 1959.

Exhibited: R.B.A., 1865 (42nd annual exhibition).

Henry Garland (*active* 1854-1890), painter of genre; born at Winchester; lived chiefly in Islington; exhibited at the Royal Academy and elsewhere between 1854 and 1890.

The hero is carried in triumph on the shoulders of his team-mates, one of whom raises aloft the flag of the Excelsior C.C.

56 Spencer Gore: *The Cricket Match* (Plate 107)

Wakefield City Art Gallery.

Oil on canvas: 16 × 18 in. 1909.

Signed (bottom right): *S.F. GORE.*

Exhibited: Arts Council of Great Britain, *Spencer Frederick Gore 1878-1914*, 1955 (18).

Spencer Gore (1878-1914), one of the founders of the Camden Town Group (1911), of which he became President; influenced by Sickert and the French Impressionists, including Pissarro (see Nos. 92, 93, Plates XXXII, 106), and exhibited at the Paris Salon des Indépendants; reflected in his later work something of the impact of Cézanne. His early death deprived England of one of its finest exponents of Impressionism.

The scene is presumably set at or near Hartingfordbury, in Hertfordshire, where the artist's family lived at the time the picture was painted. The match is viewed from over the fence near the boundary, and owing to the impressionistic style the details of the game are rather difficult to make out: yet the picture remains a fine "impression" of a characteristically English scene. There are resemblances in design to Pissarro's *Cricket at Bedford Park* (No. 93, Plate 106).

57 Sir Francis Grant, P.R.A.: *Cricketing Scene*

Present whereabouts unknown.

Pen and wash.

At one time ascribed to Constantin Guys.

Provenance: Ferrer Gallery, 9 Piccadilly Arcade, London.

Sir Francis Grant (1803-1878), Scottish portrait painter who is also known for his hunting scenes; born in Perthshire; began as an amateur painter (until 1830); became one of the leading portraitists of his time, scoring a notable success with his large canvas of *Queen Victoria and Lord Melbourne riding in Windsor Park*; married a niece of the Duke of Rutland, and worked frequently in Rutland and Leicestershire; exhibited regularly at the Royal Academy from 1834; elected A.R.A. in 1842, R.A. in 1851, and President of the Royal Academy in 1866, when he was knighted

This is an extremely animated impression of a cricket match around the middle of the nineteenth century, and conveys an idea of the bustle and excitement of the crowd of fashionable spectators, with their elegant attire and their carriages. The players are dressed in white. The suggestion of a curved bat in the hand of the right-hand batsman would be anachronistic if it is deliberate.

58 J. Cole *after* **Hubert Gravelot:** *The Second Part of Youthfull Diversions* (Plate 9)

Engraving: 13 × 17 in.
Lettered: *Engraved and sold by J.Cole, published 7 May 1739.*

Hubert François Bourguignon Gravelot (1699-1773), French-born Huguenot engraver and draughtsman; a close associate of Francis Hayman and William Hogarth at the St Martin's Lane Academy.
Youth Playing Cricket is one of a group of designs arranged as a decorative border. The French rococo character of these designs led to their being transfer-printed on various jugs, sugar bowls and plates, examples of which are in the Victoria and Albert Museum (*C.* 60-1932), the Fitzwilliam Museum, Cambridge, and the Melbourne Cricket Club (from the collection of Anthony Baer, Esq).

59 George Halse: *Young England* (Plate 54)

Collection of Andrew Sanders, Esq.

Parian ware cast: 15½ in. high. 1874.

Inscribed (around the base): *G. Halse Sc. YOUNG ENGLAND copyright reserved COPELAND F.74.*

Another cast is at M.C.C. (Memorial Gallery).

George Halse, a sculptor working in London, exhibited at the Royal Academy from 1855 to 1888.

60 Francis Hayman, R.A.: *"Cricket in Marylebone Fields"* (Plates II-IV, 10, 11)

M.C.C.

Oil on canvas: 28½ × 36½ in. Mid-1740s. Perhaps dated (lower right): *1747.*

Provenance: ?Thomas Lord; by 1825 in the possession of William Ward (who purchased Lord's ground and pictures); J.H.Dark (proprietor of Lord's Cricket Ground from 1835 to 1864); from whom purchased by M.C.C. in 1867.

Exhibited: R.A., 1881 (6); 1934 (389); London, Grosvenor Gallery, 1980 (111); Wembley Exhibition, 1925 (v.26); London, The Iveagh Bequest, Kenwood, and Nottingham University Art Gallery, *Francis Hayman*, 1960 (27).

Literature: E.R. Wilson, "Early Cricket Prints", *The Cricketer Spring Annual*, XXII (1941), 74 ff.; M.H. Grant, *Old English Landscape Painters*, (8 vols. Leigh-on-Sea, 1957), II, 35, Pl. 25; Lawrence Gowing, "Hogarth, Hayman and the Vauxhall Decorations", *The Burlington Magazine*, XCV (1953), 4 ff., 15 (No. *49*).

Engraved by C. Grignion, 16 July, 1748 (Plate 11).

Francis Hayman (1708-1776), foundation member of the Royal Academy, 1768; became Librarian in 1771; like Hogarth, had a great interest in the theatre, and was a close associate of his, e.g. at the St Martin's Lane Academy (where Gravelot was also teaching); painted numerous canvases for the supper-boxes in Vauxhall Gardens. Hayman was much influenced by French rococo art, but produced highly original and varied works which are quintessentially English.

There appear to be no eighteenth-century records of cricket in "Marylebone Fields", and Thomas Lord's first ground, on the site of what is now Dorset Square, was not established until 1787.

This painting of the full double-wicket game is the most important of all the early visual records of cricket, and was to become the most frequently reproduced, providing a source for the illustrations which accompanied successive editions of the laws of the game. It appeared on the handkerchief identified by Rait Kerr (*op. cit.*, pp. 13 ff.) as bearing the 1744 Laws; it then reappeared, with changes to the dress of the spectators, with three stumps, and with the urban background of White Conduit Fields, on another handkerchief of 1785. It was later the basis of the illustrations to the Laws published by J. Wallis in 1789, 1800, 1809 and so on. If Rait Kerr is correct in dating the handkerchief he discusses to *c.* 1744, it follows that this painting predates the handkerchief, even though Grignion did not produce his engraving until 1748. It is the only surviving autograph painting of cricket by Francis Hayman. There is an oval version (10¼ × 11½ in.), painted *c.* 1790, in the Paul Mellon Collection (J. Egerton, *The Paul Mellon Collection: British Sporting and Animal Paintings* [1978], pp. 185 f.).

There is a slightly larger painting, *Cricket at Brading, Isle of Wight* (M.C.C.), which, in a more grandiose way, is also indebted for the arrangement of its figures to this design: the handling is quite unlike Hayman's and, indeed, the style of the landscape would seem to indicate that it was painted in the nineteenth century and that the picture is a *pastiche*.

In view of the seminal influence of Hayman's painting and the number of engravings and copies made from it–and especially its association with the Laws–it seems that this painting was always held in especial esteem as a correct record of the game. It also has a remarkable *provenance*. It was almost certainly in Thomas Lord's possession, a fact suggestive of the high regard in which it was held at an early date. It is not difficult to imagine its having been given or sold to Lord by one of the early members of the M.C.C. It is certain that it came into the possession of William Ward in the year that he bought Lord's lease, and that it was then passed on with the lease until M.C.C. got possession of it in 1867, the year after the Club gained the freehold, its last owner having been J.H. Dark, the last individual proprietor of Lord's. The small size and intimate character of the picture suggest that it was a special commission, a private record. The careful rendering of every detail, especially of the costume and caps, indicates a specific club. The painting is quite different in character from the frivolous, large-scale, public canvas of single-wicket which Hayman executed for the Vauxhall pleasure gardens, the original of which is now lost (see No. 61, Plate 14).

There are signs of *pentimenti* (alterations by the artist), for example an adjustment to the height of the stumps at the striker's end, which suggest that Hayman was careful to be as accurate as possible. Confusingly, this picture has also been known as *The Royal Academy Club in Marylebone Fields*, but this club existed only briefly as an informal group of artists after the foundation of the Royal Academy in 1768, some twenty years after Hayman's picture was painted. This title seems to have been associated with the oval version made about 1790 which is referred to above.

61 C. Benoist *after* **Francis Hayman:** *Cricket* (Plate 14)

Engraving: 13¾ × 11¼ in. Published 4 April 1743.

Lettered: *F. Hayman Pinxt. Published according to Act of Parliam^t April 4^t 1743. Benoist Sculp^t. after the Painting in Vauxhall Garden./ Printed & Sold by Tho. Bowles in S^t. Paul's Church Yard & Jno. Bowles at Y^e. Black Horse, Cornhill.*

In the centre is the title *CRICKET*, on either side of which are the following verses:

To exercise their Limbs, and try their Art
Forth to the verdant Fields the Swains depart:
The buxom Air and chearfull Sport unite
To make Hulse *useless by their rough Delight.*

Britons, whom Nature has for War design'd
In the soft Charms of Ease no Joy can find:
Averse to wast in Rest th' inviting Day
Toil forms their Game, & Labour is their Play.

Literature: *Norwich Mercury*, 7 May 1743; *Ambulator* (1807), p.294; E.R.Wilson, "Early Cricket Prints", *The Cricketer Spring Annual*, XXII (1941), 74 ff.; E. Parker, "The Noble Game of Cricket through Two Centuries", *The Connoisseur*, CIX (1942), 86 (repr.); Lawrence Gowing, "Hogarth, Hayman, and the Vauxhall Decorations", *The Burlington Magazine*, XCV (1953), 4 ff., 15 (No. *49*); D. Coke, *The Muse's Bower: Vauxhall Gardens 1728-1786* (Sudbury, 1978), repr.; P. Wynne-Thomas, "The Artillery Ground and its Paintings", *The Cricket Statistician*, Issue 35 (October 1981), pp. 9 ff.

The painting from which this engraving was made, Francis Hayman's *The Play of Cricket*, hung in a supper-box at Vauxhall Gardens, but has since been lost. (A painting after this engraving, with the title of *Cricket in the Artillery Ground*, is in the M.C.C. collection [No. 62, Plate 15].) The single-wicket form of the game is shown. A second, smaller form of this engraving (made by B. Cole) appeared above a printing of the 1744 Laws in *The New Universal Magazine* of November, 1752–from which the very doubtful identification of the site as the Artillery Ground derives. The wicket-keeper in Benoist's engraving has traditionally been identified with William Hogarth, who, with Francis Hayman, planned the decoration of Vauxhall Gardens. Hogarth's features are well known from contemporary portraits, and no resemblance to him can here be detected. (There seems to be no great antiquity to this tradition.)

The *Hulse* referred to in the verse was Sir Edward Hulse, Bart., physician to George III. (His direct descendant, also Sir Edward, in the middle of the nineteenth century sold to Hampshire C.C.C. the land in Southampton on which the county had long played cricket.)

62 Unknown copyist *after* **Benoist** (*after* **Hayman**): *"Cricket in the Artillery Ground"* (Plate 15)

M.C.C.

Oil on canvas: 20 × 40 in.

Provenance: Colman Gift.

For comments on this dubious picture see No. 61 and pp. 7ff.

63 *ascribed to* **Francis Hayman, R.A.**: *Playing Cricket*

Present whereabouts unknown.

Oil on panel: 17¼ × 24 in.

Provenance: George Stoner; Sotheby's, 27 November, 1974 (24) (repr.).

The attribution to Francis Hayman is not convincing.

In 1921, when with Agnew's, this painting was identified as a representation of Burton Court, Chelsea, which is still the home ground of the Guards Cricket Club. The picture displays some curious features: for example, the scorers, even if we allow for eighteenth-century practice, are improbably close to the wicket. One of them also holds a bat to score on instead of a stick– presumably indicating a misunderstood copying by the artist of another source. The clothes worn by the umpires are also unusual: the two men are apparently wearing waistcoats with sleeves. The bats are of a shape and size unknown in the history of the game. Some doubt, therefore, must hang over the status of the picture.

64 Thomas Henwood: *The Scorer* (Plate 98)

M.C.C.

Oil on canvas: 14 × 12 in. Painted in 1842.

Signed (bottom centre): *T. Henwood/Pinxit 1842.*

Inscribed: *The Scorer William Davies at Brighton.*

Lithographed by the artist in 1842, with the Chesterfield tape and the stumps omitted.

Exhibited: London, Hayward Gallery, *British Sporting Painting 1650-1850*, 1974-5 (216).

Literature: Sir Pelham Warner, *Lord's 1787-1945* (London, 1946); G. Bernard Hughes, "Hob-nob Goblets of the Georgians", *Country Life*, 10 September 1970, pp. 648-650.

Thomas Henwood, a Sussex artist, supplied the drawings for most of the plates in Horsfield's *History of Sussex*, to which he was also one of the subscribers. He is recorded in *Kelly's Directory* for 1855 as "Thomas Henwood, Artist, Keene Street, Lewes", and the same address is given in 1858. He was probably dead by 1862. Only one other oil-painting by him, *"The Dripping Pan" at Lewes*, would appear to be known.

The sitter is William Davies, scorer to the Lewes Priory Club and Sussex County Cricket Club: he died in the year this portrait was painted. He is shown with his claret bottle and "hob-nob" goblet, a glass to be used by more than one person at a time, often for hot toddy. It is possible therefore that he has not already drunk the bottle lying on the grass all by himself.

The table is a flip-top tripod table which would be easily portable. A score-book is being used, while on the ground are a couple of bats, a ball, and three stumps of flat section with notches for the bails. There is also a wind-up tape-measure on the table, for measuring out the pitch and the creases, a ritual which was not handed over to the groundsman (and thus incorporated in the Laws) until later.

65 George Elgar Hicks: *Three Young Cricketers* (Plate 35)

Southampton Art Gallery.

Oil on card: 11¼ × 8½ in.

Probably painted in 1883.

Provenance: Miss Annie Hicks, by whom presented to Southampton Art Gallery in 1942.

Exhibited: London, The Geffrye Museum, *George Elgar Hicks: Painter of Victorian Life*, 1982-3 (38).

George Elgar Hicks (1824-1914), painter of genre, portraits and crowded scenes of Victorian life such as *Billingsgate* and *Dividend Day at the Bank of England*. He had trained as a doctor. Later, he added "history" and Biblical subjects to his vigorous portrait practice.

Hicks was a fine draughtsman, and this preliminary sketch for a portrait group displays his facility. The sitters are probably the three sons of the Earl of Dudley, for the Earl is known to have commissioned their portraits from Hicks in 1883 for no less than 1000 guineas. They are: Viscount Ednam (*left*); the Hon. John Hubert Dudley (*centre*); and the Hon. Robert Arthur Dudley (*right*). Unfortunately for us, as well as for Hicks, the commission was repudiated by the Earl's widow or his executors on his death, which took place immediately before the painting of the large picture was due to begin: "a most unprincipled action" according to Hicks. There would have been no equivalent large-scale portrait group in cricket art.

66 Joseph Highmore: *The Revd John Duncombe*

The Master's Lodge, Corpus Christi College, Cambridge.

Oil on canvas (feigned oval): 30 × 25 in.

Signed and dated (bottom left): *Jos: Highmore / pinx: 1766.*

Provenance: Probably presented to the College by a Fellow.

Exhibited: London, The Iveagh Bequest, Kenwood, *Paintings by Joseph Highmore*, 1963 (42).

Literature: J.W. Goodison, "Two Portraits by Joseph Highmore", *The Burlington Magazine*, LXXIII (September, 1938), 125f., repr. p. 127 (Pl. D).

Joseph Highmore (1692-1780), painter of portraits and subject-pictures, which include a series of twelve illustrations to his friend Samuel Richardson's novel *Pamela* (Tate Gallery, London; Fitzwilliam Museum, Cambridge; National Gallery of Victoria, Melbourne); studied at Kneller's Academy for ten years after first being trained to the Law. Along with Hogarth, Highmore was a pioneer of the English portrait, and like Hogarth he was much influenced by the work of Gravelot (see No. 58, Plate 9) and French rococo taste.

The Revd John Duncombe, who was an undergraduate at Corpus and from 1751 to 1758 a Fellow of the college, was the author of the poem *Surrey Triumphant, or the Kentish-men's defeat* (1773), which describes a match between Surrey and Kent played at Bishopsbourne, near Canterbury, for no less than £2,000. Kent won the return match played at Sevenoaks, provoking a "return poem" by John Burnby–*The Kentish Cricketers: A Poem*. Duncombe married Highmore's daughter Susanna. In 1766 he was appointed one of the six preachers in Canterbury Cathedral, which probably accounts for the fact that in Highmore's portrait he is wearing the black scarf normally denoting a Doctor of Divinity (which Duncombe was not).

67 Thomas Hudson: *The Family of the 3rd Duke of Marlborough*

Collection of the Duke of Marlborough, Blenheim Palace.

Oil on canvas: 119¾ × 193 in. *c.* 1754.

Provenance: By family descent.

Literature: Theodore Crombie, "Hudson at Blenheim", *Apollo*, XCV, No. 119 (January 1972), 48-9 (repr.).

Thomas Hudson (1701-1779), portrait painter; studied under Jonathan Richardson (1665-1745), the portraitist and influential writer on art, whose daughter he married; established himself in the 1740s as the most employed portrait-painter working in London; painted little from about 1760, when the stars of Ramsay and Reynolds were in the ascendant; numbered Reynolds and Wright of Derby among his pupils.

From left to right the sitters are: George, Marquess of Blandford (later 4th Duke of Marlborough); Lord Charles Spencer; Charles Spencer, 3rd Duke of Marlborough; his wife, Elizabeth Trevor, Duchess of Marlborough; Lady Elizabeth Spencer; Lord Robert Spencer; and Lady Diana Spencer (later Lady Diana Beauclerk).

The sheer scale of this painting, which hangs in the Great Hall at Blenheim Palace, makes the inclusion of the cricket bats and ball even more remarkable as evidence of the place occupied by cricket at this time. The portrait of *The Courtenay Brothers* (M.C.C.) (No. 71, Plate 25), attributed to Hudson, is derived from the left-hand section of this painting. Hudson's sketch for the Marlborough group survives in a private collection in London (No. 68, Plate 24).

68 Thomas Hudson: *The Family of the 3rd Duke of Marlborough* (sketch) (Plate 24)

Private Collection.

Oil on canvas: 22½ × 34¼ in. *c.* 1753.
Study for No. 67 (q.v.).

Provenance: ?Hudson's sale, Christie's, 26 February 1785 (14); by family descent in the Spencer family to Lady Oliphant, second wife of Victor, 1st Viscount Churchill, and sold by her, Christie's, 20 December 1940 (61), as by Arthur Devis; bought by Gabriel Harrison.

Exhibited: London, The Iveagh Bequest, Kenwood, *Thomas Hudson*, 1979 (54).

Literature: S.H. Pavière, *The Devis Family of Painters* (Leigh-on-Sea, 1950), p. 62, no. 164; Theodore Crombie, "Hudson at Blenheim", *Apollo*, XCV, No. 119 (January 1972), 48-9 (repr. in colour, Pl. VIII).

Hudson made various changes to the composition and to details in the full-scale portrait (No. 67). The influence of Joshua Reynolds's portrait of *Commodore Keppel* (National Maritime Museum, Greenwich) (Fig. 8) is discussed in the text (see p. 25). (Reynolds's painting is therefore more likely to have been painted in 1753 than in 1754 as is sometimes suggested.)

69 Thomas Hudson: *Mrs Matthew Michell and her Children* (Plate 26)

Leicester Museum and Art Gallery.

Oil on canvas: 76 × 64 in. *c.* 1757-8.

Provenance: Trenchard family of Stanton Fitzwarren, Highworth, Wilts., descendants of Mrs Matthew Michell; Agnew's, from whom purchased by the Museum in 1938.

Literature: Benedict Nicolson, *Joseph Wright of Derby : Painter of Light* (London, 1968), p. 26; Anon, "Two Paintings by Sir [*sic*] Thomas Hudson", *Cricket Quarterly*, Vol. 7, No. 2, 1969, p.67; Joyce Boundy, "An unpublished conversation piece by Thomas Hudson", *Apollo*, CVII (October 1978), 248 ff. (repr.).

Mrs. Matthew Michell, *née* Frances Ashford, daughter of John Ashford of Cheshunt, married Matthew Michell of Chelton in 1749. She is shown with her two children, Matthew and Anne. Her husband became M.P. for Westbury. Nicolson (*op. cit.*) suggests that Hudson's pupil Wright of Derby may have collaborated on this picture.

70 *ascribed to* **Thomas Hudson:** *The Boy with a Bat (Walter Hawkesworth Fawkes)* (Plate 27)

Collection of Sir Westrow Hulse, Bart.

Oil on canvas: 48 × 40 in. *c.* 1760.

Provenance: By family descent from the Mason family of Copt Hewick Hall, Yorkshire.

The attribution to Thomas Hudson is not convincing.

Walter Ramsden Beaumont (1746-1792) assumed, first, the name of Hawkesworth on his marriage and, secondly, the name of Fawkes on succeeding to Farnley Hall, Yorkshire, under the will of his cousin, Frances Fawkes. His son Walter became the chief patron of J.M.W. Turner. Newark Castle and Bridge, Nottinghamshire, can be seen in the background of this painting, which is of especial interest in that it shows the two stumps of the period not as forked twigs but as flat pieces of wood with notches carved in their tops. The sitter carries his bat on his shoulder, as was customary, and wears a hat of a kind to be seen in other cricketing portraits of this period. Newark Castle, from the same side of the river, can be seen in a painting of *A Cricket Match at Newark-on-Trent* by J.D. Curtis, of 1823 (No. 35). It seems clear, therefore, that Walter Fawkes has been playing on the same field, which is still in use as a cricket-ground.

71 *circle of* **Thomas Hudson:** *The Courtenay Brothers* (Plate 25)

M.C.C.

Oil on canvas: 50 × 40 in.

There are weaknesses in the execution of this painting which suggest that it may not be by Thomas Hudson (1701-1779), notably the painting of the right arm of the boy on the right and the line of his cheek. The picture is, in effect, a half-length copy of the left-hand section of Hudson's *Family of the 3rd Duke of Marlborough* (No. 67: see Plate 24) although the sitter's features are different. The repetition of a pose from one portrait to another was a common practice with Hudson and other painters of the period. The Courtenay family of Powderham Castle were indeed patrons of Hudson, but it is difficult to ascertain precisely which Courtenay brothers these two boys could be. (Cf. Ellen G. Miles and Jacob Simon, *Thomas Hudson 1701-1779, portrait painter and collector: a bicentenary exhibition* (exhibition catalogue). (The Greater London Council, The Iveagh Bequest, Kenwood, London, 1979, no. 22).

72 William Henry Hunt, R.W.S.: *The Boy Batsman* (Plate 73)

M.C.C.

Watercolour: 15½ × 10 in.

Literature: Sir Jeremiah Colman, *The Noble Game of Cricket* (London, 1941), Frontispiece.

William Henry Hunt (1790-1864), painter in oils and watercolour, specializing in still-life, rustic genre and landscape; often referred to, in allusion to his favourite subject-matter, as "Bird's Nest Hunt" and "Hedgerow Hunt"; a cripple, he studied under John Varley before entering the Royal Academy Schools in 1808; elected A.R.W.S. in 1824 and R.W.S. in 1826; first exhibited at the Royal Academy in 1807; best known from 1827 for his small watercolours of fruit and flowers, which earned him the praise of Ruskin and became extremely popular.

This watercolour, like another of *The Boy Cricketer* (15½ × 10½in.) (M.C.C.) (Plate 74), is typical of Hunt's technique of stippling over a white ground. The attitude of the boy batsman has been borrowed from Watts's lithograph of *The Cut* (No. 128, Plate 72).

A mezzotint by W. Bromley after W. H. Hunt, entitled *Done Up* and published in 1841, shows a boy asleep in a chair with a cricket bat and ball lying on the floor (M.C.C. Collection).

73 Robert James: *Tossing for Innings*, I (Plate 77)

M.C.C.

Oil on canvas.

Painted *c.* 1843.

Literature: Sir Pelham Warner, *Lord's 1787-1945* (London, 1946), p. 268 (Appendix II: "The Long Room Pictures", by Viscount Ullswater); repr., Frontispiece.

Robert James (1809-1853), a Nottingham painter, evidently born at Burton-on-the-Wold in Leicestershire; first exhibited at the Royal Academy in 1841, having already established a local reputation as a portraitist; died suddenly in November, 1853. James is best remembered for his pictures of children, and especially for *Tossing for Innings*, which is his masterpiece.

A group of ragged chimney-sweeps are about to play a game of cricket on an open common. Two of them toss for innings with a bat, which has been thrown high in the air. Another boy is piling up crates to construct a makeshift wicket.

A smaller version of this painting (oil on canvas: 25½ × 19½ in.) (exhibited: Arts Council of Great Britain, *British Sporting Painting 1650-1850*, 1974-5 [215]) is also in the M.C.C. collection: this has been referred to in the literature as a study for the larger painting. It is signed or inscribed (bottom centre): *R.JAMES/NOTT^m^*. A horizontal version of this painting is in a private collection (see No. 74, Plate XX).

74 Robert James: *Tossing for Innings*, II (Plate XX)

Private Collection.

Oil on canvas: 35½ × 57 in.

Signed (bottom right): *R.James/Nottingham.*

Provenance: Bought by the present owner from a dealer in Nottingham in 1969.

Exhibited: M.C.C. Memorial Gallery, 1969.

The picture was cleaned and restored in 1969. It is larger than the similar painting at Lord's (No. 73, Plate 77), which is earlier; it is also horizontal rather than vertical in form, has more figures in it, and shows Nottingham Castle in the background. One of the most curious features of this painting is the way in which the bat–the throwing of which into the air is the most striking invention of the composition–disappears behind the frame.

75 William Jefferys: *Cricket at the Free School, Maidstone* (Plate 22)

Maidstone Public Library.

Pen and wash: Plate 247 of an album.

William Jefferys (1723 or 1730-1805), a Maidstone artist and coach painter, was the father of the brilliant James Jefferys (1751-1784), whose early death in Italy deprived England of one of her supreme and most promising historical painters and draughtsmen (cf. the catalogue of the exhibition *The Rediscovery of an Artist: The Drawings of James Jefferys*, Victoria and Albert Museum, 1976). Edward Edwards wrote of William Jefferys: "The father was much employed at Maidstone, being what is called a painter in general, and therefore frequently engaged in decorating coaches. He also painted landscapes and fruit pieces: of the latter he produced some good specimens" (*Anecdotes of Painting in England* [London, 1808], p. 96).

The drawing shows two stumps, which form a low wicket. Maidstone was one of the centres of early cricket and provoked puritanical rage in the middle of the seventeenth century: "Maidstone was formerly a very profane town inasmuch as I have seen Morris-dancing, Cudgel playing, Stoolball, Crickets, and many other sports openly and publicly on the Lord's Day."
([George Swinnock,] *The Life and Death of Tho. Wilson, Minister of Maidstone*, 1672, referring to *c.* 1653; cf. F.S. Ashley-Cooper, *Highways and Byways of Cricket* [London, 1927], p. 175.)

76 *attributed to* **Charles Landseer, R.A.:** *The Duke of Wellington batting, with the Three Graces as the Wicket* (Plate 82)

M.C.C.

Etching: 3 × 5 in.

Provenance: Sir Jeremiah Colman.

The attribution to Charles Landseer (1799-1879) (elder brother of Sir Edwin Landseer) is questionable, and the monogram (bottom left) may or may not be *CL*. The artist was possibly the E.H.L. whose drawings were etched by George Cruikshank (1792-1878) in 1817 (*see* British Museum no. 12922-3).

The Duke of Wellington has the Owl of Wisdom for a cap. The ball seems to be a cock representing France or Napoleon and is inscribed *out*. The Three Graces hold a banner on which is written *à bas le tyran* ("down with the tyrant").

77 Sir Edwin Henry Landseer, R.A.: *The Lord's*

M.C.C. (formerly).

Sketching board: 11 ⅞ × 7¼ in.

Signed and inscribed on the back: *The Lords. E. Landseer.*

Sir Edwin Henry Landseer (1802-1873), the eminent animal and portrait painter and sculptor of the bronze lions in Trafalgar Square. Landseer lived near Lord's at No. 1, St John's Wood Road, from 1826 to 1873.

78 Edward George Handel Lucas: *When We Were Boys Together* (Plate 93)

Private Collection.

Oil on board: 11¾ × 10 in.

Signed (upper left): *E.G. Handel Lucas*. Dated (to the right): *1881*

Provenance: Sotheby's Belgravia, 27 March 1973 (88); Sotheby, King & Chasemore, Pulborough, July 1982.

Edward George Handel Lucas (1861-1936), a painter of still life, landscape and genre who worked in poverty at Croydon; exhibited at the Royal Academy, the Society of British Artists and the Grosvenor Gallery (which had been established in Bond Street by Sir Coutts and Lady Lindsay, and which was associated especially with the "Aesthetic Movement" of the 1880s, dominated by Burne-Jones). He is best known for still life paintings which, as in the case of *When We Were Boys Together*, carry moralistic overtones, often relating to the temptations of drink and the evils of tobacco, typical titles being *Silent Advocates of Temperance* and *Companions of Vice*.

Here the still life group includes a cricket bat, a cricket ball (with a noticeably raised seam), a slate bearing a chalk sketch of a schoolmaster, books and marbles; and a tawse hangs from the wall, on which the signature and date appear as *graffiti*.

79. David Martin: *John Campbell of South Hall* (Plate 38)

Present whereabouts unknown.

Oil on canvas: 66½ × 53¾ in.

Signed and dated 1771.

Provenance: Col. Parker of Browsholme Hall, Lancs.; inherited by K.E. Kissack; Christie's, 23 March 1979 (121), bought McInnes.

David Martin (1737-1797), Scottish portrait-painter; became a pupil of Allan Ramsay (1713-1784), whom he later joined in Italy in 1756-7, and whose principal assistant he remained until the late 1760s; set up practice on his own in London before moving to Edinburgh in the mid-1780s, becoming the leading Scottish portrait-painter in the period before the advent of Raeburn; appointed (1785) Portrait Painter to the Prince of Wales in Scotland.

John Campbell (1758-1817) became Captain in the 21st Light Dragoons, a Colonel in the Argyll Militia, and a rather notorious Deputy-Lieutenant of Argyll. He is shown in Van Dyck dress and cannot therefore be about to play. The cross-legged pose may have been introduced into Britain by Ramsay, since it is found as early as *c.* 1740 in his full-length of *The Hon. John Bulkeley - Coventry*. This portrait is of particular significance as evidence of the extent to which cricket had become fashionable in Scotland by this time. It is thought that the landscape background shows part of Argyll.

80 *attributed to* **James Miller:** *Carmalt School, Wandsworth Lane, Putney* (Plate 23)

Museum of London.

Watercolour: 11¾ × 19½ in. *c.* 1780.

James Miller (*fl.* 1773-1791), watercolourist, whose many views of London are of great topographical interest. His figures are usually awkwardly drawn.

The school was founded in 1684 to educate the sons of Putney watermen. A game of single-wicket is shown. The wicket itself is noticeably low for the suggested date of the picture. In top-class cricket three stumps were in use by this time, and also straight, rather than curved, bats. Straight bats appear to be in use here, but the somewhat primitive quality of the figures suggests that this drawing has dubious documentary value. Nonetheless, the use of a coat to stop the ball behind the wicket can often be seen in depictions of single-wicket and explains, for example, the matador-like figure in Sablet's portrait of Thomas Hope (No. 105, Plate XXIV). In Walton's painting of *A Cricket Scene at Harrow School* (No. 124, Plate 30) a boy is using his hat for a similar purpose.

81 John Morgan, R.A., R.B.A.: *Ginger Beer* (Plate 92)

Present whereabouts unknown.

Oil on canvas: 40 × 27 in.

Signed: *J. MORGAN*.

Provenance: Anon sale, Sotheby's Belgravia, 9 March 1976 (82).

Exhibited: R.A., 1860 (572).

John Morgan (1823-1886), a genre painter specializing in pictures of children as well as biblical and historical subjects, in the former respect owing much to the example of Thomas Webster, R.A. (1800-1886) (Nos. 129-131); exhibited at the Royal Academy, the Society of British Artists and the British Institution.

82 John Morgan, R.A., R.B.A.: *The Fight* (in the country) (Plate XXVI)

Formerly with Roy Miles, London.

Oil on canvas: 27 × 41 in.

Signed and dated 1869.

Provenance: M. Bernard; Roy Miles.

Exhibited: R.A., 1869 (472).

Literature: *Apollo*, LXXVI (December 1962) (advt.).

A cricket match is taking place in the distance; some players are all in white, but others wear coloured jackets. The scene is set in the country; an urban *Fight* was in the collection of the Duke of Norfolk, and also shows a cricket bat and stumps.

The boy at the centre, it may be noted, holds his cricket bat over his shoulder, in the traditional manner already seen in the eighteenth century in works by Hudson and others (see Plates 24-27).

83 Richard Morris: *The Regent's Park*

Museum of London.

Brown wash over etching: 4⅞ × 18⅞ in.

Dated 1831.

Published by R. Ackermann.

Richard Morris (*fl.* 1830-1844) was a painter of landscapes who exhibited occasionally at the Society of British Artists, at the Royal Academy and at the British Institution.

Harrow and Little Primrose Hill can be seen beyond the Park, which had been laid out for the cricket-loving Prince Regent by John Nash. This is a section from Morris's *Panoramic View round the Regent's Park*.

84 Sir David Murray, R.A., R.S.A., R.S.W., R.I.: *Cricket on the Village Green* (Plate 104).

Rutland Gallery, London.

Oil on canvas: 12 × 14 in.

Signed and dated (bottom right): *David Murray 91*.

Sir David Murray (1849-1933), Scottish landscape painter; born in Glasgow; entered on a career in business before devoting himself to painting; elected A.R.S.A., 1881; settled in London in 1882; elected A.R.A. in 1891, R.A. in 1905; exhibited at the Royal Academy, the Old Watercolour Society, the Royal Scottish Academy and elsewhere; left a bequest to the Royal Academy for the encouragement of landscape painting.

The treatment owes much to French Impressionism, whose principles were developed in England especially by the members of the New English Art Club (founded in 1886), such as Whistler, Clausen, Wilson Steer and La Thangue.

85 Algernon Newton, R.A.: *A Cricket Match at Bournville* (Plate 105)

Cadbury Schweppes, plc.

Oil on canvas: 38½ × 50½ in. 1929.

Provenance: see below.

Exhibited: Sheffield, Plymouth and R.A., *Algernon Newton*, 1980 (19).

Algernon Newton (1880-1968), painter of landscapes and buildings, and grandson of Henry Charles Newton, the founder of the firm of Winsor and Newton (Artists' Colourmen); educated at Clare College, Cambridge, but left after a year; trained as a painter at Frank Calderon's School of Animal Painting in London, at the Slade School, and at the London School of Art in Kensington; lived for some time in Switzerland and also on his uncle's ranch in British Columbia; volunteered for the Army on the outbreak of the First World War; after being invalided out, went to Cornwall, where he renewed his earlier acquaintance with the painter Lamorna Birch; in 1918 moved to Berkshire, and in 1938 to Suffolk; later settled at Beck Hole in North Yorkshire; elected A.R.A. in 1936 and R.A. in 1943. Algernon Newton was a profound student of the work of Canaletto, adopting the eighteenth-century master's use of a monochrome underpainting, and emulating the precision of his style and his effects of lighting.

The painting was presented to Messrs Cadbury Ltd in 1929, as a Jubilee gift, by William Cadbury, Director of Cadbury's from 1899 to 1937. It was then known as *Cocoa Block from Men's Grounds*. During the Second World War Algernon Newton painted a further picture of the same view which showed the camouflage on the "Cocoa Block" and soldiers drilling on the field.

86 Sir William Nicholson: *A Cricketing Jug* (Plate 85)

Signed (bottom right) with a monogram.

Frontispiece to *A Hundred Years of Trent Bridge*, edited by E.V. Lucas (privately printed for Sir Julien Cahn, Bart., President of the Nottinghamshire County Cricket Club, 1938).

Sir William Nicholson (1872-1949), painter of portraits, still lifes and landscapes, and graphic artist; born at Newark, Nottinghamshire; studied at the Académie Julien in Paris; collaborated with his brother-in-law James Pryde (1866-1941) in designing posters under the name "The Beggarstaffs"; a founder member of the National Portrait Society in 1911; knighted in 1936; father of the painter Ben Nicholson. Besides his great distinction as a painter of uncommon facility and stylishness, Nicholson became widely known for his lithographs and woodcuts (his *Alphabet* being the most famous of his works in the latter medium).

The jug represented (see Plate 84) was in the artist's possession. It is a famous example of Staffordshire ware, of about 1840, and the figures around it are portrayals of Fuller Pilch (the batsman), William ("Old") Clarke (the bowler), and (not visible in Nicholson's Frontispiece) Thomas Box (the wicket-keeper).

Cricket also features in Nicholson's series of coloured woodcuts *An Almanack of Twelve Sports* (1898), in which the month of June is represented by a portrait of Alfred Mynn, the great Kent and England all-rounder. The *Almanac* was published by Heinemann in a *de luxe* edition and in "Library" and "popular" editions. Each of the twelve illustrations was accompanied by a set of verses by Rudyard Kipling. The lines for *June* read:

Thank God who made the British Isles
  And taught me how to play;
I do not worship crocodiles
  Or bow the knee to clay!

Give me a willow wand and I,
  With hide and cork and twine,
From century to century
  Will gambol round my Shrine.

87 John Nixon: *Harwich, with a Game of Cricket in Progress* (Plate 41)

Present whereabouts unknown.

Pen and grey ink, and watercolour: 4 ⅛ × 7 in.

Signed: *J Nixon 1784*. Inscribed: *Harwich*.

Provenance: Christie's, 4 March 1975 (47).

John Nixon (1760-1818), amateur artist, etcher and caricaturist (not to be confused with the earlier John Nixon [*c.* 1706-1760]); by profession a merchant in the City of London; best known as the principal author of a series of views of country seats in England and Ireland published by Watts (the engraver) from 1779 to 1886; exhibited frequently at the Royal Academy.

What we see is a game of single-wicket cricket. Nixon went on a visit to the Netherlands in 1784, and so this drawing was presumably executed on his departure or return (there is a ship in the background).

88 W.W. Ouless, R.A.: *A.N. Hornby*

Lancashire C.C.C.

Oil on canvas: 56 × 41 in. Painted in 1900.

Provenance: Originally presented to A.N. Hornby by Lancashire C.C.C.

Walter William Ouless (1845-1933), portrait painter born at St Helier, Jersey; a prolific and immensely successful society artist. In 1897 Ouless was commissioned by M.C.C. to paint Sir Spencer Ponsonby-Fane, who had for many years been treasurer of the Club, and who had built up the Club's collection of pictures.

For A.N. Hornby see under No. 30. He is shown here at three-quarter-length, dressed in his flannels, and holding a bat.

89 A.F. Payne: *A Cricket Match at Cowley, Oxford* (Plate 83)

Collection of Peter Rook, Esq.

Watercolour: 5⅕ × 7⅕ in.

Painted in June 1857.

Provenance: Covent Garden Art Gallery.

Arthur Frederick Payne (1831-1910) exhibited etchings and a work entitled *The Burial of the Lord of Rosslyn* at the Royal Academy between 1858 and 1873. He was born in the Newarke, Leicester.

He and his twin brother Alfred went up to

Trinity College, Oxford, at the age of 19, and both won cricket Blues, Alfred being captain of the University XI in 1856. The twins then played cricket for Leicestershire, but evidently Arthur Payne's love of painting was disconcerting to the supporters of Leicestershire cricket: as the author of one history of Leicestershire cricket observed, "Arthur F. Payne although a useful cricketer devoted much of his time to Art and lived in Paris for long periods."

One of the brothers was singled out by Ranjitsinhji in his *Jubilee Book of Cricket* (London, 1897, p.321):

"In 1852 Mr A. Payne, a very fast left-hand bowler and successful bat, appeared [at Oxford]."

A man of independent means, Payne was an accomplished amateur artist, and in possessing an apparently equal facility for both art and cricket he resembles his rather older contemporary "Felix". He himself was painted by Millais: he bequeathed the portrait to his daughter Lillie, wife of Major William Augustus Fox-Pitt. His own father, a lawyer, had been a keen collector, his most notable purchase being William Etty's *The Destroying Angel*, which he bought from the artist in 1832, and which is now in the Manchester City Art Gallery.

An exhibition of works by Payne was held at the Covent Garden Art Gallery in the spring of 1982.

This tiny picture is crammed with detail, including a good view of the tented pavilions which were a feature of the game throughout the eighteenth and nineteenth centuries. There is a black, red and gold flag flying; we are in the era of the newly founded touring clubs, and perhaps I Zingari (founded 1845) may even be indicated.

Cowley Marsh was "the cradle of Oxford University cricket": it was a large common stretching some way beyond the Cowley end of Magdalen Bridge to Shotover Hill: the move to The Parks was not made until 1881. The continuous series of annual matches between Oxford and Cambridge began in 1838.

90 Edward Penny, R.A.: *Sir William Benett of Fareham at the age of 12* (Plate V)

Laing Art Gallery, Newcastle-upon-Tyne (E 1160). Oil on canvas: 20 × 14 in. *c.* 1743-4.

A label on the back is inscribed in an eighteenth-century hand: *Sir William Benett at twelve years old.*

Provenance: By family descent to G.R. Brigstocke; Dr John Dockray; purchased by the Gallery from Leger Galleries in 1960.

Edward Penny (1714-1791), foundation member of the Royal Academy and Professor of Painting from 1769 to 1783; was a pupil of Hudson and then studied in Rome, returning in 1743. His gifts were considerable but essentially domestic. As a result, he created a personal and influential form of "history painting" which looks forward to nineteenth-century subjects (where everything has a moral, if only you can find it). *The Death of Wolfe* used to be his most famous work.

A superscription on the original label on the back identifies the picture as being in the possession of W.B.P. Brigstocke in 1865. The Brigstockes are descended from the Player family; the Benetts and Players were at least twice related by marriage: the William Benett (the spelling with one "n" is that used on the label) of Fareham of *c.* 1700 had two daughters who married into the Player family, in 1692 and 1712.

This picture was formerly attributed to Arthur Devis. The basis of our attribution of it to Edward Penny is its resemblance to three portraits of the Nevel family by Edward Penny, all of which are identical in size to this painting. The date can be established by the costume, but also by reference to Penny's other portraits. Benett stands by a wicket – of which this is one of the earliest representations. He was to become first a Steward (1778) and then President (1786) of the Hambledon Club. Benett was at one time Sheriff of Hampshire, and was knighted in 1760: his known career therefore agrees with the suggested date of the painting. A figure climbs a stile in the background, having laid his red kerchief bundle on the ground. Benett holds a red kerchief prominently in relation to the wicket, an action which must refer to some specific incident. He is not dressed ready to play, for he has his tricorn hat under his left arm and is wearing his coat. In the background there is a cottage with a figure in the doorway, beside a stream or river, as well as a church with a spire.

91 Robert Edge Pine: *The Revd Robert Waugh as a boy* (Plate 39)

Present whereabouts unknown.

Oil on canvas: 51 × 40½ in. *c*. 1777.

Provenance: Christie's, 17 March 1978 (85).

Robert Edge Pine (*c*. 1730-1788), painter of portraits and history pictures; a friend of the actor David Garrick, who sat for him frequently; pioneered the portraiture of actors in character parts; worked in London and, in the 1770s, in Bath; emigrated to America in 1783 and settled in Philadelphia.

The Revd Robert Waugh was born in 1767 and is shown here at about the age of ten: the portrait would therefore have been painted about 1777. He died in 1810. He wears an open-necked shirt such as was common for cricket, a coat and waistcoat, and shoes with buckles.

92 Camille Pissarro: *Cricket on Hampton Court Green* (Plate XXXII)

The Ailsa Mellon Bruce Collection, National Gallery of Art, Washington (2425).

Oil on canvas: 21½ × 29 in.

Signed and dated (bottom left): *C. Pissarro, 1890.*

Provenance: Durand-Ruel, Paris; presented by Mr Paul Mellon to the National Gallery of Art, Washington, in 1981.

Literature: Lodovic Rodo Pissarro and Lionello Venturi, *Camille Pissarro: son art – son oeuvre* (2 vols., Paris, 1939), no. 746.

Camille Pissarro (1830-1903), French Impressionist painter, born at St Thomas in the Danish West Indies the son of a Portuguese-Jewish father and a Creole mother; entered the Ecole des Beaux Arts in Paris in 1855; came under the influence of Corot, calling himself his pupil; later met Monet and joined the Impressionists' circle, exhibiting at all the eight Impressionist exhibitions (1874-1886); also exhibited at the Salon and the Salon des Refusés; during the Franco-Prussian War of 1870-1, when Prussian troops occupied his house at Louveciennes (turning it into a butchery and using his finished canvases as duckboards in the garden), Pissarro joined Monet in London. When his sons were subsequently living in London, Pissarro made numerous visits to England.

The style of this painting is so impressionistic that it is impossible to tell what is going on "in the middle". Compare the British School painting of the same cricket ground in 1836 (No. 155).

93 Camille Pissarro: *Cricket at Bedford Park* (Plate 106)

Jeu de Paume, Paris.

Oil on canvas: 21 × 26 in.

Signed and dated 1897.

Provenance: Durand-Ruel, Paris; Leicester Galleries; Broun & Philips, London.

Literature: Lodovic Rodo Pissarro and Lionello Venturi, *Camille Pissarro : son art–son oeuvre* (2 vols., Paris, 1939), no. 1008.

Pissarro painted another picture in 1897 from the same point of view, *Fête en Jubilée à Bedford Park*, which also shows a large and festive crowd with tents and marquees: evidently the cricket match was part of the same celebrations, which marked the sixtieth anniversary of Queen Victoria's ascent to the throne, and which gave the name to Prince Ranjitsinhji's *Jubilee Book of Cricket* published in the same year.

94 James Pollard: *A Cricket Match at Copenhagen House, Islington*

Present whereabouts unknown.

Oil on panel: 9¼ × 11¾in.

Provenance: Christie's, 11 April 1980 (22).

Literature: N.C. Selway, *James Pollard* (Leigh-on-Sea, 1965), p. 59 (no. 331) (probably).

James Pollard (1792-c.1859), sporting painter and engraver; specialized in coaching subjects; son and pupil of Robert Pollard (1755-1838), an engraver and publisher; was encouraged by the great wood-engraver Thomas Bewick (1753-1828); worked at first with his father, achieving independence in 1825, when he married; exhibited occasionally at the Royal Academy and elsewhere, but worked chiefly for private patrons and dealers. Pollard never recovered from the death of his wife and younger daughter in 1840.

There was another version, small, in the collection of G.H. Weston, Esq. The view is of particular interest since it confirms the building in a watercolour portrait of Edwin Paul (No. 159), of *c.* 1850, as being Copenhagen House. A pavilion and flag-pole are also in the same position in each picture. The portrait of Edwin Paul was also in the collection of Mr G.H. Weston. The James Pollard of the same scene owned by Mr Weston was given by him to Handel Davis, M.D.

A strip of shorter grass runs between the wickets, though to one side of them, and extends along the bowlers' run-ups. There are two tents, or "pavilions", on opposite sides of the ground; the players would therefore emerge from them as from opposing camps. Most of the players wear white shirts, and some are dressed entirely in white. A ball has just been bowled, and the batsman has raised his bat to meet it; the wicket-keeper crouches expectantly. Two of the fielders stand with their hands placed at the front of their hips–a posture sometimes seen in other cricket pictures.

95 John Robertson Reid: *A Country Cricket Match* (Plates XXVII, 96)

Tate Gallery, London (T.1557).

Oil on canvas: 41½ × 71½ in. 1878.

Signed and dated (bottom left): *John R Reid 78.*

Provenance: Tate Gift, 1894.

Exhibited: R.A., 1878 (77).

Literature: George R. Halkett, "John R. Reid", *Art Journal*, 1884, pp. 265 ff., repr. p. 268 (engraving by J.C. Griffiths); Sir Edward J. Poynter, *The National Gallery* (London, 1900), III, 229.

John Robertson Reid (1851-1926), Scottish landscape and genre painter; pupil of George Paul Chalmers (1883-1878) (an artist influenced by Turner) and William McTaggart (1835-1910), the Scottish Impressionist; settled in England but maintained contacts with the members of the Glasgow School, which he influenced; exhibited at the Royal Academy.

This is not to be thought of as just a picture of a rustic team so much as of grand visitors playing a village: thus the men beside the pavilion wear a variety of cricket caps of a type to be seen in the portrait by Mary Drew of *A Woolwich Cadet* (No. 41): they are coloured pink and white, red and black, blue and white, red and yellow.

The detail of the match at the top right shows a batsman taking strike. It is noticeable that the square-leg umpire still holds a bat–a practice by this time abandoned in the first-class game but surviving in the country long after the need for touching the bat to score a run had passed. In another intriguing detail, there is a still-life of bat, pads, gloves and ball in the lower right-hand corner. The picture was painted at Ashington in Sussex.

96 John Ritchie: *Village Cricket* (Plate 65)

M.C.C.

Oil on canvas: 31½ × 49½ in.

Signed and dated (bottom left): *J Ritchie 1855.*

Provenance: Colman Gift, 1947.

Exhibited: Tate Gallery, 1934; National Book League, 1950; Arts Council of Great Britain, *British Sporting Painting 1650-1850*, 1974-5 (218).

Literature: Sir Norman Birkett, *The Game of Cricket* (London, 1955); Diana Rait Kerr and Ian Peebles, *Lord's 1946-1970* (London, 1971): Appendix 3 ("MCC and the Arts", by Diana Rait Kerr).

John Ritchie (*fl.* 1858-1875), genre painter; specialized in costume pictures set in the seventeenth or eighteenth century; exhibited at the Royal Academy, the British Institution and the Society of Artists.

This painting has been wrongly described (as have so many paintings of country cricket matches) as *Cricket at Hambledon*. The bowler appears to be about to deliver a no-ball.

97 George R. Roller, R.P.E.: *W.E. Roller going out to bat* (Plate 108)

Surrey County Cricket Club.

Oil on canvas: 96 × 57½ in.

Provenance: Presented to the Surrey County Cricket Club by the batsman's mother in 1883.

George R. Roller (*fl.* 1887-1896), presumably the son of the painter George Conrad Roller (1856–*c.* 1904) and brother of the sitter; member of the Royal Society of Painters and Etchers; exhibited at the Royal Society of British Artists.

W.E. Roller played for Surrey in the latter part of the nineteenth century, his most notable achievement being to score 204 (batting at No. 6) and perform the "hat trick" in the match against Sussex played at The Oval on 29, 30 June, 1 July 1885.

In this picture, Roller is seen descending the pavilion steps at The Oval as he walks out to bat during the the second innings of a County match between Surrey and Lancashire, played on 23, 24 and 25 August 1883. Roller, who was then an undergraduate, was batting when Surrey needed 112 runs to win, with only three wickets standing. On the last day 56 runs were still needed and Roller hit the winning run, being not out for 55. In the painting a scorecard of the match lies on the ground.

98 Henry Rossi: *The Batsman* (Plate 52)

The Marquess of Tavistock, Woburn Abbey.

Marble: 28 in. high. *c.* 1825.

Provenance: By family descent.

Exhibited: see below.

Literature: R. Gunnis, *Dictionary of British Sculptors, 1660-1851* (London, 1951); *Cricket Quarterly*, 1965, pp. 34-5 (repr.).

Henry Rossi (1791-1844), sculptor, son of the sculptor John Charles Felix Rossi, R.A. (1762-1839), whom he assisted in 1819 with the sculptural decoration of St Pancras on the Marylebone Road (the well-known caryatids on the exterior of which were made too tall and had to have their middles cut out to make them fit). In the same year he exhibited the first versions of his models of figures of cricketers at the Royal Academy.

This marble statuette, together with its companion, *The Bowler* (No. 99, Plate 53), was, according to Gunnis (*op.cit.*), commissioned by the Duke of Bedford after Rossi's exhibition of models of the two subjects at the Royal Academy in 1824 and 1825 respectively.

However, Graves (Algernon Graves, *Royal Academy Exhibitors* [London, 1906], VI, 371) cites the following details of Rossi's exhibiting at the Royal Academy:

1819 (1182): Model for a statue of a cricketer [i.e., a batsman]
(1183): Model for a statue of a bowler
1823 (1100): Statue in marble of a cricketer [i.e., a batsman]
1824 (1024): Model for a statue of a bowler to be carved in marble.

It is conceivable therefore that the Duke bought the statue of the batsman exhibited in 1823, and commissioned the statue of the bowler after seeing the model for that sculpture exhibited in 1824. Mention is made in the literature of "replicas" or "copies" of the two sculptures, either in marble or plaster, in the possession of the Merchant Taylors' Company and at Stourhead. The plaster copies or versions at the Merchant Taylors' Company were destroyed in the Second World War; the National Trust has no record of such sculptures at Stourhead.

The versions of the sculptures formerly with the Merchant Taylors' Company were perhaps those models by Rossi exhibited at the Royal Academy in 1819 (1182) and 1824 (1024) respectively.

The Bedford family (the Russells) were keenly interested in cricket: the 6th Duke, for example, was present at one of the earliest games at the first Lord's ground, when the White Conduit Club beat Middlesex by ten wickets on 5-6 June 1787. The 4th Duke and the Earl of Sandwich were recalled by the poet Thomas Gray earlier in the century as "dirty boys playing at cricket".

Lord Charles Russell, son of the purchaser of these sculptures, became President of the M.C.C. in 1835, and his brother Lord John (later 1st Lord Russell) was a brilliant first-class cricketer.

It is recorded that William Ward of Lord's, in the middle of the nineteenth century, "had a beautiful marble statue of a 'Cricket player' made by the sculptor Rossi" (*Scores and Biographies, cit.*, I, 361).

No. 98, unfortunately, was dropped in 1978 on

its return from an exhibition in Australia: it broke into ten pieces, but has since been well restored.

99 Henry Rossi: *The Bowler* (Plate 53)

The Marquess of Tavistock, Woburn Abbey.

Marble: 34½ in. high. *c.* 1825.

Provenance: By family descent.

Exhibited: see under No. 98.

Literature: R. Gunnis, *Dictionary of British Sculptors, 1660-1851* (London, 1951); *Cricket Quarterly*, 1965, pp. 34-5 (repr.).

This sculpture and its companion *The Batsman* (No. 98, Plate 52) are very Neoclassical in style. *The Bowler* is all the more interesting, therefore, when we compare it with the description by John Nyren (in a passage almost certainly written by his "ghost", Charles Cowden Clarke) of David Harris of Hambledon; the Classical Greek sculptor Phidias is referred to in this famous passage:

> It would be difficult, if not impossible, to convey in writing an accurate idea of the grand effect of Harris' bowling; they only who have played against him can fully appreciate it. His attitude when preparing for his run previously to delivering the ball, would have made a beautiful study for the sculptor. Phidias would certainly have taken him for a model. First of all, he stood erect like a soldier at drill; then, with a graceful curve of the arm, he raised the ball to his forehead, and drawing back his right foot, started off with his left. The calm look and general air of the man were uncommonly striking, and from this series of preparations he never deviated. I am sure that from this simple account of his manner, all my countrymen who were acquainted with his play will recall him to their minds. His mode of delivering the ball was very singular. He would bring it from under the arm by a twist, and nearly as high as his arm-pit, and with this action *push* it, as it were, from him. How it was that the balls acquired the velocity they did by this mode of delivery I never could comprehend. (*The Young Cricketer's Tutor*, etc., reprinted London, 1974, pp. 80 f.)

Rossi's sculptures of *The Batsman* and *The Bowler* were very popular, and several casts were made of them. Nyren's book was first published in 1833, and it seems possible, therefore, that his description of Harris owes something to the inspiration of Rossi's Neoclassical sculpture.

100 Thomas Rowlandson: *Cricket in White Conduit Fields* (Plate 57)

M.C.C.

Pen and watercolour. *c.* 1790.

Thomas Rowlandson (1756-1827), satirical draughtsman and caricaturist; studied in Paris and at the Royal Academy Schools in London; having gambled away an inheritance from a French aunt, recouped his losses by producing hundreds of satirical and humorous drawings of the contemporary scene, working much for Ackermann and other publishers, his illustrations to *The Tours of Dr Syntax* (1812-20) being his most famous series.

White Conduit Fields is seen from the west, and this drawing can be compared with that by Robert Dighton (No. 41, Plate 56), where the same post-and-rail arrangement (visible in the background here) is to be seen. Even if we allow for artistic licence on Rowlandson's part, little can be made of this view of a game of double-wicket cricket in which so few players are taking part. Certainly, nothing is recorded of the White Conduit Club itself after 1787, in which year some of its members founded the M.C.C. Three stumps and bats of uncertain design are being employed.

101 Thomas Rowlandson: *Rural Sports, or a Cricket Match Extraordinary* (Plate 91)

Coloured print: 8⅞ × 13⅜ in. 1811.

Literature: Marjorie Pollard, "Women as Cricketers", in *The M.C.C. 1787-1937* (London, 1937); Mary Dorothy George, *Catalogue of Political and Personal Satires preserved in the Department of Prints and Drawings in the British Museum*, IX (London, 1949), 60 (no. 11790).

Ladies' cricket was already well developed by the last quarter of the eighteenth century. This humorous print represents a match played at Newington Green, Middlesex, for 500 guineas. On 3 October 1811, the *News* announced:

CRICKET MATCH EXTRAORDINARY

On Wednesday last a singular Cricket match commenced at Ball's pond, Newington. The players on each side were twenty-two women: eleven Hampshire against eleven Surrey. The match was made between two Noblemen of the respective counties, for five hundred guineas a side. The performers in this singular contest were of all ages and sizes, from 14 years old to upwards of 40; and the different parties were distinguished by coloured ribbons: Royal purple for Hampshire; orange and blue, Surrey. The weather being favourable on Wednesday, some very excellent play, and much skill was displayed; but the palm of that day was borne off by a Hampshire lass, who made a 41 innings before she was thrown out.....The game, it is expected, will be concluded tomorrow; but the general opinion is, that Hampshire will gain the victory.

Besides its interest in documenting women's cricket in this period, Rowlandson's print supports other evidence that in the early nineteenth century cricket continued to be played in the month of October. Otherwise, as Marjorie Pollard has put it, this match "savours of exploitation" (*op. cit.*, p.120).

The watercolour from which this print was taken (9 × 14 in.) is now in the possession of M.C.C.

102 *ascribed to* **Thomas Rowlandson:** *Lord's Cricket Ground, St John's Wood*

M.C.C.

Pen and watercolour.

Inscribed (lower left): *Lord's Cricket Ground St John's Wood 1827.*

Provenance: Dr Crichton Starkey; Christie's, 1963.

The attribution to Rowlandson (1756-1827) is very doubtful, although there are some hints of his style. The arrangement of the figures is also unusually vague, even cursory; the presence of only five players for double-wicket cricket and, for example, the absence of any indication of bounds to the ground (although we know that Lord could exclude people when he wished) make this drawing of very little documentary value. It was possible for *hoi polloi* to pay for the use of the ground. The old pavilion had been burnt down in 1825, and its replacement can be seen, for example, in the background of the anonymous portrait of *George Whieldon at Lord's*, painted in 1845 (No. 157, Plate XXI). The fact that the building shown in No. 102 has a very different appearance must cast further doubt on the status of this drawing.

103 John Russell, R.A.: *The Revd John H. Chandler as a Boy*

Private Collection.

Oil on canvas: 49 × 39 in. Painted in 1767.

Provenance: By family descent.

Literature: G.C. Williamson, *John Russell, R.A.* (London, 1894) pp. 90, 139.

John Russell (1745-1806), portraitist in oil and in pastel, had already won premiums from the Society of Arts when he was 14 and 15 years old. In the year in which he painted this portrait he was finishing his study of crayon painting (i.e. pastel) with Francis Cotes, whose famous oil of *Lewis Cage with a bat* (No. 33, Plates XVI, 17) was painted in 1768. He published *Elements of Painting with Crayons* in 1772 and was made "Crayon Painter to the King and to the Prince of Wales" in 1790.

A red cricket ball with a hemisphere seam is shown and the boy holds a curved bat. It is interesting to compare this picture with Russell's later portrait, *The Sons of Thomas Pitt*, 1804 (No. 104, Plate 45), in which the shape of the bat has changed, and which is much more sentimental and Romantic. The severity of the portrait of John Chandler, painted in 1767, may conceivably be related to Russell's conversion to Methodism three years earlier. However, as Sir Ellis Waterhouse (*op. cit.*) has remarked, although religion played a large part in Russell's life it "is oddly little reflected in his highly fashionable crayon portraits" (of which his portrait of the Pitt brothers is such a fine example).

104 John Russell, R.A.: *The Sons of Thomas Pitt* (Plate 45)

Private Collection.

Pastel: 30 × 25in. Signed and dated 1804.

Provenance: Christie's, 19 June 1979 (88); John Mitchell & Son.

Exhibited: Royal Academy, 1804 (423).

Literature: G.C. Williamson, *John Russell, R.A.* (London, 1894), p. 130.

Thomas Pitt, of St James's, Westminster, married the younger daughter of Henry Cornwall Legh, of High Legh, Cheshire, in 1788.

It is probable that Russell painted this portrait during one of his annual trips around the provinces. In addition to his much earlier cricket portrait of *John Chandler* (No. 103), there is a portrait by Russell of *The Hon. Edward Rice as a young boy* (Sotheby's, 18 November 1976 (147), repr.): the sitter has been identified as "holding a racket handle", but in fact he is holding the top of the handle of a cricket bat, identical in appearance with that shown in the portrait of the Pitt brothers.

105 Jacques Sablet: *Thomas Hope of Amsterdam playing Cricket at Rome* (Plate XXIV)

M.C.C.

Oil on canvas: 24½ × 19¾in.

Signed and dated, lower left: *J. Sablet Roma 1792.*

Provenance: Hope Heirlooms at Deepdene; sold Christie's, 20 July 1917 (69); bought by 7th Duke of Newcastle, by whose Trustees it was sold at Christie's, 21 June 1968 (89), to Leggatt acting for an anonymous private bidder; bought for M.C.C. in July 1968 *via* Leggatt for 9,500 guineas with the help of grants from the V. & A. Grant-in-aid fund and the N.A.-C.F. together with private subscriptions.

Exhibited: Nottingham Castle Museum and Art Gallery, *Clumber House Collection*, 1929; *Exhibition of Cricket Pictures*, 1930 (43); M.C.C. (permanent loan), 1957-68; Grosvenor House, Antique Dealers' Fair, N.A.-C.F. stand, 1970; Paris, Grand Palais, *David à Delacroix*, 1974-5 (162).

Literature: *National Art-Collections Fund, 65th Annual Report, 1968* (2329), repr. in colour; Roland Bowen, *Cricket : A History of its Growth and Development throughout the World* (London, 1970), pp. 71-2, 267, ill. 10.

There were two Sablet brothers, Jean François (1745-1819) and Jacques (1749-1803). Jean François Sablet was, like his brother, a Swiss-born, French-trained artist resident in Rome; he was known as "Le Romain". The ascription of this picture to him has been convincingly challenged (*David à Delacroix*, *loc.cit.*), and the picture has instead been identified as the work of his brother Jacques. The signature shows the initial letter "J." only, rather than "J.F.", and Jacques it was who struck up a friendship in Rome with the sitter, Thomas Hope: he advised Hope on the decoration of his London house in 1800. Jacques Sablet was known as "le peintre du soleil", evidently because of his predilection for distributing a few foreground figures in front of a brightly lit sky, an effect enhanced by the low viewpoint he usually adopted. This painting is a good example of his style.

Thomas Hope (1769-1831) was on the Grand Tour, and in Rome in 1792, when this picture was painted. He came from a family of Scottish bankers based in Amsterdam, but had to leave Amersterdam in 1796. He settled in Deepdene in Surrey, where he formed a celebrated collection of antiquities. He was one of the great patrons and connoisseurs of the Neoclassical era. His granddaughter, Henrietta Adèle, married the 6th Duke of Newcastle.

The curved, old-fashioned bat is unusually long and slender, and the three-stump wicket is rather small–details which suggest a rather makeshift game. Despite recent suggestions that Vesuvius is depicted in the background, the form of the signature seems to confirm the traditional view that the picture was painted in Rome, although some poetic licence has presumably been taken with the landscape. However, Hope did travel down to Sicily in 1792–a journey which would normally have taken him *via* Naples and Vesuvius. For Thomas Hope see David Watkin, *Thomas Hope and the Neoclassical Idea* (London, 1968).

See also under No. 80.

106 Paul Sandby, R.A.: *Landscape with a Cricket Match*

M.C.C.

Gouache: 12 × 17¾in. Painted in 1774.

Provenance: J.M.W. Turner, R.A., who presented

it to Samuel Dobrée; Dobrée family until about 1928; Ackermann; bought in 1928 by Sir Jeremiah Colman; Colman Gift, 1952.

Exhibited: Nottingham Castle Museum, *Exhibition of Cricket Pictures*, 1930 (36); Tate Gallery, London, 1934; London, National Gallery of British Sports and Pastimes, Hutchinson House, *Cricket Exhibition*, 1950; Reading and Bolton, 1972.

Literature: Sir Jeremiah Colman, *The Noble Game of Cricket* (London, 1941), p. 20, Plate 2.

Paul Sandby, (1731-1809), watercolourist, topographical draughtsman and occasional landscape painter in oil; worked in gouache for many of his grandest compositions; born in Nottingham; younger brother of Thomas Sandby (see under No. 107), with whom he moved to London in 1741; assisted in the survey of the Highlands undertaken by the Government after the Forty-five Rebellion; spent much time working at Windsor, where his brother was Deputy Ranger; founder-member of the Royal Academy in 1768. Sandby was the leading English watercolourist before the advent of Girtin and Turner.

This picture, which was in the possession of J.M.W. Turner (see Nos. 121, 122), is the most famous of several cricket scenes by, or ascribed to, Sandby. A similar drawing, which may not be autograph, was bought by M.C.C. in 1942; a *Landscape with a Cricket Match in Progress* (perhaps representing the Yorkshire Moors) of *c.* 1743, is recorded; and there is also a line engraving by M.A. Rooker after Paul Sandby, *Knole Park in Kent, the seat of His Grace, the Duke of Dorset*, dated 1 September 1775.

The attribution of No. 106 to Paul Sandby is no longer generally accepted, and an alternative but untenable attribution to Richard Wilson (1713-1782) has been proposed.

107 Thomas Sandby, R.A.: *Cricket in front of an Old Mansion*

Nottingham Castle Museum and Art Gallery.

Watercolour: 13½ × 21 in.

Provenance: W.A. Sandby, by whom bequeathed to the Museum in 1904.

Exhibited: Sheffield, *Two Centuries of Cricket Art*, 1955 (96).

Thomas Sandby (1721-1798), topographical draughtsman and watercolourist, elder brother of Paul Sandby, R.A. (*q.v.*); Deputy Ranger of Windsor Great Park under the Duke of Cumberland. Sandby was in Scotland during the period when the Duke ("Butcher" Cumberland, as he became known as a result of his ruthlessness) was putting down the Forty-Five Rebellion. He was a founder member of the Royal Academy, of which he became the first Professor of Architecture.

108 Robert Scaddon: *William Rice* (Plate 18)

M.C.C.

Oil on canvas: 59 × 42½ in.

Signed and dated 1744.

Provenance: Christie's, 31 March 1933 (104).

Literature: Ellis Waterhouse, *The Dictionary of British 18th Century Painters* (London, 1981).

Robert Scaddon (*fl.* 1743-1774), portrait painter; perhaps a pupil of Hudson; was also a miniaturist: a miniature by him dated 1774 is known. A mezzotint published in 1743 confirms the spelling of his name as it is given above, as distinct from "Scaddan", as it often appears in the literature.

The sitter, who holds a bat in his left hand, is fashionably dressed in a brown coat and frilled white waistcoat, each with gold buttons; the urn on the left is a common feature of eighteenth-century portraits, especially those of the 1740s. A game of cricket is being played in the distance, to the right; the scale is not very accurate, and the two-stump wicket therefore appears rather too large.

The picture was repaired and revarnished in 1980-1; it had been retouched in 1950.

109 Charles Schwanfelder: *William and Charles Chadwick at Burley Lodge* (Plate 76)

Art Gallery and Temple Newsam House, Leeds (No. 30/36).

Oil on canvas: 39⅝ × 33⅝ in.

Signed and dated (bottom left): *C.H Schwanfelder/*

1824.

Provenance: Presented by Miss Agnes Lupton in 1936.

Charles H. Schwanfelder (1773-1837), born in Leeds, where he mainly worked; painted picturesque landscapes, animals and occasional portraits; appointed animal painter to George III, and afterwards to the Prince Regent.

The elder boy stands with a pony; the younger kneels on one knee with a bat (straight and child's size) and a ball. The bat handle is strung in the lower part only, the top bound with tape (?); the top itself is bare. Compare the portrait of *Lord Hay* (No. 151, Plate XVII), where the bat, though bigger, has similar features. The kneeling boy is presumably about to knock the stumps into the ground with his bat.

110 Samuel Shelley: *Two Children*

Present whereabouts unknown.

Miniature: 4 × 3½ in. (oval).

Provenance: Christie's, 11 October 1977 (62) (repr.).

Samuel Shelley (1750-?1808), miniaturist and watercolourist; founder-member of the Old Watercolour Society.

Miniatures like this one were often mounted as brooches. The composition ingeniously incorporates a curved cricket bat within the oval.

111 George Shepheard: *Twelve Cricketers in Characteristic Attitudes* (Plates 5-8)

M.C.C.

Pen and wash: 8 × 10 in. *c.* 1795 (?).

Inscribed with the names of the cricketers.

George Shepheard (1770?-1842), watercolourist, genre painter and engraver; studied at the Royal Academy Schools; exhibited at the Royal Academy between 1811 and 1841, and also at the British Institution, the Royal Society of British Artists, the Old Watercolour Society and elsewhere; published in 1814-15 a set of *Vignette Designs*, etched by G.M. Brighty. Shepheard is especially known for his landscape views in Surrey and Sussex, which are often peopled by well-drawn rustic figures.

This sheet of studies of famous cricketers of the late eighteenth century is particularly valuable in giving us portraits of such great players as Lord Frederick Beauclerk, Captain the Hon. E. Bligh, David Harris, Thomas Lord, William Beldam and the Hon. Charles Lennox (afterwards Duke of Richmond).

It may be noted that Captain (later General) the Hon. E. Bligh - known as "Skirmish" Bligh - was the brother of the 4th Earl of Darnley and an ancestor of the Hon. Ivo Bligh (later 8th Earl of Darnley), of "Ashes" fame.

112 Thomas Hosmer Shepherd, *Pensioners' Hall, Charterhouse* (Plate 58)

Museum of London.

Brown wash and pencil: 3⅝ × 5⅝ in. *c.* 1830.

Engraved by J. Rogers (engraving published by Jones and Co., 25 September 1830).

Thomas Hosmer Shepherd (1792-1864), who was evidently the son of the watercolourist George Shepherd and the brother of the topographical artist George Sidney Shepherd (d. 1858), specialized in topographical views of London, and was employed by Frederick Grace (1779-1859) to make drawings of the old buildings before they were pulled down. His importance is very largely due to the fact that we can see old London through his eyes. His *Metropolitan Improvements: or London in the Nineteenth Century; displayed in a Series of Engravings of the New Buildings from Original Drawings by T.H. Shepherd* (published in 1827) contains 160 steel engravings of parks, streets, bridges, river scenery etc., and forms the best and most comprehensive pictorial record of London as it was just before Queen Victoria came to the throne.

The scene is set in the City of London, between St John Street on the west, Goswell Street on the east, Long Lane on the South, and Wilderness Row on the north. The drawing affords attractive evidence of the way in which cricket, in its informal single-wicket form, flourished as an everyday activity in the heart of the City.

113 Jane Sophia Clarendon Smith, N.W.S.: *Four Children in a Summer Landscape*

Present whereabouts unknown.

Watercolour: 19 × 25 in.

Signed and dated (lower right): *J.S. Clarendon Smith. Sep^ter 1869.*

Provenance: Sotheby's Belgravia, 23 April 1974 (363) (repr.).

Jane Sophia Clarendon Smith (Mrs H. Clarendon Smith), *née* Egerton (*fl.* 1858-1877), genre painter in London; exhibited at the New Watercolour Society.

The cross-legged stance of the boy on the left, with his cricket bat over his right shoulder, is an interesting survival of a traditional pose. See p. 24.

114 Ruskin Spear, C.B.E., R.A.: *F.S. Trueman* (Plate 109)

The Lord's Taverners: on loan to the M.C.C.

Oil on canvas: 82 × 26½ in. 1963.

Exhibited: R.A., 1963.

Ruskin Spear (born 1911), painter of portraits and other subjects; studied at the Hammersmith School of Art and under Sir William Rothenstein at the Royal College of Art; first exhibited at the Royal Academy in 1932; President of the London Group, 1959-60; taught at the Royal College of Art until 1976. Ruskin Spear is particularly well known for the distinction of his portraiture, which, as in this full-length of Trueman, often combines expressive drawing with richness of colour.

F.S. ("Fiery Fred") Trueman, Yorkshire and England fast bowler who broke all records by taking 307 wickets in Test matches; in his first season with England in 1952, took 29 wickets against India, including a paralysing 8 for 31 at Old Trafford; with Brian Statham of Lancashire, provided England with perhaps its finest-ever opening bowling combination; now one of the wisest and most perceptive of cricket commentators.

Ruskin Spear's painting, while being unable by the very nature of portraiture to evoke the classic beauty of Trueman's bowling action, admirably expresses the duality of his menacing aggressiveness as a player and his attractiveness as one of the great personalities of the game.

115 Robert Streatfeild: *Cricket at Spa, Belgium* (Plate 86)

Collection of William Drummond, Esq.

Watercolour: 4¼ × 8 in. *c.* 1840.

Robert Streatfeild (1786-1852), landscape artist; chiefly known for views in Belgium and France.

For cricket in Belgium see pp. 43f. See also No. 162 (Plate 87).

116 Albert Chevallier Tayler: *Gilbert Jessop*

Cheltenham Art Gallery and Museum.

Chalk on dark grey paper: 21 × 14 in. 1905.

Albert Chevallier Tayler (1862-1925), genre and portrait painter; exhibited at the Paris Salon in 1891, and at the Royal Academy from 1884; he was capable of very attractive oil paintings which show the influence of contemporary French Impressionism, such as his painting of *Lord's Ground during an Eton and Harrow Match* (No. 117).

One of a series of forty-eight drawings for Tayler's *The Empire's Cricketers*, published by the Art Society in 1905 in weekly parts, and later as a bound edition, with a text by G.W. Beldam. These prints, on dark grey paper, are well known and readily recognizable, but are rather unappealing in comparison with Tayler's other work. Nonetheless, they are an invaluable record by a gifted artist of the giants of "the Golden Age". This portrait of Jessop demonstrates why he was feared as a cover-point almost as much as for his devastating batting.

G.W. Beldam, who wrote the text for Tayler's illustrations, was a pioneer of action photography, and produced a famous series of photographs of cricketers in the same year as Tayler's *Empire's Cricketers*, among them the immortal image of Trumper leaping out to drive. It seems more than likely that Tayler's drawings of cricketers were based on Beldam's action photographs.

Gilbert Laird Jessop (1874-1955), known as "The Croucher", was an immensely hard-hitting batsman and brilliant cover-point who played for Gloucestershire and England: many of his feats of fast scoring remain unsurpassed. "Jessop's Match" was the Oval Test Match against Australia in 1902, when, on a difficult wicket, he scored 104 in 75 minutes, to snatch victory from impending defeat.

Jessop's own copy of a print of this portrait of himself survives in a private collection in London, as do other cricket pictures and prints which he had collected.

117 Albert Chevallier Tayler: *Lord's Ground during an Eton and Harrow Match*

M.C.C.

Oil on canvas: 8¼ × 11½ in.

Signed and dated (bottom right): *A. CHEVALLIER TAYLER 1886.*

Provenance: Presented by the artist.

The picture shows a view of the "A" enclosure and the old pavilion at Lord's. The artist displays a delightful touch in this little painting, which demonstrates how far the lessons of French Impressionism had been absorbed within his own distinctive style. It was executed in the year which saw the foundation of the New English Art Club, a group of artists dedicated to introducing the principles of Impressionism into English painting.

118 Lawrence Toynbee: *Cricket at Hovingham Hall* (Plate 110)

Collection of Sir Marcus Worsley, Bart., J.P., D.L.

Oil on board: 36 × 56in. 1978.

Signed with initials, *LLT*, and dated *78.*

Provenance: Commissioned by Sir Marcus Worsley, Bart.

Lawrence Toynbee (born 1922), painter and formerly Director of the Morley Gallery and Art Centre, Morley College; educated at New College, Oxford, before studying art at the Ruskin School of Drawing at Oxford. Lawrence Toynbee's masterly draughtsmanship and the subtlety of his feeling for light and tonal values are distinctive enough in their own right, but what is to the point here is the manner in which, in his various cricket pictures, these qualities make possible a true, as well as an evocative, expression of the essential character and charm of the game. His better-known *Hit to Leg*, in the Memorial Gallery at Lord's, portraying a West Indian batsman, was purchased by the M.C.C. with the aid of the Victoria and Albert Museum's Purchase Fund, the National Art-Collections Fund, and private subscriptions. A smaller painting of *Cricket in The Parks, Oxford* (1953) is also in the M.C.C. Collection.

No 118 shows a cricket match at Hovingham Hall, Yorkshire, the home of the Worsley family. Colonel Sir William Worsley, 4th Bart. (1890-1973), who was President of the M.C.C. in 1961-2, was one of the great names in Yorkshire cricket. As Captain W.A. Worsley, he was captain of Yorkshire C.C.C. in 1928 and 1929. He had played as a boy in the Eton XI. A right-handed batsman, he also captained the Hovingham Cricket Club, of which he was President until his death. He took enormous pleasure in cricket, and spent much time maintaining the ground in front of Hovingham Hall which is represented in this picture. He marked his Presidency of the M.C.C. by presenting the Club with a painting by Adrian Allinson of backyard cricket at Stoke-on-Trent, with the aim of encouraging the acquisition by the M.C.C. of modern works.

119 Henry Scott Tuke, R.A., R.W.S.: *W.G. Grace* (Plate 100)

M.C.C.

Watercolour: 8¼ × 5¼ in. Painted on 15 April 1905.

Signed; autographed by W.G. Grace. Companion to a portrait by Tuke of Spofforth.

Provenance: Presented by G.W. Beldam.

Henry Scott Tuke (1858-1929), painter of portraits and genre subjects; studied at the Slade School and subsequently in Florence and Paris; settled in Cornwall, first at Newlyn and then at Falmouth; developed a vigorous *plein-air* style; exhibited at the Royal Academy, the Society of British Artists, the New English Art Club and elsewhere. His studies of nude boys bathing tended to cause offence in Victorian England.

G.W. Beldam, the donor of this picture, played for Middlesex, and was a pioneer of action photography (see under No. 116): a watercolour portrait of him by Tuke survives in a private collection.

120 Henry Scott Tuke, R.A., R.W.S.: *W.G. Grace in Ranjitsinhji's turban*

Private Collection.

Watercolour. Painted in 1908.

Literature: Bernard Darwin, *W.G. Grace* (illustrated edition, with an introduction by John Arlott, London, 1981), p. 103 (repr.).

"W.G."posed in Ranjitsinhji's turban after a match played at the great Indian batsman's Sussex home of Shillinglea Park in 1908.

121 J.M.W. Turner, R.A.: *Wells Cathedral with a Game of Cricket* (Plate XVIII)

The Lady Lever Art Gallery, Port Sunlight (327).

Watercolour: 16 × 21 in. *c.* 1795.

Signed (lower right): *W. Turner.*

Provenance: ? John Allnutt sale, Christie's, 18 June 1863 (25); Abel Buckley; Anon sale, Christie's, 27 May 1910 (47); bought Wallis; Agnew, 1912; Lord Leverhulme.

Exhibited: Cooke's Gallery, 1822 (45).

Literature: Andrew Wilton, *The Life and Work of J.M.W. Turner* (London, 1979), p. 314 (no. 134 [repr.]).

Joseph Mallord William Turner (1775-1851), landscape painter in watercolour and oil; described by John Ruskin in *Modern Painters* as "the greatest painter of *all* time": born in London in humble circumstances; studied at the Royal Academy Schools and worked also with Thomas Girtin (1775-1802) at the house of the amateur Dr Monro; elected A.R.A. as early as 1799 and R.A. in 1802; made frequent visits to Italy, France and other parts of Europe; in his will, left nearly 300 of his oil-paintings and nearly 20,000 of his watercolours to the nation.

A game of double-wicket cricket is taking place before the West front of Wells Cathedral. The players are using long curved bats and two-stump wickets, both surviving in rural areas after being superseded at the main cricket centres by straight bats and three-stump wickets. A number of hoops and sticks can be seen, and these and the cricket together lend a "picturesque" touch to this topographical view. The rather uncertain perspective is characteristic of Turner's works at this early stage in his career.

122 J.M.W. Turner, R.A.: *The Lake, Petworth; Sunset, bucks fighting* (*Plates XIX, 48*)

Collection of H.M. Treasury and the National Trust (Lord Egremont Collection), Petworth House (132).

Oil on canvas: 24¼ × 57 in. *c.* 1829.

Engraved by J. Cousen in 1859 for *The Turner Gallery* (as *Petworth Park*).

Provenance: Commissioned by the 3rd Earl of Egremont for the dining-room at Petworth; by family descent to the 3rd Lord Leconfield, who in 1947 conveyed Petworth to the National Trust; in 1957 accepted with the State Room contents by the Treasury in part-settlement of death duties.

Literature: Martin Butlin and Evelyn Joll, *The Paintings of J.M.W. Turner* (Yale University Press, New Haven, for the Paul Mellon Centre, 1977), no. 288; Andrew Wilton, *The Life and Work of J.M.W. Turner* (London, 1979), no. P 288.

In the late 1820s and 1830s Turner stayed frequently with the Earl of Egremont at his Sussex home at Petworth, where he was given a painting-room and allowed a free run of the house. During these visits, Turner made numerous watercolours of interiors at Petworth, besides views over the splendid park, which had been laid out by the great landscape designer Lancelot ("Capability") Brown (1716-1783). In this wonderful sunset scene the prospect of the spacious park is enlivened by the large herd of deer on the right and the balancing figures of cricketers on the left. As is so often the case in "cricket pictures", shadows steal over the grass as the day's play draws to a close. The field-placing seems a little speculative, but conceivably in Lord Egremont's day there was some fast bowler in action at Petworth who required more than one long-stop, as indeed appears not to have been unusual in the early history of cricket.

123 Francis Jukes *after* **John Walker:** *The Back of the Salvadore House Academy, Tooting*

London Borough of Wandsworth Public Library.

Aquatint. Published 2 April 1787.

The print carries the following legend: *This back view of Salvadore House Academy Tooting Surrey is inscribed to the Parents and Guardians of the young gentlemen educated at the Academy by their humble servant John Walker, Drawing Master.*

Francis Jukes (1747-1812), painter and engraver working in London.

John Walker (late eighteenth century), drawing master at the Salvadore House Academy at Tooting; son of the engraver William Walker (of Thirsk) (1729-1793), a number of whose plates he completed after his father's death.

Some of the "young gentlemen" are busily engaged in a game of double-wicket cricket, and are equipped with up-to-date straight bats; others prepare to fly their kites. There is no doubt that cricket was a fully accepted and approved part of school life in and around London by this date (1787).

124 Henry Walton: *A Cricket Scene at Harrow School* (Plate 30)

Private Collection.

Oil on canvas. Painted in 1771.

Literature: William Gaunt, *The Great Century of British Painting: Hogarth to Turner* (London, 1971), Fig. 72.

Henry Walton (1746-1813), portrait and genre painter; a pupil of Zoffany; possessed of a private income, as a practising artist he was more of a "gentleman" than a "player", and retired to Brome, Suffolk, in 1779, in which year he ceased to exhibit. He was an elegant and highly original artist, both in conversation pieces–of which this picture is an excellent example–and in genre pieces (which had a marked influence on Francis Wheatley and George Morland).

The scene is set at Harrow School, and the boy batsman is evidently being coached by a formidable master. It is interesting to note that the boy behind the wicket is using his hat to stop the ball. The habit of using a hat or cloak for this purpose is depicted in other cricketing scenes in the eighteenth century, where informal games or practice sessions are taking place: the painting by Sablet of *Mr Hope of Amsterdam* (No. 105, Plate XXIV) is an example.

125 Sir Leslie Ward ("SPY"): *W.G. Grace*

Lithograph: 12½ × 7½ in. Published by Vincent Brooks, Day & Son.

Cartoon for *Vanity Fair*. Published on 9 June 1877.

Literature: Russell March, *The Cricketers of Vanity Fair*, with an introduction by John Arlott (Exeter, 1982), p. 28.

Leslie Ward (1851-1922), caricaturist; eldest son of Edward Matthew Ward, R.A., and of the latter's wife Henrietta Ward (otherwise not related), an artist who was the granddaughter of the painter James Ward, R.A.; discovered by John Everett Millais; studied architecture under Sidney Smirke, R.A., and Sir Edward Barry, R.A.; was encouraged by W.P. Frith to become a painter and so entered the R.A. Schools; exhibited a bust at the Royal Academy at the age of sixteen; worked as a portrait painter and caricaturist, becoming most famous for his cartoons for *Vanity Fair*, which in turn published in 1889 a cartoon of Ward by "Pal".

The original drawing for the cartoon of *W.G. Grace* is in the M.C.C. Collection (12¾ × 6½ in.).

126 Sir Leslie Ward ("SPY"): *Lord Hawke* (Plate 102)

Lithograph: 12½ × 7½ in. Published by Vincent Brooks, Day & Son.

Cartoon for *Vanity Fair*. Published on 24 September 1892.

Literature: Russell March, *The Cricketers of Vanity Fair*, with an introduction by John Arlott (Exeter, 1982), p. 46.

Martin Bladen Hawke, 7th Baron Hawke (1860-1938); educated at Eton and Magdalene College, Cambridge; entered the Army; captain of Yorkshire; played for England. Lord Hawke was a strict disciplinarian but there was a softer side to his nature, evidently, which was recalled by Sir Osbert Sitwell, who, as a child, came to know Lord Hawke through the visits of the Yorkshire team to the annual Scarborough Festival:

> Unappreciative of the game though I was, I derived much pleasure from the company of Lord Hawke, for many years captain of the team. A man of great charm and character, I often as a child reflected how apt was his name, for, indeed, his features, his shrewd, sharp eyes and dark brows and sunburnt face made him, by some process of name-magic, resemble a hawk; but further than that, no likeness could be traced, for he was very tall and broad, with a slightly shambling gait, and the whole atmosphere round him, and for which he was responsible, was genial and human. Year after year he returned to Scarborough with his team, and when it was not actively engaged he would watch the other matches, and in the intervals of play wander round the ground, seeking out his innumerable young friends and admirers–among whom, in spite of my lack of interest in cricket, I was proud to count myself–and distribute to them peppermint humbugs of an especially vast size out of an enormous paper bag. His personality provided a background for the team, and together with my grandfather's universal presence, gave to the whole week a certain quality, an atmosphere of kindliness that, I believe, distinguished it from other festivals of the same kind.

(Sir Osbert Sitwell, *Left Hand Right Hand!* [London, 1941], p. 145.)

127 George Frederick Watts, O.M., R.A.: *The Cut*

M.C.C.

Pencil, on light green paper, heightened with white: 13¾ × 9 ¾ in. 1837.

Signed (lower centre): *G.F. Watts.*

Inscribed (lower centre): *The Cut / Dedicated with permission to William Ward Esq.*

Provenance: Presented by the artist to Lord Harris, President of M.C.C., in 1895.

Literature: Sir Pelham Warner, *Lord's 1787-1945* (London, 1946), p. 36; Wilfrid Blunt, *"England's Michelangelo": a biography of George Frederick Watts, O.M., R.A.* (London, 1975), pp. 10f.; Gerald Brodribb, *Felix on the Bat: being a memoir of Nicholas Felix* (London, 1962), Appendix C.

George Frederick Watts (1817-1904), portrait and allegorical painter and sculptor, who aspired (in his own phrase) to be "England's Michelangelo"; studied at the Royal Academy Schools, and then, being acutely aware of his lack of formal education, attended the school at Blackheath run by Nicholas Wanostrocht, who, as "Felix" (see Nos. 49, 50, Plate 75), pursued a parallel career as an England cricketer, and who commissioned from him a series of lithographs illustrating batting strokes, first exhibited at the Royal Academy in 1837; after travelling in Italy achieved great fame as a portrait painter and as a painter of moral allegories, such as the well-known *Hope* and *Love and Death* (both in the Tate Gallery); elected R.A. in 1867; made an O.M. in 1902; in 1864 married the actress Ellen Terry, but after the failure of this marriage remarried in 1886. Of all the painters of the Victorian period Watts was the most revered by his contemporaries, not least for the "high seriousness" of his allegorical compositions.

This is a preliminary drawing for one of the five lithographs commissioned by Felix (see Nos. 49, 50, Plate 75) in 1837. For the lithograph itself see No. 128 (Plate 72). Felix himself posed for all the drawings. Other drawings in the possession of M.C.C. in the same series are *The Draw* (Plate 79), *Forward*, *Leg Volley*, and *Play* (Plate 78) (on the *verso* of *Leg Volley*). On the latter sheet is the inscription: *No. II Drawing from Life by G.F. Watts. "The Leg Volley" / portrait of Felix.* Around the main study of *Play* there are several studies by Watts for a group of a mother and two children, sketches of riders, and slight details of *Play*.

Felix dedicated all Watts's lithographs to prominent members of M.C.C. As the inscription on the drawing for *The Cut* already indicates, this one was dedicated to William Ward, the saviour of Lord's in 1825. The old pavilion had been burned down after the first Harrow *v.* Winchester match, of 28 July, 1825, and when to the loss of priceless records and subscription accounts there was added

Thomas Lord's anxiety to retire, it seemed as though the ground was doomed to building speculation. Ward, however, bought the lease, presenting Lord with a cheque for £5,000, and so enabling him to retire to Hampshire.

See also the discussion on pp. 38 ff.

128 George Frederick Watts, O.M., R.A.: *The Cut* (Plate 72)

Lithograph: 13 × 10 in. 1837.

Inscribed, with signature (below): *drawn from life & on stone by me, G.F. Watts.*

Literature: as under No. 127.

One of five lithographs illustrating batsmanship which were commissioned from Watts by Nicholas Wanostrocht (Felix) (see Nos. 49, 50) in 1837. The lithograph was developed from Watts's pencil drawing of *The Cut* (No. 127) and,as the inscription states, was drawn directly on the lithographic stone by Watts himself. Although Felix posed for all five of the lithographs in the series, they were not intended to be portraits–as were, for example, two further lithographs by Watts of *Fuller Pilch* and *The Batsman: Portrait of Alfred Mynn*, which were also commissioned by Wanostrocht (at a date unknown). For this reason Watts was content to draw the left-handed Felix on the stone, knowing that, when printed, the image would be reversed and would therefore show the more common right-handed batsman. In addition to the five original lithographs in this series, Felix published a derivative set bearing only the initials *G.F.W.*, rather than the full signature. One set of these five later lithographs (measuring 11 × 9 in.) (*The Cut, The Draw, Forward, Play, Leg Volley*) is in the M.C.C. Collection. The differences in style from Watts's originals suggest to us that these prints were the work of Felix himself, expecially since several of their physiognomic characteristics (including a tendency to increase the size of the head) are found in Felix's own watercolour drawings.

Watts's pencil study for his lithograph of *The Batsman: Portrait of Fuller Pilch* (see above) is also in the M.C.C. Collection. This lithograph was "dedicated to the lovers of the noble game by N. Felix".

129 Thomas Webster, R.A.: *The Boy with Many Friends* (Plate 94)

Corporation Art Gallery, Bury.

Oil on panel: 24½ × 35½ in.

Signed (in a monogram) and dated: *TW 1841.*

Provenance: Jonathan Peele sale, Christie's, 11 March 1948 (65), bought by Colls; John Hargreaves of Broad Oak, Accrington; Hargreaves sale, Christie's, 5 June 1973 (313), bought Agnew; Thomas Wrigley; presented to the Gallery by the latter's children.

Exhibited: R.A., 1841 (65); Manchester Art Treasures, 1878; R.A., *British Art*, 1934 (430); Arts Council, *Victorian Paintings*, 1962 (66); R.A., *Bicentenary Exhibition*, 1968-9 (194) (repr.); Bolton Museum, *Presents from the Past*, May-June 1978 (5).

Literature: Graham Reynolds, *Painters of the Victorian Scene* (London, 1953), p. 52, Pl.8; Christopher Wood, *Victorian Panorama* (London, 1976), p. 77, Pl.75.

Thomas Webster (1800-1886), painter of genre subjects; sang as a boy in the Chapel Royal Choir, his father–who wished him to become a musician–being a member of George III's household; after the death of George III in 1820, realized his ambition to be a painter, studying at the Royal Academy Schools, where he was a Gold Medallist in 1824; was much influenced by the genre subjects of Sir David Wilkie (1785-1841) and William Mulready (1786-1863), who had found their inspiration in Teniers and the seventeenth-century Dutch masters; exhibited at the Royal Academy, the British Institution and the Society of British Artists; elected A.R.A. in 1840 and R.A. in 1946; in 1856 settled at Cranbrook, in Kent, where he remained for the rest of his life, becoming the leading member of the Cranbrook Colony–a group of artists who gathered there each summer to paint scenes of everyday life. Webster specialized in pictures of children, of which *The Boy with Many Friends* is one of the most famous.

In a classroom a pampered boy with a hamper of goodies becomes the focus of attraction for the other boys, and even the cricket bat is forgotten in the rush, while, in the background, a boy waving a cricket bat seeks in vain to encourage his friends to join him in a game outside.

130 Thomas Webster, R.A.: *A School Playground*

Collection of C. Lloyd Lockinge, Esq.

Oil on panel: 30 × 59¾ in.

Exhibited: R.A., 1852 (60).

The setting is similar to that in Webster's painting of *A Rough and Tumble* (No. 131), and again a cricket bat and ball lie on the ground (to the left of centre).

131 Thomas Webster, R.A.: *A Rough and Tumble*

Present whereabouts unknown.

Oil on panel: 8½ × 18¼ in.

Signed and dated 1854.

Provenance: Christie's, 17 December 1965 (171), bought Newman.

Exhibited: M. Newman, 4-21 May 1966.

Piggy-back, football and other games are being played. A cricket bat and ball lie on the ground to the left. A similar setting appears in Webster's painting of *A School Playground* (No. 130).

132 Carel Weight, C.B.E., R.A.: *The First Cricket Match of Spring*

City Art Gallery, Manchester (1945-270).

Oil on canvas: 16 × 20 in.

Provenance: Purchased from the Leicester Galleries, London, in October 1945, for the Rutherston Collection.

Professor Carel Weight (born 1908), studied at Goldsmiths' College, University of London; first exhibited at the Royal Academy in 1931; taught at the Royal College of Art, becoming Professor of Painting in 1957. Retrospective exhibitions of Professor Weight's work were held at Reading in 1970 and at the Royal College of Art in 1973.

In a northern mining village children and their elders engage in a game of street cricket.

133 Carl Werner, R.I.: *A Cricket Match at Rome* (Plate 88)

Present whereabouts unknown.

Watercolour: 6¾ × 10⅞ in. Printed in 1850.

Signed and dated: *C. Werner f. 1850. Rom.*

Provenance: Christie's, 16 May 1978 (228) (Pl. 3).

Carl Friedrich Heinrich Werner (1808-1894), German landscape and architectural painter; born at Weimar; travelled widely in Europe and the Middle East, making watercolour views of the cities and scenery of many countries; visited England, exhibiting at the Royal Academy from 1860 to 1878 and also at the New Watercolour Society, of which he became a member until his resignation in 1883; elected a member of the Royal Institute of Painters in Watercolour and of the Venetian Academy.

This watercolour was sold at Christie's in 1978 (see above) along with a sheet inscribed with the following: *List of people on the ground at the Cricket Match at Rome in the Pamphili Doria Villa–1850. Lord Balgowie / Honble West / Mr Owen / Mr King / Mr Franks / Mr Oswald Augustus Smith / Sir Francis Scott / Mr Martin Tucker Smith / Mr Martin Ridley Smith / Mr Nicholl / Mr George Ridley / John Berridge (footman to Mr T. Smith).* Three further names presumably identify the spectators: *M^{r} and Mrs Crawford / Mrs Lowther.* Lord Balgowie (1831-57) was the elder son of the 8th Earl of Leven and Melville.

The far batsman seems to be calling for a run. A scorer in a top-hat is seated at a table, accompanied by the small group of onlookers. Cricket is still played in the grounds of the Villa Doria Pamphili: cf. the delightful volume by P.G.G. Labouchère, T.A.J. Provis and Peter S. Hargreaves, *The Story of Continental Cricket* (London, 1969), pp. 28 f.

Cricket had been played by Englishmen in Rome in the eighteenth century, notably in the Borghese Gardens (which had been redesigned by Prince Marcantonio Borghese). We learn, for example, that Englishmen were "permitted by the Borghese family to repair [there] twice a week, and play at cricket and football" ([Lady Anne Riggs Miller,] *Letters from Italy, Describing the Manners, Customs, Antiquities, Paintings, &c., of that Country, in the years MDCCLXX and MDCCLXXI* (3 vols.,

London, 1776), III, 155). British artists who were resident in Italy or making the Grand Tour were among those who joined in such games, and in March 1780, during his long period of study in Rome, the eminent Welsh landscape painter Thomas Jones (1743-1803) recorded a cricket match in the Villa Borghese between "The English Cavaliers with as many of their Country men among the Artists as they could muster" ("Memoirs of Thomas Jones", *The Walpole Society*, XXII [1946-8]).

See also No. 134.

134 Carl Werner, R.I.: *Cricketers taking Refreshments* (Plate 89)

Present whereabouts unknown.

Watercolour: 6⅞ × 10¼ in. Painted in 1850.

Signed and dated: *C. Werner f. 1850. Rom.*

Provenance: Christie's, 16 May 1978, p. 435 (repr.).

The occasion is an interval for luncheon in the match represented in No. 133. Several of the players are in their white cricketing gear.

135 Benjamin West, P.R.A.: *The Cricketers* (Plate 34)

Private Collection, England.

Oil on canvas: 38⅞ × 49 in. Painted in 1763.

Provenance: By family descent.

Exhibited: Allentown Art Museum, Pennsylvania, 1962 (5); Royal Maritime Museum, Greenwich, *1776*, 1976 (336) (repr.).

Literature: *Proceedings of the Lehigh County Historical Society*, xxiii (Allentown, Pennsylvania, 1960), 10-13, repr. p. 31.

Benjamin West (1738-1820), American-born history and portrait painter born in Pennsylvania, trained in Philadelphia; went to Italy in 1760 and arrived in London in 1763; appointed Historical Painter to George III; succeeded Sir Joshua Reynolds as President of the Royal Academy in 1792, when he refused a knighthood on account of his Quaker principles. West leapt into fame in 1771 with his *Death of Wolfe*, and, although a pioneer of the Neoclassical style, he later anticipated the dramatic emotionalism of the Romantics.

This conversation piece is one of the first paintings executed by West after his arrival in England from Italy. He found his erstwhile American patron William Allen already in England, and two of the sitters are Allen's sons. The sitters are five American students pursuing their education in England. They are (*from left to right*): Andrew Allen of Philadelphia, who was at the Middle Temple (1761-5); James Allen, younger brother of Andrew Allen, also at the Middle Temple; Arthur Middleton of South Carolina, who had been at school in Hackney and went on to St John's College, Cambridge, and the Middle Temple; Ralph Izard of South Carolina, educated for twelve years in England altogether, and at this time at Trinity College, Cambridge; Ralph Wormeley of Virginia, Eton and Trinity Hall, Cambridge. The unity displayed by the group in their common love of cricket was not to last, and their loyalties were variously divided in the American War of Independence which followed. Arthur Middleton was a signatory of the Declaration of Independence. Ralph Izard commissioned a replica of the painting from West which now hangs in the Brook Club in New York.

136 The Revd James Wills: *The Andrews Family* (Plate 43)

Fitzwilliam Museum, Cambridge (657).

Oil on canvas: 43¼ × 56⅞ in.

Signed and dated (lower left): *J. Wills pinxit. 1749.*

Provenance: By family descent at Shaw House; by inheritance to H.J.A. Eyre; Christie's, 9 December 1905 (29), bought by Charles Fairfax Murray; by whom presented to the Museum in 1908.

Literature: J.W. Goodison, *Fitzwilliam Museum, Cambridge: Catalogue of Paintings*, Volume III: *British School* (Cambridge University Press, 1977), 284 f. (no. 657); Ellis Waterhouse, *Painting in Britain 1530 to 1790* (Harmondsworth, 1953), Pl. 120 a.

The Revd James Wills (*fl.* 1740-1777), painter of religious subjects and conversation pieces; a member of the circle of Hogarth, Hayman and Gravelot; assisted at one time in the running of the St Martin's Lane Academy; in 1746 he was one of four artists–the others being Hogarth, Hayman and Highmore–who painted large religious compositions for the Foundling Hospital. In later life he was ordained, becoming Vicar of Cannons. His *Andrews Family* is his best-known conversation piece, and reflects the influence of Francis Hayman (1708-1776) (*q.v.*).

Seated at the right is Joseph Andrews (1691-1753), who was appointed Paymaster to the Forces in 1715, and who bought Shaw House, Newbury, in 1751. His second wife Elizabeth, whom he married in 1736, and their son James Pettit Andrews stand beside him. On the left is his elder son Joseph (1727-1800), afterwards Sir Joseph Andrews, Bart. The lady seated next to him has not been identified. It is not certain which game is indicated by the long flimsy bats and small ball, but these items of equipment can be seen in other eighteenth-century paintings, e.g. in *The Cathcart Family* by David Allan (No. 2, Plate 42). But it does seem that the game was at least closely related to cricket.

137 John Wollaston: *Warner and Rebecca Lewis*

Private Collection: on loan to the College of William and Mary, Williamsburg, Virginia, U.S.A.

Oil on canvas. *c.* 1760.

Provenance: Judge Taylor Collection, Gloucester, U.S.A.; G.A. Greaves, U.S.A.

Exhibited: Richmond, Virginia, Virginia Historical Society, Virginia House, *Historical Portraits*, May 1929.

Literature: *American Magazine of Art*, XX, No. 7 (July 1929), 374 (repr.).

John Wollaston (*fl.* 1738-1775), portrait painter, son of the London portraitist John Woolaston (*c.* 1672-1749); about 1749 left England for the American colonies, where he developed a large practice in a number of cities from New York to Virginia; may have moved to the West Indies in 1758 before returning to America; came back to England in 1767.

The sitters are the children of Warner and Eleanor Lewis, whose portraits were also painted by Wollaston. The boy is holding a cricket bat, and there is a ball lying on the ground beside his tricorn hat.

138 Archibald Stuart Wortley: *W.G. Grace at the Wicket* (Plate XXV)

M.C.C.

Oil on canvas: 48 × 34 in.

Signed (in monogram) and dated (lower right): *1890*.

Engraved.

Provenance: Commissioned by the M.C.C. by means of £1 subscriptions in 1888-1890. The artist was paid £300.

Exhibited: R.A., 1890 (1003).

Archibald J. Stuart Wortley (1849-1905), portrait and sporting painter; had lessons in painting from Sir John Everett Millais; exhibited at the Royal Academy, where by 1875 his work had attracted the admiration of John Ruskin; enjoyed considerable popularity.

The scene is Lord's Ground. The old tennis court can be seen in the background.

139 Joseph Wright, A.R.A. (Wright of Derby): *The Wood Children* (Plate X).

Derby City Museum and Art Gallery.

Oil on canvas: 66 × 53 in.

Signed and dated (below Robert Wood's foot): *I.W.P./1789*.

Provenance: By descent in the Wood family until 1934; sale, Christie's, 1 June 1934 (62) (repr.), but withdrawn by consent of the owner, R.H. Wood, who sold it to the N.A.-C.F.

Exhibited: Derby, 1934 (34); Tate Gallery, 1958 (28).

Literature: Benedict Nicolson, *Joseph Wright of*

Derby: *Painter of Light* (The Paul Mellon Foundation for British Art, London, 1968), I, 227 (no.151); II, Pl. 279.

Joseph Wright of Derby (1734-1797), painter of portraits, landscapes and genre subjects; born in Derby; studied in London under the portraitist Thomas Hudson (1701-1779) before setting up practice as a portrait painter in Derby in 1758; made a visit to Italy; after an unsuccessful attempt to succeed to Gainsborough's former practice at Bath, returned to Derby, where he was much employed on commissions for portraits, landscapes and genre subjects, and where the scientific and industrial revolution associated with such men as Erasmus Darwin, Arkwright and Wedgwood had already inspired such pictures as *The Orrery* of 1766 and the *Experiment with an Air Pump* of 1768; exhibited at the Royal Academy from 1778, being elected A.R.A. in 1781; later declined election as R.A. Wright of Derby is celebrated for his interest in striking effects of light, notably moonlight and candlelight, which he painted with an essentially scientific curiosity, and for the uncompromising realism of his style.

The children, whose parents were Hugh and Sarah Wood, of Swanwick, Derbyshire, are (*left*) Robert, (*centre*) John, (*right*) Mary. Robert Wood kneels on the ground to knock a stump in with his bat. John Wood adopts an elegant cross-legged pose, often found in fashionable portraiture of the eighteenth century. The picture shows the different sizes of bat available.

140 Joseph Wright, A.R.A. (Wright of Derby): *The Thornhill Children* (Plate 31)

Private Collection.

Oil on canvas: 57 × 48½ in. *c.* 1790.

Provenance: By family descent.

Exhibited: Derby, 1870 (256); 1883 (78); 1934 (124).

Literature: Benedict Nicolson, *Joseph Wright of Derby: Painter of Light* (The Paul Mellon Foundation for British Art, London, 1968), I, 223 (no.136), II, Pl. 278.

The two boys were the sons of Bache Thornhill (1747-1830), of Stanton-in-Peak, Sheriff of the County of Derby in 1776. The older boy, Henry Bache, was born in 1780, and seems here to be about ten years old; the younger boy, William, was born in 1781. A date of *c.* 1790 for the picture can be presumed.

Haddon Hall, Derbyshire, can be seen in the background.

141 Johan Zoffany, R.A.: *The Sondes Children* (Plate XI)

Collection of Commander Michael Saunders-Watson.

Oil on canvas: 38 × 48 in. *c.* 1764-5.

Provenance: By family descent.

Exhibited: London, National Portrait Gallery, *Johan Zoffany*, 1976 (27).

Johan Zoffany (1733-1810), portrait painter specializing in conversation pieces, of which this picture is a fine example; born near Frankfurt-am-Rhein; came to London, probably in 1760; was taken up by David Garrick, the great actor, and in 1762 painted views of Garrick's house at Hampton Wick; elected R.A. in 1769; came to the notice of George III and Queen Charlotte, by whom he was much employed in the years around 1770; visited Italy from 1772 to 1776, executing there, for Queen Charlotte, his famous *Tribuna of the Uffizi*, in which he showed off all his skill in the rendering of meticulously studied detail; worked in India from 1783 to 1789.

The children in this picture are the sons of the first Lord Sondes and his wife Grace, daughter of the Rt. Hon. Henry Pelham. Their ages suggest a date of *c.* 1764-5. The children are: (*left*) Henry (1755-1833); (*centre*) Charles (1761-1769) (still in skirts); and (*right*) Lewis (1754-1806). The eldest child holds aloft a red cricket ball, and he has a bat in his right hand; but his younger brothers are absorbed in the feeding of a red squirrel with nuts carried in the youngest brother's basket. Charles's cricket bat lies discarded for the moment in the foreground. Both curved bats are proportionately small. The landscape is perhaps not a literal rendering of a view near the family home of Rockingham Castle, despite certain similarities, for there appears to be a sea-inlet visible in the distance, such as could not be seen from that Midlands height. There is, however, a suggestion of a statue in a niche to the left, which would seem to indicate that the scene is indeed set in the park of a country house. This conversation piece is one of the loveliest of all "cricket pictures".

One of Zoffany's paintings of Hampton Wick (Collection of Lord Egremont, Petworth) includes a view of Molesey Hurst (on the opposite bank of the Thames), the site of many famous cricket matches, where Garrick himself patronized games, offering on occasion silver cups as prizes. In the same picture there can be seen a horse in the grounds of Garrick's house pulling a lawn-roller of a type which is still in use on cricket grounds today.

142 Anon: *Boy with curved stick and ball (PUERITIA)*

Stained-glass window, Canterbury Cathedral. *c.* 1180.

Literature: Bernard Rackham, *The Ancient Glass of Canterbury Cathedral* (Canterbury, 1949), pp. 63 ff.; Madeline H. Caviness, *The Early Stained Glass of Canterbury Cathedral, circa 1175–1220* (Princeton, 1977), pp. 126 f.

This figure is from the "Six Ages of Man" depicted in a window in the north-east transept. It represents Boyhood, and is labelled *PUERITIA*. It is interesting that the game chosen to represent childhood at this early date should be so like cricket, which certainly filled the same role in the art of later centuries. This is evidently the earliest representation of a bat-and-ball game resembling cricket. Dr. Caviness observes of the series of which this is a part: "The Six Ages of Man are standing, holding genre objects that could have been invented for the scene; no parallel has been found elsewhere. The boy has a ball and curved stick...Labels are provided...as if it were feared the attributes alone would not serve to identify the figures" (*op. cit.*, *loc. cit.*). The implication is that the figure symbolizing Boyhood is the work of a native artist–which would suggest the peculiarly English character of the game even at so early a date. A similar figure is to be found, nearly two centuries later, in the east window of Gloucester Cathedral (No. 145, Plate I). The Gloucester figure has been known, in recent years, as "the golfer": but doubt must be cast on that identification by the similarity of the Canterbury figure, which is identified as *Pueritia*; for while cricket has been perennially identified in art and literature with boyhood, golf never has been. It may be added that in early times golf and even tennis were thought of as foreign games and in that sense as being very distinct from cricket–a sentiment that lies behind an apologetic couplet of the seventeenth century, referring to:

Cricket which to some men is
As pretty a game as Gauffe or Tennis.

143 Schilling MS.: *"A Game of Cricket"* (Plate 2)

Private Collection.

Manuscript illumination: 4¾ × 3¼ in. *c.* 1300.

Literature: L.M. Randall, *Images in the Margins of Gothic Manuscripts* (California Studies in the History of Art) (Berkeley, California, 1966), p.36.

144 MS. Bodley 264 f.22r: *"A Game of Cricket"* (Plate 3)

Bodleian Library, Oxford.

Manuscript illumination: 17⅛ × 12½ in. *c.* 1340.

Literature: L.M. Randall, *Images in the Margins of Gothic Manuscripts* (California Studies in the History of Art) (Berkeley, California, 1966), p.30.

Illustration to a manuscript of *The Romance of Alexander*, illuminated by Jehan de Grise, Bruges, 1338-1344.

145 Anon: *Man with curved stick and ball* (Plate I)

Stained-glass window, Gloucester Cathedral. *c.* 1350.

Literature: D. Veney and D. Weland, *Gloucester Cathedral* (London, 1979), pp. 114 f., Pls. LXX, LXXIII.

This figure is from the great east window (the Crécy window), and is usually known as "the golfer". There is, however, less justification for that title than for one designating any other bat or club and ball game. A similar figure appears in Canterbury Cathedral at an even earlier date (No. 142).

See the discussion under No. 142.

146 British School: *A Boy of the (?) Lansdowne Family with a Cricket Bat (The Lansdowne Boy)* (Plate 19)

Private Collection.

Oil on canvas: 78 × 42 in. *c.* 1740-5.

Provenance: This painting and the companion portrait of the boy's sister (and a half-length of their father [?] of earlier date) were apparently in the house (which had belonged to the Marquess of Lansdowne) when it was acquired by the present owner's grandfather in the mid-nineteenth century.

The artist would seem to have been influenced by Thomas Hudson. It is hard to date this picture much later than *c.* 1745. It is an early example of the cricket-bat portrait, and is rather more elegant than the closely contemporary portrait of William Rice by Robert Scaddon, signed and dated 1744 (No. 108, Plate 18). In each picture the bat appears disproportionately large. As both sitters are young boys, that would be natural if the bats were full-size men's bats, some of which (e.g., one of *c.* 1750 surviving at Lord's, and weighing no less than 5 lbs. 5 oz.) could be very big. In fact, smaller bats were available for men, and there were also bats for children.

The painting was recently restored, and repainting is evident in the area of the right side of the boy's face.

147 British School: *Thomas Lord as a boy* (Plate VII)

Private Collection.

Miniature (oval). *c.* 1765.

For Thomas Lord see pp. 30 and No. 153. He is also represented in Plate 5.

148 British School: *Cricket at Kenfield Hall* (Plate 49)

M.C.C.

Oil on canvas: 30½ × 46½ in. *c.* 1780.

Provenance: Sir Jeremiah Colman; Colman Gift.

Exhibited: Nottingham Castle Museum, *Exhibition of Cricket Pictures*, 1930 (3).

Literature: The Illustrated London News, 18 October 1919; *The Field*, 25 October 1919.

Kenfield Hall is at Pelham, near Canterbury. The picture illustrates the close relationship which has often existed between cricket ground and country house.

149 British School: *Boy with a Cricket Bat*

M.C.C.

Oil on canvas.

Literature: Viscount Ullswater, "The Long Room Pictures," in Sir Pelham Warner, *Lord's 1787-1945* (London, 1946).

The picture was at one time believed to be by Gainsborough. There are no apparent grounds for the erstwhile identification of the sitter with George IV as Prince of Wales. The picture has some odd stylistic features, and the painter seems to have misunderstood the design of a cricket bat of the period.

150 British School: *John Nyren*

M.C.C.

Oil on canvas: 9¼ × 6¾ in. *c.* 1805-10.

Provenance: Purchased in 1931 (see below).

Exhibited: National Book League, 1950.

John Nyren (1764-1837) published *The Young Cricketer's Tutor and Cricketers of my Time* in 1833. For comments on this influential work see pp. 10f.

This is presumably the picture mentioned in a letter of 25 March 1926, from Miss Mary Nyren (granddaughter of John Nyren) to F.S. Ashley-Cooper, in which she refers to an oil-painting of her grandfather in the possession of her sister and herself at Hythe, Kent.

151 British School: *Lord Hay as a Cricketer* (Plate XVII, Fig. 9)

Private Collection.

Oil on canvas: 66 × 42 in. *c.* 1810.

Provenance: By family descent.

The style has certain affinities with that of John Hoppner (1758?-1810). The sitter, James, Lord Hay (1797-1815), was the elder son of the 17th Earl of Erroll. The picture can be dated from the age of the sitter, who was born in 1797. He went to Eton, probably in 1811, and was killed in 1815 at Quâtre Bras. It was formerly assumed that the picture was painted while he was at Eton, and that the background shows a view of Windsor. The view, however (Fig. 9), seems likely to be of Slains Castle, the home of the Earls of Erroll, especially as the outline of the castle in the painting is similar to that of a nineteenth-century engraving of Slains Castle, after W.H. Bartlett. The painting shows the sea rather than a river, and the landscape, with its Scotch pines, seems altogether more typical of Scotland than the Home Counties.

This distinguished and charming painting is one of the last of the line of portraits of aristocratic youths with cricket bats painted on a large scale. There is a cricket ball at the bottom right. There are parallels for the thickness of the bat, notably in David Allan's *Cathcart Family* of 1784-5 (No. 2, Plate 42) and in Heny Edridge's *Young Cricketer* of *c.* 1810 (No. 45, Plate 64). Lord Hay was present at the famous ball on the eve of Waterloo given by the Duchess of Richmond, wife of the cricketing 4th Duke, famous as Col. Charles Lennox (who died of hydrophobia after he was bitten by a pet fox). It is possible that Lord Hay played in the cricket match held earlier that day. He was A.D.C. to General Peregrine Maitland, commanding the Brigade of Guards in the Waterloo campaign. During the Quâtre Bras engagement he was acting as Adjutant to Lord Saltoun and riding beside him outside a wood when something fell across Lord Saltoun's horse. "What was that?" Lord Saltoun asked. "That was Lord Hay, my lord," replied a private soldier, "but I have shot the Frenchman that did it."

Lord Hay had been presented to the Prince Regent a few days earlier and shaken the royal hand firmly instead of kissing it. The Prince was much amused and observed that "he had never seen so handsome a young soldier in the uniform of the Guards" (*The Reminiscences and Recollections of Captain Gronow* [1892], II, 254 f.).

152 British School: *Kennington Oval when a Nursery*

Collection of Simon Tindall, Esq.

Oil on composition painting panel: 20 × 29 in. *c.* 1810.

Provenance: Painted for F. Laundensark; Rutland Gallery, London, from which purchased by the present owner in 1980.

The view is from the Vauxhall end, towards what is now Harleyford Road, showing the site of The Oval before it became a cricket ground. There is an engraving of The Oval in 1846 (Surrey C.C.C.) showing the same view when it had become a cricket ground, as also a painting of 1847 by C. Rosenberg, junior (*fl.* 1844-1848). Inscribed on the back of this latter picture are the words *Kennington Oval, with the Market Gardeners' Dwelling turned into a Club House.*

153 British School: *Thomas Lord*

M.C.C.

Oil on canvas: 30 × 25 in. *c.* 1810.

Provenance: Presented by Miss Florence Lord in 1931.

Literature: Lord Harris and F.S. Ashley-Cooper, *Lord's and the M.C.C.: A Cricket Chronicle of 137 years, based on official documents, & published, with the knowledge and sanction of the Marylebone Cricket Club, to commemorate the centenary of the present ground* (London, 1914), repr. (Frontispiece); the *Morning Post*, 17 December 1931.

This well-known portrait of Thomas Lord (1755-1833), the founder of Lord's Cricket Ground, represents him in middle age. He wears a green coat with a white stock. The picture was formerly ascribed to George Morland (1763-1804). See also No. 147.

154 Anon: *An Eleven of Nottingham v. Leicester*

M.C.C.

Oil on canvas: 16 × 27½¼ in. *c.* 1829 (?).

Provenance: V. Jourado, 21 October 1931; Sir Jeremiah Colman, Bart.; Colman Gift, 1947.

Exhibited: Tate Gallery, 1934.

Literature: Sir Jeremiah Colman, *The Noble Game of Cricket* (London, 1941), Pl. 43.

Colman observes: "As the first County Match of Nottingham took place in 1835, the match here portrayed is presumably an XI of Nottingham or the 'Old Nottingham Cricket Club' *v.* Leicester. Such a match was played on July 27th, 1829, between The Town and an XI of Leicester...The contour of the hills suggests the ground on which the Notts. Forest Football Team now play. The notice on the board prints 'LEICESTERSHIRE' in capital letters. We may presume, therefore, that Notts. were the home team." (*The Noble Game of Cricket.*)

155 British School: *The First Grand Match of Cricket Played by Members of The Royal Amateur Society at Hampton Court Green on Wednesday, August 3rd, 1836*

Yale Center for British Art, New Haven, Connecticut, U.S.A. (921).

Oil on canvas: 22 × 33¼ in. 1836.

Provenance: John Mitchell in 1964.

Literature: J. Egerton, *The Paul Mellon Collection: British Sporting and Animal Paintings* (London, 1958), no. 353.

The "Royal Amateur Society" does not seem to be known: the main club at Hampton was the Royal Clarence Club, founded in 1828 under the patronage of the Duke of Clarence. The view is from the Cavalry Barracks, with "The Chequers" inn and the Royal Mews in the background on the right. Cricket at Hampton Court Green was painted some sixty years later by the French Impressionist Camille Pissarro (No. 92, Plate XXXII).

156 British School: *Portrait of a Batsman* (Plate 50)

Private Collection.

Oil on canvas: 24 × 20 in. *c.* 1840-50.

A characteristic and charming example of a small-scale cricket portrait of the mid-nineteenth century. The batsman is wearing a cap of the type found in representations of Felix of about the same time, i.e. *c.* 1840. The newly-invented splice of the bat is shown. In the background there is a tented pavilion of a kind seen in cricket pictures from early times. Attention may be drawn to the fact that the use of the word *pavilion* in relation to cricket appears as early as 1687 (*O.E.D.*). Confirmation of the fact that this was a tent is found in a newspaper report of 15 June, 1737: "There was a Pavillion [*sic*] erected for the Reception of His Royal Highness [Frederick, Prince of Wales], who was accompany'd by several Persons of Distinction." Indeed the word used for the tournament and campaign tents of medieval chivalry survived to be adopted as the appellation for the permanent structures which were ultimately to grace more modern cricket fields. In David Allan's *Cathcart Family* (No. 2, Plate 42) the cricket pavilion is in fact a military tent, which Lord Cathcart had borrowed from his regiment for the duration of the game. Thus there is nothing, we would suggest, to connect the word *pavilion* in its cricketing usage with the pleasure-buildings common in nineteenth-century country houses, in which Mark Girouard has seen its origin (cf. Mark Girouard, *The Return to Camelot* [Yale University Press, New Haven and London, 1981], pp. 238 f., p. 304, note 27).

157 British School: *George Whieldon at Lord's* (Plate XXI)

Collection of Simon Tindall, Esq.

Oil on board: 8½ × 6½ in. 1845.

Inscribed on the back: *George Whieldon, Wyke Hall Gillingham Dorset 1845, b. 1817, d. 1871.*

Provenance: Rutland Gallery, London, from which bought by the present owner in 1980.

George Whieldon played for Derbyshire in 1858. The picture is of particular interest because it has a good view of Lord's pavilion in the background. The sitter holds a spliced bat, a recent innovation.

158 British School: *Sir Emilius Bayley, Bart., as a boy* (Plate 51)

Private Collection.

Oil on canvas: 26 × 14 in. *c*. 1840.

Provenance: David A. Cross Fine Art Gallery, Bristol.

The painting is characteristic of cricket portraits of the middle of the nineteenth century in its small size, but is unusual in including an imposing column more customary in large-scale portraits.

Sir Emilius Bayley was the son of Sir John Bayley, Bart., President of M.C.C. in 1844. He is depicted while a schoolboy at Eton. He played in three successive Eton *v*. Harrow matches, and went on to play for Oxford and Kent.

159 Anon: *Edwin Paul of Middlesex*

Formerly in the collection of G.H. Weston, Esq.

Watercolour.

Edwin Paul (1822-1858) played for Middlesex, opening the innings at Lord's on 20 and 21 May 1850. He is buried in Highgate Cemetery. He was probably the owner of the Tufnell Park Cricket Ground, of which a drawing from this time survives (No. 160).

The flag in this picture carries the word *Copenhagen*, thus identifying the ground as that at Copenhagen House, Islington: the latter building is shown here, as also in James Pollard's painting of *A Cricket Match at Copenhagen House* (No. 94).

160 Anon: *Tufnell Park Cricket Ground*

Formerly in the collection of G.H. Weston, Esq.

Watercolour. Mid-nineteenth century.

This ground in north London was porbably owned by Edwin Paul, of whom a watercolour portrait survives (No. 159). It is noticeable that the ground evidently possessed permanent buildings in addition to pavilion tents (which are of a kind familiar from cricket pictures throughout the nineteenth century).

161 British School: *Charles Dickens bowling the first ball at a Charity Match at the back of Gad's Hill Place, near Rochester, September 16th, 18(68?)* (Plate 99)

M.C.C.

Oil on millboard: 11½ × 15½ in. *c*. 1868.

Provenance: Charles Dickens, Gad's Hill; Sotheby's, 17 February 1921, bought by Sir Jeremiah Colman; Colman Gift, 1947.

Exhibited: Nottingham Castle Museum, *Exhibition of Cricket Pictures*, 1930 (1); London, Victoria and Albert Museum, *Charles Dickens*, 1970 (M15).

Dickens lived at Gad's Hill Place from 1856 to 1870. A letter of 11 November 1931, from his son, Sir Henry E. Dickens, enclosed in the frame of this picture, gives the following information: "I cannot recall the 'Charity Match' which it represents; but it may have taken place when I was away at school or college. My father used to take the part of 'scorer' at the games we played there, and was sustained in that arduous job by the 'cooling drinks' provided for the guests who were staying in the house at the time or for the neighbours who came to see the games".

Dickens is shown bowling the first ball. If the ball was hit to the boundary it was his custom to present the batsman with a guinea. Another painting showing a cricket match at Gad's Hill was painted in 1860 by J. Shaw, and is also in the M.C.C. Collection. This is known as *Henry Dickens's XI v. Men of Kent*, and shows Dickens as the scorer.

Dickens's interest in cricket is also reflected in his ownership of No. 36 (Plate 101).

162 Anon: *Vallon des Anglais, Bois de la Cambre, Brussels* (Plate 87)

M.C.C.

Watercolour: 12 × 9¼ in. *c*. 1870.

For this watercolour see p. 44.

The identification of the site was made in 1946 by M.A. de Geradon, whose opinion was confirmed by Dr Bommer, formerly Keeper of the Royal Museums (Belgium), and by M. Lyna, head of the Bibliotèque Royale, Brussels.

See also No. 115.

163 British School: *W.G. Grace* (Plate 97)

National Portrait Gallery, London (2112).

Oil on canvas: 33½ × 27½ in.

Provenance: Given by the M.C.C. and other cricket clubs in 1926.

Acknowledgements

The authors and publishers wish to express their gratitude to the following for various forms of help or advice in the preparation of this book and of the exhibition **The Art of Cricket**:
Thos. Agnew & Sons Ltd., London; Mr. Brian Allen, The Paul Mellon Centre for British Art, London; Mr. Bert Avery, Gloucestershire County Cricket Club; Mr. Anthony Baer; Mr. I. Bartfield, National Gallery of Art, Washington, D.C.; Mr. Graham Beal; Mr. Stephen Blake, Cheltenham Art Gallery and Museum; Miss Domenica Blenkinsop, Bridgeman Art Library, London; Mr. J.W.G. Boucher, O.B.E., Headmaster, Thames County Primary School, Blackpool; Professor Alan Bowness, C.B.E., Director, The Tate Gallery; Mr. James Boyes, Headmaster, City of London School; Mr. Christopher Burgess, Surrey County Cricket Club; Cadbury Schweppes, plc; Professor Kenneth Cameron, F.B.A.; Mrs. Anne Campbell; Dr. Colin Campbell; Mr. David Clarke, Curator, Carlisle Museum & Art Gallery; Mr. Derek Clifford; Mr. Timothy Clifford, Director, City Art Gallery, Manchester; Mr. William Collier; Dr. Patrick Conner, Keeper of Fine Art, Royal Pavilion, Brighton; Mr. Michael Croker, Surrey County Cricket Club; Mr. David A. Cross, Fine Art Gallery, Bristol; Paul Deaville, Photography, Ltd., Blackburn; Mrs. Violet Dobson; Mr. William Drummond; Mr. Martin Drury, The National Trust; Mrs. Anthea Dundas-Bekker; Mr. J.A. Field; Dr. Celina Fox, Curator, Department of Paintings, Prints and Drawings, The Museum of London; Mr. David Fraser, City of Derby Museum and Art Gallery; Miss Janet Freeman; Mr. D.W. Fuller, Arthur Ackermann & Sons Ltd., London; Mr. Mark Girouard; Mr. Timothy Goodgue, Yale Center for British Art, New Haven, Conn., U.S.A.; Mr. Stephen Green, Curator, Memorial Gallery, M.C.C., Lord's Ground; Miss Sonia Halliday; Mr. Simon Harrison; Miss A.C.M. Hay; Miss Gill Hedley; The Laing Art Gallery, Newcastle upon Tyne; Dr. James Holloway, National Museum of Wales; Sir Westrow Hulse, Bart.; Mr. Robin Hutchison; Mr. Gervase Jackson-Stops; Mr. Richard Kendall; Mr. Keith Kissack; Mrs. Caroline Krzesinska, Assistant Keeper, Fine Art, City of Bradford Metropolitan Council; Mr. Peter Laws, Mr. Adrian Lewis and Mr. A.M. Llewellyn, Blackburn Museum & Art Gallery; Mr. Michael Liversidge, University of Bristol; Mrs. Cecily Lowenthal; Mr. Michael Lucey, Memorial Gallery, M.C.C., Lord's Ground; Miss Laura Lushington; Miss Margaret Macfarlane, Hampshire County Museum Service; Mr. F.J. McCarthy; Mr. John Millard, Curator, Laing Art Gallery, Newcastle upon Tyne; Sir Iain Moncreiffe of that Ilk; Mr. B.G. Murray, Archivist, Cadbury Schweppes, plc; Mrs. Evelyn Newby; The Nottinghamshire County Cricket Club; Mr. John Nutting; Mr. H.A. ("Ossie") Osborne, Sussex County Cricket Club; Mrs. Robin Paisey, Leicester City Museum and Art Gallery; Mr. C.G.A. Paris; Mr. David Phillips (formerly of the Castle Museum, Nottingham); Sir John Carew Pole, Bart.; Mr. Martin Postle, Institute of European Studies, London; Mr. Benedict Read; Mr. Joseph Rishel, Philadelphia Museum of Art; Mr. Duncan Robinson, Director, Yale Center for British Art, New Haven, Conn., U.S.A.; Mr. & Mrs. Peter Rook; Mr. John Rowlands, Keeper, Department of Prints and Drawings, The British Museum; The Rutland Gallery, London; Dr. Andrew Sanders; Mrs. Janet Saraty; Mr. E. Rotan Sargent, C.C. Morris Cricket Library, Haverford College, Pennsylvania, U.S.A.; Mr. Ian Searle; Mr. James Sellick; Mr. Jacob Simon, The Iveagh Bequest, Kenwood; Dr. Michael Smith, University of Bristol; Mr. Julian Spalding, Sheffield City Art Galleries; Miss Caroline Stapylton-Thorley, Thos. Agnew & Sons Ltd., London; Mr. Timothy Stevens, Director, Walker Art Gallery, Liverpool; Mr. C. Strange, Barclays Bank Trust Co. Ltd.; Miss Miranda Strickland-Constable, Temple Newsam House, Leeds; Mr. Patrick Strong, Eton College; Mr. John Sunderland, Witt Librarian, Courtauld Institute of Art, University of London; Mr. Simon Tindall; Mrs. Rosemary Treble; Mr. Michael Trinnick, The National Trust; Mr. Stanley Warburton, Lancashire County Cricket Club; Mr. Roger Webb, Petworth; Mr. G.H. Weston; Sir Richard Baker Wilbraham, Bart., and Lady Baker Wilbraham; Mr. Stephen Wildman, Birmingham City Art Gallery; Miss Victoria A.G. Williams, Hastings Museum & Art Gallery; Mr. Cedric Wood; Mr. John Wood, Gallery Framers, Nottingham; Sir Marcus Worsley, Bart.; His Honour Judge Christopher Young and Mrs. Christopher Young.

Photographic Acknowledgements.

The authors and publishers desire to thank the following for permission to reproduce works of art in their possession or care, or to reproduce photographs for which they hold the copyright:

The Marylebone Cricket Club and the Bridgeman Art Library:
Plates 5,6,7,8,9,10,11,12,13,14,15,18,20,21,25,47,49,57,59,60,61,65,69,70,73, 74,75,77,78,79,82,84,98,99,100,101,103,VI,XXIV,XXV.
Alinari, Florence, and the Mansell Collection, London: Figs. 5,6,7. Messrs. Arthur Ackermann and Son Ltd., London: 37. Thos. Agnew & Son Ltd.: 64. Blackburn Museum and Art Gallery: XXXI. The Bodleian Library, Oxford: 3. Thames County Primary School, Blackpool: XXX. The University of Bristol: 29. The Corporation Art Gallery, Bury: 94. Cadbury Schweppes, plc, Bournville: 105. Carlisle City Art Gallery: 63. The Rt. Hon. The Earl Cathcart: 42. Robert Chapman Photography, Plymouth: 28, XIII. The City of London School: 55, Fig. 10. Arthur Cooper Ltd., London: 46,88,89. The Witt Library, Courtauld Institute of Art, University of London: 22, 71. Mr. David Cross, The Fine Art Gallery, Bristol: 51. Prudence Cuming Associates Ltd., London: 40. Paul Deaville Ltd.: XXXI. Derby City Museum and Art Gallery: X. Mr. William Drummond: 86 English Life Publications: XI. The Provost and Fellows of Eton College: XXII. The Fitzwilliam Museum, Cambridge (University of Cambridge): 43. Mr. Charles Goater, Nottingham: XXIX. The National Maritime Museum, Greenwich: Fig. 8. Sonia Halliday Photographs: I. Harvert Consultancy (Holdings) Ltd, Dundee: 95. Sir Westrow Hulse, Bart.: 27. The Jeu de Paume, Paris: 106. The Lady Lever Art Gallery, Port Sunlight, and the Walker Art Gallery, Liverpool: XVIII. The Laing Art Gallery, Newcastle upon Tyne: V. Temple Newsam House, Leeds (Leeds City Council): 76. Leicester Museum and Art Gallery: 26. The Lord's Taverners: 109. Maidstone Public Library: 22. The Paul Mellon Centre for British Art and British Culture, London: 31,32. The Paul Mellon Collection: 56. Mr. Roy Miles: XXVI. John Mitchell & Son, Ltd.: 45. The Museum of London: 23,58. The National Portrait Gallery, London: 97. The National Trust: 1, 48, XIX. Nottinghamshire County Cricket Club: XXIX. Mr. John Nutting: XVI. Phaidon Press, Oxford: 30. Sir John Carew Pole, Bart.: 28. Mr. Peter Rook.: 83. Mr. Robin Ross and Morgan Wells Associates Ltd.: 17, XVI, XVII, Fig. 9. The Rutland Gallery, London: 104. Dr. Andrew Sanders: 54. Commander Michael Saunders Watson: XI. Southampton Art Gallery: 35. Surrey County Cricket Club: 108. The Tate Gallery, London: 16, 33, 96, VIII,IX,XII,XXVII, Fig. 4. The Most Hon. The Marquess of Tavistock: 52,53. Mr. Simon Tindall: XXI. The Victoria and Albert Museum, London: 62. The Wakefield City Art Gallery: 107. The National Gallery of Art, Washington, D.C., U.S.A. (The Aisla Mellon Bruce Collection): XXXII. Sir Marcus Worsley, Bart.: 110. The Yale Center for British Art, New Haven, Conn., U.S.A.: 36, 44.

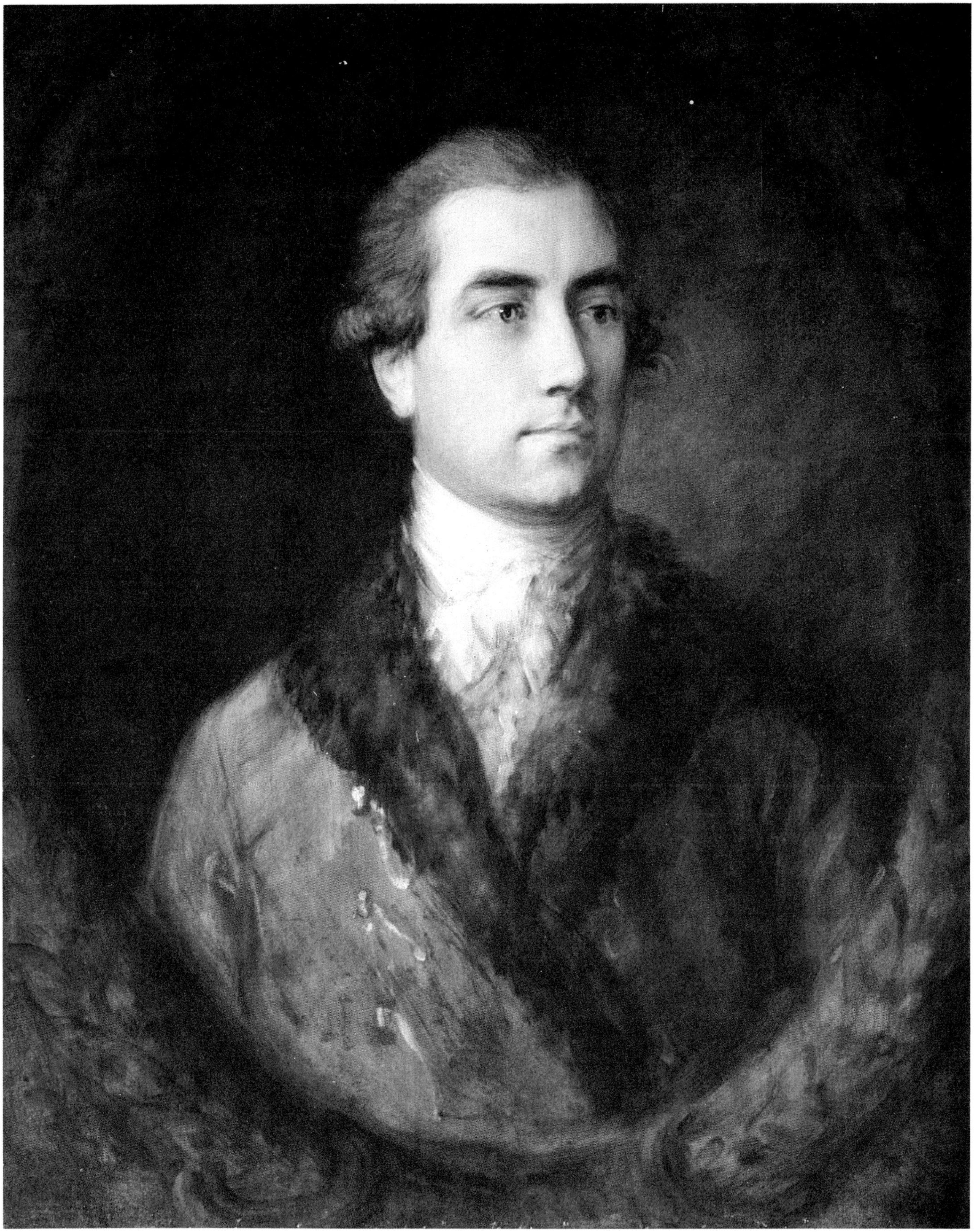

1. Thomas Gainsborough, R.A.: *John Frederick Sackville, 3rd Duke of Dorset* (1782) (Lord Sackville, Knole Park).

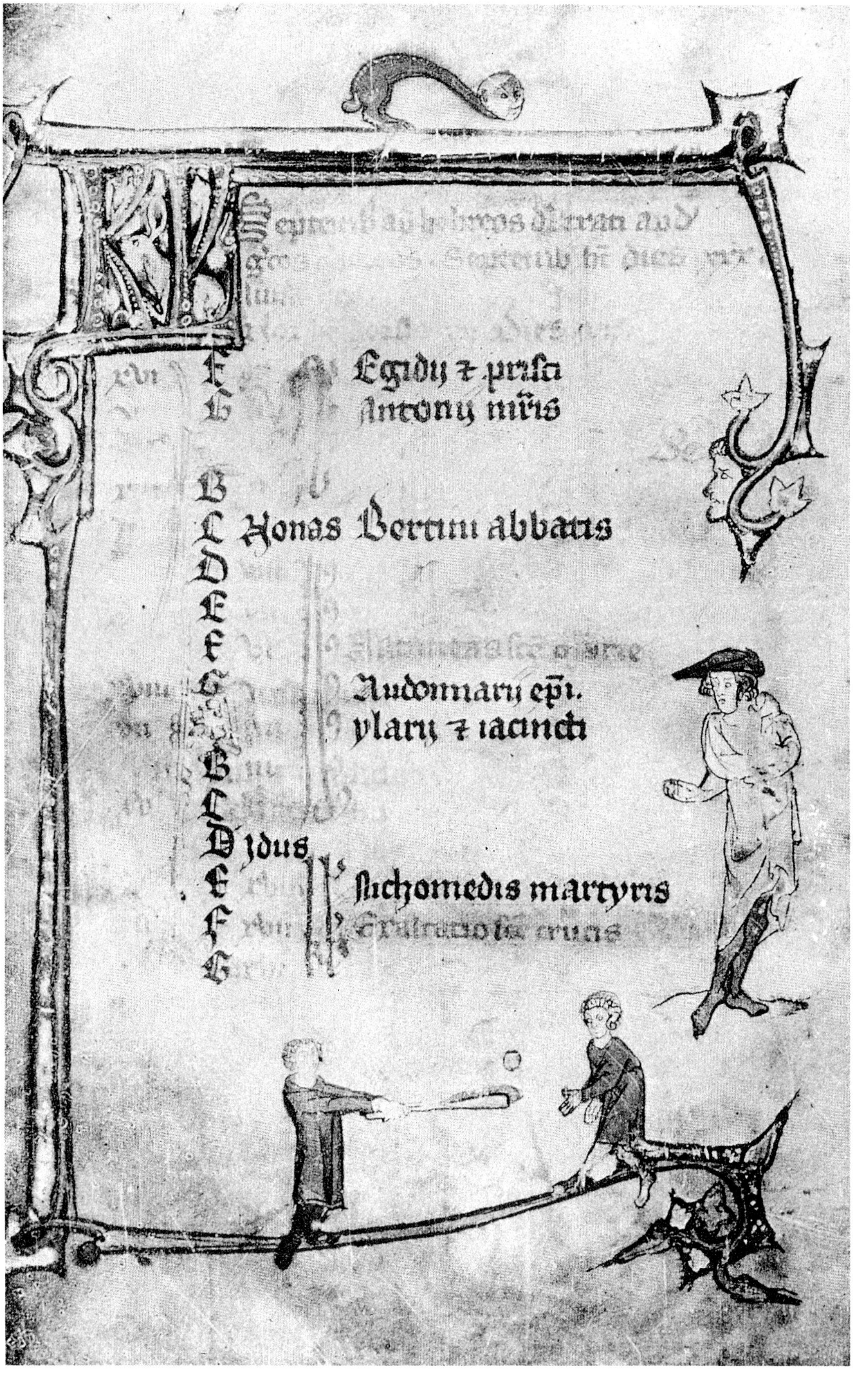

2. *"A Game of Cricket"* (*c*. 1300): Schilling MS. (Private Collection).

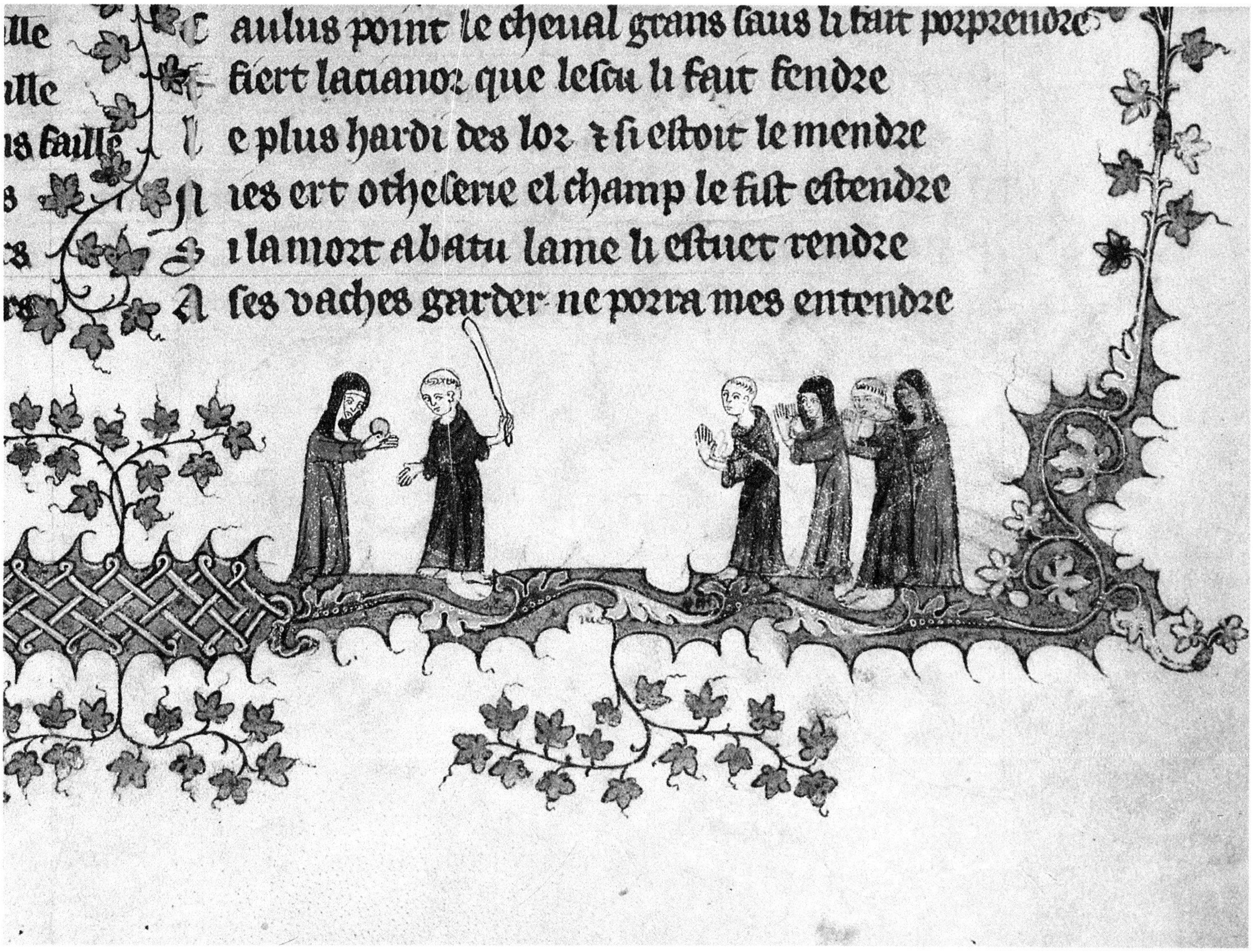

3. *"A Game of Cricket"* (*c*. 1340): MS. Bodl. 264, fol. *22r* (Bodleian Library, Oxford).

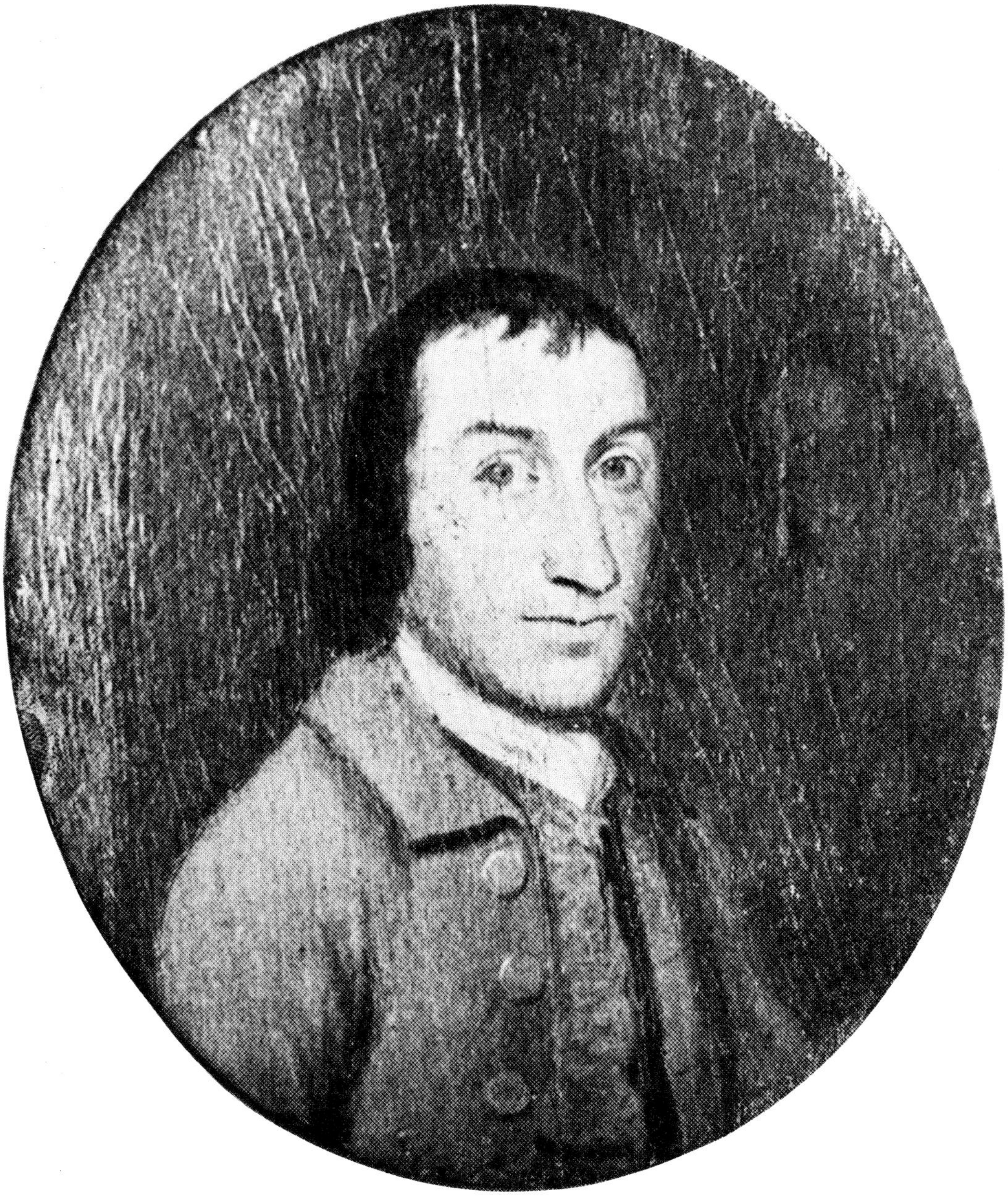

4. Almond: *Edward ("Lumpy") Stevens* (1783) (Lord Sackville, Knole Park).

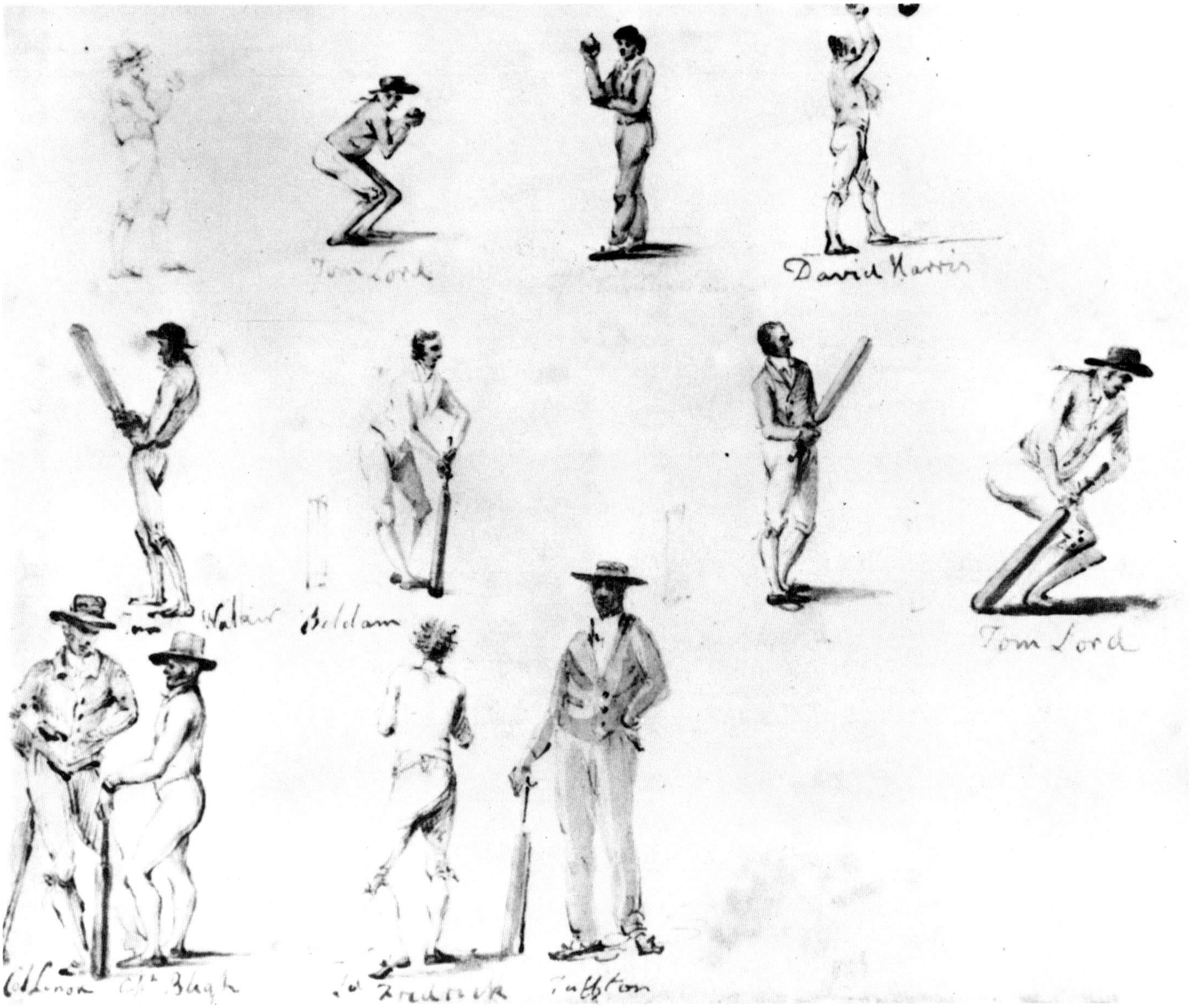

5. George Shepheard: *Twelve Cricketers in Characteristic Attitudes* (M.C.C.).

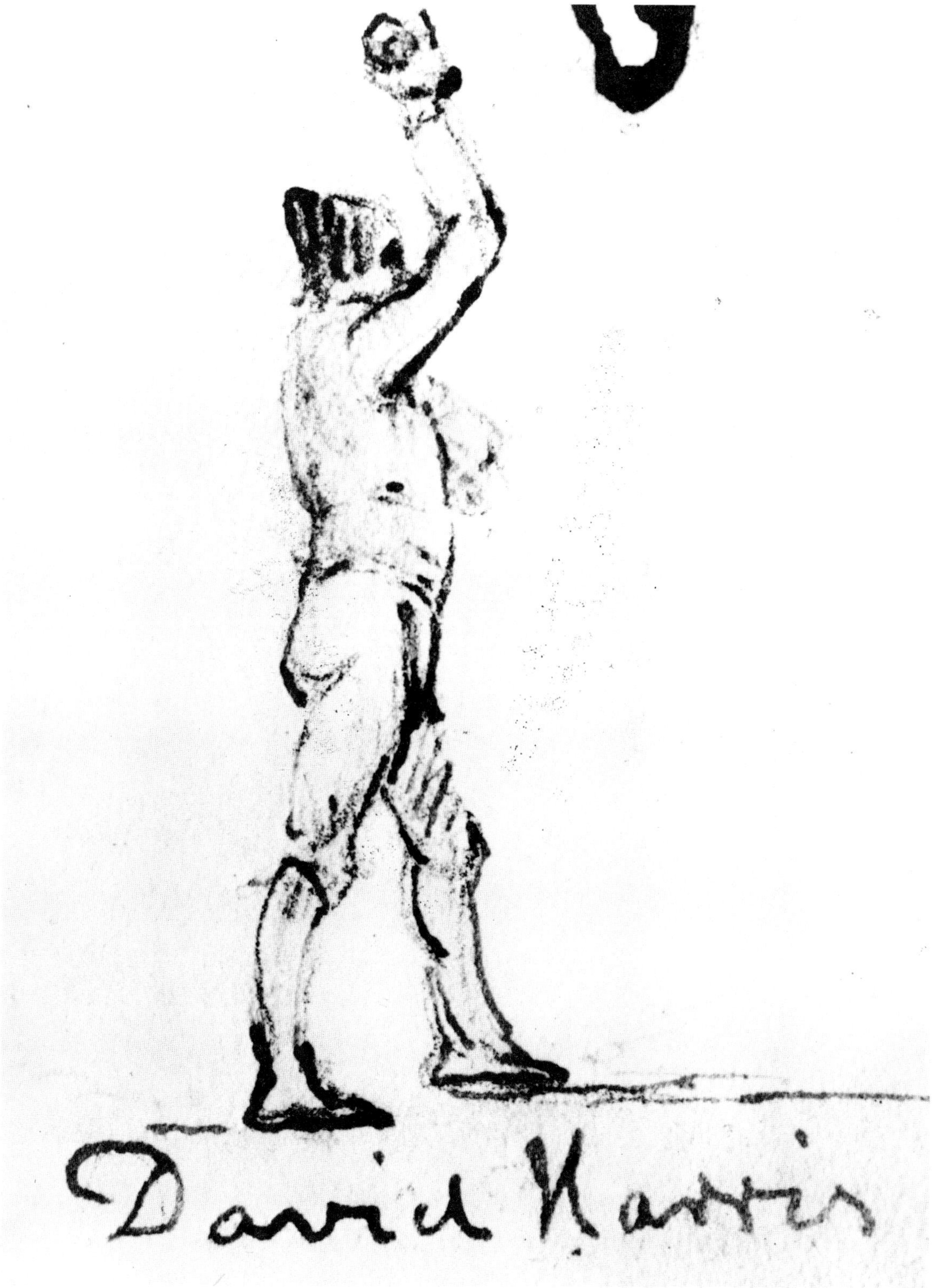

6. George Shepheard: *David Harris* (detail of Plate 5).

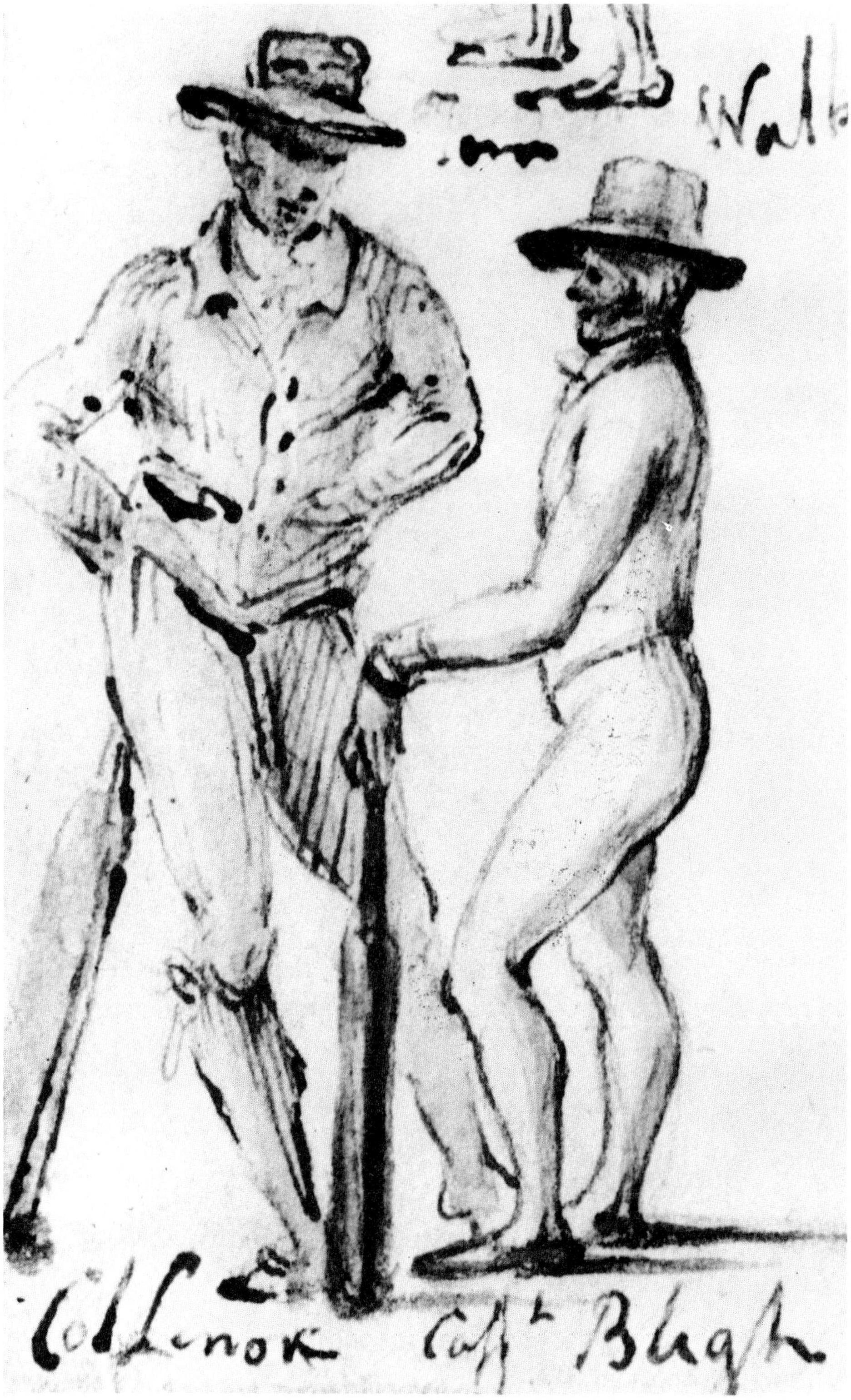

7. George Shepheard: *Charles Lennox and Captain Bligh* (detail of Plate 5).

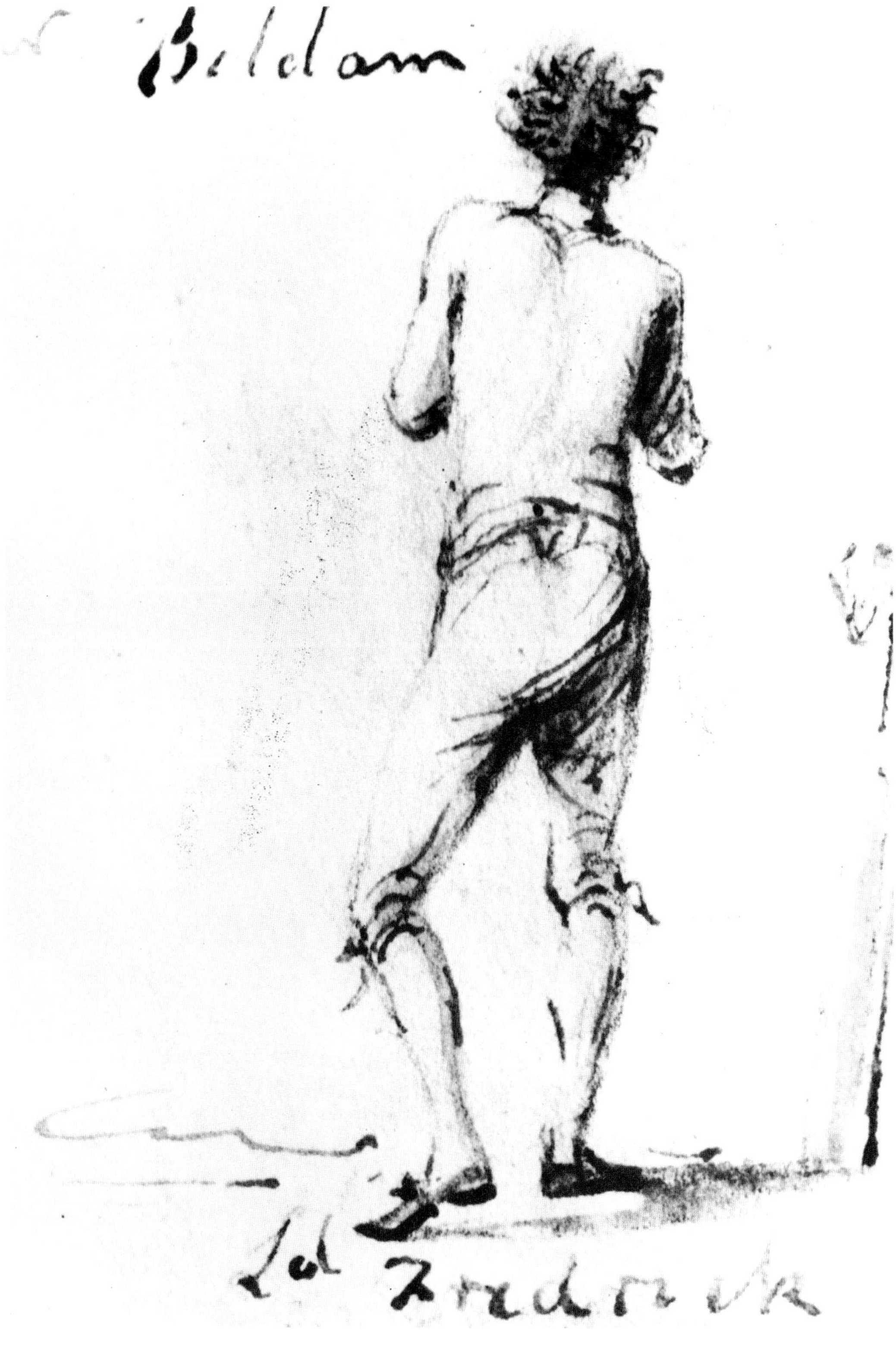

8. George Shepheard: *Lord Frederick Beauclerk* (detail of Plate 5).

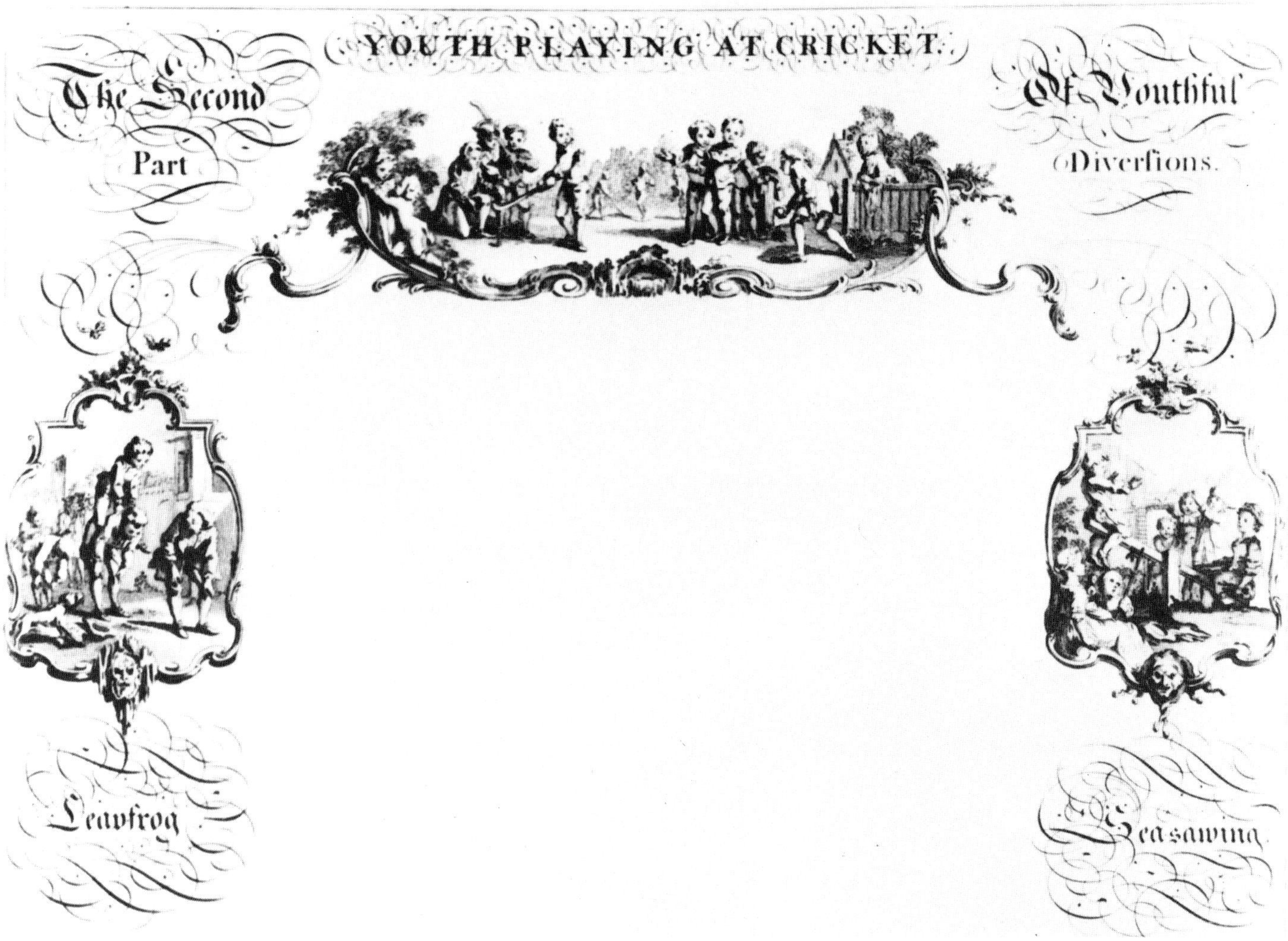

9. J. Cole *after* H. F. B. Gravelot: *Youth playing Cricket.*

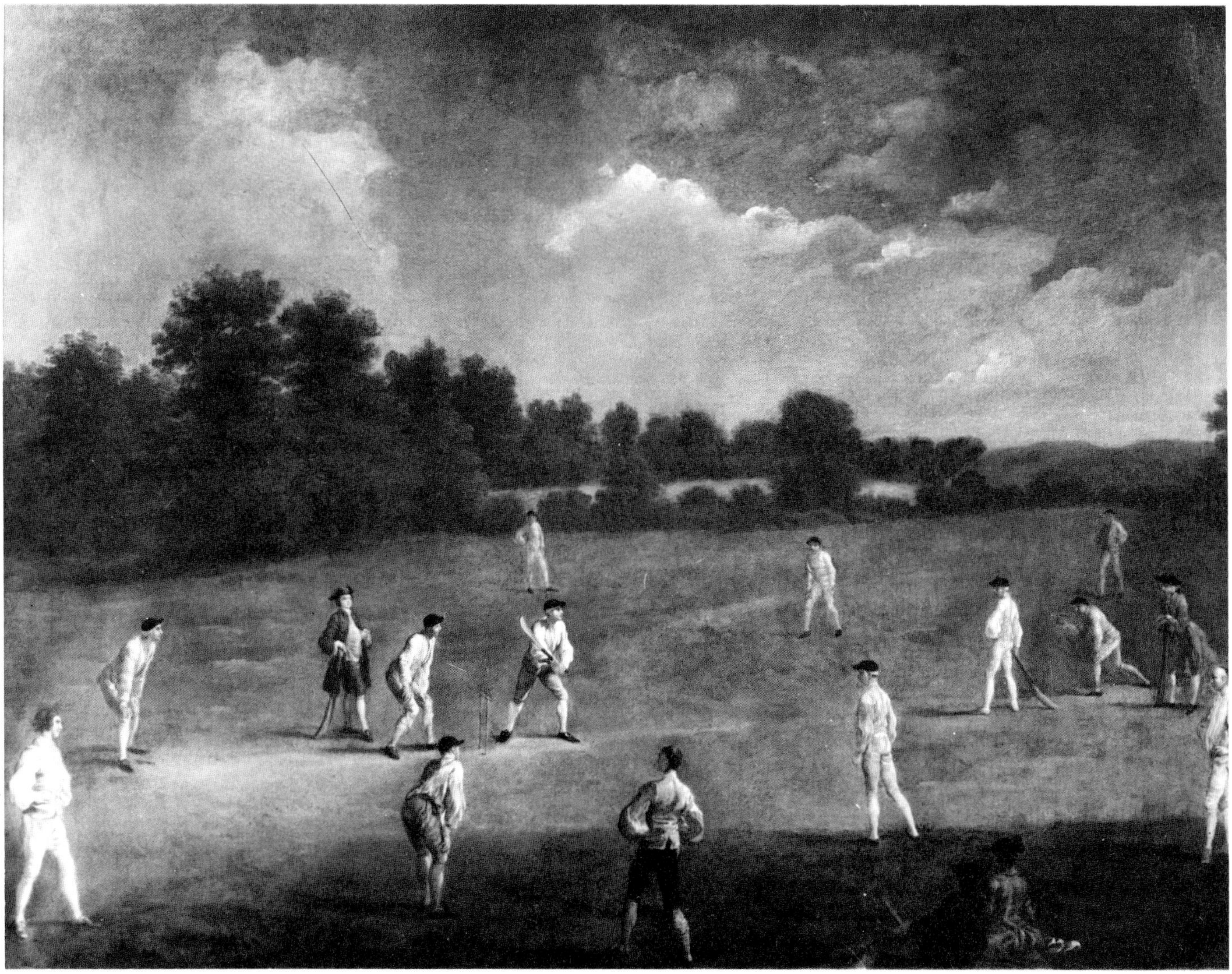

10. Francis Hayman, R. A.: *"Cricket in Marylebone Fields"* (*c*. 1743-7) (M.C.C.).

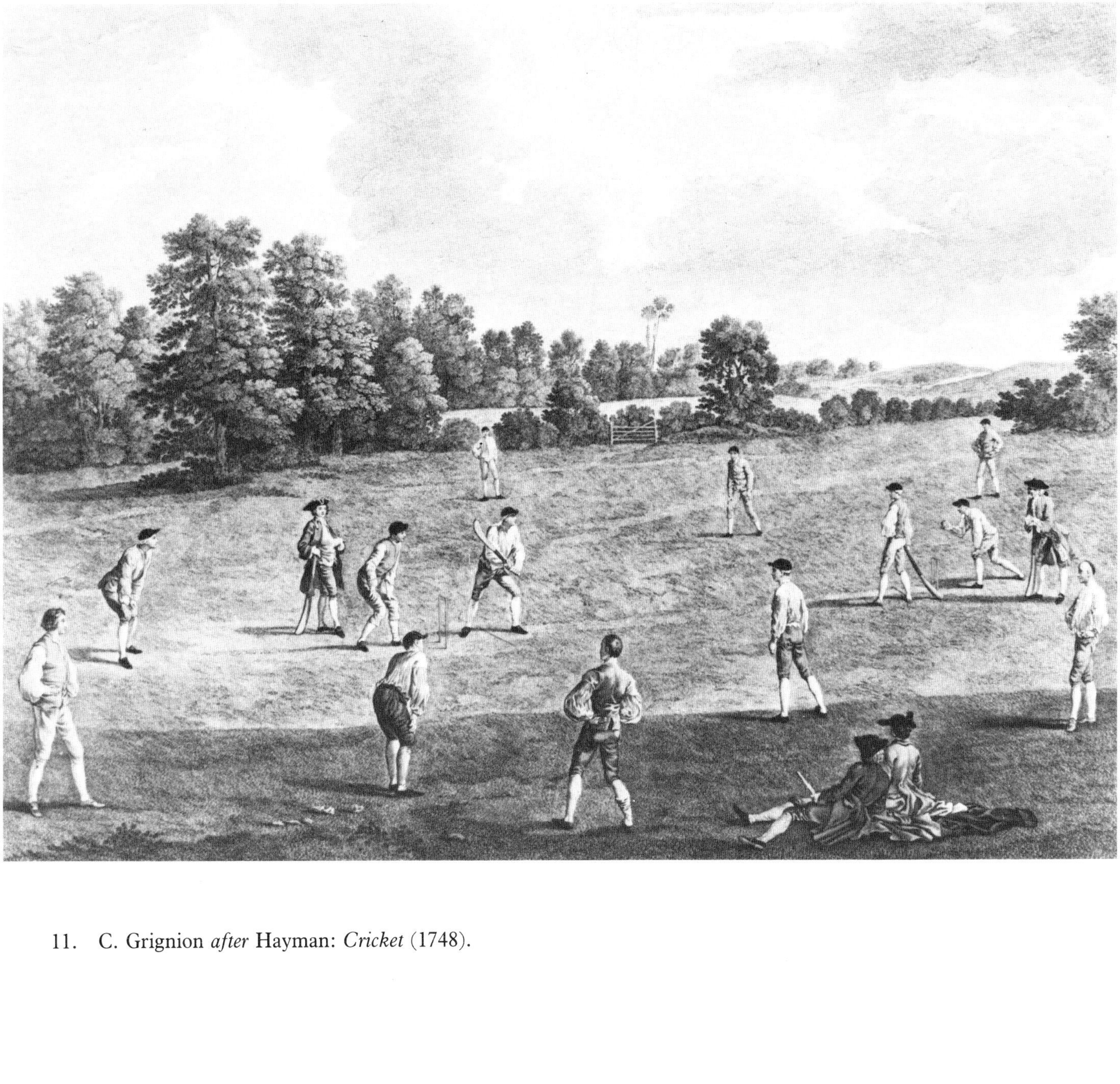

11. C. Grignion *after* Hayman: *Cricket* (1748).

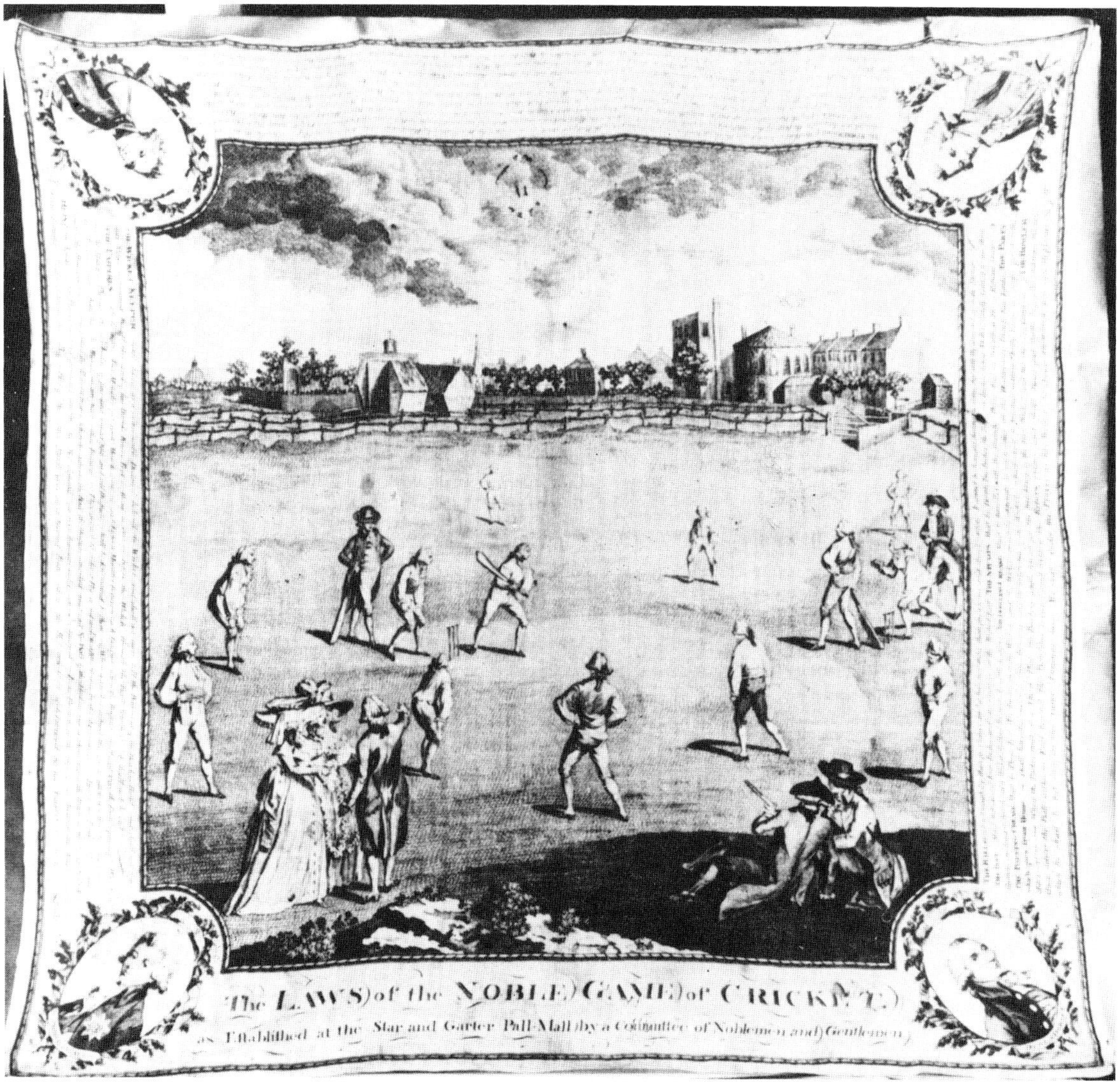

12. Handkerchief with *The Laws of the Noble Game of Cricket* (M.C.C.).

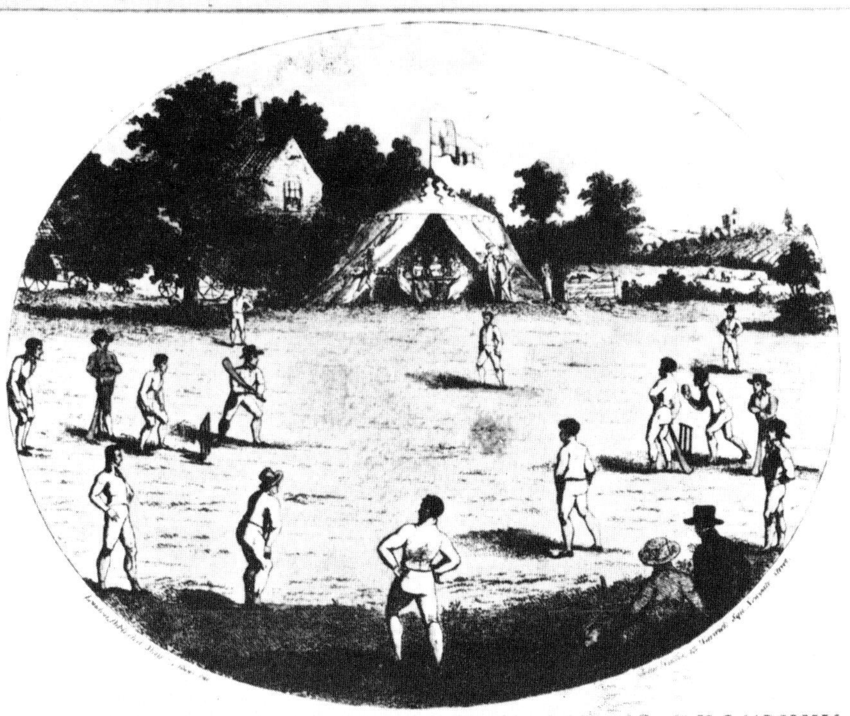

The LAWS of the NOBLE GAME of CRICKET

as revised by the Club at St Mary-le-bone

THE BALL muſt weigh not leſs than Five Ounces and a Half, nor more than Five Ounces and Three Quarters. At the beginning of each Innings either party may call for a New Ball.

THE BAT

Muſt not exceed Four Inches and One Quarter, in the wideſt part.

THE STUMPS

Muſt be Twenty-four inches out of the ground, the BAILS Seven Inches in length.

THE BOWLING CREASE

Muſt be in a line with the Stumps, three Feet in length, with a Return Crease.

THE POPPING CREASE

Muſt be Three Feet Ten Inches from the Wicket, and parallel to it.

THE WICKETS

Muſt be oppoſite to each other, at the diſtance of Twenty-two yards.

THE PARTY WHICH GOES FROM HOME

Shall have the choice of the Innings, and the pitching of the Wickets, which ſhall be pitched within Thirty Yards of a center fixed by the Adverſaries.

When the Parties meet at a Third Place, the Bowlers ſhall toſs up for the pitching of the Wickets, and the choice for going in.

It ſhall not be lawful for either party during a Match, without the conſent of the other, to alter the Ground, by rolling, watering, covering, mowing, or beating. This rule is not meant to prevent the Striker from beating the ground with his Bat near where he ſtands during the Innings, or to prevent the Bowler from filling up holes, watering his ground, or using ſawduſt, &c. when the ground is wet.

THE BOWLER

Shall deliver the Ball with one foot behind the Bowling Crease, and within the Return Creaſe, and ſhall bowl four Balls before he changes Wickets, which he ſhall do but once in the ſame Innings.

He may order the Striker at his Wicket, to ſtand on which ſide of it he pleaſes.

THE STRIKER IS OUT

If the Bail is bowled off, or the Stump bowled out of the ground.

Or, if the Ball, from a ſtroke over or under the Bat, or upon his hand, (but not wriſts) is held before it touches the ground, although it be hugged to the body of the Catcher.

Or, if in ſtriking, or at any other time while the Ball is in play, both his feet are over the Popping Creaſe and his Wicket put down, except his Bat is grounded within it.

Or, if in ſtriking at the ball he hits down his Wicket.

Or, if under pretence of running a Notch, or otherwise, either of the Strikers prevent a Ball from being caught, the Striker of the Ball is out.

Or, if the Ball is ſtruck up, and he wilfully ſtrikes it again.

Or, if in running a Notch the Wicket is ſtruck down by a throw, or with the Ball in Hand, before his Foot Hand or Bat is grounded over the Popping Crease. But if the Ball is off, the Stump muſt be ſtruck out of the ground.

Or, if the Striker touches or takes up the Ball while in play, unleſs at the requeſt of the other Party.

If with his foot or leg he ſtops the Ball, which the Bowler in the opinion of the Umpire at the Bowler's Wicket ſhall have pitched in a ſtraight line to the Wicket, and would have hit it.

If the Players have crossed each other, he that runs for the Wicket which is put down, is out; if they are not croſſed, he that has left the Wicket which is put down, is out.

When a Ball is caught, no Notch to be reckoned.

When a Striker is run out, the Notch they were running for is not to be reckoned.

If loſt Ball is call'd, the Striker ſhall be allowed four, but if more than four are run before loſt Ball is call'd, then the Striker to have all they have run.

When the Ball has been in the Bowler's or Wicket-keeper's hands, it is conſidered as no longer in play; and the Strikers need not keep within their ground, till the Umpire has called Play, but if the player goes out of his gronnd with an intent to run before the ball is delivered, the Bowler may put him out.

If the Striker is hurt, he may retire from his Wicket, and have his Innings at any time in that Innings.

If a Striker is hurt, some other Perſon may be allowed to ſtand out for him, but not go in.

If any Perſon ſtops the Ball with his Hat, the Ball is to be conſidered as dead, and the oppoſite Party to add Five Notches to their Score; if any are run, they are to have five in all.

If the Ball is struck up, the Striker may guard his Wicket either with his Bat or his Body.

In single Wicket Matches, if the Striker moves out of his ground to strike at the Ball, he shall be allowed no Notch for ſuch ſtroke.

THE WICKET KEEPERS

Shall stand at a reaſonable diſtance behind the Wicket, and ſhall not move till the Ball is out of the Bowler's hand, and ſhall not by any noiſe incommode the Striker; and if his hands, knees, feet, or head, be over, or before the Wicket, though the Ball hit it, it ſhall not be out.

THE UMPIRES

Are the sole judges of fair and unfair play, and all diſputes ſhall be determined by them; each at his own Wicket: but in caſe of a Catch, which the Umpire at the Wicket cannot ſee ſufficiently to decide upon, he may apply to the other Umpire, whoſe opinion is conclusive.

They ſhall allow Two Minutes for each man to come in, and Fifteen Minutes between each Innings; when the Umpire ſhall call *Play*, the party refusing to Play ſhall loſe the Match.

They are not to order a player out, unless appealed to by the Adverſaries.

But if the Bowler's foot is not behind the Bowling Creaſe, and within the return Creaſe, when he delivers the Ball, they muſt, unasked, call *No Ball*.

If the Striker runs a ſhort Notch, the Umpire muſt call *No Notch*.

The Umpire of the Bowler's Wicket, ſhall be first applied to decide on all Catches.

The Umpires are not to be changed during the Match, but by the consent of both Parties.

BETS.

If the Notches of one Player are laid against another, the Bets depend on the First Inning, unless otherwiſe ſpecified.

If the Bets are made upon both Innings, and one Party beats the other in one inning, the Notches in the First Inning ſhall determine the Bet.

But if the other Party goes in a ſecond time, then the Bet must be determined by the number on the Score.

Published by John Wallis, 13, Warwick-Square, London.

13. Broadsheet of *The Laws of the Noble Game of Cricket as revised by the Club at St. Mary-le-bone* (John Wallis, publisher: London, 1809) (M.C.C.).

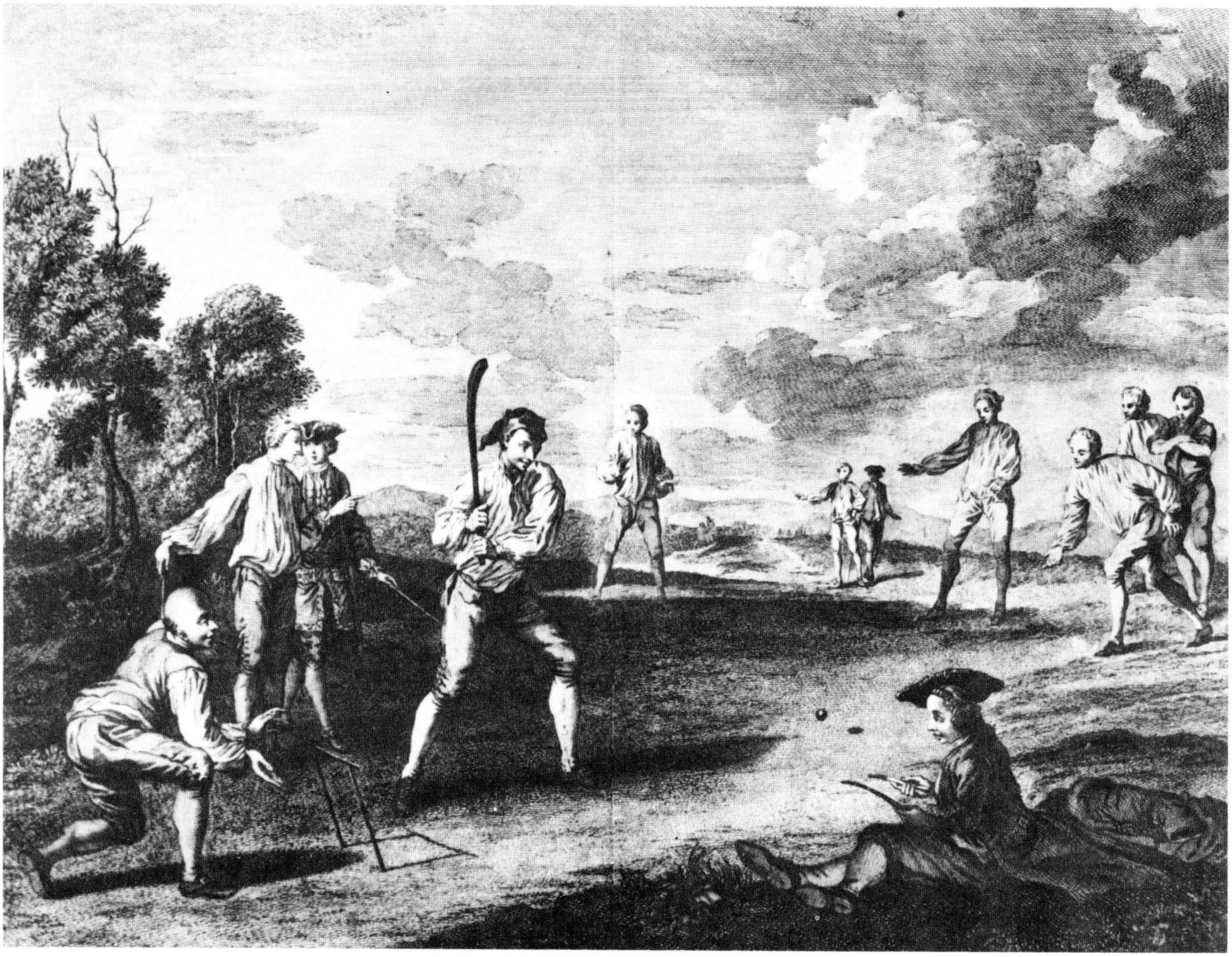

14. C. Benoist *after* Hayman: *Cricket* (1743).

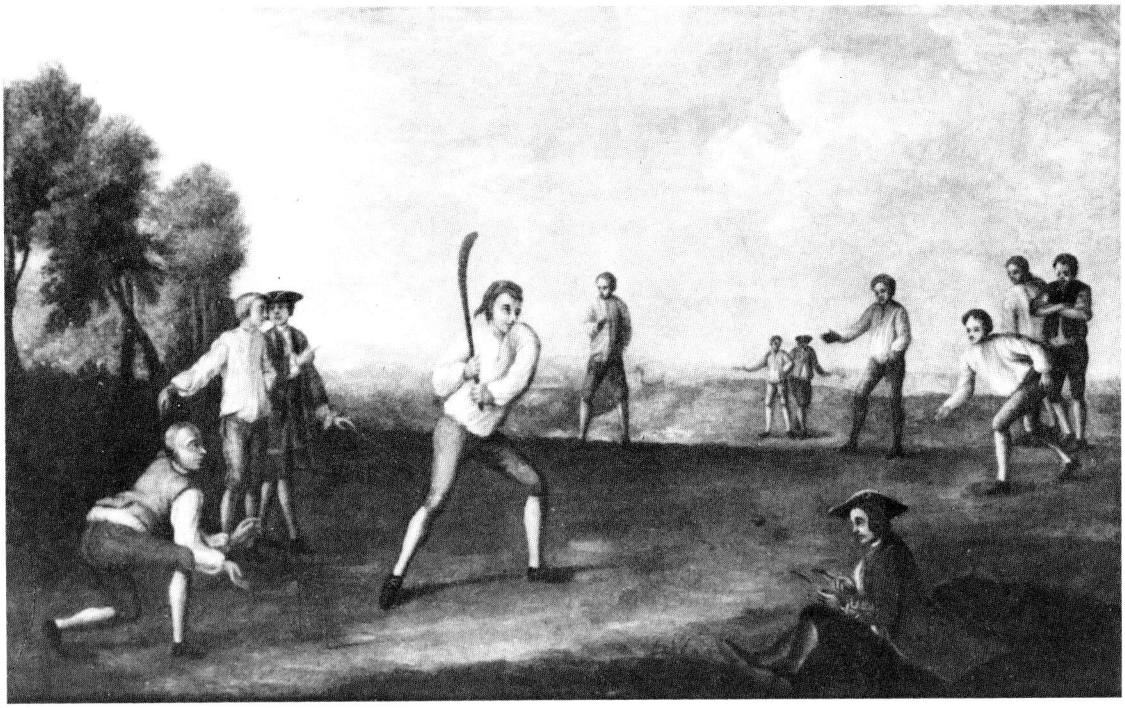

15. Unknown copyist *after* Benoist (*after* Hayman): *"Cricket at the Artillery Ground"* (M.C.C.).

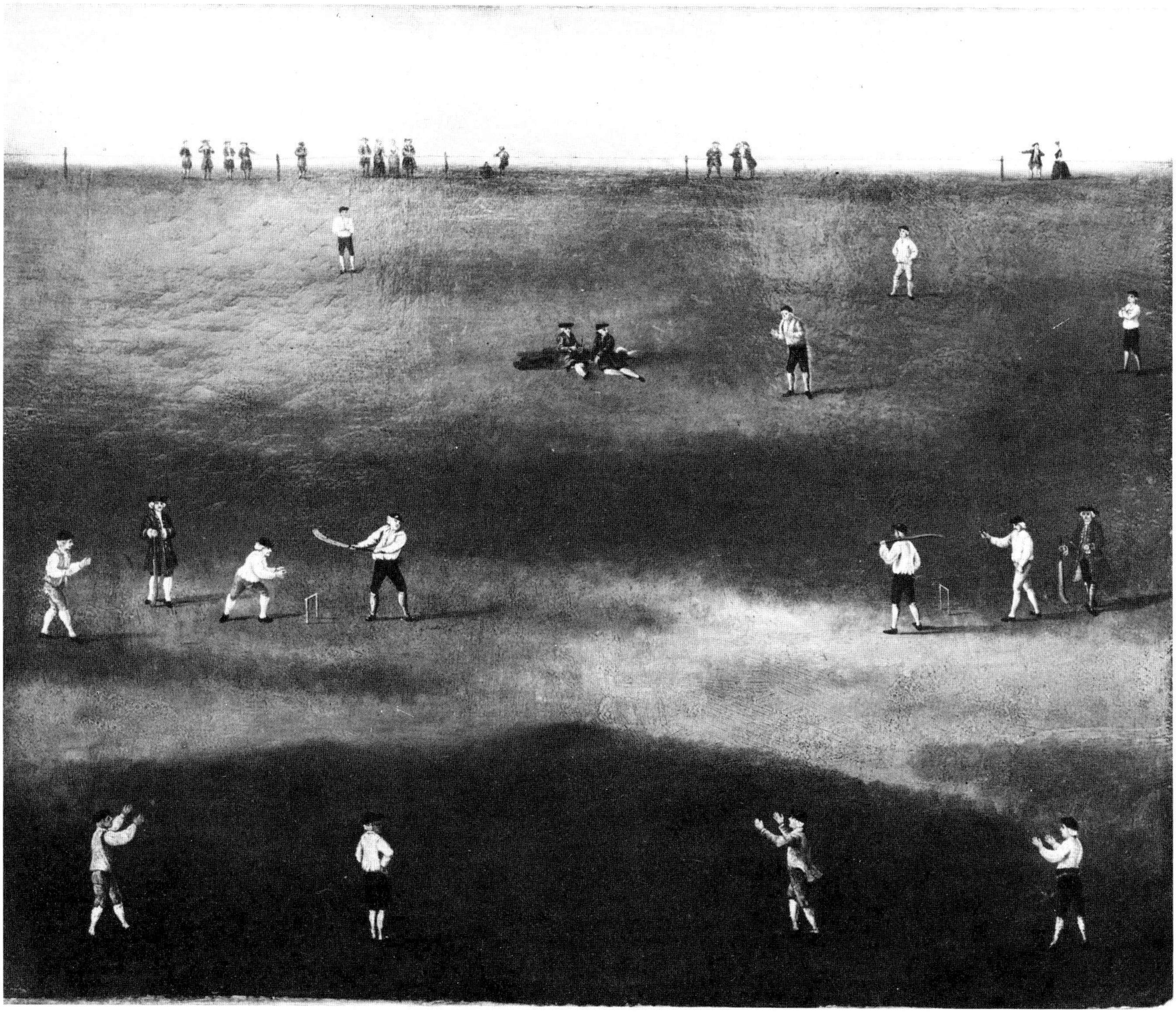

16. *Attributed to* W.R. Coates: *A Cricket Match* (*c.* 1743-5) (Tate Gallery, London).

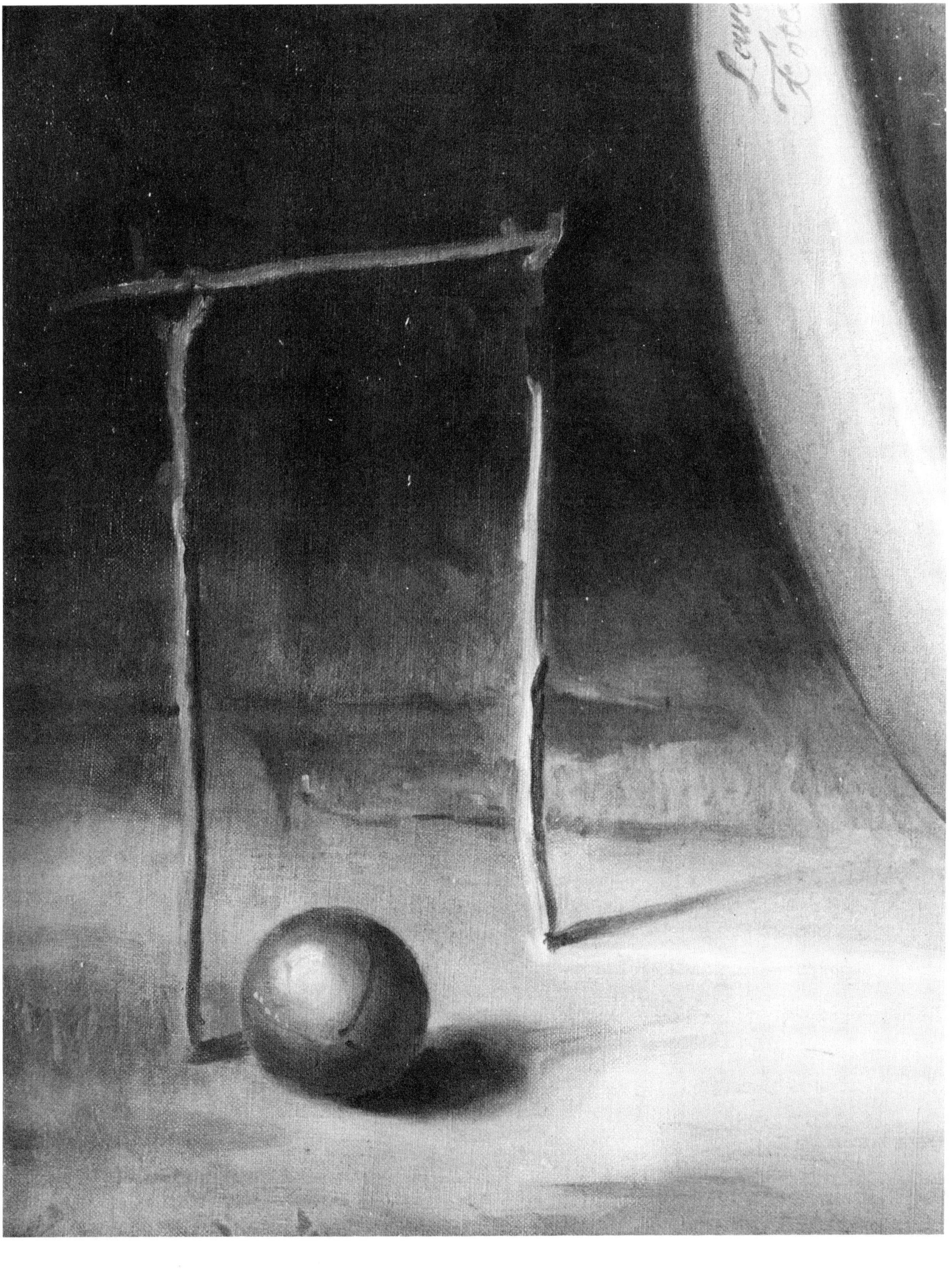

17. Francis Cotes, R.A.: Wicket and ball (1768): detail of Plate XVIII.

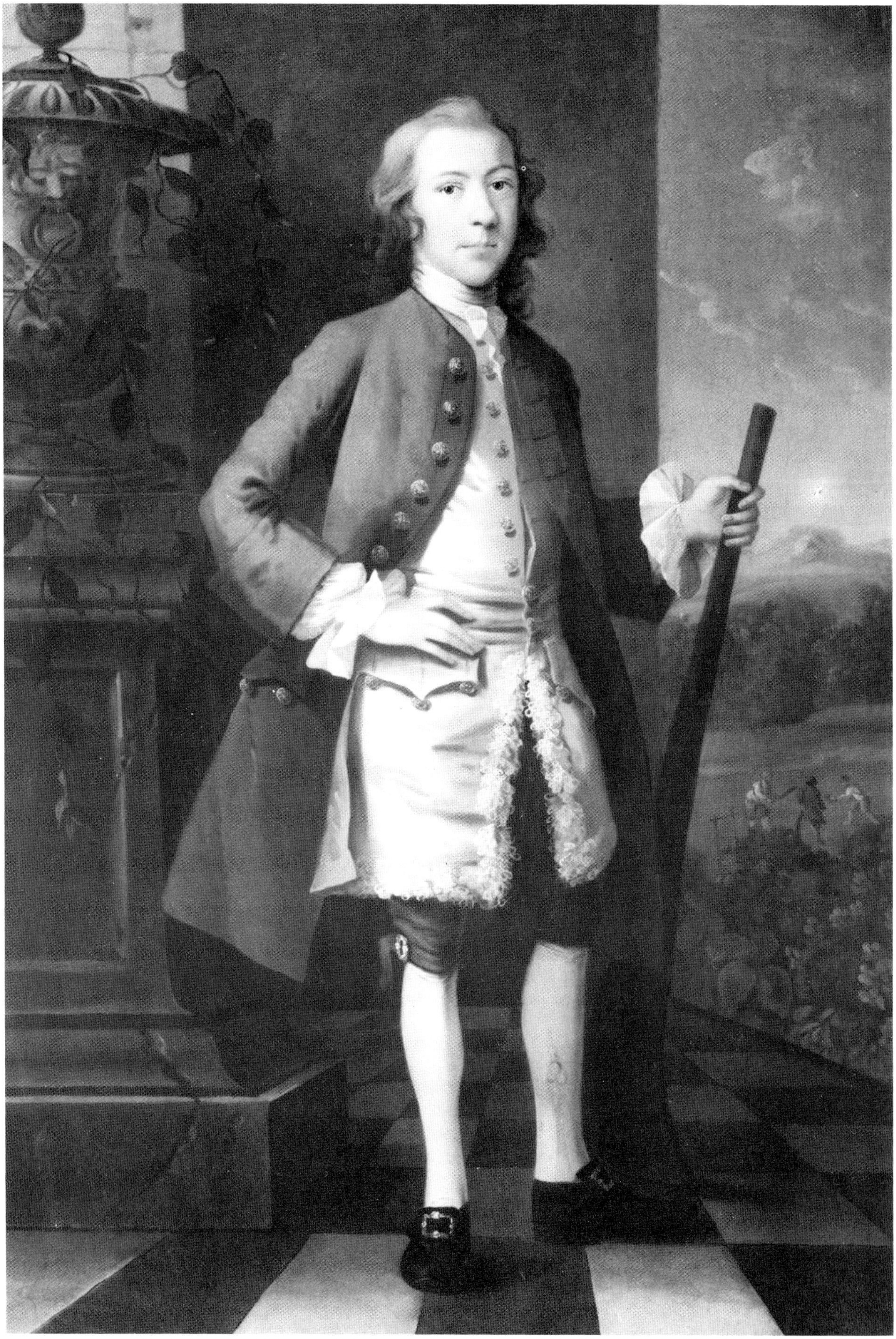

18. Robert Scaddon: *William Rice* (1744) (M.C.C.).

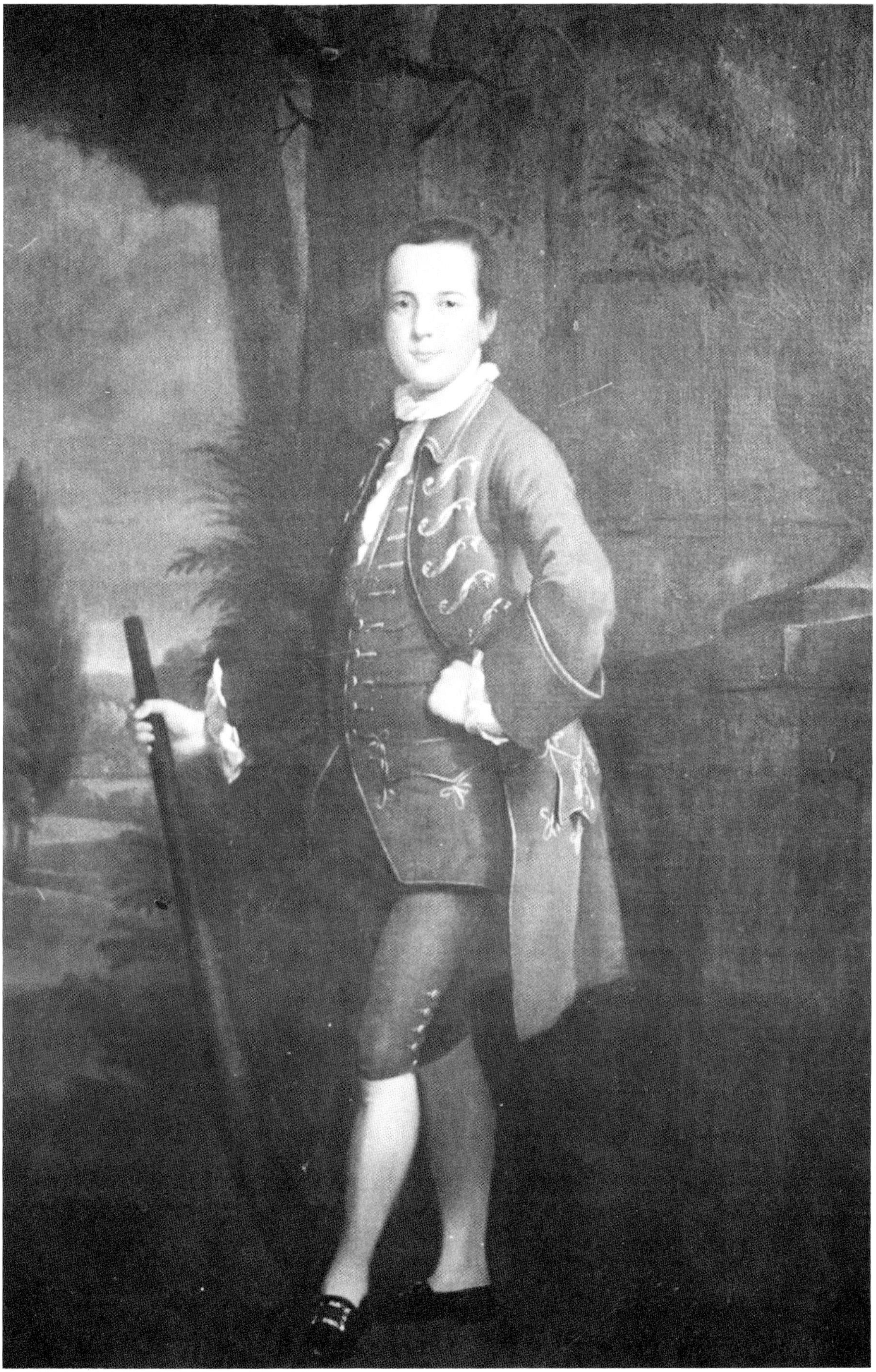

19. British School: *The Lansdowne Boy* (*c*. 1740-5) (Private Collection).

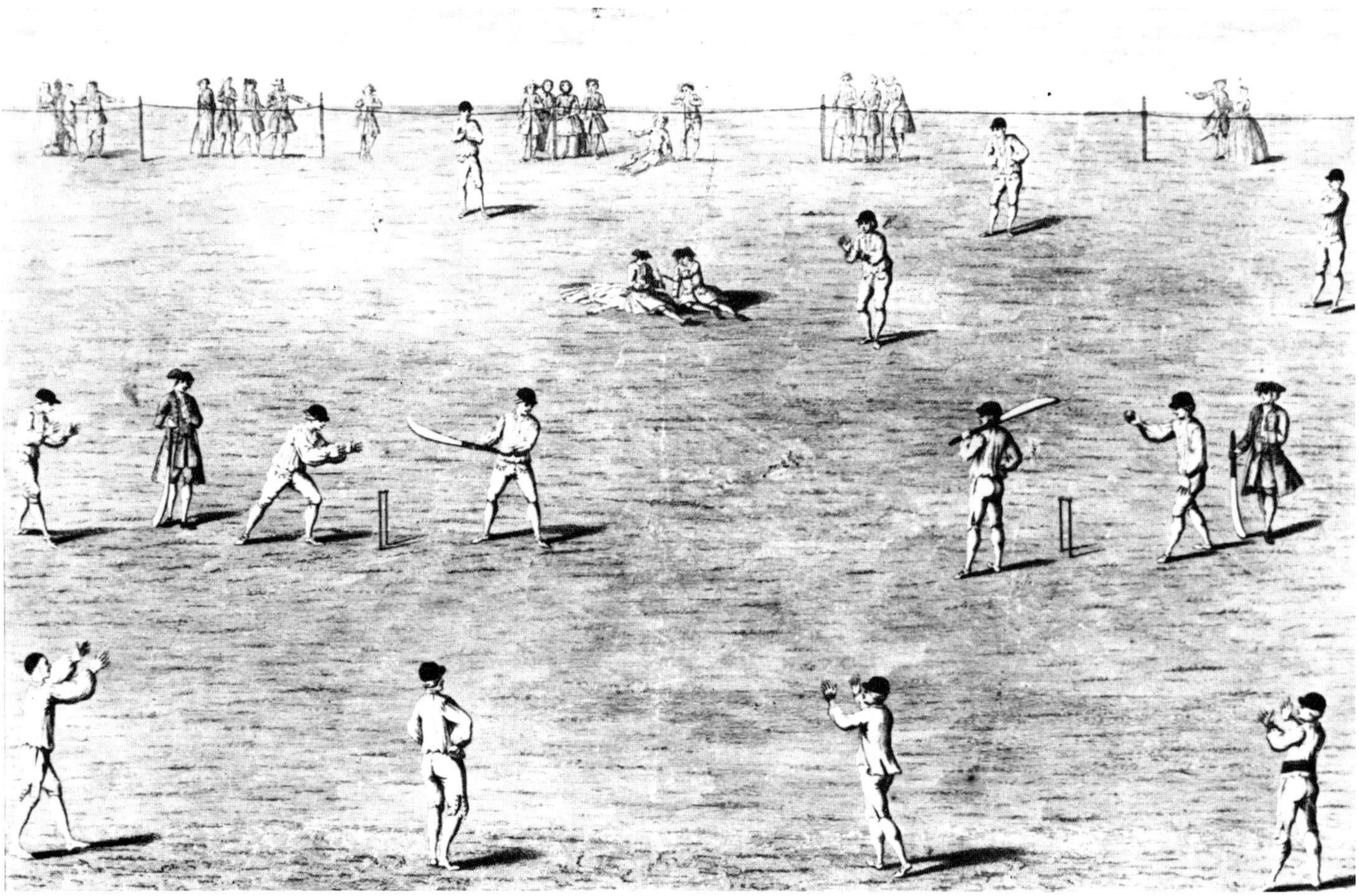

20. H. Roberts *after* L.P. Boitard: *An Exact Representation of the Game of Cricket* (1743).

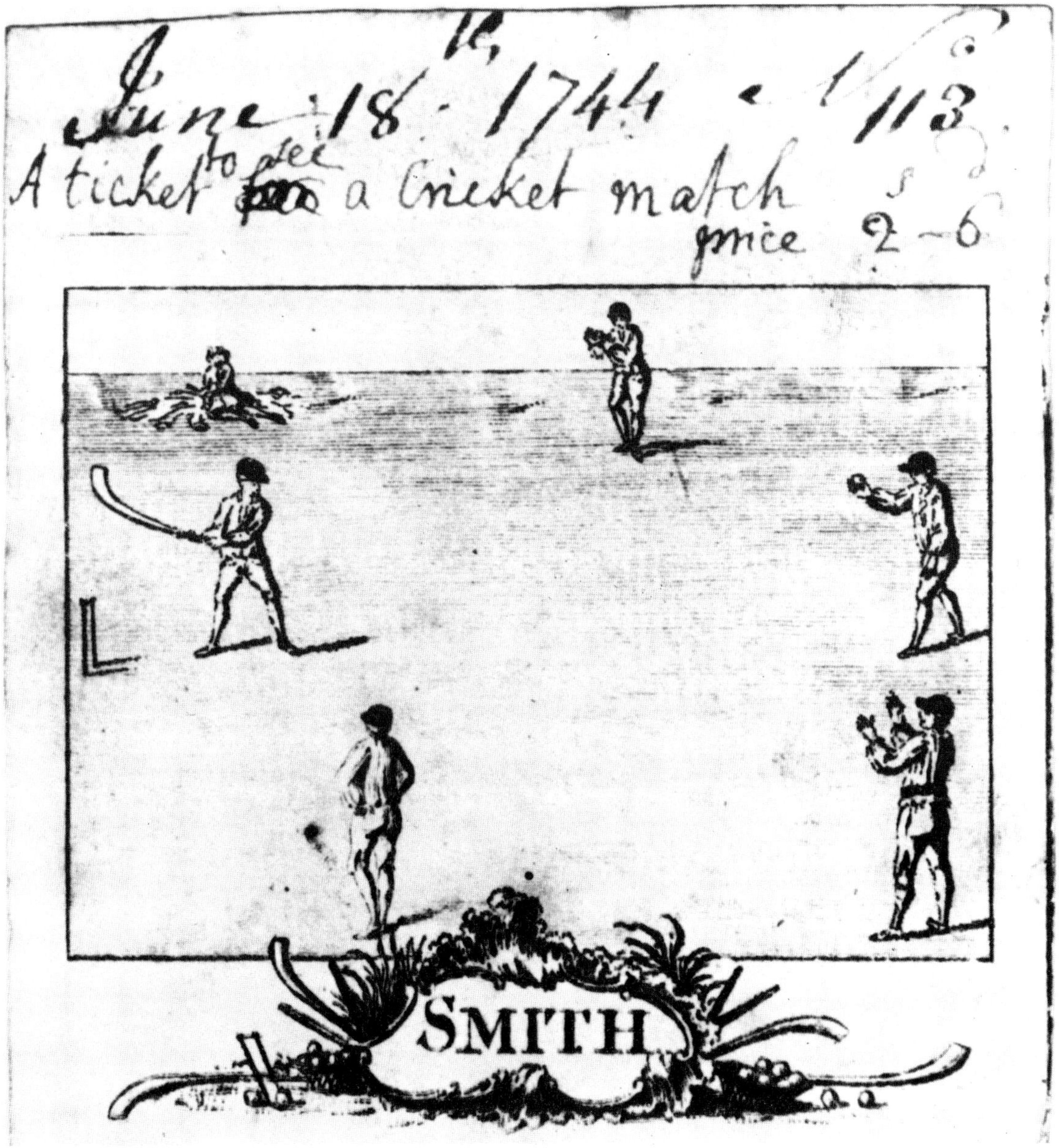

21. Match Ticket of 1744 (M.C.C.).

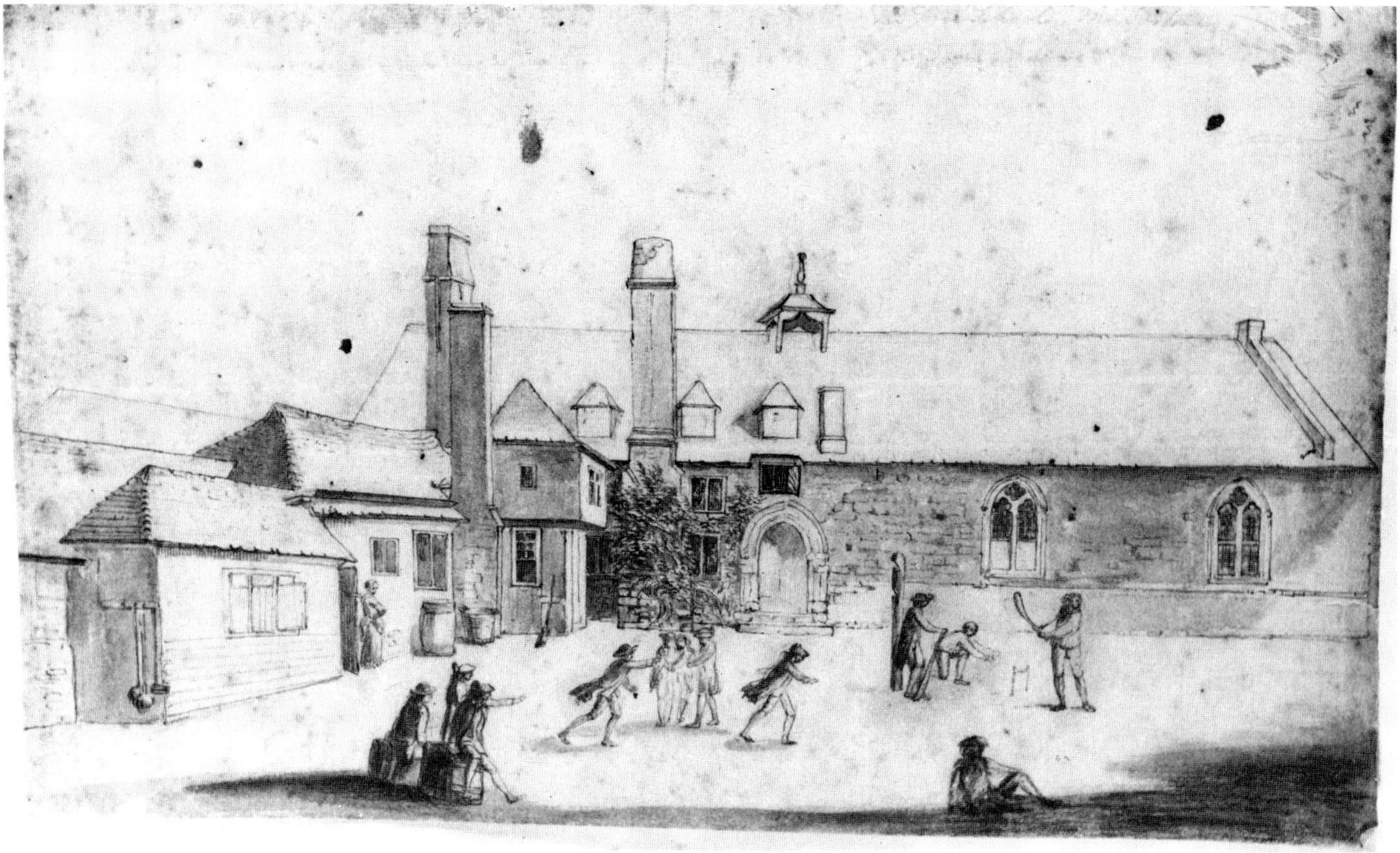

22. William Jefferys: *The Free School at Maidstone* (Maidstone Public Library).

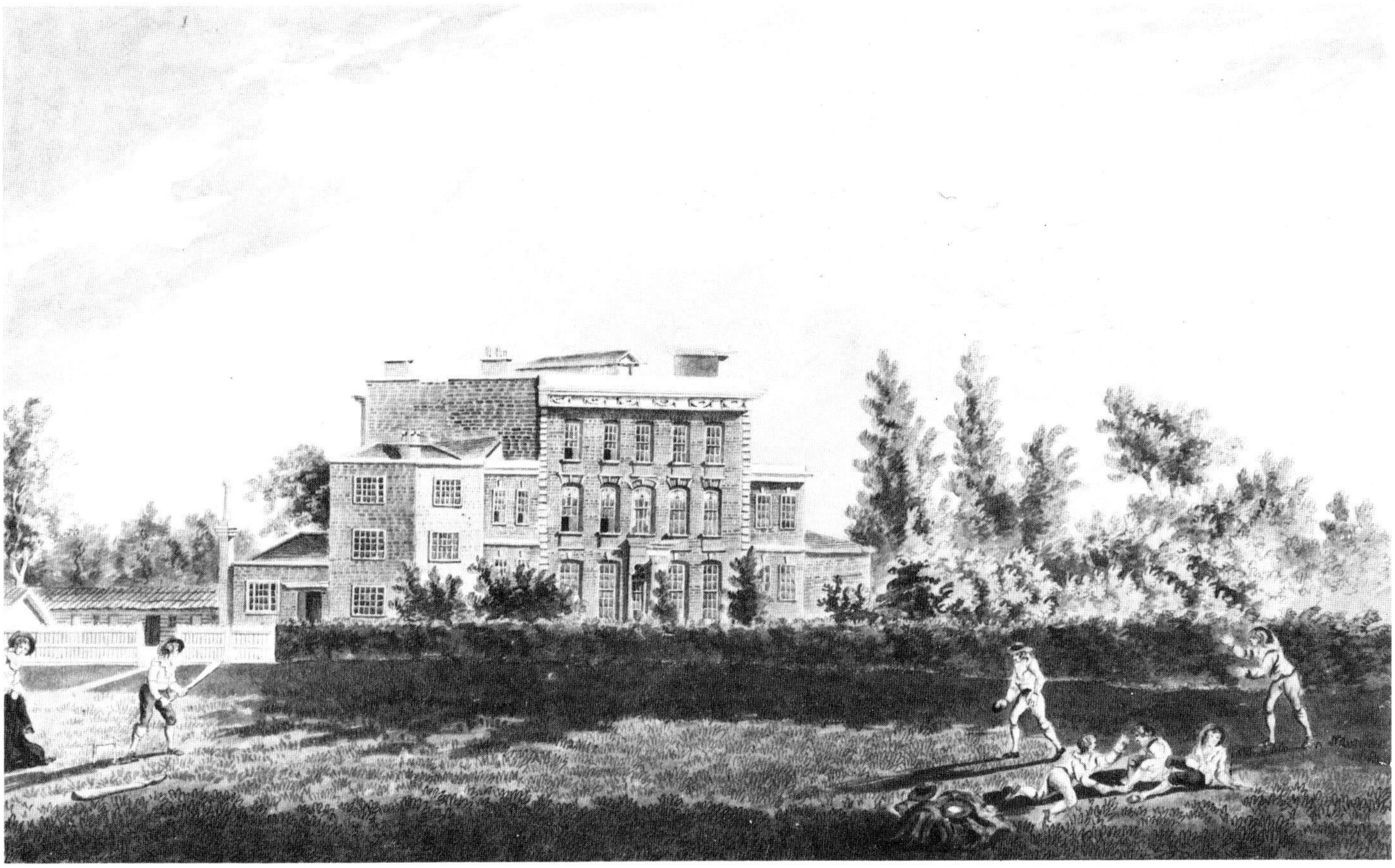

23. *Attributed to* James Miller: *Carmalt School, Putney* (*c.* 1780) (Museum of London).

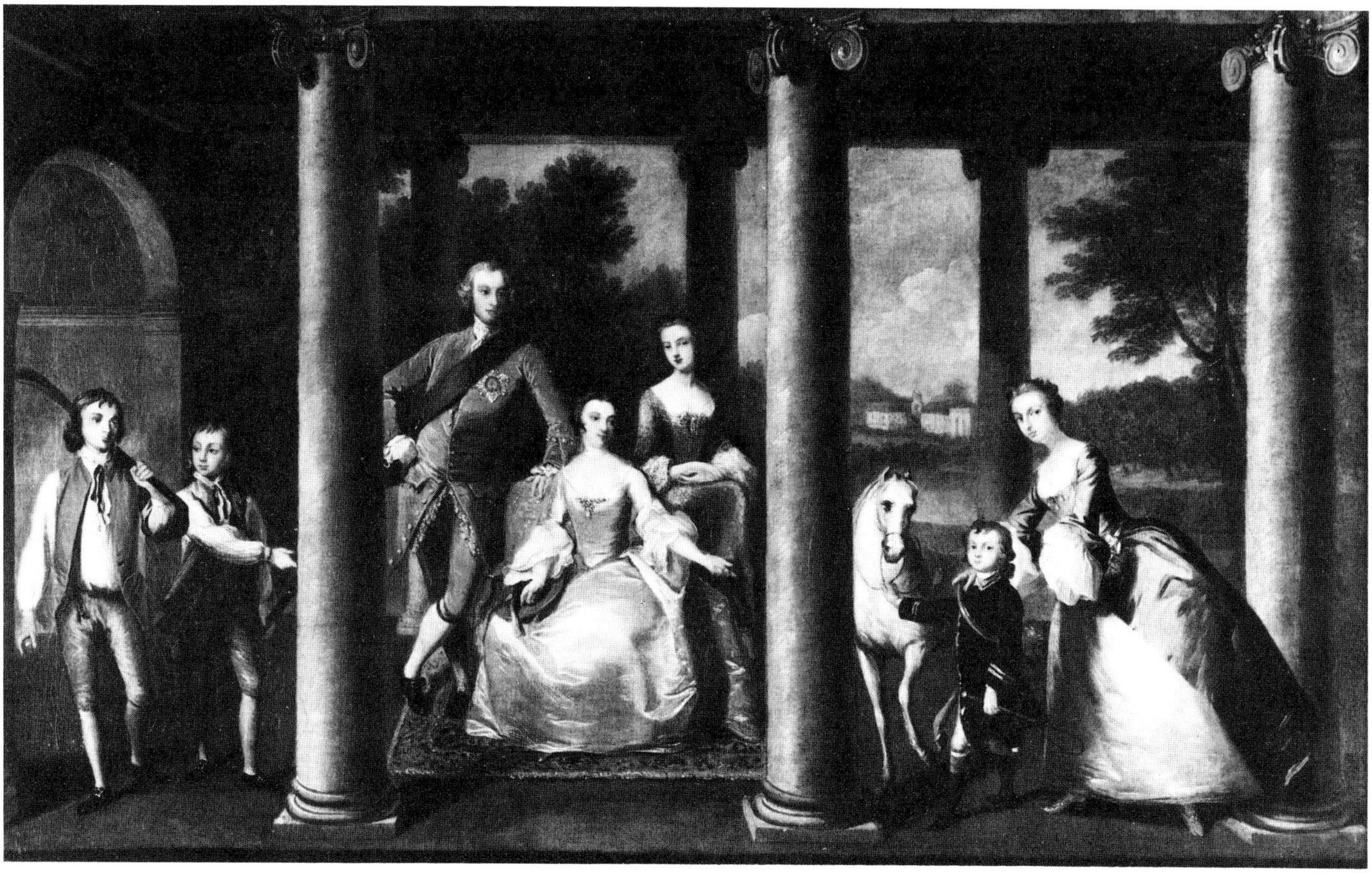

24. Thomas Hudson: *The Family of the 3rd Duke of Marlborough*: oil sketch for the portrait-group at Blenheim Palace (*c.*1753) (Private Collection).

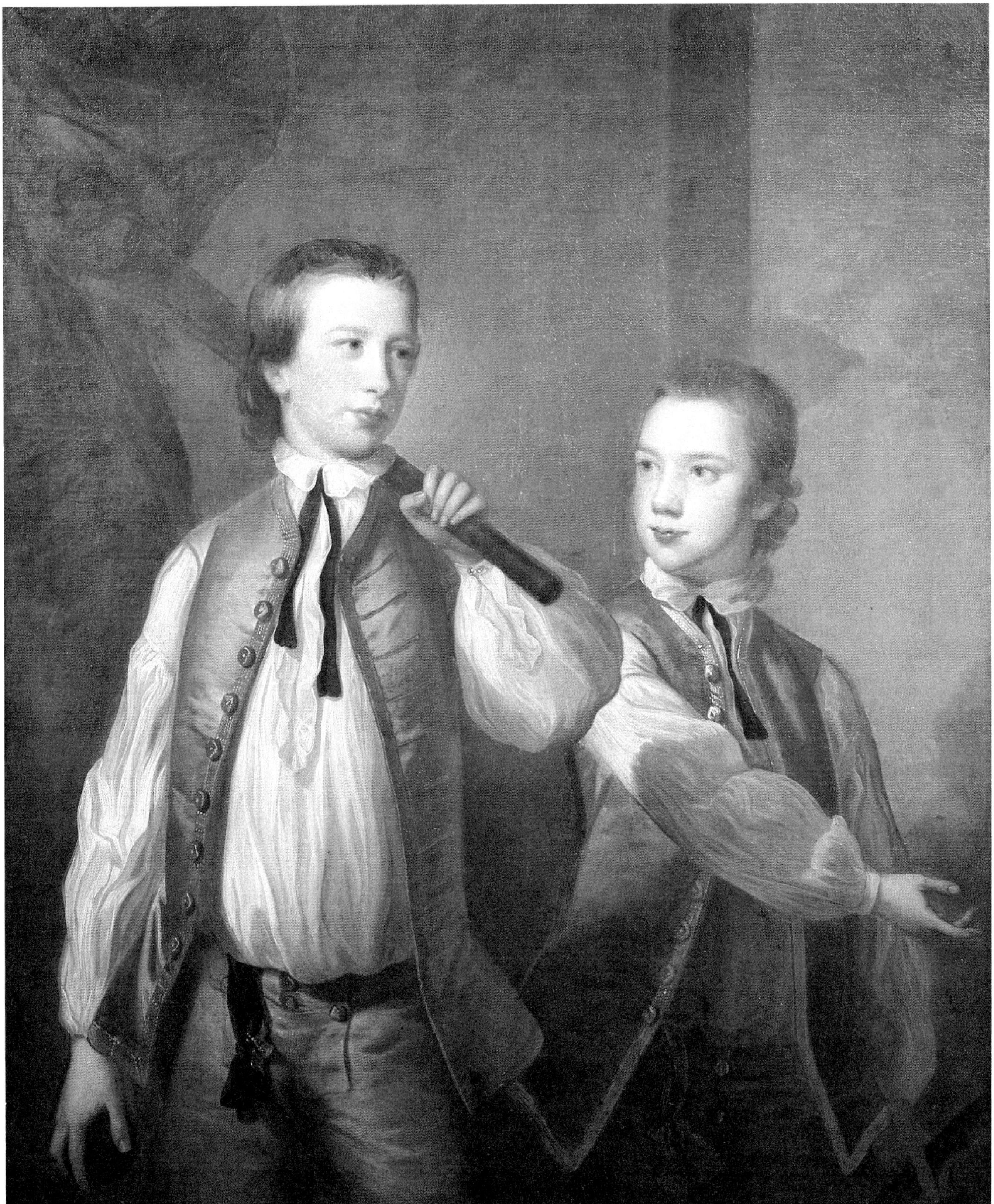

25. *Circle of* Thomas Hudson: *The Courtenay Brothers* (M.C.C.).

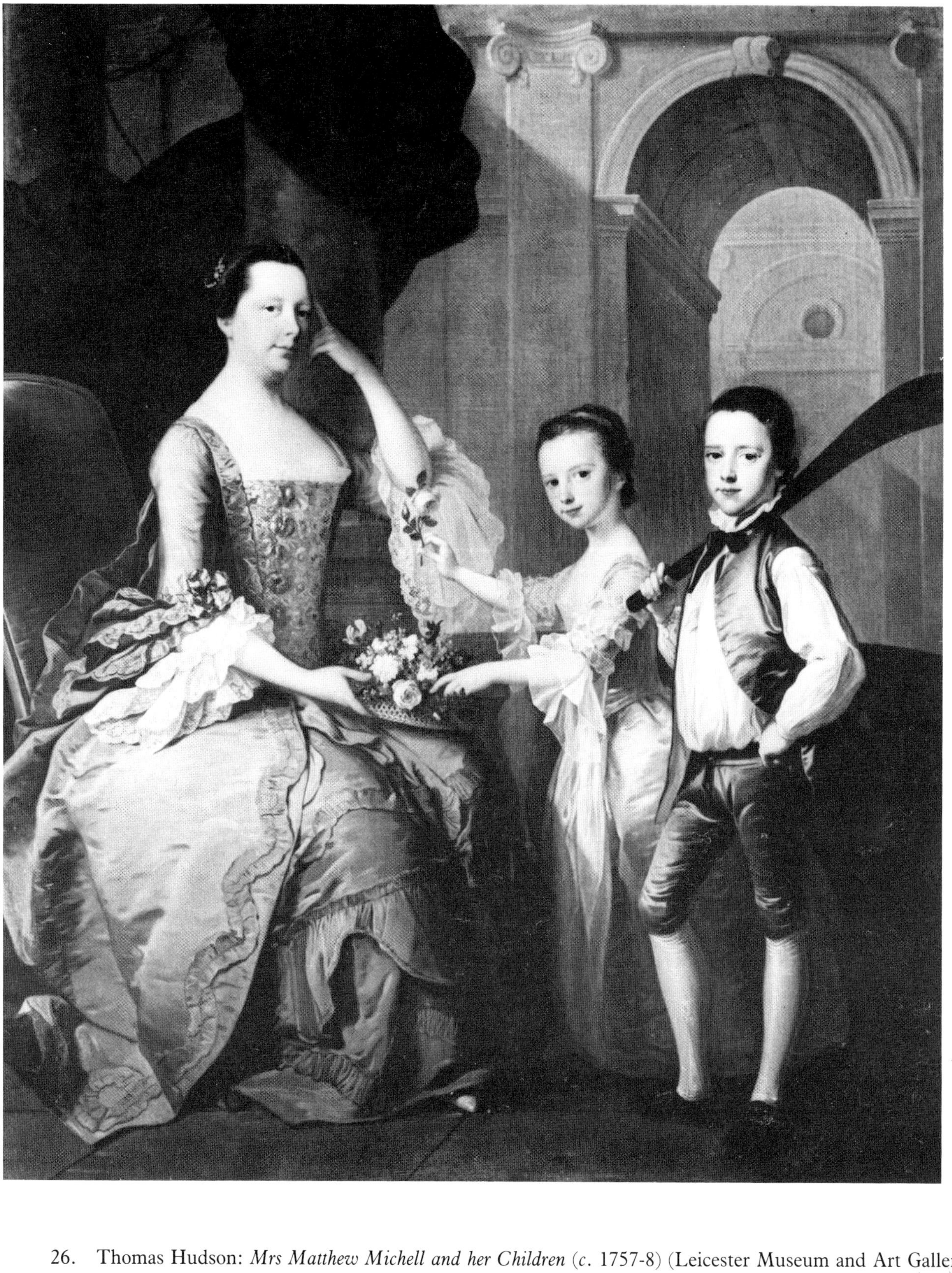

26. Thomas Hudson: *Mrs Matthew Michell and her Children* (*c.* 1757-8) (Leicester Museum and Art Gallery).

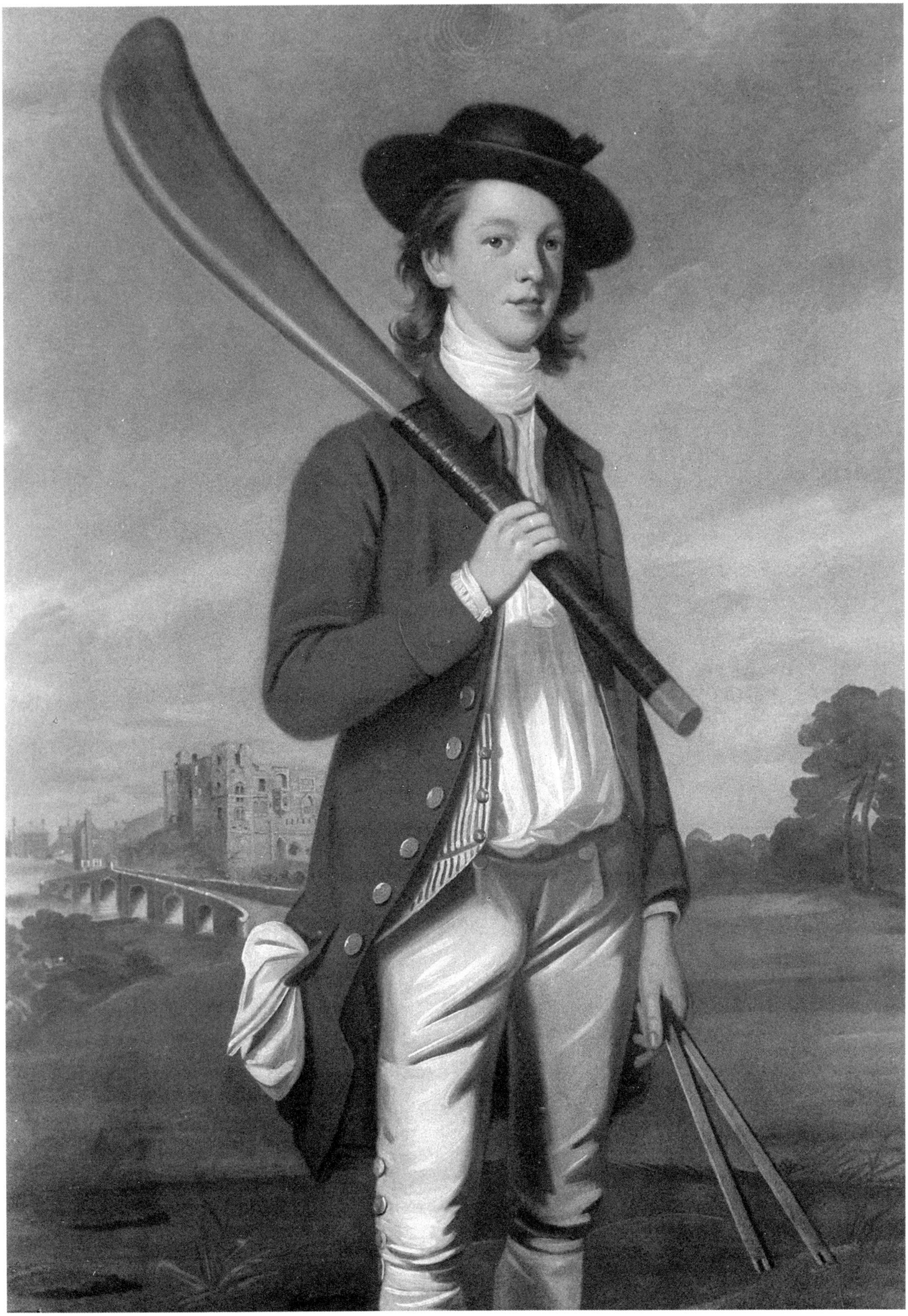

27. *Ascribed to* Thomas Hudson: *The Boy with a Bat (Walter Hawkesworth Fawkes)* (*c*. 1760) (Sir Westrow Hulse, Bart.).

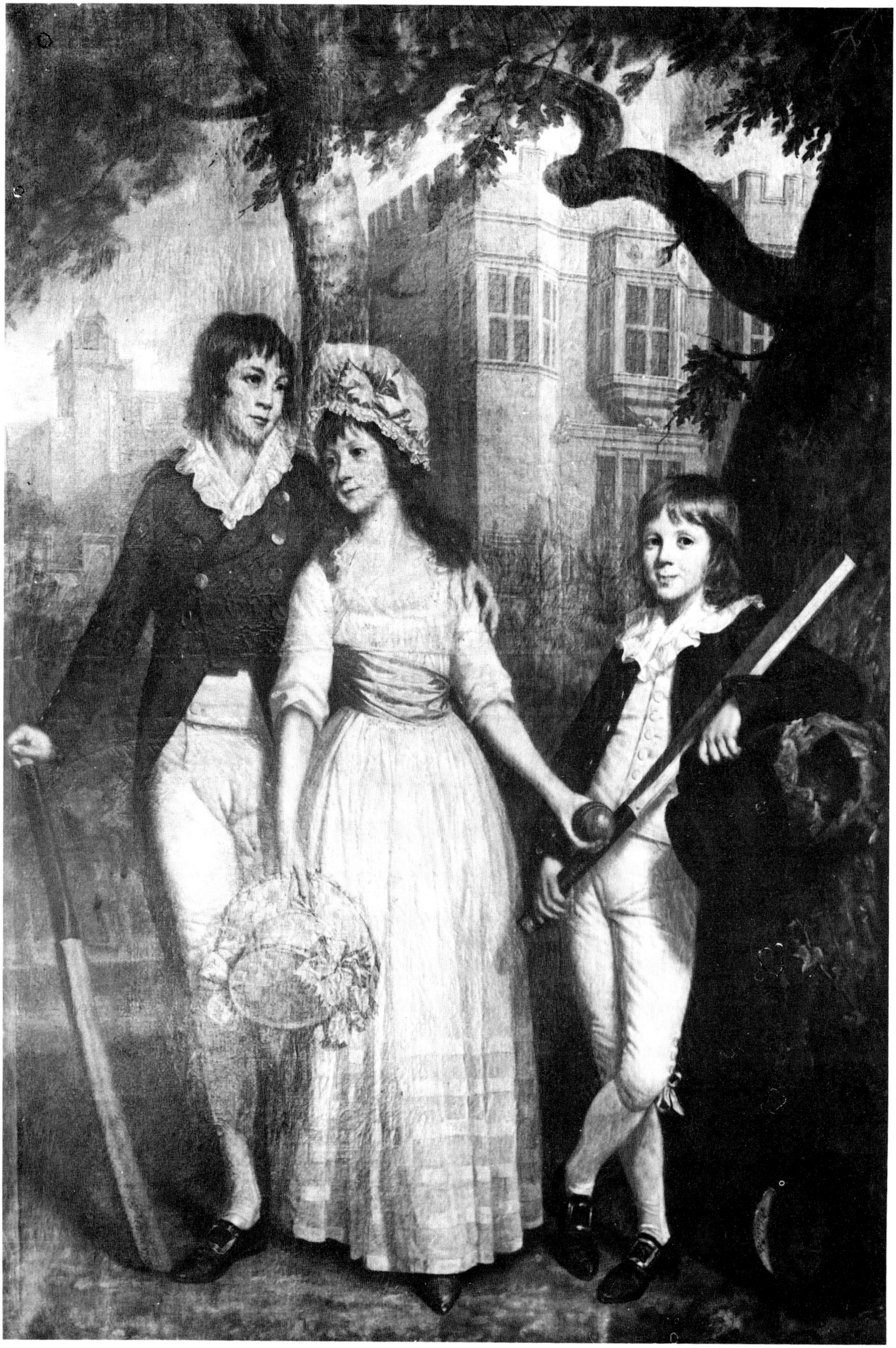

28. Thomas Beach: *The Children of Sir John William de la Pole* (1793) (Sir John Carew Pole, Bart.).

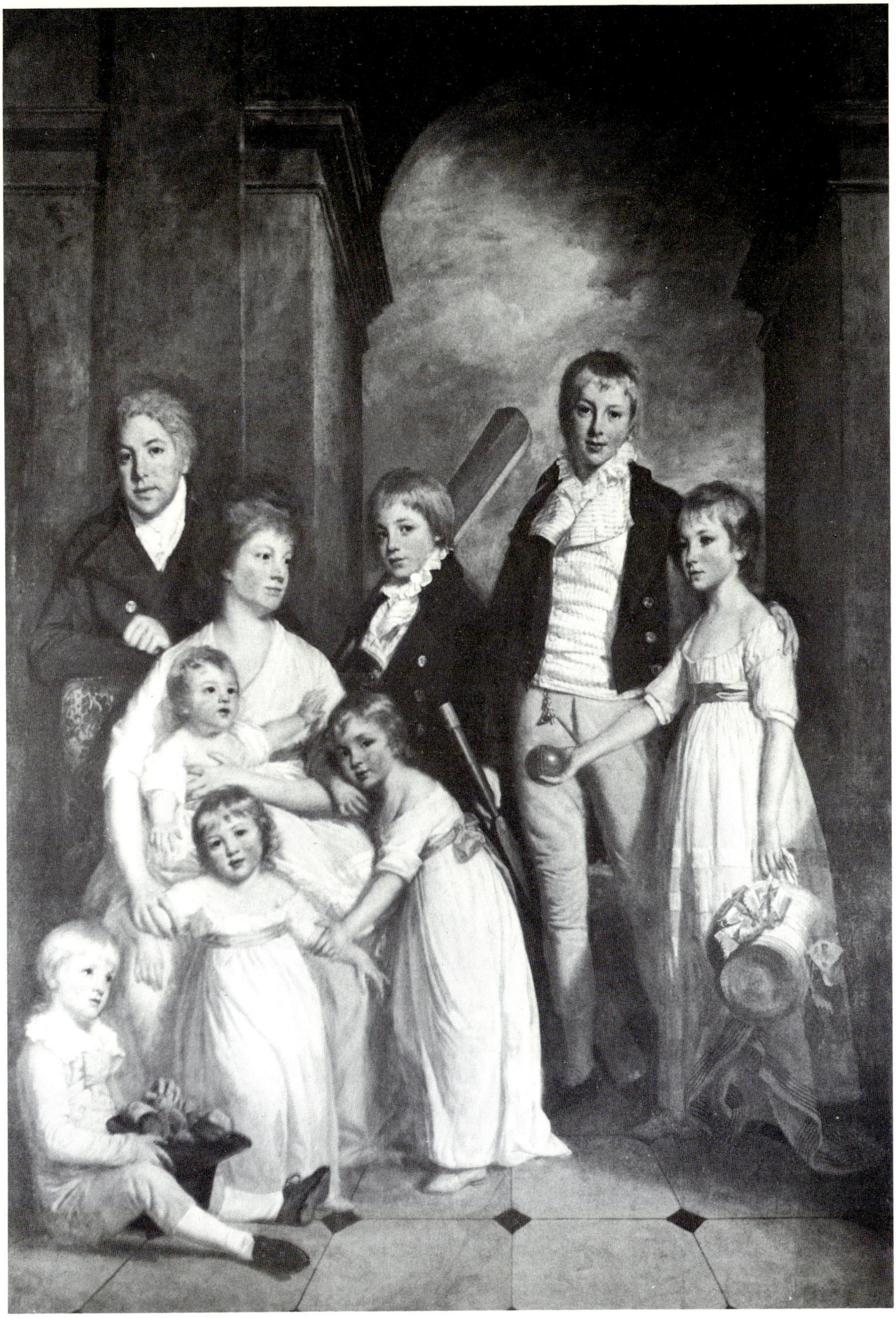

29. Thomas Beach: *The Tyndall Family* (1797) (The University of Bristol).

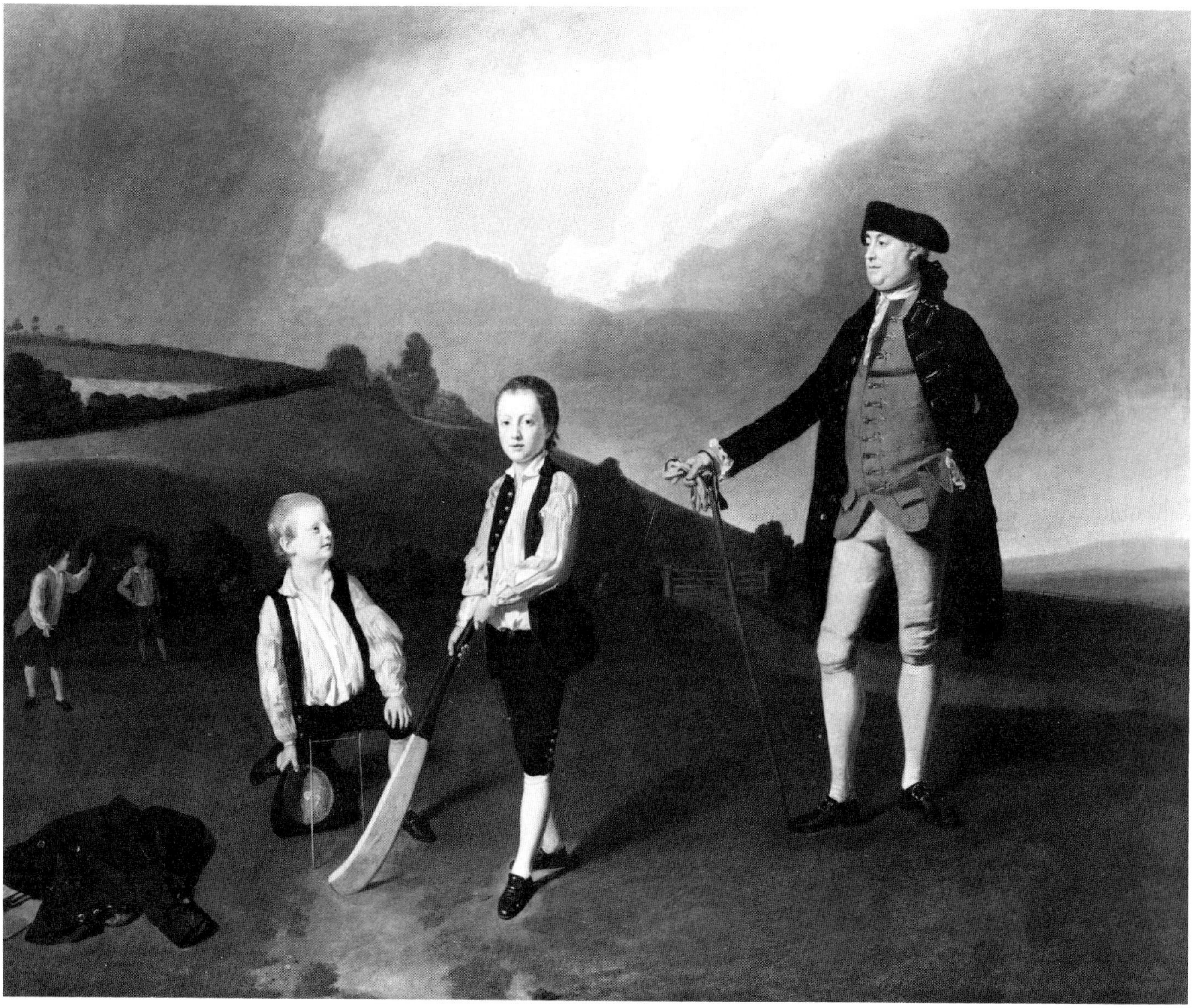

30. Henry Walton: *A Cricket Scene at Harrow School* (1771) (Private Collection).

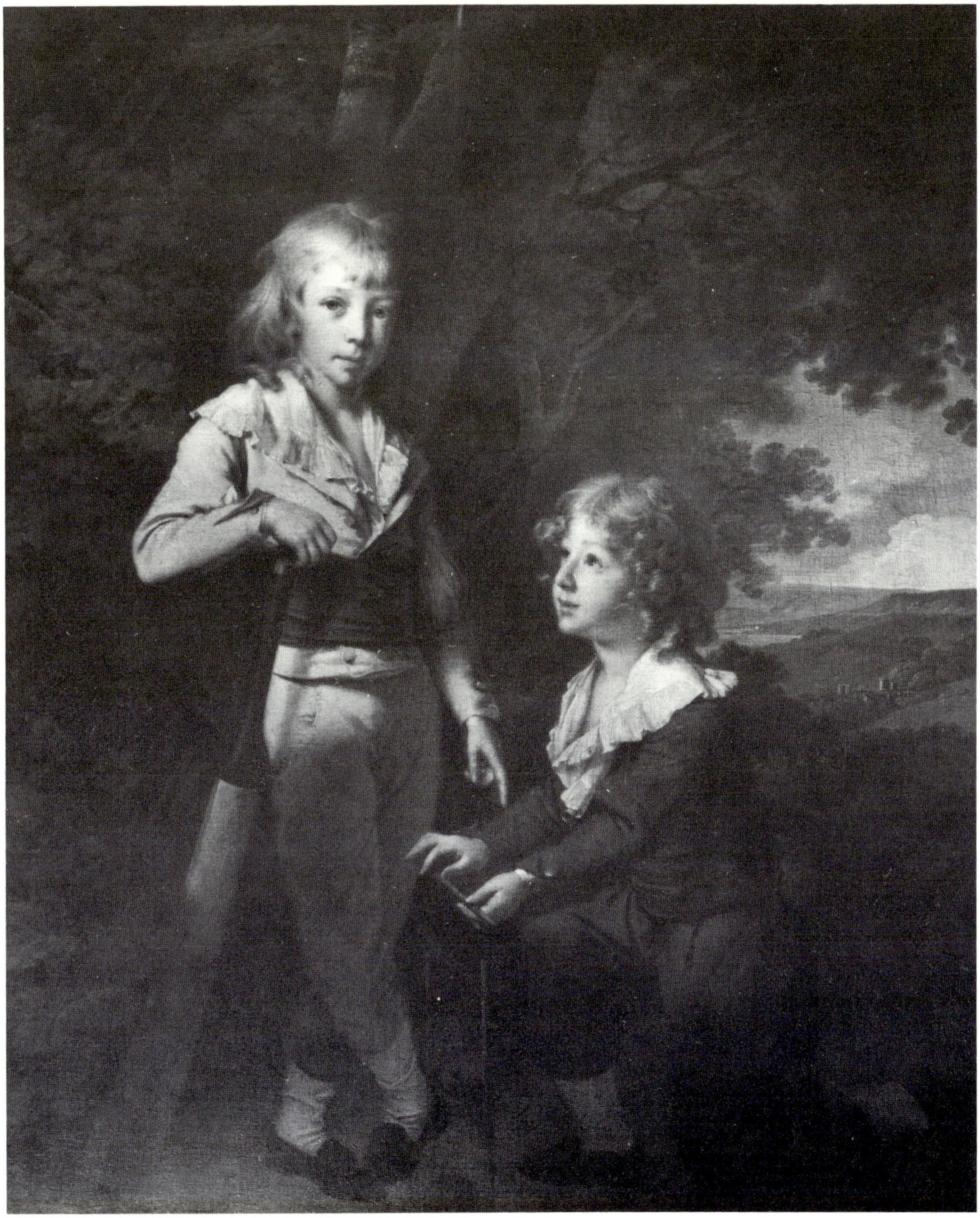

31. Joseph Wright of Derby, A.R.A.: *The Thornhill Children* (*c.* 1790) (Private Collection).

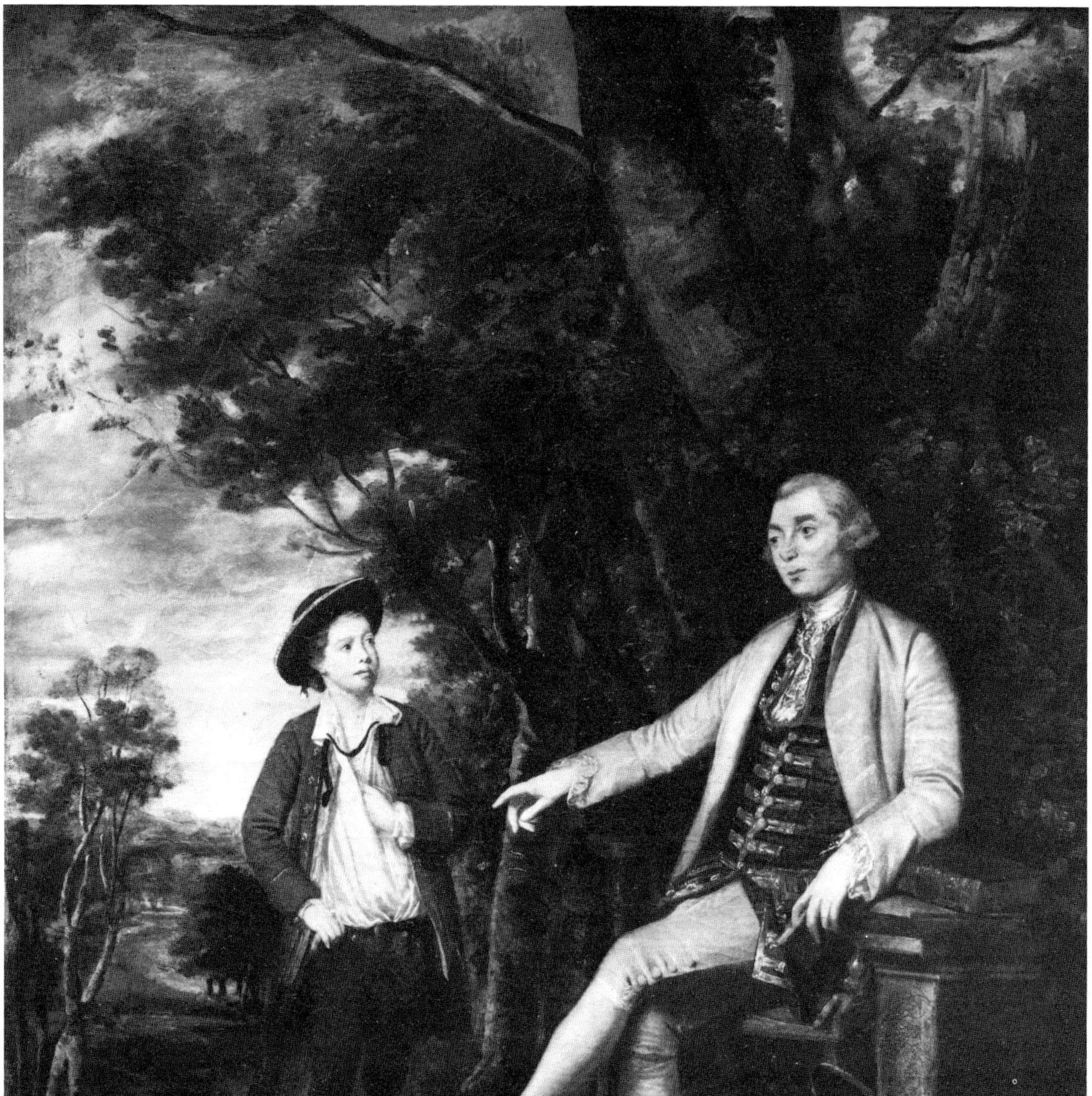

32. *Attributed to* Hugh Barron: *Edmund Butler and his son* (*c.* 1767-8) (Private Collection).

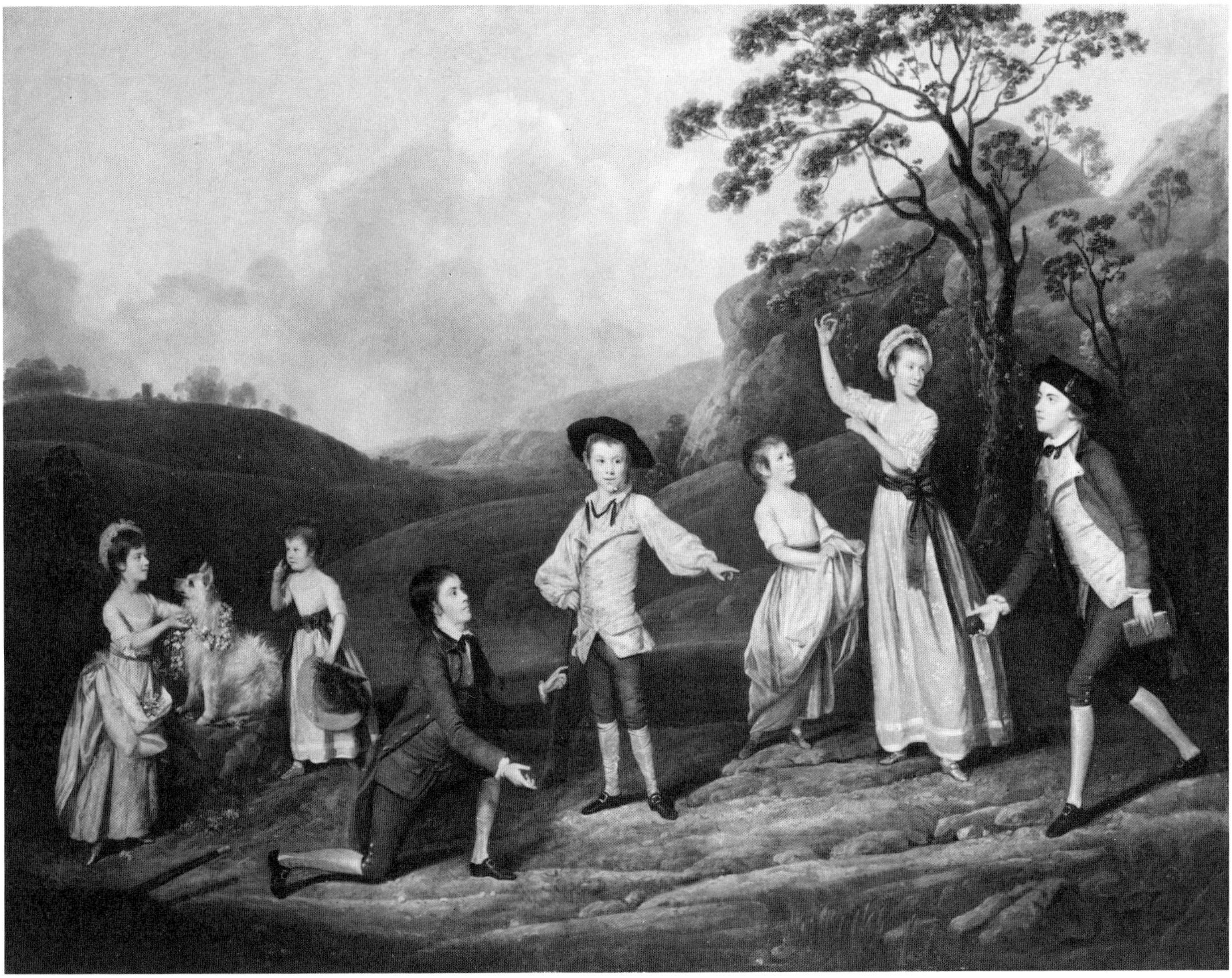

33. Hugh Barron: *The Children of George Bond of Ditchleys* (Tate Gallery, London).

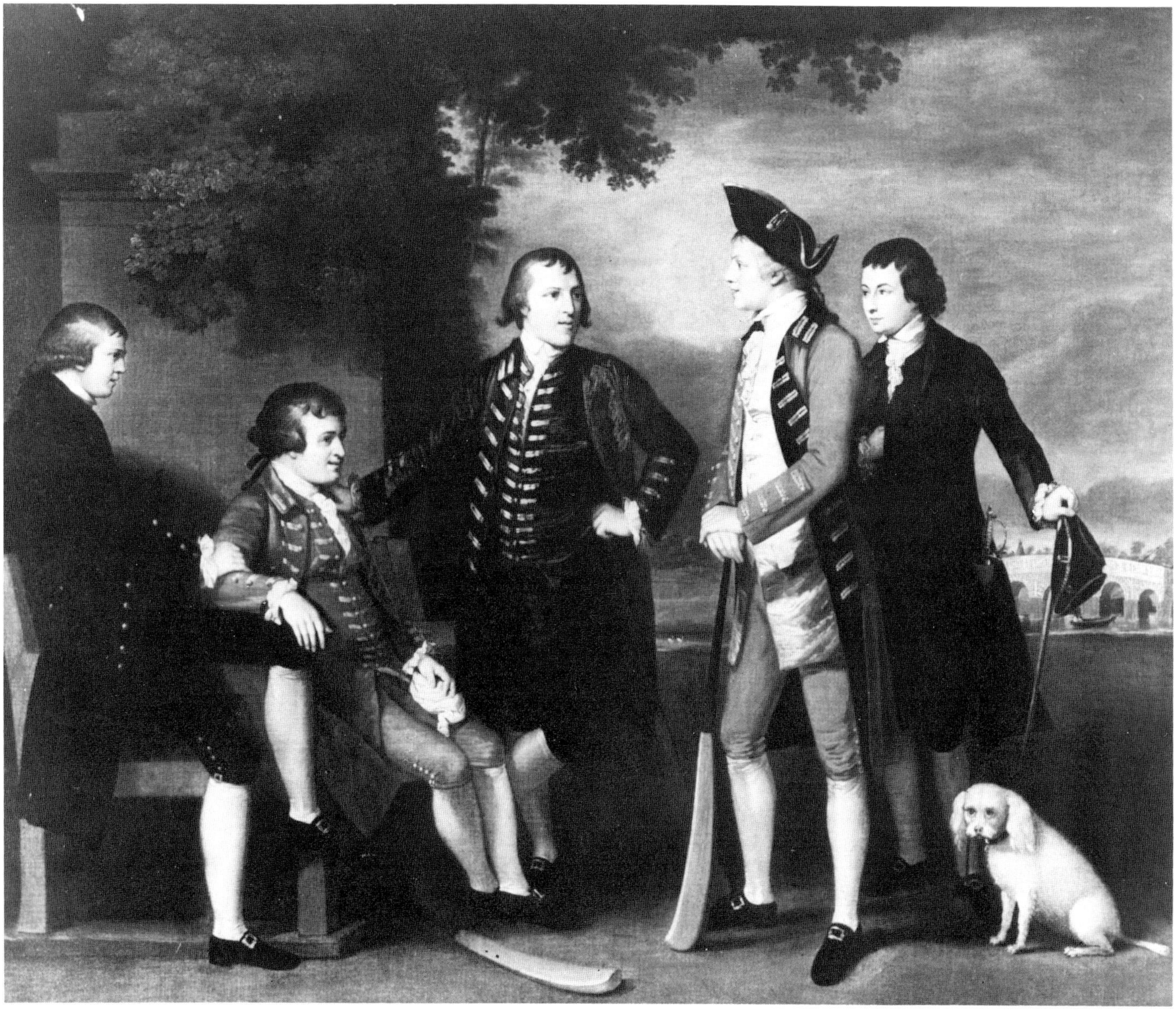

34. Benjamin West, P.R.A.: *The Cricketers* (1763) (Private Collection).

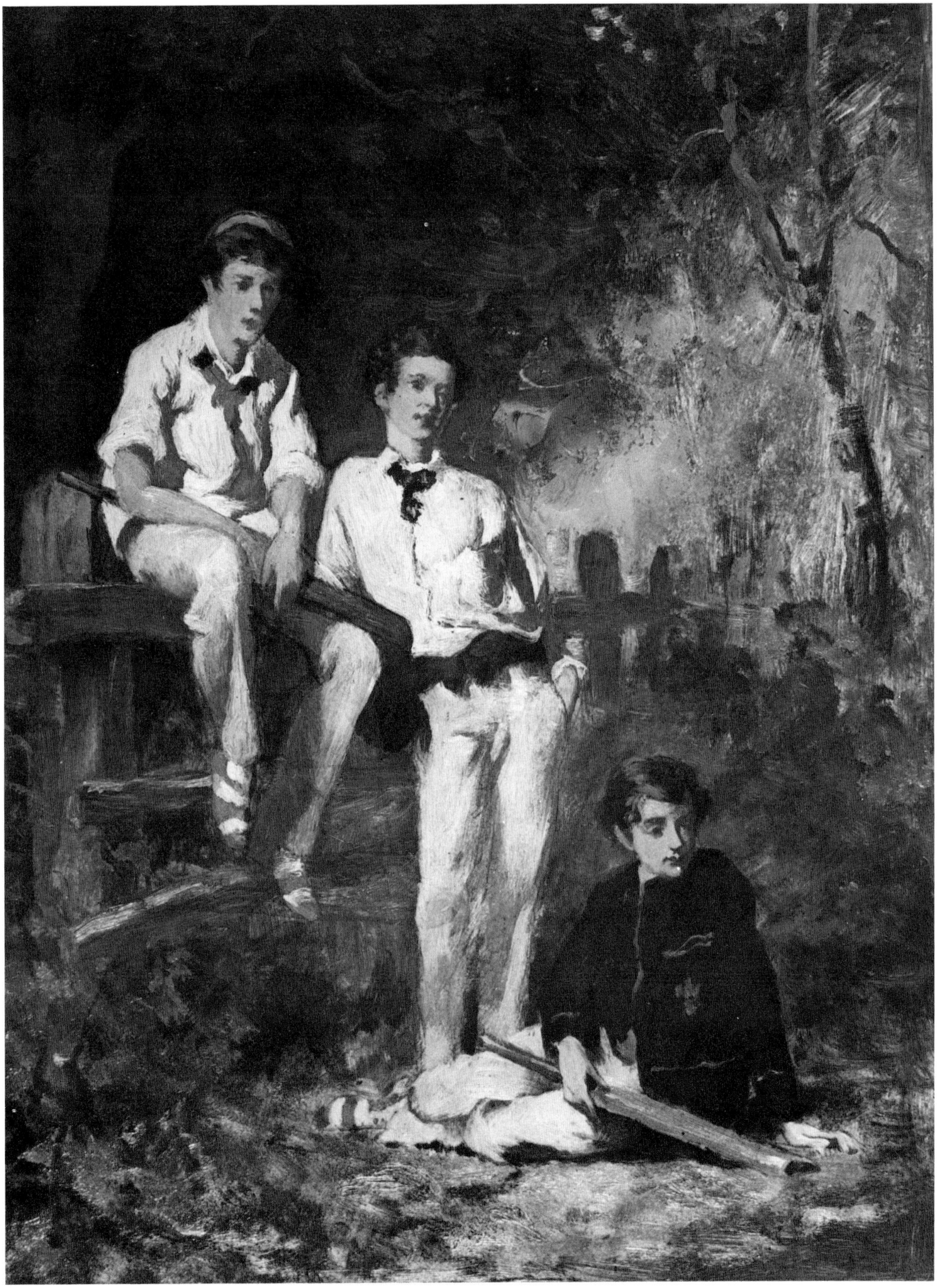

35. George Elgar Hicks: *Three Young Cricketers* (Southampton Art Gallery).

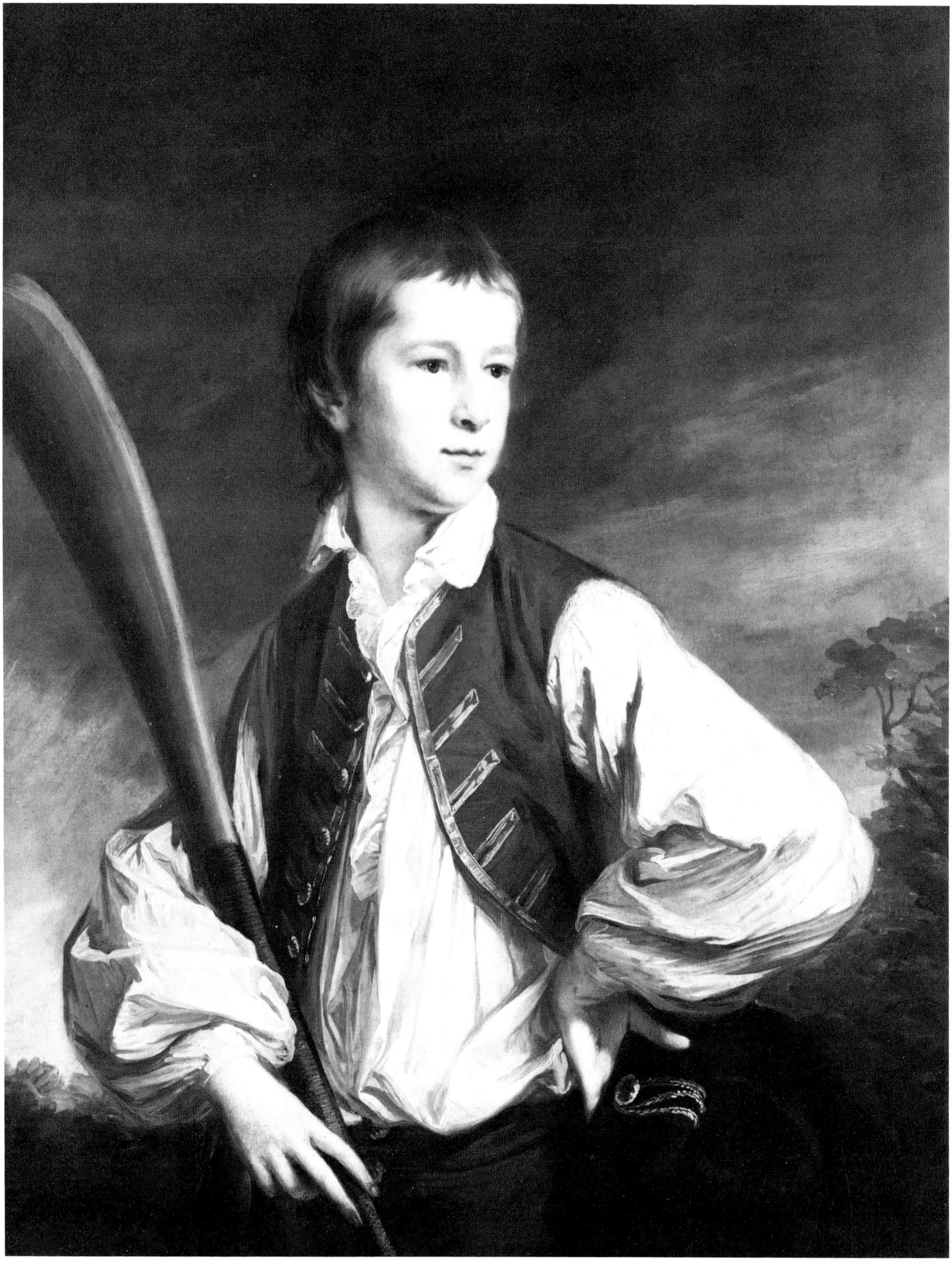

36. Francis Cotes, R.A.: *The Revd. Charles Collyer as a boy* (Yale Center for British Art, New Haven, Conn., U.S.A.).

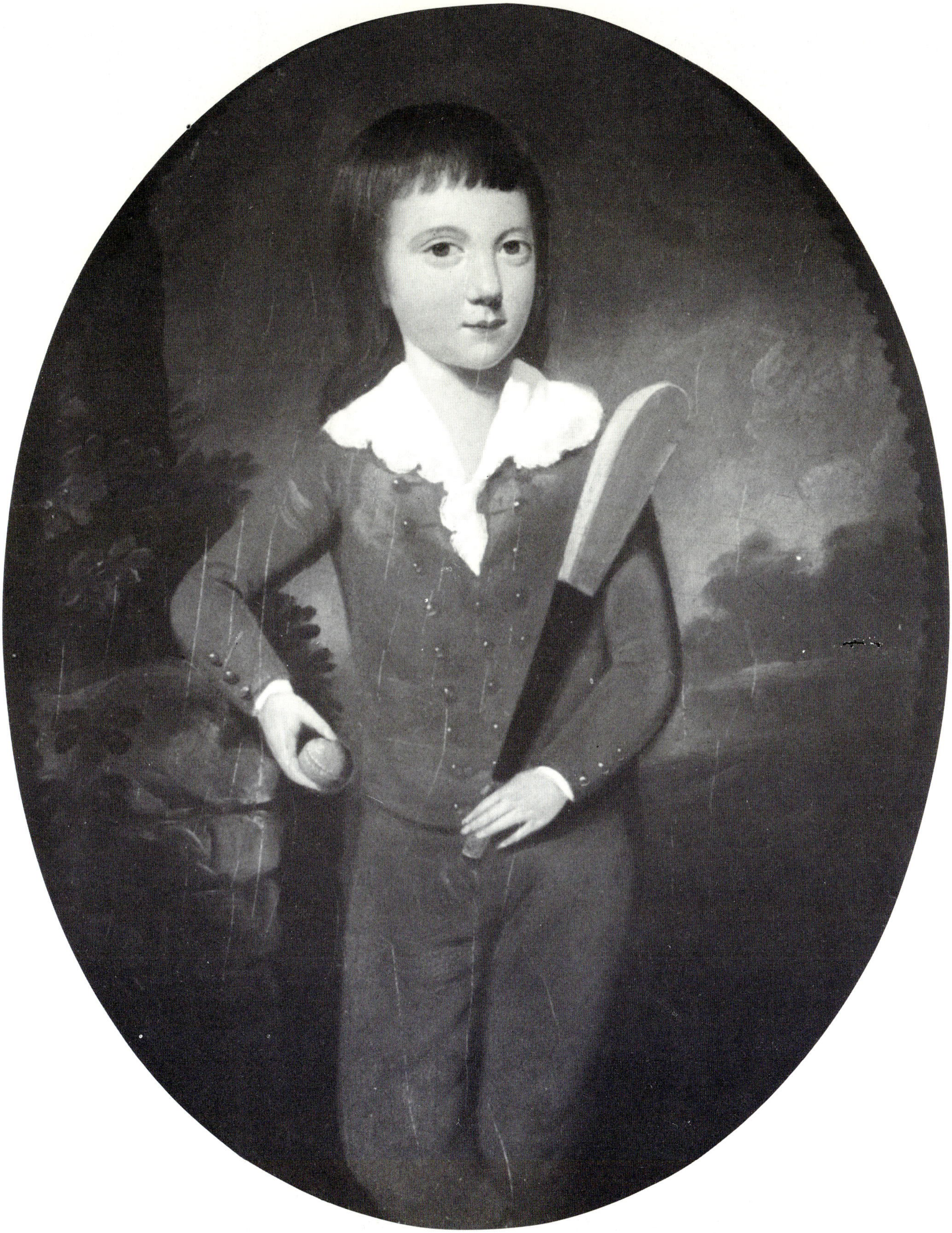

37. Francis Alleyne: *John Call with Bat and Ball* (Messrs. Arthur Ackermann and Son, Ltd., London)

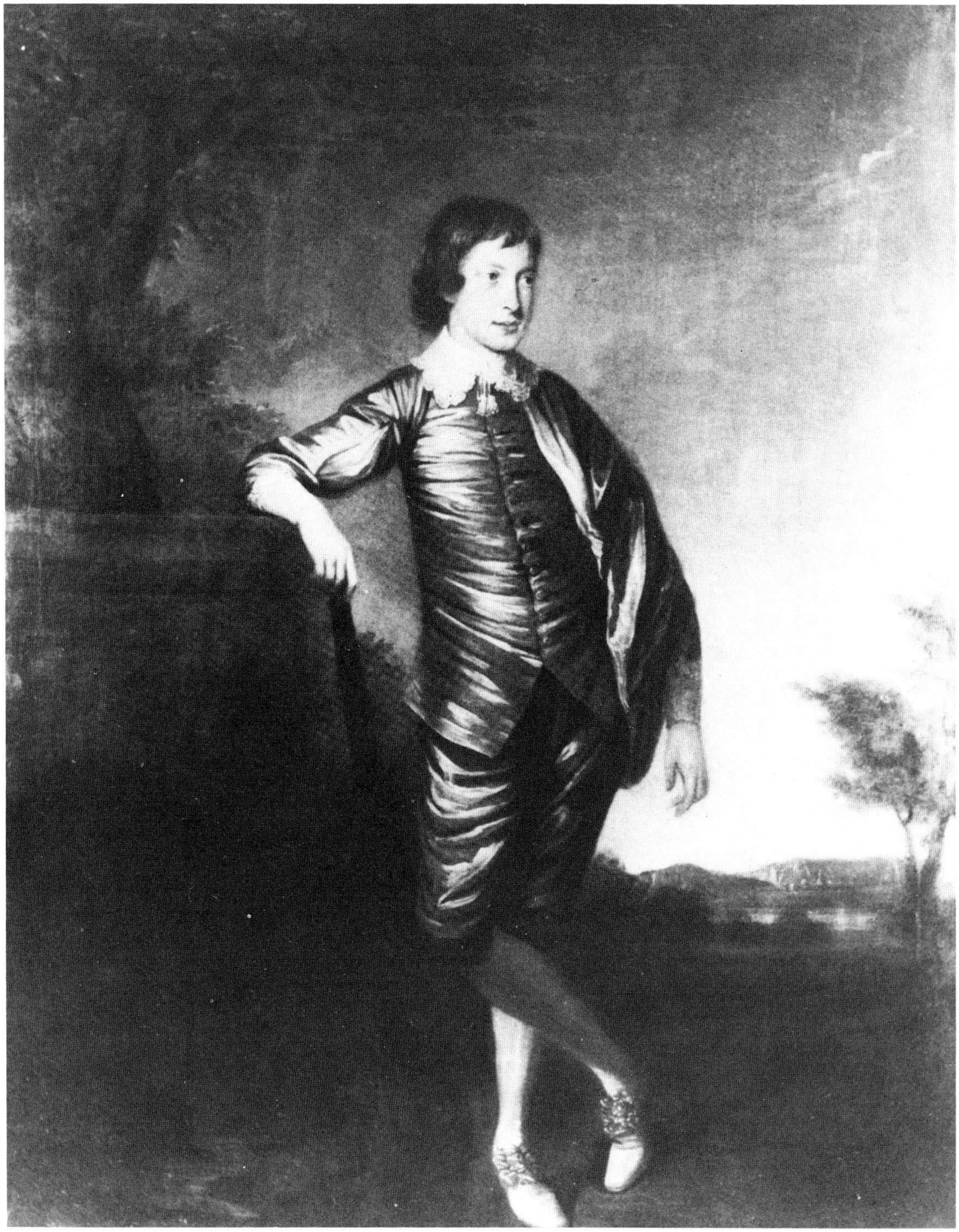

38. David Martin: *John Campbell of South Hall* (1771) (present whereabouts unknown).

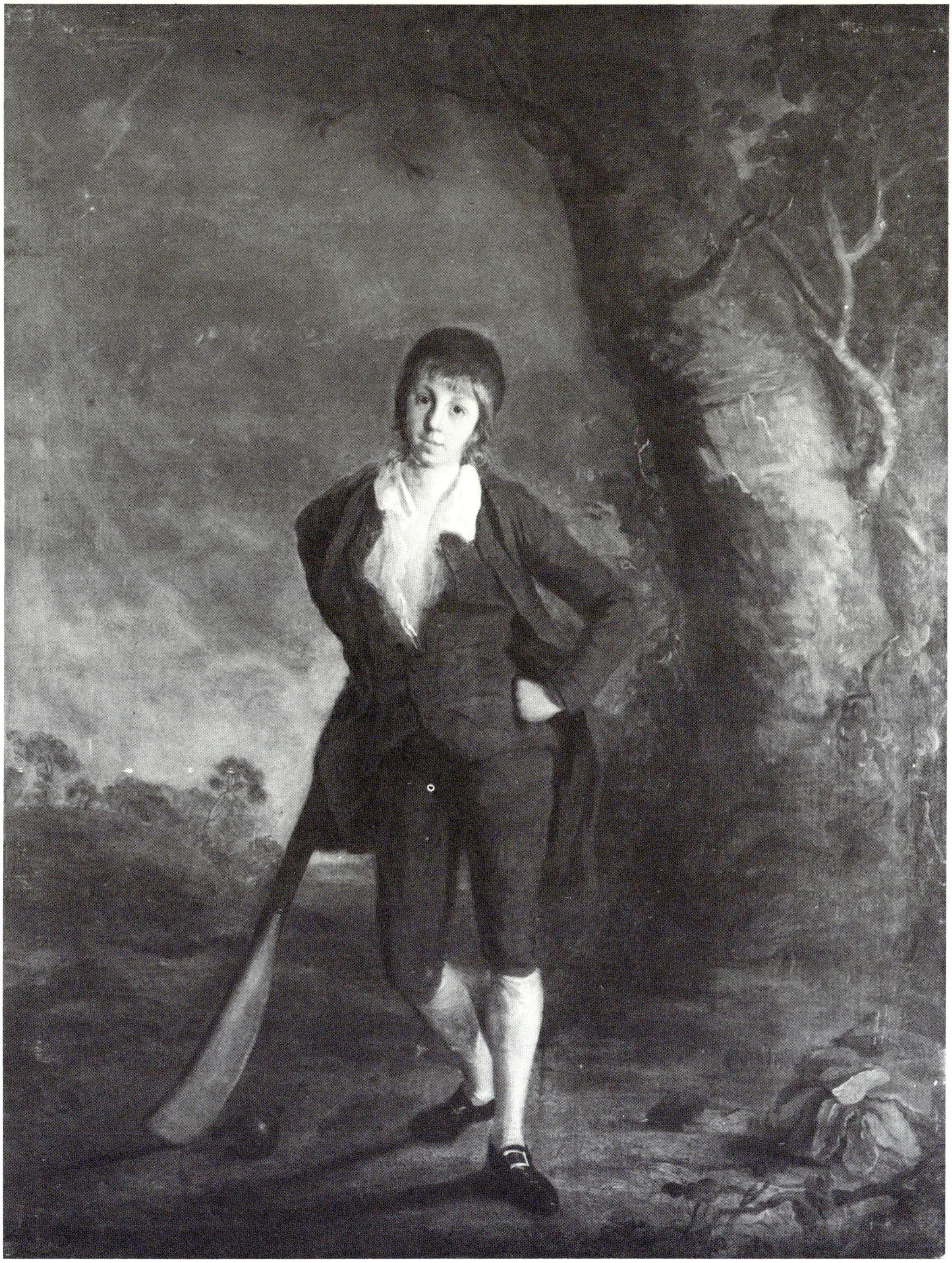

39. Robert Edge Pine: *The Revd. Robert Waugh as a boy* (*c.* 1777) (present whereabouts unknown).

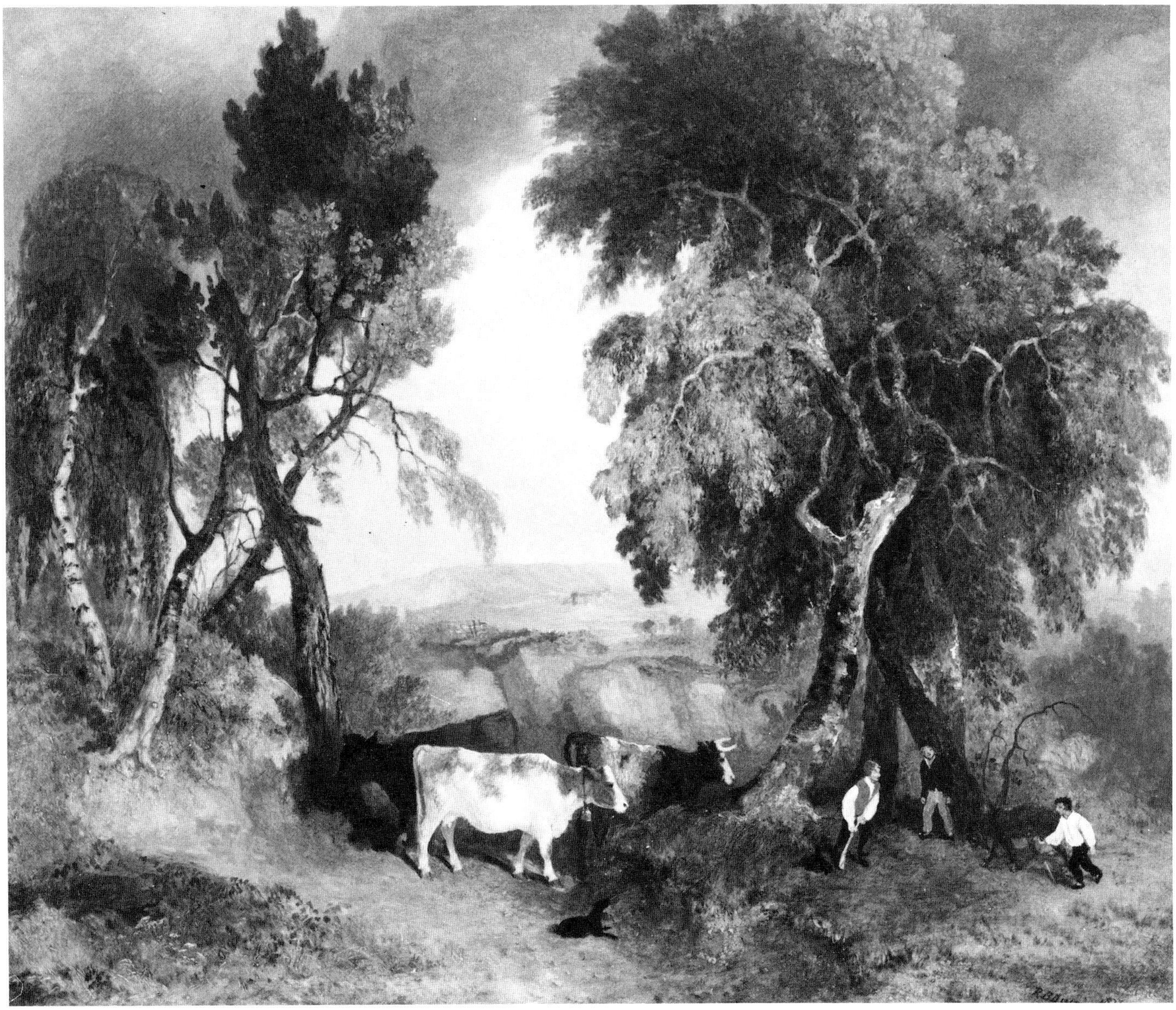

40. Richard Barrett Davis: *Landscape with Children playing Cricket* (1827) (present whereabouts unknown).

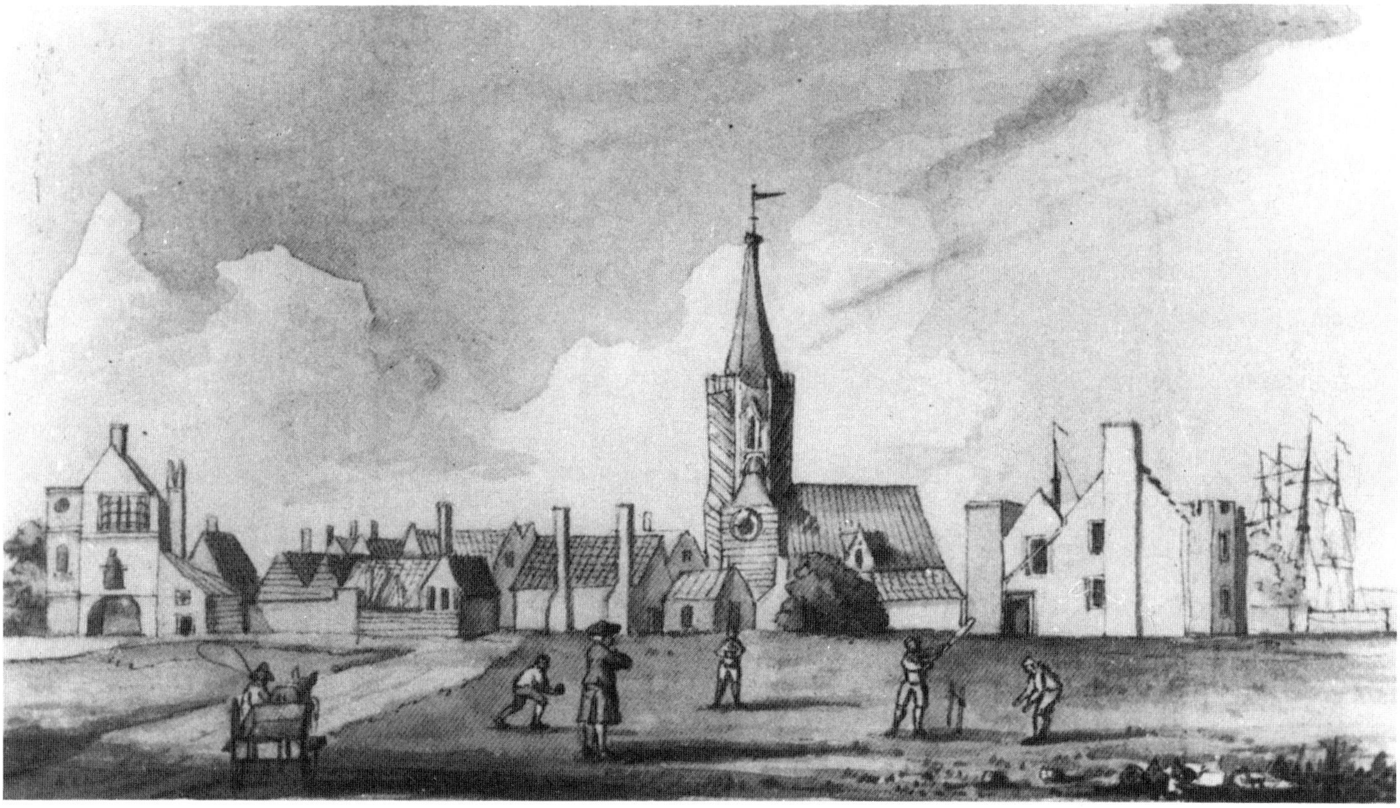

41. John Nixon: *Harwich, with a Game of Cricket in Progress* (1784) (present whereabouts unknown).

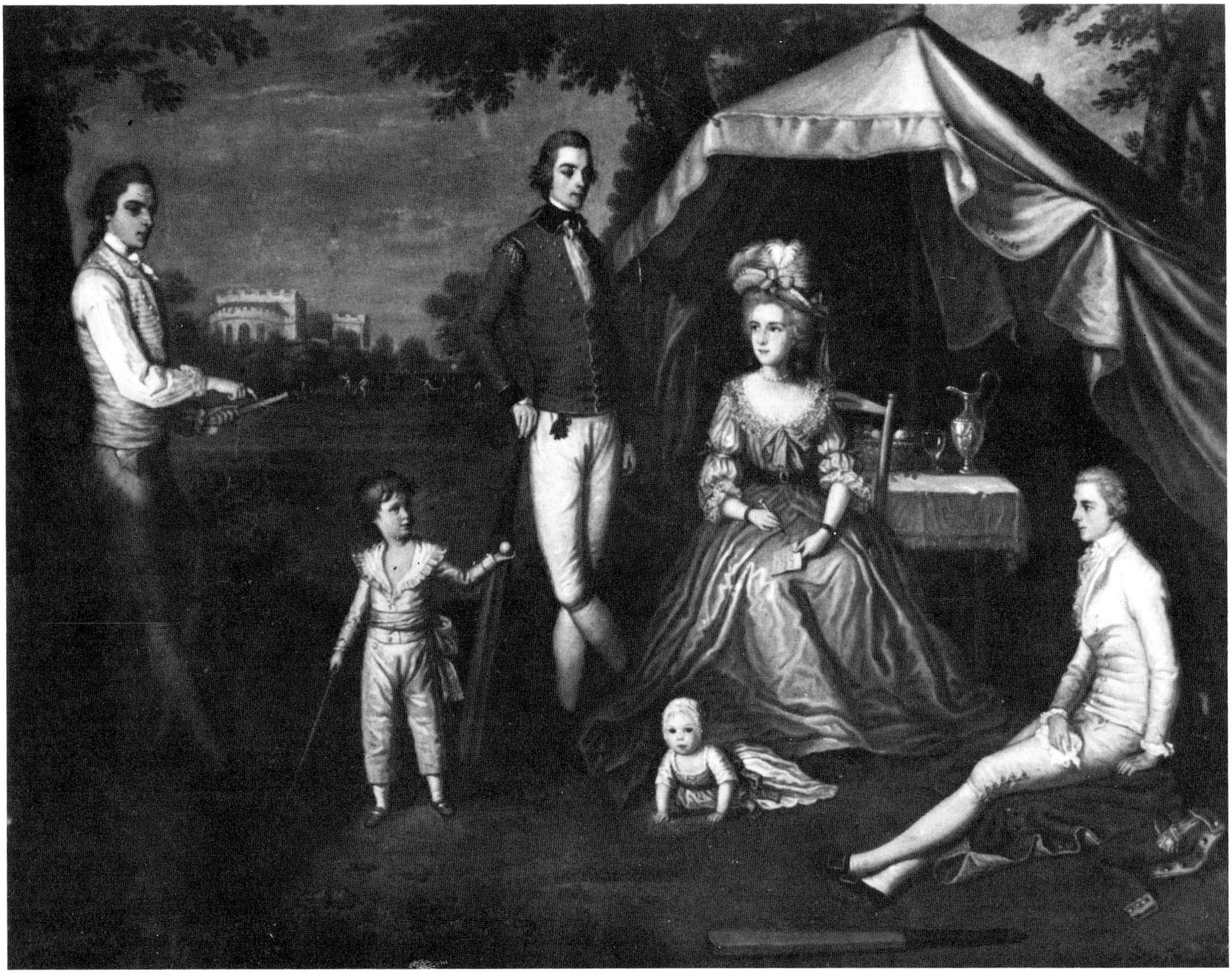

42. David Allan: *The Cathcart Family* (1784-5) (The Earl Cathcart).

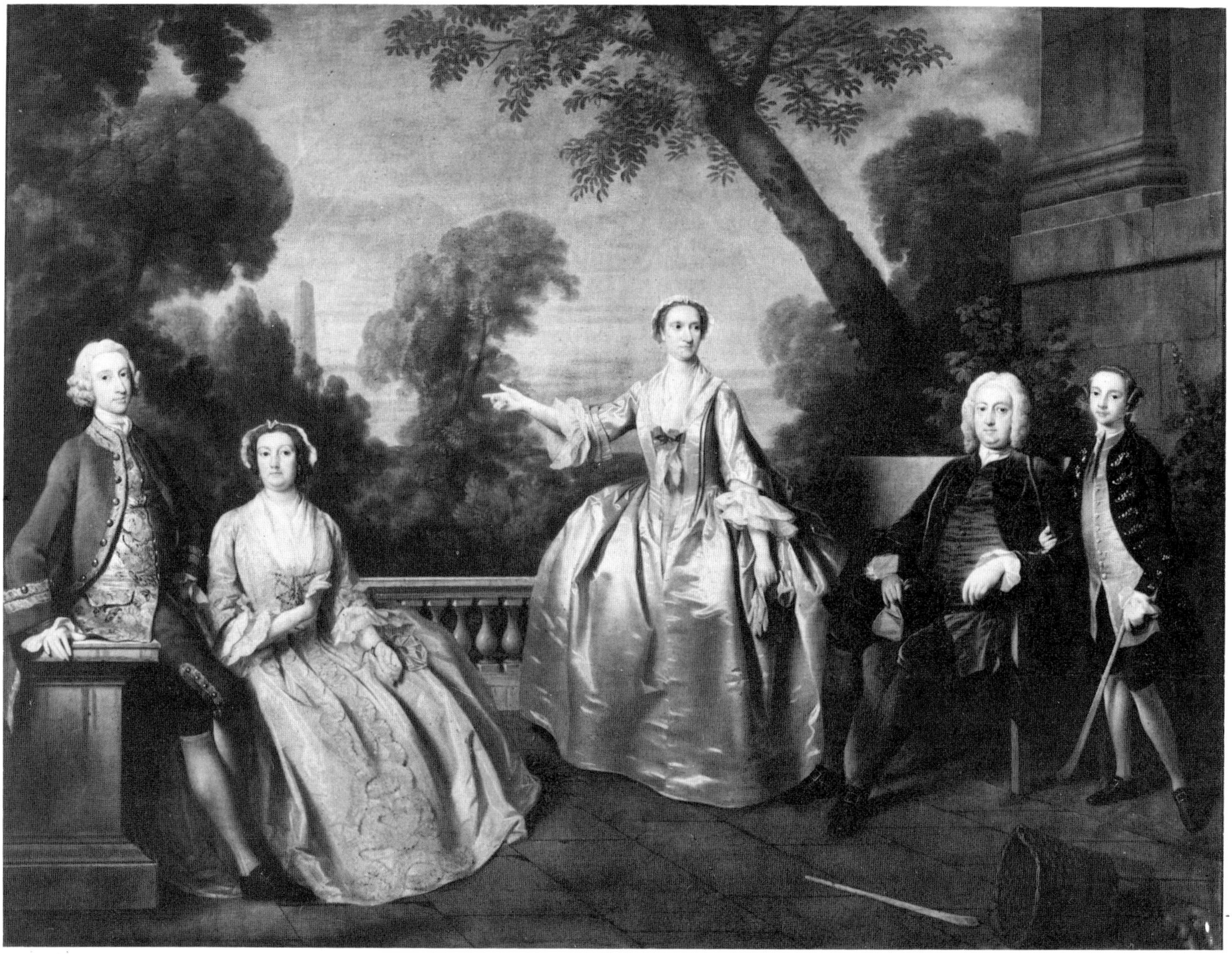

43. The Revd. J. Wills: *The Andrews Family* (1749) (Fitzwilliam Museum, Cambridge).

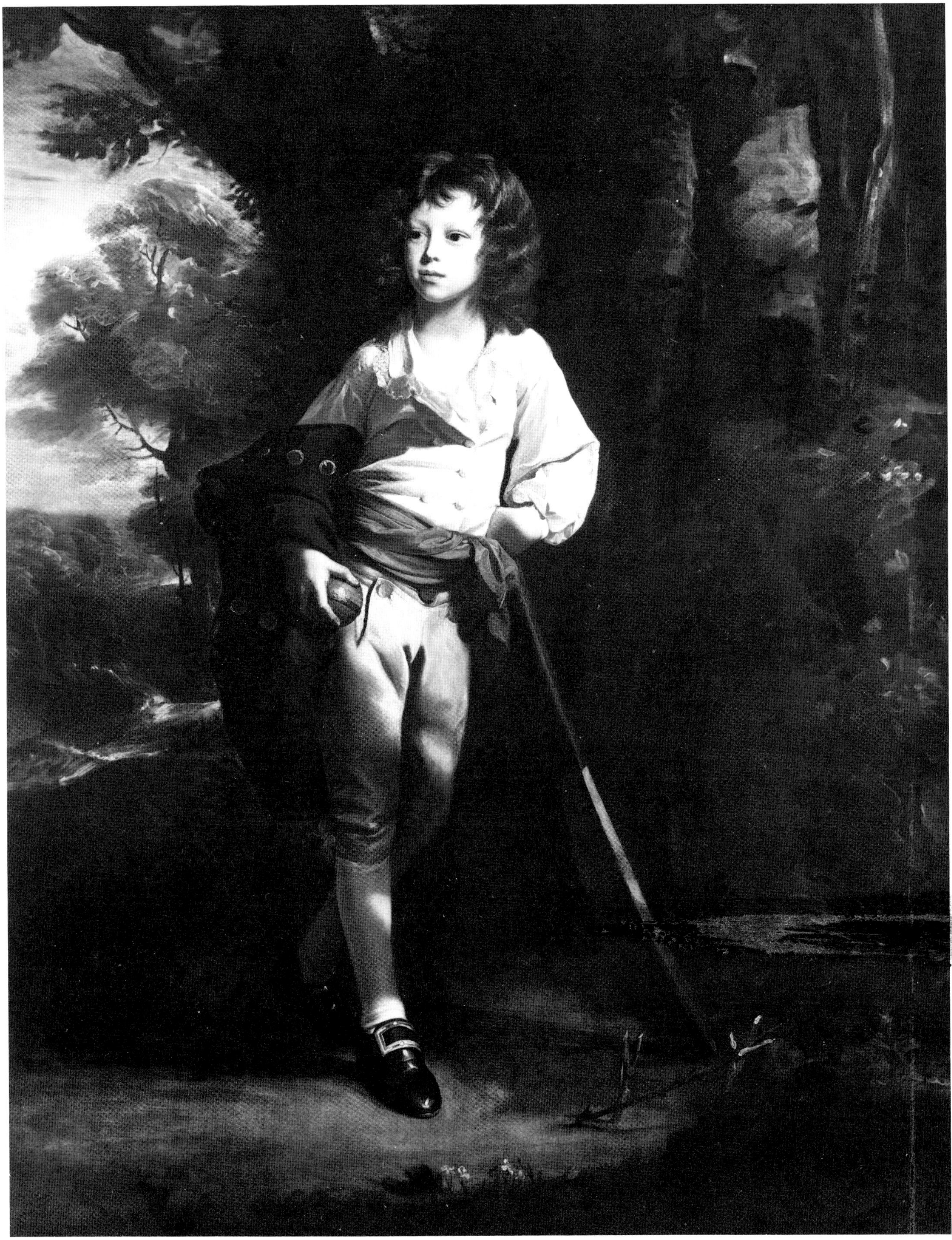

44. John Singleton Copley: *Richard Heber as a boy* (Yale Center for British Art, New Haven, Conn., U.S.A.).

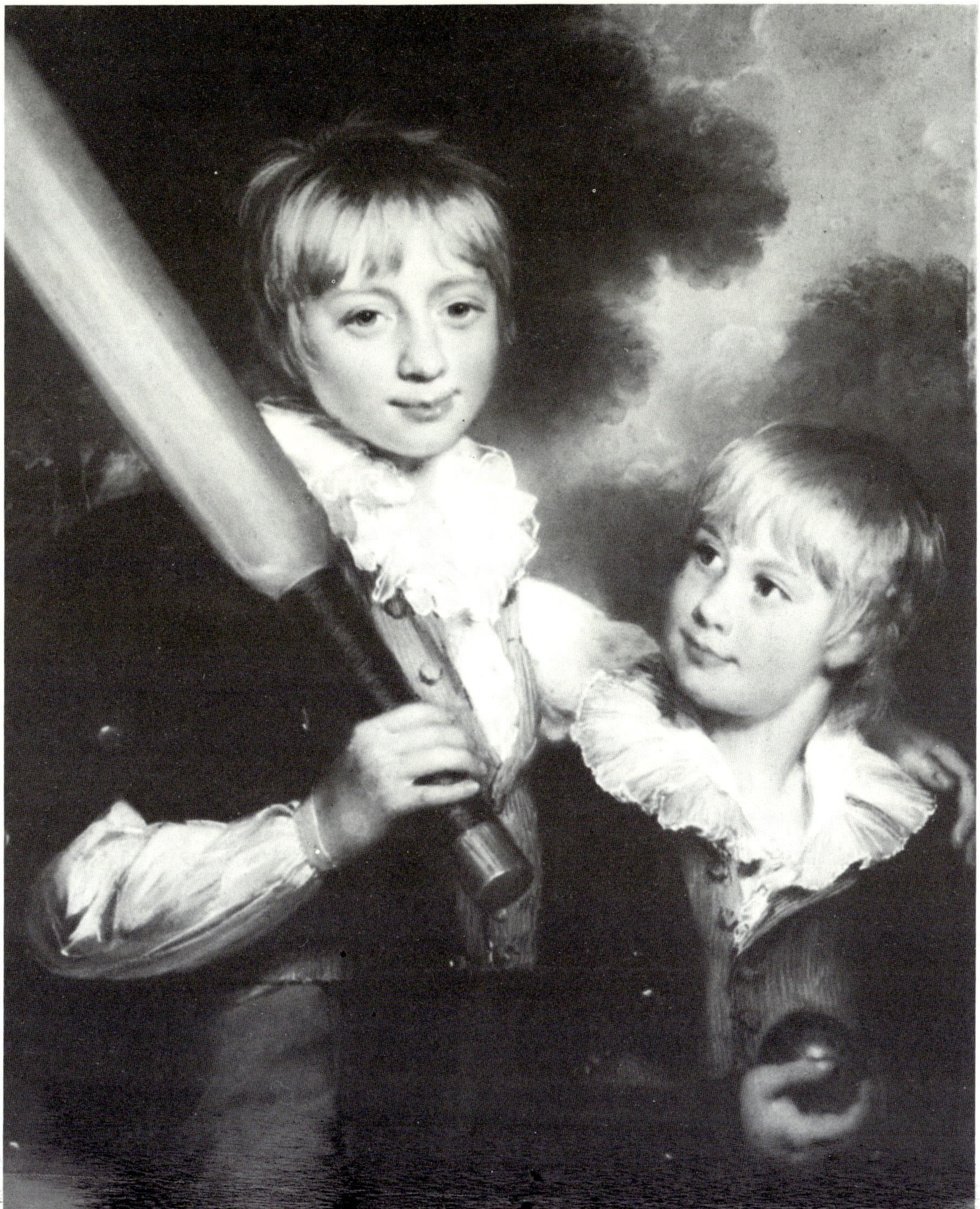

45. John Russell, R.A.: *The Sons of Thomas Pitt* (1804) (Private Collection).

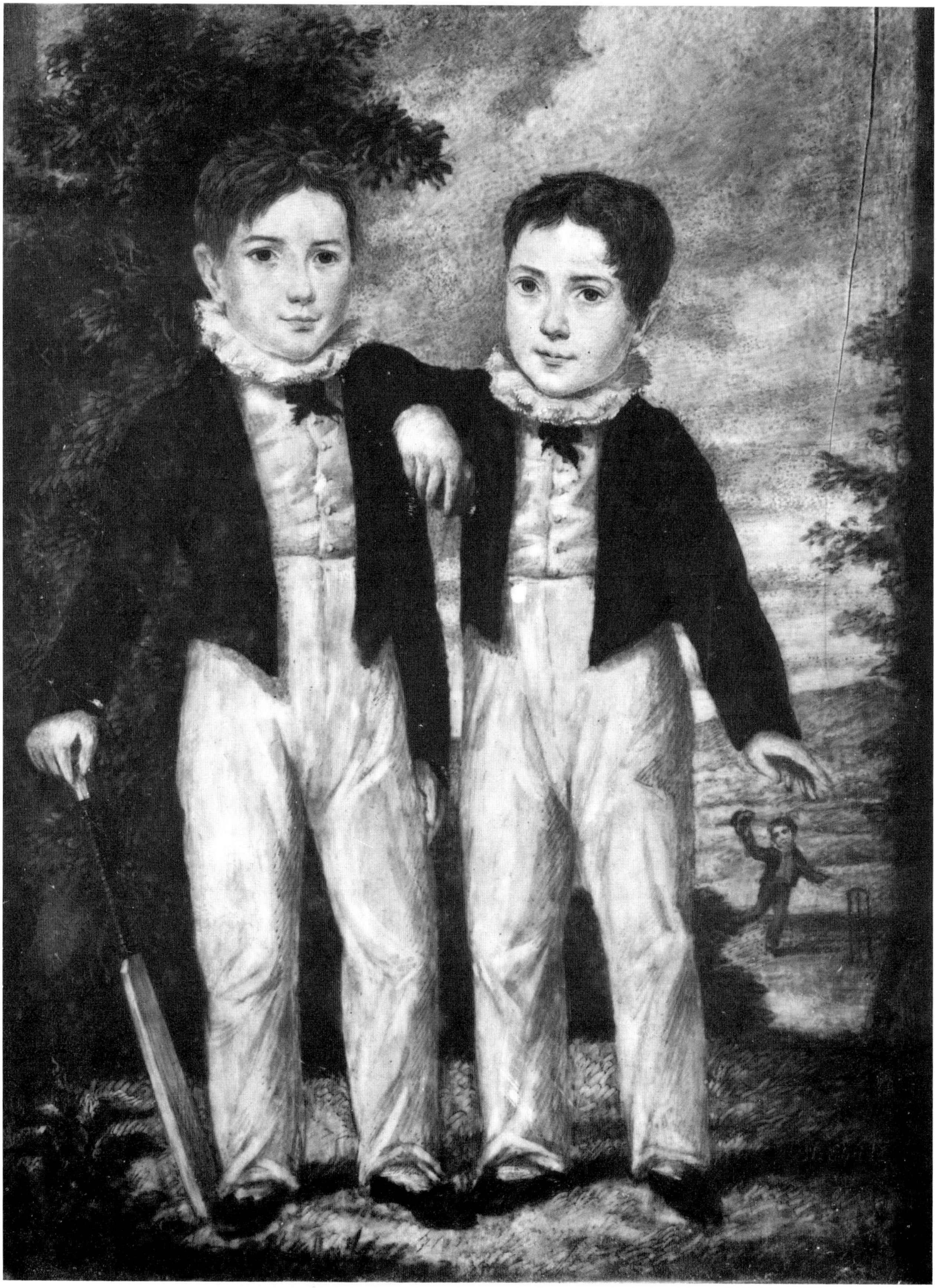

46. James Warren Childe: *Two Young Cricketers* (present whereabouts unknown).

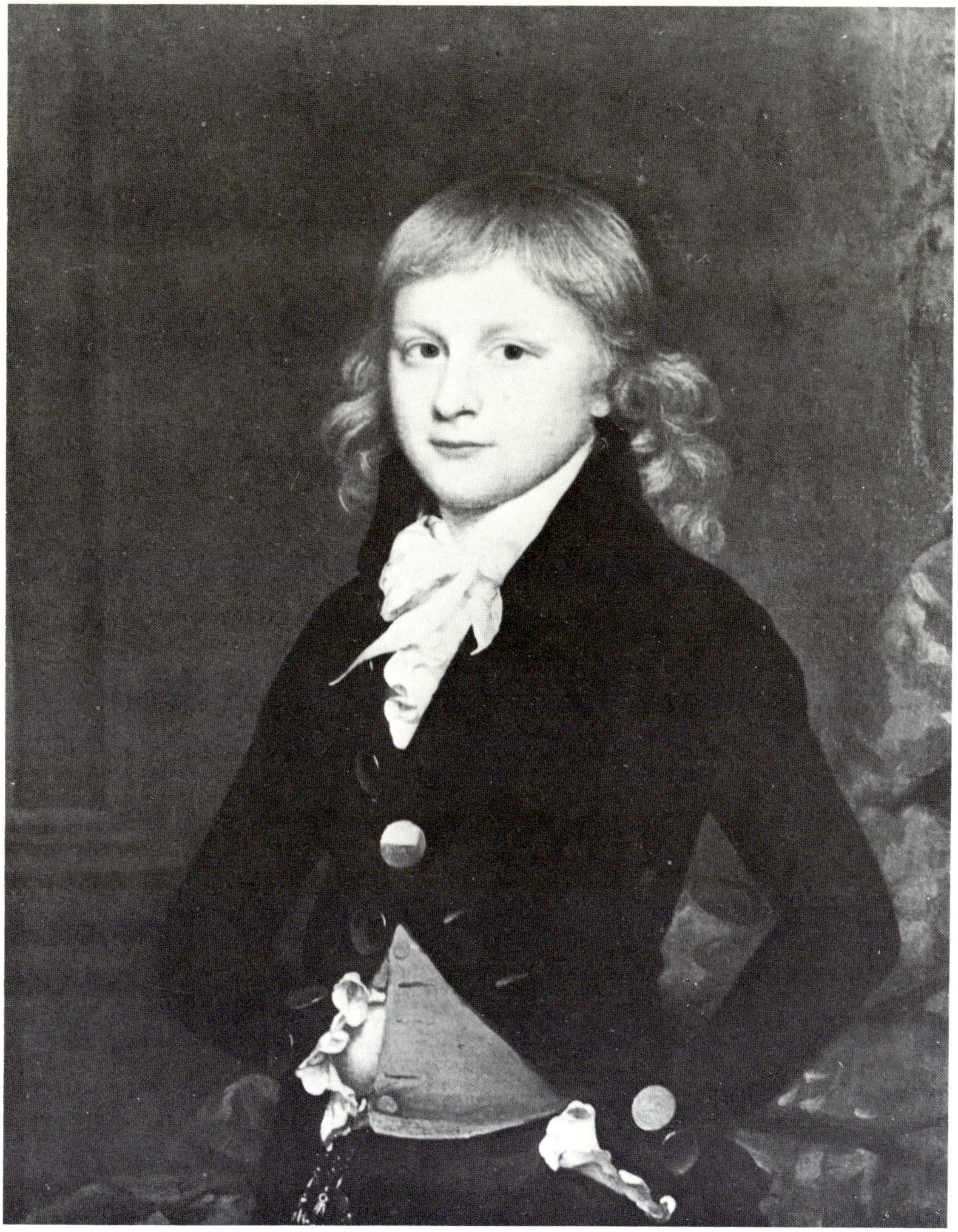

47. Sir William Beechey, R.A.: *The Revd. Lord Frederick Beauclerk as a boy* (M.C.C.).

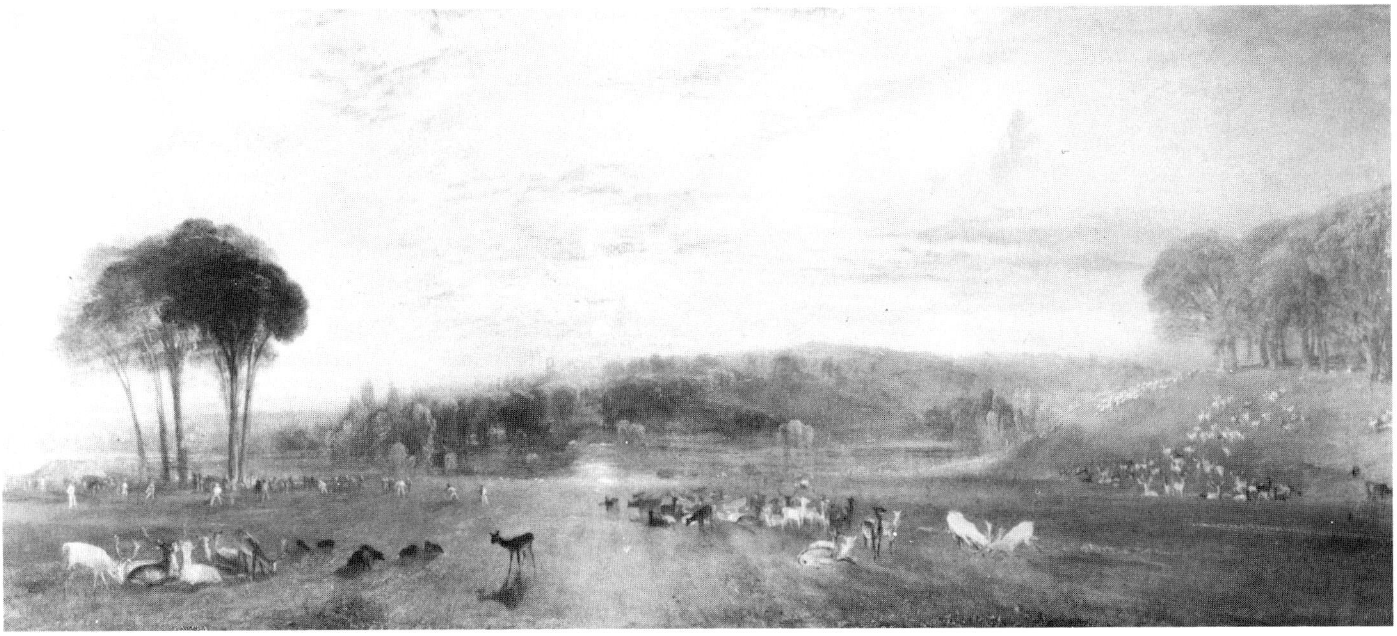

48. J. M. W. Turner, R.A.: *Petworth Park: Bucks Fighting* (*c*. 1830) (Petworth: National Trust).

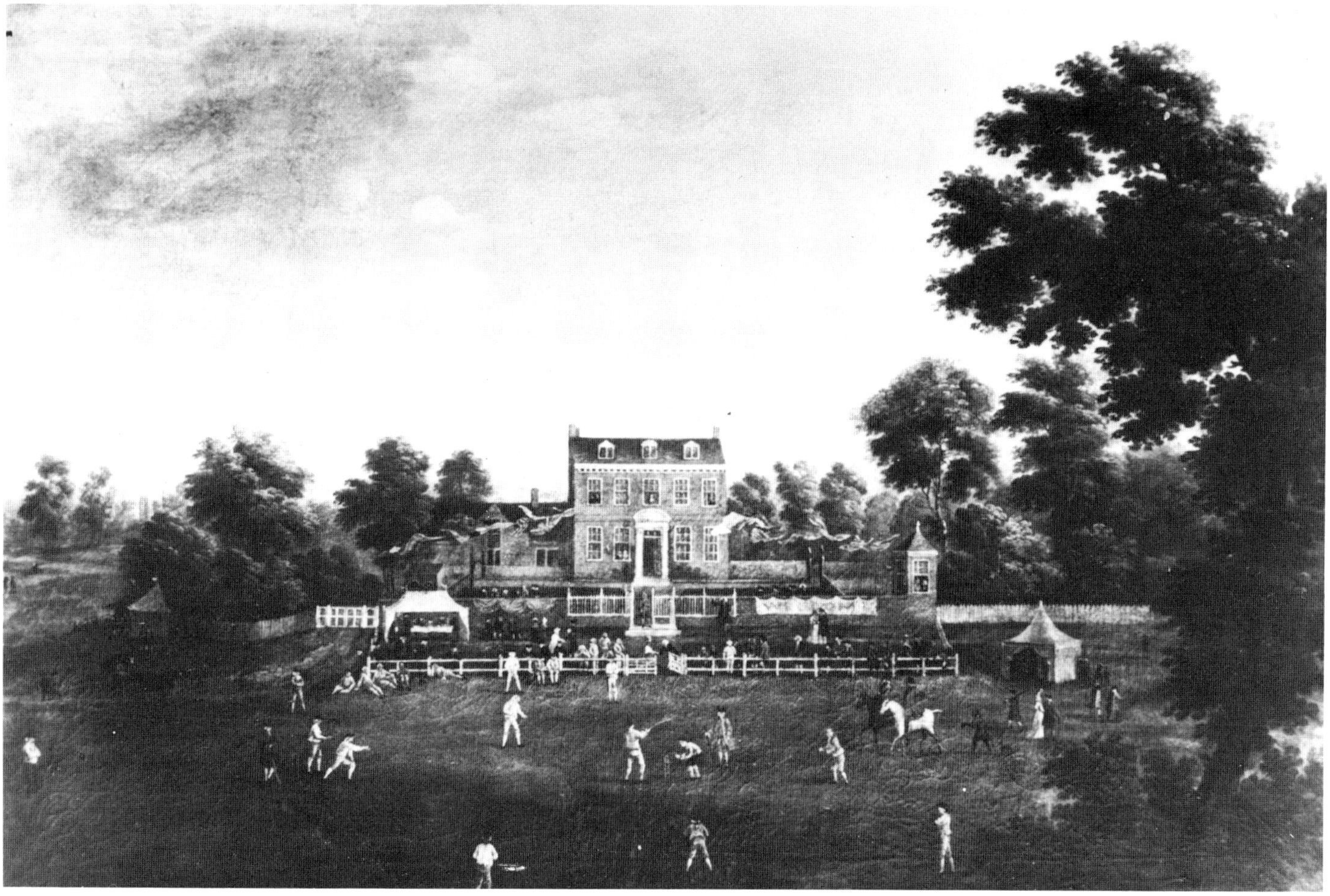

49. British School: *Cricket at Kenfield Hall* (1780) (M.C.C.).

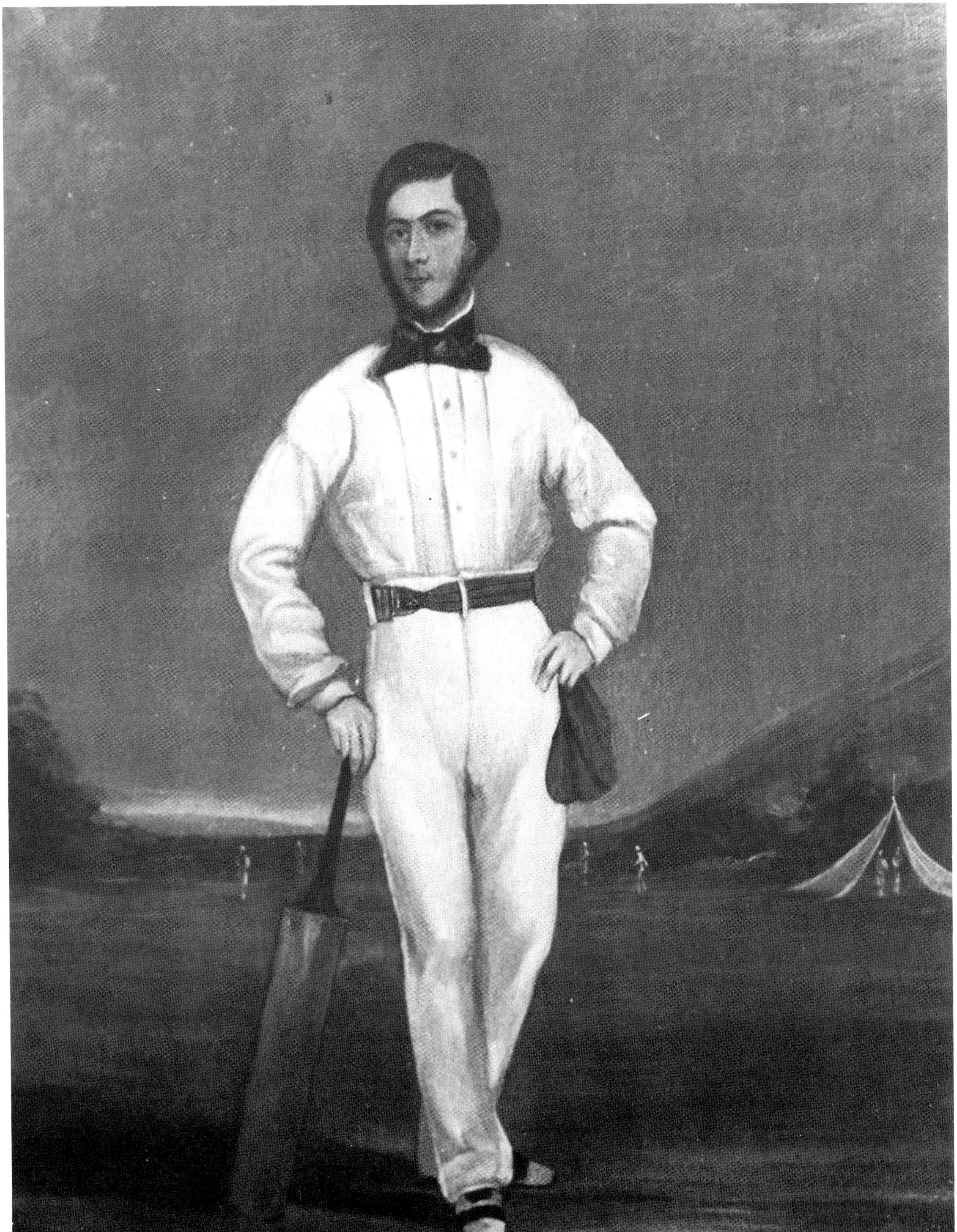

50. British School: *Portrait of a Batsman* (*c*. 1840) (Private Collection).

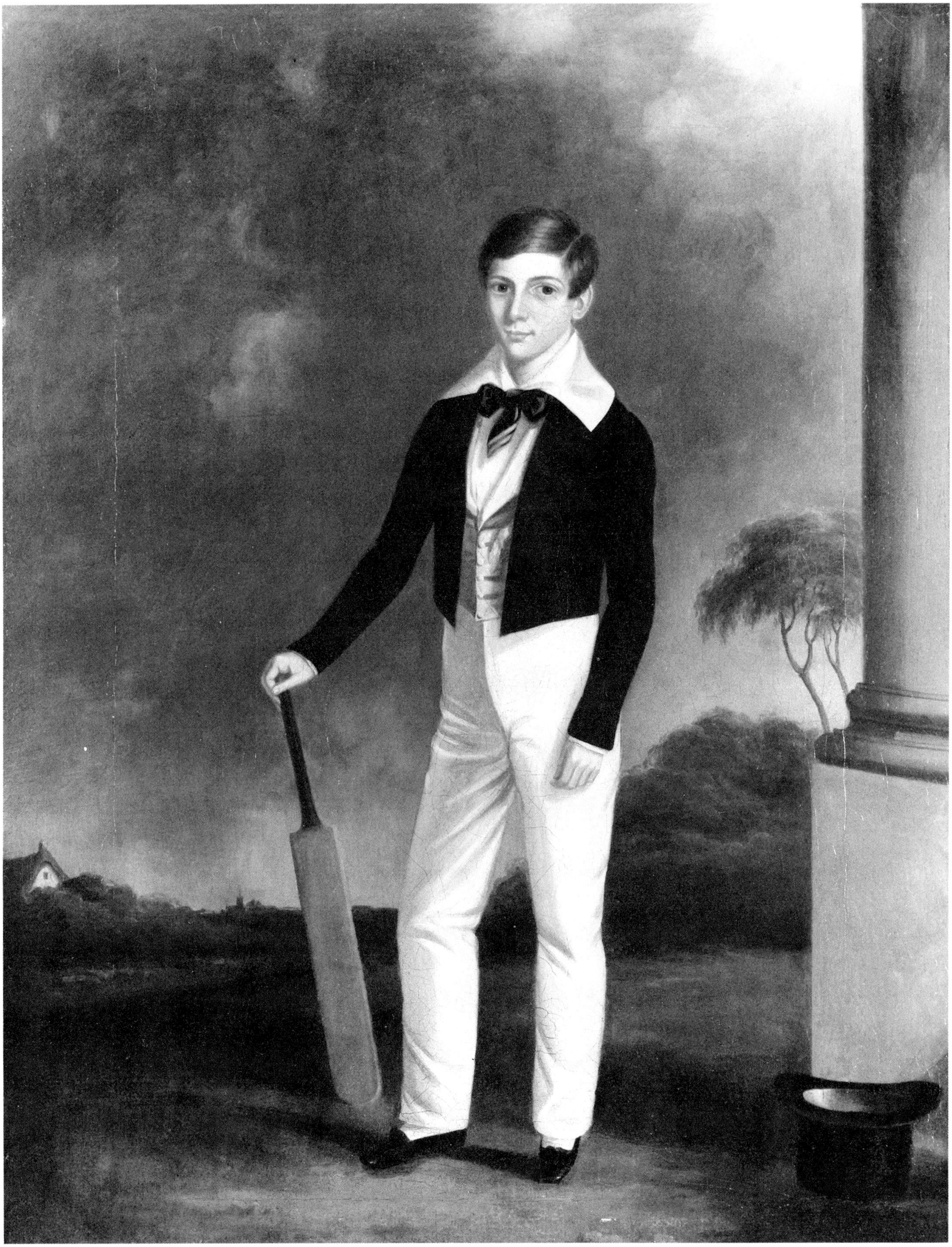

51. British School: Sir Emilius Bayley as a boy (*c.* 1840) (Private Collection). (Photograph: David Cross, Fine Art Gallery, Bristol).

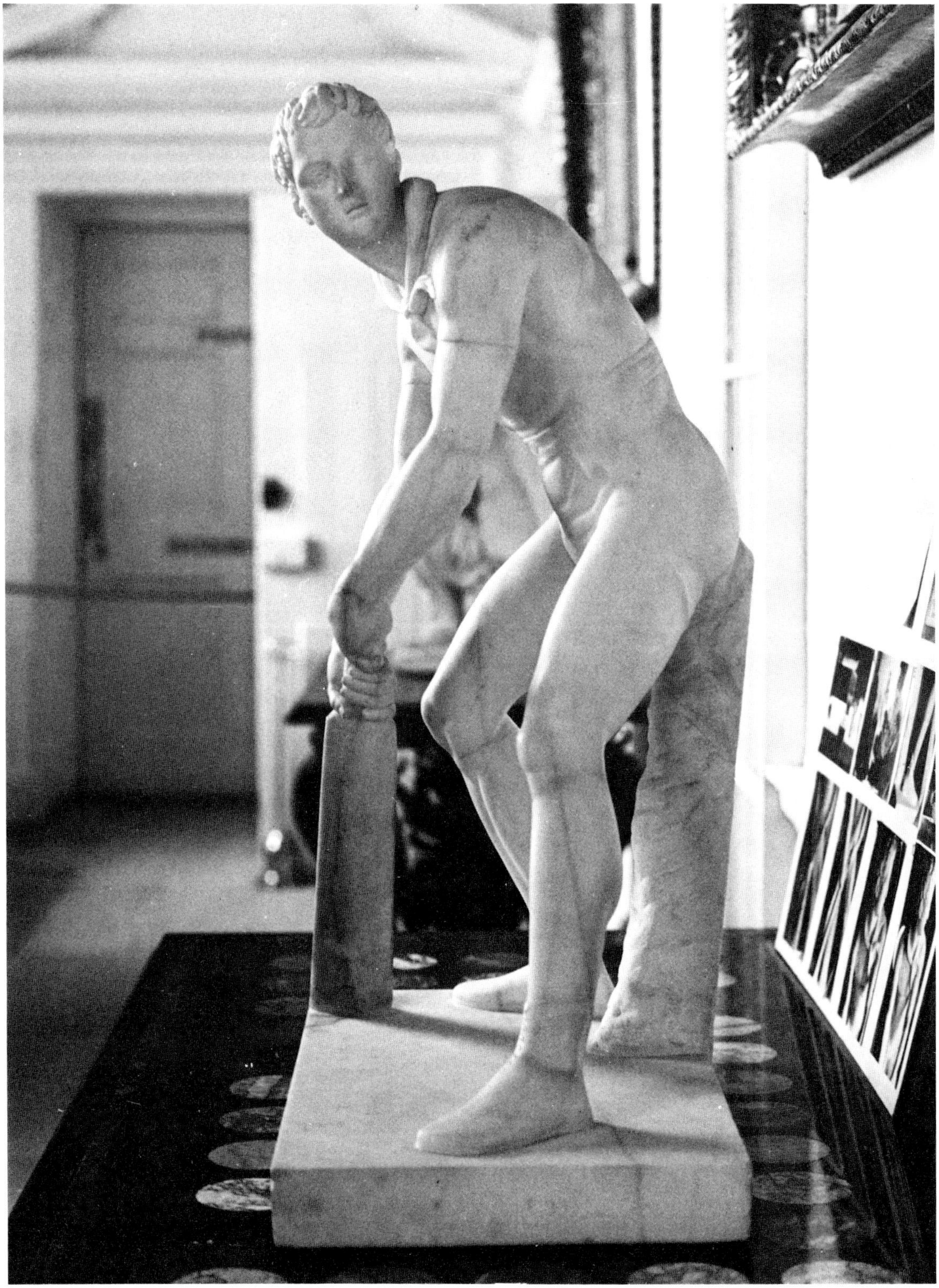

52. Henry Rossi: *The Batsman* (marble) (1825) (The Marquis of Tavistock).

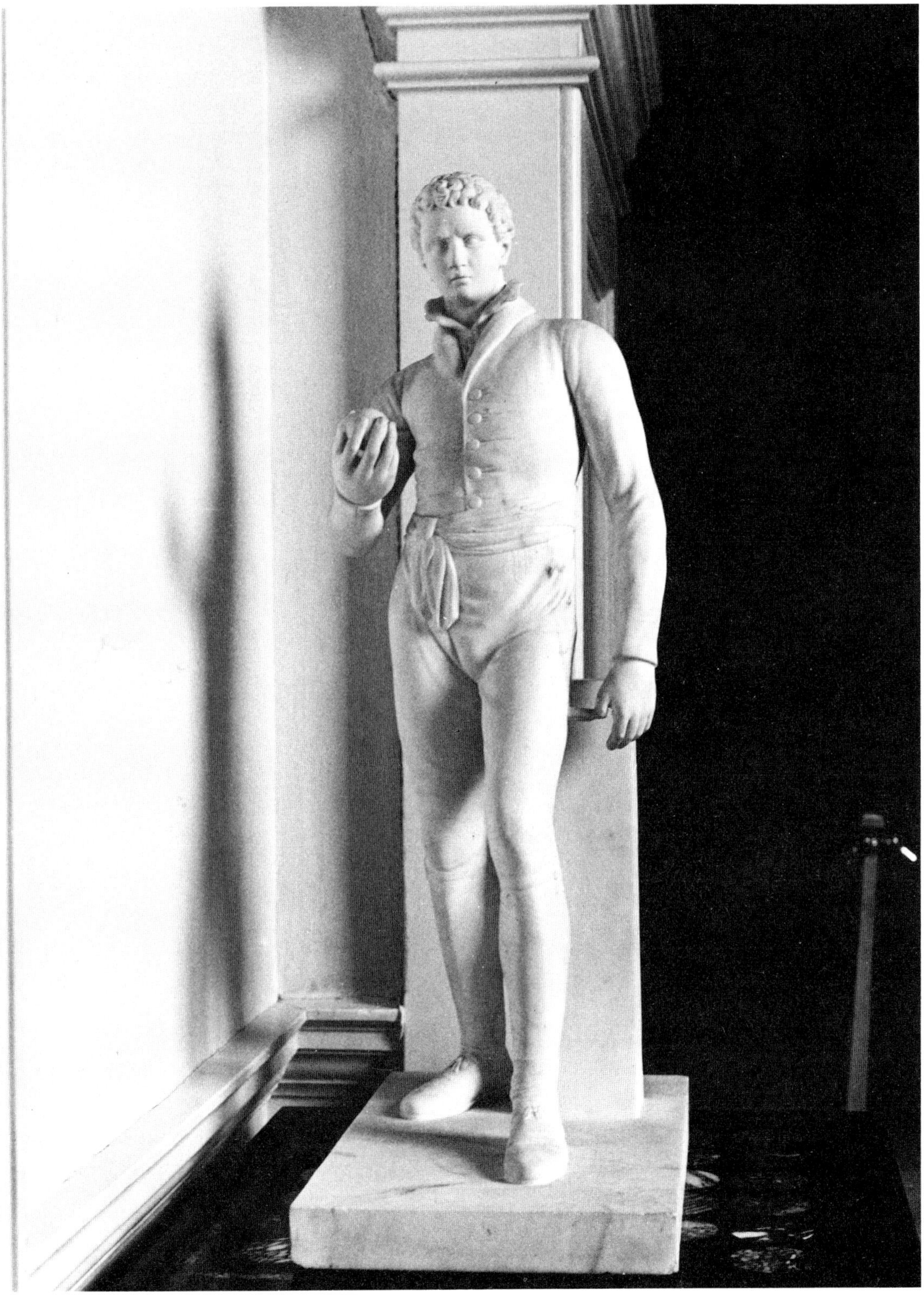

53. Henry Rossi: *The Bowler* (marble) (1825) (The Marquis of Tavistock).

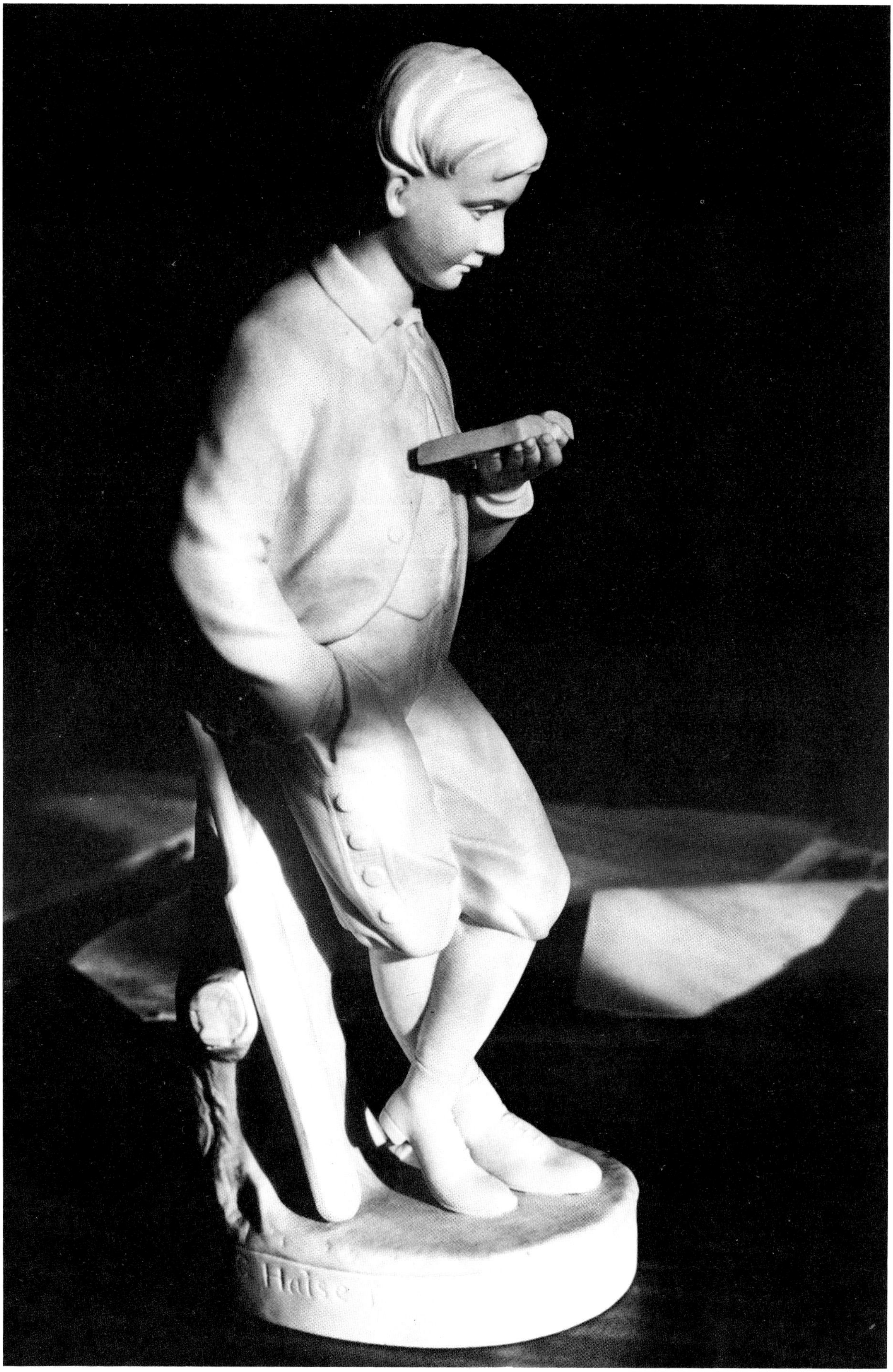

54. G. Halse: *Young England* (1874) (Dr. Andrew Sanders)

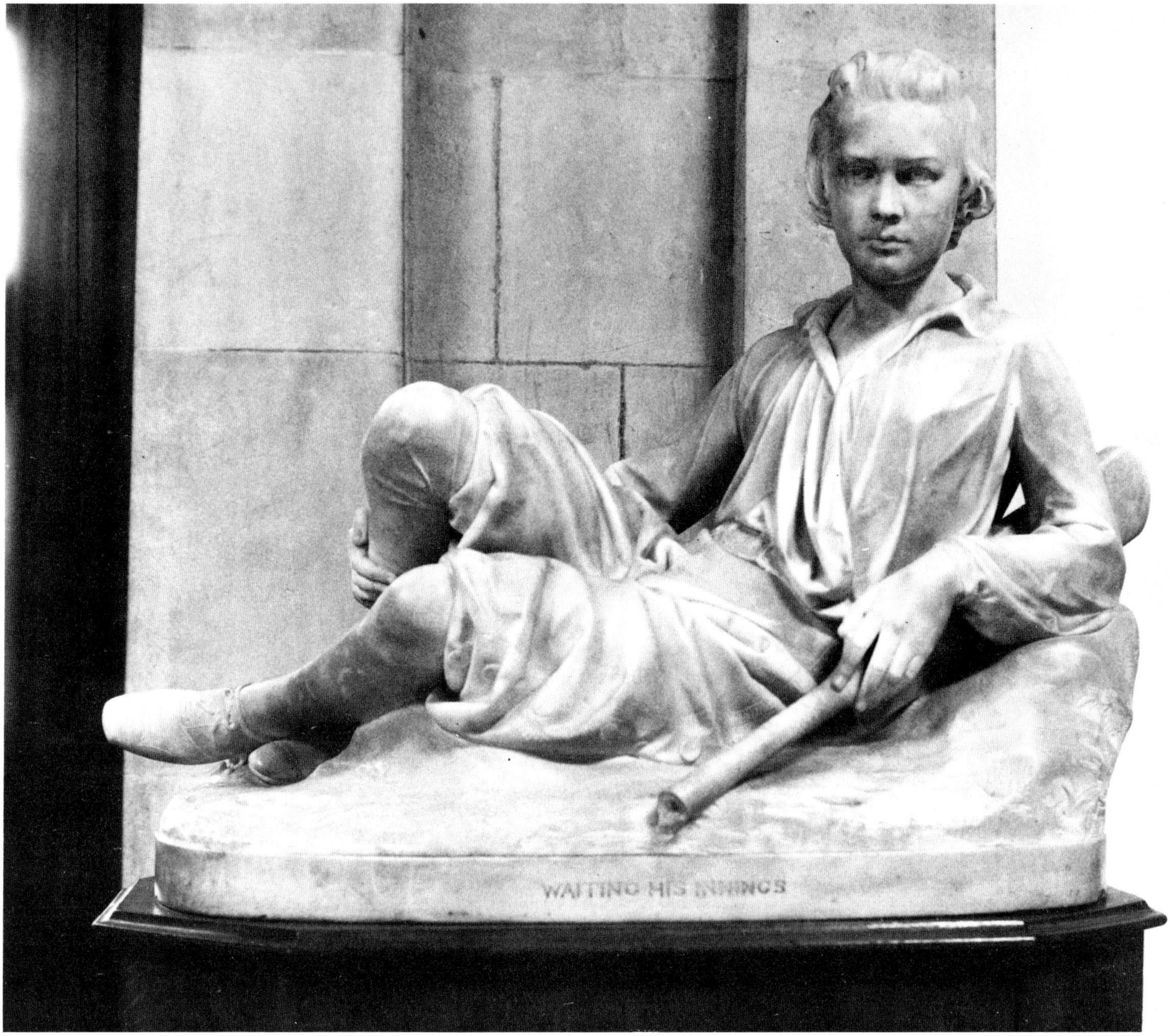

55. Joseph Durham: *Waiting his Innings* (marble) (1866) (City of London School).

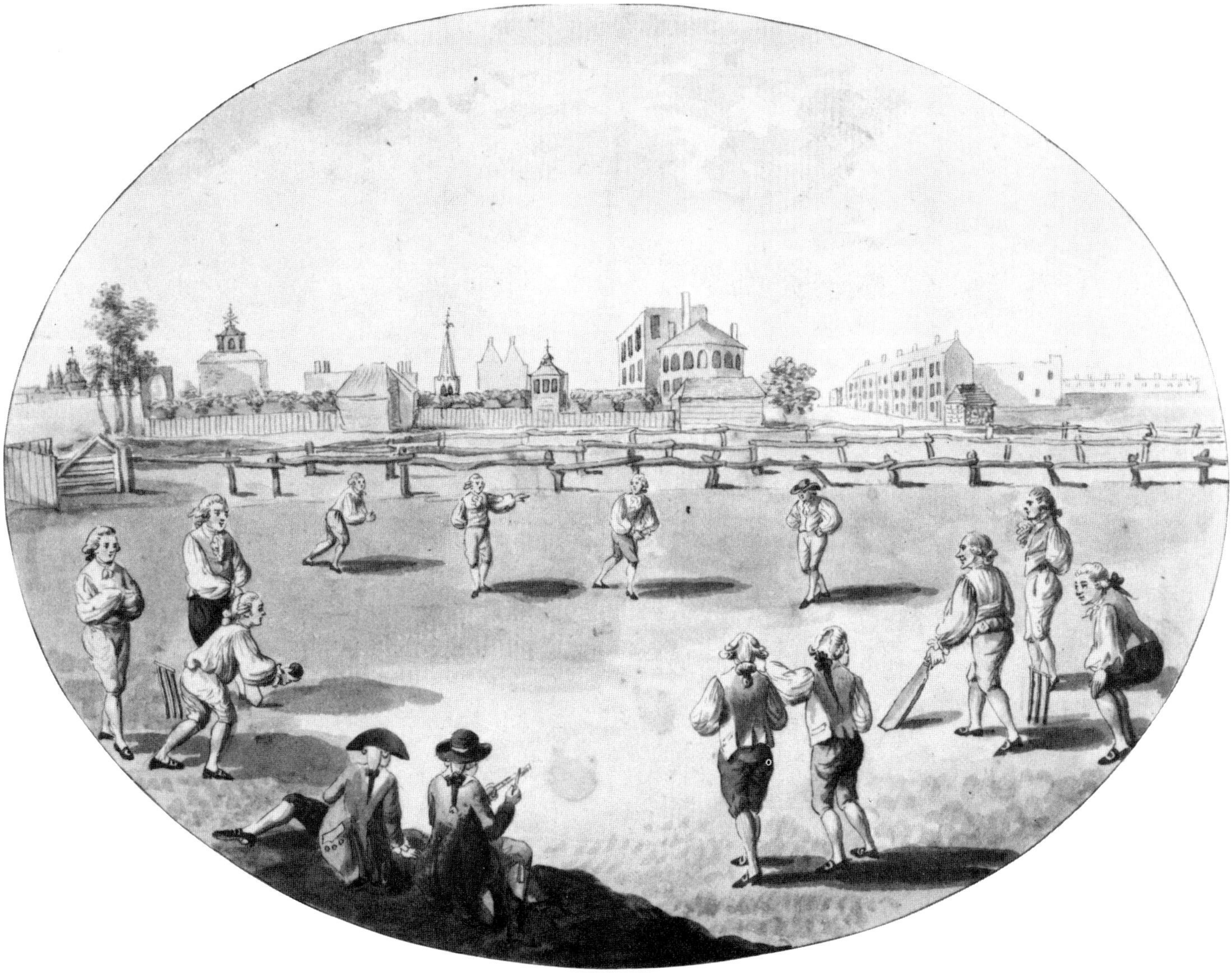

56. Robert Dighton: *Cricket played by the Gentlemen's Club, White Conduit House* (1784) (Paul Mellon Collection).

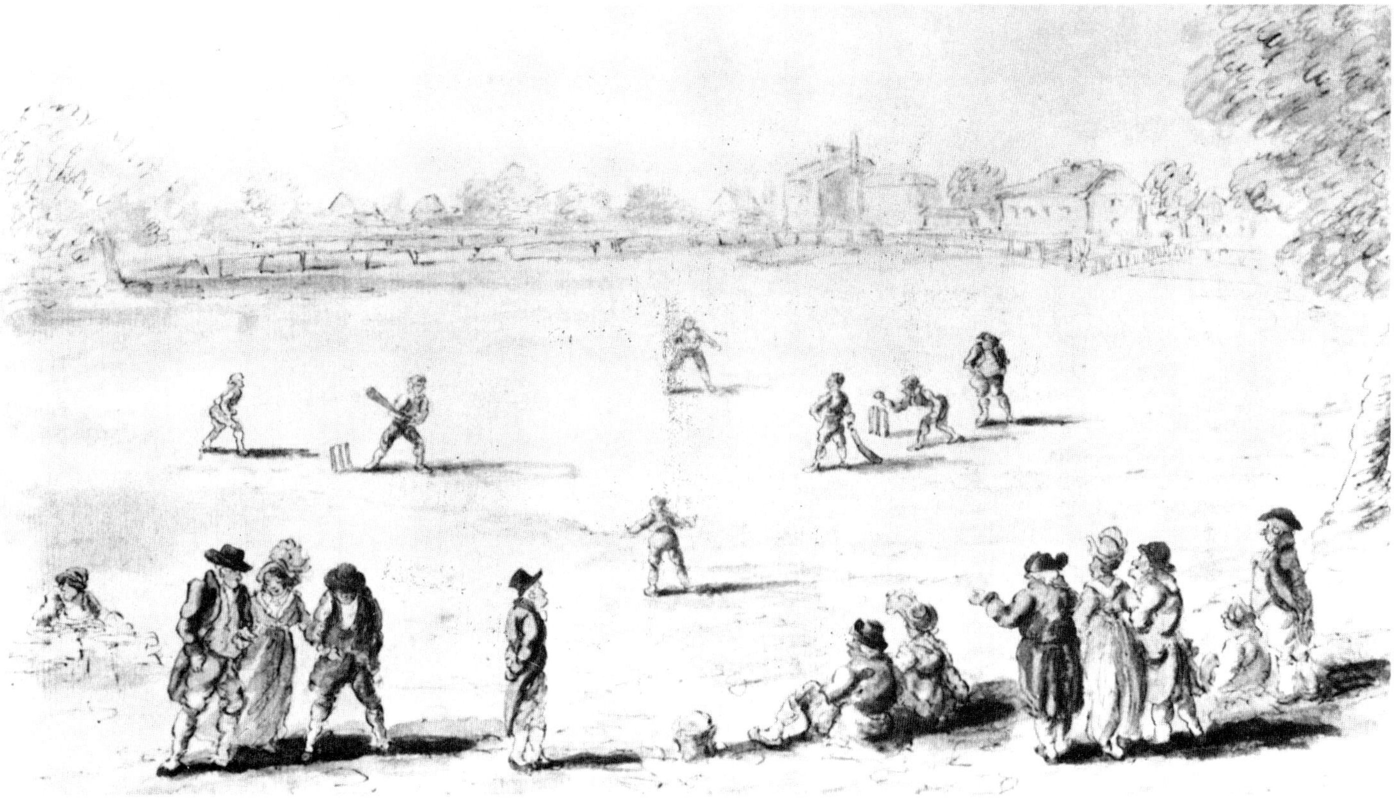

57. Thomas Rowlandson: *Cricket in White Conduit Fields* (*c*. 1790) (M.C.C.).

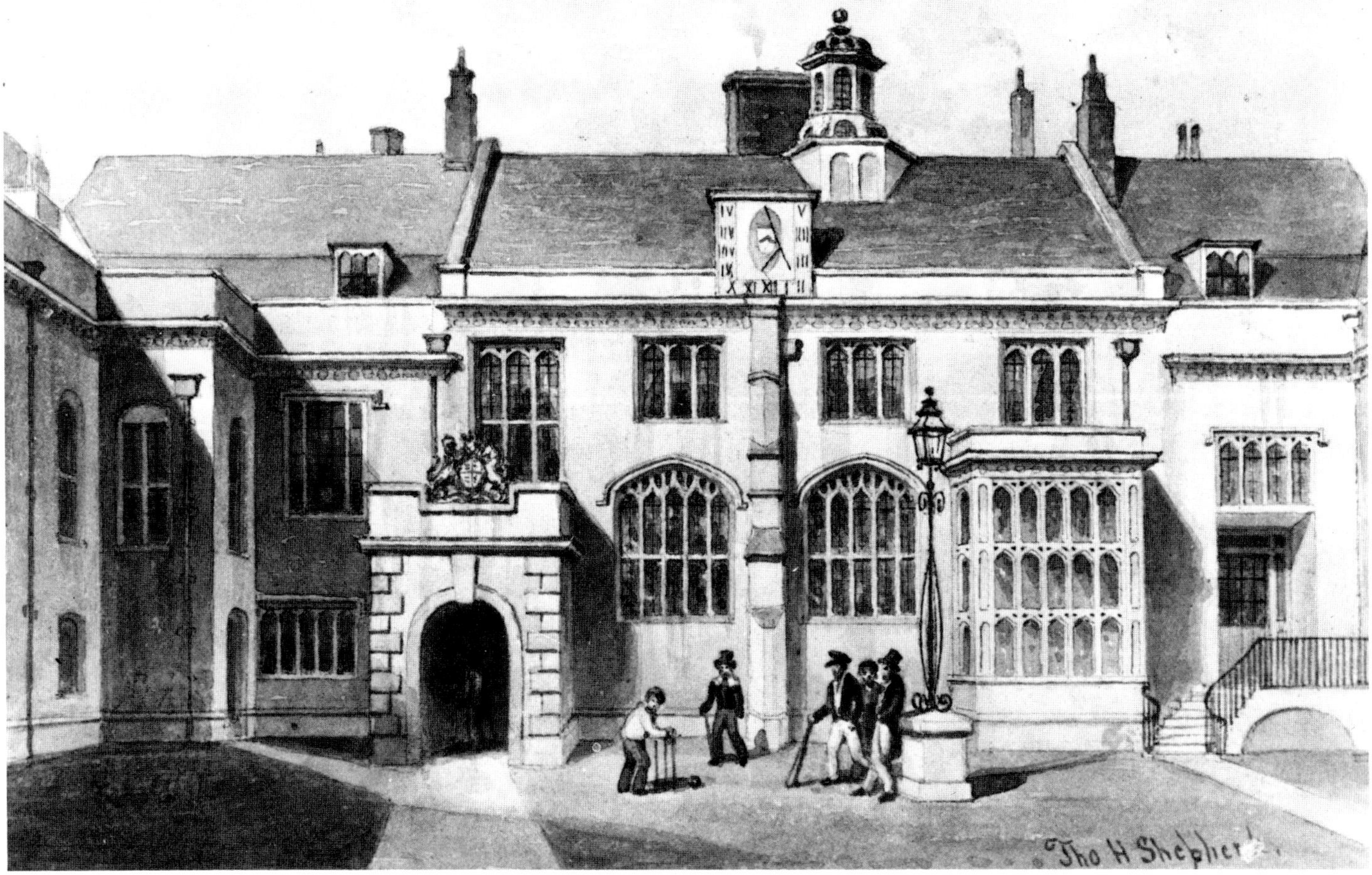

58. Thomas Hosmer Shepherd: *Pensioners' Hall, Charterhouse* (Museum of London).

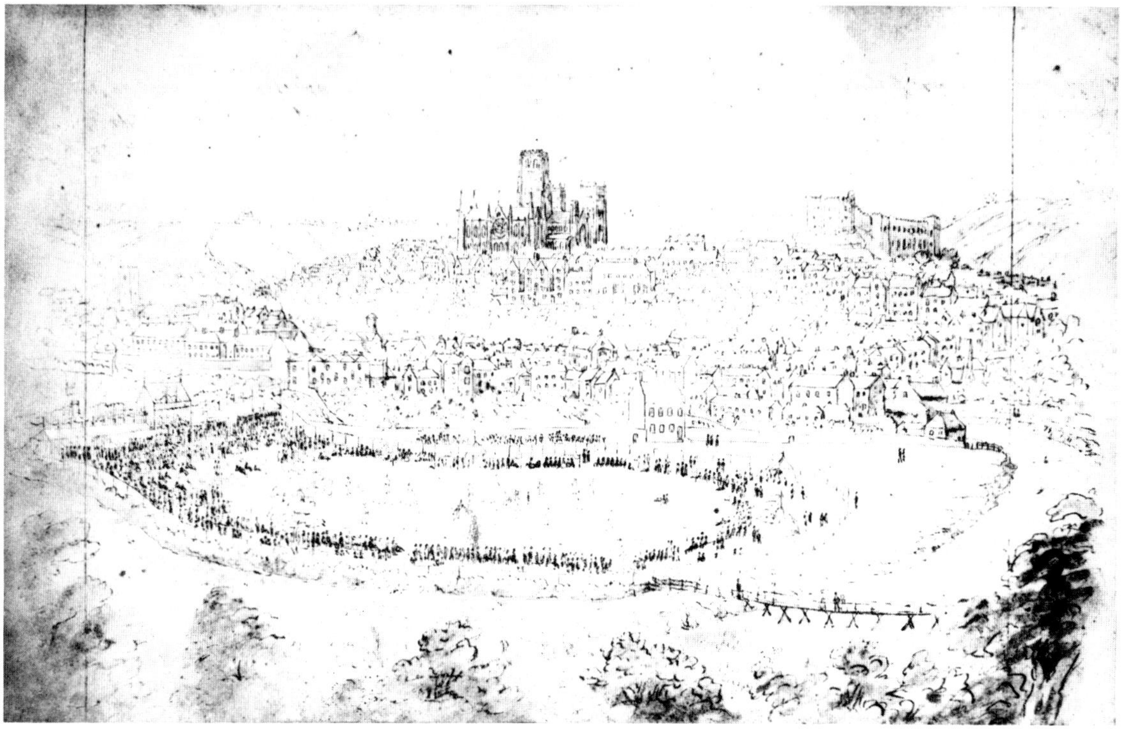

59. Edward Bradley: *Durham* (1849) (M.C.C.).

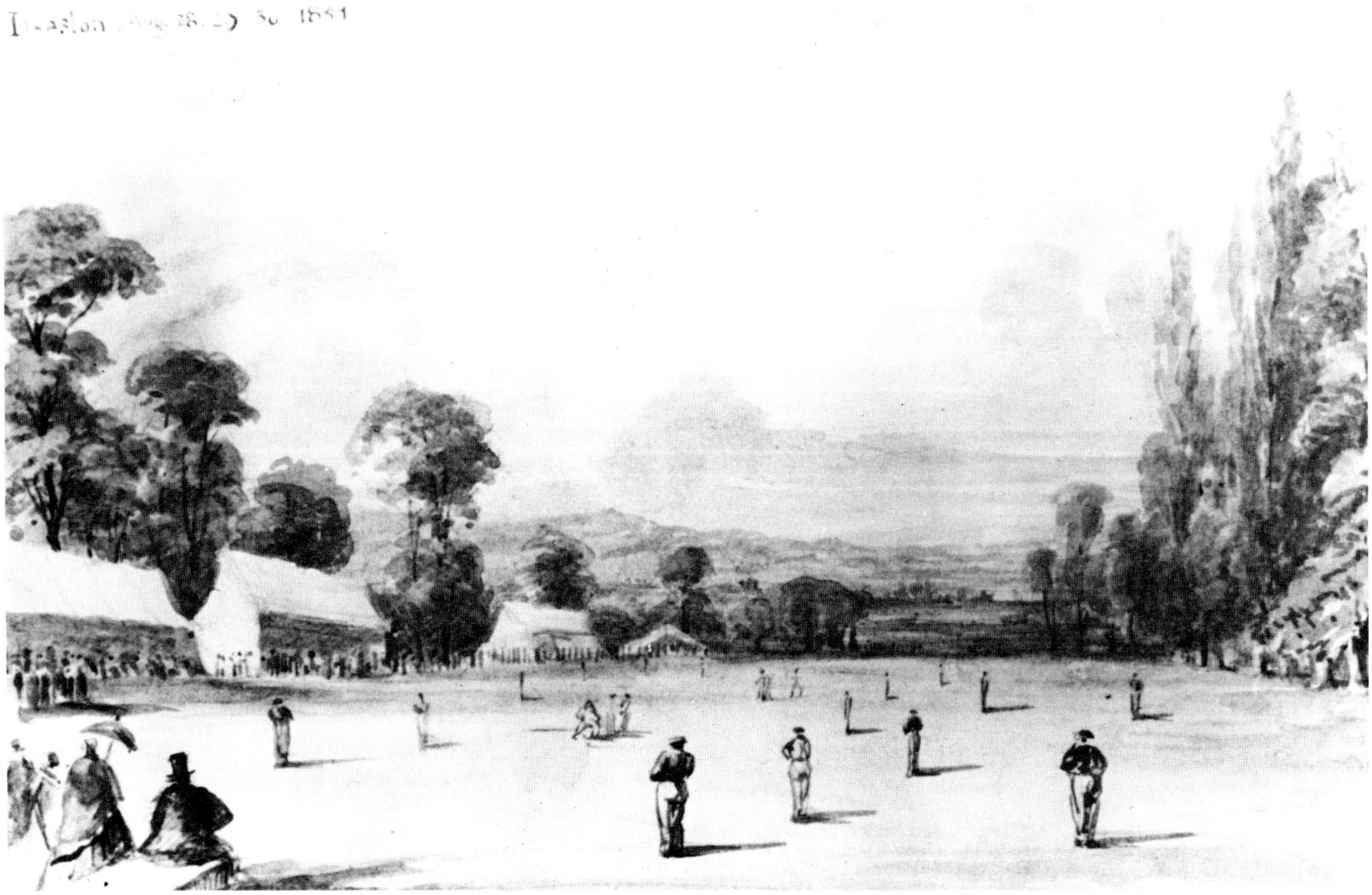

60. Felix: *Cricket at Ilkeston* (1851) (M.C.C.).

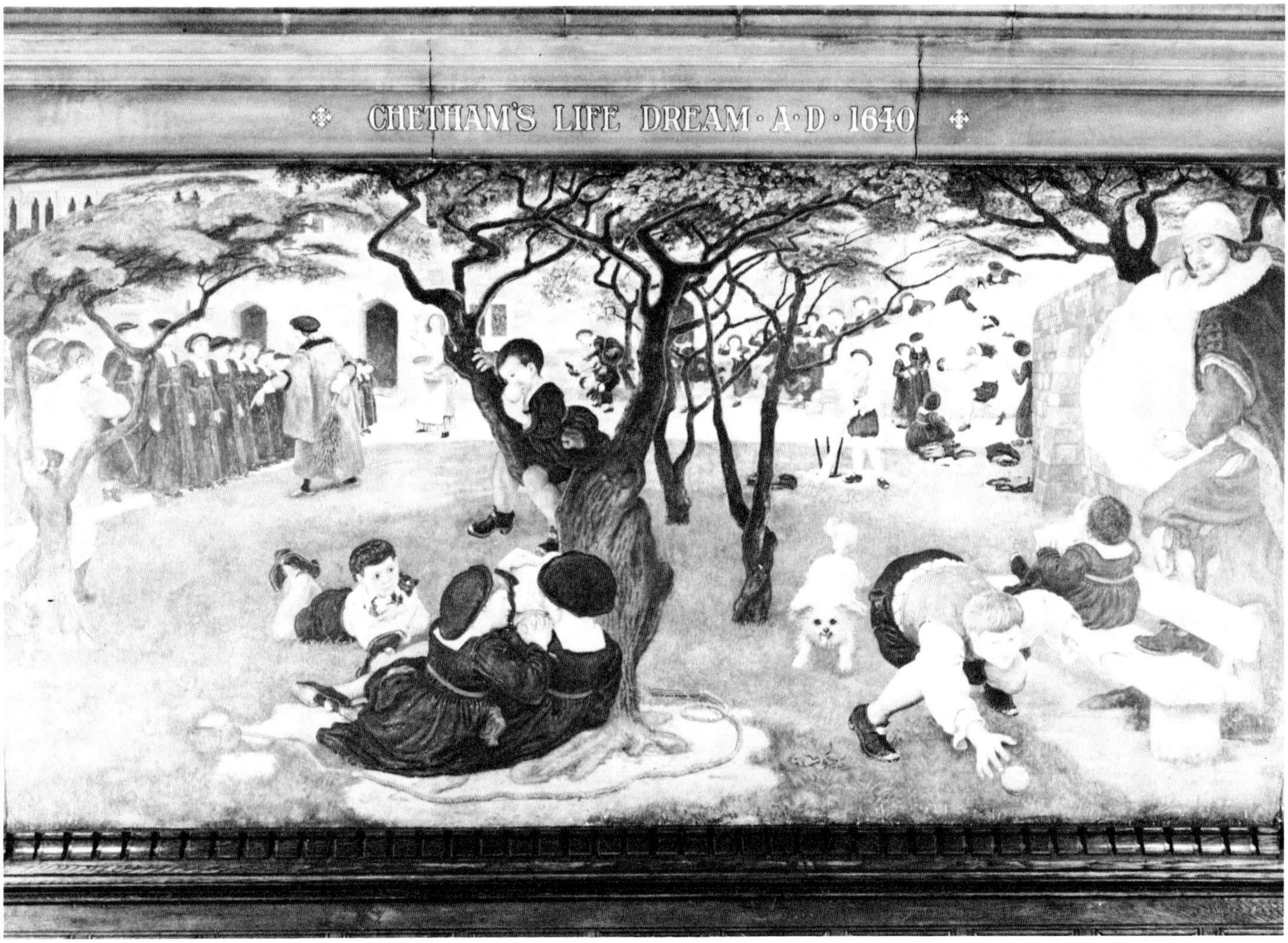

61. Ford Madox Brown: *Humphrey Chetham's Life Dream* (Manchester Town Hall).

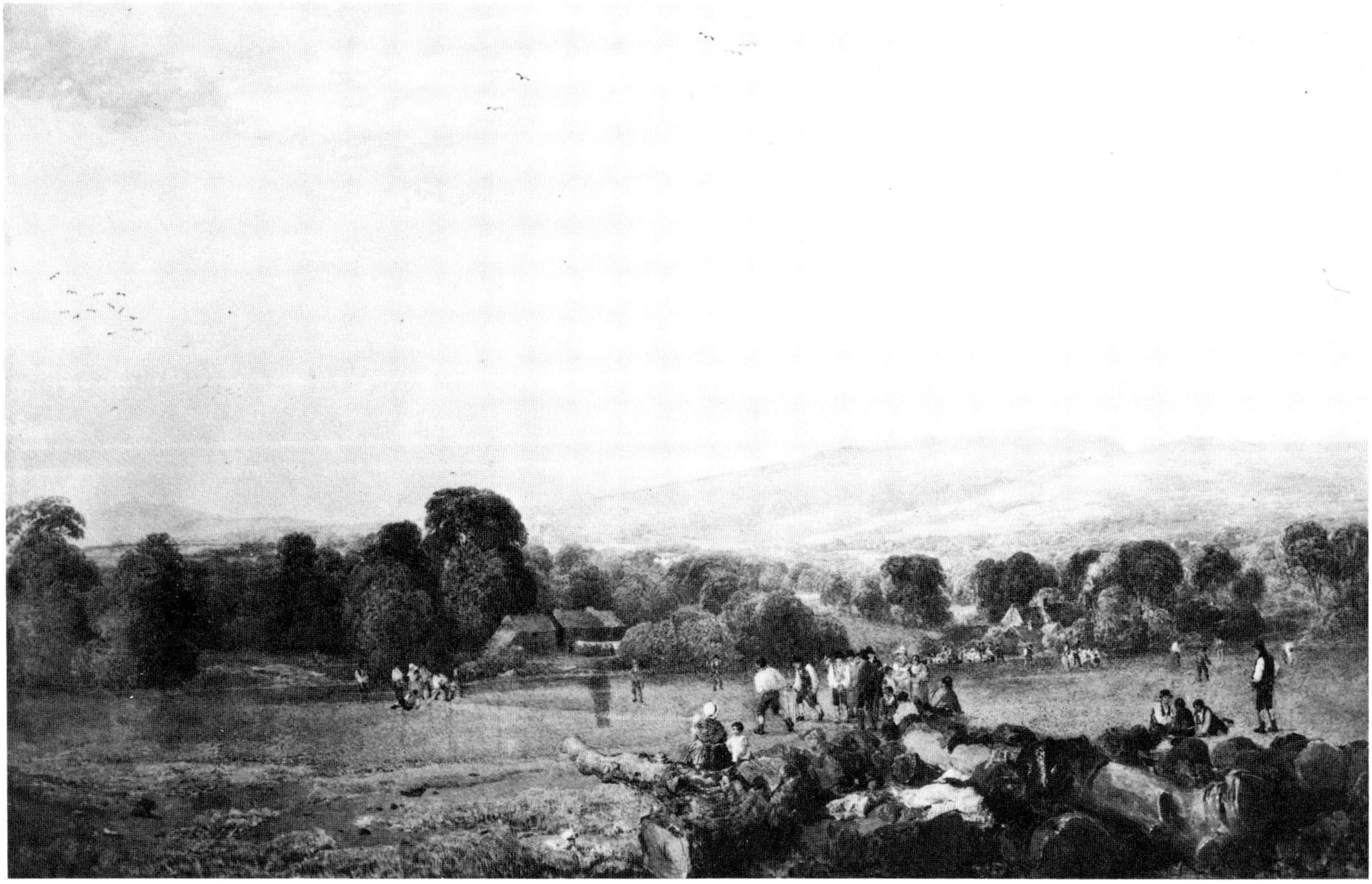

62. Peter De Wint: *The Cricketers* (Victoria and Albert Museum, London).

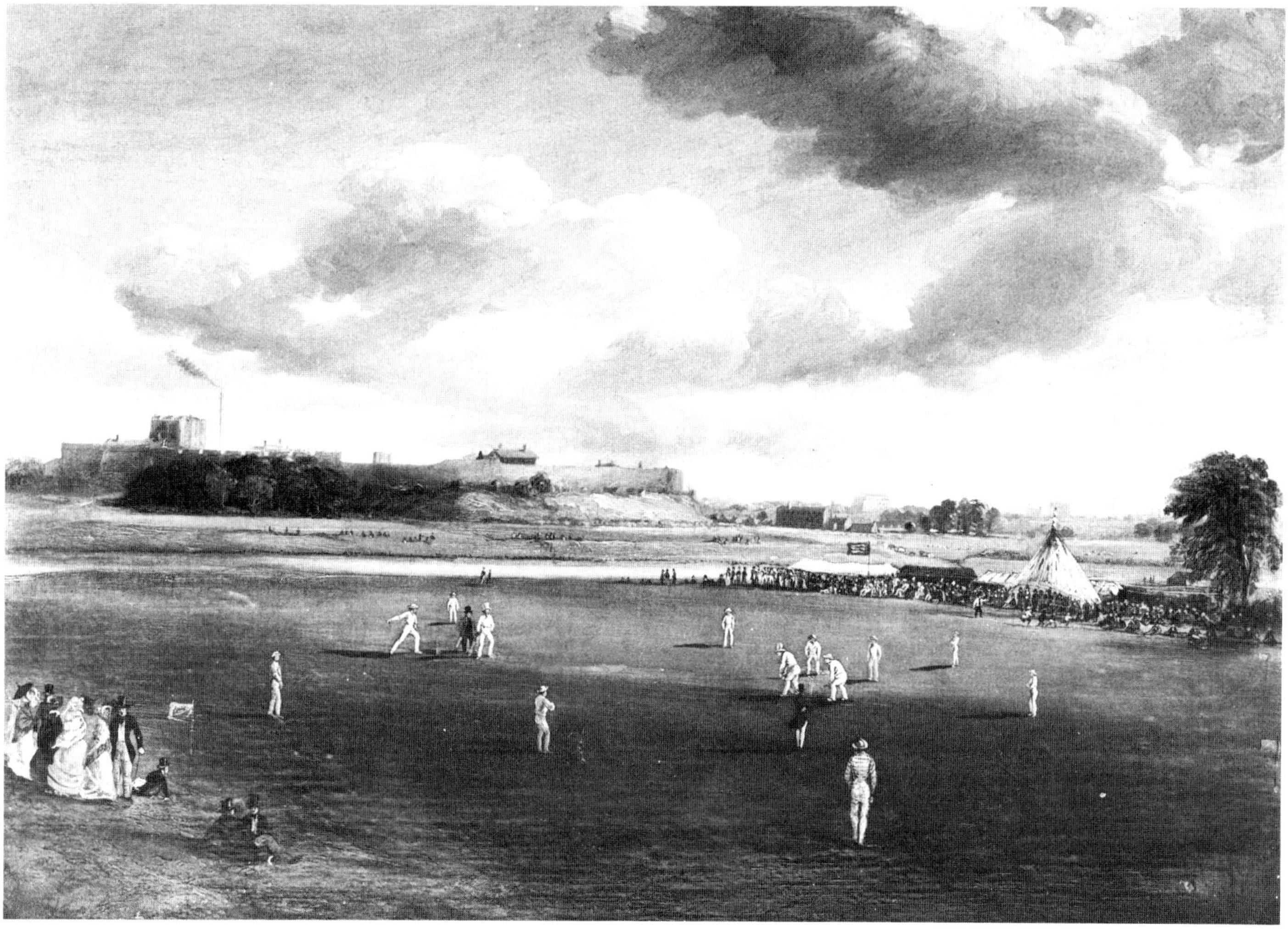

63. Sam Bough: *Cricket at Edenside, Carlisle* (Carlisle City Art Gallery).

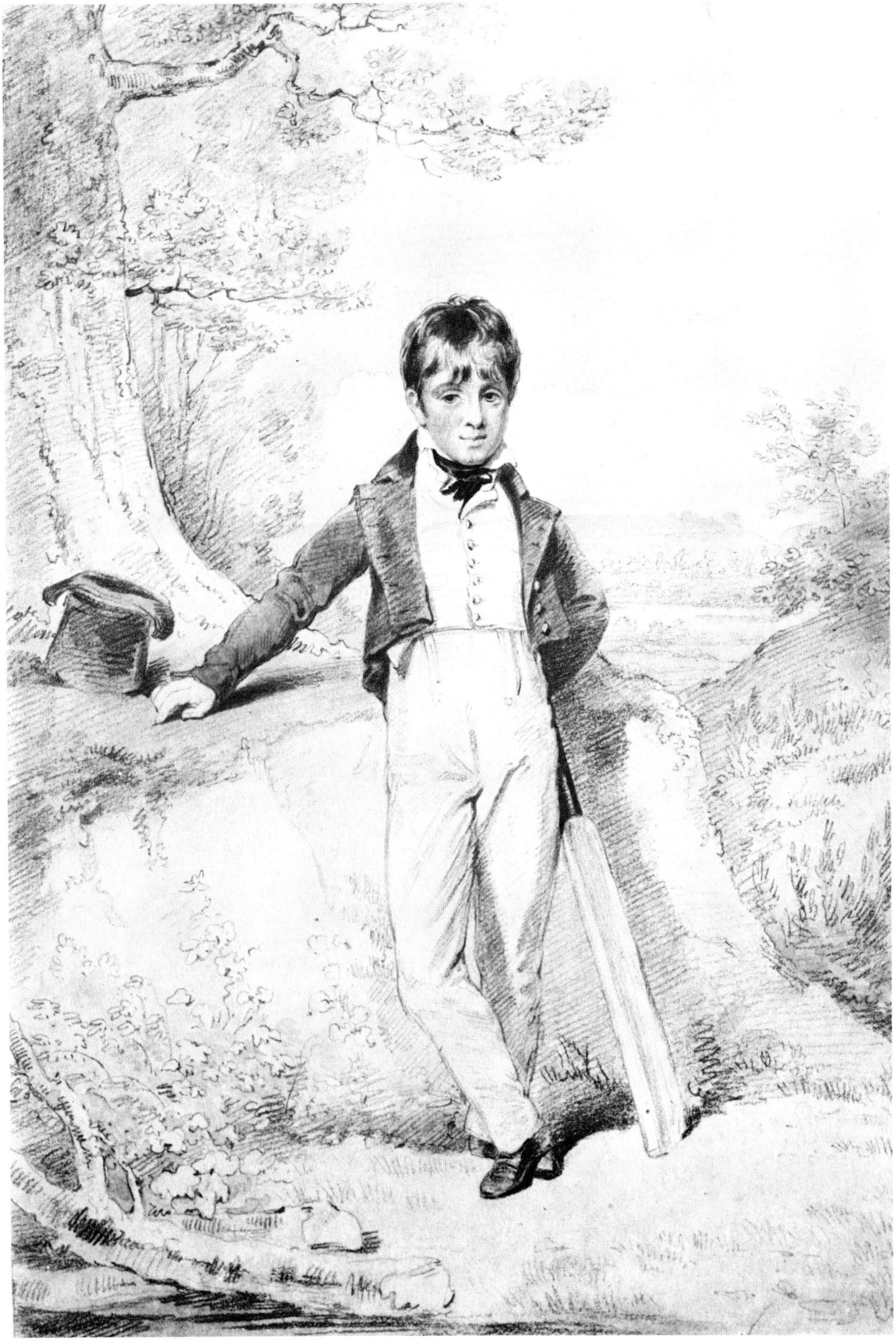

64. Henry Edridge, A.R.A.: *A Young Cricketer* (Private Collection).

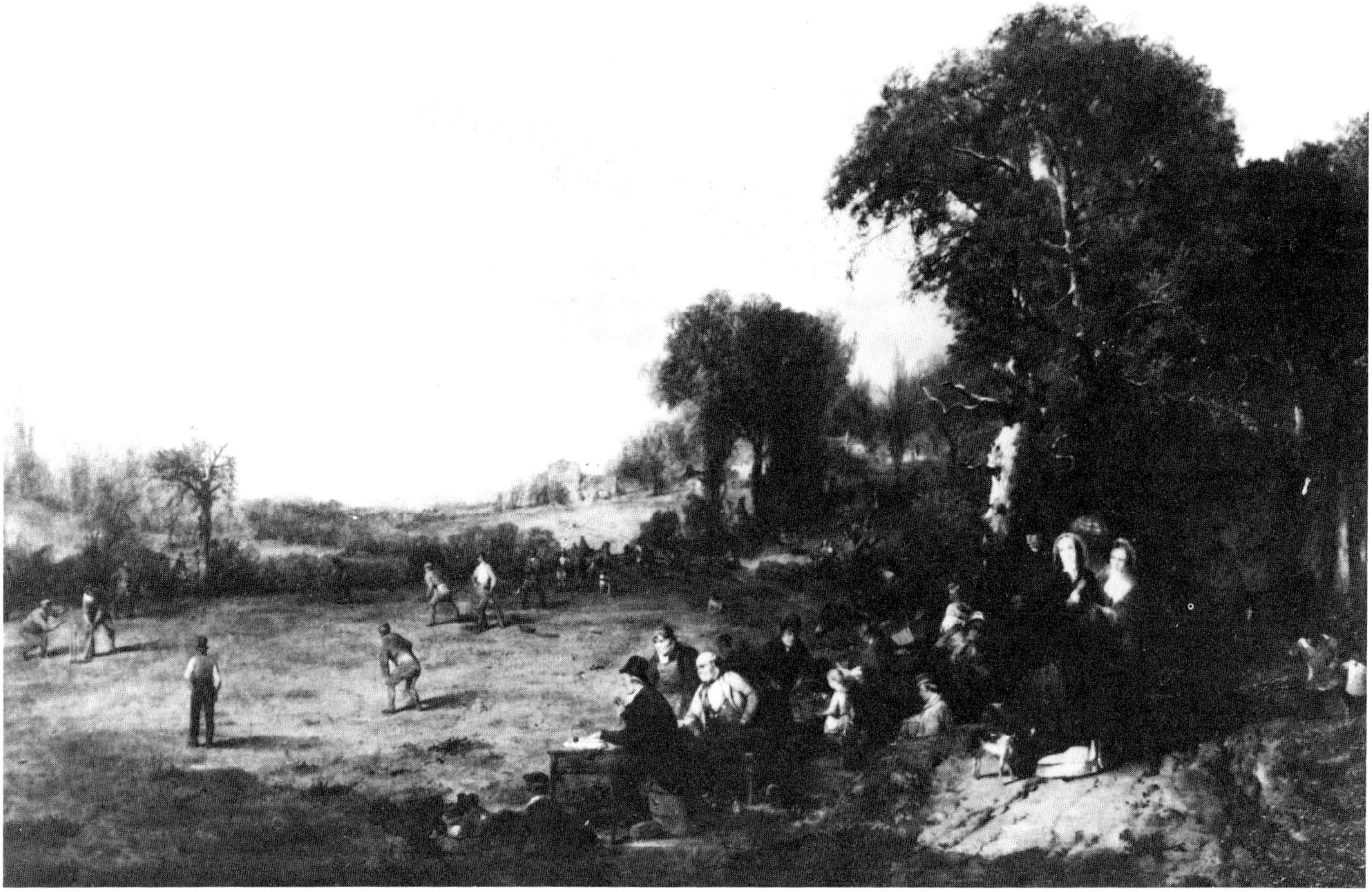

65. John Ritchie: *Village Cricket* (1855) (M.C.C.).

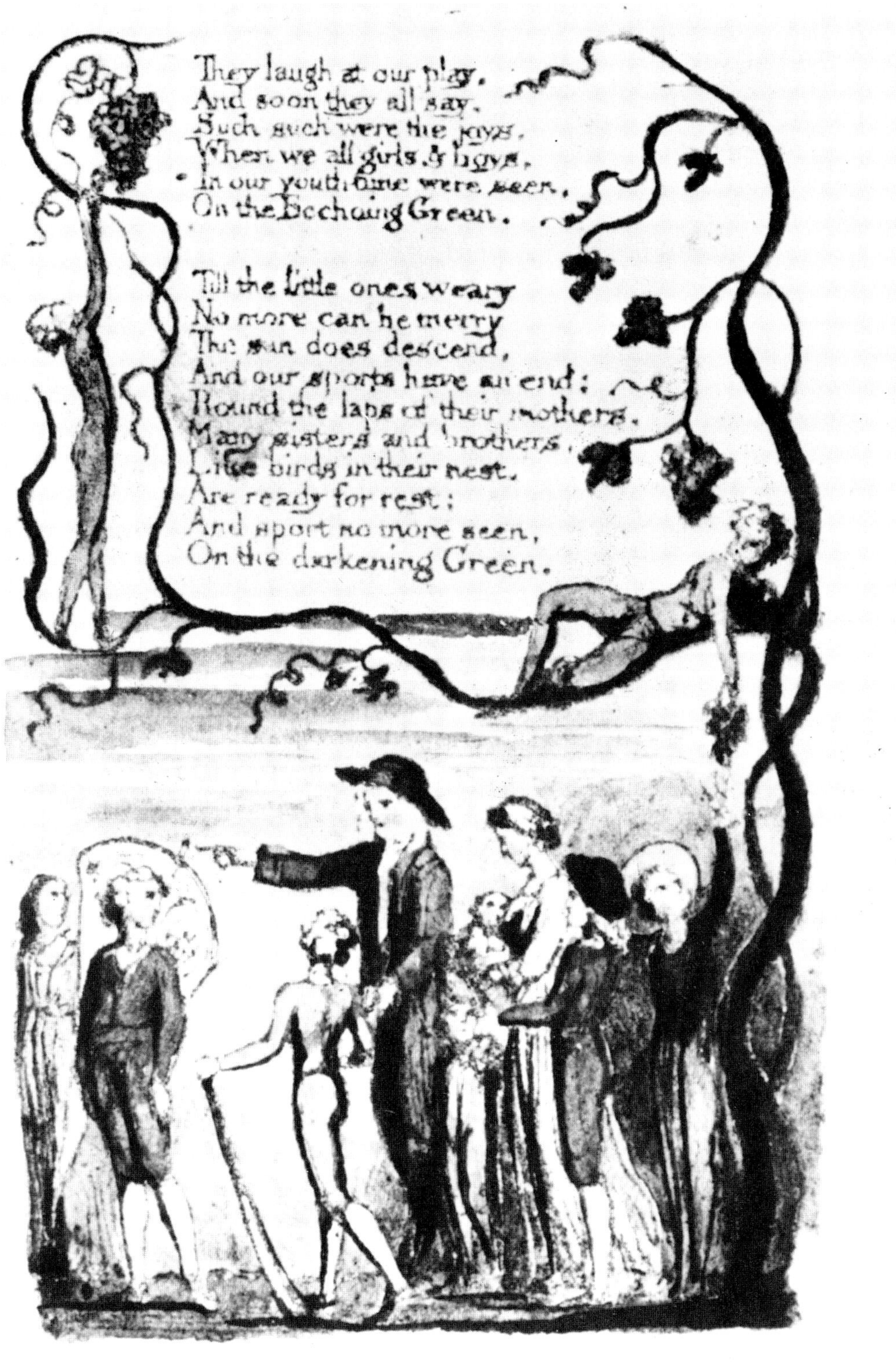

66. William Blake: *The Echoing Green*, I (1789).

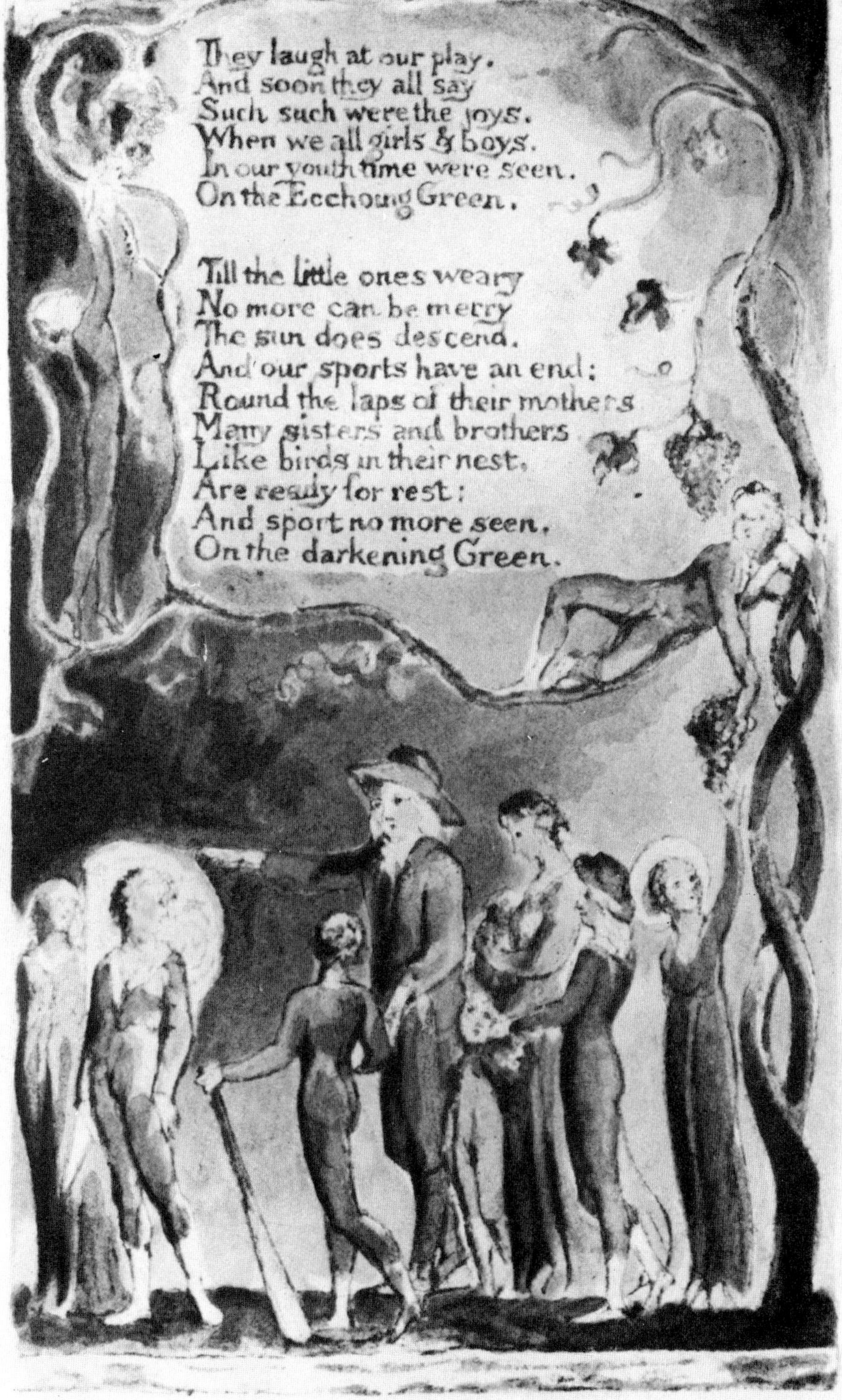

67. William Blake: *The Echoing Green*, II (1820s).

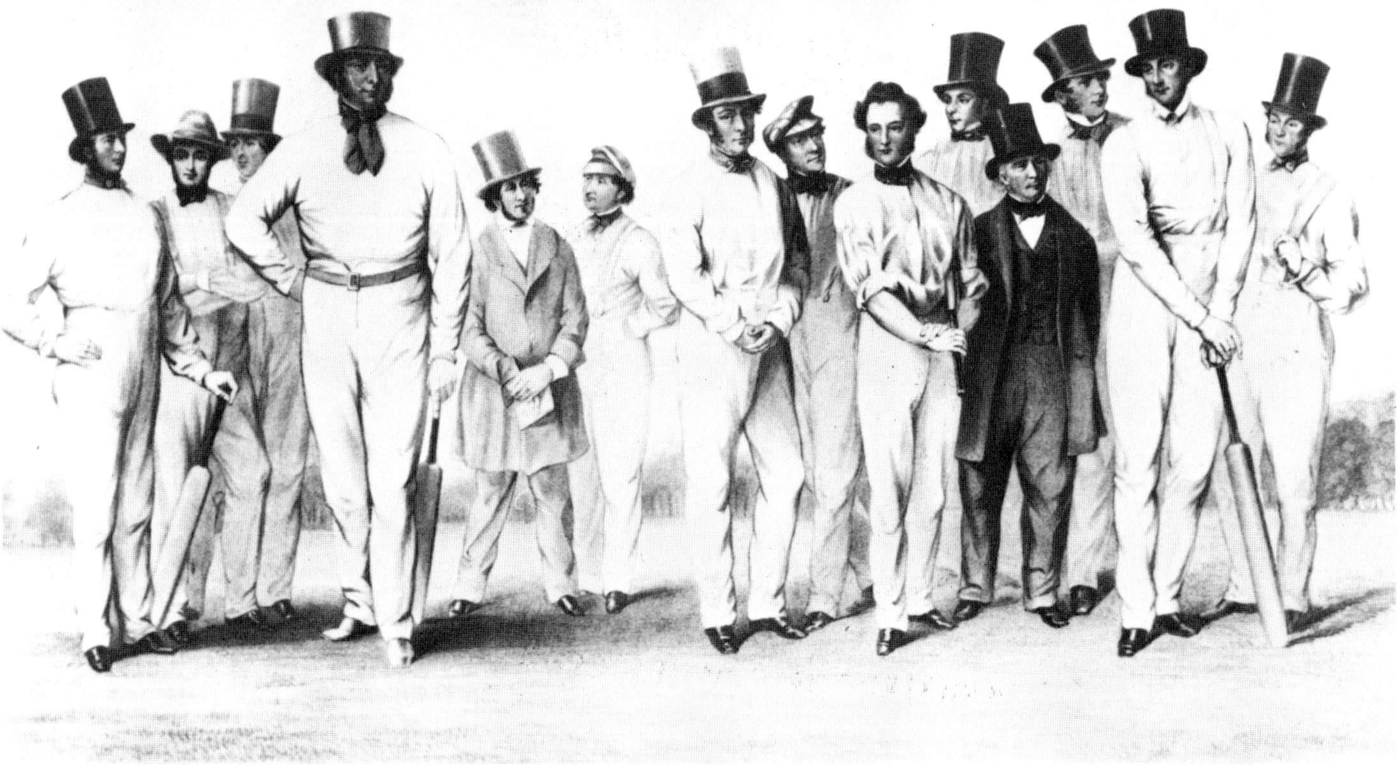

68. N. Ploszczynski *after* Felix: *The Eleven of England* (1847).

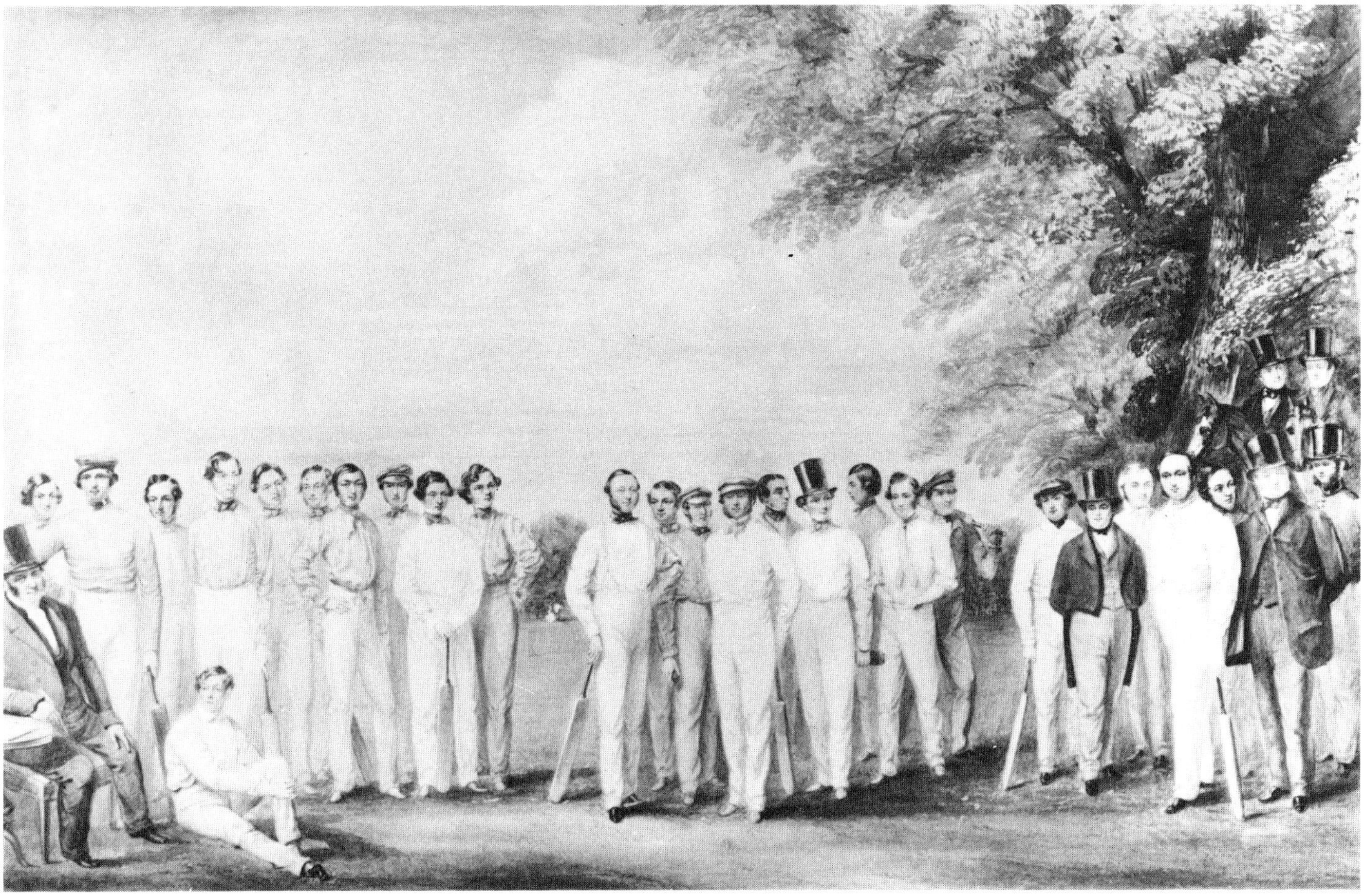

69. Felix: *The Two Elevens of the University of Cambridge* (1847) (M.C.C.).

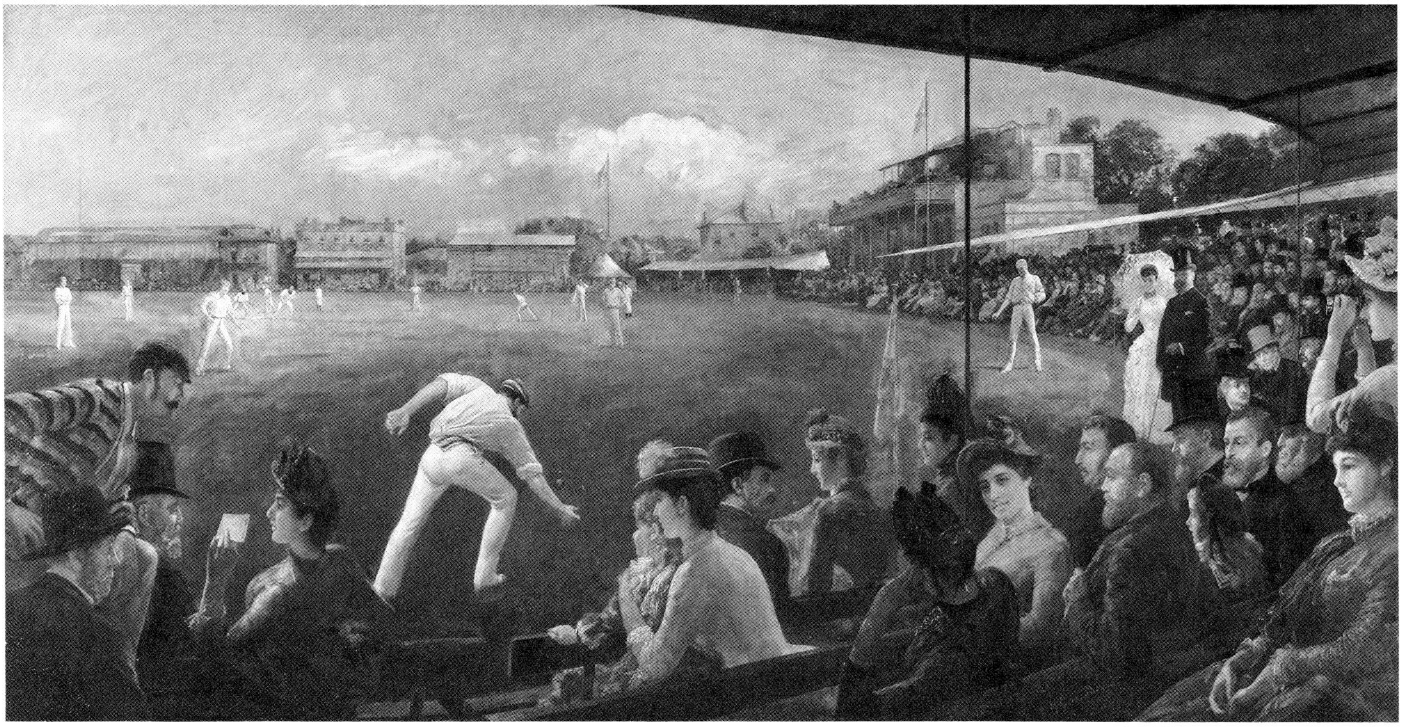

70. George Hamilton Barrable and Sir Robert Ponsonby Staples, Bart.: *England v. Australia at Lords's* (1887) (M.C.C.).

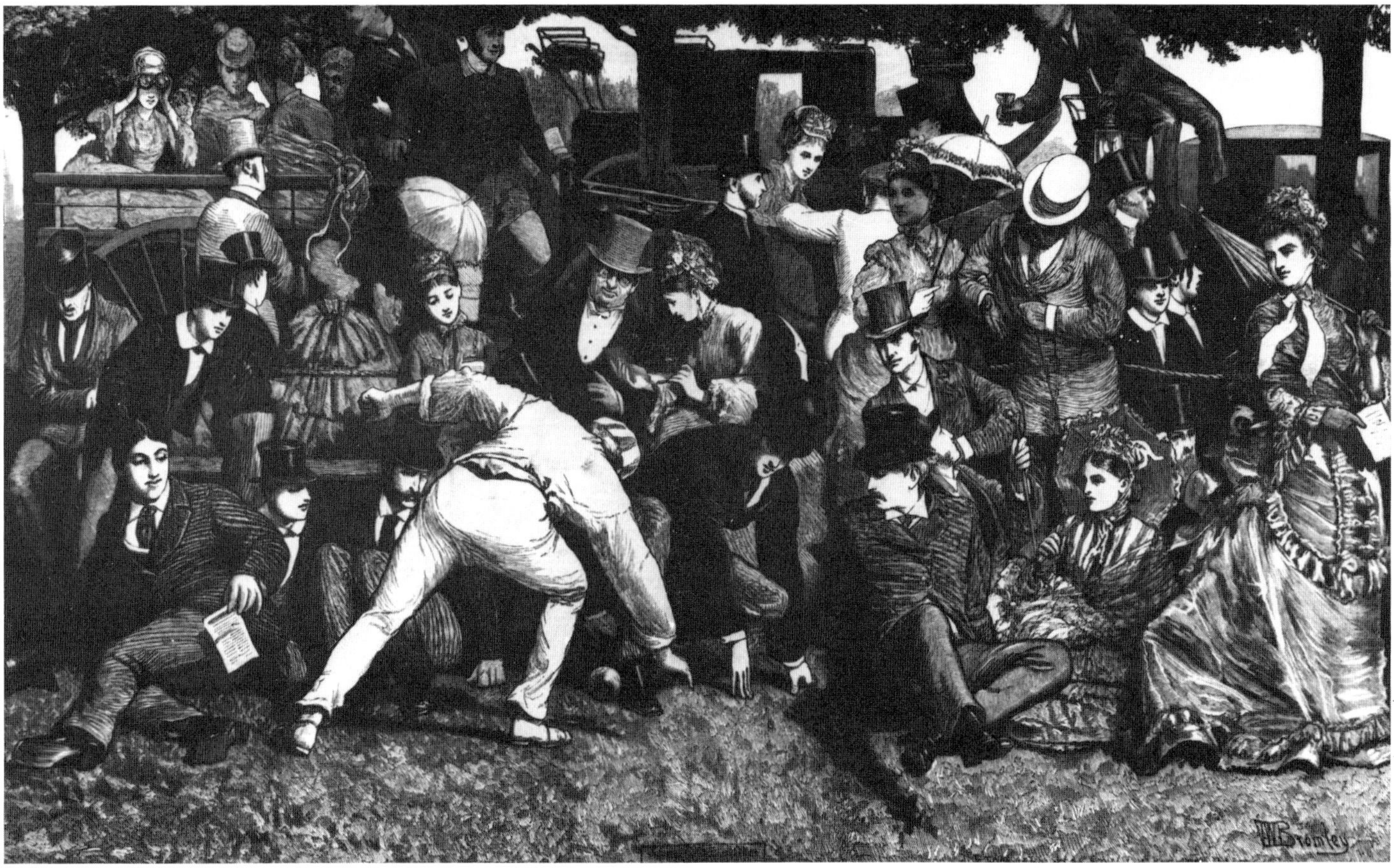

71. Valentine Walter Bromley: *At the Eton and Harrow Match* (1878).

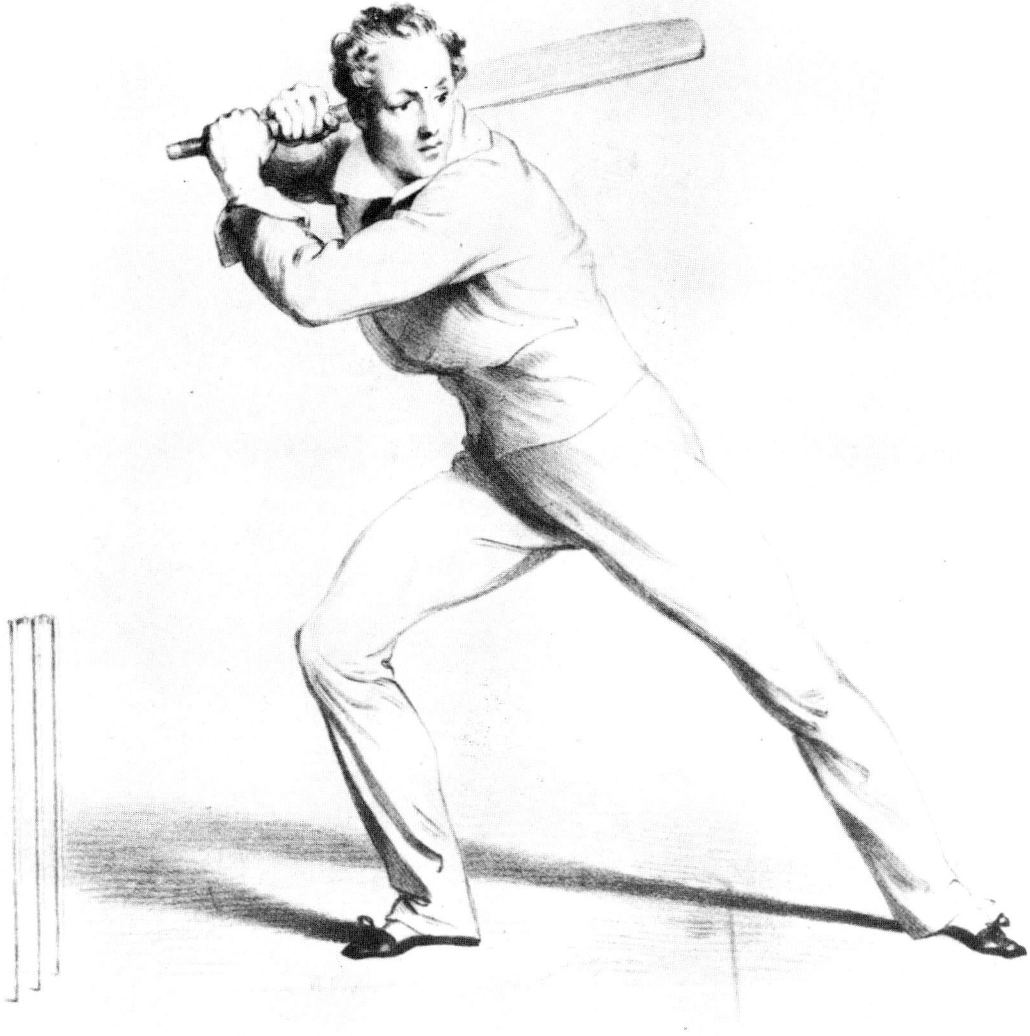

72. George Frederick Watts, O.M., R.A.: *The Cut* (lithograph) (1837) (M.C.C.).

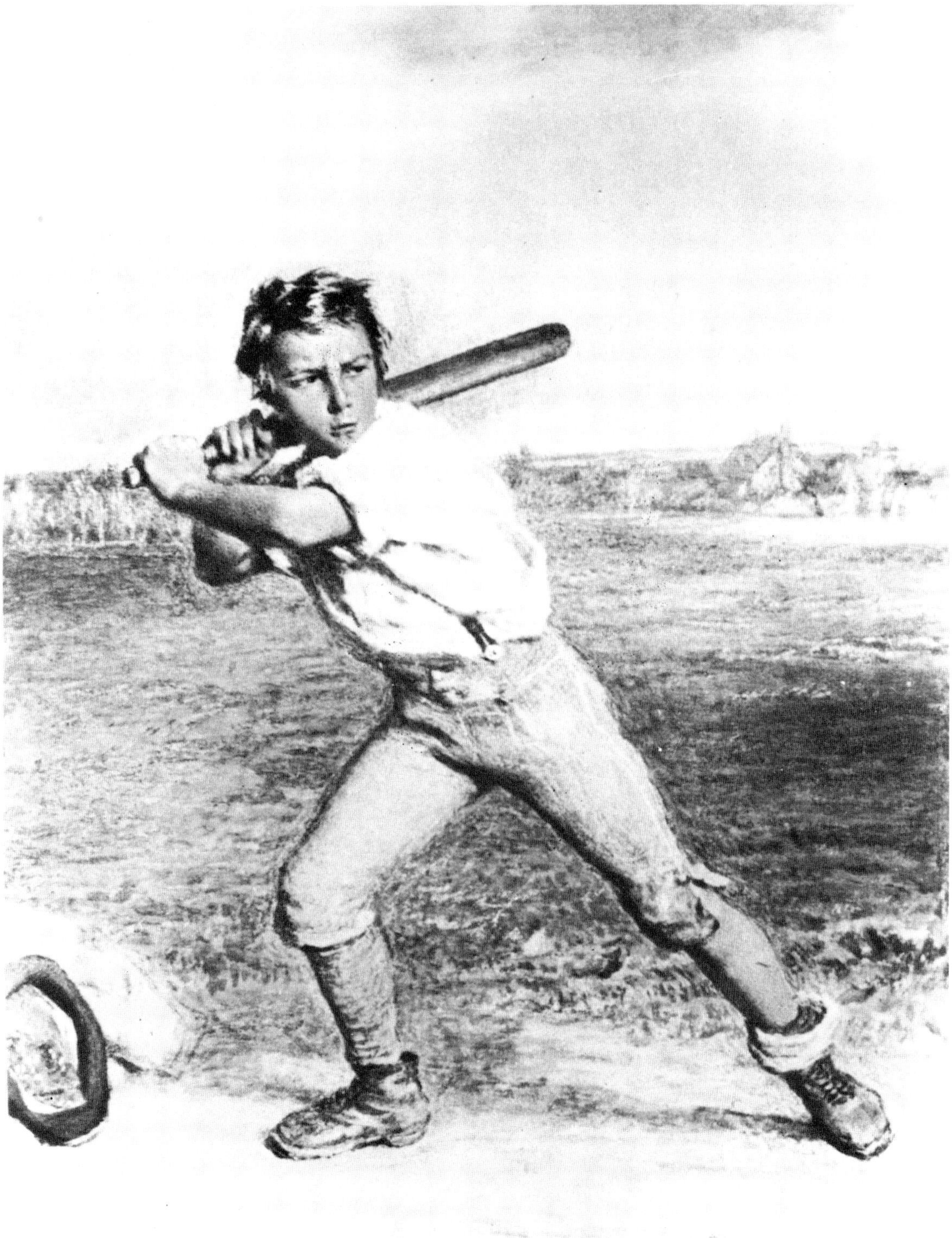

73. William Henry Hunt R.W.S.: *The Boy Batsman* (M.C.C.).

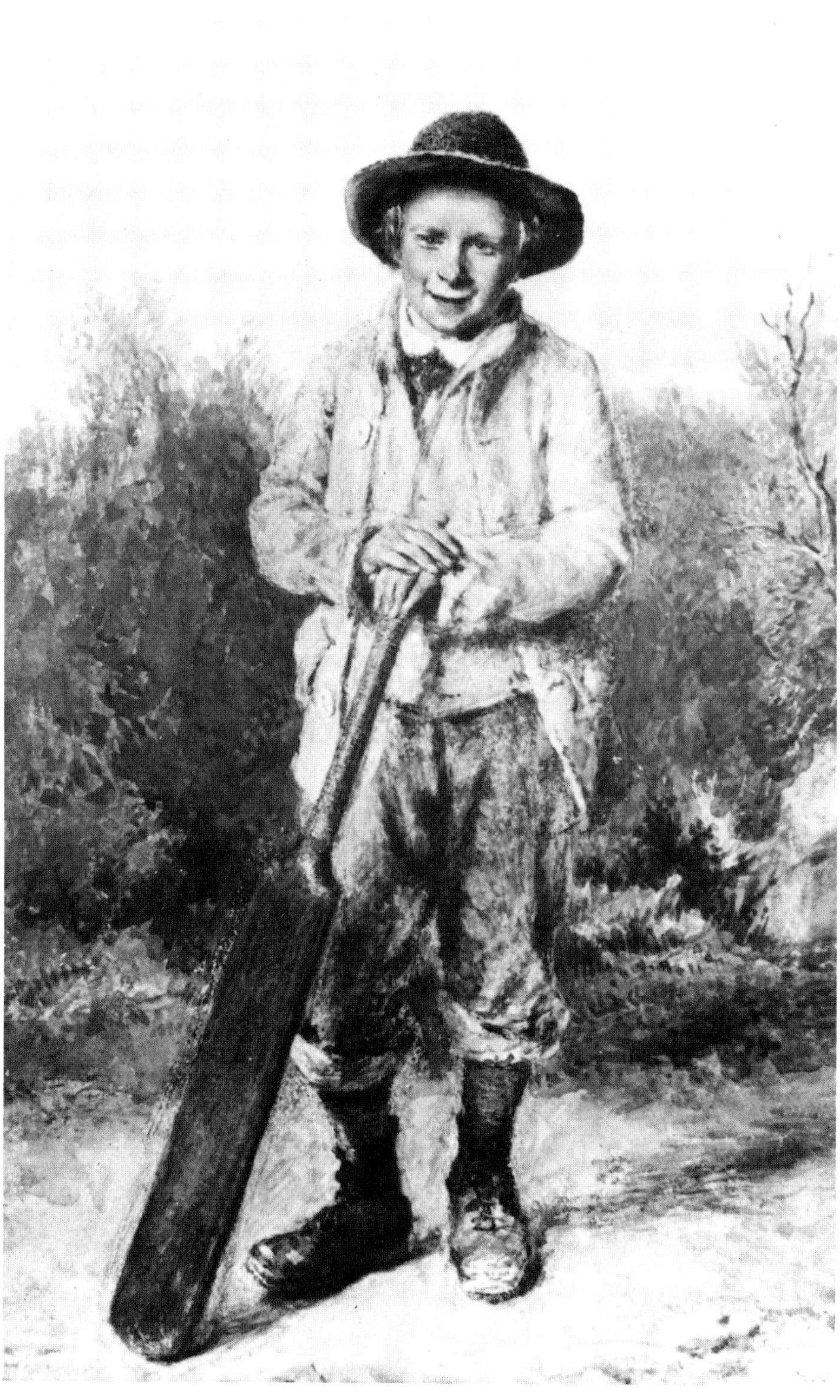

74. William Henry Hunt R.W.S.: *The Boy Cricketer* (M.C.C.).

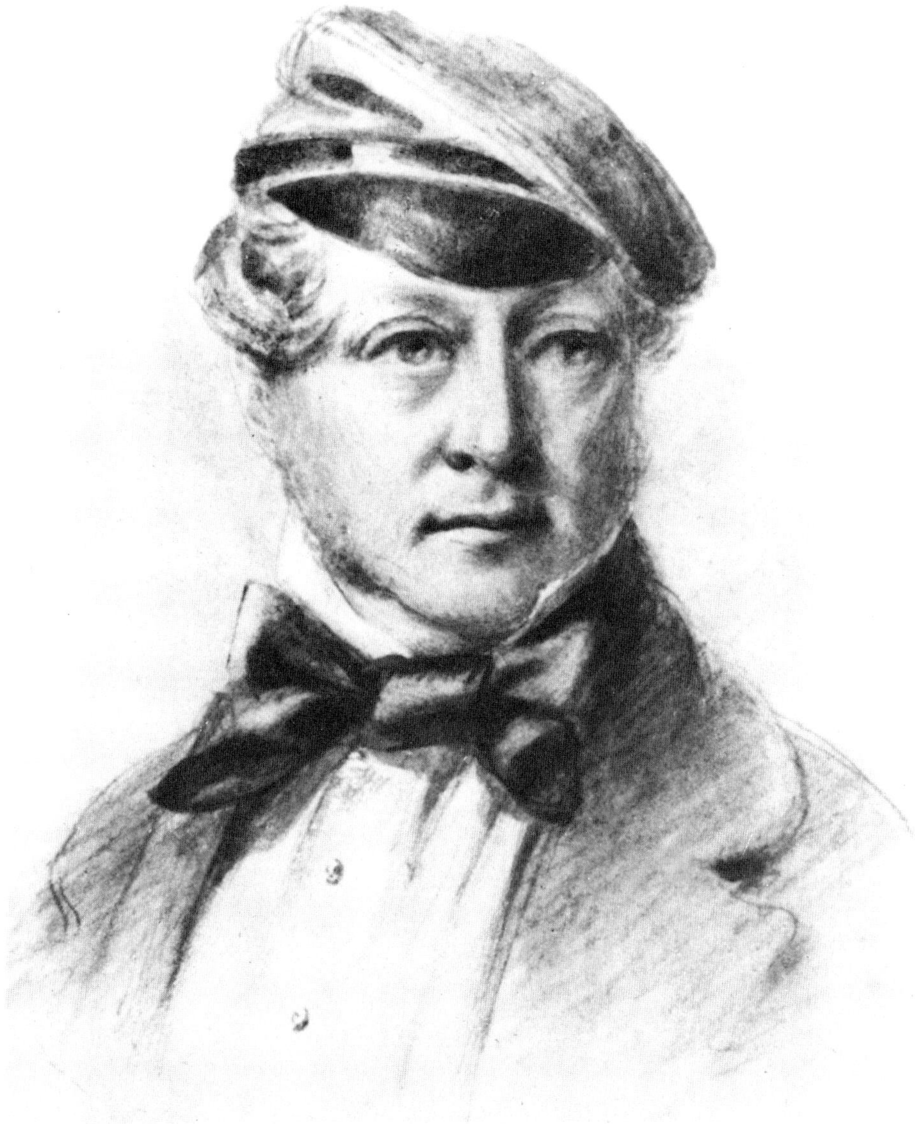

75. Felix: *Self-Portrait* (M.C.C.).

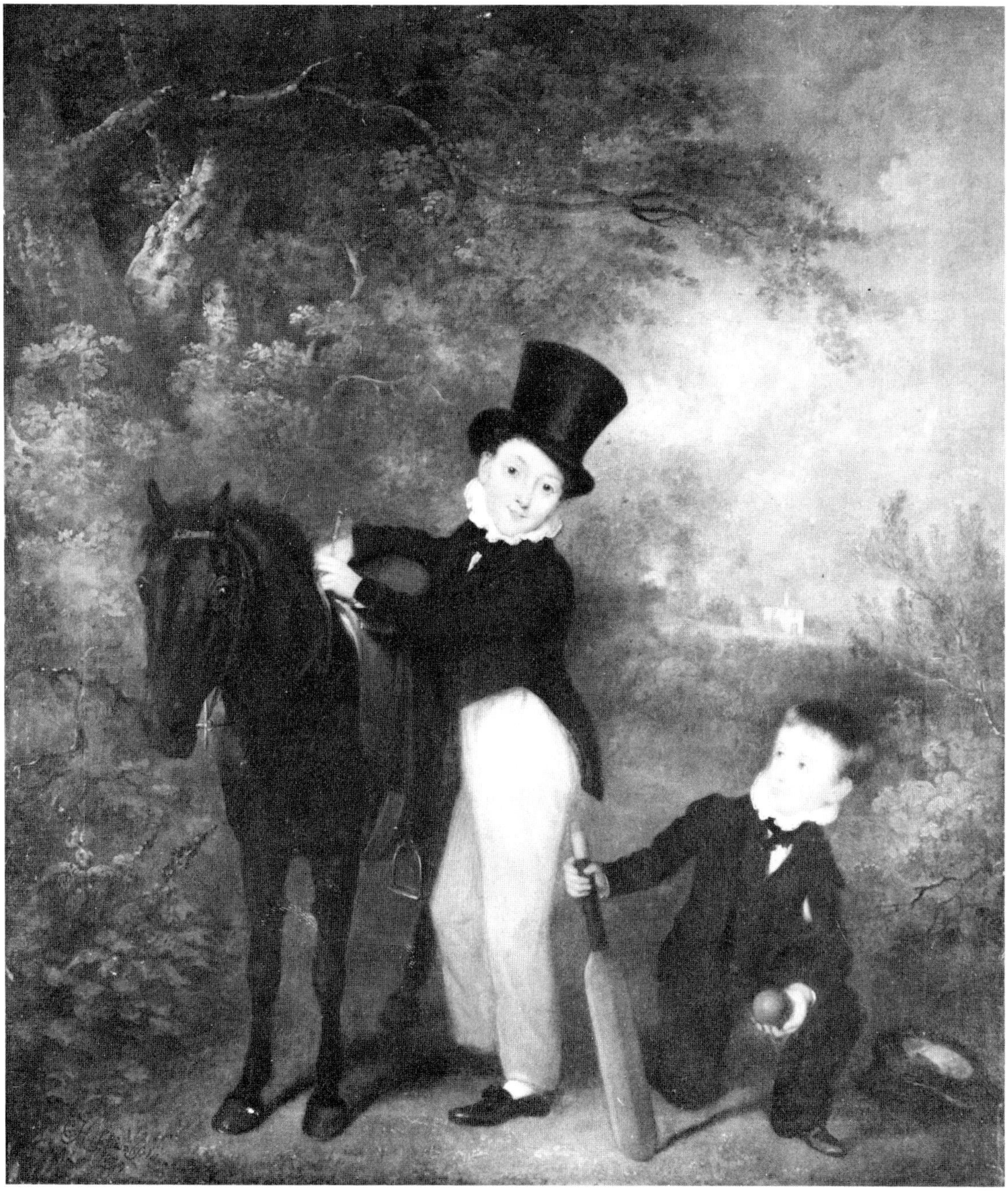

76. Charles Schwanfelder: *William and Charles Chadwick* (1824) (Temple Newsam House, Leeds).

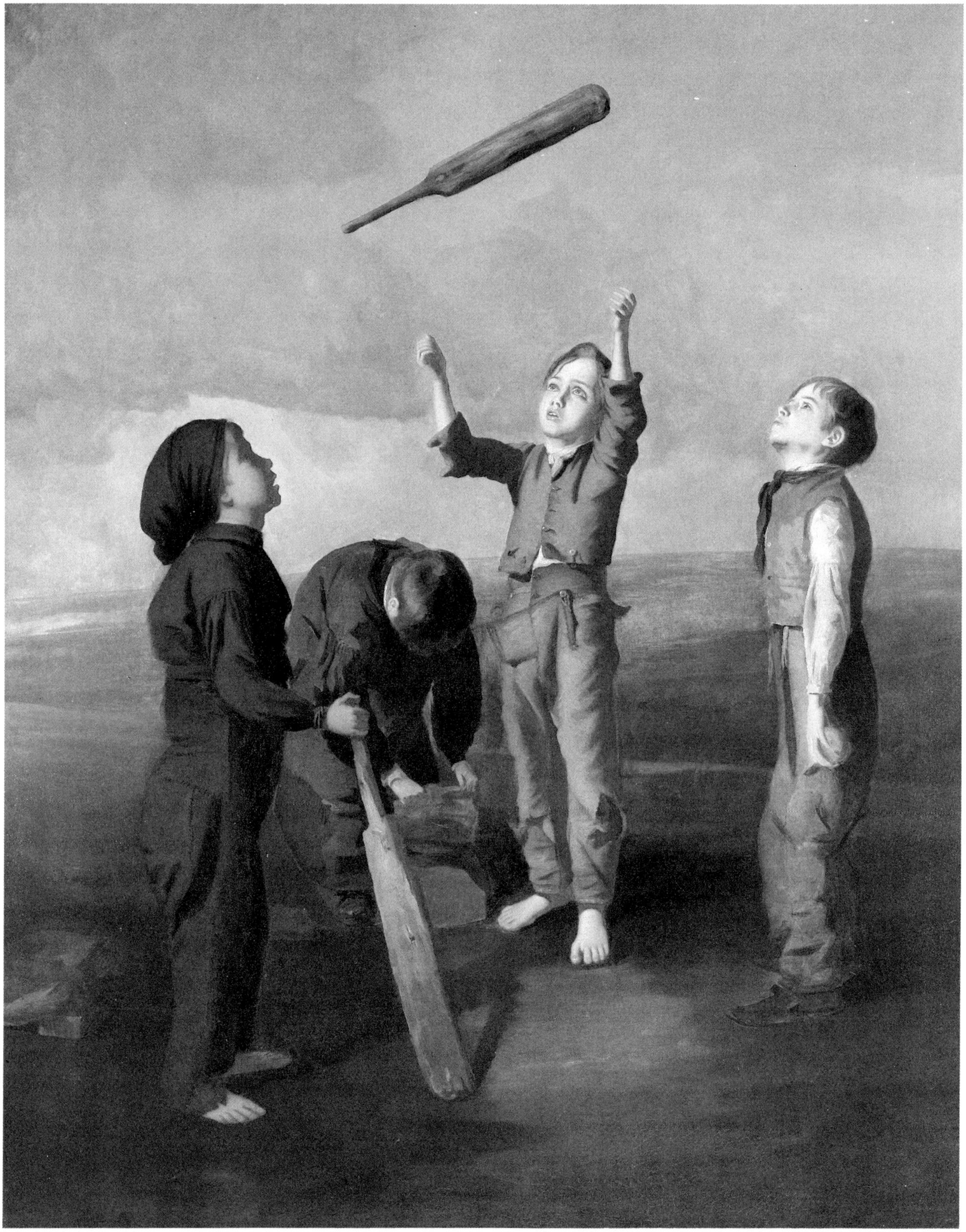

77. Robert James: *Tossing for Innings*, I (M.C.C.).

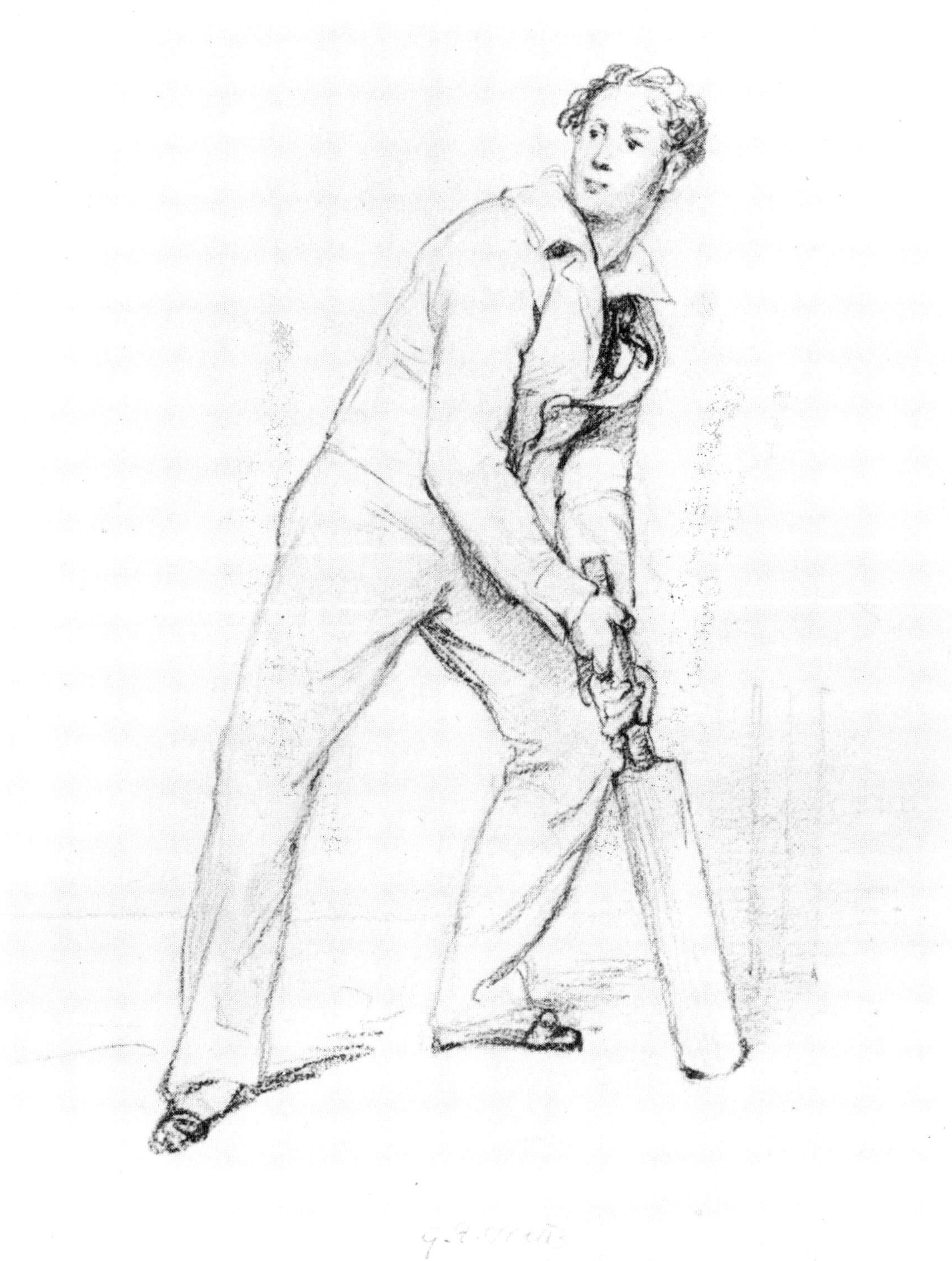

78. George Frederick Watts, O.M., R.A.: *Play* (M.C.C.).

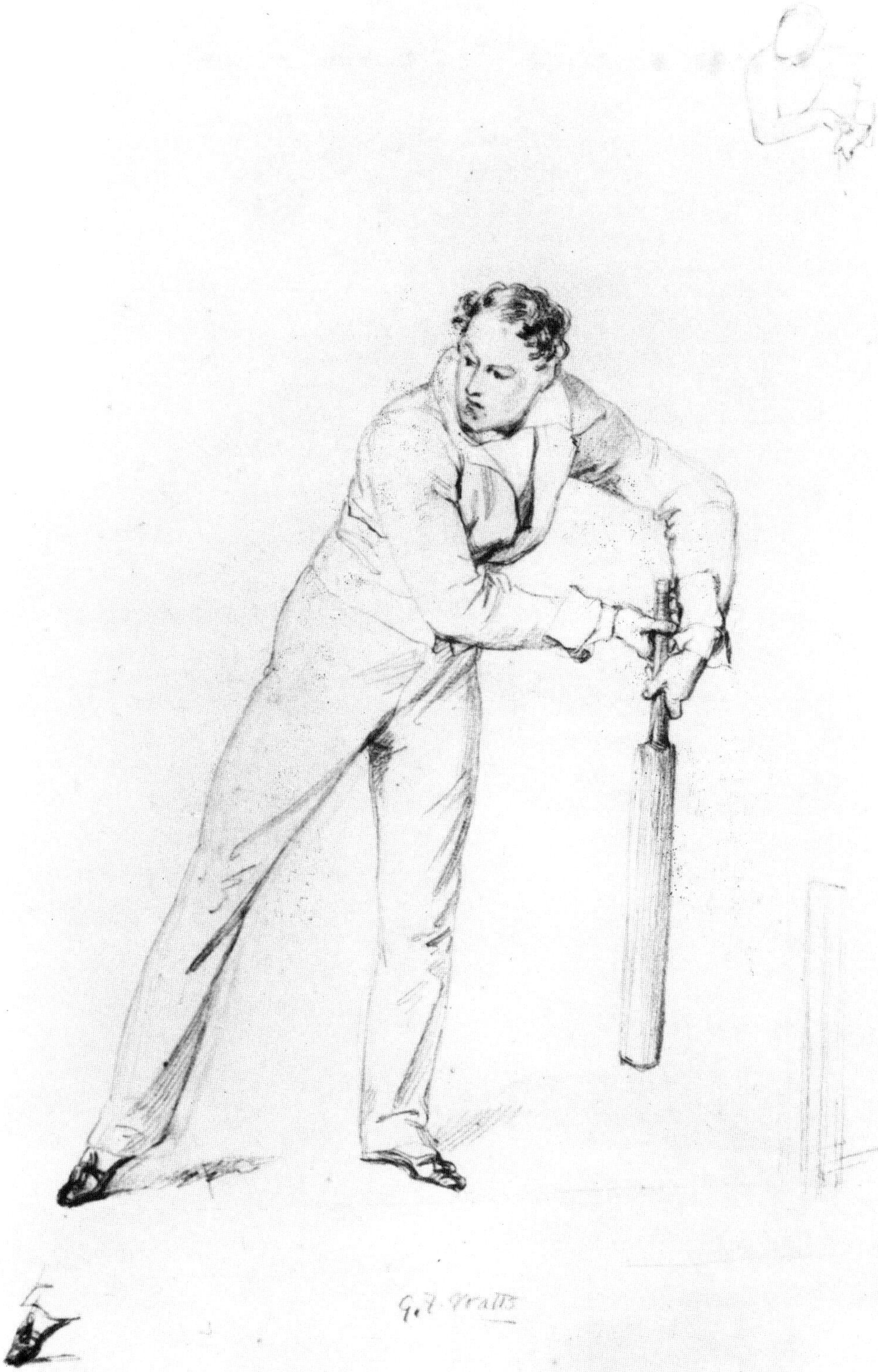

79. George Frederick Watts, O.M., R.A.: *The Draw* (M.C.C.).

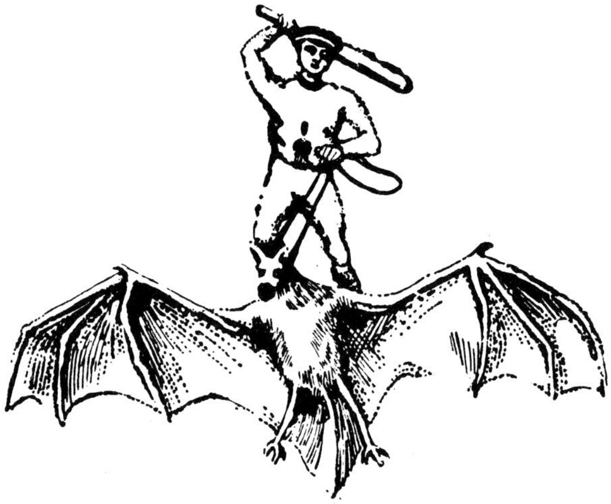

Felix on the Bat

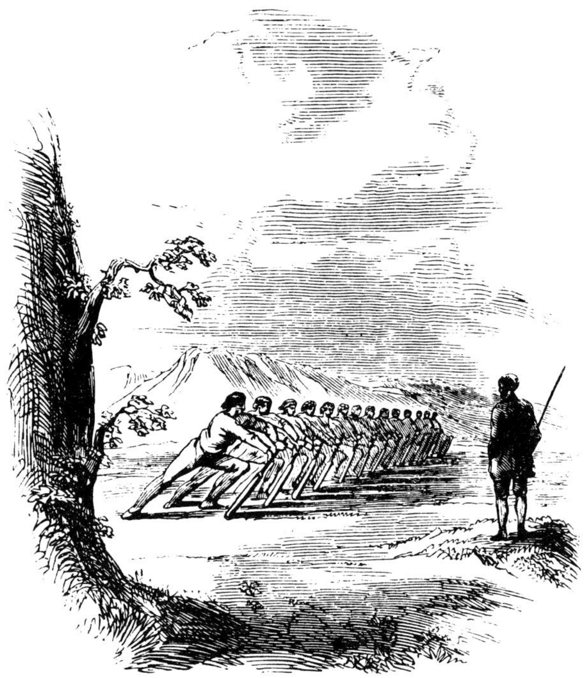

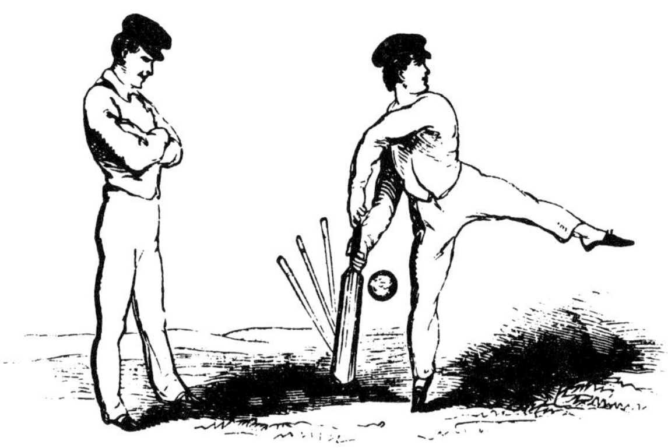

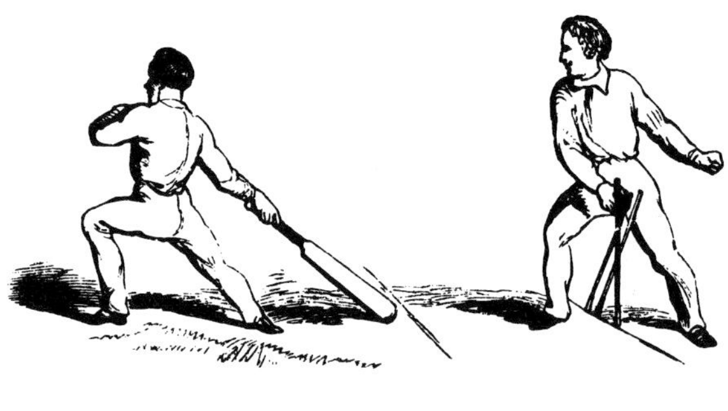

80. "Things you ought not to do". N. Felix: illustrations to *Felix on the Bat* (1845).

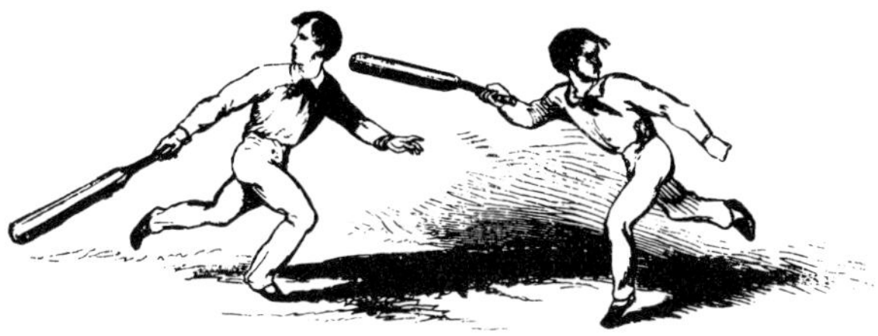
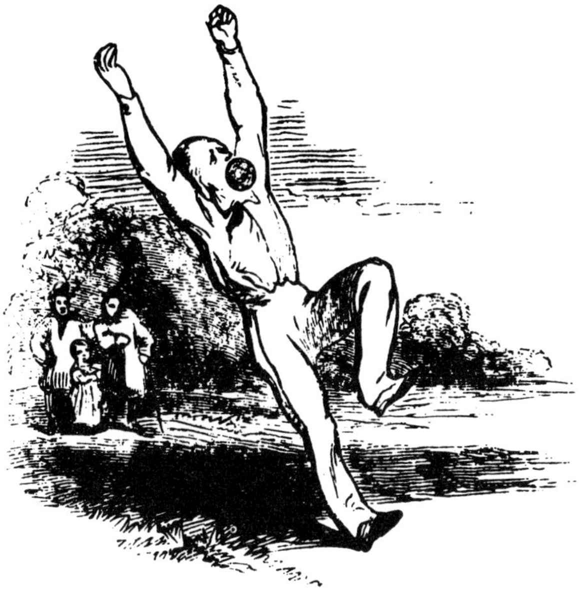
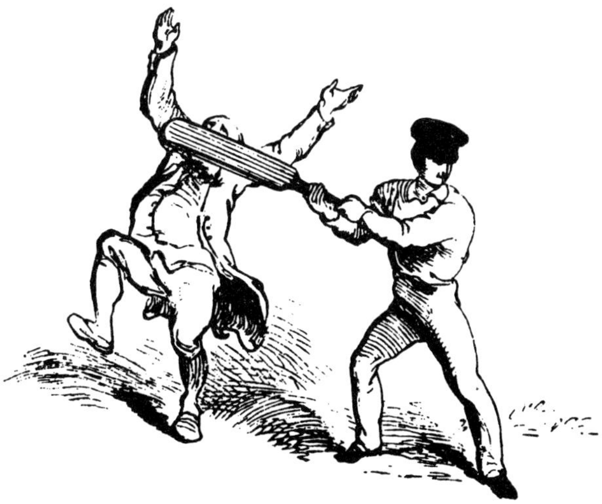
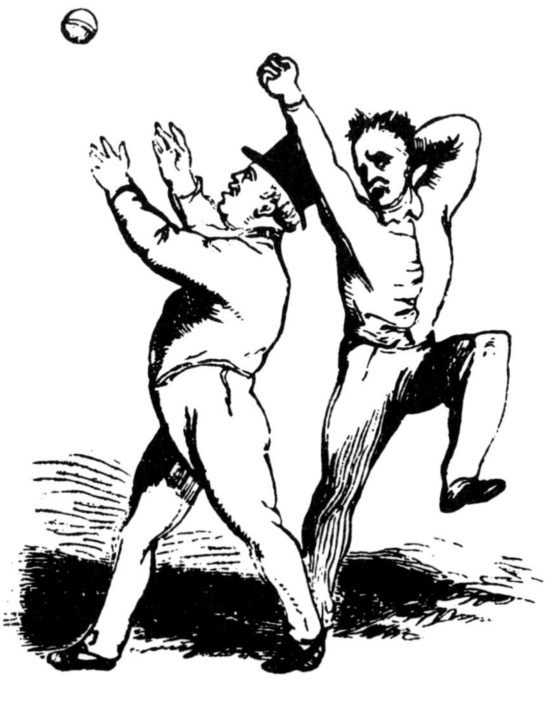

81. Further "Things you ought not to do".

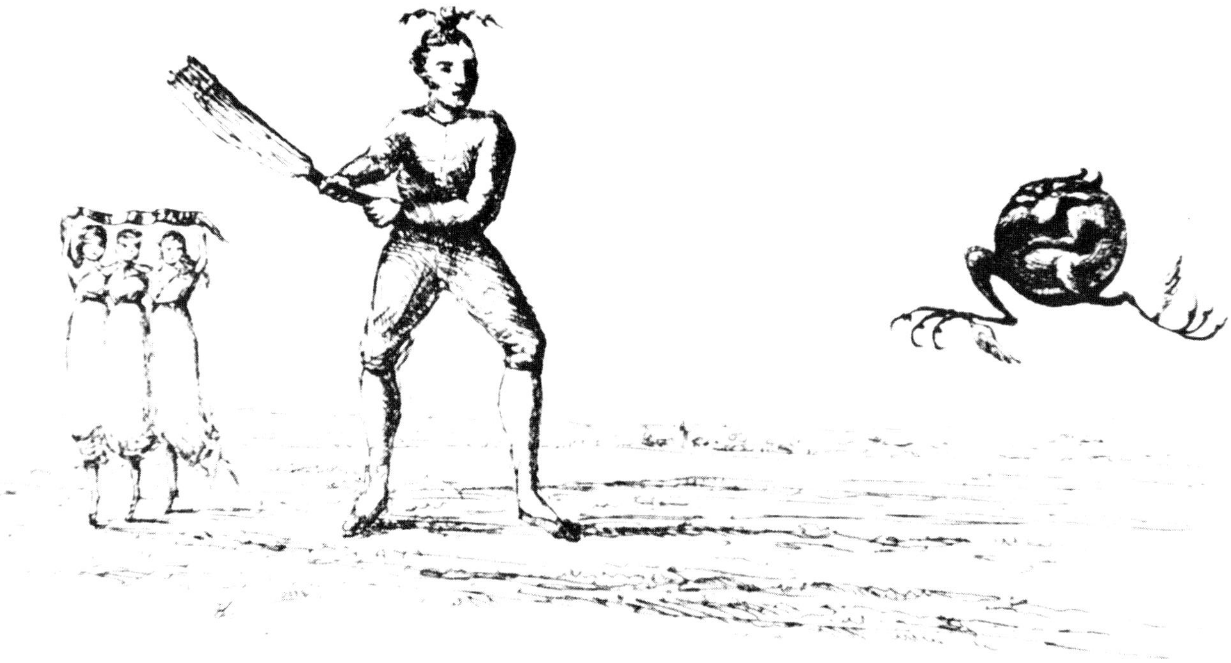

82. *Ascribed to* Charles Landseer: *The Duke of Wellington batting, with the Three Graces as the Wicket* (M.C.C.).

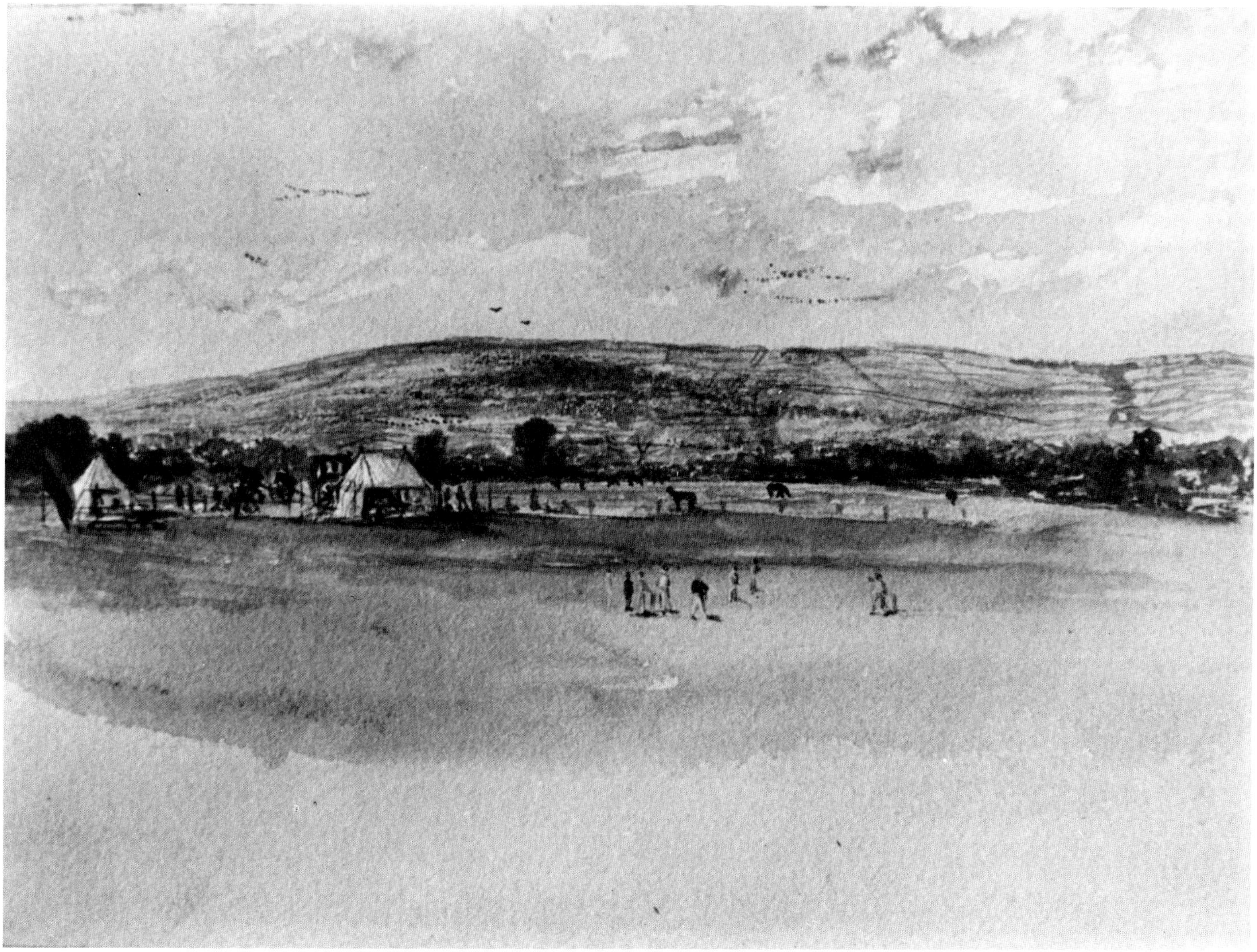

83. A.F. Payne: *A Cricket Match at Cowley, Oxford* (1857) (Peter Rook, Esq.).

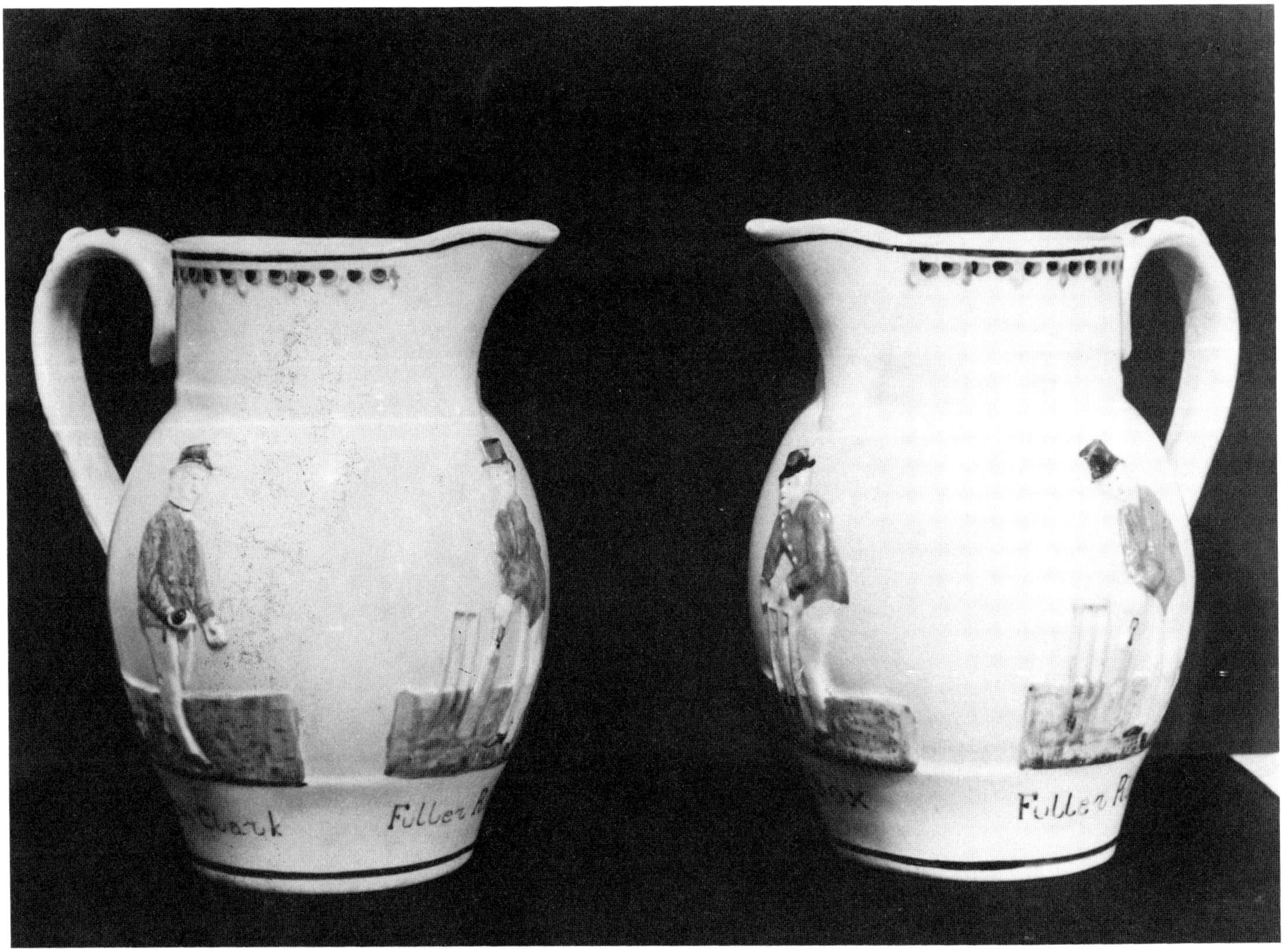

84. Staffordshire Ware: jug with *Clark, Pilch and Box* (*c.* 1840) (M.C.C.).

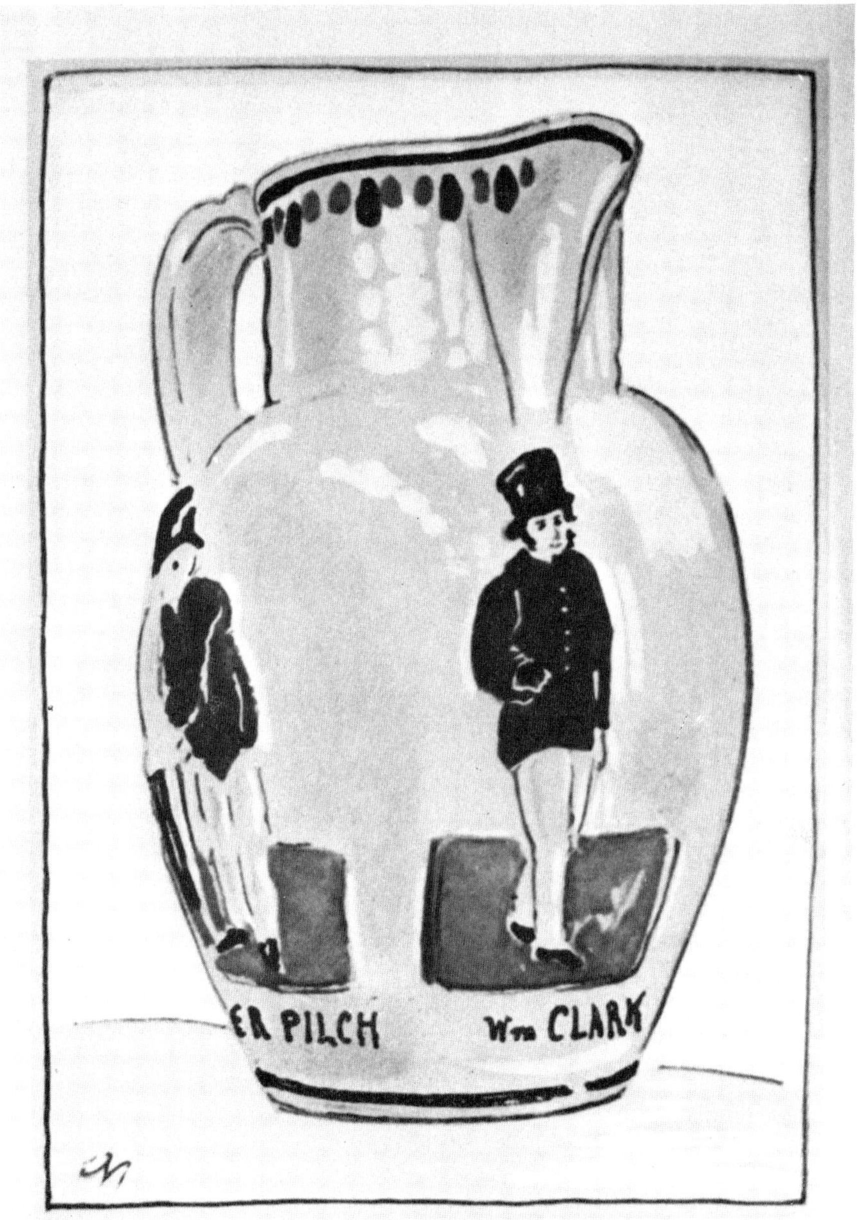

85. Sir William Nicholson: *A Cricketing Jug*: Frontispiece to E.V. Lucas, *A Hundred Years of Trent Bridge* (1938).

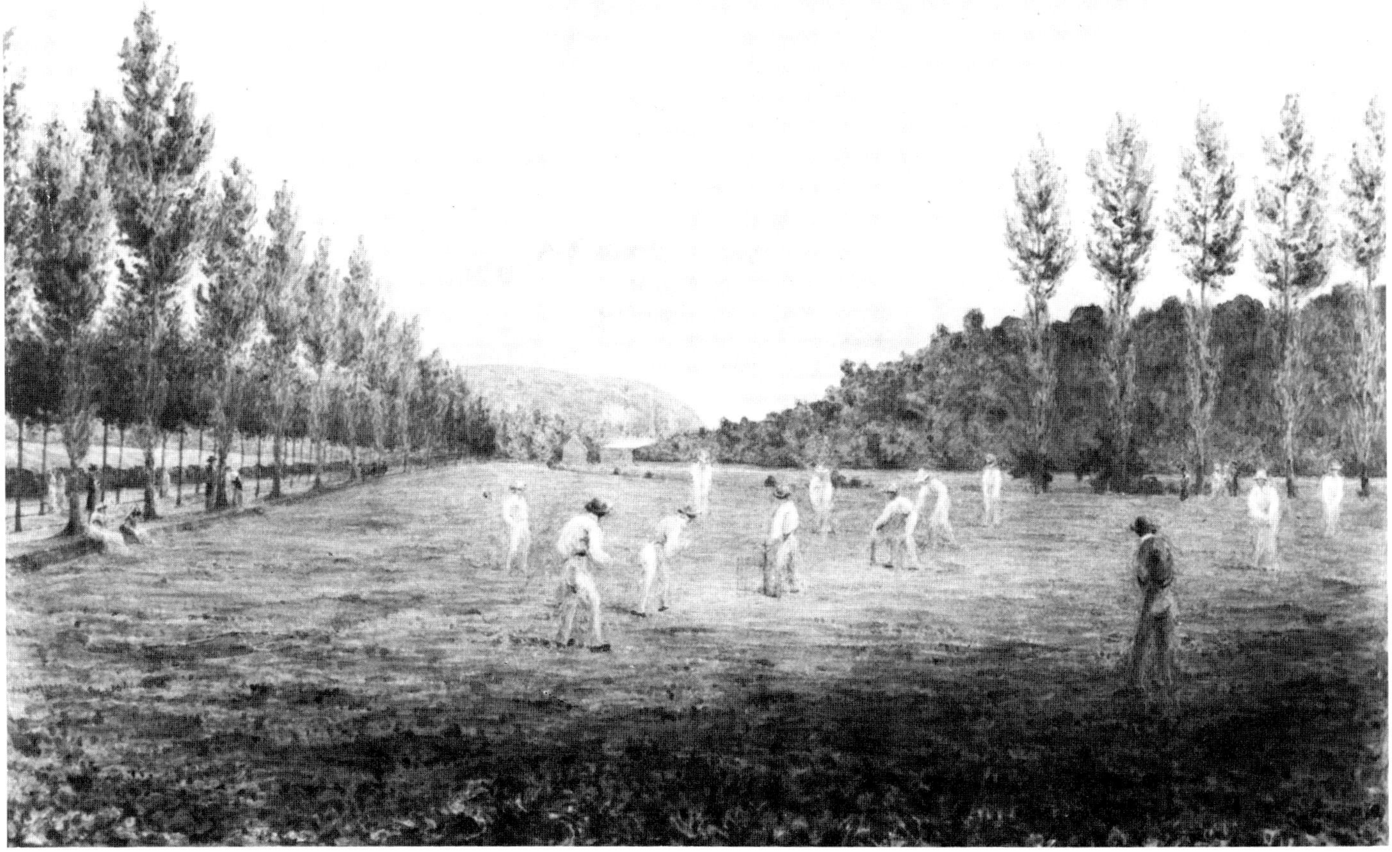

86. Robert Streatfeild: *Cricket at Spa, Belgium* (*c.* 1840) (William Drummond, Esq.).

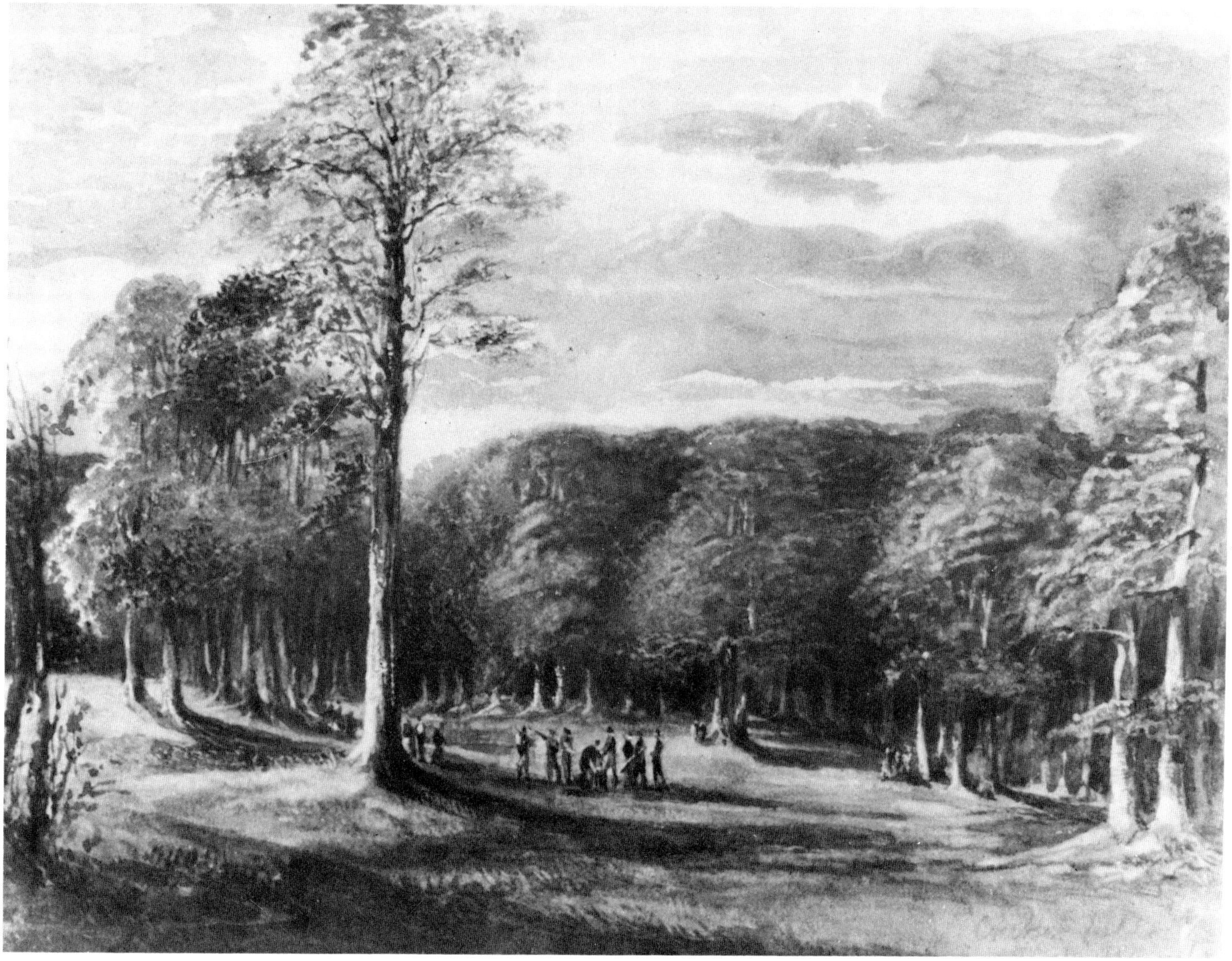

87. Anon: *Vallon des Anglais, Bois de la Cambre, Brussels* (*c*. 1870).

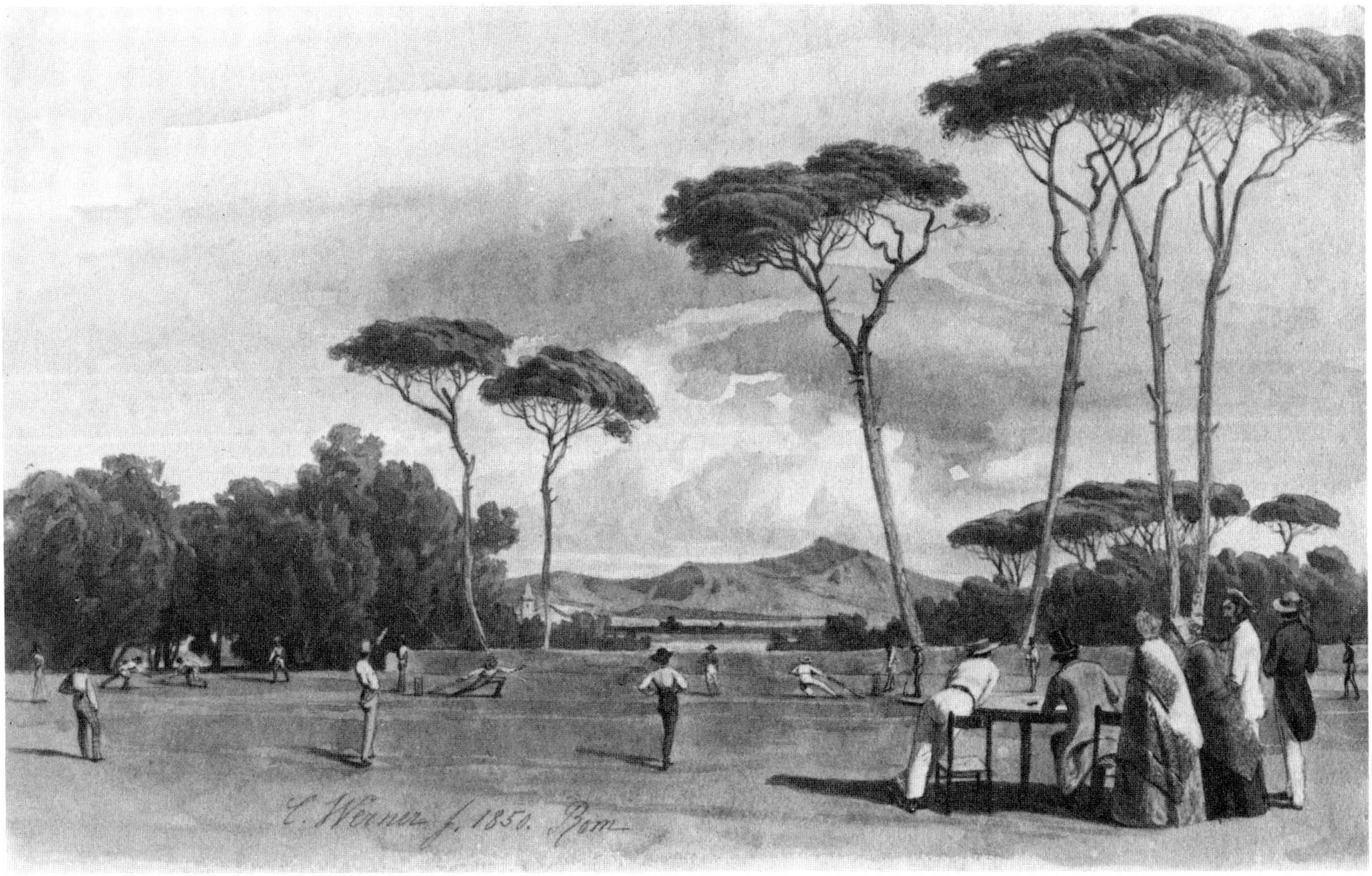

88. Carl Werner: *A Cricket Match at Rome* (1850) (present whereabouts unknown).

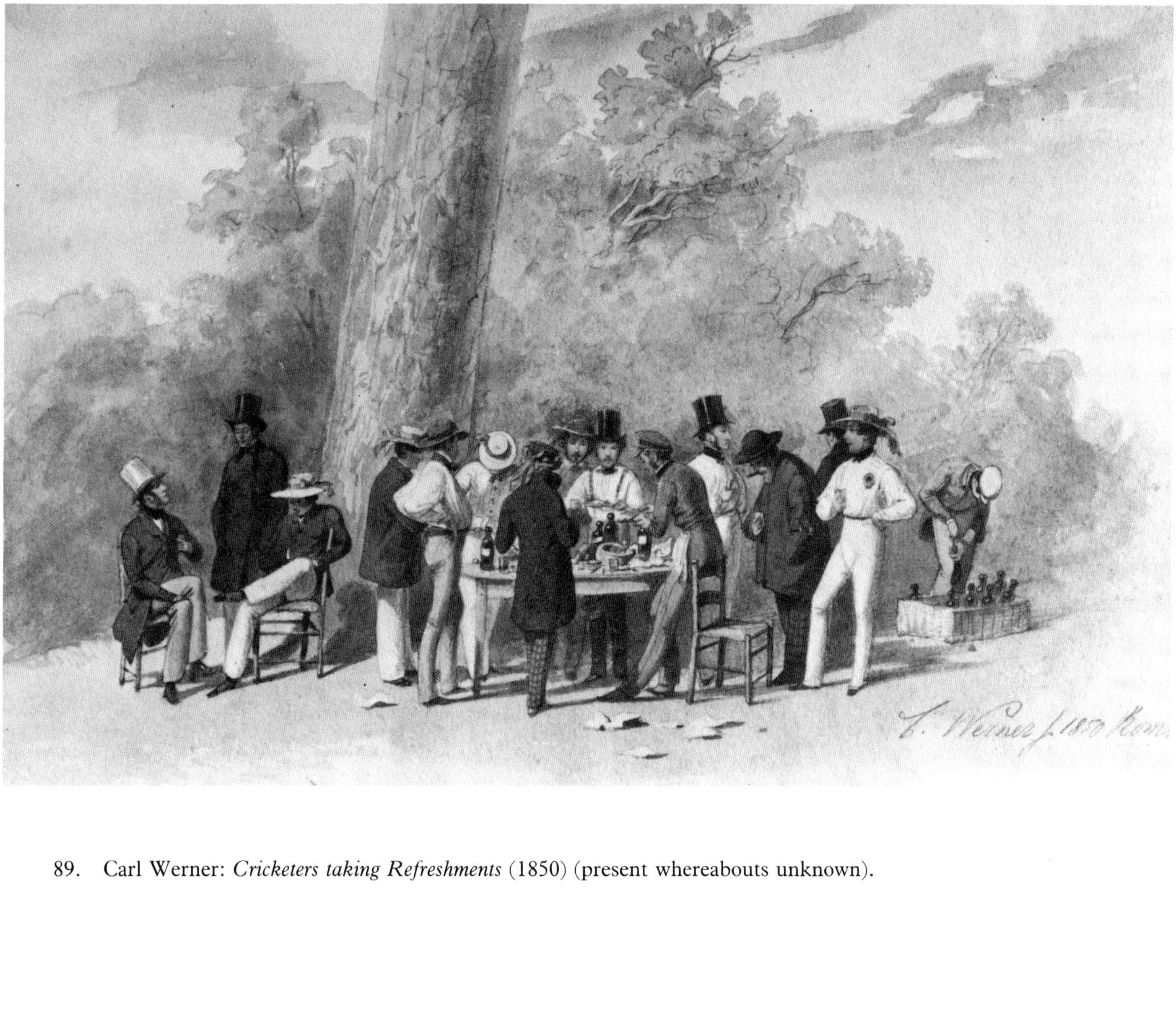

89. Carl Werner: *Cricketers taking Refreshments* (1850) (present whereabouts unknown).

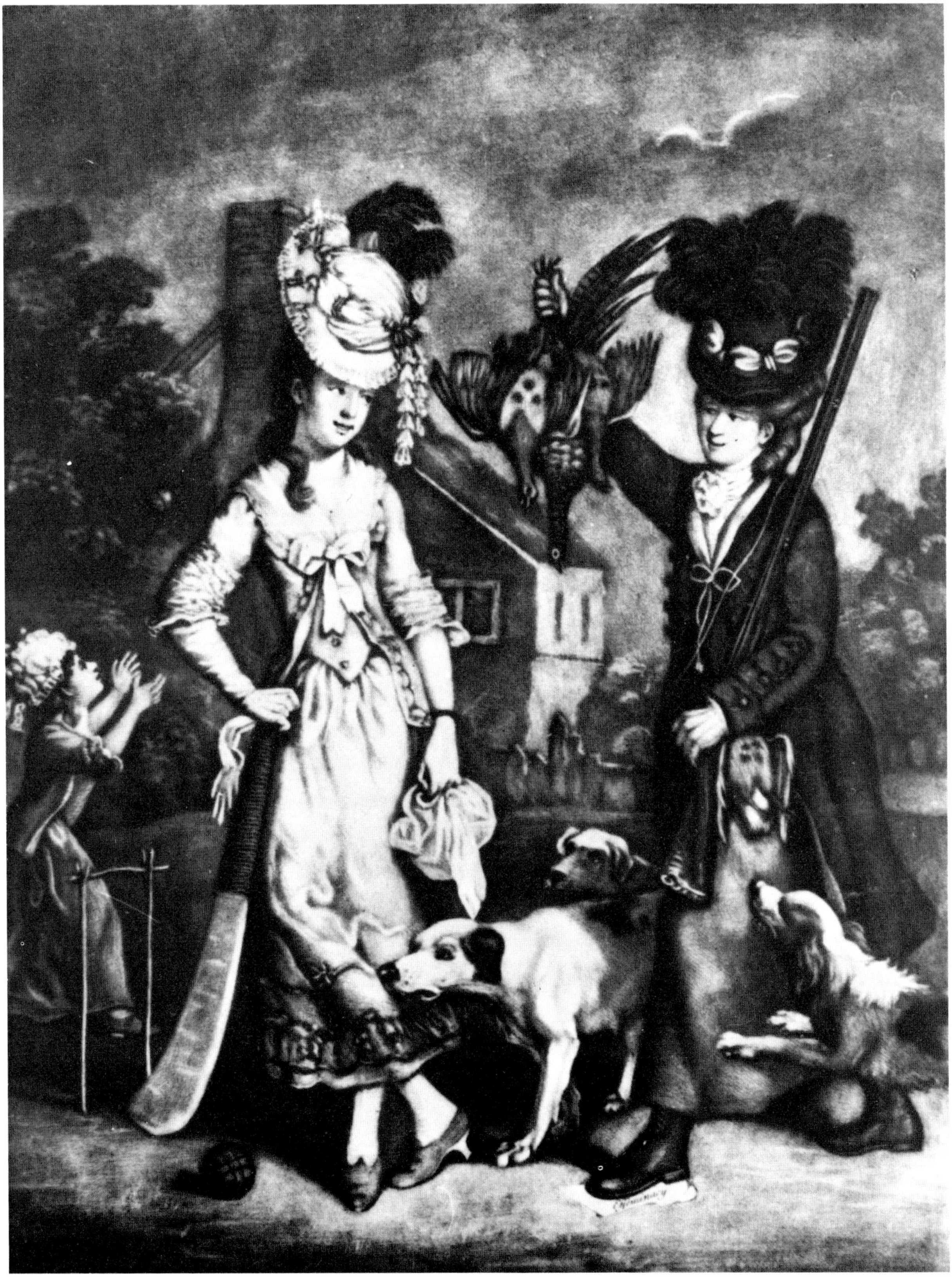

90. *After* John Collet: *Miss Wicket and Miss Trigger* (1778).

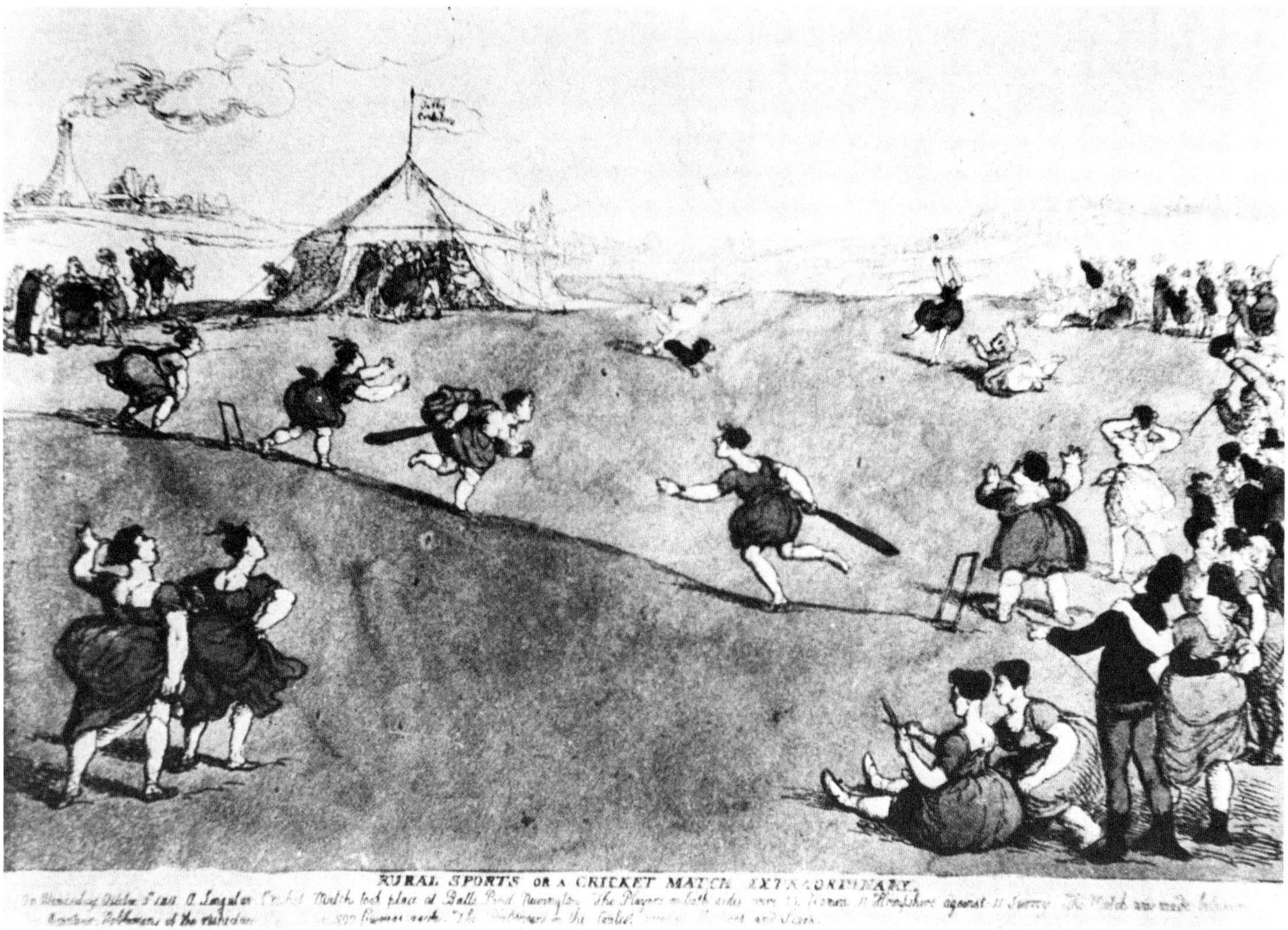

91. Thomas Rowlandson: *Rural Sports, or A Cricket Match Extraordinary* (1811).

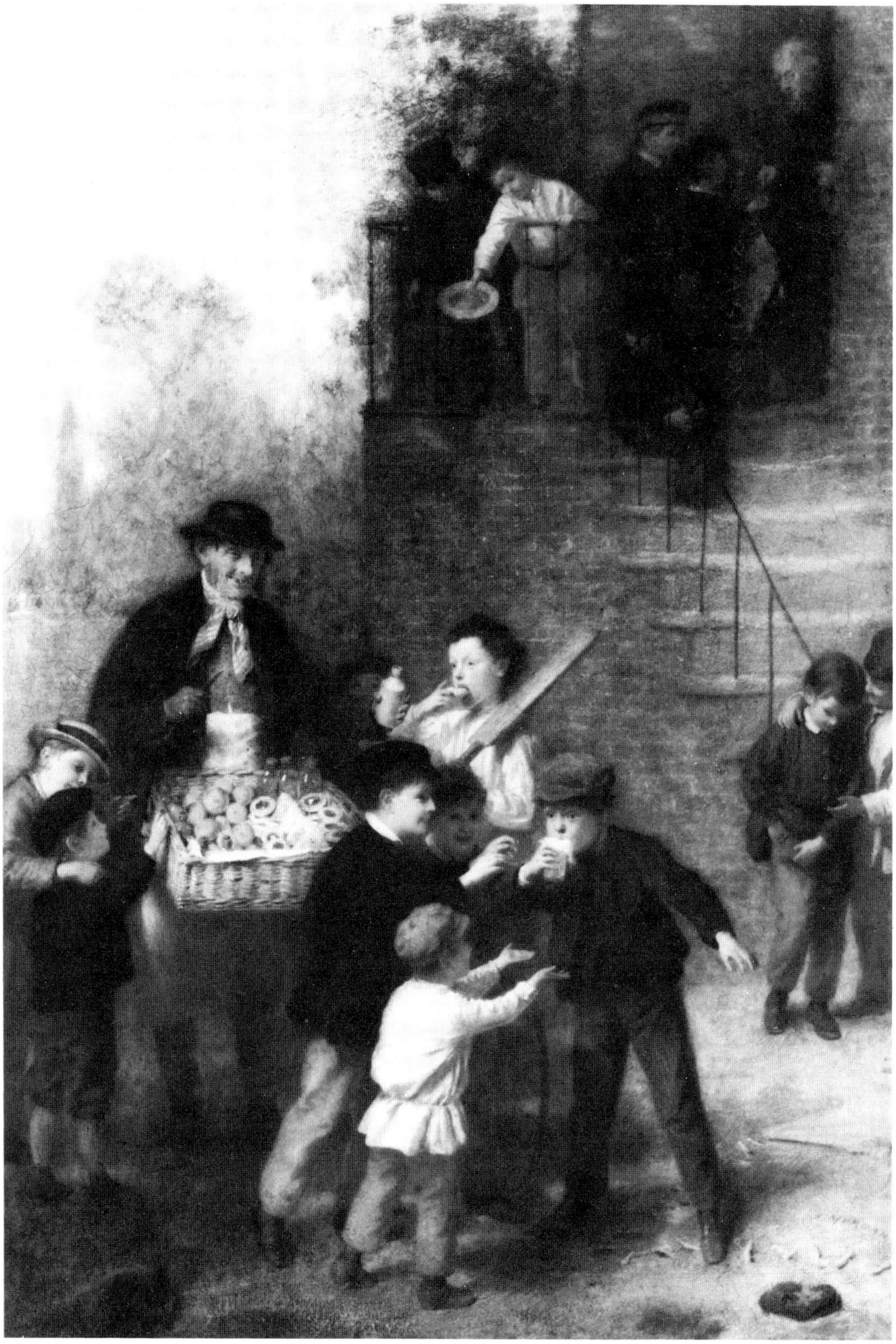

92. John Morgan R.A., R.B.A.: *Ginger Beer* (1860) (present whereabouts unknown).

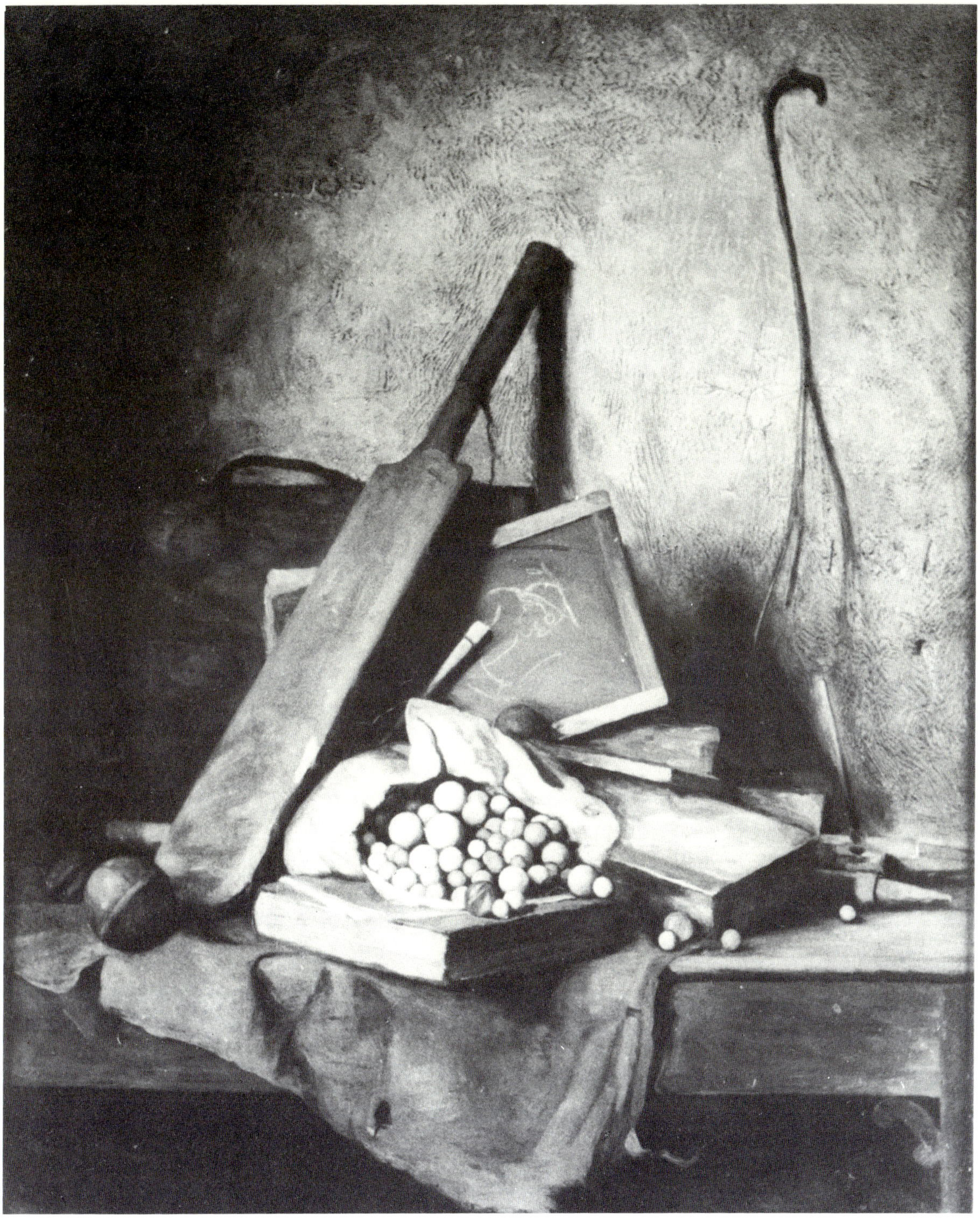

93. Edward George Handel Lucas: *When We Were Boys Together* (1881) (Private Collection).

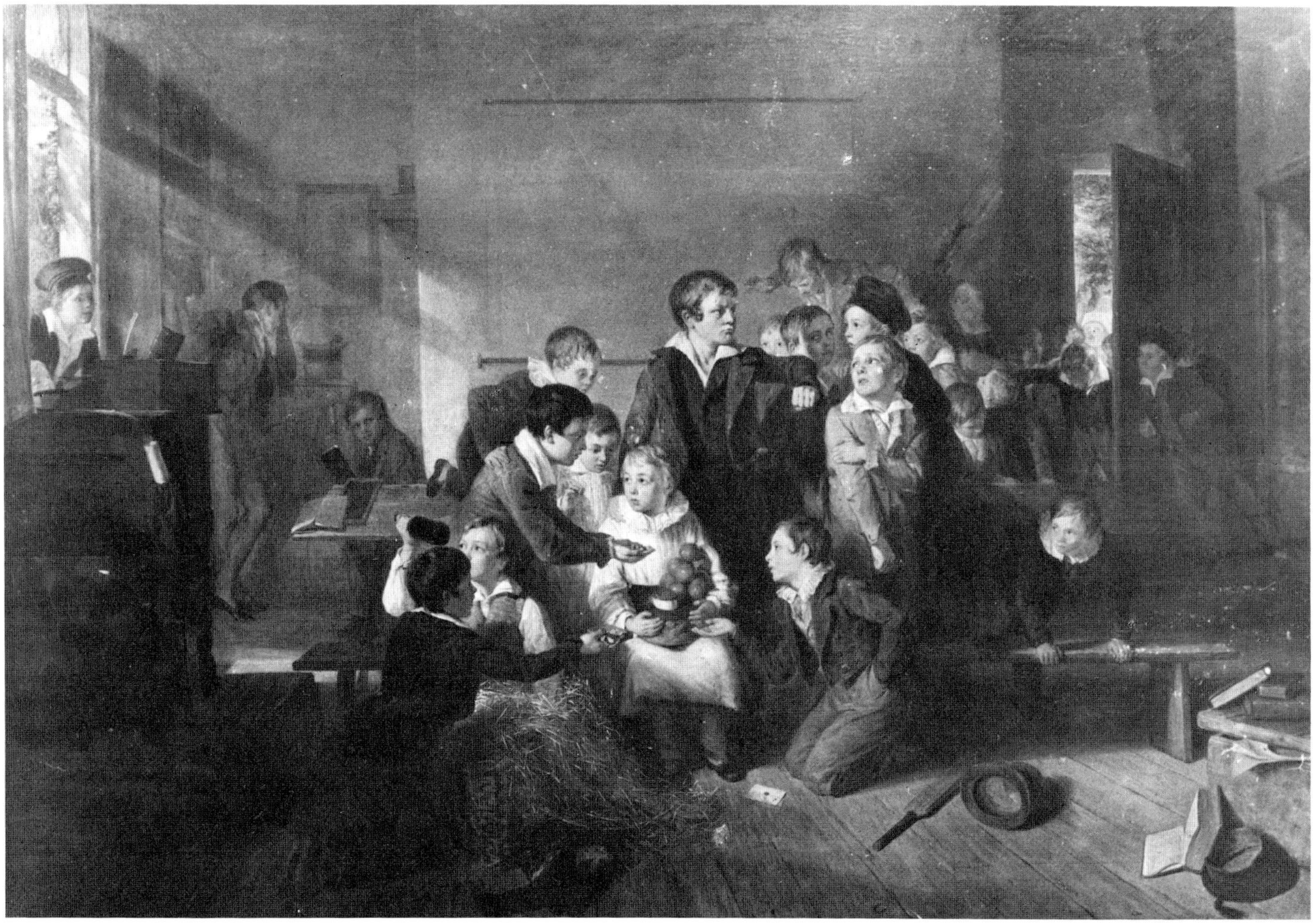

94. Thomas Webster, R.A.: *The Boy with Many Friends* (1841) (Corporation Art Gallery, Bury).

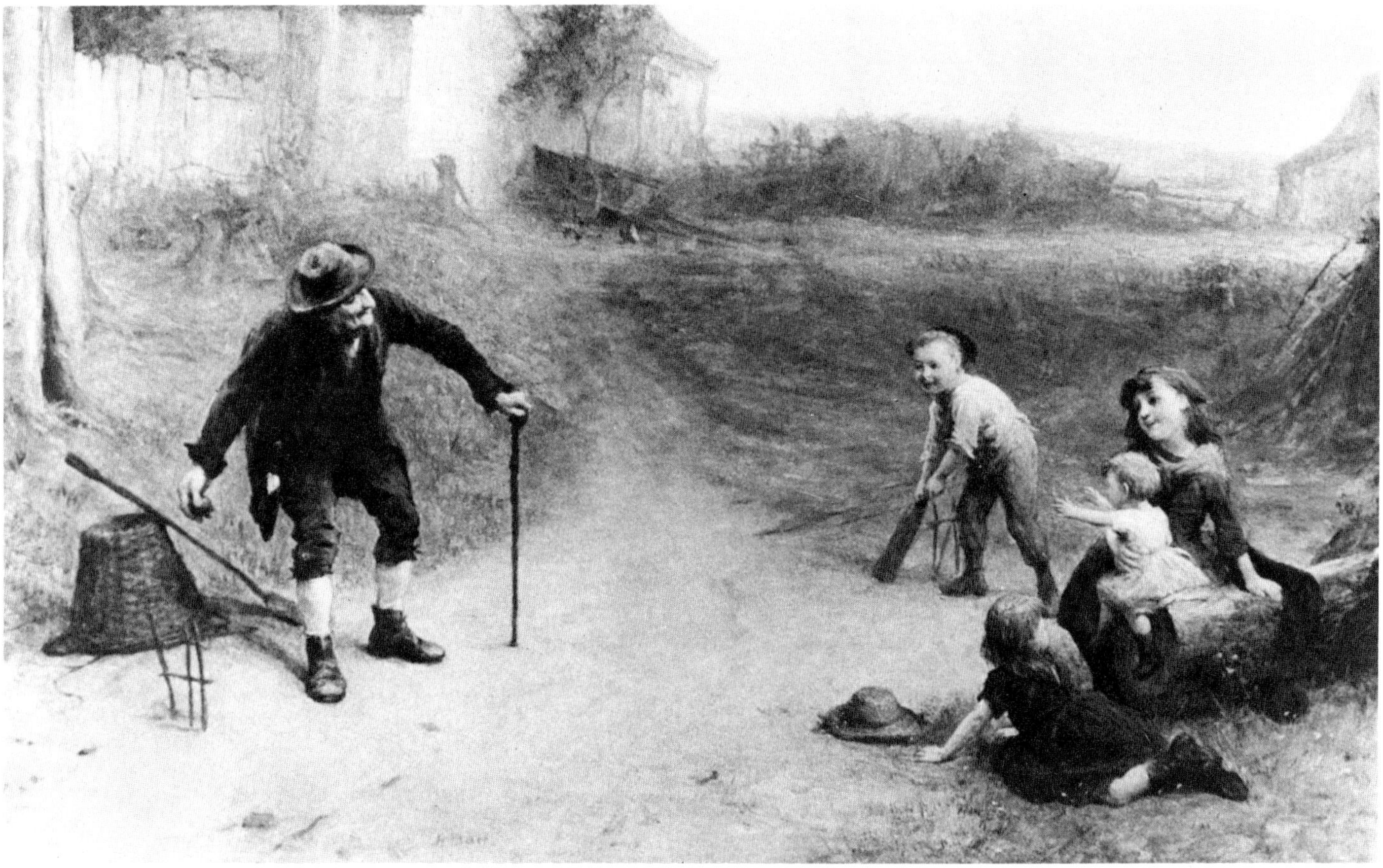

95. Alexander H. Burr: *A Game of Cricket: Youth and Age* (*c*. 1860-70) (Harvert Consultancy (Holdings) Ltd., Dundee).

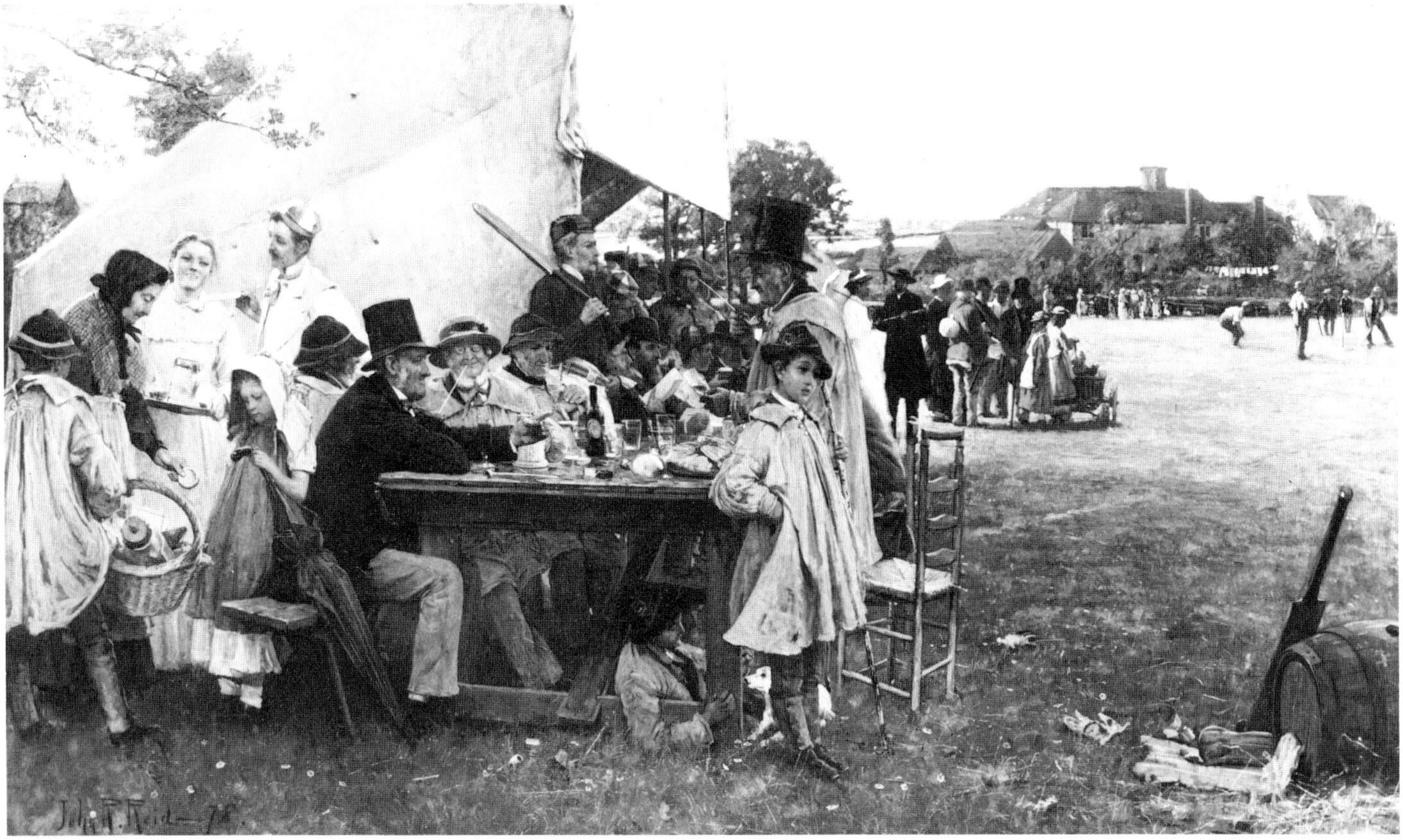

96. John Robertson Reid: *A Country Cricket Match* (1878) (Tate Gallery, London).

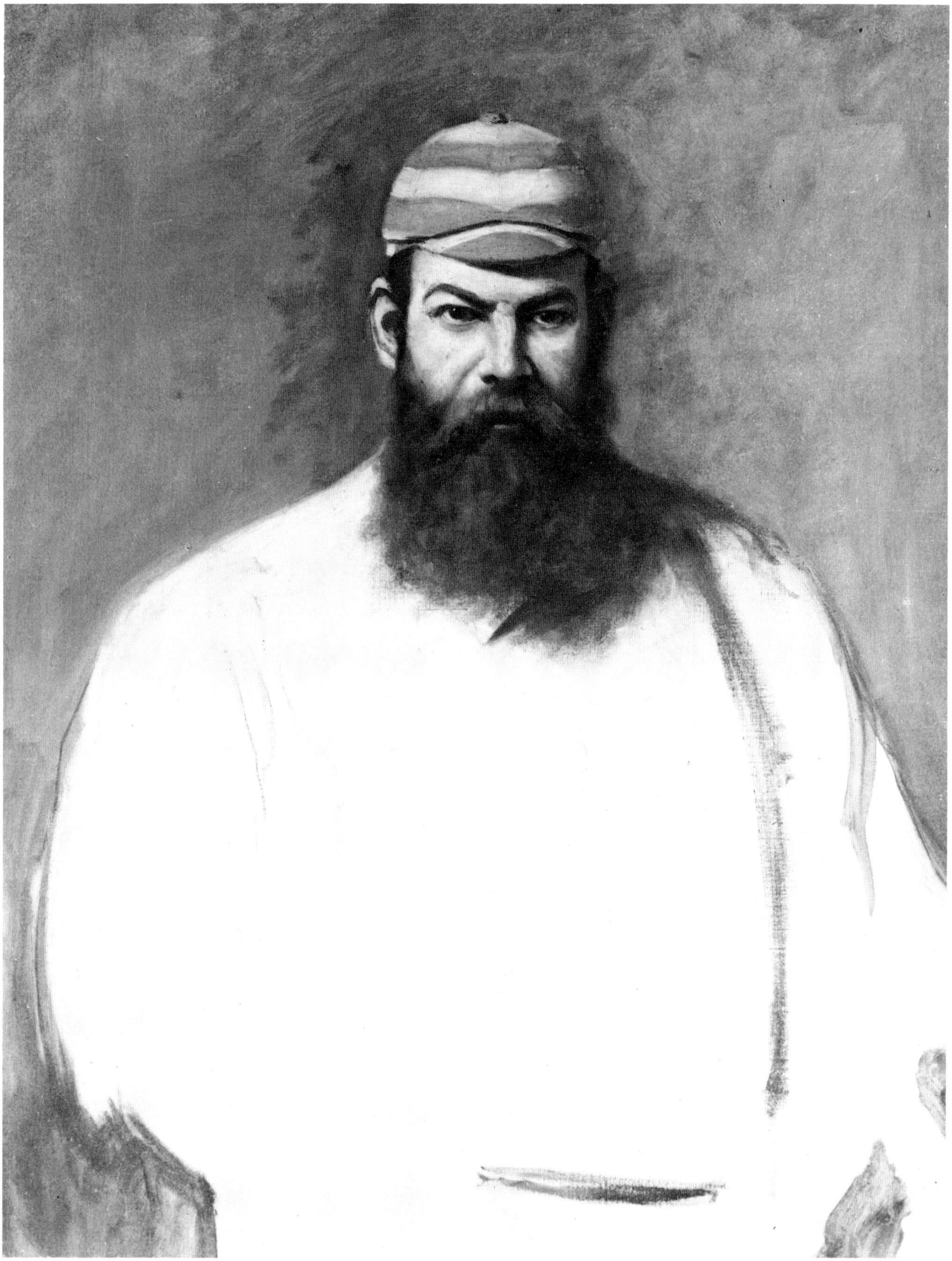

97. British School: *W.G. Grace* (National Portrait Gallery, London).

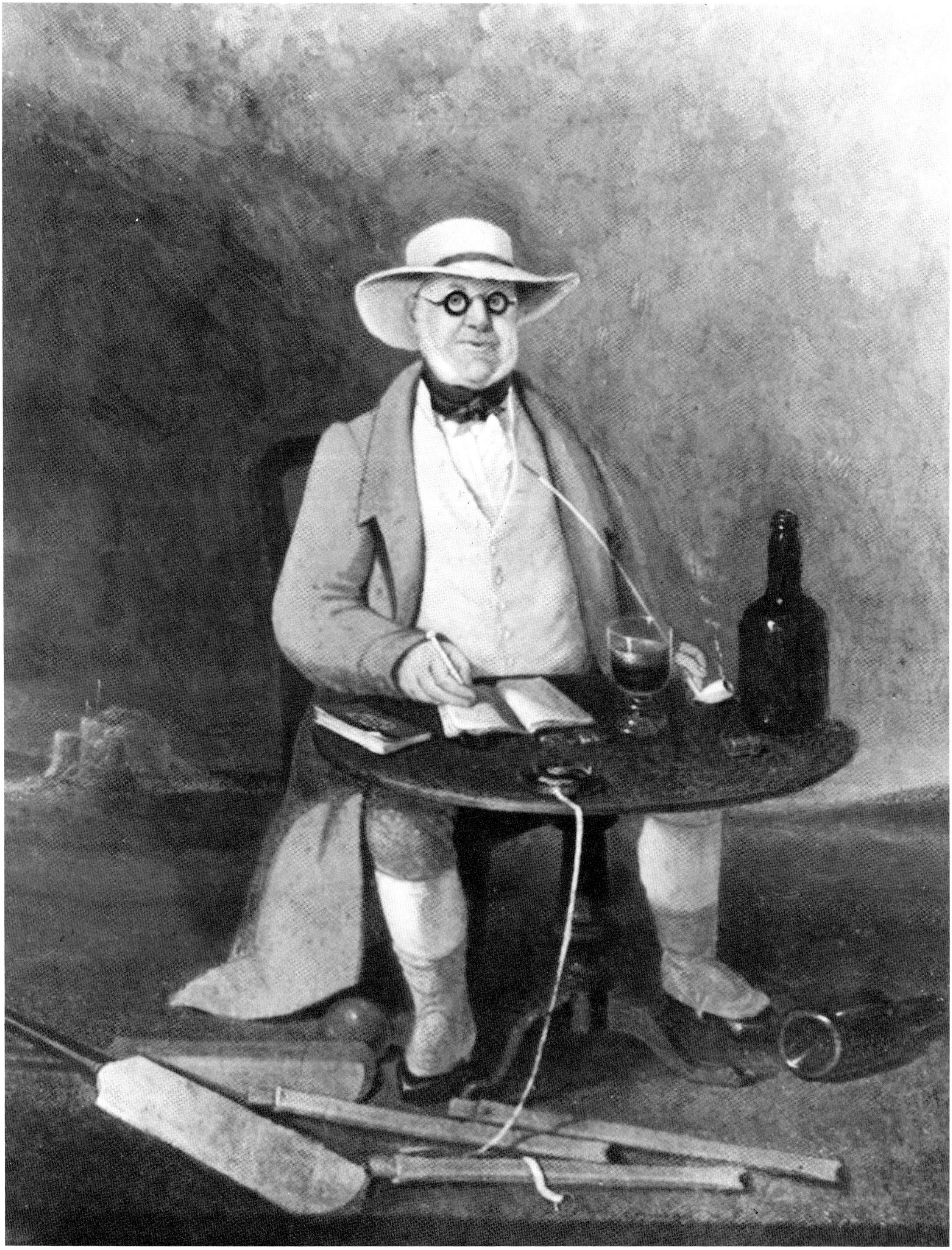

98. Thomas Henwood: *The Scorer* (1842) (M.C.C.).

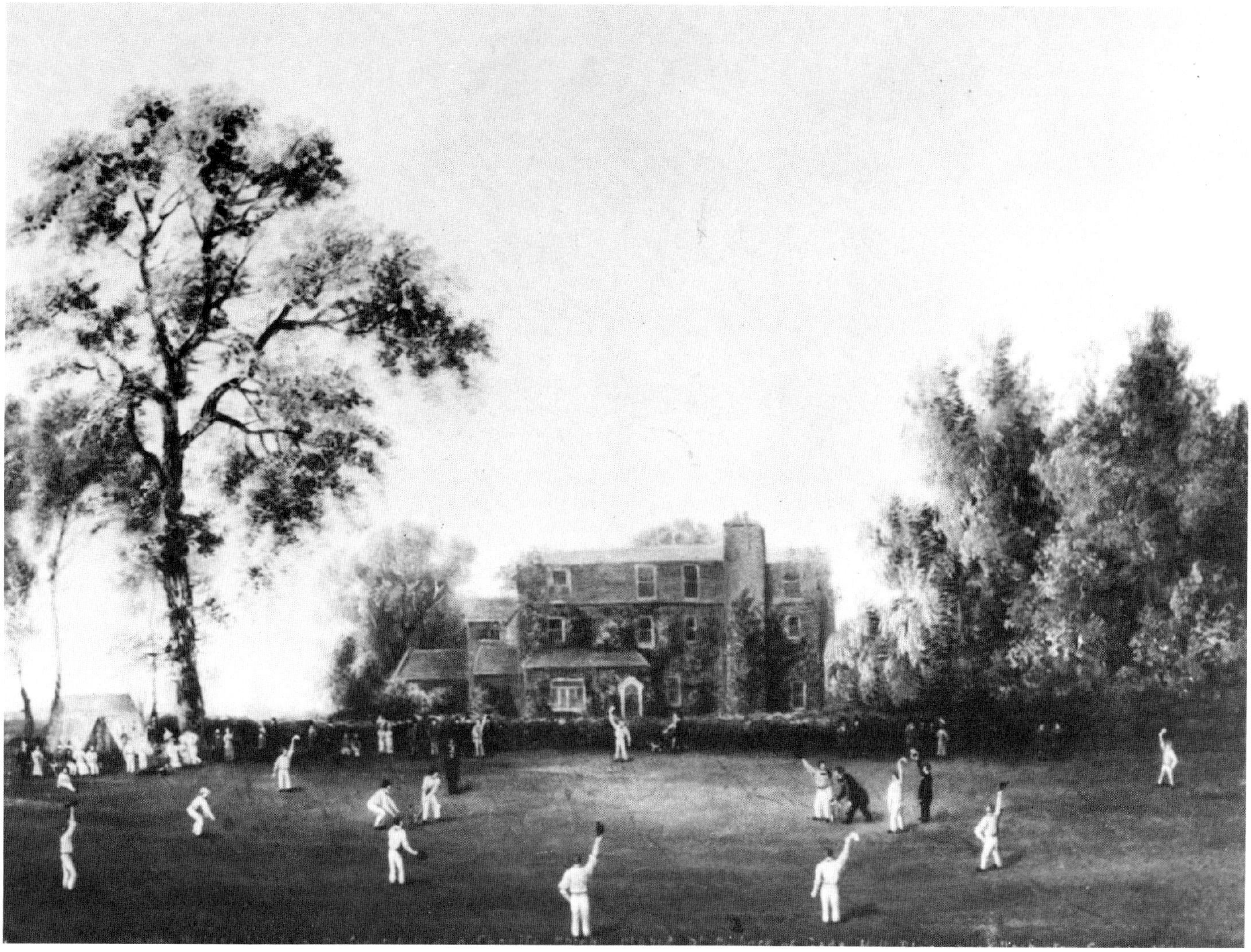

99. British School: *Cricket at Gad's Hill: Charles Dickens bowling the first ball* (M.C.C.).

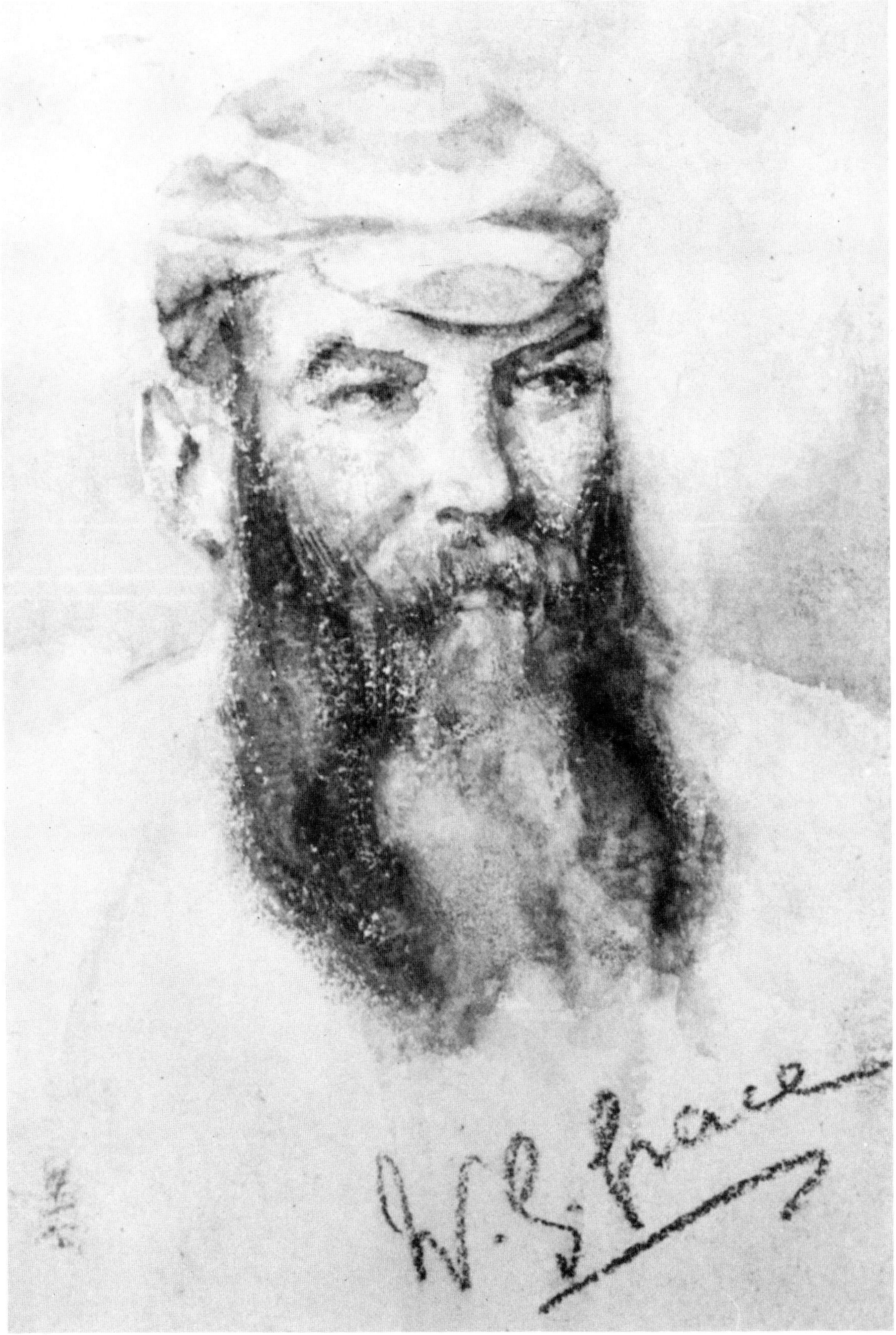

100. Henry Scott Tuke, R.A., R.W.S.: *W. G. Grace* (1905) (M.C.C.).

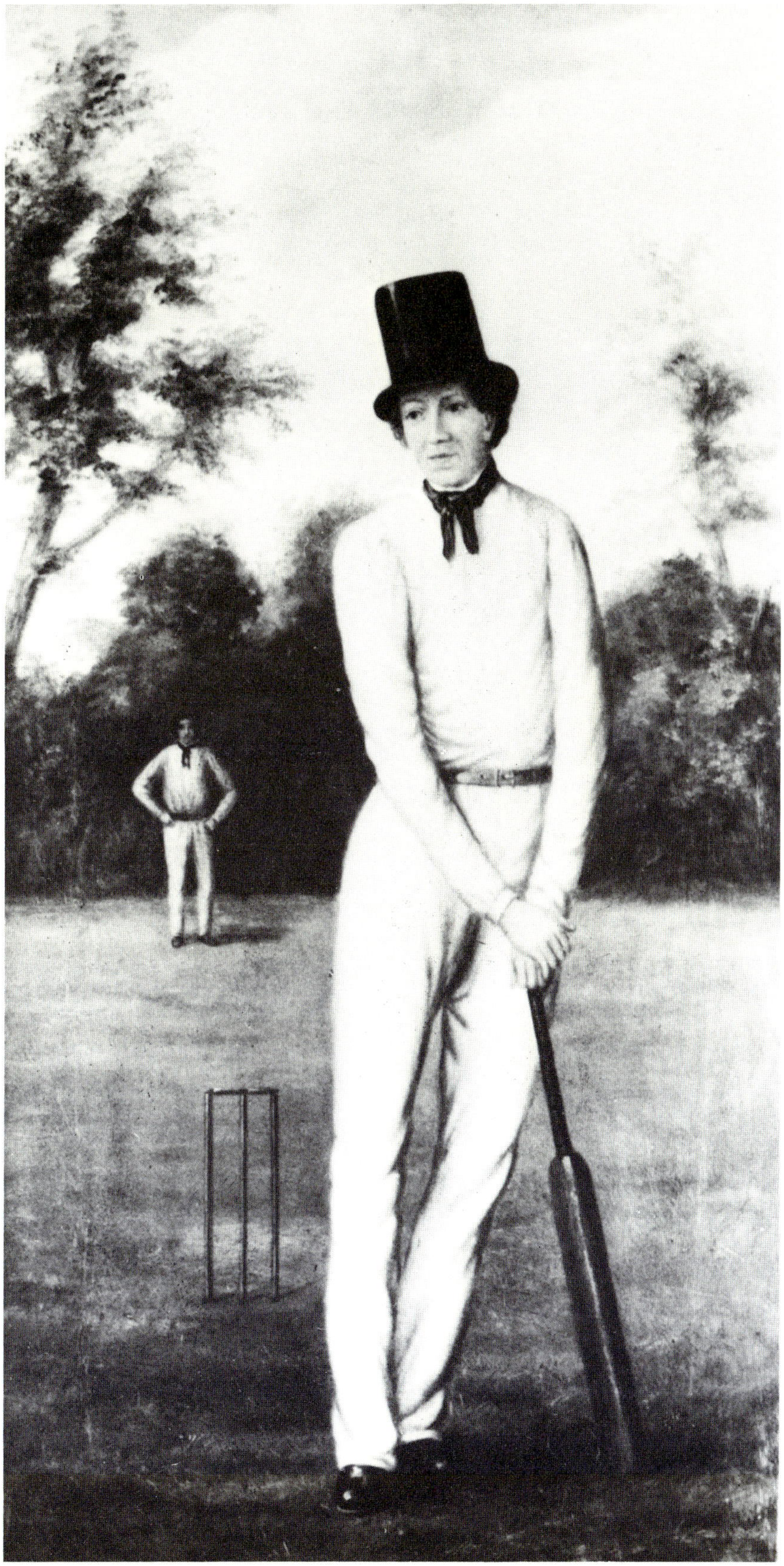

101. R. D. [Richard Dagley]: *Benjamin Disraeli at the Wicket* (1824) (M.C.C.).

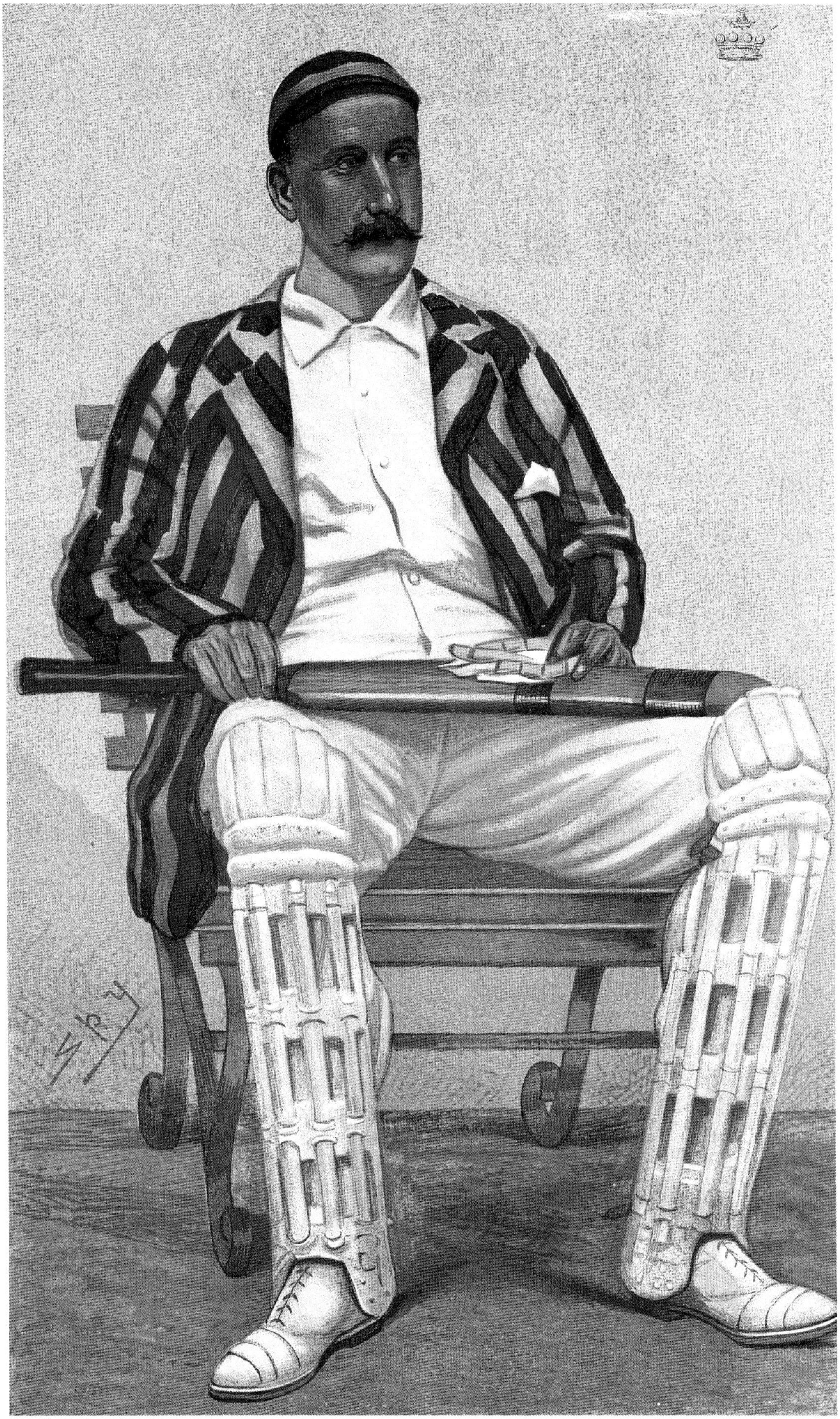

102. Sir Leslie Ward ('SPY'): *Lord Hawke* (1892).

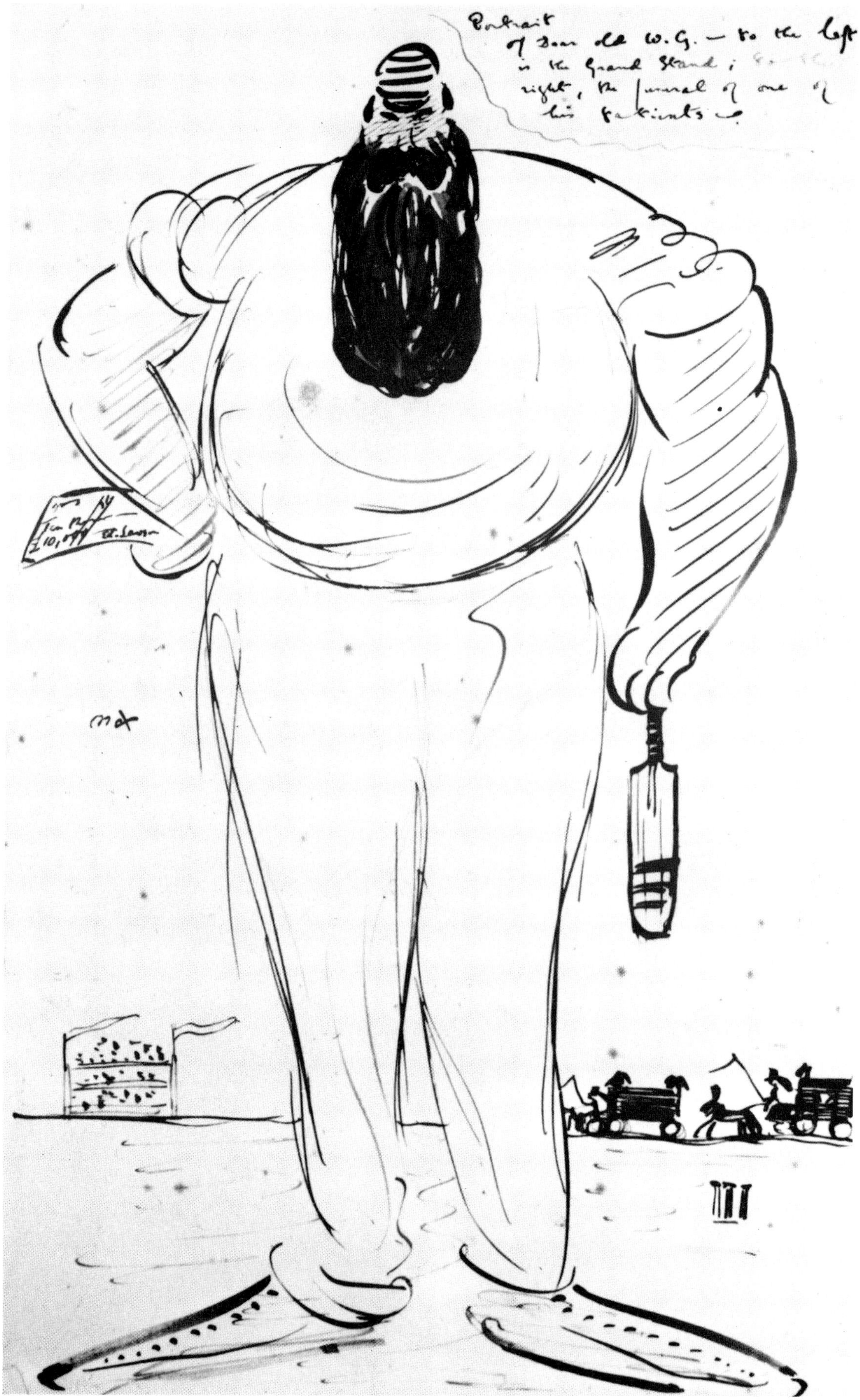

103. Sir Max Beerbohm: *W. G. Grace* (M.C.C.).

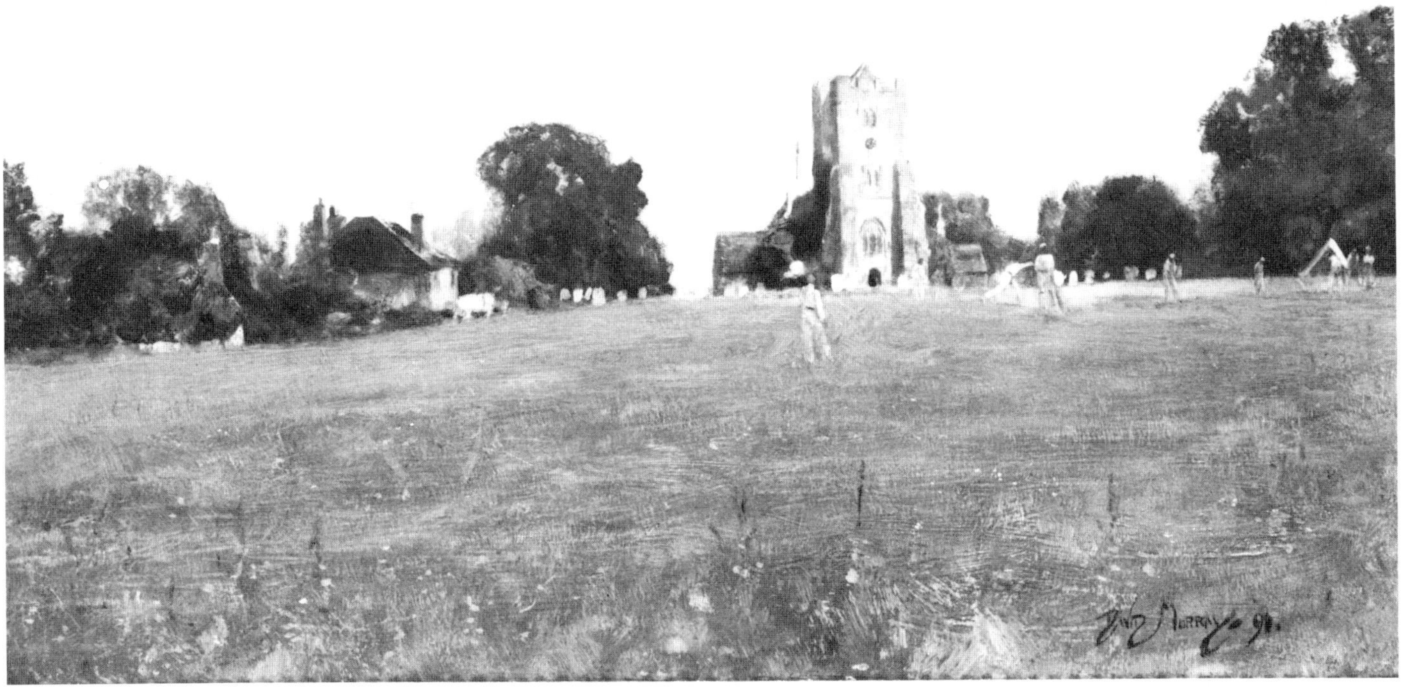

104. Sir David Murray, R.A., R.S.W., R.I.: *Cricket on the Village Green* (1891) (Rutland Gallery, London).

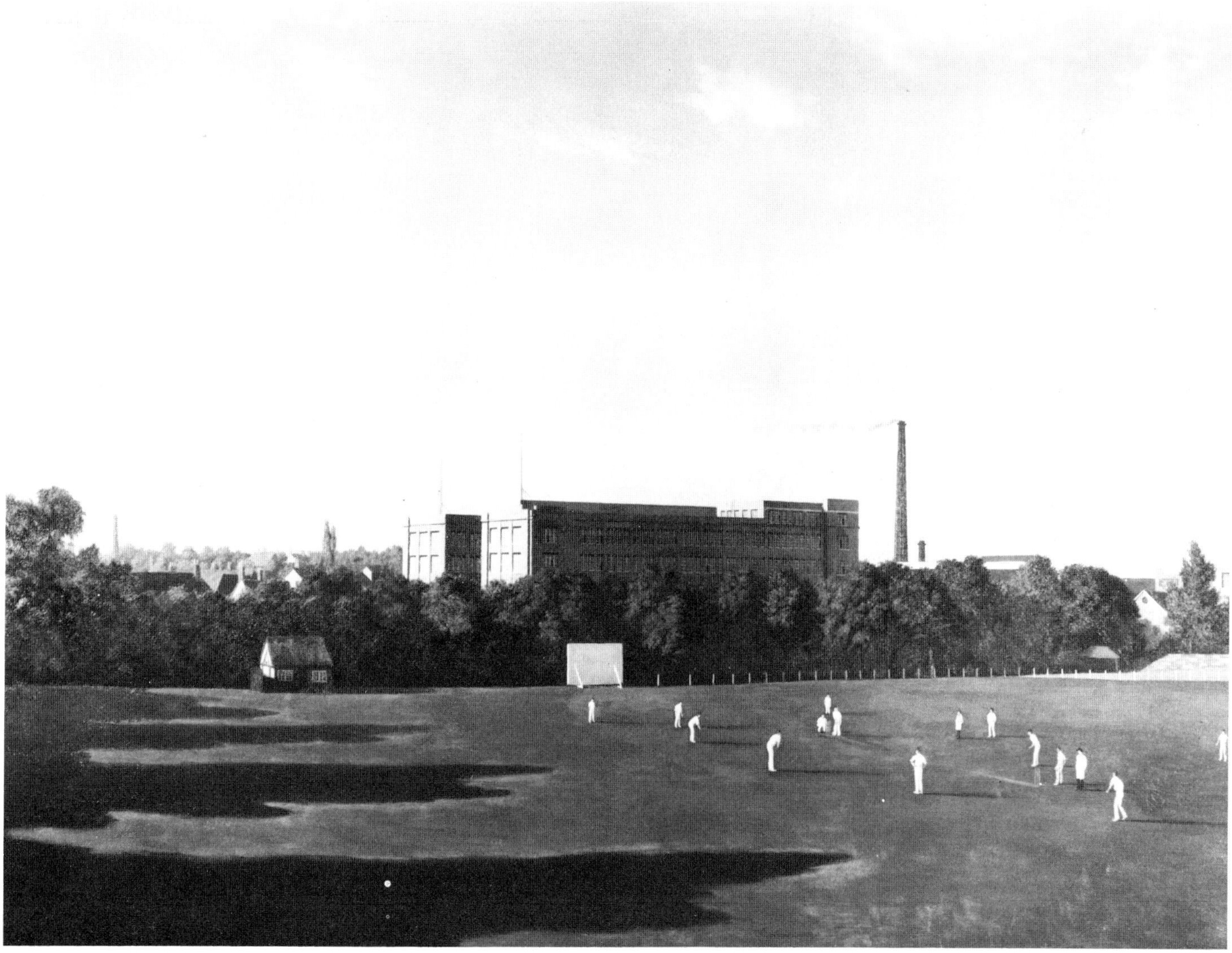

105. Algernon Newton, R.A.: *A Cricket Match at Bournville* (1929) (Cadbury Schweppes plc, Bournville).

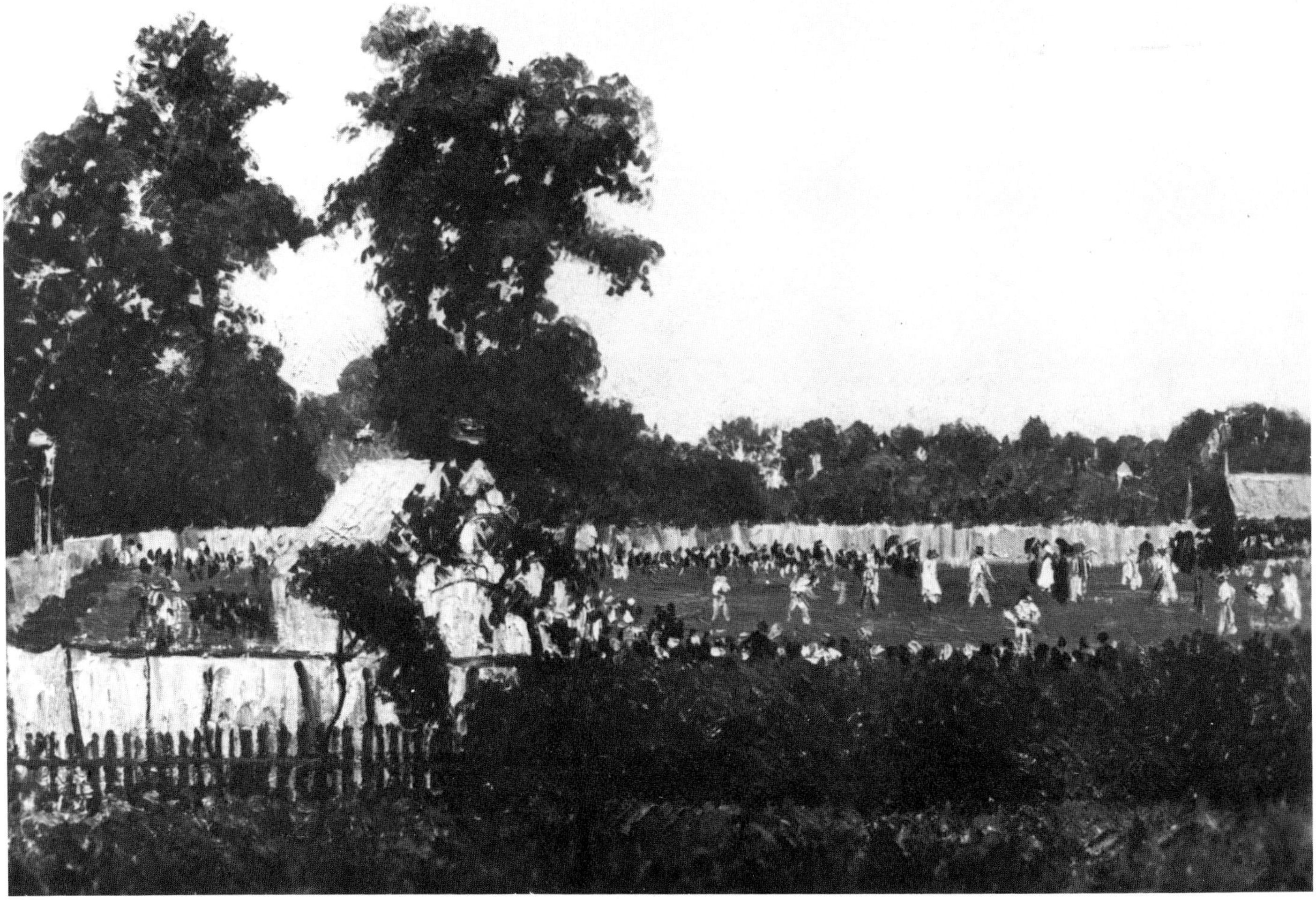

106. Camille Pissarro: *Cricket at Bedford Park* (1897) (Jeu de Paume, Paris).

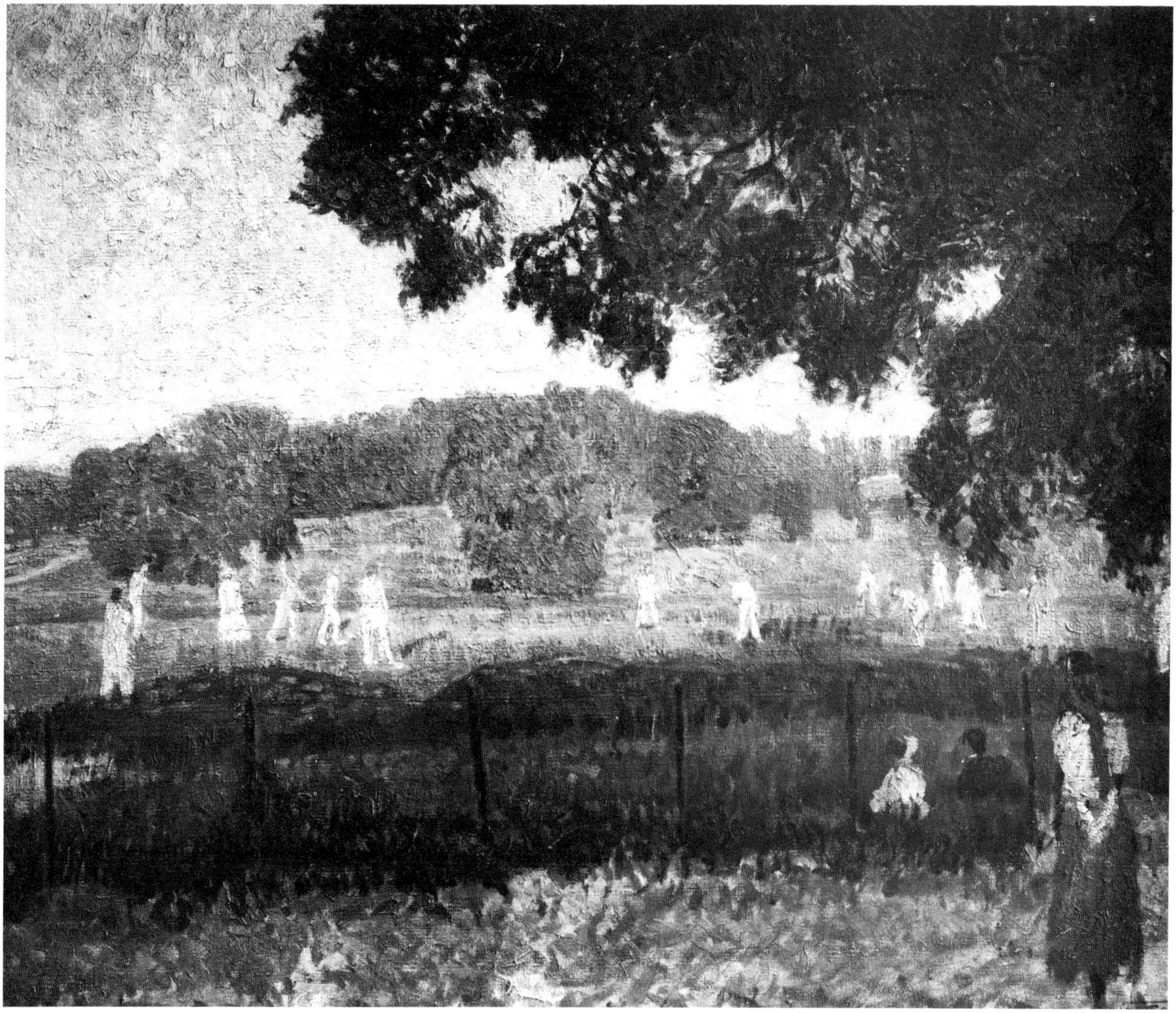

107. Spencer Gore: *The Cricket Match* (Wakefield City Art Gallery).

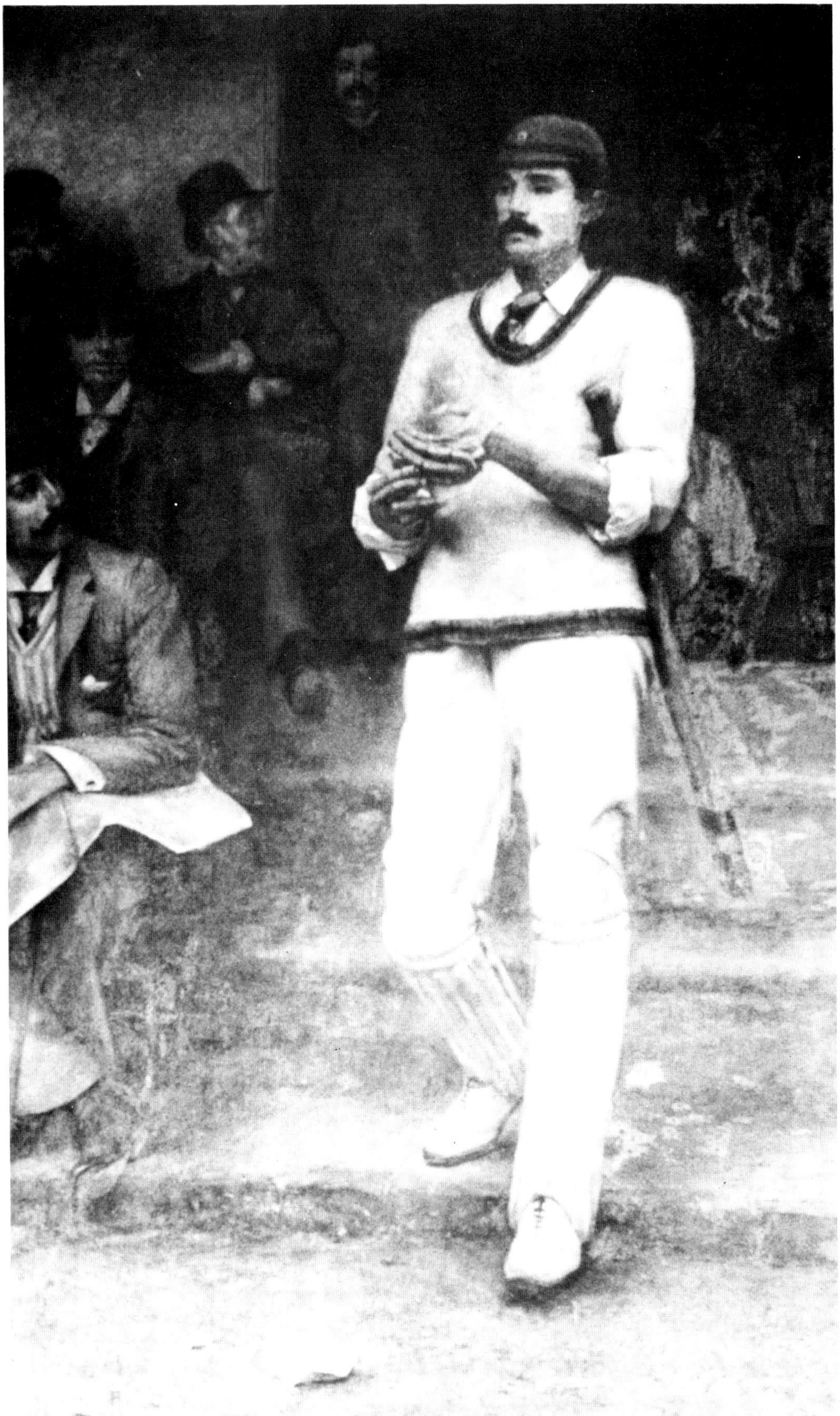

108. George R. Roller, R.P.E.: *W.E. Roller going out to bat* (Surrey C.C.C.).

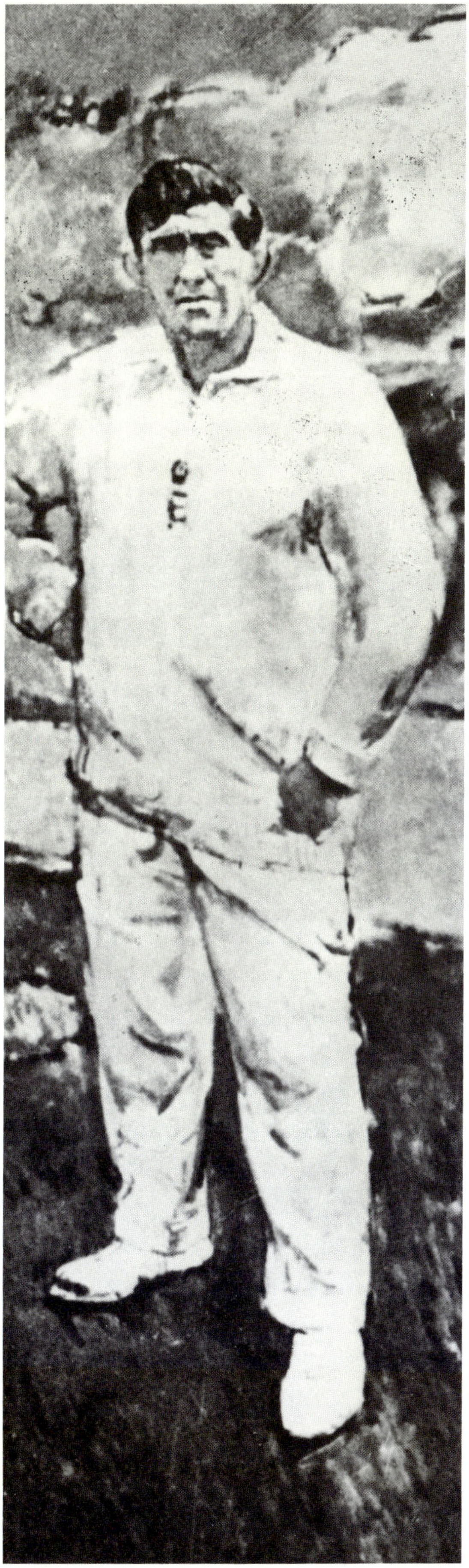

109. Ruskin Spear, R.A.: *F.S. Trueman* (M.C.C.).

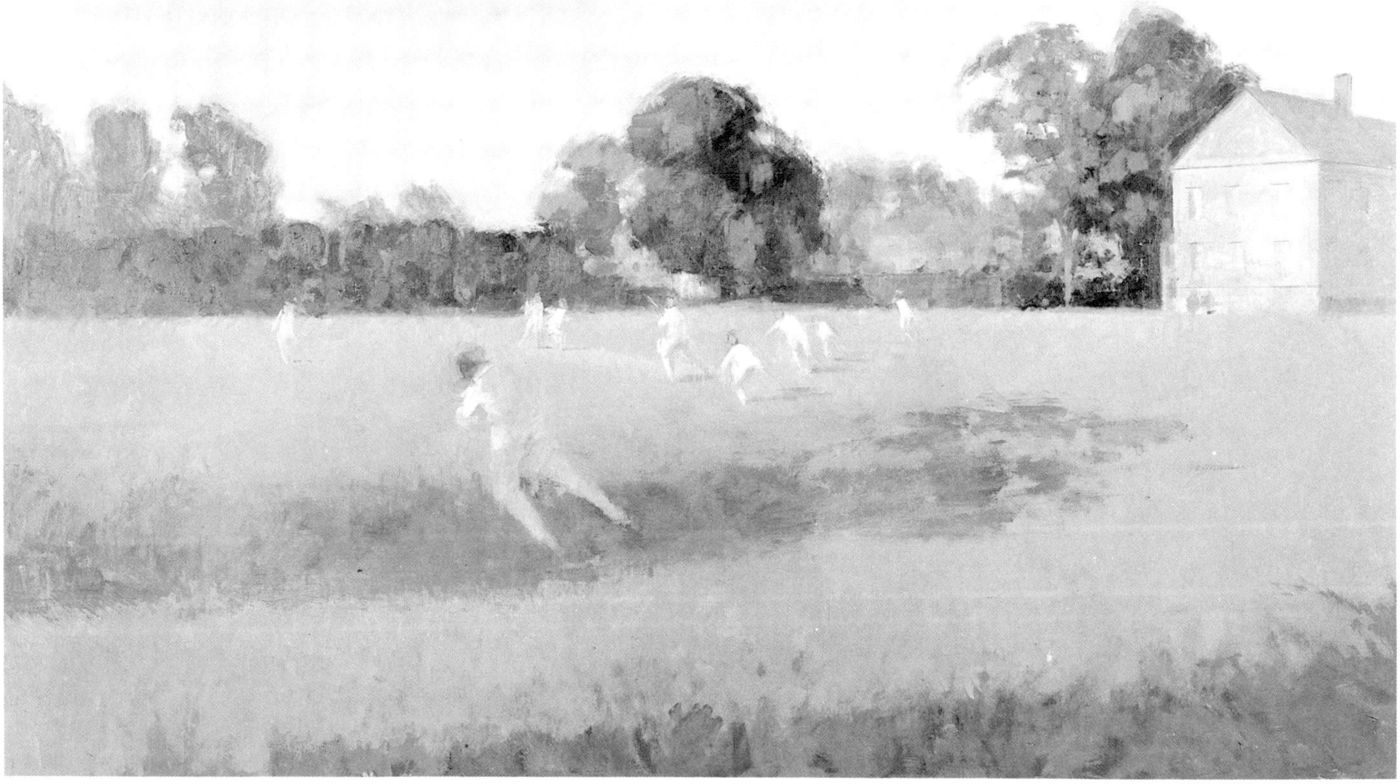

110. Lawrence Toynbee: *Cricket at Hovingham Hall* (Sir Marcus Worsley, Bart.).

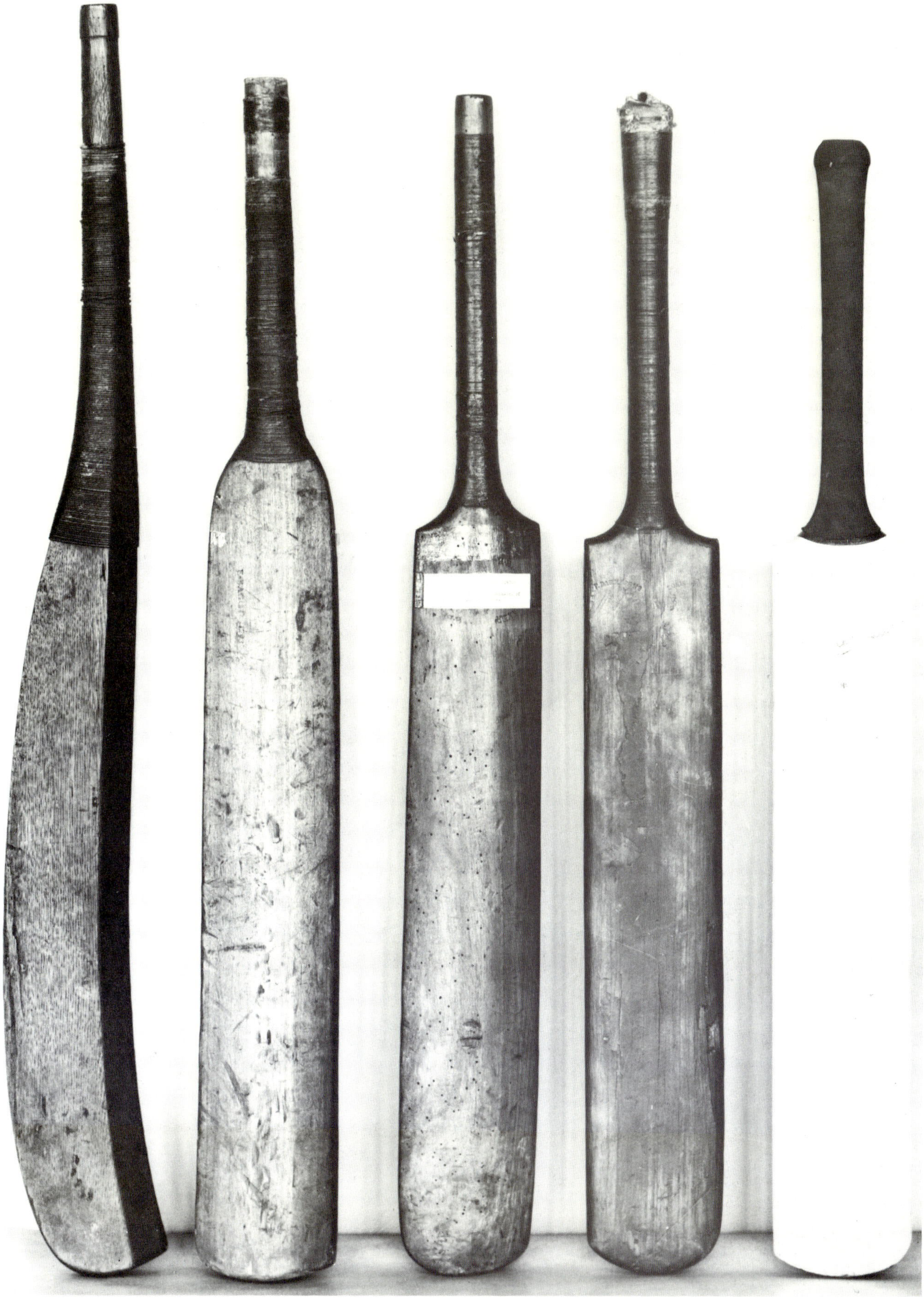

1. Cricket bats of early and modern times (M.C.C. Collection): (i) curved bat, *c.* 1750-70; (ii) early straight bat, 1793; (iii) bat used by Fuller Pilch (1803-1870); (iv) bat owned by W.G. Grace (1848-1915); (v) bat used by Sir Donald Bradman in England in 1948.

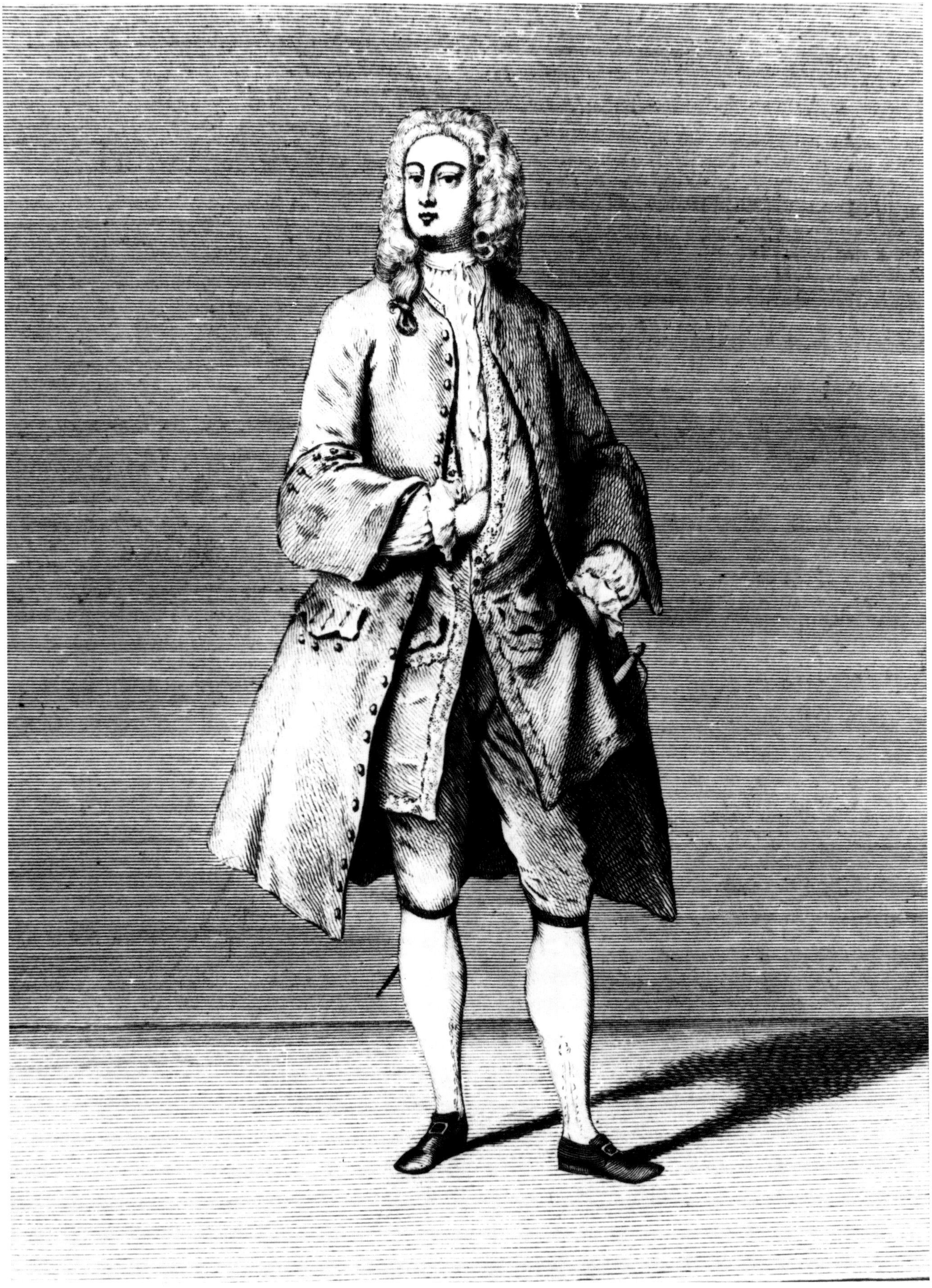

2. L.P. Boitard *after* Bartholomew Dandridge: Plate 1 from F. Nivelon, *Rudiments of Genteel Behavior* (1737).

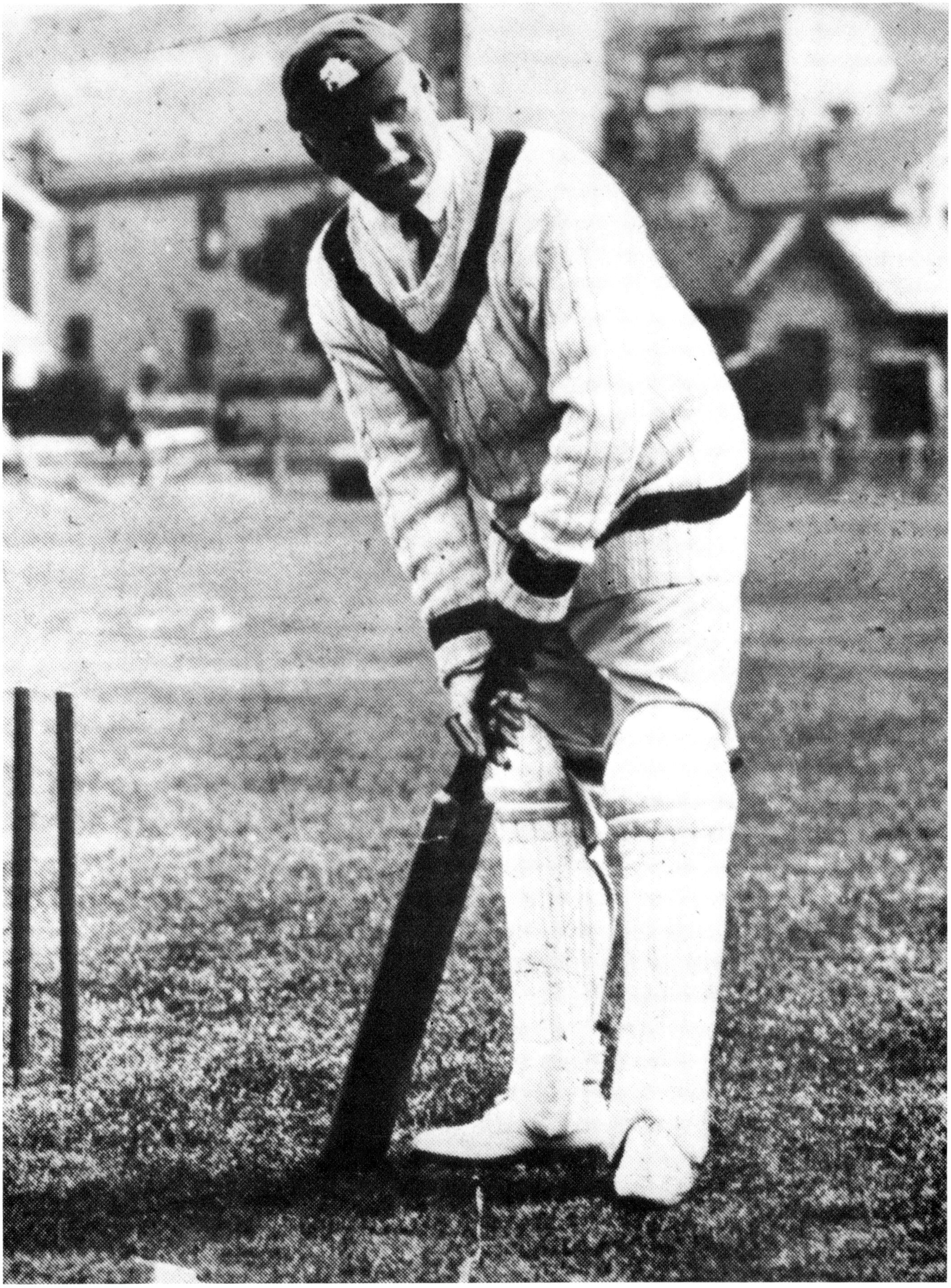

3. A.C. MacLaren at the wicket.

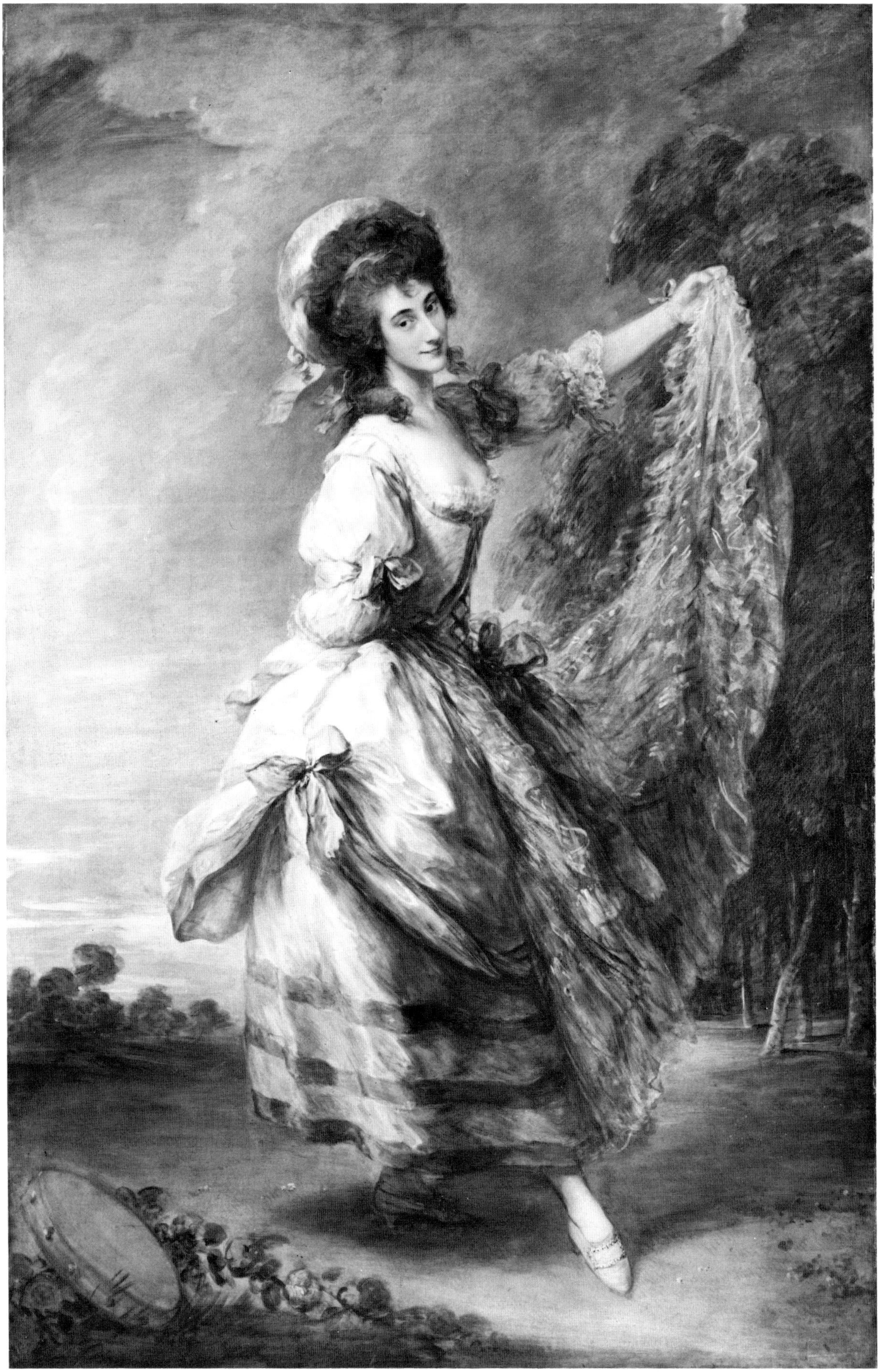

4. Thomas Gainsborough, R.A.: *Giovanna Baccelli* (Tate Gallery, London).

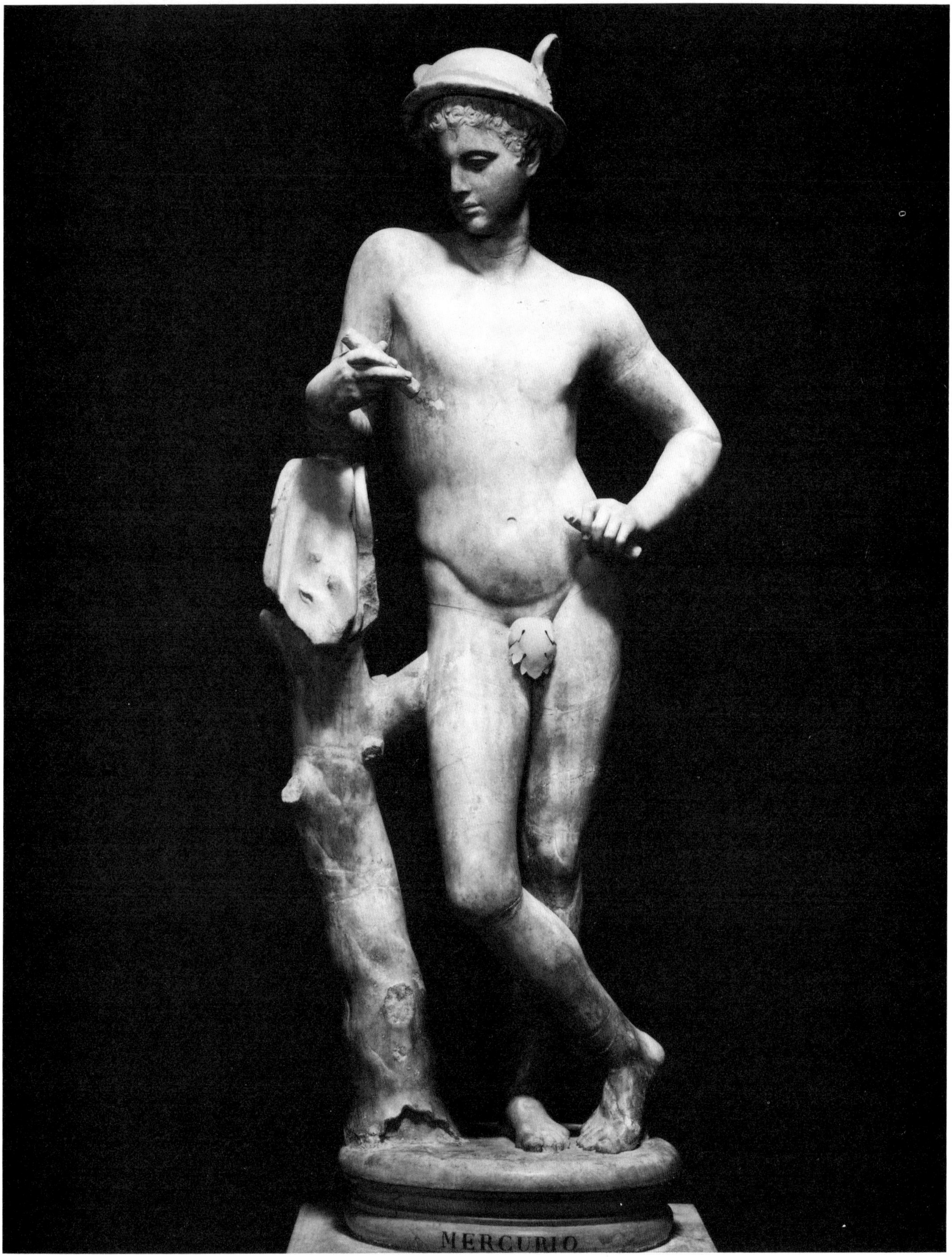

5. *Mercury* (Uffizi Gallery, Florence).

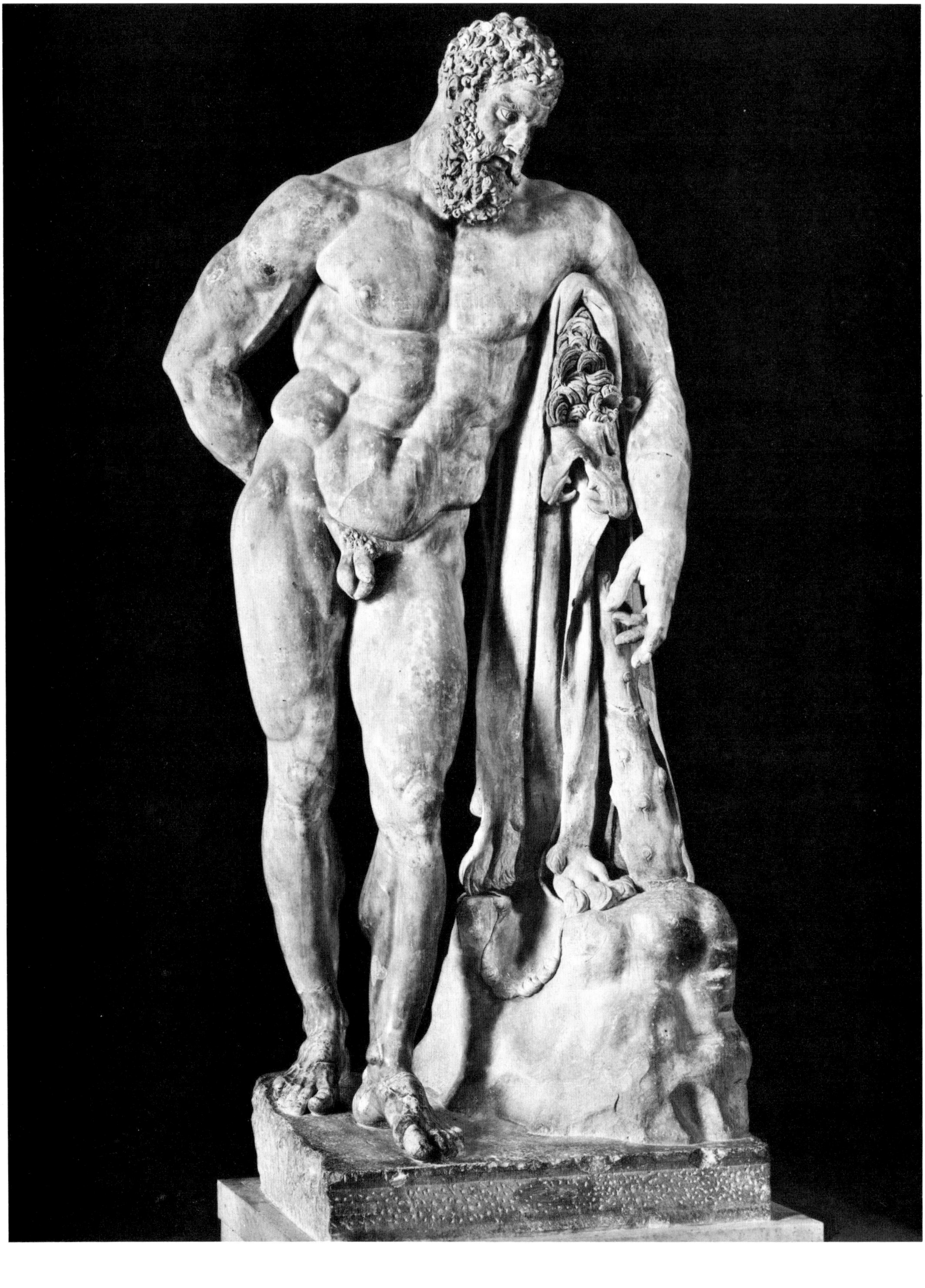

6. *The Farnese Hercules* (Museo Nazionale, Naples).

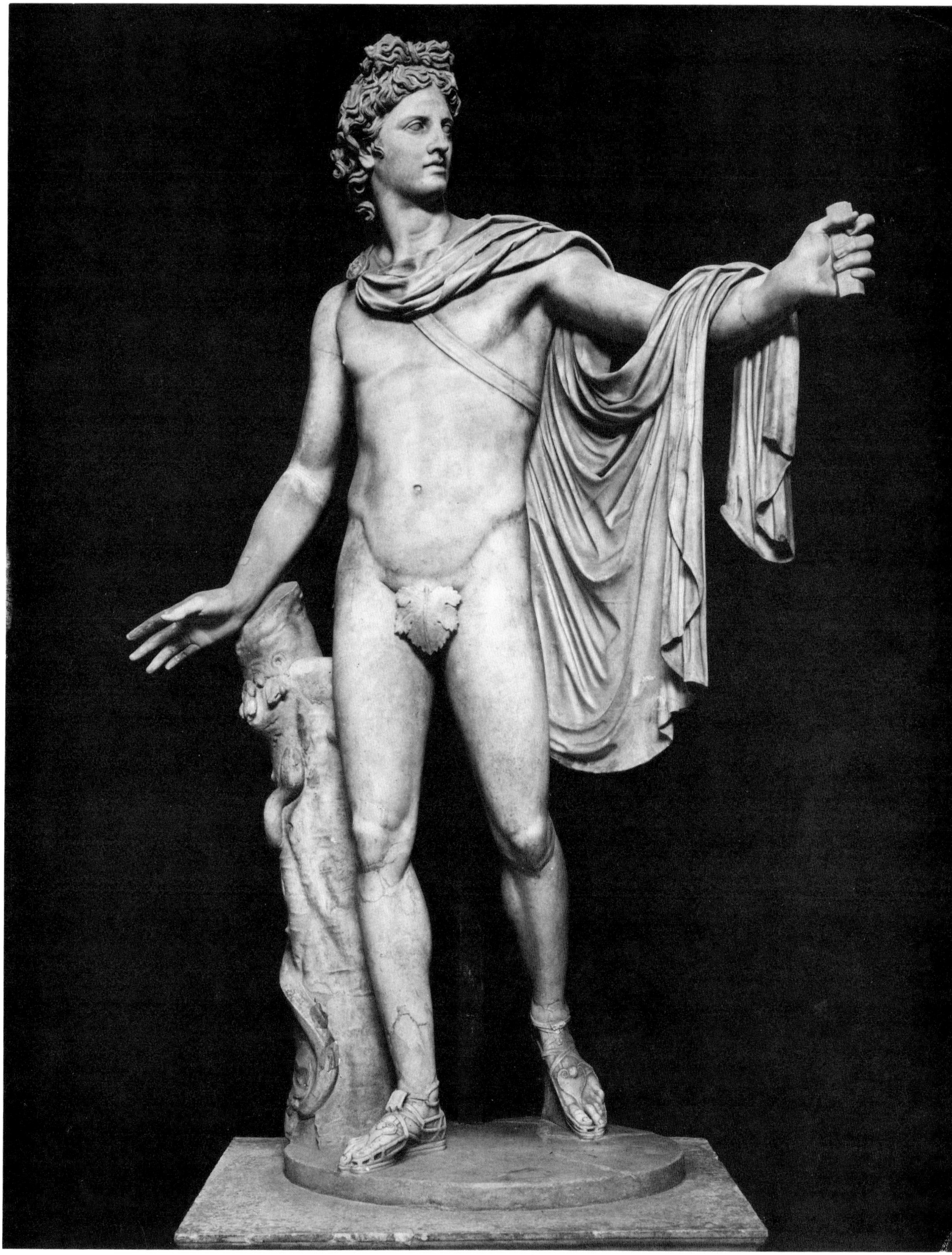

7. *Apollo Belvedere* (Vatican, Rome).

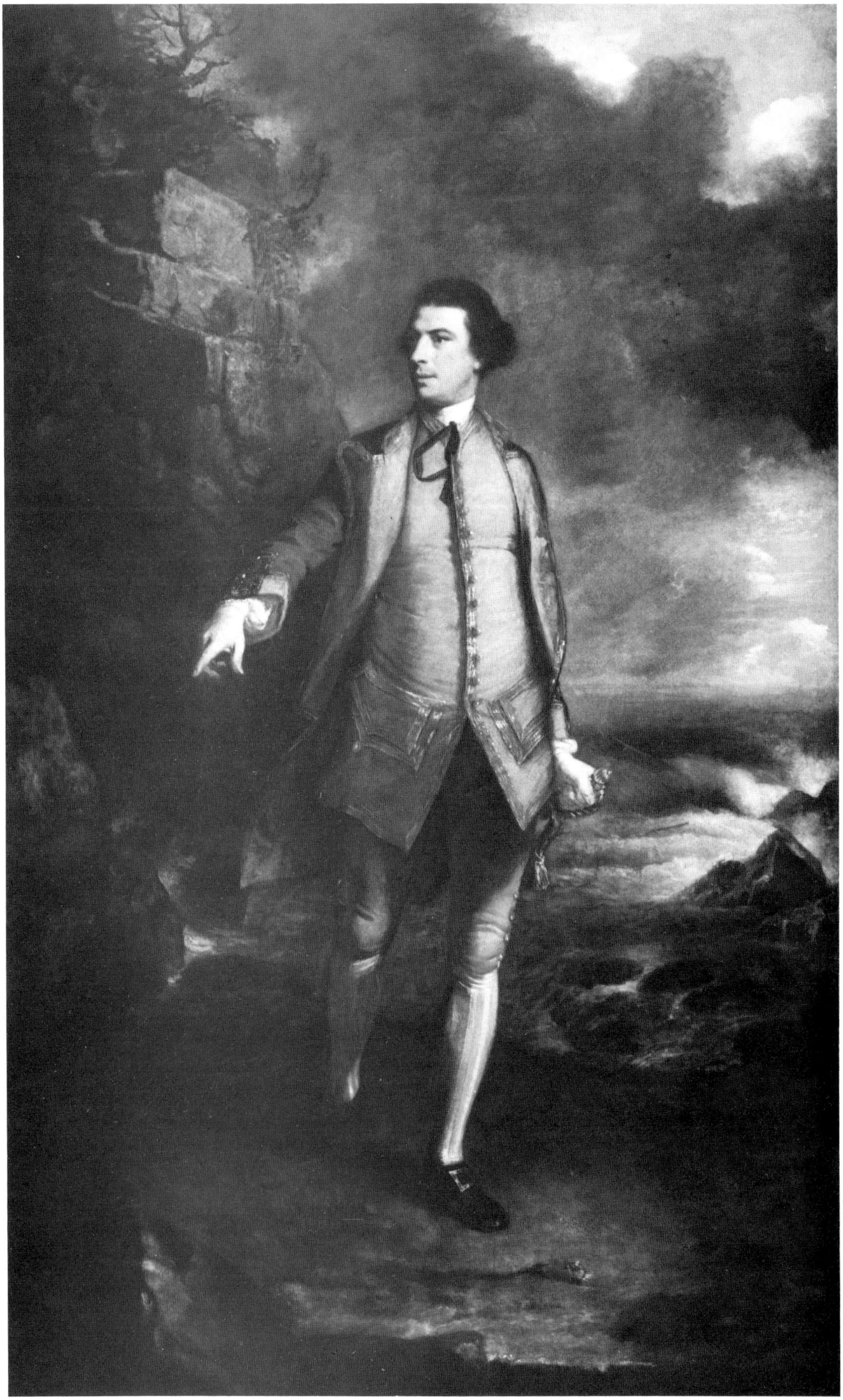

8. Sir Joshua Reynolds, P.R.A.: *Commodore Augustus Keppel* (Royal Maritime Museum, Greenwich).

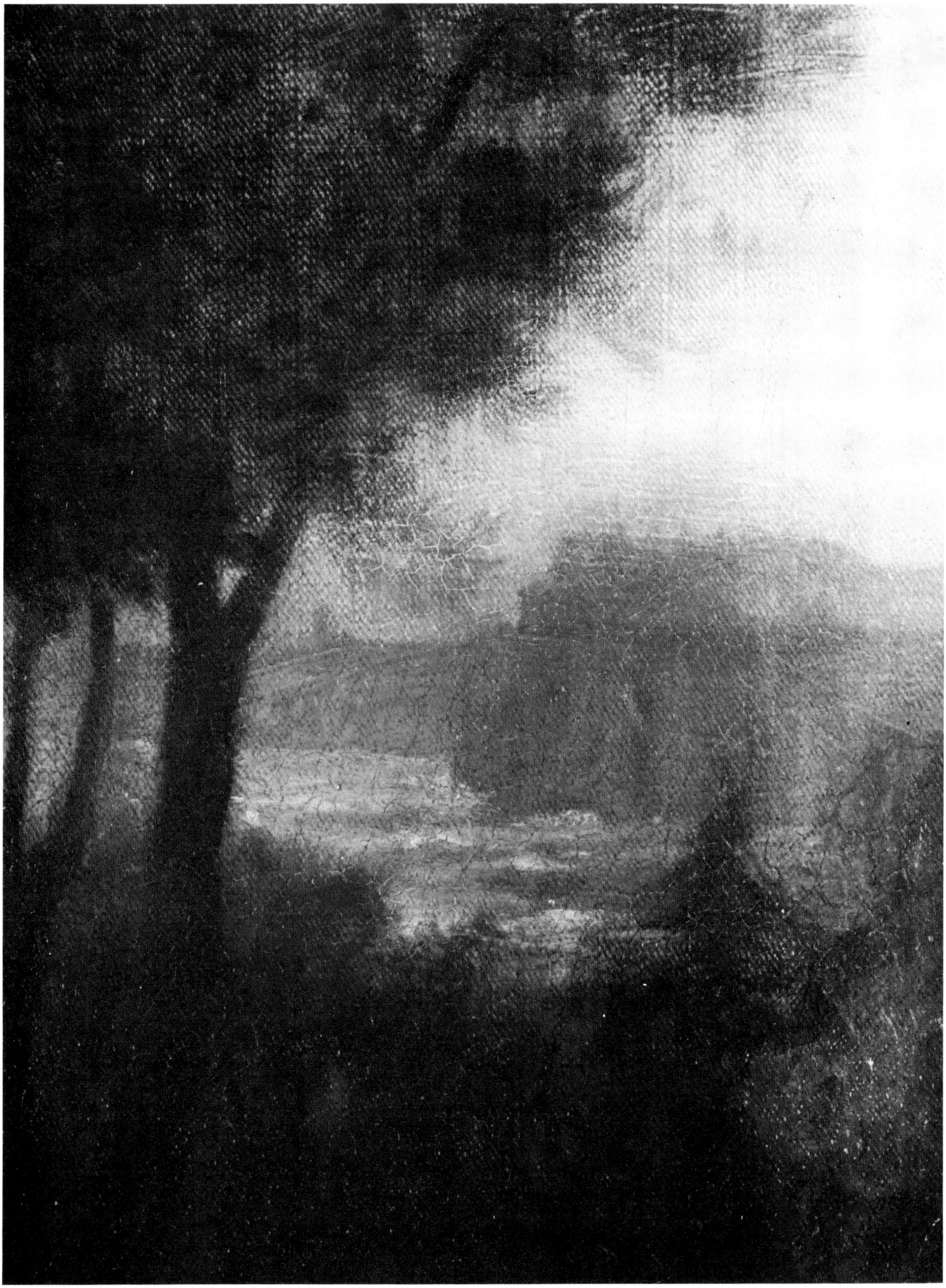

9. Slains Castle: detail of Plate XVII.

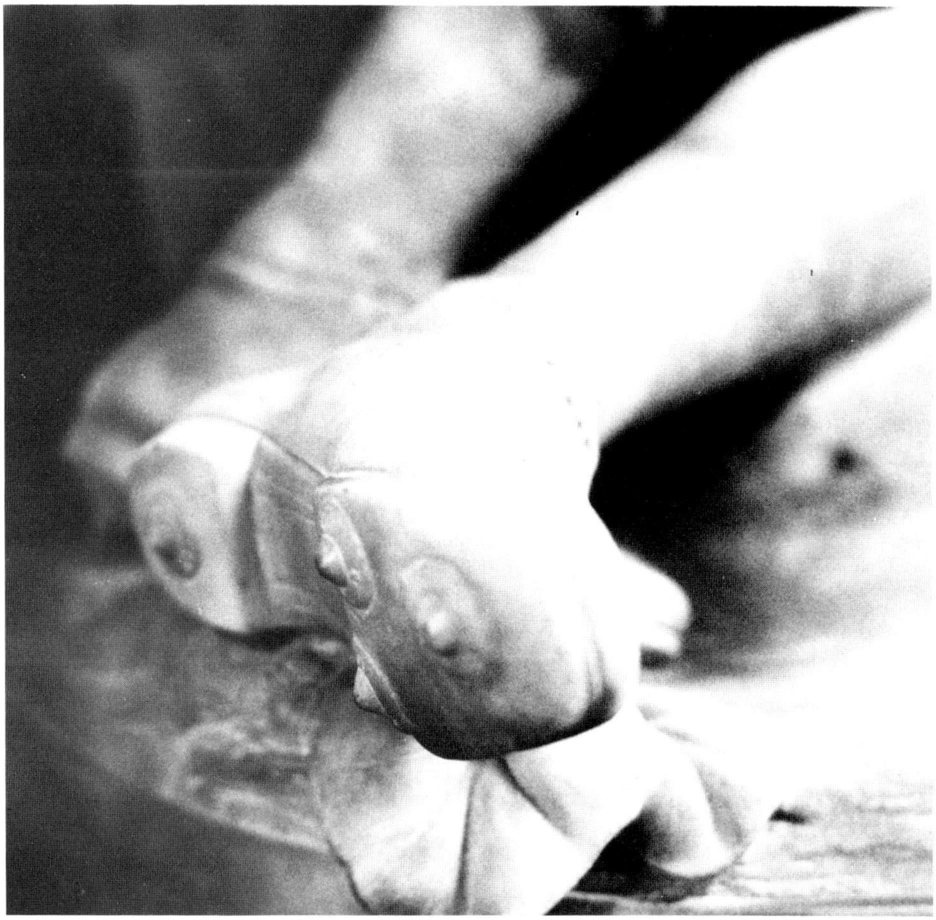

10. Cricket-boot of 1866: detail of Plate 55.

Index

Roman numbers in parentheses refer to colour plates and arabic to black and white plates. Page references to the text are given in roman, Catalogue numbers in italics. The index incorporates the subjects of works of art mentioned in the text and Catalogue (e.g. the sitters in cricket portraits and the places represented in pictures of cricket matches), and also provides an index to collections.